NEW GREEN PAGES

Compiled by John Button

A Directory of Natural Products, Services,
Resources and Ideas

An OPTIMA book

© John Button 1990

Green Pages first published in 1988 by Macdonald Optima,
a division of Macdonald & Co. (Publishers) Ltd.
New Green Pages first published in 1990 by the same publisher

A member of Maxwell Macmillan Pergamon Publishing Corporation

British Library Cataloguing in Publication Data

Button, John
    New green pages.
    2nd ed.
    1. Great Britain. Environment. Conservation
    I. Title   II. Green pages
    333.720941

ISBN 0-356-19109-5

Macdonald & Co. (Publishers) Ltd
Orbit House
1 New Fetter Lane
London EC4A 1AR

Typeset in Garamond and Futura by the compiler
and Saxon Printing Ltd, Derby, and designed by the compiler

Recycled paper supplied by Paperback Ltd, London

Printed and bound in Great Britain by
Mackays of Chatham PLC, Chatham, Kent

CONTENTS

HOW TO USE THIS BOOK

There has recently been a spate of books suggesting specific ways in which we might live more lightly, taking real care of ourselves and our environment. There have also been television programmes on particular environmental issues, and a steady stream of technical reports and surveys.

Until *Green Pages* was published two years ago, however, the wide range of issues raised by the rising tide of green awareness had not been brought together in a single volume. Preceding the phenomenal success of books like *The Green Consumer Guide* and the Green Party's amazing showing in the 1989 European elections, it provided the first detailed and practical guide to what many people now call a 'green lifestyle'.

Here now is *New Green Pages*, a completely updated and enlarged version of the original book. On page 8, if you are interested, you can read about how the book came into being; for the time being I simply hope that *New Green Pages* will make it easier for you to find out about the things and ideas which will help all of us to live a healthier, happier and more fulfilling life, and ensure that we minimize the harm we do to the environment in the process.

Green Pages is a book for dipping into, not necessarily for reading from cover to cover. You can find the sections that most interest you by checking the contents page, where the broad outline of each section is given. For more specific subjects, like 'ionizers' or 'walking holidays', the subject index on pages 349 and 350 will help you find the relevant entries. If you know the name of a supplier or organization and want to find out more about them, there is an index of companies and organizations on pages 350-352.

One or two readers of the first edition said that they weren't clear which sections were my own original thoughts and which were quotations; the convention I have used is to put all quoted material in italics. Now you know which bits to blame me for!

Each of the twelve subject areas is prefaced with a short thought-provoking introduction, in which I have attempted to provide a context for the decisions we make within each aspect of our lives. Any discussion about the changes that are necessary to bring about a better world will inevitably be controversial, a fine line between vision and realism. Positive change rarely comes from the wholesale demolition of an entire social and economic structure, yet — as is becoming ever clearer — fundamental change is crucial if we are to weather successfully the tempestuous times in which we live.

This is the spirit in which *New Green Pages* is written and presented.

As with the first edition of the book, the production of *New Green Pages* would have been impossible without the help of the enormous number of people who provided information and advice. Special thanks are due to Sarah Eno and Sue Francia for working alongside me in the final hectic weeks; also to Gail Chester, Gerard Darby, Peter Lang, Jan McHarry, Declan McHugh, Val Oldaker, Marion Paul and John Rowan. I want to thank again the friends who helped with specific sections of the first edition, much of which has been incorporated into *New Green Pages*: Roz Elphinstone, Soo Goodwin-Downes, Clare Hill, Adrian Judd, Bernard Little, Pat Kirby, Mitra and Liz Shephard. Finally thank you to Philippa Stewart and Erica Smith, the mainstays of the Optima imprint when the project was first conceived and produced, and to Jayne Booth and Harriet Griffey who have kept the project on course following their predecessors' promotions elsewhere.

INTRODUCTION

'Weave real connections, create real nodes, build real houses.
Live a life you can endure . . .'
Marge Piercy

We live in exciting and dangerous times. Some cynics have suggested that green concern will before long turn to green boredom, but there are now few days when the media do not have something to report on green-tinted issues. Too often it is yet another disaster, another scare, another example of gross inhumanity. Yet seemingly all-pervasive negativity is increasingly being tempered with the human thoughtfulness, concern and intelligence that green activists have believed in all along. Who would have believed that on one eventful Friday in November 1989 the Berlin Wall would fall on the same day that Britain effectively abandoned its civil nuclear power programme?

British politicians, following their leaders' conversion to the green cause (their own interpretations, of course), are now working desperately to be greener-than-thou. Their business colleagues are running neck-and-neck to display their green credentials. Despite their protestations, little is yet happening at the centre of British public life. In their review of the government's record to the end of 1989, Friends of the Earth showed that only in one area — the unleading of petrol — had the government made any major policy commitment to the greening of Britain.

But in many ways the people of Britain are streets ahead of their political and economic leaders. From neighbourhood recycling projects to school wildlife gardens, the grassroots greening of Britain is to a large extent happening *despite* the system. The compiling of *Green Pages*, especially of this new edition, has convinced me that a very great deal is going on in Britain as we enter the critical 1990s, and that a very large number of people now want to make the conscious shift to a more sane, humane and ecological lifestyle.

There is a lot going on, and the purpose of *New Green Pages* is to inspire you to find out more about what is happening where, who is doing it, and how you can be involved in a future for our planet which is truly life-enhancing, for all human beings and for all the life with which we share a common home.

Why 'green'?

Until the mid-1980s the label 'green' in relation to politics or lifestyle would have meant very little to most people. With the growth of green parties around the world and a rapidly increasing awareness of the importance of environmental issues — using 'environmental' in its widest sense — 'green' has taken on a vast range of implications and understandings, so that it is now possible in many circles to use the word 'green' as shorthand for a whole array of ideas and beliefs centred on the importance of a deep respect for all life on earth.

Jonathon Porritt of Friends of the Earth calls this perspective 'seeing green' (see page 253). Ways of seeing green vary a great deal from observer to observer, but most green-seers would probably agree at least in outline with the following list, which is adapted from Jonathon's book.

The sort of person that I would expect to get a great deal from *New Green Pages* is likely to think of the following as being very important:

▶ A respect for all life, including all other human beings.

▶ A willingness to live as lightly as possible, taking and using only what is really necessary for their nourishment.

▶ A willingness to waste as little as possible.

▶ A recognition of the rights of all people to have access to what they need regardless of sex or colour or beliefs, and a willingness to uphold and implement these rights in every aspect of daily life.

▶ A willingness to share and co-operate with other people, rather than assuming that competition is the only way to get on in the world.

▶ An emphasis on the participation of people in decisions which affect them, and on giving people the practical tools to help them make their own decisions, both as individuals and as groups.

▶ A recognition of the rights of future generations to enjoy their planet, involving the conscious choice of the present generation to use non-renewable resources as sparingly as possible.

▶ An emphasis on self-reliance — looking at ways of providing people with what they need within their community, rather than relying too much on national and international organizations and trade networks.

▶ A belief that work should be useful, rewarding, and properly rewarded.

▶ A belief that material possessions are only part of a person's real wealth, and that real wealth involves access to those things and qualities which are truly life-enhancing, such as a healthy environment, peace, and relaxation.

▶ A rejection of institutionalized violence and warfare, and of weapons of mass destruction.

What to include . . .

From the very beginning of the *Green Pages* project, I knew that big though the book is it could not contain everything remotely green-tinted and therefore that it had to be selective. Despite its name, I wanted it to be much more than a simple *Yellow-Pages*-style listing of names and addresses. It had to be discriminating and informative, and ensure that whatever subject was covered, it was described in sufficient detail for the information to be of real and lasting use to the reader.

A great deal of useful information is included in books and guides which have already been published; this is increasingly the case as the green movement grows and gathers momentum. This explains why as much as a third of *New Green Pages* is devoted to reviews of books and other publications. Around 30,000 new book titles are published in Britain every year, so deciding which are the very best of their sort is not easy. In general I have selected books which are thought-provoking, easy to read, available in reasonably-priced paperback editions, and share — more or less — the philosophy of *Green Pages*. Most of these books have been published in the last two or three years and so contain up-to-date and relevant resources. Though I have included some 'classics' which are sadly (and I hope temporarily) out of print, I have tried wherever possible to ensure that the books I have included are still in print and so readily available.

One feature of recent years has been the rapidly growing number of guides and directories to different aspects of greenness — guides to vegetarian restaurants, communities, wildlife groups, health practitioners, self-help workshops and courses. Some are published as books, others as leaflets or booklets by the relevant umbrella organization. The existence of these directories has made my task much easier, since it means that there is no need to list every vegetarian bed and breakfast or every homeopathic doctor in the country — all I need to do is point you in the direction of the relevant listing, many of which are held by (better) public libraries. Thus to a large extent *New Green Pages* is a resource of resources. It might not tell you the name and address of your nearest chiropractor or paper recycling scheme, but I would be surprised if such local information were more than one phone call away when you have *New Green Pages* at your elbow.

Then there are the organizations. Monica Frisch's *Directory for the Environment* lists nearly 1,400 organizations involved in one aspect or another of the environment; then there are organizations concerned with health, children, peace, trade associations, the Third World, poverty ... In *New Green Pages* I have included those organizations which I feel are the most relevant to the everyday concerns of green-minded people, particularly those which can supply useful information or which are involved in particularly exciting or important campaigns.

Finally, but by no means least important, are the suppliers. When *Green Pages* first appeared in 1988, before 'green consumerism' was invented, it broke new ground in bringing together details of some of the many small businesses now offering environment-friendly goods. 'Environment-friendly' and its synonyms have sadly (but predictably) become the stock-in-trade of multinationals and their advertising agencies, which makes the need for discrimination ever more acute. As you will read in the next section, a crucial aspect of a green lifestyle is cutting consumption of all material things to what is really needed for our wellbeing. Yet *New Green Pages* recognizes that we all need food, clothing, shelter, warmth, and a certain number of physical objects to keep us company and help make our lives more enjoyable, and that if we are going to consume we can at least consume awarely, causing as little damage as possible to the earth and its inhabitants — including ourselves.

As with everything else in *New Green Pages*, it is neither possible nor desirable to include *every* producer of clothes in natural fibres, *every* organic grower or *every* maker of wooden toys. What I have done is describe a representative selection of some of the best and most worthwhile sources of environmentally and socially kind products, and as with the other sorts of information in *New Green Pages* I have wherever possible included places where you can find more information.

Consumer or Conserver?

The back cover of *New Green Pages* says that one of the categories that booksellers can put it under is 'consumer interest'. 'Consumer' is a very two-edged word. We are all consumers, and as such there are certain rights and safeguards that we should expect and demand — that what we buy is fit for its purpose, safe, and reasonable value for money. Yet the consumer ethic rampant in our society — the belief that all growth, expansion and increase in material wealth is unquestionably a good thing — is a morality which can neither be sustained nor supported in the long run. Beyond a certain (and fairly modest) level of ownership, it is very obvious that increased wealth does not lead to increased fulfilment. The deep questioning of what we really need for our wellbeing is central to green philosophy and practice: conservation, which means the careful and sensitive management of all resources, must take precedence over blind consumerism — even over blind 'green consumerism'! As Henry Thoreau once said, 'Every superfluous possession is a limitation upon my freedom.' However natural, additive-free, environment-friendly and healthy a product is, the first thing to ask — every time — is 'But do I really need it?'

How *New Green Pages* came about

Several strands went into the weaving of *New Green Pages*. The earliest and probably the most formative is the American *Whole Earth Catalog*, which first appeared in 1968 and has since spawned numerous offspring, the latest of which is *The Essential Whole Earth Catalog* which appeared in 1987. Because *WEC* has done its job so well, *New Green Pages* has unashamedly (but with due respect) borrowed many of its stylistic and design features.

Green Pages was first used as a title for the regional directory of the Ozark Area Community Congress in the USA in 1978; it has since been used for similar directories both in North America and in Britain. The first British *Green Pages* was the *Oxford Grapevine* (which uses *Green Pages* as its subtitle), though *The Gloucestershire Directory*, which serves a similar purpose, was first published a year earlier in 1985 (you will find both of these directories on page 341).

More immediately, the impetus for this book came from Philippa Stewart of Optima, who suggested that in my capacity as a freelance commissioning editor I might like to commission a guide to positive alternatives in Britain. It didn't take me long to decide that the obvious person to work on the project was myself, and I'm very glad that Philippa agreed.

Green Pages was first published in May 1988, and of the twelve thousand copies that were printed sales have continued to rise month by month as green issues become ever more crucial. By mid-1989 it was clear that the book would have to be reprinted early in 1990. Rather than simply update addresses and phone numbers, Optima took the plunge and decided to go for a complete overhaul of the book. Although it has meant an enormous amount of work in a very short space of time, I knew that this was the only real option in the light of the pace of developments in the past two years.

Around a third of the material in *New Green Pages* is either completely new or radically revised. I have added nearly a hundred reviews of important books published since the first edition appeared, and every address and telephone number has been checked to ensure that all is as relevant and up-to-date as possible.

The first edition of *Green Pages* was typeset on a 1981-vintage Commodore Pet, a solid metal-boxed 8-bit word processor that has now found a good home with a novelist friend. Though it wasn't easy, our typesetters were able to convert the disks from the first edition, so that they could be used again (brilliant idea this recycling) on an Amstrad 2386 system using WordPerfect as a word processing package and Ventura desk-top publishing. Yes, I know what I said about DTP on page 293 of *Green Pages*: appropriate technologies have changed and I have (as the assertiveness people remind us) the perfect right to change my mind.

WHOLEFOODS

'When eating or drinking, become the taste of the food or drink, and be filled'
Paul Rep (ed.), *Zen Flesh, Zen Bones*

'Food is vital, the most basic commodity in the world,' says Colin Spencer, food correspondent to *The Guardian*, in the introduction to his book *Good and Healthy* (Robson, 1983, £6.95). 'The lack of it is used as a form of torture or of self-martyrdom, while the preparation of it is extolled as an art form. Food (or its lack) can be used as political blackmail to subjugate under-developed countries. The richer countries use food supply as a persuasive tactic to keep their favoured regimes in power in less rich countries. While millions die from diseases associated with a lack of food (and what food there is poor in quality), in the richest third of the world people die from diseases associated with too rich a diet, a surfeit of fats and sugars. Government subsidies ensure that the rich stay rich. Mountains of food are allowed to rot away under EEC food policies.' Oh, sorry. Were you about to put the kettle on? And did you mention chocolate biscuits?

What Is Food?

Most people don't give the question a second thought, the answer seems so obvious. What is food? Stuff you eat, of course — stops you being hungry, keeps you going. But we very rarely eat simply because we are hungry, and often give little thought to what sort of foods we really need. A great deal of eating is to do with habit and social pressure. Food is what you do at lunchtime; food is special offers at the supermarket.

Not convinced? Then try keeping a record for a few days of what you eat, why you think you eat it, and what you feel about it. This isn't in order to make you feel guilty or to start you worrying about the starving millions, simply to help you become aware of what you are doing in an area where the habits of decades are probably the most powerful.

At the most fundamental level, food is a basic physical need; it is nutrition for our physical bodies. There can be few people today who do not have some idea of the basic guidelines for healthier eating; these have been known about for decades, but until recently were systematically denigrated as cranky and faddish by a well-organized food lobby. The breakthrough came in 1984 when Caroline Walker and Geoffrey Cannon (*The Food Scandal* — see page 11) revealed that an important report by NACNE, the National Advisory Committee on Nutrition Education, had been suppressed by the government for three years because it said with a strong and unified voice all the things which enlightened nutritionists had been saying for years.

The massive publicity that followed explains why supermarkets have recently become very interested in additives, nutritional labelling and organic produce — they couldn't afford to ignore it. The message was strong and clear — Britons eat far too much sugar, too much salt, too much saturated fat, and far too many additives; they don't eat anything like enough fibre, fruit and vegetables. It couldn't be simpler.

The stranglehold of the food processing industry isn't just keeping millions of Britons unhealthy; it is starving hundreds of millions the world over, and impoverishing land in countries both rich and poor. The tangled web of food production isn't easy to understand and is deliberately kept tangled, but people today are far less trusting than they once were; with pioneers like Frances Moore Lappé and Susan George on the international scene and Geoffrey Cannon monitoring the national situation the industry knows that the balance of power is shifting in favour of the consumer.

Consumer Power

The food industry has done its best to mystify things, to hook us on its soothing promises and caring smiles, but we are not stupid. People ate more or less healthily for millennia before being told by food experts how and what to eat, and given accurate information and supplies of the right foodstuffs at affordable prices there is nobody who would actively choose debility in preference to health.

You only have to look at the massive steps that have already been taken by every major supermarket chain (see pages 21-23), or the explosion in the number of health food shops (pages 15-16), to see what a change has already taken place. Here are some highlights from a press release issued by Tesco as early as May 1987: 'Sales of fish have doubled in the last year; combined sales of semi-skimmed and skimmed milk have grown seven times faster than full-fat milk; over the last two years sales of wholemeal bread have virtually doubled; fresh fruit, salad and vegetables have all seen 15-20% growth in sales over the last year; longlife unsweetened fruit juice has seen an increase in volume sales of a staggering 30 per cent.'

Why did this happen? Because people started voting with their purses and are now actively choosing healthy food instead of unhealthy food. And given the awareness of what food really is and how it is produced, consumer pressure can do a great deal more. It can insist on organic produce, less wasteful packaging, alternatives to produce from countries with tyrannical regimes like South Africa and Chile.

A few closing words from *Food First* (see page 12): 'One final reminder when talking about changing our lifestyle for the better. Consuming less, wasting less, growing our own foods and living more simply are all constructive for ourselves. It is certainly worthwhile. It loosens the grip of our consumerist environment on us. But there is no magic mechanism which transfers what we have saved to those who are hungry and powerless. What they ultimately need are the effective means that will give them a voice in the global market place.'

Another biscuit?

This Food Business

By the beginning of the 1980s, 70 per cent of the British diet comprised processed foods. This food revolution has brought great change, and some benefits. The vast choice of foods on the shelves bears witness to the end of overcooked meat and two veg. That is the good news. The bad news is that this revolution in food production has brought with it concern about exactly what we are putting into our bodies.

Miracles of technology tickle our tastebuds. Synthetic colours replace those lost in processing and give the illusion of real ingredients that may not be there. Taste enhancers seduce our palates.

Many new food technologies have been introduced to suit the manufacturer or seller of food, rather than the consumer. Consider the issue of water being added to food. This is a very old form of fraud, yet it goes on today — soaking fish in polyphosphate salt solution to increase the water it holds, for example, or 'double glazing' prawns which are frozen and then rolled in more ice to pick up extra weight. Why sell food when you can sell water?

*

This Food Business is a concise introductory booklet to many of the issues now facing food manufacturers and consumers — and that includes you. Produced to accompany a Channel 4 series in late 1989, it explains the problems from pesticide residues and irradiation to labelling and the challenge of an open European market. Clear tables and diagrams give up-to-date information about the causes of diet-related illness, pesticides which are banned in other countries but still used in Britain, which supermarket chains and multinationals control the marketplace, and much more. The 'To Eat or Not To Eat' chart at the back could usefully be pinned on every kitchen wall in the land.

For just £1.75 including postage (from the Food Commission, see page 28), this is a cheap and easy way to educate yourself about the intricacies of the food business.

This Food Business
London Food Commission
New Statesman and
Society/Channel 4, 1989
£1.75

The Politics of Food

Geoffrey Cannon's Politics of Food is a real humdinger, a book that the food industry is finding it hard to ignore. He shows conclusively that the British diet is one of the unhealthiest in the Western world, with lax controls, official untruths and industry sponsored 'independent research' all doing their best to maintain food industry profits at the cost of our health. He gives a mass of evidence — more than 550 pages of it — but in a very readable and often highly amusing form, and also includes detailed lists of politicians and advisers so you can see the fine detail of the web of deceit.

*

There is general agreement among scientists around the world that in the last few generations the food supplies of Western countries such as Britain have become dangerously unbalanced. In Britain we have special problems. The national palate has been insulted by mass-manufactured 'store' food ever since the Industrial Revolution; corrupted by the confections of fats and sugars available to the middle classes since Victorian days; and then in the last generation, after the 1939-45 war, degraded as increasingly uniform, cheapened, artificial food.

Successive governments have encouraged a Euroglut of saturated fats and processed sugars, and would if anything like to see more sweet fat poured down the national gullet. The food manufacturing and retailing industries are now concentrated in the hands of fewer firms than in any other country in the developed world.

The Politics of Food
Geoffrey Cannon
Century, 1988
£5.95

The Food Scandal

When it was published in 1985, The Food Scandal blew the whistle on official suppression of information about the deleterious effects that the 'normal' British diet was having on the British public. It told how NACNE had agreed its set of sensible dietary guidelines and how the government, kow-towing to the combined pressure of the food and agriculture industries, had done its best to block a shift towards healthier eating. Caroline Walker and Geoffrey Cannon's trailblazing book then went on to explain the relative importance of each element of our diet — meat, bread, salt, sugar, vegetables and so on — and what we could do to move towards a healthier way of eating.

The Food Scandal probably did more than anything else to help bring about the dietary changes that we are now witnessing, the revolution which has brought organic wholemeal bread and additive-free foodstuffs to shops and supermarkets which until recently were convinced that 'there was no call for them'. It's a minor scandal that this important book is no longer in print, but look out for it in your library. Look out too for The Great British Diet, a practical guide to ways of implementing the NACNE diet, which was published as a companion volume to The Food Scandal and is also now out of print.

The Food Scandal
Caroline Walker and
Geoffrey Cannon
Century, 1985
out of print

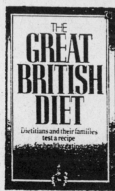

The Great
British Diet
British Dietetic
Association
Century, 1985
out of print

Healthy Eating: Facts, Figures and Fiction

When so many different people have so many points of view to sell about healthy eating, it can be hard to know who to trust. A good (and free) start is the Health Education Authority's *Guide to Healthy Eating*, produced as part of their 'Look After Your Heart' campaign—you should find this in your local health centre or library. This 32-page booklet covers the whole range of dietary concerns from fats and sugars to alcohol and additives, with pretty pictures and clear diagrams to boot.

Which? magazine has put together a well-written book called *Healthy Eating: Fact and Fiction*. In trying to take every viewpoint into account it sometimes veers towards the bland, but it is a good and readable introduction to diet and health. At the end is a questionnaire which the enthusiastic can fill in to assess their weekly energy and nutrient intake; I gave up because I can't think exactly what I do eat in an 'average week'.

Food Facts and Figures is another primer, again with a fill-it-in-yourself questionnaire (this one is slightly easier to use but tells you less in the end). The thirty pages of 'food composition tables' are clear and comprehensive, the rest of the text rather patronizing with far too many exclamation marks! On the other hand it is fairly cheap.

Healthy Eating: Fact and Fiction
edited by Anna Bradley
Hodder and Stoughton, 1989
£5.95

Food Facts and Figures
Jill Davies and John Dickerson
Faber, 1989
£3.99

Gluttons For Punishment

James Erlichman, scientific correspondent to *The Guardian*, has produced in *Gluttons For Punishment* a concise and very approachable account of the links between the food, agricultural and chemical industries. Like Geoffrey Cannon, he shows how the government is continuing to play blind and deaf to some of the worst excesses.

*

Before we start pointing fingers at too many people, we ought to look at ourselves. As consumers we too have become unwitting addicts to chemical agriculture. We have come to expect cheaper, more attractive looking food. We grumble, but on the whole we get what we pay for, thanks to the growth boosting properties of pesticides, antibiotics and hormones. In real terms fresh foods have never been cheaper or apparently more appealing. We now choose from rows of unblemished, polythene wrapped chickens at reasonable prices, stacks of lean minced beef, and lettuces so pristine in appearance that their acquaintance with insects, or even soil, seems remote.

Gluttons For Punishment
James Erlichman
Penguin, 1986
£2.95

from *Food for Beginners*, Susan George and Nigel Paige (Writers and Readers, 1982)

The Hunger Machine

The Hunger Machine was written to accompany another Channel 4 television series, 'The Politics of Food', and using specific examples from all over the world it shows very clearly that it is our policies relating to food pricing and distribution that affect patterns of starvation in the world. The inspiring conclusion, 'What We Can Do', makes it plain that it is only understanding and compassion that will ultimately change things: when 'we can take our common humanity seriously'.

Food First is a brilliant and eloquent appeal for a sane approach to the world food issue. It makes it abundantly clear that hunger and famine are not the inevitable result of lack of food in the world or climatic shifts, they are the result of greed and the myopic pursuit of profits on a global scale. Although the emphasis is on the Third World, much of what the authors have to say about land ownership, the productivity of small farms, the tyranny of the petrochemical giants and national and international price fixing will ring many a bell for the small farmer in Britain. Since its publication in 1980 *Food First* has become a widely quoted source for new and positive thinking about ways of breaking the mould of greed and famine, and the practical suggestions at the back of the book show what you can do to play your part.

The Hunger Machine: The Politics of Food
Jon Bennett and Susan George
Polity, 1987
£5.95

Food First
Frances Moore Lappé and Joseph Collins
Abacus, 1982
£3.50

Holistic Cookery

On now to the practicalities of wholefood cooking, and what Janet Hunt's *The Holistic Cook* has going for it is a very clear and concise eighty-page wholefood glossary which tells you exactly where each ingredient comes from, its nutritional importance, and how to store and use it. It covers every ingredient you are likely to come across, from buttermilk and ghee to aduki and borlotti beans — including all the alternative names like okra/ladies' fingers/bamia/bindi/gumbo. *The Holistic Cook* isn't really a recipe book, though it does have a useful smattering of basic recipes, which as anyone who feels at home with cooking knows is all you need to start experimenting. The glossary is sandwiched between chapters about nutrition, the worldwide tradition of wholefood cooking, kitchen planning, basic physiology, and food additives and pollutants.

YOGURT

What it is: A thick creamy substance usually made from cows' milk, either full fat or skimmed. It is one of the finest natural foods, but is often sold with artificial colourings, flavourings and preservatives. Nowadays yogurt made with goats' and ewes' milk is also becoming more popular, the advantage being that the milk is produced on a small scale and less likely to be contaminated with antibiotics and hormones. Yogurt can also be made with soya milk.

Origins: Yogurt is thought to have been used first by the nomads of eastern Europe at least a thousand years ago. Other names for yogurt include tako, laben raid, zabady and kefir, and the taste and texture of these traditional yogurts can vary considerably.

Principal nutrients: Yogurt is high in protein, and low-fat varieties are widely available. Some nutritionists believe that the bacteria and enzymes in yogurt help to maintain a healthy intestinal environment. The main thing to remember is that yogurt is as good as the milk it is made from, especially where the fat content is concerned. There is no difference in nutritional terms between live and pasteurized yogurt, though you may prefer your yogurt to be bacteriologically alive rather than sterile.

Buying and storing: Yogurt is sold just about everywhere these days, though live unflavoured varieties are usually only available from health food and wholefood outlets. Those sold in supermarkets may still be live—it depends whether they have been pasteurized after bacterial action or not. Never buy flavoured yogurts. You can always flavour plain yogurt using natural ingredients of your choice.

The Holistic Cook
Janet Hunt
Thorsons, 1986
£7.95

On Food and Cooking

On Food and Cooking is a thick and encyclopedic book in which in which anyone really interested in food will always find something new. Not only does Harold McGee describe each ingredient in detail, he explains why cooking works the way it does — why mayonnaise sticks together as an emulsion, why dough expands, even why the surface tension on a glass of strong wine creates moving 'tears' of liquid on the inside of the glass. One thing I particularly like is that he says when he doesn't know something — like why adding oil should help bread to rise in the oven. *On Food and Cooking* is not vegetarian, is not a crusade against additives and pesticide residues, and includes alcoholic drinks and confectionery, yet as mainstream food writers go he is remarkably honest where the benefits of good diet are concerned. Harold McGee also writes very well, which makes the book a pleasure to read.

*

The point of most egg cookery is to bond a liquid, whether the egg itself or a mixture of egg and other liquids, into a moist, delicate solid. This means avoiding such extensive coagulation that the proteins squeeze out the liquid they are supposed to retain. Either a rubbery texture or curdling — solid lumps floating in the wrung out liquid — is the unhappy result of overcooking egg dishes. To understand this, we must descend once more to the molecular level. Water is held both within and around the coiled proteins by relatively weak hydrogen bonds, which are easily broken as the energy of both water and protein molecules increases. Only the stronger ionic and covalent bridges between proteins last for any amount of time as the solution is heated. Heat, then, automatically favors protein-protein bonds over protein-water bonds.

On Food and Cooking: The Science and Lore of the Kitchen
Harold McGee
Unwin Hyman, 1988
£12.95

Eating Cheaply

Bernadine Lawrence lives with her husband and four children in a Chelsea council flat; like five million other households in Britain today their main source of income is the weekly benefit order. Several studies have shown that cheap food tends to be unhealthy food, with white bread, jam and fatty meat costing a lot less than wholemeal bread, fresh fruit and lean meat. Bernadine, however, concerned about the nutrition of her own family and others like them, sets out to show that with a bit of foresight and effort eating cheaply does not necessarily mean eating badly. *How To Feed Your Family For £4 A Day* is a very practical book, full of tips and recipes which, if everybody took note of them, would ease both our health and environmental prob lems considerably. Nor does Bernadine Lawrence overlook the political consequences of the advice she gives: she recognises the contradictions inherent in providing poor people with information about how to live better on less.

*

It was only upon reading a most upsetting feature about the problem of malnourishment, not in any Third World country but here in our own back yard, that I felt compelled to do something on a larger scale. I wrote to the director of a major anti-poverty pressure-group. What I suggested was that they publish either a diet card or a sheet upon which there would be seven of my recipes for main meals: something different for each day of the week, and a smaller number of recipes for breakfasts and lunches, with all ingredients costed and all attainable within £28 per week. The response of the group's director was to point out that were such information put out by themselves, certain politicians would seize upon it to use as hard evidence that benefit levels were abundant, a truly paradoxical catch-22 situation.

How To Feed Your Family For £4 A Day
Bernadine Lawrence
Thorsons, 1989
£3.50

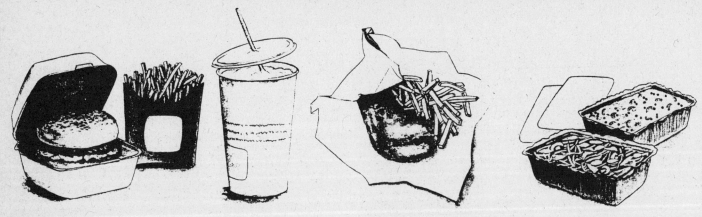

Fast Food

The major fast food chains in Britain, like their American counter-parts, are now working very hard to green-tint their inherently ungreen act. Wimpy have come up with a Wimpy Food File about 'healthy eating', which proves rather conclusively that Wimpy's version of it is highly suspect — even the sesame buns have four different additives in them, including the suspect flavour enhancer bromate. At least we now know what goes into their products, so thank you Wimpy.

Not to be outdone, McDonalds have also produced a thirty-page booklet called The Facts, together with a series of McFact Cards, available in all their outlets. The three cards explain that 'only lean forequarter and flank' are used in their hamburgers (where does the rest of the cow go?), that they've stopped using CFCs in packaging (now how about the volume of packaging?), and that they don't use beef that threatens rainforests (no, but someone does, and who hooked us onto beefburgers in the first place?). The Facts also shows conclusively that vegetarians needn't bother with McD's: even the hash browns are fried in beef and vegetable shortening.

Environment Now, October 1989

As Britain has become ever more Americanized fast food has become part of most people's way of life. Between us we now eat more than seven billion 'fast meals' every year, but do we stop to think what we are doing to ourselves and to our envir-onment when we buy over-processed over-packaged 'con-venience foods'? It isn't that all fast food is bad food — a cheese and tomato pizza, for example, is a pretty balanced meal — but it will almost certainly be wrapped up in layers of unrecycled and unrecyclable packaging, and will be very expensive for what you get. With little help from the fast food chains themselves, Tim Lobstein has brought together a mass of fascinating information in *Fast Food Facts*: he explains what fast foods have in them and what they don't, what nutritional needs they do and don't fulfil, and how fast foods contribute to ill health, litter, low-paid work and political inertia. Everything is substantiated in a mass of easy-to-read tables, and at the end are diagrams showing nutritional information and addi-tives for more than 300 of our favourite fast foods.

Fast Food Facts
Tim Lobstein
Camden Press, 1988
£4.95

Real Food Directories

Over the last thirty years, what we eat has changed dramatically. We have been encouraged to buy a whole new generation of foods. Most food manufacturers have been concerned with uniformity and mass availability, with levelling out variety and choice. It is the Coca-Cola principle — devise a miracle product that nearly everyone in the world will drink. Foods have been promoted on the basis of cosmetic appearance, yield, and ease of picking rather than flavour. Whether it is a pint of beer, a loaf of bread or a piece of cheese, the principle has been that it should taste the same in Bradford as it does in Truro. In the same way that environmentalists have bemoaned the loss of hedge-rows and the habitats for wild animals so, and in many ways far more relevantly, is there cause to bemoan the bulldozing of the small craft food industry, to be replaced by the factory with its barrels of additives.

*

So wrote Drew Smith and David Mabey in the last edition to be published — in 1986 — of *The Good Food Directory*. In the last few years, with wholefood shops and restaurants opening in most towns and more growers and food producers becom-ing aware of environmental and health issues, it has become steadily easier in Britain to buy foods which are wholesome, relatively unadulterated, relatively unprocessed, and relatively lightly packaged.

Now that everybody is getting in on the healthy eating scene there is no longer a single reference source that you can use to find out where to buy wholefoods. In some ways this is good news, since it reflects the fact that compared with even five years ago the number of shops selling wholefoods has in-creased enormously. Today there is hardly a corner shop, let alone a supermarket, that doesn't sell wholewheat bread and pasta, and at least some packaged 'health food' lines.

The bad news is that it isn't easy to find out which are the best places to find a good range of real wholefoods. If you live in one of the places covered by a recently-published 'green directory' (see pages 341-343), it will almost certainly include up-to-date information on wholefood shops and restaurants; otherwise *Thorsons Organic Consumer Guide* (page 31) is the best nationwide guide, insofar as if a shop or supermarket goes to the lengths of stocking organic produce the chances are that it will be serious about wholefoods in general.

Wholefoods

Such has been the confusion between health foods and wholefoods that many people now make a clear distinction between the two. While all wholefoods are healthy foods, certainly not all health foods are wholefoods. Though their manufacturers may well make an effort to keep your health in mind, 'health foods' are often over-packaged, expensive and supplement-ridden; this is why many people still say that they can't afford to eat healthy food — they are thinking of the rows of packaged products in the health food shop with names like Healthilife and Nutrinut.

Wholefoods are very different. Wholefoods are whole, unadulterated, unrefined staple foods. They include wholegrains, pulses, nuts, fruits and vegetables as they come off the plants, wet fish, humanely reared meat, free range eggs. As you start refining, separating out, adding and packaging, the less whole such 'wholefoods' become, even though they may still be healthier than most processed foods.

You can live on wholefoods. They are not boring, they are not tasteless, and when the complete food budget is taken into account, they are no more expensive than an average diet (see Bernadine Lawrence's book on page 13 if you need proof).

What To Buy

A good wholefood shop will stock far more different products than you'll ever need and, interesting though they may be, you don't need to keep sixteen sorts of bean and eleven sorts of flour on your shelves. In the end you'll simply feel guilty about not using them more often, and when you find maggots in the buckwheat flour you may have second thoughts about these preservative-free wholefoods.

You probably know already what you like in the way of wholefoods; if so, ignore the next section. These are my suggestions for a basic wholefood larder, from which, with the addition of fresh fruit and veg (plus eggs, cheese, fish and a little meat if you eat it), you will always be able to concoct an appetizing meal.

Grains and Flours

▶ 100% wholemeal flour (organic stoneground if possible)
▶ Brown rice
▶ Millet (convenient since it is very fast to prepare)
▶ Barley (for soups)
▶ Rolled oats (for crumbles, buns, etc.)

Pastas

▶ Wholewheat spaghetti
▶ Wholewheat lasagne/pasta shapes

Beans and Pulses

▶ Lentils
▶ Split peas (very cheap)
▶ Kidney beans (especially for chilli dishes)
▶ Haricot beans (for baked beans)

Nuts and Dried Fruits

▶ Peanuts (the cheapest of the nuts)
▶ Sultanas
▶ Raisins

Oils

▶ Pure vegetable oil (soya is cheapest; sunflower not much more; a small amount of olive wonderful for some dishes)
▶ Vegetable margarine (see page 39)

Other Things

▶ Honey (cheaper if bought 7lb at a time; buy named-origin honey if you are concerned about countries of origin)
▶ Peanut butter (again cheaper in bulk — 2kg at a time)
▶ Tamari/shoyu (real soya sauce)

A 'starter pack' of these twenty basic ingredients will cost less than £20, and even if you haven't yet ventured into wholefoods you will almost certainly have many of them in your kitchen already.

As for quantities, there are definite pros and just as definite cons to buying in bulk. If you live miles from the nearest shop and can be cut off for days in the winter, buying in bulk means that you can survive quite comfortably for several weeks. Careful storage should ensure that your bulk-bought foods stay fresh and bug-free. On the other hand, nearly all foods will deteriorate over time even if they are well-stored, and bulk buying means finding relatively large sums of money each time you do it.

If you live a long way from your nearest wholefood shop (and even if you don't) you will probably find that somebody in your area has organized a bulk food-buying co-operative. Buying food in this way makes your food bill as much as 30% cheaper for the things you bulk buy, though you mustn't at the same time grumble that all the small wholefood shops are going out of business — you can't have it both ways. See page 19 for more about food-buying co-operatives.

Wholefood Shops

Even ten years ago real wholefood shops were very thin on the ground, and sent orders halfway across the country to lone outposts of the diet revolution. Now every population centre of any size has its wholefood shop, from Scoop in Lerwick to Jenny's Wholefoods in Penzance, selling a range of grains, flours, mueslis, beans and pulses out of hessian and paper sacks, herbs from a line of hand-painted sweetie jars, and a rack of books about health and diet. Some also sell organic vegetables and fruit, free range eggs, and wholegrain bread and bakes.

It's impossible to tell how many wholefood shops there are, partly because new ones open every week, partly because it's hard to tell where a wholefood shop shades into a health food store, and with more and more supermarkets and delicatessens starting to sell wholefood lines (you can even get a range of wholefood snacks at stations, garages and airports), the wholefood business is becoming veritably mainstream.

As the supermarkets take over an increasing amount of the trade, however, you are in danger of losing your friendly local wholefood shop. It's not that the prices don't compare well; they usually do. It's usually because it appears to be easier to buy your wholefoods at the supermarket while you're doing the rest of the shopping. Do try to resist this temptation. Small independent wholefood shops have worked hard on your behalf, so don't forget them as everybody cashes in on the trend.

If by 'wholefood shop' is meant an independent business that sells a complete range of wholefoods and doesn't sell an inordinate amount of prepackaged health foods, there are probably around 1,800 in Britain. Here are descriptions of one or two to give you an idea of what is available.

Harvest Natural Foods, Bath

37 Walcot Street, Bath (0225 465519)
Eighteen years ago a few friends took over a small vegetable shop in Bath and started selling a range of wholefoods from it. Now Harvest is a twenty-strong workers' co-operative (officially called the Bath Wholefood Co-operative), running a thriving business, and using their three lorries to supply shops as far as 75 miles away with a full range of healthy foods (see page 19). Harvest is generally considered to be a model wholefood shop, and anyone setting up in the business would be well advised to see it in action. The prices — especially when you buy in bulk — are very reasonable, the staff friendly and helpful. Fresh fruit and vegetables, tofu (soya bean curd), herbs, bread, a reading corner, and a large playpen with a range of toys complete the services offered.

Scoop Wholefoods, Lerwick

Scoop Wholefoods, Old Infant School, King Harald Street, Lerwick, Shetland (059 571 392/059 584 428)
At the other end of the scale, but no less a model for a small wholefood co-operative, is Scoop (Shetland Co-op), Britain's northernmost wholefood shop. Here Vicki Coleman and Mariane Tarrant sell the usual range of wholefoods, plus organic vegetables when available, herbs and spices, biodegradable washing products, and natural cosmetics; but Scoop is much more as well. In such a widely-flung community as Shetland, those who have to make a whole day of coming into Lerwick to shop use Scoop as a meeting place to discuss (as their bulk order is prepared) everything from nuclear power and the oil industry to playgroups and breastfeeding. A notice board keeps customers aware of the latest in the Dounreay waste-dumping plans, local activities, and a range of topics from animal liberation to CND. A friendly, dependable, and very important service to a lively rural community.

Wholefood

Wholefood has a special mention because it is one of the old originals, now thirty years old; because it does so much more than just sell wholefoods; and because they take their job seriously. It was started in 1960 by members of the Soil Association (see page 66) in premises in Baker Street, and when the rent got too much they moved round the corner (though some people still refer to Wholefood of Baker Street). The emphasis is on natural organically grown food, and the shop stocks a wide variety of organic fruit and vegetables (though they will stretch the point with crops like citrus fruits where 100% organic is almost impossible to obtain — then they go for guaranteed sun-ripened and unwaxed fruit). The bakery range is still growing (all from organic grains), and the bookshop carries an excellent range of titles on nutrition and health (mail order too — send for a booklist). The staff at Wholefood are very helpful, and though you are inevitably paying London and organic premiums, basic foods are not expensive.

Wholefood

24 Paddington Street
London
W1M 4DR
0(7)1-935 3924

Natural Food Trader

Natural Food Trader is the trade magazine of the still-rapidly-expanding wholefood and health food market. Published by the prolific Argus Health Group (which also publishes *Here's Health* — page 142), it's a twenty-page newspaper-format monthly with information about new products and suppliers, book reviews, news stories within the trade and some interesting product comparisons. The December 1989 issue, for instance, carried the story of the resignation of the chairwoman of Regina, the controversial royal jelly company, and a profile of the newly-refurbished Wild Oats wholefood shop in West London. *Natural Food Trader* is fairly essential if you're in the trade (which is why it is circulated free to retailers), but is also interesting inside information for anyone interested in the natural food marketplace: a subscription for non-retailers costs £18.50. Argus also publishes an annual *Health Food Buyers Guide* each December, subtitled 'The A to Z of UK Products, Manufacturers and Wholesalers' and telling you exactly who makes and distributes what. The 1990 edition costs £4.

Argus Health Publications Ltd

Victory House
14 Leicester Place
London
WC2H 7NB
0(7)1-437 9011

Food Preparation and Cooking

This section on food preparation basics is intended to help demystify the 'holistic approach' to food and eating. Preparing food can be both simple and satisfying, and very often new ways of cooking don't so much involve learning as deliberately forgetting. There is a skill to cookery just as there is to doing anything well and efficiently, and great pleasure to be had from a special dish lovingly prepared and beautifully presented, but many cookery techniques are largely the inventions of the manufacturers of foodstuffs and appliances, designed to encourage you to use more of their products and spend more of your time in the kitchen.

I have deliberately put kitchen equipment on a page of its own (page 104) in the 'Home' section, sandwiched between ionizers and filters on one hand and furniture on the other, and you will find things like washing-up liquid at the end of the recycling section on page 114

Do You Need to Buy Food?

Everybody has to buy food, but do you actually need to *buy* all of it? There are at least three ways of obtaining some of your food without having to spend hard-earned cash.

The first way is to grow it. If you have garden space and a little time, growing a few salad crops and herbs will almost certainly save you money; if you have more time or can share the work with friends it may well be worth thinking on a slightly larger scale and looking at working an allotment (see the gardening section on pages 75-84 for more ideas). But you don't even need a garden in order to grow a little of your own food.

You can grow herbs on a windowsill — they will provide greenery and a pleasant non-chemical aroma as well as being handy when it comes to chopping some fresh herbs for a salad or a stew. Just as easy is the sprouting of seeds and beans in a jam jar or plastic container: for a beautiful photographic essay on sprout growing (and the basic instructions too) see *The Findhorn Family Cook Book* by Kay Lynne Sherman (Findhorn Press, 1981, £3.50). All you do is soak the seeds (mung beans, alfalfa, aduki beans, fenugreek seeds, lentils, wheat: almost any natural wholegrain will sprout) overnight, then leave them in covered jars in indirect light, rinsing them twice a day until they're ready. This way you can have salads and beansprout stir-fries year-round from your own kitchen-grown bean sprouts.

The second way is to barter it.

Many allotment and garden growers have excess produce in season, and may well be open to giving you some in exchange for babysitting, mending their car or whatever. You won't know until you ask.

The third way is to find food in the wild. This is tricky if you live in a city (though chickweed and lambs lettuce grow wild in many urban gardens), but even if you only go into the countryside now and again you will find a wealth of edible plants growing there. As Richard Mabey says in *Food for Free* (Collins, 1989, £6.95 — the essential book if you want to explore this possibility): 'Every single one of the world's vegetable foods was once a wild plant.'

Another extremely useful reference source to both wild and cultivated crops which you will find in Britain is G.M. de Rougemont's *A Field Guide to the Crops of Britain and Europe* (Collins, 1989, £14.95); it includes full details of where each can be found and what it can be used for, and a colour illustration of each main species. Resistance to wild foods is amazing; when I offer some people chantarelles from my local beechwood they turn their noses up and say 'How do you know where it's been?'. What do you say?

Do You Need to Cook It?

Some things you have to cook, of course: gnawing your way through a large bag of rice may take some time. But fruit and vegetables almost never *have* to be cooked. With few exceptions, cooking always leaches nutrients from fruit and vegetables as well as using more energy (electricity or gas) in the preparation. The Inuit of North America, among other tribal peoples, still eat a great deal of their meat raw, which is thought to contribute to their high level of health. Eating more food raw keeps your teeth in good trim, though it takes more time to eat because you have to chew it for longer. On the other hand, eating more raw food helps to ensure that you don't eat more than you need.

A good policy is to have something raw with every meal — carrot sticks, salad, an apple at the end. This gives you essential nutrients, roughage, and something for your teeth to work on.

Some Guidelines for Holistic Cookery

First, some basic considerations:
▶ Waste as little as possible.
▶ Use as much fresh food as possible, preferably locally grown.
▶ Use as little packaged food as possible, especially food packaged in materials that are difficult to recycle.
▶ Use leftovers in preference to new ingredients.
▶ Use what you have in the kitchen before going out to buy more.
▶ Use as few utensils as possible — this saves on your energy and the energy used to heat the washing up water, and it probably means you need less equipment in your kitchen.

Having dealt with the basics, here are some more detailed thoughts:

Plan Ahead

Healthy wholefood cookery doesn't take very much time, but there are some things you do need to think about in advance. Beans, pulses and wholegrains take a while to cook, but once cooked, will keep for a few days. I usually make more than I need of these ingredients, then have them in the fridge to add to stews and stir-fries as needed. Most beans and pulses need to soak for a while before cooking; putting them to soak takes hardly any time, but you do need to remember to do it. Any good cook book will give you soaking and cooking times.

Preparing Vegetables and Fruit

Never peel fruit or vegetables unless you have to — many of the nutrients lie just under the surface. Do give them a good scrub, however, especially if they are not organic, since the chemical sprays and waxes used on them while they are growing will almost certainly still remain.

Cooking Vegetables

The general guideline is: cook them as little and as quickly as possible. Where did I read about a trainee cook whose first job every morning at nine was to put the lunchtime cabbage on to boil? No wonder British cooking had a bad name.

Steam leaf and other green vegetables (including broccoli, cauliflower, peas and beans) in preference to boiling them. A folding steamer is useful, or you can simply steam them in an ordinary saucepan with a little margarine or oil and about half an inch of water, brought to the boil with the lid firmly on, then simmered for ten to fifteen minutes (less for spinach and peas).

Another quick way to cook things and retain both nutrients and flavour is stir-frying. You don't need a wok, though it helps. All the ingredients are cut fairly small, then cooked in a small amount of oil and soya sauce over a hot heat. Stir-frying works for all vegetables — even potatoes and other roots — and you can add little bits of meat and fish as you want.

Basic Soups

Soups are an ideal way of using leftovers. All you do is cook everything in sufficient liquid until it's all tender. A little tomato purée, soya sauce or a stock cube will add flavour if it needs it.

Basic Sauces

A good stir-fry will always produce its own delicious sauce. For a basic sauce for things like cauliflower cheese or leeks in mushroom sauce, heat a little margarine in a saucepan, add a little flour to the melted marge and stir it well to form a 'roux' (paste); remove it from the heat, then add liquid (the vegetable water is excellent), stirring all the time until your sauce is the thickness you want it. Add things like cheese, herbs or chopped mushrooms near the end, and make sure it doesn't stick. There is obviously a great deal more than this that you could learn about cookery, but these basics alone would provide you with a varied and tasty diet.

Eating Out

While packet meals neatly turned under the microwave dominate the fast-food end of the market, many restaurants in Britain now recognise that good wholefood cookery is what many people want, and go to some lengths to provide it.

There are all sorts of new and interesting places to eat out, and most large towns have a vegetarian restaurant for the growing number of people who are choosing not to eat meat. Even though you risk life and limb getting in and out of Food for Thought in London's Neal Street during busy times, the food is always excellent; the same applies to Henderson's in Hanover Street, Edinburgh. Huckleberry's in Bath knows how to lay on a stylish dinner with an imaginative choice of international dishes, while Rainbow's End in Glastonbury produces some wonderfully gooey puddings.

To whet your appetite, here are a couple of entries from the guides mentioned elsewhere in *New Green Pages*:

Good Taste

44 Market Street, Llangollen, Clwyd
'This vegetarian tea room is a real find. It is small but spotlessly clean, and serves only home-made food. Although it is described as a tea room, Good Taste has plenty more than simply afternoon tea on offer. There are starters of mushroom paté or egg mayonnaise. The main courses include vegetable cobbler, mushroom vol-au-vents with jacket potato, savoury pancake or quiche. For more of a snack, there are filled or open sandwiches, jacket potatoes, scones, and buttered toast with a choice of breads. Traditional-style sweets include apple or lemon meringue pie, pear belle hélène and ice cream.'
Sarah Brown, *Best of Vegetarian Britain*

The Falafel House

95 Haverstock Hill, London NW3
'The surroundings are simple and the atmosphere casual at this popular little restaurant. The friendly staff are prepared to find out exactly what is vegetarian on the menu, which turns out to be an excellent choice of side dishes that easily make up a substantial meal. All the classic Middle Eastern offerings are available, such as falafel, hummus, aubergine dip and pitta. There are also some main-course dishes such as guvetch (a ratatouille type of stew) or savoury rice and beans. It's quite cheap and a good place to go with a party. They also do take-aways.'
Sarah Brown, *Vegetarian London*

There are several nationwide guides to good wholefood eating places. The ones I trust the most are Sarah Brown's *Best of Vegetarian Britain* and *Vegetarian London* (see page 46), which include a number of omnivorous restaurants that also specialise in vegetarian cuisine. The other vegetarian guides on page 46 are also useful, though just because somewhere is vegetarian it does not necessarily guarantee quality and value for money. Other guides worth consulting are the *Which? Good Food Guide* (Hodder and Stoughton, 1989, £11.95) and the *Which? Good Pub Guide* (Hodder and Stoughton, 1989, £10.95); neither is a 'real food' guide by any means, but do contain a lot of information about establishments which provide reasonably good food at fairly reasonable prices.

Wholefood Wholesalers

As with any other product, food does not — with rare exceptions — arrive in the shop directly from the place where it was grown or prepared. For every two people employed in food retailing, another is employed in wholesaling and distribution, and these functions are just as vital to the wholefood industry as they are to its bigger siblings, the giant food chains.

In the early years of wholefood shops, finding regular suppliers of things they could be proud of selling was a headache, so the arrival of the first wholefood wholesale co-operatives, Arjuna in Cambridge in 1976 and Suma in Yorkshire in 1977, was most welcome. There are now more than ten such operations in Britain, and because they are such an important part of the wholesome 'food chain' in Britain (and because you might well find cause to contact them), full details are given below, together with an expanded portrait of the one I know best, Green City in Glasgow.

The range of products carried by each of the wholesalers is pretty much the same, though some carry lines not carried by others. They all work closely together, for several reasons which are worth explaining. They believe in co-operation rather than competition, which in practice means collective buying when appropriate, mutual advice and support, and a general agreement not to work in ways that would prejudice each other. Thus they agree to cover different parts of the country, and work together to support initiatives such as Third World producer groups, or even to raise joint capital where necessary.

The Federation of Wholefood Wholesalers is probably further down the path of aware commerce than any other business network in Britain, and with more than a dozen year's experience has a great deal to teach any other group wanting to explore different ways of working together. The problem is that they are always so busy keeping everything going that they won't have much time to tell you about it!

Wholefood Co-operatives

When wholefood shops were thinner on the ground, many people (following American precedents) got together in groups to buy good food in bulk and distribute it amongst the members, thus ensuring high quality at the lowest possible prices. Food co-ops have always come and gone with almost alarming regularity, since they are nearly always run voluntarily, and few people have the staying power to support a co-op as it needs to be supported to be efficient and effective.

As the number of wholefood shops has grown, several of the wholesalers have stopped trading with food co-ops altogether, arguing that it is more important for them to encourage shops in their area, that consumer co-operatives undermine such businesses, and that if consumers do want to buy in bulk they should make the necessary approaches to their local wholefood shop.

In rural areas, however, the wholesalers who cover such areas will in general encourage and help consumer food co-operatives where there is no local wholefood shop, and where it is a genuine co-operative group open to new members (not just a family or a few friends).

If you want to check out the possibility of joining such a group, the best thing to do is to ask your nearest wholefood wholesaler: they will be able to tell you if there already is one. If there isn't, then and only then think about starting your own.

Most of the wholesalers will give advice about setting up a food co-op in appropriate circumstances, and they will also tell you their trading guidelines. Those currently operated by Green City, for instance, mean that you must buy at least £75 worth at a time (£150 if you don't want a small order surcharge), you must pay on delivery, and you must pay with a single cheque drawn on a co-op account. If you do become part of the organization of a food co-op you will find that it involves a lot of work, taking the orders, making sure they get distributed, sorting out the money: don't take it on lightly!

The Wholesalers

Arjuna, Cambridge

Arjuna Wholefoods Ltd, Unit 7, Dales Brewery, Gwydir Street, Cambridge CB1 2LJ (0223 313861)

Arjuna started in 1973 as a macrobiotic shop and restaurant, turning into a co-op and starting the wholesale side in 1976. Arjuna's shop at 12 Mill Road (0223 64845) is still central to life in alternative Cambridge, and the warehouse processes bulk orders which can be collected (at 24 hours notice) or delivered.

Bramble, Braintree

Bramble Wholefoods Ltd, Unit 1, The Mazes, East Street, Braintree, Essex CM7 6JJ (0376 42337)

A nineteen-strong co-operative formed in 1978 to warehouse and deliver wholefoods in the northern home counties and East Anglia. Not keen on supplying bulk buyers as they want to support local wholefood shops.

Green City

Green City Wholefoods, 23 Fleming Street, Glasgow G31 1PH (041 554 7633/4)

(see description on the next page)

Harvest, Bath

Bath Wholefood Co-operative Ltd (trading as Harvest Natural Foods), Unit 2a, Riverside Business Park, Bath, Avon BA2 3DW (0225 336474)

The wholesale arm of the shop described on page 15.

Highland Wholefoods, Inverness

Highland Wholefoods, Unit 6b, 13 Harbour Road, Longman Estate, Inverness IV1 1SY (0463 712393)

A recently formed workers co-operative, stocking 1,200 lines including many organic products. They operate a cash-and-carry and a distribution service, and will gladly supply wholefood co-operatives.

Infinity, Brighton

Infinity Foods Co-op Ltd, 67b Norway Street, Portslade, Brighton, East Sussex BN4 1AE (0273 424060)
A workers' co-operative, Infinity started as a small shop, expanding in 1979 into a wholesaling operation. It now employs twenty people and has expanded into producing some of its own lines, including 100% natural jams.

Leicester Wholefood Co-op

Leicester Wholefood Co-operative Ltd, Unit 3, Freehold Street, off Dysart Way, Leicester LE1 2LX (0533 512525)
A new co-operative, founded in 1989 to distribute wholefoods throughout the Midlands. The co-op specializes in organic groceries (they supply Ryton Gardens — see page 78 — for example), and their 'supermarket' is open to the public. They are also happy to organize a wholefood stall at local events.

Nova, Bristol

Nova Wholefoods Co-operative Ltd, Unit 3, Lodge Causeway Trading Estate, Fishponds, Bristol BS16 3JB (0272 583550)
Nova started life in 1981 as the reincarnation of a private wholesaling business, since when it has increased its turnover four-fold and now employs twenty people, which makes Nova one of the biggest wholesalers in the country, delivering as far afield as South Wales, the Midlands, Oxford and Cornwall. In 1983 they expanded to provide 'cash and carry' facilities, and are starting to supply schools and hospitals with healthy food. They encourage food co-ops where there is no shop.

Suma, Halifax

Unit 1, Dean Clough Industrial Park, Halifax, West Yorkshire HX3 5AN (0422 345513)
Alongside Green City and Nova, Suma are the big league of the wholefood trade, as well as being one of the first off the ground way back in 1974. It became a co-op in 1977 and has moved twice to larger premises, taking over its present warehouse in 1986. Suma employs thirty people, and its six-truck fleet carries Suma produce all over England and Wales, from the Scottish border to Northamptonshire. They produce a range of their own-brand products, including the popular Suma margarine. Suma also co-publish *The Wholefood Express*, a book of quick healthy recipes (see page 48).

Wholesome Trucking, London

Wholesome Trucking, Unit 9, Higgs Industrial Estate, 2 Herne Hill Road, London SE24 0AU (0(7)1-733 2614/737 2658)
Wholesome Trucking fulfils an important role in distributing wholefoods in London and the home counties, and as far west as Birmingham. Employing eight people, it is the smallest of the main wholesalers, but no less efficient for that.

Green City

GREENCITY wholefoods

The Scottish Wholefoods Collective Warehouse was born out of the needs of co-op retailers for a locally based, reliable distribution service, and was founded in 1978. Our name, Green City Wholefoods, is derived from our home city — the name Glasgow originally meant 'the dear green place'. From our current premises in the east end of the city we aim to promote the healthier aspects of life in Scotland.
A Green City Leaflet

Now employing 27 full-time workers and with a turnover of £2.7 million in 1989, Green City has transformed the wholefood scene in Scotland, and there can be few co-operative organizations as innovative as they are. Their catalogue is a learned volume in itself. They have started producing their own range of organic produce and their own label — 'Now' — in collaboration with other Scottish wholefood businesses. They encourage direct trade with Third World producer groups, working with Equal Exchange (see below) to distribute Central American honey, Mozambiquan cashew-nut butter and Nicaraguan peanut butter. In line with their desire not to become one mega-co-op, Green City has recently started another co-operative — Green City Earthcare — which will run parallel with GCW to become a major supplier of recycled paper products and other non-food items.

After a large exodus of staff in 1988 they took a long hard look at the needs of the people in the business, and now have training sessions, a new management structure of work teams, and an elected small management team to co-ordinate and speed up decision making. Green City plays a major role both in the Federation of Wholefood Co-operatives and in ICOM (see page 275), and together with Nova Wholefoods in Bristol they are currently working out a set of ICOM model rules designed specifically for consumer co-operatives. Green City will happily supply food co-operatives where there is no shop nearby, and have advice sheets on how to start one.

Equal Exchange

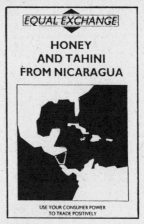

What a long way the wholefood and 'alternative' food movement has come since the late 60s. The ideals of those early years are now being realized as the wholefood wholesalers become ever more firmly established and consumer pressure grows for more just and sustainable sources of wholefoods. Edinburgh-based Campaign Coffee (see page 41) is one very active group that has succeeded and diversified so well that they have recently decided to split into two organizations, a trading arm called Equal Exchange Trading and a campaigning and educational arm (registered as a charity) called Equal Exchange Ltd.

Equal Exchange Trading is a workers' co-operative dedicated to the promotion of coffees, teas and foodstuffs from collective organizations of democratic countries in the Third World. They pay above world market prices, guarantee that the proceeds do actually reach the producers, and use the packaging on the products to inform consumers about political and social conditions in the country of origin. They have honey from women's groups in Mexico; olive oil from Palestine; peanut butter, tahini and instant coffee from Nicaragua; and from the frontline African states there is dark tahini, cashew-nut butter and coffee. Equal Exchange Ltd will continue to produce their informative newsletter *Coffee Times*. You can help to support their work by becoming a member of Equal Exchange Ltd for £5 a year; you can buy Equal Exchange products from all good wholefood shops.

Equal Exchange Trading/Equal Exchange Ltd
29 Nicolson Street
Edinburgh
EH8 9BX
031 667 0905

Supermarket Chains

At the other end of the spectrum of food distribution and retailing from the wholefood wholesalers are the supermarket chains. Nova (see page 20), one of the largest wholefood wholesalers, has a turnover of about £2.5m a year; in 1989 Marks and Spencer's had a turnover of £5.1 billion, with profits in excess of £540 million. This may help you to understand why the supermarkets have such buying and selling power in the marketplace.

The power in buying and selling works both ways, however. It is reckoned that the real profitability in a particular product is in the last ten per cent of sales; that is, if ten per cent of the customers for a product change their minds, or demand a change in the nature of that product, then the supplier will think very hard about changing or withdrawing it.

'People need to be told of the need to change their regular eating habits,' said Tesco's Managing Director at a recent press conference, but the truth is that it is we, the consumers, who are telling the food industry what we want. This, together with some very necessary investigative journalism (see the books reviewed on pages 11-14), is what has 'encouraged' the supermarket chains to change their selling policies. To be fair to many of them, as they have seen sales of more healthy food rocketing they have produced literature which explains to us how we can eat more healthily, but nothing changes selling policy like consumer pressure.

Whatever the reasons, things are much better than they were: you can truly buy a healthy and balanced range of ingredients from most supermarkets today, an impossibility only five years ago.

Yet there are some basic considerations to bear in mind when you choose whether to buy your healthy food at the supermarket or at the wholefood shop. The main one is economic: does it make any difference to you whether you put your money into a multinational food company creating large profits for its shareholders, or into an independent co-operative venture exploring different ways of dividing the world's resources?

What follows is an assessment of each of the seven largest supermarket chains in Britain, based on information received from their press offices in December 1989. Things are changing all the time, but this will give you some idea of the relative virtues of each of them, and some basis for making your consumer decisions.

Co-op

Co-operative Wholesale Society Ltd, PO Box 53, New Century House, Manchester M60 4ES (061 834 1212). The Co-op, unlike the other supermarket chains which are centrally owned and organized, is actually a collection of autonomous shops which they describe as consumer (as opposed to worker) co-operatives. This means that although many promotions, including their current green campaign, are centrally organized, policies can vary from store to store. This is a pity, since otherwise they would score an unqualified plus for being, for example, the only supermarket not to stock South African produce, a policy which the central Co-op wholesalers have had for many years. That proviso apart, the Co-op has recently been very active on the green front, launching its *Action Guide To The Environment* and the children's 'Mission Earth' pack with photographs of David Bellamy liberally sprinkled throughout. To the extent you could expect from a national chain of 5,000 stores, the Co-op has also been pretty good at matching words with actions, though their claim that they have redeveloped all their products to such an extent that 'they do not damage their customers or the environment in any way' is just a teensy bit over the top.

FOOD ADDITIVES
The Co-op has a policy to remove artificial additives and replace them with natural preservatives and flavourings 'wherever we can.' They are reducing the amount of sugar in many products and say they will phase out many products with sugar if customers demand it.

LABELLING
They label food 'suitable for vegetarians' if there could be doubt, and are introducing nutrition labelling to full EC standards.

ORGANIC FOODS
Could do a lot better here. So far organic fruit and vegetables are only being stocked in 100 of their superstores, though the Co-op has recently become involved in an organic farming project in Leicestershire.

SOUTH AFRICA
No own-brand goods originate in South Africa, but a few stores do stock South African fruit and vegetables — not always clearly labelled as such.

PACKAGING AND RECYCLING
Around 150 bottle banks are in place, but no plastic or can banks as yet. All branches have the option of using Co-op recycled paper bags, but most don't. Egg boxes are nearly all now made from recycled pulp. The Co-op led the way in banning CFCs from their own-brand products, and have also introduced plastic container labelling so that when plastic recycling gets under way it will be possible to identify what sort of plastic a container is made from.

EDUCATIONAL LITERATURE
The Co-op is very good on educational literature. Look out for the Co-op *Action Guide To The Environment* (on recycled paper) and the 'Mission Earth' pack (not all on recycled paper, and packed in a non-recycled plastic 'briefcase' — a fact pointed out to me by an aware and annoyed eight-year-old).

Gateway

Gateway Foodmarkets Ltd, Gateway House, Hawkfield Business Park, Whitchurch Lane, Bristol BS14 0TJ (0272 780629)
Not a terribly impressive record from this supermarket chain which has been rapidly expanding in recently years, though they are now beginning to make important changes under pressure from consumers and green supermarket front-runners. The only policy area in which Gateway have led the way is in the banning of CFC-containing aerosols, otherwise changes tend to have been cosmetic and 'as-little-as-we-can-get-away-with'.

FOOD ADDITIVES
A poor record so far, though they are 'developing products without using unnecessary artificial additives'. All meat is free from tenderizers and colourings.

LABELLING
Again a poor record, especially on nutritional labelling.

ORGANIC FOOD
150 of their 830 stores now carry organic fruit and vegetables; larger stores carry some organic grocery lines.
SOUTH AFRICA
Some South African products sold, always labelled as such. 'We always try to offer an alternative.'
PACKAGING AND RECYCLING
70% of egg boxes made from recycled pulp. CFC aerosols banned from July 1989. Gateway say they recycle all their waste cardboard and are exploring the reclamation of polythene. 190 stores have bottle banks. They print a message on their carrier bags 'urging customers to re-use them'.
EDUCATIONAL LITERATURE
No in-store green educational literature.

Marks and Spencer
Marks and Spencer plc, Michael House, Baker Street, London W1 1DN (0(7)1-935 4422)
Marks and Sparks are justifiably known for the clothes, but if you want green food you'll do better elsewhere. For the first edition of Green Pages they said it was 'difficult' for them to comment on how green they were. Now that they have seen other supermarkets taking the lead in this important area they've appointed an adviser on environmental issues, but their food is still overpriced and overpackaged, with virtually no recycling facilities available at their stores. On the other hand, they treat (and pay) their staff better than other supermarkets, and none of their stores is out-of-town, only to be reached by those fortunate enough to have the use of a car.
FOOD ADDITIVES
They say they have always used as few artificial additives as possible, and have reduced the number they do use. 'Our approach has been to take a cautious and well-balanced view.'
LABELLING
M&S introduced proper nutritional labelling in late 1989, complying in almost every respect with the 1988 EC draft directive.
ORGANIC FOODS
Having stalled for a long time on organics, M&S gave way early in 1989 and now stock a limited range in most branches.
SOUTH AFRICA
South African produce stocked alongside everything else: 'We do not believe that we should impose any specific view on our customers; they should be free to choose as they wish.'
PACKAGING AND RECYCLING
M&S say their pre-packed ready-to-eat foods such as salads demand the excessive packaging they use; I say it makes it look as though you're getting more for your money than you are. They have been phasing out CFCs.
EDUCATIONAL LITERATURE
Nothing much beyond a single-sheet handout or two, though they will supply nutritional information sheets on their products on request.

Safeway
Safeway Food Stores Ltd, Beddow Way, Aylesford, Maidstone, Kent M20 7AT (0622 712000)
Safeway are one of the market leaders in environmental issues: they've been phasing out most of the most dangerous food additives from their own label products, organic produce is available in all of their 220 stores, and they have been saving money and energy through an extensive energy conservation programme. Safeway have moved beyond the usual issues of CFCs and bottle banks, and are also looking at issues such as phasing out bleach from the paper bags used in their bakeries, plastic bottle and can recycling, and becoming actively involved in organic farming initiatives. Not for nothing have they come top in the Green Consumer Guide's star rating; can they keep up the innovation?
FOOD ADDITIVES
Safeway has removed the fifty most dangerous additives from all its own-brand products, based on advice from the Hyperactive Children's Support Group (see page 216).
LABELLING
There is no recycling information on their packaging, though they do sometimes use the 'Keep Britain Tidy' logo. They label 'Nutritional Information' on many packaged goods, showing energy, protein, carbohydrate and fat content.
ORGANIC FOODS
Safeway have organic food in all their stores, and have been justifiably winning trade awards for this policy. The company has recently combined with the EC and the Scottish Development Agency to co-fund an organic farming research centre on Tayside in Scotland.
SOUTH AFRICA
No policy on South African products: Safeway 'is not in a position to make international political decisions'.
PACKAGING AND RECYCLING
Recycled paper bags are now available at checkouts (though they don't do a lot to discourage the plastic alternative), and they are considering introducing biodegradable plastic carrier bags. Under a fifth of stores have bottle banks, and they don't use returnable bottles. They recycle cardboard used for bulk packaging, and plan to use recycled paper for head office stationery.
EDUCATIONAL LITERATURE
A very good series of eleven Healthy Living booklets. Number 4 on nutritional guidelines is especially good; Number 8, on sugar, fudges the issue in deference to the sugar industry.

Sainsbury's
J. Sainsbury plc, Stamford House, Stamford Street, London SE1 9LL (0(7)1-921 6000)
Sainsbury's have a well-deserved reputation for variety and quality of food and for customer service. Innovative and responsive, they still have some ground to make up on Safeway and the Co-op on overall policies, but have recently started to sell an 'environmentally-friendly' range of cleaning products called Greencare, routinely recycle cardboard packaging, and have recently opened a prototype energy-efficient store at Streatham Common in South London. Sainsbury's could well end up being one of the best supermarket choices for the more aware consumer.
FOOD ADDITIVES
A major review of additive policy is currently taking place, with artificial additives being removed wherever possible.
LABELLING
Around 1,800 (out of 3,000) of their packaged products now have 'Nutrition' panels (which include added sugar and salt), together with flashes like 'High Fibre' and 'No Added Sugar'.
ORGANIC FOODS
Both the number of outlets carrying organics and the range are steadily increasing; all is grown to Soil Association standards. Many stores also stock organic bread, grains, cheese, yogurt, coffee and wines.
SOUTH AFRICA
Where South African goods are stocked, Sainsbury's say they make 'every attempt also to stock alternatives'.

PACKAGING AND RECYCLING
Sainsbury's (unlike Safeways) have found can banks to be successful at a handful of sites and a programme is underway to introduce bottle banks to at least one fifth of their stores. They are also experimenting with newspaper collection points, and are looking at the potential for plastic recycling. Sainsbury's is also using recycled packaging 'wherever this is appropriate'.

EDUCATIONAL LITERATURE
Produces a good series of *Living Today* leaflets, including *Your Food and Health*; *Understanding Food Labels*; and *Keeping Food at its Best*. Number 9, *You and the Environment*, is printed on recycled paper (why not the rest?). An *Environment Friendly Shopping at Sainsbury's* leaflet includes a wide range of phosphate-free cleaners, organic groceries and recycled paper products.

Tesco
Tesco, Tesco House, PO Box 18, Delamare Road, Cheshunt, Waltham Cross, Hertfordshire EN8 9SL (0992 32222)

In late 1988 Tesco made headline news across the country as the first supermarket to 'go green'. As a public relation exercise the launch of 'Tesco Cares' was highly successful, and their publicity office was able to flourish a hundred pages of press cuttings, showing how they had stolen a march on their competitors. They phased out CFCs from their own brand aerosols and published booklets about how they were protecting the environment, but there was a high hype-to-action ratio. Currently in the second league behind Safeway, Sainsbury's and the Co-op, Tesco are trying very hard, selling organic produce in most stores, using recycled packaging 'whenever possible', and introducing a special range of logos to make recycling easier.

FOOD ADDITIVES
Unnecessary additives are being removed from all own-brand products, although this isn't as strict a policy as Safeway's, for example. A list of 400 additive-free products is available.

LABELLING
The 'Tesco Cares' campaign completely changed the company's labelling policy. They now have a range of 'environment friendly' labels to back up the nutrition labels they introduced some years ago. A nutrition panel appears on many packaged lines, showing energy, fat (divided into saturated and unsaturated), protein, carbohydrate, vitamins and minerals.

ORGANIC FOODS
Great improvements here, with organic produce now widely available. A few stores also have a limited range of packaged organic goods.

SOUTH AFRICA
No plans to avoid South African produce, though consumer pressure has led to two inner city stores not stocking them.

PACKAGING AND RECYCLING
The company says it uses recycled packaging wherever possible and avoids 'excessive packaging', although biros and batteries still come in bubble packs. 64 stores have bottle banks and ten have can banks.

EDUCATIONAL LITERATURE
Some of the best: a *Tesco Guide to Healthy Eating* series; plus a detailed guide to the nutritional value of each of their lines, a good *Tesco Guide to Healthy Eating on a Budget*, and a *Paper and the Environment* leaflet.

Waitrose
John Lewis Partnership, 171 Victoria Street, London SW1E 5NN (0(7)1-828 1000)

One of the smaller chains, though as committed as any of the others to change towards healthier eating. It was second only to Safeway in the shift towards organic produce, and a wide range of organic and vegetarian food is now on sale. Other initiatives include the banning on Alar-treated apples from 1989 onwards, and the availability of relatively naturally-reared pork in some of their outlets.

FOOD ADDITIVES
Many unnecessary additives have been removed, though Waitrose are vague about which and how many.

LABELLING
A small but growing number of packaged goods now carry nutritional labelling, showing fat, protein, energy and carbohydrate. A few also show sugar and salt content. Lists of additives and additive-free products are available on request.

ORGANIC FOODS
All 88 Waitrose branches now carry organic fruit and vegetables, and you can also buy organic bread and cereals.

SOUTH AFRICA
No policy to avoid or provide alternatives to South African produce.

PACKAGING AND RECYCLING
Cardboard boxes are offered for customers' use at all branches; other cardboard outers are recycled. There are bottle banks at about 40% of stores, sixteen can banks and one experimental newspaper collection point. Waitrose also uses recycled packaging where possible, 'but not in contact with food for fear of contamination' — very recycledpaperist.

EDUCATIONAL LITERATURE
A leaflet called *Waitrose Products and the Environment* is available, and they will also send a ring-bound tome called *Additive Free Foods and Nutrition Information* to interested teachers, nutritionists and other professionals.

South African Brands

If avoiding South African goods is part of your buying strategy, here are some of the labels to avoid:

FRESH, TINNED AND DRIED FRUIT
Cape, Copper Leaf, Del Monte, Gants, Goddess, Golden Glory, Golden Jubilee, Gold Reef, IXL, Jardin du Cap, John West, Kat, Kit, Koolkat, Outspan, Pendant, Princes, S&B, Safari, Shelford, Silver Leaf, Sun Fresh, Sweet Nell, Tambor, Turban.
CANNED MEATS AND FISH
Apex, Armour Star, Bull, Glenryck, John West, Lucky Star, Princes, Puffin, S&B.
WINES AND SPIRITS
Koopmans Sckloof, KVW, Lanzerac, Rembrandt, SA Burgundy, SA Hock, SA Sherry, Stellenburg, Zonnebloem.
JUICES AND BEVERAGES
Appletise, Cap d'Or, Ceramin, Citruseal, Divec, Juicy Lucy, Koo, KVW, Lemax, Liquifruit, Natur Fruit, Pot o' Gold, Southern Sun, Valor.
HEALTH FOODS
Koo, Packo Spices, Rooibosch Tea.

Food Additives

INGREDIENTS
Raspberry Flavour Jelly Crystals
Sugar, Gelling Agents (E410, E407, E340, Potassium Chloride),
Adipic Acid, Acidity Regulator (E336), Flavourings, Stabiliser
(E466), Artificial Sweetener (Sodium Saccharin), Colour (E123).
Peach Flavour Custard Powder
Starch, Flavourings, Salt, Colours (E110, E124).
Sponge, with Preservative (E202), Colours (E102, E110).
Decorations, with Colours (E110, E132, E123).
Trifle Topping Mix
Hydrogenated Vegetable Oil, Whey Powder, Sugar, Emulsifiers
(E477, E322), Modified Starch, Lactose, Caseinate, Stabiliser
(E466), Flavourings, Colours (E102, E110, E160a), Antioxidant
(E320).
    from the label of Birds' Peach and Raspberry Flavour Trifle

The label says it all — fifteen different food additives, of which at least five (the azo dyes E102, E110, E123 and E124 and the antioxidant BHA, E320) are highly suspect and not advised for children. Britain is possibly the least safety-conscious of all Western countries when it comes to food additives.

A Thames Television booklet written to accompany two programmes called 'Good Enough to Eat' (and requested by more than 35,000 viewers) had this to say about food additives: 'An imaginary food scientist with an understanding of the very latest in food technology can create a vast range of textures, shapes, flavours and colours, and produce them to order as cakes, biscuits, snacks, drinks and sauces. These are made with varying proportions of refined starches, sugars and fats, and a few wholesome ingredients - all blended together with additives. . . Britain allows more additives and has weaker controls than any other major industrialised country'.

The use of food additives has grown tenfold in the last three decades. Two hundred thousand tonnes a year of nearly four thousand different additives are added to our food, and processed food, which makes up three quarters of the British diet, is rarely free from them.

Many food additives are naturally-occurring ingredients, such as alginates made from seaweed, natural gums, beeswax and natural minerals; many of the additives currently used in the British food industry, however, are known to be suspect. A growing number of concerned people believe that the present system of safeguards, whereby an additive can be used as long as it has not been proven conclusively that it does harm, should be replaced by a system which does not allow the use of an additive whenever there is evidence that it may do harm.

Since information about additives is considered in Britain to be an 'industrial secret' (nobody knows, for example, the volume of specific additives going into food manufactured in this country), it can be a real problem finding out which additives are potentially dangerous and which are harmless, though there is now a handful of useful guides.

One frightening development is that some companies which reduced their use of dangerous food additives in the wake of customer concern are now putting them back in, often under different names and numbers. Thus Mars has recently reintroduced carcinogenic azo dyes into lines such as Smarties and Opal Fruits, a move which should be strenuously resisted.

Taking The Lid Off

The best introduction to food additives, straightforward and pulling no punches yet acknowledging that the food industry is not 'out to poison us', Erik Millstone's book tells us what food additives are, in whose interests they are added to food, and how they are tested for 'safety'. The final chapter, called 'What is to be done?', makes it clear that consumers must have more say in monitoring additives, that research must be independent, and must look at the hazards of the 'additive cocktails' in many processed foods rather than at single isolated additives. An appendix lists those additives implicated in hyperactivity, and in their advert at the back of the book the publishers list *The Penguin Book of Horror Stories* — pure coincidence?

*

Time and again the British food industry has claimed that consumers are receiving better value for money and a healthier diet than ever before. If this were true it would not have been either necessary or possible to write this book. There is clear evidence that there have been earlier times when we were better fed, and plenty of evidence proving that we could be better fed. The food supply in Britain is inferior in many respects to that available in other countries. Despite the oft-repeated and bland assurances of the Government and the food industry, there is a great deal wrong with that industry. Our diet, as determined by the industry which supplies it, does not serve the interests of customers as well as it could or should. The use of food additives is, furthermore, both crucial to and symptomatic of much that is wrong with our food.

Food Additives
Erik Millstone
Penguin, 1986
£2.95

The Soil Association (see page 67) has produced a handy twelve-page two-colour leaflet (Look Again at the Label, 1984, 65p (+ 30p postage if ordered from the Association)), with a complete list of additives under the headings 'safe', 'suspect' and 'beware', together with brief notes as to why they may be dangerous and to whom. This is a good deal more convenient to cart about with you when shopping than *E For Additives*.

BEWARE	SUSPECT	SAFE	
AZO DYES			
E100		E100 Turmeric	E100
E101		E101 Vitamin B2	E101
E102	E102 Tartrazine		E102
E104	E104 Quinoline Yellow		E104
107	107 Yellow 2G		107
E110	E110 Sunset Yellow		E110
E120		E120 Cochineal²	E120
E122	E122 Carmoisine, Azorubine		E122
E123	E123 Amaranth		E123

The New E For Additives

The 'old' E For Additives sold over half a million copies, and has probably done more than anything else to alert food producers and retailers to the fact that consumers do want to know what their food contains. Now a new edition, more expensive and twice as thick, gives updated information on every additive found in processed food in this country. To my mind the new edition has more in it than even the interested consumer needs to know; the copious documentation and cross-referencing at the end of the book is more than is strictly necessary and could have been in very small print. The introductory chapters, however, make fascinating and alarming reading, covering subjects like additives in wines and medicines, hyperactivity, and a very useful list (pages 57-59) of the 57 additives that are best avoided (photocopy it and keep it in your purse or pocket):

102	210	310	407	621	924
104	211	311	450	622	925
107	212	312		623	926
110	213	320		627	
120	214	321		631	
122	215	385		635	
123	216				
124	217				
127	218				
128	219				
131	220				
132	221				
133	222				
142	223				
150	224				
151	226				
153	227				
154	250				
155	251				
173					SUSPECT
180					ADDITIVES

(E numbers are omitted — 107, 128, 133, 154, 155, 385 and 621-926 have not yet been allocated the 'E' prefix)

*

Since 1 January 1986 most foods have had to carry a relatively complete list of ingredients. Flavourings do not have to be declared, except by the word 'flavourings', but all the other ingredients, including water, have to be listed in descending order by weight. . . It is very important to take this into account when reading the label. Many soup or dessert mixes have remarkably similar lists of ingredients in which sugar, starch or flour of some sort, and hydrogenated vegetable fat are high up on the list of ingredients, and sometimes the designated variety of the product such as tomato or strawberry is present in small amounts, or may be altogether absent.

The New E for Additives
Maurice Hanssen
Thorsons, 1987
£3.50

Understanding Additives

Another useful book about additives has recently been added to the *Which?* series published by Hodder and Stoughton. Called *Understanding Additives*, it provides clear and detailed information on the subject, including a full list of additives with their uses and numbers. While it explains the functions and dangers of additives very straightforwardly, the style is sometimes reminiscent of a well-meaning doctor who keeps saying 'There, there, everything's going to be all right.' It's pretty bland when it comes to the political context of necessary change, and when it quotes research such as a 1983 study which estimated that cancer risks associated with diet were up to thirty times as great as those associated with additives, it doesn't take much deep cogitation to wonder how you can possibly separate one from the other when our food is so universally contaminated.

Understanding Additives
A Which? Book
Hodder and Stoughton, 1988
£4.95

Additive-free Products

There has never been a time like the present when so much money could be made out of telling customers how few 'enhancers' were in your food product, or how (like Heinz baked beans or Weetabix) you had never put them in in the first place. 'Additive-free' is blazoned across packets of everything from bread to sausages, and it is becoming much easier than it was to buy ingredients for a relatively additive-free diet from your local chain store or supermarket. For a complete range of organically produced and entirely additive-free foods, however (especially valuable for people with particular allergies), it is well worth knowing about an organization called Foodwatch International.

Foodwatch International

After many years in the food industry, Peter Campbell set up Foodwatch in 1982 to supply a wide range of additive-free foodstuffs. He sees his main market as people suffering from allergy, though increasingly people looking for otherwise difficult-to-find additive-free products are finding that Foodwatch, with its excellent and speedy mail order service, is a useful supplier for a wide range of products. Many of the Foodwatch lines are produced exclusively for them, including natural jelly mixes, mousse mix, burger mix and other additive-free treats for children, a wide range of flours including water chestnut and yam flour, unfortified white wheat flour (for which Foodwatch has a special Ministry dispensation), and even additive-free flavourings and colourings (red from beetroot, yellow from saffron, green from chlorophyll and blue from grapeskins) — additive-free additives! Prices are not outlandish but, as you might expect, a good deal more than the supermarket equivalents. Foodwatch also sell non-food products including non-toxic clingfilm, cleaning products and books, including the *Foodwatch Alternative Cookbook* by Peter's wife Honor (Ashgrove Press, 1990, £5.95). Send an sae for a catalogue and pricelist.

Foodwatch International
Butts Pond Industrial Estate
Sturminster Newton
Dorset
DT10 1AZ
0258 73356

Food Adulteration

Food Adulteration is possibly the most important book to come out of the London Food Commission (see page 28); indeed, possibly the most important book about the state of Britain's food and food industry that you can read. For just £4.95 you will get in-depth background to additives, pesticides, nitrates, irradiation, food colourings, food poisoning, government policies and the official secrecy surrounding the food industry — all in the LFC's readable style and with a very complete bibliography and resource sections if you want to take things further. An essential book for any green bookshelf. 'Food matters to everyone,' say the authors; 'We deserve the best.'

*

The food industry has persuaded government that secrecy is needed for commercial reasons. Companies argue that commercial rivalry necessitates secrecy over such matters as ingredients, market share and technology. the government claims companies will only share such secrets with the Civil Service if it agrees to keep them confidential.

This confidentiality also extends to the results of safety studies done by companies. Since there is little safety testing done by government, this is often the only data available for deciding whether additives, pesticides and food processes are safe. Given the widespread concern over safety of some products that have been approved, this secrecy is no longer acceptable. The public's health and safety is too important to allow hearings behind closed doors. Cross-examination of company evidence, in public, is essential to rebuild public confidence.

Food Adulteration And How To Beat It
London Food Commission
Unwin Hyman, 1988
£4.95

Food Scares and Food Safety

Richard Lacey, Professor of Clinical Microbiology at Leeds University, has been appearing on our television screens with increasing regularity over recent months, because he is *the* media expert on food scares. And what with salmonella, listeria, viruses, Chinese rice poison, campylobacter, botulism, staphylococcus and clostridium (did you know there were so many things to worry about?) his services are certainly needed. This recently-published slim paperback contains everything you need to know (rather too much for many) about the growing prevalence of food poisoning and how to avoid it. If you followed all Richard Lacey's advice you'd spend your whole life being careful, a very counterproductive activity — surely it would be much easier simply to avoid the main food culprits like meat products and other overprocessed foods and maintain commonsense kitchen hygiene. A timely book nonetheless.

*

If only 2,000 cattle out of hundreds of thousands have been affected by BSE, is it really a serious matter? Unfortunately, yes — very serious. The real worry for the human population is the risk of catching BSE from infected animals. A rare brain disease in human beings, Creutzfeldt-Jacob disease, has been known for some years and is similar to BSE in cattle and scrapie in sheep. Perhaps the most reassuring fact is that while scrapie has been occurring in sheep for many years, there is no proof that we can catch it. BSE in cattle is too new for us to be certain that we cannot catch it from infected cows, although that is unlikely.

Safe Shopping, Safe Cooking, Safe Eating
Richard Lacey
Penguin, 1989
£2.99

A government-sponsored food hygiene agency called Food Sense has produced a free leaflet called *Food Safety: A Guide from HM Government*; most libraries and local government environmental health departments will have copies, otherwise you can write to Food Sense at London SE99 7TT.

DON'T SCREW AROUND, WARNS EDWINA
Evening Standard

Life Lines

There are two sorts of reactionary politicians — the ones whose tough public image fits their narrow thinking, and the ones who smile and soothe and nod while enumerating the additional hardships they have chosen to impose on the bulk of the electorate. It must be said that Edwina Currie is among the most endearing of the latter, winning faint but deserved applause from radical greens for her stance on issues such as smoking, drink-driving, and food quality, not to mention her unwillingness to capitulate on the salmonella issue even when her ministerial post was at stake.

Her autobiography of the three years she spent as Junior Health Minister is chatty and frequently condescending, displaying a welcome concern about a wide range of health issues but lacking real understanding of the root causes of ill health. The last chapter about the egg showdown, 'Endgame', is the one we shall hear most about in the reviews, but as an insight into the workings of an intelligent Tory mind the whole book is worth reading.

*

There was an AIDS advert for girls, too, warning them of the dangers lurking in a syringe offered by a friend, with the powerful image of a wax doll, stabbed over and over again with pins, falling dying at the end. My twelve-year-old daughter Debbie saw it on television at her boarding school and wrote me a long letter — 'it was awful, Mum; we talked about it for ages, and we all said we'll never, never try drugs. Did you have anything to do with it?'

*

All politicians, all public speakers, occasionally fail to make their meaning absolutely clear. But if you live by the word and stand by the word, you die by the word. The industry did not collapse because of my words; it was already in trouble, at least in part because of the worries expressed by many others that there might be something lurking in the eggs — or at least in some of them, with no way for the customer to tell which. The difference the interview made was that afterwards everyone knew about it.

Life Lines
Edwina Currie
Sidgwick and Jackson, 1989
£13.95

Packaging

There is no denying the ritzy appeal of the Ferrero Rocher chocolate box — a supreme example of 'perceived added value'. The chocolates are individually wrapped in metallic paper and a cup. They are set into two layers separated by a plastic tray. To top everything off, the outer container is a thick and heavy plastic box whose ultimate destination, after its admired position on the shop shelf, is the ignominy of the bin.

Adrian Judd, *Creative Review*, April 1987

Packaging makes up more than a third of all household waste in Britain — in the USA it's nearer a half. 42% of paper products used in Britain and more than 25% of plastics are used for packaging, to be thrown away as soon as whatever was inside the packaging has been unwrapped.

What is packaging really for? Is it to tell you about the product? If you are buying a basic foodstuff you hardly need to be told what it is: an apple is an apple; brown rice is brown rice. You might appreciate being told the variety and place of origin, but all that needs is a sign in the shop. At the very most all you really need is a simple label.

Is the packaging to prevent the product from being damaged? Then how do you justify Kerrygold's Cream for Coffee — ten small plastic cups, each with a foil lid, set in another plastic dish and finished with a thick card lid? All this to stop the cream being damaged? Many products come in the form of a package within a package — even such unbreakables as sultanas and rolled oats come with all this unnecessary paraphernalia.

What can you do about it?

Hard though it is, the most important thing you can do is buy as little packaging as you can in the first place. If you buy your food in a wholefood shop, the chances are that they will be very happy for you to bring in your own bags and containers. If you shop in a supermarket, take your own carrier bags and don't be tempted to take another just because it's there. Use boxes rather than plastic bags.

Try to prevent check-out assistants giving you plastic bags you don't need — they do it unconsciously, but will rarely object if you say simply 'I don't need a bag, thanks.'

Buy things which come in recyclable packaging — paper and glass — in preference to things wrapped in plastic and foil. Avoid plastic egg boxes — you'll rarely find a free range egg in a plastic box, and if you feel up to it, encourage your local shop or supermarket to switch from plastic to cardboard. Buy milk in milk bottles wherever you can; and buy milk and juices in cardboard rather than plastic containers — you shouldn't keep drinkable liquids in plastic containers for more than a few days anyway, since plastic is slightly porous and the liquid may start to evaporate or become contaminated.

Avoid buying tins — most of the time you don't need to (see page 111) — and above all avoid buying aerosols (see below).

Whenever you have the chance, recycle the packaging you do have to buy. For more information and ideas about recycling the materials that packaging is made of, see pages 109-113.

You don't need to be fanatical about packaging, just aware. Although that every bit of packaging avoided is helping to reduce the problem of pollution in the world, the most potent prod into action is usually the thought that it's us who are paying for the packaging we buy.

Aerosols

800 million aerosol cans are produced in Britain every year, more than ten for every inhabitant of the country. They are bad news in almost every way.

An aerosol is a minute particle of a substance, so light that it floats freely in the air, and so small and even in size that you can spray an aerosol on to a surface and be guaranteed to end up with a very even coating. Aerosols thus have their uses, but people managed to spray their hair, retouch their cars, make cream cakes and deal with insect pests perfectly well before the aerosol can was invented. To produce an aerosol, you have to seal the substance into a can under high pressure together with a 'propellant' which is liquid under pressure, but expands and evaporates when you press the button and release it and the substance it is carrying.

Here is the bad news:

▸ The cans are unrecyclable.
▸ They are dangerous because they are under such high pressure. Butane, one propellant which is used, is highly flammable and can turn an aerosol can into a flaming torch.
▸ Even though the ozone-destroying chlorofluorocarbons (CFCs) which were until recently used in most aerosols are rapidly being phased out, some of the CFC replacements — hydrofluorocarbons (HFCs), halons, methyl chloroform and carbon tetrachloride — are just as damaging to the ozone layer. Ozone is what protects life from dangerous ultra-violet radiation from the sun.
▸ They are expensive.

If you must use an aerosol, try to ensure that it is one that doesn't use a CFC as its propellant. Better still, don't use aerosols at all — the Swedes have banned them completely except for medical and other approved purposes.

INCPEN

INCPEN was formed in 1974 as a coalition of industry interests 'to further the protection of the environment insofar as it is affected by packaging'. It collects and disseminates information about packaging, attempts to explain to the media and the public just how concerned the industry is about green issues, and does its best to feed public concerns back to the industry. INCPEN produces a monthly *Journal* and some interesting reports, including — would you believe — one called *Packaging Saves Waste*. Write for an information pack.

**The Industry Council for
Packaging and the Environment**
Premier House
10 Greycoat Place
London
SW1P 1SB
0(7)1-222 8866

The Food Commission

The advent of the Food Commission, until April 1990 called the London Food Commission, was one of the best things ever to befall the British food consumer.

The Commission was established in March 1985, with a grant from the Greater London Council, to be Britain's foremost independent and authoritative source of advice, information and research about food, and it has been fortunate in bringing together many people who both know what they are talking about and who are not prepared to kowtow to food industry giants and politicians. In the first four years of its existence the Commission has published more than two dozen major reports and five important books, reviewed elsewhere in this 'Wholefoods' section. The Commission also produces the influential bi-monthly *Food Magazine* (see below), and acts as an independent consultancy.

The Food Commission
88 Old Street
London
EC1V 9AR
0(7)1-253 9513

The Food Magazine

Even if you don't read *The Food Magazine* you are unlikely to have missed the scandals it has unearthed since it first appeared in 1988. Fruit drinks with no fruit in them, ice sold as frozen prawn, milkshakes containing 22 lumps worth of sugar, burgers with 40% fat, chips covered with textile dye — all this and very much more in an attractive well-written magazine that aware greens really ought not to miss. *The Food Magazine* costs £12.50 for a year's subscription.

*

'Mummy, can we have sausages?' 'No.'
'Why?' 'Because they could be contaminated with BSE.'
'What's that?' 'Well, you see some sheep got this brain disease . . .'
'Why?' '. . . and they fed those sheep to some cattle . . .'
'Why?' '. . . and the cattles' brains got made into pies and sausages. . .'
'Why? Ooh, Yuk!!!' Exactly.
　　　　　　　from 'Pamela Stephenson's Diary', September 1989

The Food Magazine
88 Old Street
London
EC1V 9AR
0(7)1-250 1021

Irradiation

Irradiation is the bombarding of food with very large doses of ionizing radiation in order to sterilize it, so that in theory it stays fresh for longer. There are so many doubts about the safety of irradiation, however, that neither the process nor the import of irradiated food is currently allowed in Britain. But this is about to change if the present government has its way, and it is vitally important that conmbined consumer pressure ensures that food distributors and retailers are never tempted to offer irradiated food for sale. In *Food Irradiation: The Myth and The Reality*, Tony Webb and Tim Lang of The Food Commission present a detailed investigation of the claims and counter-claims for irradiation, showing how very little is still known about the long-term effects of this potentially dangerous technology. They show quite conclusively that irradiation has more to do with the nuclear industry looking for a use for its rapidly-becoming-redundant technology than the widening of consumer choice, that the safety of irradiation has not been proven, and that — probably most importantly in the long run — very few people actually want irradiated food.

Food Irradiation
The Myth and the Reality
Tony Webb and Tim Lang
Thorsons, 1990
£5.99

The Food Commission is co-ordinating a national Food Irradiation Campaign; for details send an sae to the Commission at the above address for an information pack and a campaigning kit.

Parents For Safe Food

(Parents for Safe Food)

'I started Parents for Safe Food,' writes Pamela Stephenson in the PfSF leaflet, 'because, like you, I am very concerned about the safety of the food I buy and prepare for my children.' This new campaigning group, with masses of celebrity support, made an early mark with its campaign about apple spraying with Alar, a known carcinogen. From being a routine treatment in many British orchards up until the 1989 harvest, public outcry has been so vociferous that several supermarket chains and fruit wholesalers have said that they would no longer buy in apples treated with Alar and the manufacturers have 'voluntarily' stopped producing it. Membership of PfSF costs £5 (or whatever more you can afford), which brings you regular information and briefings; from early 1990 a *PfSF Kit* will be available for £6, containing 'fun items for the kids' as well as an organic directory and a *Safe Food* booklet.

Parents For Safe Food
Britannia House
1-11 Glenthorne Road
London
W6 0LF
0(8)1-748 9898

Daily Bread

According to a press release issued by Tesco in May 1987, sales of wholemeal bread had virtually doubled in the previous two years. The wholemeal bread market is booming — and about time too. Anybody who knows anything about nutrition knows that we need the fibre that whole-grain bread provides, and that the bran in wholemeal bead (missing from white bread) is an important source of vitamins and minerals.

Bread that is sold as 'wholemeal' must by law contain 100% of the grain, but 'nowt taken out' isn't the same as 'nowt put in'. It's true that packaged bread doesn't have the array of additives in it that it boasted in the pre-additive-awareness days, but it usually still contains emulsifier and preservative, and it always contains a lot of air and water, which means that although your bread might be soft and spongy for the first couple of days, it won't keep for long without going mouldy. Home-baked loaves, on the other hand, which rely entirely on the action of yeast, oil and gluten to make them rise, are fine to eat a week after they've been baked (though there will never be anything to beat fresh bread). Incidentally, staling happens fastest at low temperatures (unless you're freezing your bread), so to keep bread for any length of time, seal it tightly and keep it in the airing cupboard, not in the fridge. To freshen days-old bread, put it in a slow oven for ten minutes.

One of the most widely-held myths about bread is that it's difficult to make, which is why less than a tenth of 1% of the bread eaten in Britain is baked at home. Which is silly, because making bread is easy, cheaper than shop-bought bread, and ensures that you know exactly what's in it.

Foolproof Bread Method

When I started making bread I failed miserably for a while — the tops fell off, loaves were dark brown on the outside and soggy in the middle, the whole thing crumbled into a heap of sawdust. But then my life changed. I was taught how to make wholemeal bread properly, and I've never had a failure since, even in the absence of measures, scales, timepieces and accurate ovens. This is how it's done.

▶ Put a little water in the kettle and boil it. Have ready a large mixing bowl, a wooden spoon, two oiled bread tins (2lb tins), honey, yeast (fresh or dried), flour and oil (plus sesame or poppy seeds if you like them).
▶ Take a little honey with the wooden spoon and put it in the mixing bowl. Add about a pint (half a litre) of boiling water and stir it until the honey dissolves. Then add the same amount of water, cold this time, until the liquid is at blood heat (stick your finger in it to test). Now add an ounce of crumbled fresh yeast or a couple of level tablespoons of dried yeast, sprinkled on to the water, and leave it for a while until it erupts (children like this bit).

▶ Now add enough flour, stirring it in with the spoon, to turn the mixture to a sponge-like consistency, thick but still easily stirrable. Leave the bowl in a warm place for as long as it takes to rise a few inches — this will take between twenty minutes and an hour, depending on how warm it is.
▶ Next, add a little oil (and I mean a little) and a little salt if you must, then enough flour to make the dough thick enough to work with your hands. Turn the dough out on to a clean floured surface, and with floured hands (keep everything well-but not overfloured all the time) knead the dough until it forms one cohesive lump, then for a bit longer — with wholemeal flour you don't have to knead for ages, though you can if you want. You should easily be able to incorporate all the flour on the work surface, and if the dough begins to feel sticky to the touch, just add a bit more flour.
▶ When you're ready, divide the dough in two and make each half into a loaf shape. If you like seeds on top of your bread, sprinkle a line of seeds on the work-surface, wet the top of the loaves, and turning them upside down, press them on to the seeds. Put the loaves in their oiled tins and leave them in a warm place to rise (I put the oven on at this point and let them rise in the grill space immediately over the oven). This will take another twenty minutes or so.
▶ Set the oven to 400°F/gas mark 6, and when the dough has reached the top of the bread tins, put them quickly into the oven before they collapse again. Give them 5 minutes at this temperature to brown the crusts, then another 30 at 350°F/mark 4 to bake thoroughly.

And there you are. Take them out carefully so you don't burn yourself in the excitement, check they're done by giving them a professional tap with the knuckle (they should sound hollow), and turn them out on to a wire tray to cool. Don't wash the bread tins (you'll lose the non-stick), but do wash the dough bowl and your work surface at this point or you'll have a real problem later. Leave the bread as long as you can resist it, then try it with Vecon (see page 38) and cucumber, or peanut butter and blackcurrant jam.

It sounds like a lot of work, but the actual work only takes ten minutes or so once you know what you're doing — the yeast does the rest. Once I knew how to do it, shop bread was never the same again.

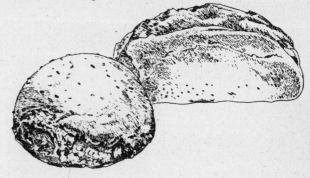

Bread Books

There are a lot of bread books about, but my favourites are Tassajara and Debbie Boater. They're both clear, informative and innovative, and there isn't much to choose between them. *The Tassajara Bread Book* comes from California, where the Tassajara operation in San Francisco is part of the Zen Centre. It was first published in 1970 and is a bit flowery at times, but some of the recipes (sourdough, bagels, candies) are wonderful. There are fewer ideas and fewer purple passages in Debbie Boater's very practical little book, but a lot of good, clear, basic recipes.

The Tassajara Bread Book
Edward Espe Brown
Shambala, 1970
about £5

The Bread Book
Debbie Boater
Prism, 1979
£2.95

Mills

Two hundred years ago, when horses, wind and water were the main sources of power for British industry and agriculture, there were in excess of twenty thousand grain mills operating in this country. Today there are fifty.

For many centuries the miller's skills were essential to the local community, but gradually milling stopped being a village industry, and is now dominated by electrically-driven roller mills, where the flour is milled at speed in large quantities. Although this produces a lot of flour, it makes for a very even and boring texture, and the heat generated in the process destroys nutrients in the grain. But the craft of milling has never been entirely lost; a handful of mills kept grinding their corn between grindstones in the time-honoured way, and now that more people are looking for stoneground wholegrain flour many of the traditional millers are finding themselves in a flourishing market.

Allinsons and Jordans are, as you might expect, the first league of the wholegrain milling line-up. Allinsons operate the largest stone grinding flour mill in the world at Castleford in West Yorkshire (tours by appointment, Tel: 0932 336366); Jordans, who manufacture a wide range of mueslis, crunchy cereals and snack bars, operate a slow rolling mill at Biggleswade in Bedfordshire (visits by appointment on Wednesday afternoons, Tel: 0767 312001).

Out of the other forty-eight operating grain mills here are four which I think are outstanding.

Little Salkeld Watermill

It really requires a book of its own to do justice to Nick and Ana Jones' incredible industry and innovation at Salkeld Mill. In the fourteen years since they took the mill over as a going concern they have expanded the range of products enormously, run an organic farm, written and published books, won a national award, shown thousands of people round the mill, and Nick still finds time to stand as a Green Party candidate for the local district council. What more to say? I sometimes buy their 100% organic wholewheat flour from my local wholefood shop — it makes excellent bread. Their other lines include an award-winning 'special blend' of wheat and soya flour, sunflower and sesame seeds, providing a unique protein balance ideal for vegans and very tasty for everyone else too; also biodynamic flour and organic animal feeds. All produce is to Soil Association symbol standard. *Mrs Doo's Watermill Story Book* is for enquiring youngsters (each 95p).

Little Salkeld offers a mail order service at retail price plus the actual cost of postage; carriage costs can be negotiated on larger orders. They deliver free within a 100 mile radius, and visitors are welcome by appointment. The prize-winning bakery in nearby Melmerby uses Salkeld flour; if you're passing through Cumbria call in on The Village Bakery for excellent home-made tea and scones — the craft shop upstairs is good, too.

The Watermill
Little Salkeld
Penrith
Cumbria
CA10 1NN
076 881 523

Doves Farm

Michael and Clare Marriage started their mill in an old tithe barn in the Wiltshire village of Ham in 1978, and moved half a mile (but across a county boundary) to their new premises in 1987. Doves Farm organic foods are now distributed nationally, and are generally reckoned to combine a quality, consistency and wide availability second to none. The flours include 100% and 85% extraction organic wheat flours, and rye, maize, brown rice, buckwheat, gram and barley flours. They also mill semolina, bran, wheatgerm and kibbled grains (grains crushed into small pieces), and sell organic whole grains. Doves Farm bread is increasingly widely available, and a recent innovation is a range of wholegrain additive-free biscuits, including gingernuts, carob bourbon and carob-coated digestives. No mail order.

Doves Farm Foods
Salisbury Road
Hungerford
Berkshire
RG17 0RF
0488 84880

Downfield Windmill

Nigel Moon started milling at the Downfield Windmill near Soham in Cambridgeshire in 1978 (though the mill itself dates from 1726), the impetus being a passion for windmills and a spell of unemployment. He mills organic and non-organic flours, 100% and 'brown' — 'flour that has been put through a sieve and had some of the larger bits of bran removed.' Wheat, oats, rye, barley and maize flour are usually available. Visitors are welcome on Sunday and bank holiday afternoons, where you can buy freshly-ground flour. No mail order.

Downfield Windmill
Fordham Road
Soham
Ely
Cambridgeshire
0353 720333

Boardhouse Mill

Boardhouse Mill at Birsay in Orkney is the islands' last remaining working water mill, specializing in the beremeal (an ancient form of barley), which was once an island staple. The Morrisons market their meals and flours throughout Scotland, and will send parcels by post anywhere in Britain — ask for a pricelist and recipe sheet, and enjoy your beremeal drop scones.

Boardhouse Mill
Birsay
Orkney
085 672 363

Organic Produce

Like the word 'natural', 'organic' means many things to many people, especially where commercial pressures are concerned. We are fortunate, therefore, that before organically grown crops increasingly became something to be asked for by the British public, the standards for organic cultivation had already been clarified by several responsible organizations. There are in fact several sets of criteria for organic produce, but they vary only in detail. The basics were clearly set out in 1981 by the International Federation of Organic Agriculture Movements:

▶ To work as much as possible within a closed system, and to draw upon local resources.
▶ To maintain the long-term fertility of soils.
▶ To avoid all forms of pollution that may result from agricultural techniques.
▶ To produce foodstuffs of high nutritional quality and sufficient quantity.
▶ To reduce the use of fossil energy in agricultural practice to a minimum.
▶ To give livestock conditions of life that conform to their physiological needs and to humanitarian principles.
▶ To make it possible for agricultural producers to earn a living through their work and develop their potentialities as human beings.

These guidelines are the basis of the Soil Association's Organic Symbol Scheme (see page 60), and of the international Farm Verified Organic Scheme (FVO), which works to ensure that organic produce not grown in Britain is truly organic. You will find the Soil Association or the FVO symbol on many organic products, and if you buy organic produce in bulk you may also come across the symbols of the Organic Growers Association and the Organic Farmers and Growers as well; this indicates that the producer of the product is a member of these very reputable organizations.

Soil Association
Organic Standard

Organic
Growers Association

Organic Farmers
and Growers

Farm Verified Organic

You may also come across the Demeter symbol of the Bio-dynamic Agriculture Association. Bio-dynamics is a system of agriculture initiated by Rudolf Steiner (founder of the Steiner Schools) in the 1920s, which takes into account the cycles of nature and the influence of the cosmos as well as the principles of good husbandry.

Seemingly blind to the fact that several long-established organic organizations already had organic labelling schemes which are recognized by customers and respected by producers alike, the British government nonetheless decided in 1988 that it would create its own labelling scheme — hence UKROFS (the UK Register of Organic Food Standards) was launched. Thus in future you may well find the UKROFS symbol alongside those of the Soil Association and the other organic growers' federations.

The Organic Consumer Guide

The first edition of the *Organic Food Guide* was published by the Henry Doubleday Research Association (see page 78) in 1983, the second by Dent in 1987. In the introduction to the second edition Alan Gear wrote: 'This could even be the last *Organic Food Guide*, for the strength of public demand for wholesome products suggests that stores selling organic food may soon be as commonplace as post offices.' Only time will tell whether the third book in the series, *Thorsons Organic Consumer Guide*, will be that last edition; I doubt it.

The *Organic Consumer Guide* (I expect just like *New Green Pages*) shows signs of having been compiled in a very great hurry, yet if it hadn't been then it would be less immediate, up-to-date and useful than it is. If you want to know what organic is all about, where we have reached in the rapid move towards healthy food, and where and what to buy to keep you and your environment healthy, then £4.99 invested in this very practical handbook will repay you quickly and handsomely.

After a rundown of why the shift towards organics is so important, 'A Shopper's Guide' looks at a wide range of foodstuffs from cereals and pasta to baby food and snacks, with accurate and detailed information about who manufactures and supplies what. Then there is a 130-page directory of where you can buy organic food, including farms, organic gardens and wholefood shops, followed by forty pages of cafés and restaurants which serve organic food, a list of organizations offering training in organic growing and a short bibliography.

*

Of course there are still enormous hurdles to overcome. Conventional farmers wishing to get off the 'chemical treadmill' are given no financial incentives to get them through the transition stage. Land needs at least two years without artificial chemicals before food grown on it can be sold as 'organic'. Crop yields drop while the soil is revitalized. And so long as there is a scarcity prices will remain high. Only when there is a great deal more organic food produced will prices begin to come down. More and more people are now concerned about the prospects for agriculture. Output is high at the moment, but how long can it last? The price that all of us pay is polluted water, degraded soil, abused farm animals, a despoiled countryside and risks to health. That is too high a price. Organic food and farming is one way — perhaps the only way — of producing safe food by methods that are in harmony with the planet. It is up to each of us to make sure that the future is organic.

Thorsons Organic Consumer Guide
David Mabey and Alan and Jackie Gear
Thorsons, 1990
£4.99

The Organic Tradition

Important ideas never spring fully-fledged from nothing, and this is as true of the organic ethic as any other. Writers and activists like Edward Hyams, Eve Balfour, George Stapledon and H.J. Massingham were pointing out the dangers of chemical agriculture, soil erosion and monoculture decades ago, and Philip Conford has brought together many of their essential writings in a carefully crafted and edited anthology called *The Organic Tradition* — excellent bedtime reading for any budding (or experienced) organic grower.

*

Ecology — the most needed of all the sciences — could in time help us to become aware that everything in heaven and earth is but part of a single whole. Then for the first time in many a century could we justifiably claim to be entering on an age of progress.

Eve Balfour, *The Living Soil*, June 1944

The Organic Tradition
An Anthology of Writings
on Organic Farming,
1900-1950
edited by Philip Conford
Green Books, 1988
£6.50

An Organic Movement Directory

Early in 1986, Working Weekend on Organic Farms (see page 290) produced an extremely useful directory of organizations and firms working in the area of organic agriculture, spreading the net very wide to include many bodies more generally involved in environmental and education issues. Already in its second printing, the directory gives annotated entries for over 200 groups, and at £1 a copy is very good value for money. An introductory essay called 'Who's Who in the Organic Movement' sets the whole thing in context, and a resources index shows clearly exactly what areas each group covers.

Directory of Organizations and Training in the UK Organic Movement
WWOOF, 1986
£1

ECOP and the Geest Connection

The organic fruit and vegetables now being sold by the supermarket chains have to come from somewhere, and in sufficient quantity. Individual farms can seldom grow enough of a particular crop to satisfy the needs of one supermarket, let alone a hundred, so an important development of the last year has been the coming together of nearby organic farmers and growers into organic producer co-operatives. One such organization is Eastern Counties Organic Producers, a seven-strong alliance of growers in central Lincolnshire, which has recently negotiated a five-year contract with another newcomer to the organic scene, the international produce giant Geest.

Seeing the need for produce preparation and packaging separate from 'contaminated' food, Geest opened a new organic packhouse in Spalding in 1987, from which they supply supermarkets all over the country. Their problem is that with supermarket chains like Sainsbury's, Safeway and Tesco asking for more and more organics, they simply can't find enough reliable supplies, and have been advertizing in the organic growers' press for farms and producer co-operatives to grow organic food which they then guarantee to buy. Could this be the beginning of a revolution in agriculture as well as one in diet?

Organics Department, Geest plc
White House Chambers
Spalding
Lincolnshire
PE11 2AL
0775 761111

Getting Organized

The growers aren't standing still when it comes to gearing up for the eating revolution. ECOP was one of the first organic marketing co-operatives to be started; a more ambitious scheme has recently been launched in the Welsh Borders, where Greengrowers' members can be found throughout Herefordshire, Worcestershire and Shropshire. Greengrowers use Organic Farm Foods in Lampeter, one of Britain's largest organics importers, as their agent and packhouse, and in their first year of business turned over nearly half a million pounds. Greengrowers are actively looking for new members, and can offer good and consistent prices, planned production schedules and centralized collection facilities, thus alleviating many of the marketing problems experienced by small growers.

Greengrowers Organic Produce Ltd
County Mills
Worcester
WR1 3NU
08854 204

Real Food Supplies

As the organic revolution gathers momentum, more and more shops are realizing that people are prepared to search out healthy food. When organic supplies come with integrity, experience and community service, moreover, a whole new way of shopping is born. This is what Phil Haughton offers in Bristol, where Real Food Supplies now operates its 'one-stop organic' shops in Bishopston and Whiteladies (6 Cotham Hill), selling a wide range of organic fruit, vegetables, meat, poultry, wine and gardening supplies, wherever possible to Soil Association standards. A member of the Soil Association Council, Phil is pioneering a new 'Retail' category of membership for shops which endeavour to maintain as high an organic standard as possible — Real Food is the first with Wholefood of London (page 16) a close second. Phil has plans to open shops in Gloucester and Somerset as soon as possible; in the meantime Real Food will deliver throughout Bristol.

Real Food Supplies
36c Gloucester Road
Bishopston
Bristol
BS7 8AR
0272 232015

Natural Foods

If you live anywhere on the northern fringes of London and are interested in organic foods, you will probably already have heard of Tim and Carol Moya's natural food service. They supply a wide range of organically grown fruit and vegetables and organic meat, cheese and wine, plus an extensive range of wholefoods (mostly not organic) and household items such as the Ecover range (see page 114). The useful thing about Natural Foods is that they deliver weekly to your door, and will even ring you up to ask what you need, all for only £1.20 a delivery. The Moyas used to grow all their organic vegetables themselves, but demand has grown so much that they now need to buy it in. Over the weeks the Natural Foods folks build up a close relationship with their customers, often seeing dramatic improvements in the health of people who switch to a wholefood diet. If you live anywhere between Dartford and Hertford, ask Natural Foods for a pricelist.

Natural Foods Ltd
Unit 14
Hainault Road Industrial Estate
Hainault Road
London
E11 1HD
0(8)1-539 1034

Ferrocrete Farm

Of the couple of hundred farms and growers listed in the *Organic Consumer Guide* I have chosen just one to give you an idea of what you can expect to find when you visit your local organic farm.

Sim and Geoffrey Fowler became interested in keeping goats — the rare English goat rather than the commoner Mediterranean goat — on their farm in the Lune Valley twelve years ago. Before long their herd grew to the point where they had more milk than they could use themselves, so started to sell it and to make yogurt and cheese. As they say, 'everything else followed on from there'. They now sell goat milk and products, sheep milk products, free range eggs, organically grown vegetables in season, herb plants, and dried herbs and spices, both from a farm shop and local retailers, and through a wholesaler in Lancaster. As demand for organic vegetables has grown, so the Fowlers have increasingly catered for it. They now have a stand on Lancaster's street market two days a week, and buy in from other local organic growers. They also sell herbs by mail order, and container-grown herbs at

the farm. Children are particularly welcome at the farm and can buy products at cost; visitors can come at any time if they ring to check in advance. A couple of years ago Derek Cooper mentioned Ferrocrete's goat milk yogurt in *The Listener* and was quoted by *Private Eye*'s 'Pseud's Corner'. Fame indeed.

Ferrocrete Farm
Arkholme
Carnforth
Lancashire
LA6 1AU
05242 21965

Organic Animal Feeds

The keeping of pets in a green world is a vexed question. For many people they provide companionship and stimulation, but there is also a high price to pay, for them and for us. Karen Christensen's *Home Ecology* (see page 95) and my *How To Be Green* (page 261) look at the keeping of pets in more detail, but here I shall concentrate on what we feed 'our' animals. Studies have shown that dogs only need a quarter of their diet, cats three-quarters, to be meat and fish, yet most people feed their pets far more than this, the bulk of it from the 2 billion petfood cans that Britons open (and throw away) every year. A great deal of petfood is based on decidedly non-organic offal, and some pets are literally hooked on the additives in certain brands.

Green Ark to the rescue, for in Alston in Cumbria this small company specializes in animal wholefoods — cereal mix, slippery elm puppy weaning food, herbal tonic, garlic powder and much more. For 75p plus an A5 sae, Green Ark will be happy to send you a copy of their comprehensive and colourful *Guide to Natural Feeding*, together with an up-to-date pricelist.

Green Ark
Low Flatt
Alston
Cumbria
CA9 3DE
0434 381766

And a Word About Soya Products

Cows' milk is thought to be a major irritant to many people's digestive systems (see allergy, page 147). If you think this is true for you or someone in your family, and cannot easily get hold of goats' or sheeps' milk (which is thinner than cows' milk and less likely to be contaminated with hormones and antibiotics), you might well consider switching to soya milk and products. Soya products are also likely to be part of any vegan diet (see page 47). It is important to remember that soya milk is not 'milk' at all, and will not work like milk in many recipes, but soya products are extremely nutritious and a wide range is now available, including soya ice cream, tofu (soya bean curd) pies, flavoured drinks and tofuburgers. Two of the main manufacturers are Sunrise (Soya Health Foods) in Manchester and Plamil in Folkestone, both of which will be happy to send you information about their range.

Soya Health Foods Ltd
Unit 4, Guinness Road
Trafford Park
Manchester
M17 1AU
061 872 0549

Plamil Foods Ltd
Plamil House
Bowles Well Gardens
Folkestone
Kent
0303 58588

Pesticides

In 1980, Edward Goldsmith wrote in The Ecologist: *'In the last thirty years there has been a veritable explosion in the use of synthetic organic pesticides. Over 800 formulations are now used in the UK alone. . .' Today, just six years later, around 4,000 different proprietary products — made up of nearly 1,000 different pesticides — are in use in Britain. . . By the early 1980s, 97-99 per cent of all main crops, cereals and vegetables were sprayed at least once. Official figures for 1983 show that one crop of lettuce was dosed 46 times with four different chemicals. Crops such as hops were receiving an average of 23 sprays a season; orchards, 17; soft fruit and glasshouse vegetables, more than eight; and cereals, at least three; and arable crops, such as peas and vegetables, an average of just under five. A third of all fresh fruit and vegetables sampled by the Association of Public Analysts in 1983 was found to be contaminated by pesticide residues.*

Chris Rose, in Edward Goldsmith and Nicholas Hildyard (ed)
Green Britain or Industrial Wasteland? (see page 58)

Worldwide, seventy thousand people die every year as a result of ingesting or inhaling pesticides. Most of these casualties are the income earners of Third World families. It has been proved that children whose parents work frequently with pesticides run six times the normal risk of contracting leukaemia (*New Scientist*, July 1987): hi-tech gardening is not such a harmless pastime as the manufacturers would like you to believe.

Fortunately you don't have to don astronaut gear to be safe in the garden — organic methods (see pages 75-84) are completely safe given a few obvious precautions. Chemicals may have their place in an emergency, but as farmer Barry Wookey of the organic farm at Rushall in Wiltshire points out: 'You don't call the fire brigade to put out the sitting room fire every night, do you?'

This Poisoned Earth

This Poisoned Earth is the most comprehensive account of the pesticide problem currently available. As well as a plethora of horrific case histories, Nigel Dudley's book provides a full checklist of hazardous chemicals, and information on identifying pesticide damage and seeking justice and compensation through the legal system. A good book which will sell very badly in Billingham.

*

On Easter Sunday 1985, a party of young canoeists were paddling along the River Avon near Evesham, when they found two adult herons floating dead in the water. The corpses reached members of Evesham Friends of the Earth, who immediately sent them to the Institute of Terrestrial Ecology (ITE) for analysis. Publicity in the local media resulted in over 50 telephone calls reporting other dead and missing birds, including more herons. In all 17 dead herons were found, and eight bodies recovered for examination. It became apparent that the birds had started to die in the River Avon early in the spring, following a hard winter. Subsequently, an important heronry has entirely disappeared. Analysis by ITE and the Hereford and Worcester county analyst showed that the birds had been killed by a lethal mixture of DDE (the breakdown product of DDT), dieldrin and polychlorinated biphenyls, although levels of each individually would have been sufficient to kill many of the birds. Scientists reported that levels of DDE were higher than they had ever seen before. The voluntary ban on DDT had already become law. Some of the pesticides could have been stored in the birds' fat and released in the very cold weather of the previous winter, but this seemed unlikely to account for all the contamination. Further investigations by FOE discovered stocks of DDT still illegally for sale in the area. Friends of the Earth members actually bought some DDT before issuing a press release about the sales. These 'banned' chemicals had wiped out a whole colony of important freshwater birds.

This Poisoned Earth
Nigel Dudley
Piatkus, 1987
£3.95

The Residue Report

Stephanie Lashford writes with a passionate, sometimes excessively passionate, fervour about the extent to which our food is being contaminated with a range of pesticides, hormones, steroids, antibiotics, metals and nitrates. *The Residue Report* brings together an enormous range of material from food companies, supermarket chains, food scientists — even the bland reassurances from Edwina Currie and Norman Fowler are included. The further reading and address lists at the back are particularly good. It's very readable, and very frightening even if only half of what Stephanie Lashford has unearthed is true.

*

No matter what you are told, there are no safe levels of residues. Everyone reacts differently to new and foreign bodies in their system and therefore with each person you are dealing with an unknown situation. This is completely and utterly unacceptable.

The Residue Report
Stephanie Lashford
Thorsons, 1988
£4.99

The Pesticides Trust

The Pesticides Trust is a pressure group which provides information and advice about pesticides to people suffering from their effects. It also aims to promote the effective regulation of pesticides, and alternatives to them. The Trust provides a forum for discussion, undertakes research, publishes the quarterly *Pesticide News* and a range of information bulletins, and works with other environmental groups both nationally and internationally.

Pesticides Trust
20 Compton Terrace
London
N1 2UN
0(7)1-354 3860

Healthy Meat

Despite claims of 'country-freshness', 'corn-fed' and 'no artificial additives', it is virtually impossible to buy meat which has not been tampered with in one way or another. Nearly all animal feedingstuffs contain additives of some sort, and most farms — including some which claim to use 'natural' methods — use a wide range of proprietary chemicals under the guise of feeds and animal welfare products. If you can buy game meats like rabbit and wild venison from your butcher, this is least likely to cause harm to you or pain to the animals involved (though post-Chernobyl caesium levels in game have in some cases risen dramatically); free-range chicken from a reputable supplier (see FREGG, page 36) is a good second best. A truly free-range hen that has reached the end of its laying life will need to be pressure-cooked or stewed for a long time — any smallish 'farm gate' chicken which you are able to roast in the 'normal' way will almost certainly have been given hormone growth promoters. Meat products like sausages may be labelled 'additive-free', but this will only refer to the manufacturing process, not to the meat that was used in the product.

Where you can buy truly additive-free meat it will be expensive, often twice as much as your local supermarket, but if you use a lot less of it mixed with vegetables, noodles, pastas, pulses and grains (which is the traditional way of using meat in all ecologically sound societies) then prices are not outlandish, chicken being around £1.80/lb, pork and lamb around £1.20-1.80/lb, and beef around £2-£3.20/lb. At last you can now buy organic meat in some supermarkets, while an increasing number of butchers are realizing that it is worth their while stocking it.

Red House Farm

'We have no qualifications, simply a lifetime's experience', says Jean Jones, who has been rearing and selling truly additive-free meat from the Red House farm shop since 1976. Red House feed their animals with traditional feeds, open graze the animals throughout the year except the depths of winter, and bed them on straw. Their meat products (sausage rolls, pasties, potted beef and haisletts) have no artificial additives, and you can choose between white flour pastry and organic wholemeal. They will send frozen meat anywhere in the country by passenger train, and deliver regularly within Lincolnshire.

Red House Farm
Spalford Lane
North Scarle
Lincoln
LN6 9HB
052 277 224

Wholefood Butchers

Started in 1983 and often called simply 'the organic butcher', Unique Butcher in north London sells only 'naturally-reared' and additive-free meat — lamb, pork and chicken, and specially-grown beef from Scotland. The sausages contain only meat and egg, and the bacon is reputed to contain only 7% water, compared with the 15-25% found in most supermarket bacon.

Owned by the same trust as Wholefood (see page 16), Wholefood Butcher is probably the closest you can get to ecologically and humanely aware meat- eating. All the meat on sale is guaranteed free of antibiotics, hormones and stimulants, and more exotic meats like Soay sheep, duck, game, venison and milk-and-grass-reared veal are sometimes available. Their patés are excellent, if pricey.

Unique Butcher
217 Holloway Road
London
N7 8DL
0(7)1-609 7016

Wholefood Butcher
31 Paddington Street
London
W1M 3RG
0(7)1-486 1390

The Real Meat Company

Founded in 1986 by two Wiltshire farmers, Gillian Metherell and Richard Guy, The Real Meat Company was created to provide the public with additive-free meat from humanely reared animals. All their meat is produced in accordance with the welfare code of Compassion in World Farming (see page 71). They sell poultry, beef, pork and lamb, both mail order and through their shops in Bath (7 Hayes Place, Bear Flat; Tel: 0225 335139) and London (61 Manor Street, Chelsea; Tel: 0(7)1-823 3509, and 3 Nugent Terrace, NW8; Tel: 0(7)1-286 3124); their range includes sausages and burgers, ice cream, free-range eggs and additive-free cheese. A list of other retailers that sell RMC meat is available on request.

The Real Meat Company
East Hill Farm
Heytesbury
Warminster
Wiltshire
BA12 0HR
0985 40436/40060

The Born-Again Carnivore

For those who like to eat healthy and humanely-reared meat now and then, Sue Mellis and Barbara Davidson's *The Born-Again Carnivore* provides a reasoned and detailed examination of every stage of meat production, both what is going wrong within the industry and the steps that are increasingly being taken to ensure that at least some of our meat is as wholesome and causes as little suffering as we would want. The book then explains exactly how to prepare and cook different sorts of meat to best advantage, and concludes with a comprehensive list of suppliers of 'real meat', giving full descriptions, information and sample prices.

The Born-Again Carnivore
The Real Meat Guide
Sue Mellis and Barbara Davidson
Optima, 1990
£5.99

Chicken and Egg

> We spray the fields and scatter
> The poison on the ground,
> So that no wicked wild flowers
> Upon our farm be found.
> We like whatever helps us
> To line our purse with pence;
> The twenty-four-hour broiler-house
> And neat electric fence
>   All concrete sheds around us
>   And Jaguars in the yard,
>   The telly lounge and deep-freeze
>   Are ours from working hard.
>
>   John Betjeman, *Harvest Hymn*

Despite the comforting pictures of cosy pastoral scenes on the egg-boxes, 96% of eggs consumed in Britain today come from intensive battery farms. 40 million birds crammed five or six to a cage produce an average of 225 eggs in their brief, dark, cramped, debeaked, medicated, miserable lives.

But things are changing. Since 1976 the Free-Range Egg Association (FREGG) has been lobbying for more humane egg production, and for legislation to ensure that eggs which are called free-range really are. Ignore claims of 'farm-fresh' eggs — it means nothing, nor are 'brown farm eggs' any guarantee of a nutritious egg from a relatively happy chicken. Since July 1985 Eurostyle egg marketing has meant that farmers selling eggs can only label them as free-range if they really are. 'Free range' eggs must now come from hens having continuous access to open-air runs, which should mostly be covered with vegetation — the maximum stocking density should be no more than 300 hens to the acre unless new ground is used each year. The next best thing, 'deep litter' eggs, must have no more than seven hens per metre of floor space with half the area covered in litter; while 'barn' eggs must have no more than 25 hens per square metre with 15cm of perch space per hen. The FREGG definition of 'free-range' is even more stringent — hens should have at least three square feet each in the henhouse, access to outside runs, and must never be debeaked or fed antibiotics.

FREGG

FREGG is a very active organization promoting every aspect of free-range egg production from farmer to consumer. The FREGG seal of approval is a guarantee of quality and compassionate poultry farming, and the number of producers and retailers interested in obtaining the seal is growing rapidly. On receipt of an sae FREGG will send you a list of approved producers, shops and restaurants; they also produce a useful little leaflet called *How To Enjoy Your Hens, or Hints on Small Flock Keeping.*

*

I couldn't wait to see their joy when I released the six battery chickens, and they realised they were free to roam wherever they chose, to dig for worms and roll in the dust, to hide their eggs — even sit on them if they wanted to. But not immediately — first they must become acclimatised. . . I put them into a chicken house with a long run and waited to see how they would respond to the comparative freedom. They reacted all right, but not the way I expected. They were absolutely terrified by all the space around them. They crawled into the further corner of the chicken house and sat there all day, huddled together and shivering with fright. If I put food under their noses they would eat it; if I scattered it in the run it just stayed there untouched. On the fourth day I left the food just outside the door of the chicken house and waited to see what happened. After half an hour one wary beak emerged, took a tentative peck at the food, and shot back in again. A few minutes later it appeared again and took another peck before disappearing inside. After another few moments two beaks emerged and then a third. Soon there were six beaks tucking in.

        FREGG Newsletter, October 1986

The Free-Range Egg Association
37 Tanza Road
London
NW3 2UA
0(7)1-435 2596

Chickens' Lib

If you feel strongly about the appalling conditions that battery hens are kept in you might consider joining Chickens' Lib, which campaigns actively for the more humane treatment of poultry. They produce newsletters and factsheets, and research the conditions experienced by chickens in battery farms. Clare Druce, one of the founders of Chickens' Lib, has written a succinct yet comprehensive overview of the current state of play in her book *Chicken and Egg: Who Pays The Price?* (Green Print, 1989, £3.99).

Chickens' Lib
PO Box 2
Holmfirth
Huddersfield
West Yorkshire
HD7 1QT
0484 861814/683158

If you have enough land (and the average garden is quite large enough) you might consider having half a dozen chickens of your own. They will eat most of your kitchen waste, fertilize your garden, and in summer at least should provide an egg each every couple of days. *Home Farm* magazine (page 74) has adverts from suppliers of day-old or point-of-lay birds; Gardencraft (see page 74) produces a range of poultry houses, folds and arks; and if you get really excited about keeping poultry you can do no better than to read Stuart Banks' *Complete Book of Poultry Keeping* (Ward Lock, 1979, £6.95), which will tell you everything you could ever want to know about mycoplasmosis, hatchability, Marek's disease and turkey manure.

Cheese

Cheese is both good news and bad news where health, nutrition and economics are concerned. Eaten regularly but in small quantities, cheese has been a staple food in Britain for at least two thousand years. It is nutritious, and easy to store and carry with you. Until a hundred years ago almost every farm made its own cheese; cheesemaking was an important part of country life, and every region had its own proudly maintained cheesemaking traditions. Cheese is an excellent source of protein, calcium and essential amino acids. There are more than four hundred varieties of cheese, so you should never get bored with it, and it is a versatile food.

Hard cheeses tend to be high in fat. This won't bother you if you only eat small quantities, but many people eat over half a pound of high fat cheeses each week — mostly Cheddar (which is around 30% fat), though Stilton at 40% is even higher. At the other end of the spectrum, cottage cheese contains only 4% fat (and 80% water!). Orange cheeses are coloured, often with Annatto or its derivative, Bixin; processed cheeses often contain a cocktail of colours, flavourings and emulsifiers. Many cheeses also have salt added, another reason for not eating too much. If you are vegetarian, you will also want to avoid the majority of cheese, which is made using animal rennet (the inner stomach lining of calves): you should be able to find vegetable rennet alternatives at your health food shop.

If you can afford it, there is lot to be said for buying a whole cheese of a basic variety (Cheddar, Cheshire or Red Leicester for example) — keep it wrapped in foil or greaseproof paper at the bottom of the fridge.

If you think you may be allergic to cows' milk products, it is worth trying a vegetarian additive-free cheese first to check whether it's the cheese itself or the additives that you are reacting to. If you still react, try goats' or ewes' cheese instead — both now come in quite a range of consistencies.

There are speciality cheese shops all over Britain, often selling wines and beers as well. Many supermarkets are cashing in too, displaying quantities of British and continental cheeses among frills of parsley and paper doilies. Don't be afraid of asking to taste before you buy — a really good shop will encourage you to.

There has been a recent upsurge in farmhouse cheese-making, and of the many cheesemakers who have re-established the art in the last twenty years I have chosen four.

Llangloffan

Leon and Joan Downey have been making their award-winning additive- free cheeses in Pembrokeshire for twelve years. Llangloffan cheeses are made from raw milk produced to Soil Association symbol standard, completely free from chemical residues and additives; at around £2.40 a pound (when bought as a complete cheese) they are not that expensive, and can be bought by post or from a growing number of shops in England and Wales. The farm shop (also selling organic produce) is open six days a week, and visitors are welcome to look round.

Llangloffan Farmhouse Cheese Centre
Llangloffan Farm
Castle Morris
Haverfordwest
Dyfed
SA62 5ET
034 85 241

Botton Village Creamery

Established in 1972 and now housed in a magnificent new creamery, the Botton Creamery is part of the Camphill Trust community at Botton in North Yorkshire. They make hard and soft vegetarian cheese, live yogurt and fresh curd, which you can buy throughout Yorkshire, from wholefood wholesalers, or by post (hard cheese only) from them. The creamery is part of a farm which is part of a village community which is part of a network of communities in which mentally disabled adults can lead a full and fulfilled life. If you are interested in finding out more, ask for details (and a product sales catalogue) from Botton Village.

Botton Village
Danby
Whitby
North Yorkshire
YO21 2NJ
0287 60871

Quicke's

Quicke's vegetarian Cheddar cheese, made by the only commercial producers of traditionally-made cheeses in Devon, is generally considered to be one of the very best. They sell their cheeses at around six months old, but they continue to mature for several months. Herb and smoked Cheddar are also available, along with single and double Gloucester, and Quicke's also make excellent additive-free low-sugar ice cream, such as apricot with yogurt or strawberry with yogurt. You can buy all of these, plus organic vegetables, eggs, chicken, duck, venison, trout, lamb, pork and even hand-made chocolates at the farm shop just north of Exeter. They don't do mail order, but you should be able to buy their cheeses at any good cheese retailer.

J.G. Quicke and Partners
Woodley
Newton St Cyres
Exeter
Devon
EX5 5BT
0392 851222

Ice Cream

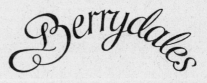

If, like me, you love real ice cream but would like to try a vegan alternative that really does give you the same sort of hit, Berrydales now make a tofu-based ice cream equivalent in four flavours: berry, maple and walnut, ginger and honey, and bitter chocolate. As well as tasting good, Berrydales' is highly nutritious and ideal for people with allergies. It contains no animal products and no additives, is low in fats and cholesterol, and is even relatively low in calories. It is sold in bio-degradable cardboard packs at 70p per 100ml tub or £2.75 for a 500ml size, and is available from Cranks and many other health food stores and delicatessens.

Berrydales
5 Lawn Road
London
NW3 2XS
0(7)1 722 2866

The Spices of Life

Mealtime, and the first bite taken. There's something missing — it just needs a bit of . . . The most common reaction is to reach for the salt or the sauce bottle. But hang on, isn't salt supposed to be bad for you, and the sauce bottle has all these Es in it?

Yes, salt is bad for you in the amounts that average Britons eat it. Here are Caroline Walker and Geoffrey Cannon in *The Food Scandal* (see page 11): 'The World Health Organisation recommends an upper limit of 5 grams a day. (Note, this is 2 grams of sodium a day.) And the WHO report points out that societies without high blood pressure problems usually consume under 3 grams of salt a day. Average salt intakes in Britain are not known. The Ministry of Agriculture estimate is 8 grams a day. Other estimates are higher — 12 grams a day. These levels are two or even four times more than the WHO guideline.' Most sauces have sugar in them, together with emulsifiers, colourings, preservatives and antioxidants.

Salt

The best advice with salt is: cut down as far as you can, and use herbs and spices instead as flavouring substitutes. There really isn't much difference between 'ordinary' table salt and 'healthy' sea salt, especially since the latter tends to come from shallow estuarine waters which are often seriously polluted (like the Mediterranean coast of France and the Essex coast). The makers of Sweet'n'Low are now marketing little fast-food sachets of Maldon Sea Salt, 'panned from tidal waters by Essex craftsmen for the connoisseur'.

Pepper

Black and white pepper come from the same tropical tree, the white berries being ripened and skinned while the black ones are the unripened fruit — this makes the white peppercorns slightly more expensive, but stronger. Pepper is said to stimulate digestion and circulation, and can't hurt you in the amounts that you can normally eat it.

Moving from peppercorns to chilli peppers, in 1986 Dounne Moore, herself from Trinidad where the best peppers grow, launched Gramma's Concentrated Pepper Sauce, the additive-free and hotter version of Tabasco, from her East Ham council flat. It isn't cheap, but a very little goes a very long way, and Dounne claims all sorts of benefits from eating hot peppers: it 'wakes up the system arousing sluggish organs to action'. Warning: 'mild' means 'hot'; 'super hot' is an understatement. Order direct from her (or if you happen to find yourself in Harrods, Fortnum and Mason . . .).

Gramma's
77 Brighton Road
London
E6 6AR
0(8)1-470 8751

Mustard

A useful, tasty and harmless addition to pickles, salad dressings, cheese dishes and so on. Coleman's of Norwich are the British mustard producers — visit their shop if you are ever in Norwich. Urchfont Mustard from Wiltshire Tracklements is wonderful stuff, but excessively expensive.

Coleman's Mustard Shop
3 Bridewell Alley
Norwich
Norfolk
NR2 1AO
0603 627889

The Wiltshire Tracklement Co. Ltd
High Street
Sherston
Malmesbury
Wiltshire
SN16 0LQ
0666 840851

Vinegar

Avoid cheap malt vinegars, which are often made from commercially-produced acetic acid. Imported wine vinegars vary enormously in quality — Dufrais is good, especially their tarragon vinegar.

Cider vinegar has all sorts of wonderful claims made about it. I don't know whether it really cures hiccups and obesity, but with honey and boiling water it is certainly extremely soothing for sore throats. Martlet and Whiteways both produce additive-free cider vinegars from English apples, but Aspalls organic cyder vinegar (about £1.80/litre) crowns them all.

Some Alternatives

Shoyu (Soy Sauce)

Any good wholefood shop will sell Japanese shoyu (at around £3-3.50/litre), which is a healthy and economical equivalent to salt if used sparingly. Most of the wholefood wholesalers bottle their own (Suma, Green City, etc. — see pages 19-20); support them rather than the come-lately multinationals.

*

This high quality shoyu is made from whole soya beans, wheat, sea salt, and well or mountain spring water; then fermented together in cedar casks using the traditional three year process which develops shoyu's characteristically rich aroma. It is rich in valuable minerals and vitamins including vitamin B12 and is also an aid to digestion. It contains no artificial colourings or flavourings and is stronger and lasts longer than many commercial soya sauces.

from the Green City Shoyu label

Vecon

An additive-free natural vegetable stock made by Modern Health Products Ltd, who will send you a free sample and recipe leaflet if you write to them. Made from vegetable protein and extracts of eleven different vegetables, it makes a good stock, hot drink, spread, or salt substitute in savoury dishes. MHP also produces a low-salt (less than 1%) yeast extract called Natex, a good substitute for Marmite — again ask for a sample sachet.

Modern Health Products Ltd
Davis Road
Chessington
Surrey
KT9 1TH
0(8)1-397 4361

Tomato Ketchup

Whole Earth produces a healthy sugar-and-salt-free tomato ketchup which will fool even children brought up on run-of-the-mill baked beans; a recent introduction is a ketchup made entirely with organic ingredients. They also do a very nice italiano sauce.

Spreads and Jams

These are what you put on slices of bread to keep you going between meals, or if you keep the farinaceous feast of teatime or high tea they may be part of one of your main meals. Spreads are a quick and useful way of turning bread into a tasty and nutritionally balanced morsel, but there are several things to watch out for.

By far the biggest danger in jams and spreads is taking in too much sugar, salt, and chemical additives, and it is wise to look carefully at the ingredients label before you buy. You can now buy healthy alternatives to every kind of spread, plus some new ones with which to treat your taste buds. Here are some of the options available.

Nut Butters

A few years ago I was taken to what I was assured was the largest wholefood supermarket in the world, Bread and Circuses near Amherst in western Massachusetts. The thing that most impressed me was an array of nut butter making machines, where you could select the nuts you wanted (peanut, hazel, almond, cashew, pecan), the texture you wanted (rough crunchy, smooth crunchy, smooth), and feed them into the machine yourself, watching them turn into the spread of your choosing.

Nut butters make a healthy and nutritious spread, and don't need anything added to them (especially sugar) to make them last quite a long time. I have heard that additive-free peanut butters sometimes contain aflatoxins, a fungal poison which can harm people, but even if this is true — which I doubt — I can't believe that they do more harm than chemical additives.

Sunwheel crunchy peanut butter has a very good taste and consistency. Meridian do hazelnut and almond butters; Equal Exchange produces a cashew butter from Mozambiquan nuts, and Whole Earth a tasty three nut butter. Eat them on their own or mixed with honey or low sugar jam. A mixture of peanut butter, honey, sesame seeds and carob, rolled in sesame seeds, makes a wicked alternative sweetmeat.

Savoury Spreads

You can buy a rapidly growing range of healthy spreads, based on yeast extract, tofu, beans and nuts. Many are very tasty, though you can often make similar spreads yourself for a fraction of the cost. Watch out for and avoid over-packaging, Tartex paté in tubes for example. Granose sandwich spreads are good, especially the mushroom and the olive, as are Living Foods' tofu spreads.

Low-Sugar Jams

Many manufacturers are now making reduced sugar jams. The point about sugar is that it is the ideal preservative because it kills all known life stone dead — and if you eat too much of it it'll kill you equally stone dead. And it's addictive. So eat low-sugar jams in moderation, and always in preference to the sickly substances traditionally passed off as jams. Danish Orchards jams in 2lb tubs are good quality and good value, and you can use the tubs afterwards — the marmalade is particularly good. You can of course make your own jam; use half the sugar it says in the recipe, don't worry if it's a bit runny, and keep it in the fridge once you have opened it. Remember that fresh fruit is always far more nutritious than its preserved variety.

Sunwheel Pear and Apple Spread

Worth a special mention, since as well as being nothing other than pure concentrated apple and pear juice which can be spread thinly on bread, it can also be used as a sweetener in baking and desserts in place of sugar. Pear and apple spread comes in pound and half-pound paper tubs at a bit more than £1 a lb.

No-Sugar Jams

When you first taste no-added-sugar jams you'll be very pleasantly surprised that you an actually taste the fruit — though you won't get the same sugar thrill (nearly all of us are addicted). Most of these jams have no added sweetener at all, though Whole Earth have recently introduced their Sweet'n' Fruity range which is sweetened with concentrated apple juice — my favourites are the Italian peach and the Scottish raspberry. Many supermarket chains are now producing own brand sugar-free jams, but the best ranges are produced by Whole Earth (try the mixed berry or the hedgerow) and Meridian (the peach and passion fruit is amazing). These are not cheap, but will save your teeth and your health. All no-sugar jams should be kept refrigerated once you have opened them, or you will find grey mould growing on them.

Margarines

All margarines have vitamins A and D added by law, and nearly all contain colourings and salt. They all contain saturated fats, too, so replacing butter with margarine will not necessarily protect you from taking too much saturated fat. In general those low in polyunsaturates are best — most are made largely from sunflower seeds. Very few margarines are guaranteed 100% vegan since they contain whey and whey products which come from cows' milk; if you want a truly dairy-free margarine look out for Granose, which now comes in a reduced salt version. The best advice is: whatever you spread on your bread, spread it thinly.

Snacks

The snack food market is a multi-million pound one, and the supreme example of how we can be persuaded to part with our money to buy overpackaged products which for the most part do us no good at all. Worse than this, children eat a higher proportion of snack foods than adults, pouring dubious additives into their growing systems while pouring their pennies into the coffers of the members of the Snack, Nut and Crisp Manufacturers Association.

Just to give you a flavour (plus colour and antioxidant) of what goes into a few of our favourite bag snacks, here's an extract from a list of products prepared by the Food Commission (see page 28) showing how many additives are put in them which are already banned from foods for babies and young children (plus those due to be banned).

Bag snacks

KP Crisps, Skips, Hula Hoops, Crunchies	MSG (621) (635) Saccharin	Sunset yellow (E110)
Smiths Square Crisps, Quavers	BHA (E320) BHT (E321) MSG (621)	Annatto (E160b)
Smiths Monster Munch	MSG (621) (635) Saccharin	
Smiths Flavour-n-Shake	MSG (621) (635) Saccharin Aspartame	
Golden Wonder Crisps, Wotsits, Ringos	MSG (621) (627) (631)	Paprika Annatto (E160b) Tumeric
Safeways Savoury Puffs	BHA (E320) BHT (E321) MSG (621)	Annatto (E160b)
Sainsburys Cheesy Nik Naks	MSG (621) Saccharin	Coal Tar Dyes (E104, E110)
Pim's Toffee Popcorn	(E310) BHA (E320)	Caramel (E150)
Osem's Bissli kosher snacks	(E310) BHA (E320) BHT (E321)	

Would you willingly feed these to your children, let alone yourself?

Healthy Snacks and Their Implications

In the last few years there has been a boom in the number and variety of healthy snack foods you can buy, from carob covered raisins and banana chips to Bombay mix and assorted nuts. Of course these are much better for you than the much-processed additive laden items I mentioned above, but do stop and think before you buy even these goodies.

Even 'healthy' foods eaten in excess will eventually make you overweight, with all the associated health risks, so always ask yourself whether you really need that crunchy bar or that tropical mix.

Then there's the question of packaging, closely linked with the perennial need to 'add value'. Whether it's made with natural ingredients or not, the bar that comes in its own wrapper neatly boxed two dozen to a carton is using an awful lot of unnecessary materials, very little of which will be recycled — and you will be paying for the privilege of throwing it away as soon as you've eaten the contents. A muesli and honey Grizzly Bar is far and away better than a packet of

Smarties with their six dangerous additives, but at 20p for 25g of muesli and honey (25g of muesli costs around 3p) it's daylight robbery. But it's your choice.

The moral is: try not to buy snack foods unless you have to, and then buy healthy ones. Otherwise make your own. Snacks in themselves are not unhealthy or immoral, and some people (including many children) seem to function much better when they eat little and often rather than tucking into three big meals a day. Mixes of nuts and dried fruit can easily be made up at home (though if you're like me you'll find it hard not to eat them all at once). Granola (the home-made version of Jordan's — and others' — Traditional Crunchy) makes a very moreish snack, as do a few pieces of dried fruit salad. If you have a more savoury tooth try sunflower seeds roasted in a little tamari. Then there is always popcorn, or even an apple.

Having said all that, we all get caught out feeling peckish now and again, so if you do suddenly feel the urge to rush into Holland and Barrett here are some favourites.

Fruit and Nut Mixes

There is a bewildering variety of mixes now available, most of which never have quite enough of your favourite ingredient (a good reason for mixing your own). 'Trail Mix' is the basic mix, with nuts, raisins and coconut slices; 'Tropical Mix' is the same with bits of mango, papaya and pineapple added. 'Festive Mix' and 'Marathon Mix' (among others) usually have even more added goodies, such as carob and yogurt coated nuts and raisins. AA Enterprises (see page 119) sell bags of Mozambiquan cashews, a tasty snack which also helps this poverty-stricken country.

Bombay Mix

A spicy savoury mixture of lentils, peanuts, soya beans, noodles, chili and curry powder (or something approximating to this).

Wholewheat Crisps

A healthier and more satisfying alternative to the mainstream variety — look out for Nature's Snack, Hedgehog (including yogurt and cucumber flavour; now also organic crisps with either sea salt or cider vinegar), and Benson's jacket potato crisps.

Crunchy and Chewy Bars

They all taste much the same, though I do like the Holly Mill carob chip bars and banana Castaway bars. Avoid Quaker Harvest Bars, which contain BHA and Sorbitol, two suspect additives.

Fig Cake

A traditional Spanish goody, made in Britain by Wilcox and Lomer in Cheltenham. Look out for the walnut and ginger and the apricot and almond.

Carob Bars

For the addicted chocolate lover prepared to make the break, Kalibu make a wide range of carob bars and yogurt-coated snack bars with no added sugar. If you're expecting chocolate, carob is obviously a different taste, but quite acceptable. Try the fruit and nut or orange carob snack bars.

Tea and Coffee

Almost all the diet and health books agree that consumption of coffee and tea should be kept to a minimum; development economists have shown convincingly that current regimes for growing and marketing these commodities impoverish both the land and the Third World workforce.

Britain is still the biggest tea importer in the world. The tea trade is dominated by British companies who make large profits by buying and selling tea all over the world. They pay the developing countries little for their tea exports and the tea workers on their estates are paid low wages and live in overcrowded and unhealthy conditions.

World Development Movement, *The Tea Trade*, 1979 (95p from WDM, Bedford Chambers, London WC2E 8HA)

Instant coffee, which now accounts for around 90% of coffee consumed, is hugely expensive in energy. Roasting, grinding and processing it takes around 18,000k/cal per kg, which makes it 10 times more energy extravagant than a fish finger and 100 times more so than ice. The coffee in your cup of instant coffee cost about 60% of the price charged by the retailer, whilst fully 10% of the price goes towards promotion.

Richard North, *The Real Cost* (see page 237)

Most teas and coffees are sold under brand names with labels that say things like 'carefully selected', 'blended from fine ingredients' and other bland promises. Such blanket platitudes disguise the true origins of the ingredients, which may be the product of Bangladeshi 'slave labour' (a phrase used by the Roman Catholic Justice and Peace Commission), the fruits of the work of poorly-paid Tamil refugees, or which may result in the massive pollution of Colombian rivers.

Most teas and coffees contain caffeine and other addictive substances, so it is hardly surprising that most people find it hard to imagine life without them. Both tea and coffee can be decaffeinated, though the health risks associated with the solvent used to extract the caffeine are considered by some nutritionists to be as great as the risks related to the caffeine. Though tea leaves are 2% caffeine by weight and coffee beans half that, the coffee is more thoroughly extracted, so a cup of coffee is likely to be about twice as rich in caffeine as a cup of tea (or, incidentally, a can of cola).

You can now buy a wide range of ingredients for hot drinks which are not based on tea or coffee, and which contain no caffeine (see the next column). If you do buy tea and coffee, however, there are now a number of ways of buying it which ensure that you know exactly what you are buying, and that the Third World producers are getting a reasonable return for their labour.

Teas and Coffees from Traidcraft

Traidcraft (see page 240 for main entry) sells the widest range of 'fair trade' teas and coffees in Britain. They started selling Campaign Coffee from Tanzanian co-operatives in 1979, and now sell a wide range of teas and coffees including loose teas and teabags from India, Sri Lanka, Mauritius and Tanzania, ground coffee from Tanzania and Nicaragua (a decaffeinated Nicaraguan coffee is also available), coffee beans from both countries, and the original instant from Tanzania (an instant called Encafé from Nicaragua is also available). Prices are only marginally higher than your local supermarket (£1.70/100g of instant coffee), and you know that you are putting money and work in the direction of the people who really deserve it.

Traidcraft plc
Kingsway
Gateshead
Tyne and Wear
NE11 0NE
091 491 0591

PURE NICARAGUAN COFFEE
After Dinner Roast

Other trading and aid organizations also sell Nicaraguan coffee, including Twin Trading (see page 241) and OXFAM. Campaign Coffee in Scotland, now part of Equal Exchange (see page 20) is a separate organization (Campaign Coffee Scotland, 29 Nicolson Square, Edinburgh EH8 9BX; Tel: 031 667 0905). Many wholefood shops and some craft/bookshops sell Traidcraft teas and coffees, the wholesale wholefood co-operatives (see pages 19-20) all sell 'aware' teas and coffees in bulk, and some coffee and tea shops with a wide range sell Nicaraguan and other origin-guaranteed beans, together with a wide range of scented and flavoured teas. The London Herb and Spice Company now sells organic Tanzanian tea at £1.29 for 40 teabags, available in health food stores or from Suma (see page 20). Two of the best tea and coffee shops — Pollards and Taylors — are in the north of England. Both produce fascinating mail order catalogues. I particularly like Taylors' fruity teas — apricot, peach, blackcurrant, apple . . . (and the old-fashioned tea room in York's cobbled Stonegate has wonderful cakes too).

Pollards
2-4 Charles Street
Sheffield
S1 2HS
0742 725460

Taylors
46 Stonegate
York
YO1 2AS
0904 622865

Tea and Coffee 'Substitutes'

There are no substitutes for tea or coffee, but there are some very good alternatives.

Where coffee is concerned you can try Barleycup, a barley-based beverage from Poland. Caro is a similar grain-based drink, tastier but more expensive. Symington's Dandelion Compound is an acquired taste. To my mind the best of the coffee alternatives, though expensive and difficult to find, is Celestial Seasoning's 'Roastaroma' blend.

Herbal teas are another alternative to caffeinated beverages. The cheapest and freshest herbs will be the ones you grow and gather yourself — grow mint and lemon balm outside the back door in pots, and gather elderflowers, chamomile and yarrow in season. More exotic herbs for tea making, like hibiscus, can be bought by the ounce from your wholefood shop. If you prefer to pay for the convenience of herbal teabags, you can now buy them in almost any health food shop or supermarket.

Water

A survey of 25 rivers, reported by the Standing Technical Advisory Committee on Water Quality, reveals that nitrate levels have, on average, doubled during the past twenty years. Levels in the Stour, said to be a fairly typical East Anglian river, exceeded the World Health organization's recommended limit of 50mg nitrate per litre of water (sometimes expressed as 11.3mg nitrate nitro-gen/litre) for 400 days in the three years from 1974 to 1977. If present land use practices continue, it is predicted that nitrate levels in the River Thames will breach this limit on an annual basis by the mid-1990s.

> Brian Price, in *Green Britain or Industrial Wasteland?*
> (see page 58)

In the US the very rich are buying 100,000-year-old water, which is presumed to pre-date pollution, trapped as it has been in Greenland's glaciers, at $7 a litre.

> Richard North, *The Real Cost* (see page 237)

It's useful to know that if you are concerned about what is in your tap-water you can ask your local authority to test it for you, and many authorities (particularly where there is a high risk of lead or nitrate contamination) will provide this service quickly and free. Friends of the Earth (see page 65) have pro-duced a leaflet which explains how to find out about the quality of your tap water and where to direct your complaints. It gives help with drafting a letter, dealing with officials who try to fob you off, and with suppliers who refuse to reveal inform-ation. It also helps you interpret what you find out about your tap water.

The main water pollution risks come from untreated sewage entering drinking water supplies, lead and aluminium poison-ing due mostly to acid rain, and nitrate pollution from agricultural chemicals.

Lead reaches the kitchen tap by means of water running through old lead pipes. There are thousands of miles of such pipework inside British homes, and lead pipes still carry water to houses all over the country. Worst affected are people who live in older houses in acid water areas. These include most of Scotland, the north of England, Wales and the West Country. Cities affected include Glasgow, Edinburgh, Birmingham, Liverpool, Manchester and Hull. It has been estimated that at least 10 million people live in areas at risk from lead in tap water, one of the most powerful brain poisons known to man.

Aluminium sulphate (alum) is leached into water from rock and soil by acid rain (see page 57). In addition, 100,000 tonnes is added to tap water in Britain every year, especially in the south-east, Yorkshire, Northern England, the Scottish Borders, and in other areas with peat-stained water. The reason is cosmetic: it is a coagulant that clarifies the water. In areas of Yorkshire the natural alum content in water can reach 3,500 micrograms per litre — the EC permitted maximum is 200 micrograms per litre. Doctors have known since the 1970s

that aluminium absorbed into the body can cause brittle bones, anaemia, and a form of dementia that is usually fatal. More recently, aluminium has been blamed for increasing incidence of the most common form of dementia, Alzheimer's disease.

Friends of the Earth estimates that in Britain about 4 million people, mainly in East Anglia, Lincolnshire, Nottinghamshire and Staffordshire, receive water supplies that sometimes exceed the EC limit for nitrates. Nitrates have been implicated in blue baby syndrome and stomach cancer. Other highly toxic pesticides and herbicides reach our drinking water from a variety of sources. In 1988 Friends of the Earth's analysis showed East Anglia, the most intensively farmed area in the country, to have the worst record for pesticide contamination of drinking water. No fewer than eleven pesticides were detected in quantities over the EC limit. The runner up was the Severn/Trent area.

Down The Drain

In the early 1980s Ken Stewart, Director of Environmental Health for Dumfries and Galloway, took it upon himself in his spare time to collect and test tapwater samples from all over his region — he discovered that two thirds of them would be deemed unfit for human consumption by the American Academy of Science. That's just one of the many frightening stories to emerge in two important new books about the state of our water. Stuart Gordon's *Down The Drain* traces the recent history of the water industry; he is particularly good on the privatization issue and on what must now happen if we are to emerge safely from the current dilemma. *Britain's Poisoned Water* is better written, with chapters on different sorts of water pollution including agricultural, industrial, sewage and toxic waste disposal, but the closing chapter about what you as a consumer can do about it all is very sparse.

Down The Drain
Water, Pollution and
Privatisation
Stuart Gordon
Optima, 1989
£5.99

**Britain's Poisoned
Water**
Frances and Phil Craig
Penguin, 1989
£3.99

Bottled Waters

Maybe I'm just not a connoisseur, but unless a bottled water has something special going for it like its fizziness I find it hard to tell the difference between them. They're all much the same price (60-80p/litre), they all come from fairly reputable sources under beautiful hills from Shropshire to the Pentlands, and they're all healthier for you than drinking polluted tap water. But bottled water is an industry like any other, and just think of all the plastic that goes into the bottles and the fuel used to get those bottles into your kitchen . . . If you do live in an area where the tap water tastes excessively chemically, however, you may have to resort to bottled water; the alternative is a water filter, details of which you will find on page 102.

Fruit Juices

One big change in grocery shops and supermarkets is that you can now buy relatively pure added-sugar-free fruit juices almost anywhere. Most of them are made from imported fruit concentrates which have been reconstituted by British soft drinks companies, and though they are much better for you than 'fruit drinks' or 'Orange C' they definitely taste reconstituted (it is useful to know that a real fruit juice must have the word 'juice' in its description — however appetizing other liquids may sound, they may never have seen the tropical fruits displayed on the packet).

The best fruit juices, however, are those that have been pressed and packed immediately. They have usually not been filtered, so they are sometimes cloudy in appearance, but once you have tasted them then reconstituted fruit juice will always be second-rate.

Among the best of the pressed juices is Aspalls' apple juice, which sells in cartons at around 97p per litre, or in bottles (made from organically-grown apples) at around £1.70. It's too expensive to drink all the time, but cold from the fridge it equals any other form of cold liquid refreshment. Aspalls also produce apple cider vinegar.

Copella produces an excellent range of English-grown fruit juices, including 'Peake's' organic apple and delicious mixes of strawberry and apple and cherry and apple; they will also send you recipe and cocktail leaflets. Leisure Drinks market the Volonté range from Belgium, which includes orange, pineapple, and a pleasant grape juice, but although these are good they do not match the English juices. They also stock the Lindavia range from Germany, which includes pear and grape, and the Eden range, also from Germany, of fruit and vegetable juices, including carrot, beetroot, bilberry and raspberry. Look out too for the new range of fruit juice concentrates from Suma (see page 20), including apple and orange, and apple and raspberry.

Aspalls
Aspall House
Debenham
Stowmarket
Suffolk
IP14 6PD
0728 860510

Leisure Drinks Ltd
24 Willow Road
Trent Lane
Castle Donington
Derby
DE7 2NP
0332 850616

Copella Fruit Juices Ltd
Hill Farm
Boxford
Colchester
CO6 5NY
0787 210348/210496

Beer and Cider

I'm not a card-carrying pub aficionado — one pint is enough for me and I can't stand clouds of cigarette smoke, let alone fruit machines and star wars in the corner. This section is thus rather a second-hand one, but if good beer in homely and comfortable pubs is part of your lifestyle you might consider subscribing to CAMRA, the Campaign for Real Ale, founded nineteen years ago to counteract the closure of neighbourhood pubs and the standardization and rapidly-falling quality of beers and ales. The CAMRA *Good Beer Guide* (£5.95), now in its seventeenth year, is a mine of information about pubs throughout Britain which serve decent beer, and though the cartoons sometimes tend towards the sexist, the good humour of the CAMRA publishing team shines through. CAMRA produces a monthly newspaper, *What's Brewing*, and has 150 or so branches throughout the country which organize social events, including brewery visits and tastings. There's a fascinating leaflet on pub sports, and 1988 saw the first publication of CAMRA's *Good Cider Guide* (£4.95). Since then they've produced a *Good Pub Food Guide*, a *Family Pub Guide*, and several guides to good pubs in different areas of the country.

Corbridge	Dipton Mill
12–3; 6–11 (12–5; 7–11 Sat)	12–3; 6–11
Tynedale Hotel	**Dipton Mill Inn**
☎ (043 471) 2149	Dipton Mill Road, Hexham
Jennings Bitter; McEwan	OS929610 ☎ (0434) 606577
80/– ⊞	**Ruddles Best Bitter, County;**
Comfortable pub beside chip	**Webster's Yorkshire Bitter** ⊞
shop Q ⇔ ⑁ ≠ ♣	Stone-built country hostelry
	with real fires and beams,
11–11 (2pm closing Sun lunch)	miles from anywhere. Guest
Wheatsheaf Hotel	beers ⇔ Q ⚠
St Helens Street	
☎ (043 471) 2020	**Etal**
Vaux Bitter ⊞	12–3; 6–11
Welcoming pub in historic	**Black Bull**
town. Camping symbol means	Turn off A1 at Lowick
caravans may park in pub car	☎ (089 082) 200
park ⇔ ⑁ ⇔ Ⓙ ⑁⑁ ⚠ ≠ ♣ P	**Vaux Lorimers Best Scotch** ⊞
	Thatched village pub near old
Try also: Lion of Corbridge	castle. Pleasant comfortable
(S&N)	interior (the pub, not the
	castle) Q

Campaign for Real Ale
34 Alma Road
St Albans
Hertfordshire
AL1 3BW
0727 67201

Non-Alcoholic (but Alcohol Lookalike) Drinks

The Germans pioneered the idea of non-alcoholic drinks that look and taste like their alcoholic counterparts but don't have the same kick or the same side-effects. A wide range of these lookalikes is imported by Leisure Drinks (see above for address), including Carl Jung's (no relation) range of alcohol-free Rhine wines and Königsaft sparkling grape juice; they also stock Palermo non-alcoholic 'vermouth' and a non-alcoholic 'anise' — send for details of the full range. A non-alcoholic drink which definitely feels alcoholic is the Original Olde Norfolk Punch, marketed by Wellbeing, which contains a wealth of herbs and spices including alchoof, feverfew and samphire to name but a handful, and is wonderful served hot on a winter's night. Send for a leaflet extolling its virtues.

Wellbeing Foods
19 Sydenham Lane
Sydenham
London
SE26 5EX
0(8)1-659 2003

Wines

As can be guessed from the proliferation of chains like Victoria Wines and Oddbins, the British are now drinking more wine than ever before. What may be less apparent is the parallel growth of the home-grown wine industry, and of the organic wine movement in Europe. 'Vins biologique' and German 'Ökowein' now have a considerable reputation, and several specialist importers carry an excellent range of wines which are guaranteed additive-free, pesticide-free, and produced without the use of any animal product. At several recent tastings an organic wine has been selected as the best of its kind, which is not surprising when you consider that the chemicals used in most wine growing and manufacture kill all the helpful organisms as well as the more obvious 'pests'. *The Organic Wine Guide* by Charlotte Mitchell and Ian Wright (Mainstream, 1987, £4.95) is the only book currently available on the subject.

Sedlescombe

Open every day from 10 to 6, April to December (winter weekends from noon to 5), Sedlescombe is Britain's only Organic Wine Centre. Here you can see an organic vineyard and winery, taste a range of English estate-bottled organics, and buy an extensive range of English and imported organic wines. You can also learn about traditional winemaking, picnic in the vineyard or lunch in the wine and salad bar — and if all this tires you out you can stay the night in their bed and breakfast accommodation. Their Soil Association approved Sussex apple wine costs £2.95 a bottle, and around a hundred imported organic wines range from £3.50 to £8.00.

The Centre for Organic Wine
Sedlescombe Vineyard
Robertsbridge
East Sussex
TN32 5SA
058 083 715

Vinceremos

Next in the list must come Vinceremos, founded five years ago, stocking an impressive list of organic wines including the award-winning English Bacchus 1984, a crisp fruity white. Vinceremos also import wines, beers and spirits from all over the world, and arrange special offers in conjunction with Third World solidarity campaigns. Thus they are the sole importers of wine from Zimbabwe — £2.75 a bottle of which £2 a case goes to the Anti-Apartheid Movement, and Flor de Ca/a Nicaraguan rum imported in conjunction with the Nicaragua Solidarity Campaign.

Vinceremos Wines
Unit 10
Ashley Industrial Estate
Wakefield Road
Osset
West Yorkshire
WF5 9JD
0924 276393

Whitakers

Whitaker's sell organic wines, liqueurs and fruit juices from their specialist wine shop in Buxton, which they believe is the only one of its kind in the country. They also sell by mail order, and supply off-licences, wholefood shops and hotels. All of their suppliers belong to some form of organic organization and are vetted by the Whitakers to ensure high standards.

Wines range from £3.80 for a Côtes du Rhone 1987, and apple, pear and grape juice is available at £1.50 per litre. Six or more cases are delivered free of charge.

Whitaker's Organic Wines
8 Market Place
Buxton
Derbyshire
SK17 6EB
0298 70241

Vintage Roots

Vintage Roots is just three years old, but already has an impressive list of organic wines from Europe, California, Australia and New Zealand. They sell only organic wines, including some vegan and biodynamic wines, believing that 'organic agriculture is the only way forward'. They will supply mixed cases, including their own selections, from around £34.50 a case of twelve, and can tell you where your nearest organic wine stockist is.

Vintage Roots
25 Manchester Road
Reading
Berkshire
RG1 3QE
0734 662569

Haughton Fine Wines

Although only three years old, Haughton Fine Wines have recently been voted Northern Wine Merchant of the Year by *Wine Magazine* and *The Sunday Telegraph*. The 125 organic wines they offer from around the world make up about half their range (the rest are good but not organic), and their catalogue is also an informed guide to organic methods and an explanation of the selection process for each wine. Bruce and Judith Kendrick have now begun wholesaling their wines and have found a ready market, but they still value their private customers.

Haughton Fine Wines
Chorley Green Lane
Chorley
Nantwich
Cheshire
CW5 8JR
0270 74 233

Three small-scale importers worth mentioning, all of which carry a small but well-chosen range of organic wines, are Elixir Wines in Oxford, Organics in London and Vinature in Birmingham. Elixir wines are remarkably good value — £3.65 for a Domaine de Maurin 1988 organic white Bordeaux. Organics import wines from Italy, and deal only with members of environmental or biodynamic organizations. Prices start at around £3.00 for a Pinot Nero del Veneto Zanette. Vinature produce organic and vegetarian wines, mostly from Europe, ranging from £3.12 for a Bordeaux Blanc Sec 1988. They deliver free in the Greater Birmingham area.

Elixir Wines
54 Rectory Road
Oxford
OX4 1BW
0865 721179

Vinature
16 Cotton Lane
Moseley
Birmingham
B13 9SA
021 449 1781/7472

Organics
290 Fulham Palace Road
London
SW6 6HP
0(7)1-381 9924

Vegetarianism

There are many reasons for eating less meat, and the fact that the average Briton is eating less meat than ten years ago may not only be because most of us can't afford to buy it any more.

The proportion of people who have given up eating meat altogether (or have never eaten it) now stands at around six per cent of the population and is rising every year. One in 14 women do not eat meat (one in eight young women), and one in 24 men. For every vegetarian, moreover, there are several other people who have drastically reduced the amount of meat in their diet. In a recent survey 35 per cent of people said they were eating substantially less meat than they were. Here are some of the reasons why you might join them:

▶ Being vegetarian is usually cheaper than being a meat-eater, especially if you eat mostly locally produced foodstuffs which are not highly packaged.
▶ Being vegetarian is certainly healthier; vegetarians have a lower incidence of many diseases than meat-eaters, especially heart and circulatory disease.
▶ You are eating further down the food chain, which means that the food you eat uses much less land and energy to produce.
▶ You are not perpetuating the cruelty to which very many farm animals are submitted, both during their lives and when they are slaughtered.
▶ You are helping people in the Third World in two ways: a great deal of the food and vegetable harvest of the Third World goes to feed meat animals for the rich West, so you are freeing land which they can use for crops for themselves, and slowing down the rate of environmental degradation in he Third World.

You don't need to become a hundred-per-cent vegetarian to have some effect on the world's food supply and land use. It is certainly true, however, that eating much less meat benefits the planet and its inhabitants considerably.

Why You Don't Need Meat

This chatty but informative book from a former director of the Vegetarian Society is a real eye-opener if you've never really thought very much about the pros and cons of eating meat. It looks at the role of meat in the British diet, how it got there, how it's kept there, and how it isn't doing anybody much good. He explains how the bulk of the meat we eat is contaminated with growth hormones and antibiotics, and shows how a non-meat diet can provide you with all the nutrients you need. If you can handle Joe the vegetarian teenager, and Kate and Mike for whom vegetarianism is the final straw in a rocky marriage, you should find this book very approachable, though ignore the over- complicated Exclusive Nutrition Checker at the back.

Food for a Future

Peter Cox explains why vegetarianism is a good idea for you and your health; these two books put the whole issue in their historical, philosophical and world setting.

Jon Wynne-Tyson's *Food For a Future* is an intelligent yet impassioned book, happily now back in print after a prolonged absence. He doesn't shun the nutritional and health aspects of vegetarianism, but his arguments from the standpoint of a compassion for all life are the most convincing. The quotations at the chapter heads are well chosen and thought provoking.

Daniel Dombrowski's *Vegetarianism* is an academic American book repackaged by Thorsons for the British market, and if you read it for the learned volume it is you will learn a great deal about the history of vegetarianism, set in the philosophical context of developing ideas about the place of human beings in the natural order of things. It isn't always easy going, but even if you're a sceptic it's an interesting read, and as useful a resource for arguing with vegetarians as having read the Bible is if you're an agnostic discussing Christianity with a fundamentalist.

*

Writers more qualified than I have written on the health aspects of a vegetarian diet in childhood, but I am convinced from life-long observation of my own children and those of both vegetarian and meat-eating friends that not only are vegetarian children of healthy stock as physically fit, mentally alert and full of high spirits as any omnivorously reared contemporaries, but that in their complexions, in the incidence of childish complaints, in the gentleness of their natures, and in their all-round air of well-being and general stability, the children who have followed the more natural eating pattern — provided it has been balanced and nutritionally sound — are ahead of the rest.

Jon Wynne-Tyson

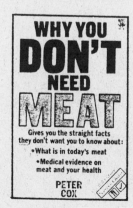

Why You Don't Need Meat
Peter Cox
Thorsons, 1986
£2.50

Food For a Future
Jon Wynne-Tyson
Thorsons, 1988
£2.50

Vegetarianism
The Philosophy Behind the Ethical Diet
Daniel Dombrowski
Thorsons, 1985
£4.95

The Vegetarian Society

Formed in 1969 as the amalgamation of two previous national societies The Vegetarian Society is the voice of vegetarianism in Britain — and a very loud voice too. They embrace every aspect of vegetarianism, emphasizing the benefits in relation to ethics, health, economics, ecology, and Third World development.

Membership of the society brings you the excellent bimonthly magazine *The Vegetarian*, which is well worth subscribing to even if you aren't a committed vegetarian, packed as it is with useful information — several of the leads for *New Green Pages* came from *The Vegetarian*. The classified advertisements at the end are extensive and comprehensive. The magazine recently became a joint production between VegSoc and the London-based publishing company ESG, and there are plans to publish monthly.

Membership also entitles you to discounts at a number of health food shops and guesthouses, and a further advantage is that you get a free copy of the annual *Vegetarian Handbook*. This useful volume includes complete lists of products which are guaranteed vegetarian, shops and suppliers, an annotated list of additives, and a section called 'Taking it Further' which gives addresses for other green campaigning groups. The Society also publishes an *International Vegetarian Travel Guide*, a county-by-county and then country-by-country handbook listing restaurants, hotels and guesthouses, holiday centres and operators, most of them with a sentence or two of description. The *Travel Guide* costs £3.99, and if you are not a member you can buy the *Vegetarian Handbook* for £2.99; the 1990 editions should be ready by the time you read this. Each volume, especially the *Travel Guide*, is worth its weight in carob-coated organic raisins.

TAL Y BONT (nr CONWY)

The Lodge (049269) 766 H D	Very modern but nicely situated hotel, maybe a bit reminiscent of 'Crossroads'! Chef and proprietors are vegetarians and offer a limited menu (Deep Fried Vegetables in a beer batter with Aoli, £4.75). Accommodation from £17.50. Open all year. Vegan & special diets catered for. Licensed. Dogs welcome. Disabled access. Seats 80, sleeps 20. 10% discount to VSUK members.

The Vegetarian Society also runs a good mail order book and merchandize service, with virtually every vegetarian cookery book currently in print, plus the usual aprons, t-shirts, badges and jewellery. And they organize vegetarian cookery courses at their Altrincham centre.

A recent success is VegSoc's youth campaign. The Education Department deals with hundreds of enquiries each week from young vegetarians, and the lively editor of the excellent magazine *Greenscene*, Juliet Gellatly, recently won one of *Cosmopolitan's* coveted 'Women of Tomorrow' awards. Following the success of the Society's SCREAM (School Campaign for Reaction Against Meat) and CHOICE campaigns, a powerful video called 'Food Without Fear' has recently been released for use in secondary schools.

VegSoc are also a well-organized campaigning group. Three years ago it succeeded in persuading tourist authorities to adopt the green 'V' to denote hotels and guesthouses offering vegetarian cuisine, and several supermarket chains are now using the symbol regularly. If you want to be part of the action, write today for more details.

The Vegetarian Society
Parkdale
Dunham Road
Altrincham
Cheshire
WA14 4QG
061 928 0793

Vegetarian Cookery Books

As you'll see if you get the Vegetarian Society publications list, there are an enormous number of vegetarian cookery books on the market. My personal favourites are the three I keep in the kitchen: *Friends of the Earth Cookbook* by Veronica Sekules (Penguin, 1980, £3.50); *Laurel's Kitchen*, a fat and comprehensive cookery book whose homey goo — the text that is, not the recipes — has to be waded through to find the gems (Routledge and Kegan Paul, 1979, £5.95); and Anna Thomas's *Vegetarian Epicure* (Penguin, 1980, £2.95 — though I have the American edition published by Vintage Books which has all the pictures and is much nicer).

A recently published book that gives you all the information you really need to know, together with some readable introductory chapters, is Alison Westcott's *Basic Vegetarian Cookery* (Ashgrove, 1986, £4.95). The pictures are attractive and the index good, too. If you're looking for a special present for a vegetarian friend who likes cooking, Deborah Madison and Edward Espe Brown's *The Greens Cook Book: Extraordinary Vegetarian Cuisine* (Bantam, 1987, £12.95) includes recipes for dishes that would turn a regular steak-eater green. It's American (the title comes from the Greens restaurant in San Francisco), but not overly so.

Vegetarian Britain

If you have the *International Vegetarian Travel Guide* (see under Vegetarian Society above) you really won't need any other guide, though it's useful to know about Sarah Brown's guides to vegetarian restaurants; one to London and one to Britain as a whole (the former is still available, though as the information has been incorporated into the British guide there are no plans to reprint the London volume). She obviously had fun putting these books together (I think I'd enjoy trying out two hundred restaurants), and it's worth keeping them handy on your travels.

Food for Living ✓

116 High Street, Chatham, Kent, ME4 4BY
☎ 0634 409 291
£3

This is a cheap and cheerful little café, linked with a wholefood shop, with significantly more to offer than the usual fast food quiche-caterers.

The main hot dish of the day is available between 12 and 2.30, otherwise there are pizzas (vegan or vegetarian) tartex sandwiches, savoury flan and jacket potatoes.

The selection of wholemeal cakes was particularly good with carrot cake, carob and peanut flapjack or carob and coconut wedge.

Although it is nothing really special, Food for Living is a welcome eatery in an otherwise typical modern shopping centre.

Open: 9-4.30 Monday-Saturday
Credit cards: none
40 seats

Pauline Davies's *Vegetarian Holiday and Restaurant Guide* is a disappointment; not only do the entries appear with no comments or annotations, but the proof-reading is pretty bad too — try asking an Edinburgh resident, for example, where Dairy Road is.

Sarah Brown's Vegetarian London
Sarah Brown
Thorsons, 1988
£3.30

Sarah Brown's Best of Vegetarian Britain
Sarah Brown
Thorsons, 1989
£4.99

Vegetarian Holiday and Restaurant Guide
Pauline Davies
Green Print, 1989
£2.99

Veganism

Of course there are vegans who live in cities and vegans who generate enough rubbish that the sanitation department wouldn't suspect anything unusual, but on the whole there is an ecological awareness among them. I did not meet one, for example, who favours nuclear power. They are genuinely concerned that non-leather belts, shoes and bags are often plastic, a petroleum derivative and source of pollution. Many conscientiously choose canvas wherever possible; some consider the entire shoe problem a difficult ethical decision, but nearly all feel that it is better to go with plastic than to use a slaughterhouse product, especially considering that the abattoir, too, is an infamous polluter.

Victoria Moran, *Compassion: The Ultimate Ethic* (see below)

Vegans seek to live as lightly as possible on the earth, which for them means the exclusion, as far as possible and practical, of any products involving the exploitation of animals. The area that this affects the most, of course, is diet, and vegans avoid all meat, fish, eggs, and non-human animal milks and their derivatives, including cheese. Some also avoid honey.

Living as I do in rural Scotland where it's fairly easy to buy truly free-range eggs and 'naturally-reared' meat, I do not for myself believe that a 100% animal-product-free life is necessarily a worthwhile goal, though I agree with nearly all that vegans hold dear. Current methods of food production are extremely harmful to the earth and to its human and non-human populations.

Each year 450 million animals are killed for food in Britain, more than two thirds of them battery hens. Most of these animals spend their entire lives under artificial conditions, unable to stretch their limbs and having no contact with other animals or with the natural earth. Cows forced to produce 6,000 litres of milk every year (a fivefold increase in the last thirty years) sometimes have udders so full that they drag on the ground. If plants were used to feed people rather than animals (nearly 85% of the world's grain harvest is used to feed animals) there would be no reason for famine in the world.

Even if you don't go the whole way and avoid animal products completely, the arguments of veganism are well worth reading about, thinking about, and acting on — even if only partly and sometimes.

The Ultimate Ethic

Books about veganism tend to be preachy and humourless: even vegans need to remember not to take themselves too seriously. There isn't one book I can recommend whole-heartedly (perhaps someone will now write it), but try starting with Victoria Moran's *Compassion: The Ultimate Ethic*. It is easy to read, and the appendices at the end covering different vegan initiatives are fascinating — though I wish she wouldn't keep talking about 'man', especially since women substantially outnumber men in the field of dietary awareness. Kath Clements' *Why Vegan* is short and straightforward, and rehearses the arguments clearly if rather pedantically. The weaning advice is particularly good, as are the pictures.

For a cookbook, Eva Batt's *Vegan Cookery* is a cheap and basic primer; Janet Hunt's *The Compassionate Gourmet* a more exciting, more expensive, and more time-consuming follow-up.

Compassion
The Ultimate Ethic
Victoria Moran
Thorsons, 1985
£4.95

Why Vegan
Kath Clements
GMP, 1985
£2.95

Vegan Cookery
Eva Batt
Thorsons, 1986
£2.95

The Compassionate Gourmet
Janet Hunt
Thorsons, 1986
£4.99

The Vegan Society

The Vegan Society, formed in 1944, follows the example of its larger sibling The Vegetarian Society (opposite) in producing very attractive literature, an excellent magazine, and campaigning tirelessly for a more compassionate world.

The Vegan comes out quarterly, a very readable magazine with a useful 'Shoparound' feature, excellent book reviews, useful classified adverts, and some good articles too. The Vegan Society's information pack (sent on receipt of an sae) is a very good mini-introduction to the politics of food and health.

The Vegan Society runs occasional day-long cookery courses, and also produces a useful handbook called *The Vegan Holiday and Restaurant Guide* which costs £2.50. The other vegan guide, *The Cruelty-Free Shopper*, has recently appeared as a book published by Bloomsbury and compiled by Lis Howlett of the Vegan Society (1989, £3.99). *Cruelty-Free Shopper* is the best available checklist of cruelty-free products, with sections covering food and drink, toiletries and cosmetics, remedies and supplements, footwear, and 'miscellaneous'.

The Vegan Society
33-35 George Street
Oxford
OX1 2AY
0865 722166

Compassionate Living

'Compassionate living is about making connections between the way we live and the way others suffer.' Thus starts the current leaflet of the Movement for Compassionate Living, a network of vegans who work actively for social and ecological harmony. Their quarterly newsletter, *New Leaves*, contains an interesting mixture of articles, recipes, reviews and adverts, and their publications include *Growing Our Own: A Guide to Vegan Gardening* (30p) and *Food for Everyone* (60p).

The Movement for Compassionate Living
47 Highlands Road
Leatherhead
Surrey
KT22 8NQ
0372 372389

Some Final Food Thoughts

A collection of books with a slightly unusual angle on food, cookery and nutrition, all readable, intelligently written, and for the most part completely sound on the ecological and political fronts too.

Stone Age Diet

The basic argument of this short and easy-to-read book is that if we ate more like our paleolithic ancestors did we would be a lot healthier. It certainly makes a great deal of sense — after all, human beings were paleolithic for nearly half a million years, have only been at all 'modern' for less than a couple of thousand, and have only been eating a contemporary Western diet for less than a century. No wonder our bodies can't take it; they weren't built for it. Leon Chaitow suggests that we might at least try eating more like our ancestors: more fruit, nuts, berries, and game animals (especially the internal organs); almost no grains and non-human milk, and no salt or alcohol. He isn't a purist, and can be quite funny at times, but he is clear that our present diet is killing us. *The Stone Age Diet* is a thought-provoking read, and includes a section of stone age recipes at the end.

*

The use of some organ meats is unappealing to many. There is little logic in this since the food value of spleen or liver, for example, is far greater than that of muscle meat. I have included some recipes for these organs, as well as some traditional Greek methods for the preparation of other parts, such as the intestines and stomach. The ambitious or brave may attempt these on their unsuspecting families. The tastes may be so delicious that they outweigh any apparent squeamishness.

Stone Age Diet
Leon Chaitow
Optima, 1987
£4.95

The Wright Diet

Books with titles like *The XYZ Diet* usually make me skip over them, but I'm glad I took a second look at Celia Wright's book. Celia and her husband Brian started the Green Farm Nutrition Centre in Kent (see page 145) nearly ten years ago, and this book sets out her philosophy that there is no one right diet that will suit everybody. If you ignore the rather tiring puns on Wright and right this is an excellent introduction to the idea that nutrition and health are intimately linked, presented in a clear and very practical way — she even shows you how to watch your faeces in a holistic light. The last section, 'The Right Food', is a good introduction to wholefoods and wholefood cookery, and the charts and resources at the end are comprehensive and well laid out. The book even smells nice, though I wish it were a £4.95 paperback instead of an £8.95 hardback.

The Wright Diet
Celia Wright
Piatkus, 1986
£8.95

Recipes for Health

I couldn't put this one under vegetarian cookbooks because it isn't quite; it has some very good fish and poultry recipes in among the other wholefood goodies. A medic, a biochemist and a nutritionist have come together with a collection of over 350 imaginative recipes which are high in fibre and low in fat, sugar and salt. The recipes are set out as clearly as any cookbook I've seen, divided in the usual way between breakfast dishes, soups and starters, and so on; at the end are some useful appendices, including three very clear pages of illustrations showing simple preparation techniques. At less than a penny a recipe this must be about the best cookbook value around.

CAPE COD OATMEAL COOKIES

1 egg
1 oz (28g) honey
3-4 tablespoons oil
1 tablespoon treacle
1 teaspoon baking soda
1 teaspoon cinnamon
1 lb (455g) rolled oats
2 oz (55g) raisins or walnuts
½ lb (225g) barley flour
Little apple juice or water to moisten, if required

1. Beat the egg lightly.

2. Add the other ingredients and mix well.

3. Drop by spoonfuls on to a buttered baking tray, and press flat with the fingers or a fork.

4. Bake at 325°F/170°C/gas mark 3, for 15 minutes.

Cook Yourself a Favour

Sheila Gibson, Louise Templeton and Robin Gibson
Thorsons, 1986
£2.99

Fast Wholefoods

There is a pernicious myth that wholefood cookery takes longer in preparation than any other variety; this is nonsense. Wholefood cookery can take a long time if you're making something complicated, but then so does beef stroganoff with a tin of ready-made sauce and boil-in-the-bag noodles.

The best of several fast wholefood books is *The Wholefood Express*, written by Sue Mellis and Maggi Sikking for the Suma wholefood co-operative (see page 20). None of these 150 recipes, even the stews and curries, takes longer than half an hour to prepare, and many can be ready in ten minutes — and there is nobody who can't spare ten minutes to prepare a meal. Their 'special fried rice' seems to be what I make when I can't be bothered to think of anything else. Great minds . . .

The Wholefood Express
High Speed Vegetarian Cookery
Sue Mellis and Maggi Sikking
Food and Futures/SUMA, 1986
£3.95

ENVIRONMENT

'Unwittingly for the most part, but right around the world, we are eliminating the panoply of life. We elbow species off the planet, we deny room to entire communities of nature, we domesticate the Earth.'
Norman Myers (ed.), *The Gaia Atlas of Planet Management*

Do you remember as a child the excitement of fishing for newts and frogspawn, or the deep involvement of making a wildflower collection? Do you remember cornfields bordered with poppies and bright blue cornflowers and grassy downs strewn with cowslips, walks in the woods and along the streams when you saw deer, maybe a badger, and if you were very lucky a kingfisher? Do you remember your favourite climbing tree? All these plants and creatures are now fighting for survival as we elbow them out of our world of tarmac and pesticides, concrete and barbed wire, 'no entry' signs and neat flower beds. Access to most of what is left is denied to us, too: today's countryside excursion is likely to require stout wellingtons, a gas mask, a pair of wirecutters, and a manual of countryside law.

But What Is 'The Environment'?

In a 1980 pamphlet called *Green Politics*, Maurice Ash cleverly defines environment as 'everything, bar something'. The 'something' is usually the intrusion that the person wanting to make the change is trying hard to justify: 'But my one little car (house, power station, missile site . . .) won't hurt the environment — it will blend in so well that nobody will notice. In fact it will even enhance it.'

In his book *The Closing Circle*, Barry Commoner tells us what 'environment' really means: 'The environment makes up a huge, enormously complex living machine that forms a thin dynamic layer on the earth's surface, and every human activity depends on the integrity and proper functioning of this machine.' Even comparing the environment with a machine overlooks the complexity of the web of nature, a complexity that we cannot hope to understand, partly because we are such an integral part of it. One thing about life that we know for certain is that the surest way to destroy it is to pull it apart in our attempts at understanding.

Our present economic system leads us to believe that the *real* world is the world of money and prices and manufactured articles, and it follows that unless something has a cash value it doesn't really signify in the order of things. Thus an industrialist looks at a valley in a national park and sees mineral reserves; a developer looks at an urban open space and sees building followed closely by money. When it comes to the crunch, politicians almost always put national accounting before conservation, because they steadfastly insist on using money value as a measure of real wealth.

Meanwhile species continue to disappear, soil to be eroded and poisoned, habitats to be destroyed. Because they have been put on an economic treadmill, farmers continue to pay for practices which they know are damaging the environment. But who is *really* paying the price of environmental degradation? Hard though it may be to imagine, it is the environment itself, the rich variety of nature, which is being mortgaged. Nature, unlike the stock market, is enormously resilient — it can take small and localized setbacks. But when human beings keep attacking it from every angle and worldwide, in the end the environment screams for help. Some people, and they are intelligent observers, not doom-mongers, believe that we may well come to this vital understanding too late. Here is the American sociologist William Catton: 'Nature must, in the not too distant future, institute bankruptcy proceedings against industrial civilization, and perhaps against the standing crop of human flesh, just as nature has done many times to other detritus-consuming species following their exuberant expansion.'

And What Did You Do in the Great Environmental Revolution?

Faced with such enormous issues you may feel that nothing you do will make any difference, but there is a great deal that each of us can do which *will* make a difference, and this section will help you to explore some of the options.

It starts with land. In *Land for the People* (see page 51), Herbert Girardet says: 'Land is constant while human life is transient on it. It is the duty of every generation to leave the land at least as vigorous and fertile as they found it.' If you have a responsibility for looking after any land at all, even if it only a small garden, this is the soundest of advice.

Land lore — the wisdom of the soil — has a centuries-long tradition in Britain, and before intervening in the cycles of nature it is as well to know something about them. The pages that follow the introduction to the land provide some basic sources of information about landforms and soils, history, birds, trees, flowers and other wildlife.

It is this wisdom that is being ignored in many land use practices, so you will also find some pretty horrifying information about pollution, agrochemicals, factory farming, acid rain and toxic waste. I'm afraid this is all part of what now constitutes the environment — 'the environment' isn't just the pretty bits.

This section closes with ten pages about organic gardening. The wise American farmer and academic Wendell Berry once wrote: 'I can think of no better form of personal involvement in the cure of the environment than that of gardening. A person who is growing a garden, if they are growing it organically, is improving a piece of the world.'

Our Land

The most fundamental resource of human beings everywhere has always been the land itself. Land is the source not only of the food we eat and the minerals from which we build shelters and shape implements, but of the space we occupy as well. When it has provided for our needs, it accommodates our pleasures. Because it is a finite resource it has always been the subject of struggle between tribes and races, nations and classes, who wish to put it to conflicting uses. Yet in otherwise strife-torn industrial Britain the land itself has been the potential theatre of conflict on which the curtain has so far failed to rise. For the last 200 years, political struggle here has largely revolved round the jobs and incomes and taxes and welfare of a population apparently firmly rooted in the towns and cities of one of the world's most industrialized countries. Eighty per cent of the land surface of Britain is countryside, but rural affairs have more or less been left to the tiny group which happens to own land. Now, however, it looks as though the land question may reassert itself. As in so many other countries today, and in our own past, the fate of the land henceforth seems likely to arouse here the most intense of political passions.

Marion Shoard, *This Land is Our Land* (see page 52)

Some facts about this land of ours:

▶ Ordinary citizens can be treated as trespassers on more than 1.2 million of the 1.5 million acres of the land area of England and Wales which is designated as common land.
▶ 9% of the area of England and Wales is designated as National Park, but the public owns only 1% of the Parks; most remains in private hands.
▶ 9% of the population of Britain own 84% of the land. Nearly 50% of the farmland in Britain is held in units of over 500 acres.
▶ According to the Ramblers' Association, around 66% of public footpaths across farmland in England and Wales are ploughed up or otherwise obstructed. A seven-month survey carried out by RA members in Buckinghamshire showed that 82% of public footpaths had been ploughed up, cultivated or crop-sown 'without so much as a tractor-wheel rut to define the line of the public path'.
▶ Countryside Commission figures show that hedgerow loss has accelerated from an average of 2,600 miles a year between 1947 and 1979 to 4,000 miles a year in the 1980s.

In an attempt to clarify issues in the area of land ownership and use, ecologist Herbert Girardet set out his ideas in a 'Land Manifesto' which was published in an important but sadly out of print book called *Land for The People* in 1976. Because it sets out the issues so clearly, and with Herbert Girardet's blessing, the *Land Manifesto* is reproduced below.

Land Manifesto

1. **Land is Life!** We must work the land for food and life. Agriculture is the one mode of production with which humans cannot dispense under any circumstances.

2. Land ultimately cannot be **owned** by anybody. Land is constant while human life is transient upon it. It is the duty of every generation to leave the land at least as vigorous and fertile as they found it, in order not to diminish the chances of future generations.

3. At present the land in Britain is 'owned' by far less than 1% of the population. Those who work it — farmers and agricultural workers represent little more than 1% of the people. Half of Britain's food is imported and yet there is enough land to feed everybody. Greater food self-sufficiency can only be achieved if agriculture ceases to be the **private concern** of a tiny minority.

4. Present agricultural practices aim at maximising **yield per person** and machine, but due to cost explosion this system is coming unstuck. Industrialised agriculture is experiencing a crisis which can only be resolved by drastic changes: agriculture can only be revitalised by more people working the land on the basis of co-operation rather than competition. But people will not 'go back' to the land if they have to look forward to a life of drudgery and subservience, on somebody else's farm.

5. In every economy a balance must be achieved between agriculture and industry, between country and town. The 'principle' that food must be imported from wherever it is cheapest is dead: nobody is prepared to sell us cheap food any longer. But greater food self-sufficiency, which is becoming increasingly necessary, cannot be achieved unless more people work the land, collectively and in the **public interest**.

6. At the present time nearly all development taking place upon the land is residential, traffic or industrial development. How the inhabitants of **new towns** are to be fed is never taken into consideration; it is taken for granted. But due to speculative land prices the gardens of the houses in new towns are usually so small as to be incapable of feeding even a rabbit. New towns are geared to their inhabitants being employed by industry.

7. With permanent redundancies in some major industries becoming very likely, a 'return' to the land by hundreds of thousands of people will become a vital necessity. **Agricultural growth** is possible and desirable as **industrial growth** is becoming unlikely and even undesirable in western countries. We must work towards a new equivalence of agriculture and industry.

8. The demand for the takeover of large areas of land for new farming villages is becoming increasingly popular. What such **new villages** shall actually look like nobody knows, only suggestions can be made at present. It must be clear to us, however, that we can no longer afford to be messy creatures, i.e. new communities must be the basis for ecologically sound activities, as far as both production and consumption are concerned.

9. Should new farming communities aim solely at self-sufficiency or, in fact, at **surplus** production? As long as towns and cities exist, agricultural villages must be able to produce more food than they require for themselves. We must aim at high **yields per acre** achieved with methods of cultivation which can be sustained for many generations to come, indeed, indefinitely. To this end liberated agriculture, science and industry must work hand in hand.

10. In new villages gardening and farming should coexist with crafts and, possibly, small-scale industry. Many **skills** should be represented among the members of every new community; at least all those skills required to build it and maintain it. Surplus production would enable new village communities to exchange their produce for necessary products of the cities.

11. The economics of the new village way of life must have the satisfaction of **human needs** at their centre, which also means that work itself must be satisfying. But every human need must be weighed up against its ecological consequences: if the fulfilment of a need or want **today** undermines the basis of human life **tomorrow**, it offers only a very dubious kind of satisfaction.

12. Some sceptics might say: "But nobody wants to leave the cities to live in farming villages." There is much evidence that they are wrong. It is well-known that many people are still being driven from the land who would love to stay if only they had the chance of a satisfactory life, economically and socially, as well as culturally. There are many people eager to live and work in the country who can't afford a few acres and a cottage.

The redistribution of land (by popular demand) is a precondition for the creation of new and viable communities. Agriculture — and industry — must be under the control of those who do the work. But without a popular movement the necessary changes cannot be brought about.

It is the task of this book to help lay the foundations for a popular movement without which the necessary changes cannot be brought about.

The Land is for Sharing

The Land! The Land! 'Twas God who gave the Land.
The Land! The Land! The ground on which we stand!
Why should we be beggars, with the Ballot in our hand?
'God gave the Land to the People!'

So sang the people of Hanley in the Potteries in 1912, during a by- election in which land tax reform had become a burning issue.

At the heart of green thinking is the belief that land cannot and should not be 'owned', denying access to anybody but the 'owner' and giving that 'owner' the right to do pretty much what he (usually) wants.

A few years ago, when Marion Shoard was commuting each day by rail from Luton to London, she glimpsed each day the magnificent Capability Brown landscape of Luton Hoo, which extends over two square miles of rolling countryside to the south of the industrial town of Luton with its 200,000 inhabitants. It is owned by a family who made their fortune from mining in South Africa. There is no public access to the grounds.

This, and the fact that the same story is repeated all over Britain, made Marion so angry that she decided to research the situation fully and write a book about it. The result is *This Land is Our Land*, a meticulously researched and damning indictment of current patterns of land ownership in Britain. Marion Shoard had already earned quite a reputation for stirring things that need to be stirred with her earlier book (see below) — then it was the agricultural establishment that rose with one voice; now it was the turn of the Country Landowners' Association, who compiled a vituperative and lengthy press release calling *This Land is Our Land* 'misguided and irrelevant'.

Landowners have a lot to lose. For a start there is the assumed right to shoot at anything on or over your land that you choose to:

One autumn day in 1982, a hot-air balloon carrying three passengers on a pleasure flight floated over a grouse moor near Ripon in Yorkshire. Viscount Mountgarrett, a major landowner in Yorkshire, who was out with a shooting party, turned his shotgun on the balloon and gave it both barrels. These hit the basket, so he reloaded and fired again.

Then there is the right to shout at and threaten anybody who wants to walk across land you own, whether or not they are doing any harm.

Broadlands estate, which is fifteen times the size of Hyde Park, overshadows the little town of Romsey. The gate at the end of Broadlands' main drive is but a stone's throw from the centre of this town of fewer than 14,000 people. Before 1977, few of these people had ever set foot behind Broadlands' enclosing wall. But in that year, the four-member family group who ran the estate decided in the face of the rising costs of maintaining and running the house they would open the house to the public. When I visited the estate and talked with Lord Romsey in 1984, the public were permitted to make their way along the private drive to the house near which they could park, and to stroll and picnic in the parking area and in a small piece of land between the house and the river — about six acres altogether. . . Lord Romsey has excepted from his general bar on access to his estate about twelve individuals and groups to whom he has granted special access permits. . . Permits are not issued to people who simply want to enjoy the beauties of the place. 'Definitely not' was Lord Romsey's reply when I asked him whether he would issue a

permit to a resident of Romsey who wrote in saying he [or she, presumably] would simply like to walk in the grounds. However, Lord Romsey has provided a piece of land on the edge of town for the exclusive use of local voluntary groups like the guides and scouts and radio amateurs. Lord Romsey told me: 'I sacrifice that piece of land totally to public use. It isn't farmed; I get not a penny of rent or whatever from it and if you like it is the concession that we wanted to make to the area.' It is . . . three acres in extent.

This Land is Our Land is a brilliant book. *The Economist* magazine said it might be as influential as Rachel Carson's *Silent Spring*.

This Land is Our Land
The Struggle for Britain's
Countryside
Marion Shoard
Paladin, 1987
£5.95

The Theft of The Countryside

This was the book which was greeted with howls of derision by the agricultural establishment, and quite understandably. Truth hurts if you've been trying to keep your secrets hidden. *The Theft of the Countryside* was the first fully-documented account of the horrendous loss of the countryside — habitats, trees, wildlife, public access — which has taken place since the war as a result of government policies which the powerful farmers themselves were instrumental in designing.

*

Although few people realize it, the English landscape is under sentence of death. Indeed, the sentence is already being carried out. The executioner is not the industrialist or the property speculator, whose activities have touched only the fringes of our countryside. Instead it is the figure traditionally viewed as the custodian of the rural scene — the farmer. . . Already a quarter of our hedgerows, 24 million hedgerow trees, thousands of acres of down and heathland, a third of our woods and hundred upon hundred of ponds, streams, marshes and flower-rich meadows have disappeared. They have been systematically eliminated by farmers seeking to profit from a complex web of economic and technological change. Speedily, but almost imperceptibly, the English countryside is being turned into a vast, featureless expanse of prairie.

The Theft of the
Countryside
Marion Shoard
Temple Smith, 1980
£4.95

The Face of The Earth

The firm ground which we tread under our feet, and long thought to be immovable, is replete with vitality, and is accentuated by incessant motion; the very mountains rise and sink; not only do the winds and ocean-currents circulate round the planet, but the continents themselves, with their summits and their valleys, are changing their places, and travelling round the circle of the globe.
                                                    Elisée Reclus, *The Earth*, 1871

If you think landscape is fascinating, find it hard to be in a new place without wanting to explore its nooks and crannies, and like to know what it is that you are looking at, here are some suggestions for books about geology, landscape and soil. There are many introductory geology primers; as good as any is Janet Watson's *Beginning Geology* (Macmillan, 1966, £7.50). If you want a book that relates geology and geomorphology (the study of landforms) to specific landscapes, Andrew Goudie et al's *Landshapes* (David and Charles, 1988, £14.95) is excellent. Andrew Goudie's earlier book, *Discovering Landscape in England and Wales* (Unwin Hyman, 1985, £14.95), written with Rita Gardner, gives more than fifty well-illustrated examples from all over the country — there hasn't been a similar volume for Scotland since Sissons' *The Evolution of Scotland's Scenery* in 1967.

Soil is not easily come by. Millions of years of baking sun, cracking frosts, wind and weather, of living things — dying, decomposing, and leaving their remains in sand and silt — are gone to make the soil we have today. It can take 500 years to create one centimetre of soil. With the current urgency to produce food, we cannot spare even a pinch of it. Yet each year 13 million hectares of arable land are lost through erosion.
                                                    Lee Durrell, *State of the Ark*, 1986

Not surprisingly, The Soil Association (see page 67) is the place to go for information about soils. A classic is Eve Balfour's *The Living Soil*, technically out of print but still available from The Soil Association — excellent value at £4 for a hardback that cost £5.25 ten years ago. Courtney and Tridgell's *The Soil* (Edward Arnold, 1984, £5.25) is a well illustrated introduction to soils, emphasizing their importance within different ecosystems. The Elm Farm Research Centre also produced a booklet called *The Soil* (£3 from the Soil Association), which specifically explains the relevance of soil analysis to vegetable growing.

The earth's atmosphere is vital to terrestrial life. It is believed to have developed in its present form and composition at least 350 million years ago when extensive vegetation cover originated on land. Its presence provides an indispensable shield from harmful radiation from the sun and its gaseous content sustains the plant and animal biosphere.
                                                    Barry and Chorley, *Atmosphere, Weather and Climate*, 1968

A good introduction to weather and weather watching, easy to read and well illustrated, is Ingrid Holford's *Looking at Weather* (Weather Publications, 1985, £1.95). As she says near the beginning, 'Books about meteorology sometimes frighten people into thinking the subject too difficult without professional qualifications. This is not so. Many fundamental weather principles are already familiar in our domestic environment, which is why my story includes such things as bicycle pumps,

refrigerators and cooking utensils.' If you are interested in becoming more actively involved in watching the weather, the Weather Watchers Network channels the observations of amateur meteorologists into a detailed local information service — they also provide basic training. As yet the network operates only in Scotland and the north of England, but there are expansion plans.

Weather Watchers Network
Laurieston
Castle Douglas
DG7 2PW
064 45 652

Survival Guides

Many years ago (thirty to be precise), Harold Gatty, an Australian navigator who among other things established Fiji Airways, wrote a wonderful book called *Nature is Your Guide*, showing you how to take your bearings from the stars, the sun, trees, anthills, and anything else you found on your travels. The book helps you to be at home wherever on the planet you might find yourself, and even if you don't plan to visit the Gobi Desert it can be useful to know which way is south even in central London. The modern equivalent of *Nature is Your Guide* is John Wiseman's *The SAS Survival Handbook* (with the SAS tastefully picked out in red). Despite its militaristic overtones, this is a fascinating volume full of useful hints — which fungi you can eat, how to make fire, knotwork, first aid in the wild, mountain rescue code — and much more. The advice is all good common sense, as it should be from the man who runs the SAS Survival School, and refreshingly direct.

*

If collision seems inevitable, stay with it and steer the car to do as little damage to others and yourself as possible. Try to avoid a sudden stop by driving into something which will give. A fence is better than a wall, a clump of small saplings better than a tree — they will eventually stop you but a tree or wall will bring you to a dead stop — and probably very dead.

Splitting logs
Stand behind a large log with feet well apart. Swing down to cut the side away from you (a).

Do NOT chop downwards (b).

To split a smaller log, angle against another log (c). DO NOT PUT YOUR FOOT ON IT.

Alternatively, hold smaller log against cutting edge of axe and bring both down together (d) on to a larger log. (Not to be tried holding too short a log for safety.)

If in doubt split larger logs with a wedge and a rock (e). DO NOT HOLD WOOD UPRIGHT IN YOUR HAND AND ATTEMPT TO SPLIT WITH AXE.

The SAS Survival Handbook
John Wiseman
Collins Harvill, 1986
£9.95

Holding Your Ground

The reasons why we value our surroundings are many. They could be described as personal, cultural, aesthetic and scientific. But increasing emphasis has been placed on the so-called scientific reasons for wishing to save something, usually because a plant, animal or landscape is rare or 'special'. If this argument is used too often the decision makers will not take seriously our parallel cultural desire to conserve the common plants and animals, vernacular buildings. It is imperative therefore that we do not let our rationale for nature conservation in particular become too biased towards such evaluations, otherwise we will end up with little pockets of nature reserves surrounded by land empty of animals and plants except monocultures of wheat, barley and conifers. These reserves, in any event, will gradually disappear as they cannot exist in isolation. Every piece of land is unique. The geology, the form of the land, the place where it is, the production processes it supports — agriculture, mining, building; the investment it represents and receives; its ownership and the rights over it; the social relationships it encourages, the politics it sustains — all are apparent in the landscape before us.

Angela King and Sue Clifford's book is a treasure chest of local conservation initiatives, and if you are concerned that nothing is being done to save Britain's heritage, then *Holding Your Ground* will give you new hope. All the way through the book are case histories of groups and projects which have successfully made a difference to the way their local environment is perceived, sometimes succeeding against all odds in the face of commercial and administrative bulldozering. From the new village sign at Potterhanworth in Lincolnshire to the planting of Little Horwood Quarry in Milton Keynes, from the Rodney Stoke Parish Footpath Volunteers in Somerset to the Perran Round festivals in Cornwall, people all over Britain are concerned about the uniqueness of their particular corners of our land, and are prepared to do something very practical about it. Every chapter has a good 'further reading' list; the practical chapters on 'How Local Government Works' and 'Money and Help' are excellent; and the book finishes with a list of organizations. The index is a weak point — individual projects aren't listed — but this is a minor grumble.

Back in September, 1981, when I enrolled on an evening course on the natural history of the Moss Valley, little did I envisage how this would develop. From an evening class introducing the natural history of the area, we have developed into a pressure group to protect the wildlife of the Valley. At first the class proceeded like any other evening class; but then the bombshell of the Sheffield Green Belt Enquiry was brought to our notice by our class tutor. From then on the seeds were sown. At extremely short notice, the class members assimilated knowledge on the natural history of the Valley from various sources, and the likely consequences of further housing development in or near the Valley. This material was then presented at the Public Enquiry. Personally I expected us to have only a minimal impact, but the Inspector took account of the wildlife interest of the Valley in his recommendations. Moreover, the importance of the Valley for wildlife was brought to the notice of the planning authorities. In respect of the Green Belt Enquiry, the Group has been extremely successful, thus proving the impact that a small determined group can have.

Mr and Mrs Egan, *The Moss Valley Wildlife Group*, June 1983,
quoted in *Holding Your Ground*

Holding Your Ground
An Action Guide to
Local Conservation
Angela King
and Sue Clifford
Wildwood House, 1987
(revised edition)
£6.95

Common Ground

The authors of *Holding Your Ground* are also the instigators of Common Ground, a sort of liaison point and catalyst for local conservation initiatives which has its offices above The London Ecology Centre in Covent Garden. Common Ground doesn't go to all the trouble of having members, but exists to foster good ideas, find funds for them whenever possible, and display the results. There is the New Milestones project, for example, which encourages artists to create sculptures to celebrate their locality. There is the Parish Maps Project to get people to really experience their local area and produce a painting, sculpture or tapestry of it and thus share their insights. Common Ground have put together a video called *The Local Jigsaw* about creating a village map, have published some important books about trees and orchards including *In A Nutshell: A Manifesto For Trees and a Guide to Growing and Protecting Them* (1989, £5.95) and *Orchards: A Guide to Local Conservation* (1989, £4.95), and organize exhibitions on countryside themes. They have also produced some very nice posters — ask for their mail order list.

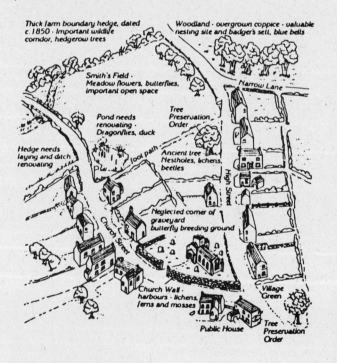

Common Ground
45 Shelton Street
London
WC2H 9HJ
0(7)1-379 3109

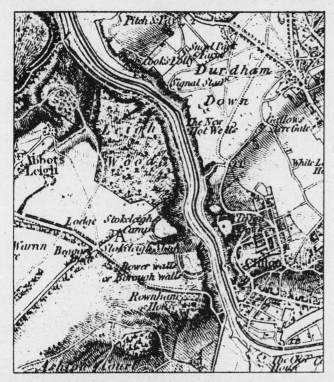

The Historical Perspective

Behind us lies the wealth of history itself, and the treasure-trove of knowledge — of successes laden with promise and failures laden with fault. We are the heirs of a history that can teach us what we must avoid if we are to escape immolation and what we must pursue if we are to realize freedom and self-fulfilment.
    Murray Bookchin, *The Modern Crisis*, Heretic, 1987, £4.95

The landscape is like a historic library of 50,000 books. Many were written in remote antiquity in languages which have only lately been deciphered; some of the languages are still unknown. Every year fifty volumes are unavoidably eaten by bookworms. Every year a thousand volumes are taken at random by people who cannot read them, and sold for the value of the parchment. A thousand more are restored by amateur bookbinders who discard the ancient bindings, trim off the margins, and throw away leaves that they consider damaged or indecent. The gaps in the shelves are filled either with bad paperback novels or with handsomely-printed pamphlets containing meaningless jumbles of letters. The library trustees, reproached with neglecting their heritage, reply that Conservation doesn't mean Preservation, that they wrote the books in the first place, and that none of them are older than the eighteenth century; concluding with a plea for more funds to buy two thousand novels next year.
    Oliver Rackham, *The History of the Countryside* (see below)

We do ourselves no good by pretending that we live independently of the past, and many people today honestly believe that if a skill or tradition is more than a few years old it must be outdated and pretty useless. They find history much more palatable when it is coloured with the pastel tints of historical romance or the bold ones of rambo violence, rarely taking the time to learn from older people's own experience, let alone from the landscape itself.
    School history teaching has a great deal to answer for. In the early 1960s we started 'doing history' in 1066 and had only reached Elizabeth I before I stopped 'doing history'; now children learn by 'doing projects', but I'm pretty horrified that children generally have little overall perspective of world or local history — they may know about the Vikings and about the Civil War, but have little idea which came first. I read that in a recent test several London secondary school children were convinced that the architect of St Paul's was Christopher Robin.

Imaginative history teaching uses primary sources to full effect, isn't afraid of untidiness, and keeps people fascinated by what they discover. In this way they begin to value their surroundings and their own place within the historical context. History, far from being bunk, is all we have to learn from.
    Here I shall concentrate on the history of the British countryside; not that urban history, national history and world history aren't important, simply that in the beginning — and in the end — it is the land that supports us. In concentrating on the countryside I want to draw attention to a vital aspect of our heritage that we are in danger of losing altogether.

A Modern Classic

First published in 1955 and never bettered, W.G. Hoskins' *The Making of the English Landscape* is still an excellent introduction to local history in England; it is surprising that nobody has ever succeeded in producing equivalent volumes for Scotland and Wales. Authoritative, poetic, very readable, the book takes you from prehistoric England and the first settlements on Dartmoor right through to the postwar landscape — though mercifully it ends while village England was still very much alive and before agriculture, industry and road improvements wrecked most of the lowlands. An excellent introduction if the whole subject of local history is new to you. Nearly a hundred photographs.

The Making of the English Landscape
W.G. Hoskins
Penguin, 1969
£4.95

The History of The Countryside

A massive tome, the result of massive wisdom, Oliver Rackham's book takes up where Hoskins leaves off, filling in and updating the details of why the countryside is the way it is. Arranged by topic — woodlands, fields, highways, ponds, marshes — he gives dozens of specific examples, wrapping everything up with wit, healthy cynicism, humour and passion. This big book is extremely good value, is fully illustrated (I like the hand-drawn maps), and well-documented — the index is particularly good.

The History of the Countryside
Oliver Rackham
Dent, 1987
£8.95

And The People?

Howard Newby's *Green and Pleasant Land?* will shatter the illusions of back-to-the-landers who dream of community, harmony with nature and other romantic notions about rural life. Life for most real country-dwellers is still feudal, with housing and public services often worse than those in inner city slums. In this intelligent study of rural life as it really is there is no mincing of words. Reg Groves' *Sharpen the Sickle*, first published in 1948 and recently reprinted, tells the story of the farmworkers' struggle to organize against appalling working conditions, starting with the Tolpuddle Martyrs and ending with the wartime recognition that we really do rely on the land to be our ultimate ally.

Green and Pleasant Land?
Social Change in Rural England
Howard Newby
Wildwood House, 1985
£5.95

Sharpen the Sickle
Reg Groves
Merlin, 1981
£2.95

Pollution

Never before in our history has the organic world around us been in so much trouble. We seem to be thriving — at least as a species we are replenishing ourselves everywhere — but not much else is. Whole forests in both the tropical and temperate zones are dying from acid rain, radiation, air pollution, timber harvesting, slash-and burn agriculture. Harbours, estuaries, seas as broad as the Mediterranean, the River Rhine are all in decline from toxic wastes. We are creating an environment of gashes, wounds, disorganization, and death.

Donald Worster, in *The Earth Report* (see page 58)

The chimneys and exhaust pipes of Europe are creating an ever more complex cocktail of chemicals in the air over the continent. Some react with sunlight to form ozone, a chemical which damages trees and crops and irritates the human lung. Ozone also speeds up the conversion of other gases to acid rain. Countries such as Britain and West Germany have banished smoke. But clearer skies only make the cocktail more reactive and increase the threat from ozone and acid rain. The familiar heat haze seen on any summer's day is made up of acid particles created by ozone. All this should frighten us. Our forests and fish, cathedrals and crops, lichen and lungs — all are under attack.

Fred Pearce, *Acid Rain* (see next page)

Richard Willson, from *Green Britain or Industrial Wasteland?* (see page 58)

More than two thirds of Britain's trees have been damaged by acid rain; 52% of Germany's trees are dead or dying. A quarter of Sweden's lakes and 50,000 of Canada's are suffering from acidification which has killed most aquatic wildlife. The most extreme case of acid rain recorded was in Scotland in 1974, where rainfall had a pH value of 2.4, equivalent to vinegar.

Thinning of the protective ozone layer around the earth was first noticed in Antarctica in 1973. By 1979 the USA had banned trade in CFC-containing aerosols, a ban which most manufacturers worldwide have now complied with. Yet almost all the CFCs we have ever pumped into the atmosphere are still there. Concentrations of ozone-destroying gasses are still increasing at more than 5 per cent each year.

More than 400 million tonnes of hazardous waste are generated worldwide each year. No one knows how many British sites contain toxic waste, but a recent independent survey estimated that there are at least 600 potentially dangerous sites.

Much of our drinking water is polluted by artificial fertilizers, domestic sewage effluent and slurry from intensive livestock units. More than a million people in eastern England receive a public water supply which exceeds EC limits for nitrates, and surveys have shown the residues of more than sixteen toxic pesticides in English tapwater.

One sign of the British government's apparent U-turn on environmental issues was Margaret Thatcher's speech to the United Nations General Assembly in November 1989. 'The problem of global climate change,' she said, 'is one that affects us all, and action will only be effective if it is taken at the international level.'

Yet only the day before this speech was given Britain, along with Japan and the USA, blocked international moves to set a target of a 20 per cent reduction in carbon dioxide emissions in the next fifteen years. And only two months earlier the British government had announced a ten-year programme for building £12 million pounds' worth of major roads to hold some of the estimated ten million additional cars they expect to be using British roads by the year 2010. How can we take seriously a government so blinkered — if not two-faced — when it comes to such a vital issue as global pollution?

In their television series *Earth*, Anne and Paul Ehrlich didn't mince words when they accused governments who ignored the evidence of the threats of pollution as being 'either blind or stupid'. Where it comes to pollution control the British government currently appears to be both blind and stupid. It remains to be seen whether they can see the error of their ways soon enough to have any real impact on the massive pollution problems we are now facing.

Reduction of pollution isn't just a matter for politicians, however. There is a great deal that you as an individual consumer can do to reduce the emission and stockpiling of dangerous substances on land, in the water, and in the air.

▶ Throw away as little as possible; recycle and re-use what you can (see pages 108-113).
▶ Keep the amount of packaging you buy to a minimum, especially packaging that uses non-renewable resources (see page 27).
▶ Use as few chemicals of any sort as possible, and where you do need to use them, use biodegradable ones (see page 114).
▶ Find out whether your car will run on unleaded petrol and use it if it can; think about fitting it with a catalytic converter; use it as little as possible (see pages 316-317). Use public transport whenever possible.
▶ Avoid using aerosols, even so-called 'environment friendly' ones. Many still use propellants and other ingredients which harm the atmosphere (see page 27).
▶ If you smoke, think about the effect this has on your environment and the people around you, and try to stop (see page 151).
▶ Use as little manufactured energy as possible by making your home and workplace energy-efficient (see pages 307-308). Bonfires and wood-burning stoves may be appropriate in rural areas, but not in cities.
▶ Buy organically-grown foods which have not been doused with polluting chemicals or grown in artificial nitrate-based fertilizers.
▶ Try to avoid polluting the environment with loud and unpleasant noise. Think about the effect it might be having on other people and other living things.

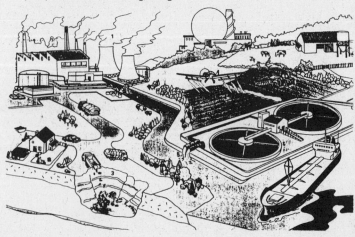

Acid Earth

Acid pollution stands as a classic example of the consequences of economic and industrial development proceeding without due regard to external costs. Acid pollution has become a test case for the lip-service paid to environmental management by more and more governments over the past decade.

John McCormick, *Acid Earth*

What is popularly called 'acid rain' — now an issue etched firmly into most people's environmental awareness — is a complex issue. We know that acid pollution is caused by the gases given off when fossil fuels are burned — sulphur dioxide, nitrogen oxides, hydrocarbons and ozone. But confirming and agreeing both the effects and the scale of acid pollution isn't easy, which has made it all the easier for governments to prevaricate 'while more research is done'.

Britain is one of the worst culprits where acid pollution is concerned — this small nation is the world's fourth largest producer of sulphur dioxide and the fifth largest producer of nitrogen oxides. We ship much of it across the North Sea to Scandinavia, safe in the knowledge that there is no equally dirty country for thousands of miles upwind to pollute our landscape to the same extent. Yet our rain is still between 100 and 600 times more acid than normal rainfall, 67% of our conifers have suffered damage, and forty-four buttresses built in 1894 to help support Westminster Abbey will soon have to be replaced as a result of acid etching.

Two very approachable books about this complex issue are well worth reading. Fred Pearce's hard-hitting account of the current state of play, called simply *Acid Rain*, is necessarily frightening. If you need yet more information to make you sit up, change your lifestyle and write to your MP, this really is essential reading (why not buy your MP a copy?).

An updated edition of John McCormick's excellent *Acid Earth* has recently appeared. John McCormick is extremely good at clarifying the issues and, like Fred Pearce, doesn't dodge the economic and political implications. The book includes chapters covering developments in different parts of the world: the chapter on the United Kingdom takes us up to Nigel Lawson's unleaded-petrol-bonus budget of 1989.

*

The Cally Estate was a small paradise for anglers. High in the Galloway hills of south-west Scotland, it attracted a small but regular group of fishermen. Annual catches in the 1950s were between 100 and 150 trout. But then the fish began to disappear.

At the time, they blamed the decline on poaching by miners from the Ayrshire coalfield forty kilometres away. Three times between 1956 and 1964 Murray Usher, who runs the estate, restocked the loch with trout. But the restocking failed and since 1960 only a handful of fish have been caught there. All over Galloway, similar stories are told.

Fred Pearce, *Acid Rain*

*

People in the middle of the next century — assuming they are more rational than we — are probably going to be looking back on the late twentieth century with a sense of awe. Why did we spend so much time and so much money, and put so much at risk, treating the symptoms of our reliance on fossil fuels rather than the disease? Why did it take us so long to realize that what we were doing was destroying the environment? Why did our institutions — government, business, universities — take so long to respond?

John McCormick, *Acid Earth*

Acid Rain
What Is It, and What Is It Doing To Us?
Fred Pearce
Penguin, 1987
£3.95

Acid Earth
The Global Threat of Acid Pollution
John McCormick
Earthscan, 1989
(2nd edn)
£6.95

Acid Magazine

A useful (and free) publication called *Acid Magazine* is produced twice a year by the Swedish National Environmental Protection Board. The Board also distributes a free newsletter published jointly by the Swedish and Norwegian environmental protection agencies (these two countries being the chief recipients of Britain's sulphur emissions), which is called *Acid News*. Write for subscriptions.

Swedish National Environmental Protection Board
PO Box 1302
17125 Solna
Sweden

Ozone and the Hole in the Sky

If acid pollution is hard to understand, what can the person in the street hope to make of ozone, a strange form of oxygen with the formula O_3 which, it seems, is poisonous if we get anywhere near it yet is absolutely vital to our wellbeing when it's ten miles up in the air? The answer is that up in the troposphere is where it should be (and where we're destroying it with a lethal dose of CFCs, halons and the like), and down here at ground level (where it's killing trees and poisoning us) is where it shouldn't be.

In his masterly way John Gribbin has sorted all this out very clearly in his study of ozone, *The Hole in the Sky*. Even though he has done his best to help his readers through this very complex and contentious issue you still (unless you have a degree in applied physics) need to read this short book slowly and carefully, but it well repays the effort.

*

A lifetime of 120 years means that 90 per cent of the CFC molecules already in the air in 1987 will still be there in 2000; 39 will still be there in 2100; and 7 per cent even in 2300. The damage we have already done to the ozone layer will be with us, and with our children and grandchildren, throughout the twenty-first and twenty-second centuries.

The Hole in the Sky
Man's Threat to the Ozone Layer
John Gribbin
Corgi, 1988
£3.95

Green Britain or Industrial Wasteland?

Though it was published four years ago, this collection of essays is still the best book currently available which covers almost every aspect of environmental pollution in Britain. It's a gloomy subject, but most of the 28 contributors manage to write about their subject in an interesting (sometimes gripping) and even humorous way, helped by some quite funny cartoons by Richard Willson. The essays cover industrial and agricultural pollution, radiation, health hazards, and government secrecy, plus some fairly newly-discovered environmental hazards such as electromagnetic pollution from high-voltage power lines. This book will provide you with enough information to counter the most reactionary arguments; I hope it doesn't give you nightmares.

*

A key Department of Health report on asbestos was kept secret for no less than eight years. When the BBC television programme Nationwide wanted a copy it had to be obtained in the USA under the US Freedom of Information Act.

*

Incredibly, under British law, there is no requirement to tell a potential buyer that a site has been used for the disposal of hazardous wastes. But, in the case of old dumps, the age-old principle of caveat emptor (let the buyer beware) takes on a new — and sinister — meaning. If housing estates, schools, or office buildings are built over contaminated sites — even in the distant future — the local population is almost certain to be exposed to a wide range of highly toxic chemicals, and heavily exposed at that.

Green Britain or Industrial Wasteland?
edited by Edward Goldsmith and Nicholas Hildyard
Polity Press, 1986
£4.95

The National Society for Clean Air

Many environmental organizations work on pollution issues, in particular Greenpeace (page 70) and Friends of the Earth (page 65). One important organization which works almost exclusively with pollution issues is the National Society for Clean Air and Environmental Improvement. The NSCA runs active campaigns on acid rain, straw and stubble burning, crop spraying, asbestos, noise, vehicle pollution and nuclear radiation among others. There are regional branches and some useful publications, including a source book of pollution statistics and legislation, *The Pollution Handbook* (1989, £12.65), a leaflet called *Air Pollution — Know Your Rights* (single copy free if you send an sae; 100 copies £3.55 to put in your library or health centre waiting room — with permission), and their newsletter which is called *Clean Air*.

National Society for Clean Air and Environmental Improvement
136 North Street
Brighton
BN1 1RG
0273 26313

Earth Reports

With so much popular concern about pollution of every kind, it is inevitable that authors and publishers have felt the need to produce *the* book that will tell you everything you need to know about every environmental problem. Three more-or-less encyclopedic volumes more or less succeed in this task.

By far the best of the bunch is *The Earth Report*, edited by the same *Ecologist* team as *Green Britain or Industrial Wasteland?*. The heart of this book consists of 400 short alphabetically-arranged articles on a host of environmental topics, though it is particularly strong on the nuts-and-bolts subjects like pollution. It's especially useful if you want to look up a particular event like Bhopal or Three Mile Island, and a clear system of cross-referencing helps you around the book. The six essays at the front of the book are an additional bonus, the illustrations are clear if a bit overstylized, and the index is good.

Next comes Michael Allaby's *Green Facts*, a repackaged version of his *Ecology Facts* of three years earlier. Michael Allaby is a good explainer, though some of his opinions take a lot of explaining away. How many other environmentalists would agree that 'action on the ozone layer may be altogether unnecessary' (page 69) or that 'for environmental reasons you should favour nuclear power' (page 133)? The pictures are pretty.

Angela Smyth and Caroline Wheater's *The Green Guide* is a timely book in desperate need of a good editor. It tries to be too many things at once, a state of affairs reflected in the misleading catch-all title — if it had been called *What's Happening to our Planet?* and had stuck to being a clear explanation of a range of vital environmental issues rather than trying (and failing) to be a 'how-to' handbook at the same time it would have been far more convincing. It is when it is explaining acid rain, the ozone layer and the greenhouse effect — which it does very well — that this book is at its best, and the added fact that many hundreds of readers of *Here's Health* magazine will buy it (and I hope read it) makes this an important addition to any green bookshelf.

The Earth Report
Monitoring the Battle for
Our Environment
edited by Edward
Goldsmith and
Nicholas Hildyard
Mitchell Beazley, 1988
£7.95

Green Facts
The Greenhouse Effect
and Other Key Issues
Michael Allaby
Hamlyn, 1989
£6.95

The Green Guide
Angela Smyth and
Caroline Wheater
Here's Health, 1990
£5.95

Wild Flowers

Seventeen species of British wild plant listed by the Nature Conservancy Council are believed to be confined to only one native site, and still there are people who believe they have the right to dig up a plant for their own garden. Unless conservation is taken seriously we may lose some species completely — among them Early Star of Bethlehem, Purple Coltsfoot and Stinking Hawk's-Beard — while other once common species like Small Fleabane and Pennyroyal now only grow in places like the New Forest where traditional forms of stock-raising continue. Plant species have as much right to survive as any other; the fact that they cannot run away and hide makes our responsibility so much the greater. Never ever dig up or pick a flower which is protected — a list of such species is included in *A Code of Conduct for the Conservation of Wild Flowers*, available if you send an sae to The Botanical Society of the British Isles, c/o The British Museum (Natural History), Cromwell Road, London SW7 5BD.

The Flowering of Britain

As agriculture becomes more and more specialized, so does the landscape which supports it. Woods and meadows are used as little more than factories for timber and grass. Commons which once supported half a dozen rights of grazing and gathering, and a range of habitats and flowers which reflected this diversity, have been turned into arable prairies. There is not much room left for wild plants, and they are not just dwindling in numbers but passing out of our lives.
Richard Mabey and Tony Evans, *The Flowering of Britain*

The Flowering of Britain is a knowledgeable and haunting introduction to the history of wild flowers in Britain, with such fascinating titbits as where snowdrops came from (they are not native), and why bluebells, a woodland flower, are often found some way from the trees. Started in 1972 as an exercise in photographing flowers in their natural setting, it grew to be the story of the flora of these islands from the Ice Age onwards. The photographs are so strikingly beautiful that you may find your eye constantly wandering from the text, poetic though the writing is. This is not a coffee table book, however: the threats of pollution and physical destruction are not overlooked, nor the need for the political will to save centuries of floral heritage.

John Fisher's *Wild Flowers in Danger* explains just how rare some of our wild flowers are, and by looking at each species in turn brings home how close we are to losing such beautiful and extraordinary flowers as the Ghost Orchid, the Snowdon Lily and the Sticky Catchfly. This is compulsive reading.

The Flowering of Britain
Richard Mabey and Tony Evans
Chatto and Windus, 1989 (new edition)
£10.95

Wild Flowers in Danger
John Fisher
Witherby, 1989
£5.95

Wild Flower Guides

When I was young I had a battered copy of Warne's *Wild Flowers of the Wayside and Woodland* with its beautiful letterpress plates. Keble Martin's painstakingly assembled *Flora* took its place in the early seventies and it looked as though it was the ultimate in flower books, but in 1981 came the Readers Digest *Field Guide*, my first choice for the original *Green Pages*; it not only illustrated each species with a painting of the plant in its setting and a photograph, but included a great deal of history, topography and general knowledge.

I still like the Readers Digest book very much, but with the publication in 1989 of Marjorie Blamey and Christopher Grey-Wilson's beautifully-produced, comprehensive and authoritative *Illustrated Flora of Britain and Northern Europe* wild plant guides enter an entirely new realm. I thought that *Green Pages* was labour of love enough, but it took Marjorie Blamey nearly a decade, working every daylight hour, to produce the thousands of paintings for the new *Flora*. Though £25 is a lot of money for a book (which also means that you won't want to use it as a field guide) any half-serious amateur botanist will surely want a copy of their own to drool over.

The *Flora* covers all species of wild plant except for grasses and rushes; thus as well as wild flowers it covers trees (including the most commonly-planted exotics) and shrubs. As well as an exquisite colour illustration of each main species there are numerous details of fruit, flowers and foliage, and at the back is a useful identification key so that you can look up any species you haven't come across before.

Field Guide to the Wild Flowers of Britain
Readers Digest Nature Lover's Library, 1983 (revised)
£8.95

The Illustrated Flora of Britain and Northern Europe
Marjorie Blamey and Christopher Grey-Wilson
Hodder and Stoughton, 1989
£25.00

Wild Seeds

The use of wild flowers in gardens, including information on seed merchants who specialise in wild flower seeds, is looked at on page 82; this section is for anyone interested in the wider implications of helping wild flowers to keep a firm hold in British soil. The Seed Bank and Exchange exists to perpetuate the seed of around 500 species of British wild flower, and though seeds can be bought from the Exchange, the basic principle is that of barter, exchanging seeds, information, advice and experience. Members receive two newsletter each year in spring and autumn, and a wild flower garden was established in 1986 to let people see the range of species helped by the Exchange.

The Seed Bank and Exchange
Cowcombe Farm
Gipsy Lane
Chalford
Stroud
Gloucestershire
GL6 8HP

Trees

Imagine an area the size of Kent, Lancashire, Nottinghamshire, Northamptonshire and Warwickshire combined: 3 million acres in all. This is the area that will be covered in new plantations by the middle of the next century if the plans of the Government and the Forestry Commission are fulfilled.
> Marion Shoard, *This Land is Our Land* (see page 52)

Technical advances have enabled the forester to create thriving woodlands on quaking peat bogs that were virtually useless and valueless.
> J. Davies, quoted in Steve Tompkins, *Forestry in Crisis* (see below)

Yet at the same time as the fir trees march across the mountains and plateaux of Scotland and Wales, we have lost 50% of our ancient deciduous woodland in the last 35 years. We import 90% of our timber requirements, but half of Britain's mixed and deciduous woodlands are unmanaged or deteriorating. Forestry in Britain today is riddled with paradox. Muddled thinking about forestry has even more drastic consequences on a global scale. The destruction of the tropical rainforests is possibly the most serious environmental threat we have ever had to face, with an area almost as large as Britain being deforested each year.

Tropical forests contain up to half of all known creatures. They are unquestionably the world's greatest treasure house of genetic diversity, a unique biological reservoir . . . Scientific authorities estimate that, at the moment, at least one wild species of animal, plant or insect a day becomes extinct. By 1990 that rate will have risen to one species an hour. By the end of the century — 15 years from now — we may have extinguished over one-quarter of all life forms.
> Charles Secrett, *Rainforest*, Friends of the Earth, 1985, £3.50

What can you do to ensure that timber and wood products, a renewable resource if harvested carefully, are used wisely? What can you do to ensure the continued existence of vital native trees and woodlands in Britain?

▶ Use as little timber and wood products as possible, though use them in preference to non-renewable resources like metal and oil- based plastics where you can.
▶ Recycle timber and paper whenever possible (see pages 108-113).
▶ Use hardwoods, especially tropical hardwoods, as sparingly as you can (see page 90).
▶ Learn about trees and their needs.
▶ Plant trees carefully and wisely in appropriate places.
▶ Do what you can to prevent the thoughtless destruction of trees and hedgerows.

The monks of Bury St Edmunds started coppicing Bradfield Woods in Suffolk in the Middle Ages. Giant coppice stools of ash and alder still exist within this 163 acre nature reserve, which continue to produce a good crop of poles. These are used by the Rake Factory in nearby Little Welnetham for scythe and rake handles, trellises and pergolas, thatching spars and wattle fencing. Wood ash is used for pottery glazes and sawdust for animal litter. Very little is wasted, and the sale of wood products pays for the upkeep of the nature reserve. 370 different plant species have been recorded within the reserve.

Forestry In Crisis

Forestry In Crisis is a timely book, authoritative and practical. Steve Tompkins, himself an experienced forester, argues convincingly that misconceived government incentives have decimated many of our uplands, especially in Scotland, with 'conifer farms'. Not only do they impoverish upland ecosystems; they provide very little employment and destroy the social and physical infrastructure of rural areas. What is needed is a very radical reassessment of forestry policy, and among other things Steve Tompkins suggests that the Forestry Commission must stop trying to fulfil two mutually incompatible functions — looking after the upland landscape and making as much money as possible. Very approachable and full of useful photographs, tables and diagrams, Brian Redhead rightly says in his introduction that this book could usefully form the basis for a more sustainable forestry policy: 'better than any White Paper, and not to be ignored'.

*

Forestry is an ancient and reputable profession, but the aberrations of ill-conceived policies have drawn a blanket of conifers across vast tracts of hill and moor, often onto the poorest ground for tree growth. But while conifer afforestation in the uplands has flourished for over 40 years, many of the lowland, broadleaved woodlands that are so important for landscape and wildlife have been neglected, replaced with conifers, or cleared for agriculture. We need to be clear why this has happened and, having established why, to then build a new approach to forestry in Britain.

Philip Stewart's *Growing Against The Grain* is an excellent introduction to the history of British forestry policy, explaining why we grow the species we do regardless of the fact that both productivity and environmental impact could be improved by growing more mixed woodland, and why the social and economic blunders of recent years continue to be perpetuated.

Forestry In Crisis	**Growing Against The Grain**
Steve Tompkins	Philip Stewart
Christopher Helm, 1989	Council for the
£12.95	Protection of Rural
	England, 1987
	£5.00

The Forestry Commission

The Forestry Commission isn't all bad, and forestry policies are slowly changing, especially under pressure from tourist authorities and conservation groups to make forests more 'user-friendly'. The broadleaf woodland grant scheme, introduced in 1985, is one such change of heart, encouraging the rehabilitation of existing broadleaf woodlands and the establishment of new ones.

The Commission publishes a wide range of literature, much of it free and all listed in their comprehensive publications catalogue. Of particular interest are the *Forest Facts* series, a series of four *Environment Leaflets* which double as posters, and their thrice-yearly free magazine, *Forest Life*. It's all a bit bland and glossy, but it's a very great improvement upon the Commission's earlier attitudes towards public interest and concern.

Forestry Commission
231 Corstorphine Road
Edinburgh
EH12 7AT
031 334 0303

Friends of the Trees

Two organizations are well worth belonging to if you are practically interested in the future of Britain's trees. Men of the Trees, on the brink of changing their rather unfortunate name, are very active, working with the United Nations to promote an international programme of careful agroforestry. Their 'new member's pack' includes a packet of tree seeds and details of local and world-wide activities. The Woodland Trust exists to conserve trees and woodlands in Britain; it owns and manages woodlands throughout Britain and is co-ordinating the 'plant a tree' scheme to replace the millions of trees blown down in the great storm of October 1987.

Men of the Trees
Sandy Lane
Crawley Down
Crawley
West Sussex
RH10 4HS
0342 712536

The Woodland Trust
Autumn Park
Dysart Road
Grantham
Lincolnshire
NG31 6LL
0476 74297

Planting Broadleafs

If you are interested in planting trees it is worth knowing that Pitney Bowes (the office equipment people) organize the 'Elms Across Europe' scheme, a research and nursery project to supply Dutch Elm Disease resistant elm saplings to help replace the 15 million elm trees lost to the disease. First-year trees of the new hybrid, a cross between a Japanese elm and a Siberian elm which will grow twelve metres in 15 years, cost £4.90 each.

British Broadleaf is a company established to plant broadleaved trees in their thousands throughout the country. The costs of the land they buy and the trees they plant are covered by inviting individuals to 'own' a particular tree or grove which will then bear their name. A good idea, perhaps, but it would be even better if they cut down on the masses of high-quality unrecycled paper they use to advertise the scheme. A 75-year lease on a 9-square-metre plot will cost you £30.

If you are even more serious about growing trees, the British Trust for Conservation Volunteers (see page 289) publishes a booklet called *Tree Nurseries* by Karl Liebscher (1984, £1.75).

Elms Across Europe
Pitney Bowes plc
The Pinnacles
Harlow
Essex
CM19 5BD
0279 37756

Traditional British Broadleaf Heritage
1 Briston Orchard
Duchy of Cornwall
Estate
St Mellion
nr Saltash
Cornwall
PL12 6RQ
0579 51195

The Fate of the Forests

Covering nearly a third of the planet's land surface, forests are crucial to its — and our — future. Yet trees are being felled at an ever-increasing rate. A fifth of the world's rainforests were felled between 1950 and 1975, and at present rates another two-fifths could be lost by the end of the century.

Not only are forests powerhouses of basic biospheric processes, notably photosynthesis and biological growth, creation of fertile humus and transfer of energy, but their exceptional contribution to the biosphere goes much further. They play major roles in the planetary recycling of carbon, nitrogen and oxygen. They help to determine temperature, rainfall and various other climatic conditions. They are often the fountainheads of rivers. They constitute the major gene reservoirs of our planet, and they are the main sites of emergence of new species. In short, they contribute as much to evolution as all other biomes.
Norman Myers, *Gaia Atlas of Planet Management*
(see page 330)

For a balanced and reasoned overview of the current state of the world's tropical forests, *No Timber Without Trees* is factual and fluent without being either blandly optimistic or numbingly sensational. The basis of the book is a report by a group of experienced researchers for the International Tropical Timber Association, and the study includes several regional surveys together with a look at what is possible in the way of sustainable forest management.

Susanna Hecht and Alexander Cockburn's *The Fate of the Forest* is a book of immense research and passionate concern, an in-depth biography of the Amazonian rainforest written by an ecologist and a radical journalist whose ancestors worked in the Amazon basin. *The Fate of the Forest* describes the political and economic reasons why the Amazon has been exploited in the way it has, and explains the human angle better than any other book has come near to achieving. Here is the real Chico Mendez story; here too are the verbatim words of the Yanomami, the rubber-tappers and the mineral prospectors. This is a rare and fascinating book, providing deep insight into the fate of a unique and vital ecosystem. It's expensive, but it's worth it.

I include Michael Goulding's *Amazon: The Flooded Forest* because, being a BBC book, it will reach many more readers than *The Fate of the Forest*, and because the photographs are stunning. Unlike the previous book it is emphatically not printed on recycled paper, and is clearly intended as a lightly (though very fluently) written natural history coffee-table book. This is the one to give your yuppie-but-slowly-turning-green friends for Christmas.

No Timber Without Trees
edited by Duncan Poore
Earthscan, 1989
£9.95

Amazon: The Flooded Forest
Michael Goulding
BBC, 1989
£15.00

The Fate of the Forest
Susanna Hecht and Alexander Cockburn
Verso, 1989
£16.95

Birds

Birds are an important indicator of the health of any habitat, and having a closely-knit network of knowledgeable birdwatchers who can draw immediate attention to changes in behaviour or distribution is a valuable aid to the taking of prompt and appropriate environmental action.

Birdwatching is a specialized art, and birdwatchers a dedicated breed. There is a lot to be learned about the habits of the different species of birdwatcher — ones that will migrate vast distances to make the acquaintance of a Rose-breasted Grosbeak, ones that will get up at five every morning to check the catching boxes, and ones who can tell a Rock Pipit from a Meadow Pipit at two hundred yards from the song alone.

The best way to start birdwatching is to go with an experienced birdwatcher. The RSPB (see below) have local groups all over the country, which organize outings and illustrated talks. At some stage you will need your own pair of good binoculars — Zeiss Deltrintem 8x30 from East Germany are generally considered to be very good value for money.

When it comes to a bird book, you will find that many full-colour guides cover Britain and Northern Europe, which is more than you will need (and covers Britain in less detail than you would like) — this is because to keep the cost down these books are published in several languages at the same time. A very good guide to British birds is *The Shell Guide to the Birds of Britain and Ireland*, with excellent illustrations by my near neighbour Ian Willis. It shows birds in their seasonal plumages, distinguishes between juveniles and adults — vitally important when it comes to species like gulls and terns, and shows the birds in their characteristic poses or flight configurations rather than in wooden rows.

The Shell Guide to the Birds of Britain and Ireland
James Ferguson-Lees, Ian Willis and J.T.R. Sharrock
Michael Joseph, 1990
£10.95

Bird Organizations

The Royal Society for the Protection of Birds is the premier bird conservation body in Britain. Sometimes criticized for being too commercially-minded, sometimes for promoting the needs of birds at the expense of other conservation issues, the RSPB has nonetheless done a great deal in the conservation field, and inspired thousands with the enthusiasm of birdwatching. It owns or manages 121 reserves throughout the country, to which membership will gain you free access. Membership also allows you to book places on their birdwatching holidays, and brings you the quarterly magazine *Birds* (along, surprisingly, with brochures advertizing guns). The RSPB also organizes a children's birdwatching group called The Young Ornithologists' Club, with a bi-monthly magazine called *Bird Life*. The RSPB has recently published an excellent book called *The Joy of Wildlife Gardening* (Geoffrey Smith, 1989, £14.95) to help you provide the conditions in your garden which will encourage birds and other wildlife. It's a delightful cross between a gardening guide and a conservationists' handbook, both thorough and detailed and with a useful address list and bibliography.

The British Trust for Ornithology is the main research and bird movement monitoring organization in Britain. As well as a useful bi-monthly newsletter they also produce technical leaflets on things like how to build and site nest boxes, and how to choose a pair of binoculars.

Royal Society for the Protection of Birds
The Lodge
Sandy
Bedfordshire
SG19 2DL
0767 80551

British Trust for Ornithology
Beech Grove
Station Road
Tring
Hertfordshire
HP23 5NR
044 282 3461

Where To Go Birdwatching

The RSPB has joined forces with BBC Books to produce a directory of all the RSPB's reserves in Britain, with maps showing the location of each one together with details about the birds found there, visiting times, facilities and how to get there. At the front is the 'Birdwatcher's Code of Conduct'; the photographs are beautiful.

Where To Go Birdwatching
RSPB
BBC, 1989
£6.50

Wildlife

With all the pressures on our countryside the conservation of wildlife has become a matter of national concern. While it is true that much of our landscape as it now stands was created by man in the first place, the increase in population coupled with the need to grow more food, to build more houses and factories and to provide space for leisure have in the last half century done immeasurable damage to our natural resources. Some of this damage was unavoidable, but some has been caused by our own greed and our lack of concern for future generations.
Prince Charles, *Britain's Nature Reserves* (see next page)

Britain's wildlife laws are a joke. Other countries laugh at us while we sit back and rest on our laurels as a 'nation of animal lovers'. We are so far behind the rest of the world that even underdeveloped nations are leaving us standing; if any effort is made to change things, the moves are somehow blocked by the very people who seem to enjoy making a travesty of the fox's life. Only recently, when moves were made by Britain to have the evils of bullfighting exposed, Spain simply sent their TV crews to film the barbarism of foxhunting as a 'pot-calling-the-kettle-black' exercise.
Les Stocker (co-founder of Britain's first wildlife hospital), *Something in a Cardboard Box* (Chatto and Windus, 1989, £7.95)

You can contact the Wildlife Hospital Trust (which incorporates the famous St Tiggywinkle hedgehog hospital) at 1 Pemberton Close, Aylesbury, Buckinghamshire HP21 7NY.

World Wide Fund for Nature

In the 26 years of its existence WWF has played a vitally important role in nature conservation throughout the world. It has helped to set up and manage wildlife reserves, worked to stop poaching, helped save particular species from extinction, and worked with governments to conserve and manage wildlife habitats. More than 4,500 species of animal and 18,000 plant species are currently threatened with extinction worldwide. Within twenty years our planet could be so impoverished that life on earth may never recover. If you want to help redress the balance, membership of WWF costs £25 a year, for which you get full details of events and campaigns together with the quarterly newsletter and the BBC *Wildlife* magazine. WWF also produces a wide range of educational resources (see page 233).

World Wide Fund for Nature
Panda House
Godalming
Surrey
GU7 1XR
0483 426444

Royal Society for Nature Conservation

With a membership of more than 165,000 and 1,680 nature reserves in their care, the RSNC is the association to belong to if you are interested in the conservation of wildlife. The RSNC keeps extensive local wildlife records, and each County Trust produces its own newsletter in addition to the national magazine *Natural World*. WATCH (see page 230) is the excellent educational wing of the RSNC.

Royal Society for Nature Conservation
The Green
Nettleham
Lincoln
LN2 2NR
0522 752326

British Association of Nature Conservationists

Founded in 1979, BANC stages regular conferences, produces reports on topics like forestry policy and local government conservation activities, and publishes an excellent quarterly journal called *ECOS* (see page 345). Through its network of local groups it aims to provide a forum for free and critical discussion, promote an exchange of views and a better understanding of nature conservation principles and their application to rural and urban planning, and further the concepts of environmental protection.

British Association of Nature Conservationists
Nature Conservation Bureau
122 Derwent Road
Thatcham
Newbury
Berkshire
RG13 4UP
0635 60478

Where To See Wildlife

If you want absolutely the most authoritative and satisfying guide to the best places to see Britain's varied wildlife, you will need to spend £24.95 on the new edition of *The Macmillan Guide to Britain's Nature Reserves*. It's a lot of money, but more than 600 pages give full details of nearly 3,000 sites throughout Britain, together with a comprehensive list of local conservation organizations. The *Guide* is divided by county, with a good introductory overview followed by reserve descriptions with full details of location, ownership and access

— a very successful combination of hard facts, beautiful photographs and a lively style.

The new Ordnance Survey *Nature Atlas* is another useful if expensive resource. Because it tries to pack a great deal into a very little space it isn't as useful as would be the previous book together with a local map of the area you're visiting, but the *Nature Atlas* is still a lovely book, with information about more than 2,000 easily accessible sites (they have deliberately left out those which could be damaged by visitor pressure).

Walks For Wildlife is a cheaper, more portable book, with information about 270 nature walks throughout Britain (though very thin in some areas). Each entry tells you how to get there, what you might expect to see, and what facilities are provided. The writing isn't very inspired, but it fulfils its function as a prod to outdoor exploration quite adequately.

The Macmillan Guide to Britain's Nature Reserves
Linda Bennett
Macmillan, 1989
(2nd edn)
£24.95

Nature Atlas of Great Britain
Pan/Ordnance Survey, 1989
£16.95

Walks For Wildlife
Ebury (in conjunction with WWF), 1989
£5.95

Bees and Other Insects

Bees are currently having a hard time, largely due to pesticides, disease and wet summers, which is why locally produced honey has recently been more expensive and harder to come by. It has been estimated that the pollination done by British bees is worth £25 million a year to agriculture alone, yet they are still too often thought of as pests. Did you know that there are 250 species of British bee, of which 241 do not possess a sting? To find out more about bees, contact the British Beekeepers Association at the National Agricultural Centre (Stoneleigh, Warwickshire CV8 2LZ; Tel: 0203 696679).

The British Butterfly Conservation Society (Tudor House, 102 Chaveney Road, Quorn, Leicestershire LE12 8AD; Tel: 0509 412 870) is our main butterfly organization, looking after the interests of Britain's much-neglected butterflies.

A good guide to British insects is Michael Chinery's *A Field Guide to the Insects of Britain and Northern Europe* (Collins, 1973, £6.95).

Other Wildlife Resources

A good though necessarily less detailed guide to all of Britain's wildlife — trees, flowers, fungi, mammals, birds and insects — is the *Collins Complete Guide to British Wildlife* by Norman Arlott and Richard and Alastair Fitter. Illustrated throughout in colour, it will fit into your pocket and costs only £5.95. The most complete book service in Britain dealing with wildlife issues is the Natural History Book Service in Totnes, whose illustrated twice-yearly catalogue is a treat in itself — write for a copy. The service is run in conjunction with the Fauna and Flora Preservation Society, a much respected international conservation organization. Their quarterly journal, *Oryx*, is excellent.

Natural History Book Service Ltd
2 Wills Road
Totnes
Devon
TQ9 5XN
0803 865913

Fauna and Flora Preservation Society
79-83 North Street
Brighton
BN1 1ZA
0273 820445

Greening the Cities

On impulse, I had snatched out of the homebound crawl after a few miles and headed down a winding suburban lane. It led to a labyrinth of gravel pits, reservoirs, and watery odds and ends. It was hardly the promised landscape, and the whole area was pocked with working quarries and car dumps. But in the mood I was in, just to have seen some murky water lapped by non-air-conditioned wind would have set me right. I had parked by the edge of a canal which curled around the western edge of this maze of water, and had stumped off, scowling, along the tow-path. I think it was my black frame of mind that made the unexpected late fruitfulness of this place strike me with such intensity I had never noticed before that the canal here was as clear as a chalk stream. Yellow water lilies dropped liked balls of molten wax on the surface. Near the edge of the water drifts of newly hatched fish hung in the shallows.

Richard Mabey (see below)

The separation so many people feel between urban living and the variety and relative tranquility of the countryside often blinds them to the simple and comforting fact that both city and countryside are part of one global ecosystem. It is only in the last two or three hundred years that city and countryside have become so apparently antagonistic to each other, and in the northern cities sheltering in the valleys of the Pennines you can still recognize the potential for the interpenetration of the two.

On a smaller scale, nature always finds ways of filling an ecological niche given half a chance, and it is only human vigilance with sprays, traps and poisons that prevents us from seeing more wildlife in our cities. Even so, for those with keen eyes and a willingness to look elsewhere than straight ahead, there is much to be seen — kestrels over London, exotic plants sprouting from discarded bird seed on rubbish tips, butterflies attracted by the buddleia in urban parks.

The Unofficial Countrside

Richard Mabey's poetic, passionate, yet highly knowledgable book about urban wildlife, *The Unofficial Countryside* (Sphere, 1978), is currently out of print, but do look out for it in your library. He shows you spotted orchids growing in dumped cars, foxes who collect golf balls, and the guelder rose bushes growing along canal banks.

In the last few years, the impetus of a growing urban wildlife movement behind it, the greening of Britain's cities has moved apace. With London and the Midlands cities leading the way, nearly 500 nature parks and wildlife gardens have been created in the last decade. This process is documented in David Nicholson-Lord's *The Greening Of The Cities*, well illustrated and engagingly written; the theme of urban greening is continued in Joan Davidson's very practical manual, *How Green Is Your City*, and Bob Smyth's gazetteer to *City Wildspace* in Britain, describing over 300 sites in detail.

*

Greening is a therapy, a technology, an art, a science and a way of recovering a lost identity. For the trapped of the cities, it represents the most direct path from halfness to wholeness, sinceit was their 'countryside' self that the city stole from them. And the neighbourhood nature park or wildlife garden proclaims the same of the community, reminds and reassures its members daily of their new enhanced identity

David Nicholson-Lord

The Greening Of The Cities
David Nicholson-Lord
Routledge, 1987
£6.95

How Green Is Your City?
Joan Davidson
Bedford Square Press, 1988
£4.95

City Wildspace
Bob Smyth
Hilary Shipman, 1987
£6.95

If you are interested in urban wildlife you could get in touch with the Urban Wildlife Group, a West Midlands based organization which promotes urban nature parks and similar projects, and encourages community groups to become actively involved in local conservation issues. They produce a quarterly *Urban Wildlife Group News*, and are also involved in the putting together of an excellent quarterly journal, *Urban Wildlife*. The Group recently produced a useful manual called *Gardening for Wildlife* (£2.50 from them), full of practical tips and with a comprehensive resource list at the end.

Think Green, 'a national campaign for greener towns and cities', was born following a Green Towns and Cities Congress in Liverpool in 1984. In the last two years it has become a very influential force for green consciousness, especially in the Midlands, where it has become involved in numerous projects including Green Festivals in Leicester and Manchester. Think Green's publications are a source of inspiration: their *Green Celebrations* (£4.99 plus £1 p+p), for example, is a treasure trove of practical suggestions for getting a community involved in and excited about their local environment.

Urban Wildlife Group
Unit 213
Jubilee Trades Centre
130 Pershore Street
Birmingham
B5 6ND
021 666 7474

Think Green
Premier House
43-48 New Street
Birmingham
B2 4LJ
021 643 8899 ext. 409

City Farms

'Helping the city grow' is the slogan of the city farms movement. In the late 1970s more than thirty city farms were established in Britain, giving city-dwellers the opportunity to experience rural activities in their own neighbourhood, and in most cases reinstating land that was derelict. Though each city farm is unique, you can expect to find chickens and ducks, goats and sheep, vegetable gardens and tree-planting schemes; some also have farm shops and restaurants. If you are interested in helping on a regular basis, you will almost certainly be welcomed. There are now more than seventy city farms, linked by the National Federation of City Farms and their bi-annual free newssheet *City Farmer*.

National Federation of City Farms
The Old Vicarage
66 Fraser Street
Windmill Hill
Bedminster
Bristol
BS3 4LY
0272 660663

Friends of the Earth

A whole page for Friends of the Earth, and they deserve it. The earth needs friends, and FoE have done their damndest to make sure it has some.

FoE started life in 1969 in the USA where David Brower, its founder, had just parted company with The Sierra Club, America's best-known environmental organization. The Sierra Club refused to be solidly anti-nuclear, and would not look beyond the boundaries of the USA to look at world problems — this wasn't good enough for David. FoE quickly became international, and now has organizations in Argentina, Australia, Austria, Bangladesh, Belgium, Brazil, Canada, Cyprus, Denmark, Ecuador, England and Wales, Estonia, France, Ghana, Hong Kong, Indonesia, Ireland, Italy, Japan, Malaysia, The Netherlands, New Zealand, Nicaragua, Papua New Guinea, Poland, Portugal, Scotland, Spain, Sweden, Switzerland, Tanzania, the USA and Uruguay.

Friends of the Earth International has consultative status with the United Nations Economic and Social Council, and produces a quarterly bulletin called *FoE-Link*. FoE global campaigns include whaling, acid rain, pesticides, tropical rainforests, marine pollution, and nuclear non-proliferation. FoE International maintains a small secretariat in The Netherlands.

All FoE groups and members are committed to the preservation, restoration, and rational use of the environment, recognizing that these aims cannot be isolated from social, economic and cultural issues. They promote citizen action and locally-accountable democracy, and promote positive alternatives like renewable energy and sustainable agricultural systems.

Friends of the Earth UK

Established in 1971, FoE UK first inhabited part of the Rowntree Trust house at 9 Poland Street in London's Soho. It then outgrew its second home in City Road and in 1987 moved into new premises alongside CND near Old Street tube station. FoE now has more than sixty full-time workers, 270 local groups and over 180,000 supporters. As Britain's best-known environmental action group, FoE finds itself co-ordinating campaigning activities on many fronts, and if somebody at FoE doesn't know (or can't find) the answer to your environmental queries, however detailed, the chances are that nobody does.

FoE's recent successes include mobilizing people to persuade aerosol and fast food companies to move to CFC-free products, enforcing EC laws on drinking water quality in Britain, and the tightening of pesticide legislation. In 1988 FoE joined forces with Greenpeace to lay down 'The Green Gauntlet', an annual report on the government's environmental record designed to test the extent to which official actions match their green words. The 1989 report (£3 from FoE, essential reading if you are concerned about Britain's record on environmental issues) gives the government 2 marks out of 30 for its progress so far — a verdict of 'not really trying'.

FoE's main current campaign areas are energy, air pollution, agriculture and countryside, rainforests, cities for people, water pollution and toxic wastes, and recycling.

In 1981 FoE set up an educational and research trust, which ensures that any donation or covenant you make to FoE is tax-deductible — you couldn't choose a better home for your millions. *Earth Matters* is FoE's excellent quarterly magazine, and membership brings you a regular mailing of important environmental campaigns and how you can get involved. I suspect most *New Green Pages* readers are already members of FoE, but if you're not then send them a cheque for £12 (£5 if you're unwaged) today and help the earth fight back.

Friends of the Earth
26-28 Underwood Street
London
N1 7JQ
0(7)1-490 1555

Friends of the Earth Scotland

FoE Scotland is proof of Friends of the Earth's commitment to local democracy. Servicing a network of twenty local groups and a rapidly growing membership, now over 8,000, their campaigning concerns include wildlife habitats, endangered species, rainforests, toxic wastes, forestry, lead pollution and fish farming. The FoE Scotland *Campaign Pack* comes out four times a year and, like FoE London, the Edinburgh office acts as a clearing house for many environmental questions from public and media alike. In 1985 FoE Scotland established an Environmental Education Trust, the first of its kind in Scotland, to meet the growing demand for information and educational materials for schools and the general public.

Friends of the Earth Scotland
15 Windsor Street
Edinburgh
EH7 5LA
031 557 3432

Friends of the Earth Handbook

The book that gives you useful and practical information on all the campaigns that FoE works on, and tells you how you can tread more lightly on this planet of ours — the best introduction to the ideas contained in *New Green Pages* too. There is a useful appendix on practical campaigning by Chris Church, the local groups co- ordinator, and lists of organizations and further reading.

Going Green isn't easy. Its possibly the greatest personal challenge you will ever take on — but what's the alternative?

Friends of the Earth Handbook
edited by Jonathon Porritt
Optima, 1990 (2nd edn)
£5.99

Agriculture or Agricide?

Our food system is unsustainable. It is based on the use of fertilisers and pesticides which depend upon fossil fuels which cause pollution, ecological damage and loss of fertility. Our demands on the Third World for feed for our intensively reared livestock and other products destroy their forest and soil fertility. Our export of surpluses are dumped on these countries thereby destroying their own food growing systems and forcing growing numbers of landless people on to marginal areas where, in order to survive, they are driven to damage the environment. Those that are dictating agricultural policy are the powerful and rich farmers and multinational agricultural industries. In Britain one half of public subsidies for supporting agriculture ends up in the hands of 10,000 farmers who are all millionaires. Meanwhile our small and part-time farmers face bankruptcy. We are heading for disaster.
Green Party press release, May 1987

Farm pollution of rivers rose last year by 6 per cent to a record 4,141 cases in England and Wales, according to a newly-pub-lished report by the Water Authorities Association and the Ministry of Agriculture. Animal slurry is the main form of farm pollution and is up to 100 times more damaging than untreated sewage. The liquor from silage — the second greatest problem — is 200 times more polluting than raw sewage. Both slurry and silage pollute watercourses, using up oxygen and killing aquatic life. Beef and dairy farming is the worst offender. Five water authority areas — North-West, Severn Trent, Welsh, Wessex and South-West — accounted for 79 per cent of all incidents. Farm-ing was responsible for 19 per cent of all pollution incidents.
The Environment Digest, May 1989

The pattern of agriculture in Britain affects the landscape we live in, the food we eat, the taxes and prices we pay, and the health of our environment and ourselves. Conventional agri-culture frequently flies in the face of both ecological and true economic considerations, and the vested interests of large-scale chemical agriculture are understandably deaf to the pleas of the organic lobby. But things are changing. Organ-izations like The Soil Association, The Organic Growers' Association and The Permaculture Association are beginning to make a real impact, with the Soil Association organic symbol turning up in supermarkets as well as the growing number of wholefood shops (see page 28).

It's true that the government doesn't believe that the public at large should have a say in agricultural policy, otherwise farmers wouldn't say that consumer pressure will have little effect on the introduction of a new biotechnology like BST. But the government is wrong. Consumers are beginning to vote with their purses, and are increasingly concerned about the environmental and health hazards of destructive farming techniques like aerial spraying, straw-burning, factory farming and hedge-grubbing. Things you can do to influence the pattern of agriculture include:

▶ Talking to farmers in your area. They often feel isolated and misunderstood, and you may find you can make arrangements to buy some of your food directly from local farms.
▶ Buying local organically-grown food; buy it from the local wholefood shop if possible, or set up a buyers' co-operative to guarantee a consistent market.
▶ Keeping an eye on your local countryside and watching for unwelcome changes (see campaigning, page 234).
▶ Educating yourself with some of the reading suggested below.

Books on Agriculture

Michael Fox's *Agricide* takes a worldwide view of the crisis facing agriculture, which has to all intents and purposes becoming a global mining company, monopolizing the world's agricultural seed stocks, bleeding soils of their nutrients, and reducing farmers with unique and important skills to the role of pawns in an uncaring multinational scramble for profits.

Unless the structure and practice of agriculture is not soon changed and made more ecologically sound, health-inducing, humane, and equitable, the next generation, argues Michael Fox, will face inevitable agricide.

A tireless campaigner for agricultural reform and Chairman of the House of Commons Agricultural Select Committee, Richard Body has access to information almost unobtainable elsewhere. He has a blind spot when it comes to the notion of 'free markets', but none of us is perfect. In *The Triumph and The Shame* he alerted the farming community to the damage we cause by subsidizing and protecting unsustainable forms of farming; *Farming In The Clouds* looks more specifically at who loses out from the present system. The list is a long one, from farmers and consumers to the poor both of this country and of the Third World. Using detailed statistics he shows that millions of pounds of public money are not only wasted; they actively create poverty and environmental degradation. Richard Body's most recent book, *Red or Green for Farmers*, looks at the stark choice facing British agriculture: 'red farming' based on chemicals and hormones, or 'green farming' based on biological methods.

Finally, *Working the Land: A New Plan for a Healthy Agri-culture* is the only book currently available to set out a realistic and practical programme for British agriculture. Easy to read and credible.

Agricide
The Hidden Crisis That
Affects Us All
Michael Fox
Schocken, 1987
£7.00

**The Triumph and
The Shame**
Richard Body
Temple Smith, 1982
£2.95

**Farming In
The Clouds**
Richard Body
Temple Smith, 1984
£3.50

**Red or Green
for Farmers**
Richard Body
Broad Leys Publishing,
1987
£3.95

Working the Land
A New Plan for a
Healthy Agriculture
Charlie Pye-Smith and
Richard North
Temple Smith, 1984
£3.95

Look at the farming magazines in the local library (if they take them) — you can learn a lot from the pages of *Farmer's Weekly* and *Farming News*. John Cherrington's regular Tuesday column in *The Financial Times* is clear and well-written, and you can do worse than listen to The Archers for current trends in agriculture.

The Soil Association

Our health depends on the quality of our food — the plant and animal products we eat. The quality of our food depends on the health of the soil. This vital relationship is crucial to the future of life on this planet.

The Soil Association was founded in 1946 to further this philosophy of interrelated wholeness. It encourages an ecological approach to agriculture, and offers organic husbandry as the long-term and only real alternative for sustainable agricultural production. The Association's symbol scheme licenses commercial food production to the highest organic standards (see page 31), and is the consumer's guarantee of organic quality. The Association published an important *Manifesto for Organic Agriculture* early in 1987 which was sent to key MPs from all political parties; the *Manifesto* is based on the straightforward *Charter for Agriculture* published a couple of years earlier. Anybody interested in organic growing can join, though obviously if you are a grower or gardener you will get more out of your membership. Local groups throughout the country organize talks, demonstrations and visits, and the Association runs a book service and publishes an excellent quarterly magazine called *The Living Earth*. Current campaigns include 'Soilwatch' to monitor soil erosion and 'The Living Earth', a consumer campaign for greater awareness about and availability of organic produce; the Association also run a 'Best Organic Garden' competition. You can obtain a list of local Soil Association members in your region, together with details about what they grow, by sending a cheque for £3 and a stamped addressed A4 envelope.

A CHARTER FOR AGRICULTURE

The current crisis of overproduction is a threat, not just to the EEC but to the stability of British Agriculture, both now and in the future. The livelihood and, indeed survival of British farmers and through them the whole fabric of agriculture and of rural society, is now seriously threatened.

Unless there is a series of fundamental reforms, the crisis will only get worse. We, therefore, call upon all who are involved in determining the future of agriculture, food quality and the environment to incorporate the principles of this Charter.

PLEDGE TO:

● 1. Ensure that all production and the management of farm resources are in harmony rather than in conflict with the natural system.

● 2. Use and develop technology appropriate to an understanding of biological systems.

● 3. Rely primarily on renewable energy and rotations to achieve and maintain soil fertility for optimum production.

● 4. Aim for optimum nutritional value of all staple foods.

● 5. Encourage decentralised systems for processing, distribution and marketing of farm products.

● 6. Strive for an equitable relationship between those who work and live on the land and, by maintaining wildlife and its habitats, create a countryside which is aesthetically pleasing for all.

The Soil Association Ltd

86-88 Colston Street
Bristol
BS1 5BB
0272 290661

Organic Growers' Associations

British Organic Farmers and the Organic Growers Association work closely together, dealing respectively with agriculturalists and with smaller-scale horticultural producers. Nearly a thousand members benefit from a network of regional groups providing local contacts, meetings, visits and training courses. Marketing advice is also available, and BOF/OGA also acts as a political pressure group and public relations forum for the organic movement. Their quarterly magazine, *New Farmer and Grower*, shows how professional the movement has now

become, with adverts from organic grain wholesalers, organic conversion programmes, organic vegetable distribution services and bulk organic grass seeds. OGA and BOF work very closely with the Soil Association, as you can see from their address, and give full support to the organic produce symbol scheme.

British Organic Farmers/ Organic Growers Association

86-88 Colston Street
Bristol
BS1 5BB
0272 299666/299800

The Permaculture Association

'Permaculture' was coined by the Australian horticulturalist Bill Mollison to describe the conscious use of ecological principles in self-sustaining food production systems. If that sounds like a lot of long words, the information produced by The Permaculture Association is both inspiring and instructive. The Association organizes lectures and training programmes, and as far as I know is the only reliable source for the two books which inspired the permaculture movement, *Permaculture One* and *Permaculture Two*, and the recently-published and encyclopedic *Permaculture: A Designer's Manual* — expensive but visionary and immensely practical.

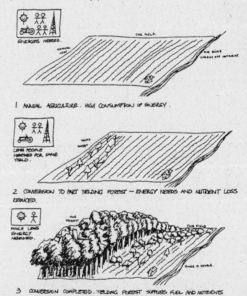

Permaculture is not about technique, it is about design. Within it, many techniques can be used — organic growing and pest control techniques; forest farming and old forestry practices such as coppicing; free-range poultry and animal raising; technology for energy conservation and the use of solar energy, and recycling of wastes. What is important is the way all the different elements are consciously designed to work together, creating an intricate web of inter-relationships which is both stable and high-yielding. In a sense this is rediscovering and developing on a conscious and informed level the wisdom of ancient polycultures which continued for centuries in balance with their surroundings.

Permaculture News, Midwinter 1989-90

The Permaculture Association

8 Hunter's Moon
Dartington
Totnes
Devon
TQ9 6JT
0803 867546

Countryside Conflicts

What kind of countryside do we want? And how can we develop the right kind of policies which will guide the British countryside into the twenty-first century? Forty years of assumptions which have influenced public policy are now coming to an end, but so far we have had little debate over what is to replace them. What is the balance we wish to see between agriculture, forestry, conservation, recreation and rural economic development?

Howard Newby, *The Countryside in Question* (see below)

Anyone who believes that what happens in the countryside is only a result of social and economic forces rather than which pressure groups have direct access to the political machine is engaging in self-delusion. Indeed, the effectiveness of controls on landscape change merely tells one about the strengths and weaknesses of the participants who attempt to influence the development of legislation relating to rural matters. The legislation speaks of the comparative success of those who exploit the rural environment for their own economic ends.

John Blunden and Graham Turner,
Critical Countryside (see below)

There can only be a limited number of botched-up compromises and one-off solutions. The whole basis of agriculture and land use must be overhauled. The present system cannot be sustained. But waiting for the wasteful, polluting, resource-hungry, ecologically- unbalanced British agricultural system to bleed itself to death is like waiting for a bull to do the same in a china shop. In its death throes, and despite its lacerations, it will do vast and irreparable damage.

Chris Rose, in *Green Britain or Industrial Wasteland?*
(see page 58)

There is no point saving butterflies, orchids or rare finches if you simultaneously allow the destruction of their habitat. Each organism is part of a complex web of life — if you destroy part of it you upset the whole. You may think you are only cutting down one tree, but that tree might be as vital to the ecology of the wood as one of its legs is to the Eifel Tower.

It isn't just agriculture, but agriculture is the main culprit. Not so much individual farmers as a government which allows itself to be pressurized by the agrochemical business and the powerful millionaire farmers into subsidizing an agriculture which ignores the value of habitat, and always puts profit before conservation. The ecological backlash is horrific — species loss is not confined to the Brazilian rainforest, and the results of an ecologically unsound agricultural system are having increasingly noticeable effects on the country's human population. Because we, too, are part of the whole. The spraying of agricultural crops poisons the whole environment: pesticides and herbicides make no distinction between a farmer's field and your garden. The felling of a tree takes place in an ecosystem within which both you and the tree have an important part to play.

The Politics of Conservation

The grim chronicle reads as follows: over the past 35 years, the nation has lost 95 per cent of lowland herb-rich grasslands, 80 per cent of chalk and limestone grasslands, 60 per cent of lowland heaths, 45 per cent of limestone pavements, 50 per cent of ancient woodlands, 50 per cent of lowland fens and marshes, over 60 per cent of lowland raised bogs, and a third of all upland grasslands, heaths and mires. . . The Large Blue butterfly became extinct in 1979, but eight more species are endangered and another twelve have declined so much that they are now officially rare — this is out of a total British list of just 55 breeding species. Of 43 species of dragonfly, three or four have become extinct since 1953 and ten have decreased to the point of becoming very rare. . . 30 lowland and six upland species [of bird] have shown appreciable long-term decline during the last 35 years. . . the otter has become extremely rare and bats are now legally protected. . . Of the 1423 native vascular plants, 149 have declined by at least 20 per cent . . .

Here is a comprehensive account of the war that is currently being waged over the countryside, presenting the historical context of the slaughter, naming and describing the adversaries, and plotting the possible course of the campaigns. Countryside Conflicts shows how powerful the landowning lobby is, gives a graphic account of the skullduggery that lay behind the enactment of the 1981 Wildlife and Countryside Act, and shows how ineffective that legislation has been in preventing further and disastrous habitat loss. The book concludes with very practical and positive proposals for reforming our agriculture and forestry.

Countryside Conflicts
The Politics of Farming, Forestry and Conservation
Philip Lowe, Graham Cox, Malcolm MacEwen,
Tim O'Riordan and Michael Winter
Temple Smith, 1986
£8.95

Critical Countryside

Although it may not be immediately apparent, great changes are taking place in Britain's countryside. Europe as a whole is producing too much food and the reduction of EC agricultural subsidies has led to the introduction of controversial schemes such as 'setaside'. Increasing pressure for suburban development in green belts has led to massive protest, while it is becoming very obvious that large-scale commercial forestry destroys both rural ecosystems and rural economies.

A few brave experiments in the revitalization of Britain's countryside are showing signs of success, but they are as yet few and far between. 'Integrated rural development' is an increasingly fashionable concept, and a few IRD schemes — as at Monyash in Derbyshire and Ardington in Berkshire — are starting to bear fruit. But as a collection of recent books about the future of Britain's countryside show, the radical policy decisions which would make real progress possible are simply not being taken.

Critical Countryside was written to accompany an Open University television series called *The Changing Countryside*, and is primarily a history of the last few decades of the British countryside, based on eight distinctive landscapes from Snowdonia to the Sussex Downs, together with a look at how the French care for their national parks. Also for the general reader who wants to explore these important issues is the Howard Newby's more recent *The Countryside in Question*, again based on a television series, with plenty of case histories — both depressing and inspiring — and some evocative photographs.

If you want more technical and legislative detail, the books to look out for are John Blunden and Nigel Curry's *A Future for Our Countryside* and Ann and Malcolm MacEwen's *Greenprints for the Countryside*. The MacEwens write more fluently and passionately, concentrating on British policy for national parks and other 'protected areas'; the resource sections and bibliographies in both books are excellent.

Critical Countryside
John Blunden and
Graham Turner
BBC, 1985
£12.95

A Future For Our Countryside
John Blunden and Nigel Curry
Blackwell, 1988
£11.50

The Countryside in Question
Howard Newby
Hutchinson, 1988
£7.95

Greenprints For The Countryside
Ann and Malcolm MacEwen
Allen and Unwin, 1987
£8.95

Countryside Commission

The Countryside Commission was established in 1968, primarily to take over the work of the National Parks Commission but with a wider brief, that of monitoring change in the countryside of England and Wales and proposing necessary legislation. The Commission's funding comes from the government, but it is an independent agency and is free to express its own point of view, even when this runs counter to the prevailing political tide. Employing 120 staff, the Commission has its headquarters in Cheltenham, seven English branches and one office in Wales.

The Commission produces a great deal of excellent printed material, from tourist brochures to detailed reports; the *Catalogue of Publications* alone has 40 pages! Many of the smaller leaflets are free, including a general introduction called *Your Countryside Our Concern*, *National Parks in England and Wales*, and *Enjoying the Countryside: Priorities for Action*. Every two months the Commission publishes *Countryside Commission News*, and *National Parks Today* appears three times a year; subscriptions to both are free on request. Countryside Commission publications should be ordered from their publications department in Manchester, not from Cheltenham.

The Countryside Commission for Scotland is based in a large country house near Perth, and fulfils the same functions in Scotland as the Countryside Commission does in England and Wales. *Scotland's Countryside* is a fascinating full-colour quarterly newsletter, which is sent free to interested groups and individuals.

Countryside Commission
John Dower House
Crescent Place
Cheltenham
Gloucestershire
GL50 3RA
0242 521381

Countryside Commission for Scotland
Battleby
Redgorton
Perth
PH1 3EW
0738 27921

Countryside Commission Publications
19-23 Albert Road
Manchester
M19 2EQ
061 224 6287

Council for the Protection of Rural England

CPRE is the foremost voluntary countryside organization in England (with a sister body in Wales), and with a combined membership of more than 30,000 is a powerful voice against ill-considered threats to the countryside. Traditionally conservative and tweedy, it has recently become more adversarial and activist, leading to the withdrawal of support from erstwhile allies like the NFU, AA and RAC — which goes to show the extent of their concern for the countryside. But all this has made the CPRE a very lively and worthwhile body, each of the 43 autonomous county groups working hard on issues ranging from pollution control and nuclear power to rights of way and land ownership. Most branches have a representative of the local authority on their committee, and are automatically notified of planning applications and development plan hearings. Their magazine, *Countryside Campaigner*, is useful, as are some of their publications — look out for *How To Help Farmers and Keep England Beautiful*. A recent book co-published with Macdonald, Derrik Mercer and David Puttnam's *Rural England: Our Countryside at the Crossroads* (Macdonald/Queen Anne Press, 1988, £14.95, sets out the threats to the English countryside region by region. The many photographs remind the reader of the heritage that we stand to lose if radical shifts in policy are not made very soon.

Council for the Protection of Rural England
25-27 Buckingham
Palace Road
London
SW1W 0PP
0(7)1-976 6433

Council for the Protection of Rural Wales
Ty Gwyn
31 High Street
Welshpool
Powys
SY21 7JP
0938 2525

RURAL

RURAL is the Society for Responsible Use of Resources in Agriculture and on the Land, a long title for a network of academics and forward-thinking farmers who meet regularly to discuss ways of developing programmes and projects which are both environmentally sustainable and help the local economy. The quarterly *RURAL News* contains news and reports about the society's activities and other titbits about positive change in the countryside.

RURAL
Home Close
High Street
Stonesfield
Oxford
OX7 2PU
099 389 686

Greenpeace

Great are the tasks ahead, terrifying are the mountains of ignorance and hate and prejudice, but the Warriors of the Rainbow shall rise as on the wings of an eagle to surmount all difficulties. They will be happy to find that there are now millions of people all over the earth ready and eager to rise and join them in conquering all barriers that bar the way to a new and glorious world. We have had enough now of talk. Let there be deeds.

Thus ends a book of native American prophecies published in the late 1960s which helped inspire a group of young Canadians to protest against American nuclear testing in Alaska. At first called the Don't Make A Wave Committee, the newly-fledged pressure group sought a name that would have a certain ring to it. Social worker Bill Darnell suggested Greenpeace, and one of the most influential environmental protests of the twentieth century was born.

Greenpeace in Britain was put on its feet in 1977: a borrowed office, £800 in donations and a great deal of determination saw to it that Greenpeace UK was soon in the vanguard of organization, the first major campaign being the anti-whaling voyage of the newly-christened *Rainbow Warrior* to Iceland.

Greenpeace has never taken the easy road, which makes for a rough ride both in its campaigns and in its internal organization. Active campaigning means dedicated and single-minded steadfastness, not always the most endearing of human traits. But, like the phoenix, Greenpeace always rises to fight another battle, and from its headquarters on Islington Green Greenpeace UK continues to campaign on the vitally important issues of whaling, sealing, nuclear testing, and dumping at sea.

Greenpeace now has more than a million members in seventeen countries, and has become the environmental action group that the media listen to — partly because Greenpeace makes the issues so immediate that they can't be ignored, partly that eighteen years' experience has given Greenpeace real standing both in scientific circles and in the popular imagination.

Greenpeace has always been action-oriented. The myth of the Warriors of the Rainbow — selfless heroism in the face of environmental threat — is lived out in the way that Greenpeacers are prepared to put themselves quite literally between the polluters and the environment, the hunters and the hunted, oppressors and oppressed. Those in authority don't like such brazenness. After many missions all over the world, for example, the *Rainbow Warrior* met her end in New Zealand at the hands of a plot masterminded by the French government in an attempt to stop the ship from interrupting French nuclear testing in the South Pacific.

Greenpeace UK co-ordinates a range of campaigns: protesting about nuclear dumping from Sellafield, trying to stop the incineration of toxic chemicals at sea, exposing the scale of pollution around Britain's coastline, campaigning for the designation of Antarctica as a World Park, and making people aware of the scale of the problem of acid rain in northern Europe. Their activities often put them at risk of breaking national and international laws, but such 'ethical illegality' is part of Greenpeace's strategy. Their campaign to block the waste pipe from Sellafield cost them a £50,000 fine; the next time they did it (there's no stopping Greenpeace) they fled to Dublin so as not to risk the impounding of the new ship, the Greenpeace. Their activities have earned Greenpeace the respect and admiration of thousands of people, and as they say themselves: 'Thank God someone's making waves!'

Greenpeace UK
30-31 Islington Green
London
N1 8XE
0(7)1-354 5100

GREENPEACE

The Greenpeace Story

1989 saw the publication of Greenpeace's semi-official 'biography', *The Greenpeace Story*, edited by journalist Michael Brown and Greenpeace activist John May. A fascinating story it is too, well-told and fast-moving, illustrated with some of the action photographs for which Greenpeace photographers are justly famed. As well as being a detailed chronicle of eighteen years of tireless campaigning, *The Greenpeace Story* can be used as an inspirational sourcebook of ideas for green activists — after all, if they can do it . . . The book doesn't buck the internal wrangles of the early years, though in fairness I would like to have seen more than a date-by-date diary of the last four years' activities. An honest assessment of the present state of the organization and a passionate clarion call to action would have been my preferred ending.

The Greenpeace Story
Michael Brown and John May
Dorling Kindersley, 1989
£7.95

Coastline

During the summer of 1986 the Greenpeace ship Beluga sailed round the coast of Britain surveying the quality of our inshore waters. Some of their findings were horrific — arsenic dumping in the Humber estuary, ammonium sulphate on Teesside, sewage sludge in the Thames, heavy metals in the Mersey, agricultural nitrates off the East Anglian coast. Partly as a result of the Beluga survey, but also to celebrate a coastline that may never be the same again, Greenpeace have put together a full-colour glossy book called *Coastline*. The photographs are wonderful, some of the text (the regional surveys and a dozen pages at the end by Greenpeace scientist Paul Johnston) fascinating and worrying by turns. All in all, however, this is rather a disappointing book — the main text reads like a tourist guidebook, but for the pictures and postscript alone *Coastline* is well worth looking out for.

Coastline
Britain's Threatened Heritage
Greenpeace
Kingfisher, 1987
£14.95

Animal Welfare

Farewell happy fields where joy forever dwells,
Hail horrors, hail.
John Milton, *Paradise Lost*

A recent report told of a broiler chicken found by the roadside, presumably having fallen from a lorry on its way to slaughter. The bird was literally being eaten alive by maggots. The vet who saw the bird was shocked, commenting that there may be many chickens in such a condition inside broiler houses during hot summer weather. Janet Hunt, *The Holistic Cook* (see page 11)

The British poultry industry can be held up as a shining example of all that is good in European agriculture.
Donald Thompson, Agricultural Parliamentary Secretary
Poultry Industry Conference, November 1986

Compassion is a vital aspect of humanity, even though it appears to be given second place whenever money or power rear their heads. Anyone who wants to live a green lifestyle will certainly have accepted that empathy and understanding are important in the way we relate to each other as human beings; do we always afford the same respect and compassion to other living things?

The exploitation of the animal realm takes many forms, from the visible cruelty of foxhunting, to the 'scientifically-justified' testing of cosmetics on the eyes of restrained rabbits, to the keeping of farm and zoo animals in conditions which do not allow them the freedom to live a happy and fulfilled life. Arguments along the lines of 'they don't mind because they're only animals' hold no sway in green circles — we and they are part of the same world. Every part of the natural world deserves respect, and has an equal right to existence.

Compassion in World Farming

Compassion in World Farming are the foremost voice in the campaign against factory farming methods, though they see this only as a first step towards reducing our dependence on farm animals as we eat less and less artificially-fattened meat. From offices above an excellent wholefood shop called The Bran Tub, CIWF campaign hard for the rights of farm animals, and their spokesperson Carol Long can often be heard on farming programmes putting a well-argued case for humane livestock rearing against the reactionary farming establishment. CIWF produce an informative bi-monthly magazine called *AgScene*, they have produced a charter for humane livestock rearing (see the next column), and their schools project, 'The Place of Animals in the Farm', has been circulated to 30,000 schools throughout Britain.

Compassion in World Farming
20 Lavant Street
Petersfield
Hampshire
GU32 3EW
0730 64208

The CIWF Guidelines for Humane Animal Farming

▶ Animals should have freedom of movement and be able to stand up, lie down, and extend their limbs without difficulty; they should not be permanently tethered or confined in stalls or cages.
▶ They should be able to exercise in a natural way every day.
▶ Housed animals should have access to clean bedding; free-range animals to clean pasture.
▶ Animals should have access to clean water at all times.
▶ Food should be adequate, regular, palatable and suitable, without added drugs or chemicals other than those prescribed by a vet.
▶ Animals should have shelter from extremes of weather and temperature.
▶ They should have adequate daylight, and not be subject to excessive artificial light.
▶ Animals should not be mutilated in any way.
▶ Transporting of live animals should be reduced as much as possible.
▶ Slaughtering should be carried out as painlessly as possible.

In 1986 the Real Meat Company in Warminster (see page 35) became the first British meat producer to adopt the CIWF guidelines; CIWF hope that others will follow their lead.

The Extended Circle

The Wynne-Tysons have been upholding the rights of animals for many years. Esmé Wynne-Tyson worked tirelessly in the field, publishing *The Philosophy of Compassion* in 1970. Her son Jon Wynne-Tyson's Centaur Press has continued the campaign, publishing in 1985 a comprehensive and inspiring collection of quotations about animal rights and the need for a humane society. *The Extended Circle* has become something of a bible for all animal welfare campaigners, containing as it does a wealth of wisdom from authors through the centuries. From the Buddhist scriptures ('Hurt not others with that which pains yourself') to Doris Day ('Killing an animal to make a coat is a sin') via Queen Victoria ('The Queen fears also sometimes from experiments in the pursuit of science') the pleas for compassion are endless and heartfelt.

*

In the long term, there is no real answer but to work for global agreement to build into educational systems the ethical basis for environmental responsibility. A compassionate philosophy — relating to all sentient life, not expediently allocated to ourselves but withheld from other life forms — must be our priority.

The Extended Circle
A Dictionary of Humane
Thought
edited by Jon Wynne-Tyson
Centaur, 1985
£7.95

Animal Experiments

A single dose of the weedkiller Paraquat (400 mg/kg up to 1,130 mg/kg) was force fed to rats using a stomach tube. Toxic effects leading to death included lethargy, loss of muscle control, shedding bloody tears, hunched posture, shivering, difficulty in breathing and bleeding from the nose.
Hazleton Laboratories, Harrogate, 1981

It has been estimated that a laboratory animal dies in Britain every six seconds as technicians inject into or spray on to them a wide range of chemicals and poisons. Many of these animals are specially bred to suffer in this way — over 12,000 mice and rats to be injected with food additives, 11,000 animals used at Porton Down to test military poisons and their antidotes. The ridiculous and outdated LD50 (Lethal Dose 50%) test — to see at what toxicity 50% of a population of animals die within two weeks — is used to test everything from weedkillers to dandruff shampoo. Not only is it cruel and unnecessary, it proves very little about the toxicity of these substances to human beings.

There are a number of organizations whose primary concern is the welfare of laboratory animals, though they may also campaign vigorously in other areas such as the abolition of bullfighting or the use of animals in circuses. The anti-vivisection organizations often work together, as in the current 'Mobilization for Laboratory Animals' campaign to persuade the government to change its basic guidelines about the use of laboratory animals.

Animal Aid

Animal Aid is the most broadly based of the anti-cruelty organizations, its campaigns including fur protests, circus animals, anti-vivisection, and better conditions for farm animals. The excellent bi-monthly magazine *Outrage* lists all the local groups, tells you what they are doing nationwide, and has detailed and informative articles about what is being done to animals in the name of science and of entertainment. Animal Aid is committed to non-violent action to achieve its ends, and has launched a 'Living without Cruelty' campaign designed to show how you can simply refuse to buy things which have involved cruelty to animals. They also have an active young people's network, and sponsor the annual 'Awards for Trivial Research' which are widely reported in the media.

Animal Aid
7 Castle Street
Tonbridge
Kent
TN9 1BH
0732 364546

Against Animal Experiments

BUAV and NAVS have similar aims, and are both part of the 'Mobilization for Laboratory Animals'. BUAV's major recent contribution to a cruelty-free lifestyle is their 'Choose Cruelty-Free' campaign, a magazine and associated nationwide bus tour (promoted by many famous names) to help people to choose products — especially toiletries and cosmetics — which have not been tested on animals. Look out for the rabbit 'Not Tested On Animals' logo, appearing ever more frequently on chemists' shelves thanks to BUAV's perseverance. BUAV

have also launched an important 'Health With Humanity' campaign to show that medical experiments on animals are both cruel and misleading; a growing number of medical professionals have joined the cause. BUAV's bi-monthly magazine is called *Liberator*.

NAVS want vivisection outlawed in all its forms. NAVS is an activist organization which seeks to expose the scandal of vivisection at every opportunity. Their bi-monthly magazine *Campaigner* tells of many varieties of animal torture and campaigns to work for the rights of these victims; each issue also contains a section of NAVS' *Campaigners' Handbook*, an excellent resource for any animal rights campaigner. One of NAVS' disclosures was the disgraceful way in which the AIDS virus was tested on laboratory animals in the 1970s with little thought given to hygiene or the welfare of the animals; they suggest that it was largely this irresponsibility that led to the current AIDS crisis.

British Union for the Abolition of Vivisection
16a Crane Grove
London
N7 8LB
0(7)1-700 4888

National Anti-Vivisection Society
51 Harley Street
London
W1N 1DD
0(7)1-580 4034

Stop the Hunt

If foxes have to be killed, as they sometimes do, a pack of hounds and bloodthirsty people on horses must be the nastiest possible way of going about it. The Hunt Saboteurs use non-violent ways of frustrating hunt meetings and publicizing the iniquity of this 'sport' of the rich. *Howl* is their quarterly magazine, full of news and ideas.

Hunt Saboteurs Association
PO Box 87
Exeter
Devon
EX4 3TX
0392 30521

And Animals in Zoos?

In Britain there are approximately 260 zoos (including bird gardens). To maintain standards of care for the animals we now have the monitoring structure of the Zoo Licensing Act — and yet conditions and situations are passed and accepted, which in the view of thousands of people, including scientists, should not be tolerated. For example — from a scientific survey carried out on behalf of Zoo Check by marine biologist Paul Horsman . . . it was discovered that 12 out of the 20 polar bears [in British zoos] were psychotic, some severely so, and that 60 to 70 per cent of cubs died before the age of one year (in the wild it is 10 to 30 per cent).
Beyond the Bars: The Zoo Dilemma (an excellent book)
Thorsons, 1987, £5.99

Zoo Check was formed by Virginia McKenna in 1984 following the death at London Zoo of the elephant Pole Pole (the story is told in graphic detail in *Beyond the Bars*) — Zoo Check, now a worldwide organization, can be contacted at Cherry Tree Cottage, Coldharbour, Dorking, Surrey RH5 6HA (0306 712091).

Back to the Land

We have goats, sheep and chickens: we eat eggs and milk puddings and muesli over summer, salted mutton and old hens over winter, along with home grown vegetables etc. We're hoping to expand into enough fodder crops — cabbages, turnips, oats — to feed the animals next winter; and to produce enough to feed us in carrots, onions etc. We're also trying a fruit garden. We currently have 15 sheep, but have hill grazing rights and could triple this, producing lots of wool and meat. We're hoping to add pigs, ducks and cows, depending on finances, very generous local grants, and our efforts to re-roof the barns. The Highlands and Islands Development Board is seen by everyone I've met as very helpful if you're a multi-millionaire, adding to your millions. If you're normal, wanting an investment of a few hundred or maybe thousands of pounds, they give you almost enough forms to set up as a scrap paper dealer and become a millionaire, but no help. . . There is a cinema in Aberdeen, but the cost of going (£200 return cheapest) left us without the cost of admission to the cinema, so . . . When I'm emptying the rinsing water in the ditch from my hand-washed clothes, in oilskins in the dark in a blizzard; when the tilleys flicker and we've run out of candles and sit in the gloom, I think about our dishwasher in Liverpool and bath and shower in Manchester. But when the sun lights up the islands over the sea, and the sheep eat out of Jody's hands, when Jody gamely rides his bike over ditches, cat and fishing nets 200 yards from me and perfectly safe, I can see me collecting my pension here, with Pam, in 28 years time.

Kevin Fleisch, 'Crofting in the Shetlands',
from *Rural Resettlement Handbook* (see page 74)

The 'we and they' syndrome experienced by many people who move from city to country in relation to the indigenous population can still be a problem, but many rural resettlers have now become established parts of their rural community, learning from the locals as the locals learn from them. In many parts of rural Britain the local economy would have stagnated into oblivion if enterprising (and usually young) people had not moved into empty houses and started working the land again.

When John and Sally Seymour published *Self-Sufficiency* in 1973 they set in motion a rush of people looking for country plots where they could grow and make everything they needed for a healthy and fulfilling life. Several lifetimes later most back-to-the-landers have dropped 'self-sufficiency' in favour of a more realistic notion of 'collective self-reliance', and John Seymour is in Ireland, writing books on more global themes.

But 'back to the land' remains a fulfilling and rewarding choice for many people, and all over rural Britain families and individuals are growing their own organic vegetables, running hens, geese and ducks, goats and a couple of sheep and maybe a milk cow — and enjoying it immensely.

The Broad Leys Empire

From her own smallholding near Saffron Walden, fifteen or so miles south of Cambridge, Katie Thear has done for smallholders what the Centre for Alternative Technology (see page 297) has done for windmill builders. Broad Leys is the home of the magazine for all small organic farmers, *Home Farm* (formerly *Practical Self Sufficiency*); The Small Farmers Association; Small Farm Services; *The Home Farm Source Book*, a one-stop reference book for all your smallholding needs (see page 74); an efficient and comprehensive Small Scale Supplies Book Service; a thriving publishing company; and open days when you can see the results of the full-time farm work that Katie does in her spare time.

Whether you need to know about dry-stone walling, maintaining an old tractor, changes in planning law, sheep shears or fancy fowl, *Home Farm* is essential reading. The magazine graduated from being a rather scruffy newssheet in 1975 and had a brief flirtation with a goat-keeping sub-title before settling down in its present format under the title *Practical Self-Sufficiency* — the change to *Home Farm* five years ago reflected misgivings about the practicality and morality of hard-line self-sufficiency. Today it carries a very readable range of articles on every aspect of small farming, and the advertisement section is the best resource which could be recommended to any budding back-to-the-lander. Katie's humour as editor shines through the pages, and whether you want to meet that special person ('Countryman, 46, needs lady to share cottage in mid-Wales; smallholding purchase in mind') or buy a goat ('Male, 8+ 133/106 Wytsend Invincible, A.N. 14569P, inoculated and insured'), *Home Farm* is for you.

I don't know when she finds the time, but Katie Thear has also written several useful little handbooks, and Broad Leys Publishing also publishes practical handbooks by other authors. For details of their own books, the book service, membership of the SFA, etc. send a (largish) sae to Broad Leys.

*

'Is there a treatment for strengthening or improving the horn of sheep's hooves? The hooves of our Frieslands split away from the soft part of the sole, and are cracked and brittle. They are on a heavy but well-drained soil at 900 feet, not in an area of excessive rainfall. No footrot is present.' Answer from the next issue: *'The horse feed supplement, Pro-Pell 22, would probably be suitable for the sheep in question. Although this product was developed and formulated for horses it contains a full range of vitamins and minerals at levels satisfactory for sheep and goats. As hoof structure is dependent on the correct balance of vitamin D, calcium, phosphorus, methionine and biotin, I would suggest that your enquirer considers using a Pro-Pell based ration. It would be much more economical than other biotin supplements. As a matter of interest, there are no anti-biotics, hormones or drugs in Pro-Pell 22 and it can be used for most animals. I have even known it to be fed to dogs (both show and pet) and pigeons, with some success.'*

Broad Leys Publishing Co./SFA
Buriton House
Station Road
Newport
Saffron Walden
Essex
CB11 3PL
0749 86688

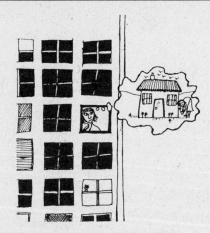

Rural Resettlement Handbook

The Rural Resettlement Handbook started life ten years ago as a 'glue-it-together-yourself book'; the amount of information grew and grew until the third edition, published in 1985 and again due for overhaul, is a thick volume of 300 pages. It calls itself 'The essential handbook for those who want to live in the country'. I don't know about essential — I'd take the Home Farm book first if the cottage roof threatened to collapse, but this is a varied and fascinating insight into the experiences of many people with first-hand knowledge of rural resettlement. It contains a wealth of information (some of it slightly, but not impossibly, dated) about everything you will need to think about if you plan to escape the rat-race and flee to the country to work and live. It deals with planning and building regulations, earning a living, countryside law, living on canal boats, living on islands, sheep, cheese, communes . . . the candid contributions from people who are actually doing it make particularly enjoyable reading.

*

I once discovered a terrace of five cottages in a wood in Derbyshire that had been derelict for several years but were still in a state where they could be refurbished. I spent a whole morning listening to the life story of the mad old man who owned them, and doing my best to admire his unique collection of garden gnomes, but he was an obdurate man and I came away empty-handed. A year or so later I went back and found the builders at work: someone had evidently been more simpatico to garden gnomes than I was.

Rural Resettlement Handbook
The Rural Resettlement Group
Prism, 1985
£4.95

Guides To The Good Life

The best guide to what is currently available in Britain for smallholders in the way of suppliers, services, organizations and courses is *The Home Farm Source Book*. The guide covers livestock, equipment, tools and all manner of supplies, and the 2,000 entries are conveniently grouped by county, with cross-referencing by subject. An updated version is on its way early in 1990, so look out for it. On the wider and more international scale, Intermediate Technology Publications produce a massive tome called *Tools For Agriculture*. More than 3,000

tools from a thousand manufacturers in fifty countries are listed, and the guide is profusely illustrated. Many of the implements described are simple and low-cost, and Tools for Agriculture is a useful ideas book as well as a guide to what is currently available. The book itself, however, is not so cheap.

The Home Farm Source Book
Broad Leys
Publishing Co.
1985
£3.50

Tools For Agriculture
Intermediate
Technology
Publications, 1985
£15.00

Smallholding Suppliers

The advertizing columns of *Home Farm* are crammed with offers of butter churns, sheep drench and kibbling plates, but two suppliers stand out by virtue of their range and service. Since 1975 Smallholding Supplies in Somerset have become one of the major suppliers of small farm and dairy equipment. Their catalogue contains drawings and details of all manner of cream separators, cheese moulds, and a beautifully-made Hungarian cheese press and curd mill. There are wire strainers, a mincer handy for those of us who like home made sausages', and an ingenious 'pig bell bristle scraper'. You can call in and buy what you need, but most of their trade is mail order.

The Smallholding and Farm Supply Company's speciality is chickens and other poultry, especially incubation equipment, while Gardencraft in North Wales can supply the poultry shed — to almost any specification. Two other good and reliable mail order companies for smallholding supplies are Meadows, who specialize in goatkeeping and dairying equipment, and Lincolnshire Smallholders Supplies, who produce a comprehensive and helpful 36-page catalogue (all these small companies appreciate an A5 sae with enquiries).

Smallholding Supplies
Pikes Farmhouse
East Pennard
Shepton Mallet
Somerset
BA4 6RR
074 986 688

Smallholding and Farm Supply Co.
Toledo Works
81 Hollis Croft
Sheffield
S1 4BG
0742 700651

Gardencraft
Tremadog
Porthmadog
Gwynedd
LL49 9RD
0766 513036

SIRE SINE LEATHER RAM HARNESS
C 181 For mating identification of ewes
C 183 Ram crayon. mild, medium grade, pack of three (red, blue and green)

Meadows' Supplies
12 Peterborough Road
Castor
Peterborough
PE5 7AX
0733 380288

Lincolnshire Smallholders Supplies Ltd
Thorpe Fendykes
Wainfleet
Lincolnshire
PE24 4QH
075 486 255

Gardening

Organic Gardening

All gardens have something to yield in the way of wisdom, whether it be a National Trust showpiece or the garden next door. Your garden does not exist in isolation, and you can constantly explore the possibilities, which are endless. Here we reach the fundamental difference between gardening and other forms of creative work, for the material of gardening is alive, constantly changing from season to season and year to year. A garden is never finished, because garden time has no end. The gardener retains the vision, chooses plants, imposes changes on the land, but the plants have a life of their own. Without the growth and cyclical changes of the living plant and soil the garden could not begin to exist.

> Margaret Elphinstone and Julia Langley,
> *The Green Gardener's Handbook* (see next page)

Organic gardening is much more than just a way of growing plants without chemical sprays and artificial fertilizers. It recognizes that the complex workings of nature have been successful in sustaining life over hundreds of millions of years, so the basic organic cultivation principles closely follow those found in the natural world. Don't be misled into thinking that these principles will have a detrimental effect on yield or quality. In fact, you are much more likely to increase both and, in doing so, you will be providing an alternative habitat for wildlife, whilst being certain that the fruit and vegetables produced in your garden are safe, flavoursome and chemical-free.

> Geoff Hamilton, *Successful Organic Gardening*
> (see page 77)

There are as many ways of gardening as there are gardens, but whether your garden is a busy lizzie and a row of herbs on the kitchen windowsill or a walled Victorian garden with a range of ornate greenhouses, gardens are a direct link with the natural world. In many cultures in the world everyone is a gardener, and life without a productive piece of land would be unimaginable. We have come a long way from that sort of connection with the land, 39% of the people in a 1986 survey said they sometimes spent time gardening (14% of teenagers; 49% of the 35+!).

Not many people now, though, grow an appreciable amount of their own food, and when we do grow it ourselves it is easy to be swayed into believing that we can't manage without the 'Easy-Spray Quick-Death', the 'Zap-Em-All Bug Killer' and the 'Nu-Lawn Weed Eradicator'. Gardeners have believed Hessayon and the chemical wizards, and your local garden centre should be very happy to show you which chemicals you need to keep your garden trim and neat. But the chemicals which have been developed to keep butterflies away from large fields of cabbages are not what you need to keep the same butterflies from eating your half dozen plants — all you need is your fingers and a jar of paraffin. Don't be fooled into believing that you can't garden without a shed full of chemical time-bombs.

When you grow your own fruit and vegetables organically you don't have to worry about the freshness of your food or the possible effects of fertilizers, pesticides or irradiation on your health.

And few people would deny the pleasure that flowers, shrubs and trees have on our environment and on our senses, adding colour and fragrance, shelter and variety. In general these need even less intervention than the vegetables and fruit, and although they still need some attention, 'wild' gardens are becoming very popular.

Even people who 'don't have time for gardening' can be surprised by the way that a pot plant or a herb-planting kit from Boots awakens a fascination they didn't know could be aroused. Perhaps this is because gardening invokes distant memories of when we were all gardeners, living much closer to nature than most of us now allow ourselves (or are allowed) to be.

Gardening is possibly the best way of holding on to, developing and celebrating a personal link with the natural world, giving you the satisfaction of knowing that you and nature have done something together for a change. Gardening is a vital part of the green revolution.

Holistic Gardening

Holistic means being part of the whole, and acting within the whole system. To be a gardener is to interact with the land, and thus to be involved with the planet in one of the most fundamental ways possible.

This is no ordinary gardening book, even though it contains in a very clear and concise format all the information you will need when you start your organic garden. The sections on vegetables, fruit, flowers, shrubs and trees are all there, together with ways of identifying and relating to all the bugs, insects and unwanted plants you will meet. You will learn how to use your tools properly, how to plan a rotation, how to sow and water and plant out.

At the same time, the authors have succeeded in that most difficult of tasks, setting the practical advice within the wider context — historical, ethical and spiritual — of gardening. There are fascinating sections about where our garden plants come from, and about the history of gardens ('Perhaps you keep your vegetables tucked away at the very bottom of the garden . . . behind a paling fence adorned with a clematis and a climbing rose because an image lurked at the back of your mind of the Victorian villa . . .'). The seed stock scandal is exposed — did you know that you can be fined £400 for growing traditional open-pollinated varieties of vegetables near a field of commercial F1 hybrids? — and the pitfalls of Latin nomenclature clarified.

The Green Gardener's Handbook is full of useful titbits of advice ('Moles can be diverted by placing slates across their tunnels'; 'Don't spend large amounts of money on machinery and then be mean towards somebody who is using their body on your behalf'). The lists of vegetables, fruit, flowers and trees provide all the information you need for looking after the basic varieties, and are laid out in a standard format, which makes the book invaluable for day-to-day use. The authors live in Scotland, so they don't always assume that south coast conditions are the norm. A comprehensive index and bibliography conclude the best all-round book currently available.

Look out too for Margaret Elphinstone's shorter (and cheaper) introduction to organic gardening, an excellent primer for any budding green gardener, to be published by Green Print in the spring of 1990.

The Green Gardener's Handbook
Margaret Elphinstone and Julia Langley
Thorsons, 1990
£6.99

Organic Gardening
Margaret Elphinstone
Green Print, 1990
£4.99

Planning the Organic Garden

This series of books takes the principles of holistic gardening a step further, and looks at the practicalities of using the space in your organic garden to best advantage. Each volume looks at a different aspect of organic gardening — vegetables, flowers, herbs — and tells you how to plan the space available, prepare the site, which varieties to grow, and effective ways of keeping unwanted pests at bay. The 'vegetable' volume is by the founder of the Rural Resettlement Group (see page 74); the other two by the head gardener at the National Centre for Organic Gardening run by the Henry Doubleday Research Association (see page 78). There are colour photographs in each of the books, and it is pleasing to see that the compost bin in the 'vegetable' volume ('an invaluable part of any organic vegetable garden'), with its corrugated iron and bits falling out at the front, is a 'real' one and not manicured like the diagrams we strive in vain to emulate — compare the one on page 25 of Geoff Hamilton's book (see opposite)!

*

Few people take a lot of trouble over the planning of their kitchen garden and very few books give planning more than the most cursory treatment. This is a pity, because although a hit and miss approach is good enough for someone who is content to use the odd corner to grow lettuces or strawberries in, it can be very wasteful for those who want to make the most of the space they have available. Eventually, however, people do realize that it is worth making quite an effort to increase the crops they are able to obtain from their plot and from the work they put in.

Planning the Organic Vegetable Garden
Dick Kitto
Thorsons, 1986
£5.99

Planning the Organic Herb Garden
Sue Stickland
Thorsons, 1986
£5.99

Planning the Organic Flower Garden
Sue Stickland
Thorsons, 1986
£5.99

These are not, of course, the only paperback organic gardening guides you can read. Many people still swear by Lawrence Hills, the founder of the HDRA (his *Month-by-Month Organic Gardening* has recently been reissued by Thorsons at £5.99); others by Jim Hay. Send an sae to the Henry Doubleday Research Association (page 78) and ask for their annotated booklist, then make your choice.

Organic Gardening magazine is a welcome newcomer to the newsstand, very practical and hands-on unlike some of the glossier gardening magazines. This small-format monthly publication is really for the experienced gardener rather than the beginner, though the variety of articles and advertisers makes it quite compulsive reading, even for novices.

Organic Gardening
PO Box 4
Wiveliscombe
Taunton
Somerset
TA4 2QY
0984 23998

For Coffee Table Organic Gardeners

Twice the price and several times glossier than the books mentioned on the previous page, this beautiful volume by the country's best-known television personality cum organic gardener is a visual treat. It doesn't actually tell you much that *The Green Gardener's Handbook* doesn't, but the colour photographs throughout are extremely helpful if you don't know what particular species of tree, vegetable and flower looks like. Even the lowly carrot and potato are here in full colour! Despite what I said on the last page, the instructions for building a compost bin are good (though shouldn't there be a lid to keep the rain out?). 'The Gardening Year' at the end is useful (you could photocopy this and put it up in the shed), and the 'useful address' list is truly useful, not just a last-minute afterthought.

*

I have been a professional gardener for thirty years and I have to admit that, up to ten years ago, I too was sceptical about organic gardening. Of course, it's hard to argue with the developments resulting from modern research: agricultural and horticultural science has increased yields dramatically, which has kept food price stable for years and increased the general well-being of the population of the Western world a thousand-fold. Indeed it would be foolish to deny that science has made, and is still making, a tremendous contribution to the art of growing both productive and ornamental plants. However perfect nature's methods may be, it was never intended that the land should be as productive as we now demand. While nature may have demanded one scraggy little wild carrot every metre, we demand a big fat juicy carrot every few centimetres. So we have needed all our ingenuity to improve on nature's methods. . . As a result of research into plants and the way in which they grow, cultivation techniques have been developed to such an extent that the Western world's larder is full to overflowing.

Successful Organic Gardening
Geoff Hamilton
Dorling Kindersley, 1987
£14.95

Wildlife Gardening

Friends of the Earth in Sheffield have transformed a corner of Sheffield Botanic Gardens into a garden specially designed to attract wildlife. The garden contains a small 'woodland' of shrubs and trees, since native tree species provide food for large numbers of associated insect species (284 different insect species feed on oak, for instance), a herb garden to attract butterflies and bees, an area of wildflower meadow, a water trough and a bird table — all within an area not much bigger than an average back yard.

Mark and Matthew Jones in Halesworth, Suffolk, will come and help you transform part of your garden into a wildlife sanctuary. They set up Wildlife Ponds and Gardens four years ago, and the small company is now booked up for several months ahead. They create ponds which look as though they have been there for centuries, the biggest of which to date has been about 90 feet by 60 feet; the cost varies according to what is needed, but you could have your garden transformed into a paradise for frogs, newts, dragonflies and birds for somewhere between a couple of hundred and a couple of thousand pounds.

The Urban Wildlife Group, a charity which exists to promote urban wildlife sanctuaries by working with landowners and local authorities (see page 64 for a fuller description), will gladly send you information about their work.

Sheffield Friends of the Earth
CVS House
69 Division Street
Sheffield 1
0742 721896

Urban Wildlife Group
Unit 213
Jubilee Trade Centre
130 Pershore Street
Birmingham
B5 6ND
021 666 7474

Wildlife Ponds and Gardens
2 White House Farm
Cottage
Spexhall
Halesworth
Suffolk
IP19 0RL
098 67 2009

Wildflower Gardening

Like Geoff Hamilton's organic gardening book, the best book on wildflower gardening is rather expensive but very beautiful. John Stevens, the author of *Wild Flower Gardening*, is one of the founders of Suffolk Herbs (see page 82), and together with his wife Caroline they are *the* experts when it comes to gardening using native species, since they have learned everything from first-hand experience. The first part of the book is a guide to species, by habitat and by season, and *Wild Flower Gardening* will almost double as a wild flower handbook, the photographs are so clear. The second part of the book is concerned with techniques — collecting seed, sowing, mixtures, planning and maintenance; it concludes with an alphabetical list of species with its site and soil requirements and cultivation details. There is a comprehensive list of suppliers and a very good index. Perhaps it's not bad value at £14.95, but perhaps there will be a paperback one day that you won't mind putting on the shelf in the potting shed.

The National Trust Book of Wild Flower Gardening
John Stevens
Dorling Kindersley, 1987
£14.95

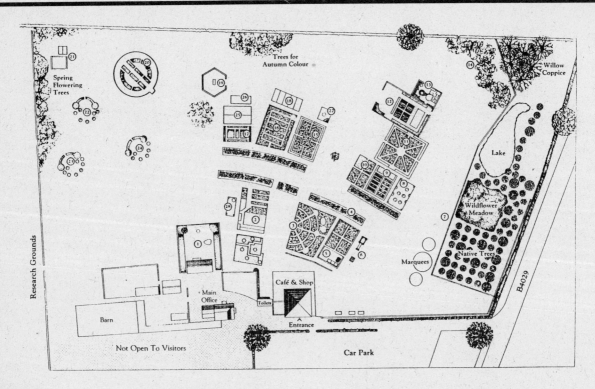

Labels on the map: Trees for Autumn Colour; Spring Flowering Trees; Willow Coppice; Lake; Research Grounds; Wildflower Meadow; Native Trees; Marquees; B4029; Café & Shop; Main Office; Toilets; Barn; Entrance; Not Open To Visitors; Car Park

The HDRA

The Henry Doubleday Research Association is Britain's largest organization concerned with organic gardening, its purpose being to investigate ways of growing vegetables and fruit without artificial pesticides and fertilizers. The emphasis is on practical improvements which are appropriate to gardeners and other small-scale growers.

Four years ago the HDRA moved from Braintree in Essex to its new site at Ryton near Coventry, which it proudly named The National Centre for Organic Gardening. The title is well deserved, for without the HDRA, organic gardening in Britain would be a pale shadow of what it has now become. Ryton Gardens have become the place of pilgrimage for organic gardeners from all over the country, and the HDRA have been quick to exploit any and all openings for organic cultivation, from books and television programmes to grant and research opportunities — and long may it flourish.

We began Ryton Gardens . . . from a run down smallholding that had been used to graze horses. All but a handful of the mature trees once surrounding the site had died a few years earlier from Dutch Elm Disease. No real hedgerows existed, consequently the site was very exposed, and indeed still is, to strong winds. Though no agrochemicals had been used by the previous owners they had bagged up and sold all the horse manure. With no fertilizer of any kind the grass was extremely poor — so much so that there was hardly a worm in the place. Many of the old field drains had become choked and water lay on the surface in many places. Not a very auspicious start, you might think, for a showpiece of organic gardening.

Though it will be a while before the trees have grown enough to make an appreciable difference to the backdrop of the 22-acre site, the Ryton gardens already look much older than their four years. A visit to the site starts with the composting display, stressing the importance of feeding the soil rather than the plants. There is an organic allotment; a large 'conservation area' with an area of woodland planted in the winter of 1985-86, a lake, a wildflower meadow, and an area of willow saplings which are coppiced every four or five years. In the centre of the Ryton plot is an area where unusual vegetables are grown — you can see cardoons (a sort of globe artichoke, except you eat the leaf stems as you would celery), skirret (a tasty root vegetable that can be used in salads), and Hamburg parsley (you can eat the roots as well as the leaves). The

bee garden illustrates how the well-run organic garden balances every aspect of the natural world, and you can even look inside the hive.

Wildflowers flourish best on soil of low fertility where there is little competition from coarse grasses. Thus the original topsoil was stripped off the meadow area and replaced with subsoil from the lake excavations. The area was sown in early October 1985 with a mixture of annual and perennial wildflowers and fine grasses. Most have now become well established. They bloom in late spring and early summer and at these times you should see cowslips, cornflowers, kidney vetch, field poppies, corn chamomile, corn marigolds, yellow rattle, ox-eye daisies and white campion. We have also planted bulbs of snakes head fritillaries and wild daffodils, and will be adding other meadow plants as they become available.

It is now illegal to sell 'unlisted' varieties of plant seed, so to keep many of the old varieties in existence the HDRA run a 'seed bank', where seeds can be donated by members and given to others, so no actual sale takes place. Certain other seeds — of rare yet unlisted species — can be bought from the HDRA under their Heritage Seed scheme. Membership of the HDRA also gives you a quarterly newsletter, advice when you need it, and participation in a national network of like-minded gardeners.

The café at Ryton is worth mentioning for its own sake — mouth-watering wholefood cookery which earned it a place in Egon Ronay within six months of opening. The shop sells books, crafts, organic produce, herbs and spices, and a whole range of organic gardening products, some of which are difficult to obtain elsewhere.

No wonder Ryton Gardens attract so many visitors. There can be few gardening clubs or Soil Association branches who haven't arranged a visit to the HDRA, and it is certainly not to be missed if you are ever in the vicinity of Coventry. Go and count for yourself how many worms now inhabit the place.

**Henry Doubleday
Research Association**
National Centre for Organic Gardening
Ryton-on-Dunsmore
Coventry
CV8 3LG
0203 303517

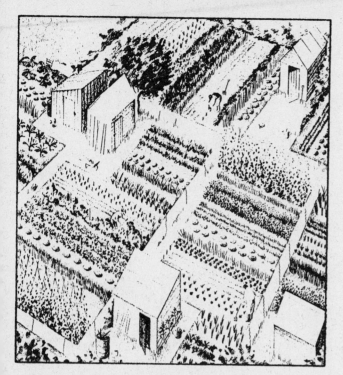

Allotments

Once an integral and everyday part of our diet, locally-grown, fresh, pollution-free fruit and vegetables are now enjoyed only by a minority of people in Britain. Supermarket shrinkwraps from distant countries are the norm, often picked weeks before and sprayed with chemicals to 'extend their shelf life'. One alternative is to grow them yourself, and demand for allotment gardens in many areas from Edinburgh to Bristol now vastly outstrips supply, proof of an upturn in interest for the first time since 1945. Looking after an allotment has its challenges, from stone-throwers to hungry pigeons, yet strolling down to the allotment with a basket and picking just enough runner beans and strawberries for supper is a most fulfilling activity.

Though you may have to wait quite a while for an allotment (depending on where you live), the procedure is not difficult, and once you have been allocated your allotment you will almost certainly find yourself in the company of experienced gardeners who are only too happy to share their knowledge (and sometimes their excess produce too).

Allotment Books

Rob Bullock and Gillie Gould's *The Allotment Book* is a handy paperback which includes everything a first-time allotment gardener needs to know. Common sense and a straightforward and clear approach to organic allotment gardening are its hallmarks, from easily remembered advice like 'the smaller the seed the shallower it should be sown', to a reminder that the presence of 'pests' is usually a timely notice that something is amiss in your land management. A useful chapter on health and safety shows exactly how to lift and dig without hurting your back, and the book includes full instructions about how to grow a wide range of vegetables and fruits. You will probably need to progress to a more comprehensive gardening book before long (see pages 76-77), but this is a good place to begin.

*

Under the 1950 Allotment Act, every local authority has an obligation to provide four acres of allotments for each thousand of its population. In reality this has never been achieved, not even in the 'Dig for Victory' and 'Dig for Plenty' campaigns during and after the Second World War. On the brighter side, however, some local authorities positively encourage the use of allotments by providing special work teams who carry out maintenance work — clearing old allotments, replacing fencing, and improving access paths and other facilities. Bristol City Council pioneered the concept of leisure gardens by opening a chalet site in 1970. Each well-fenced plot is provided with a cedarwood chalet, and the tenants are encouraged to cultivate the plots with lawns, herbaceous plants and shrubs as well as vegetables. The site is provided with a good road, car park and toilets. In 1987, Hounslow Borough Council opened a similar site to provide for council tenants who do not have a garden of their own.

*

Many allotment gardeners have areas to store odd bits of metal and wood, and an unknowing visitor could be forgiven for wondering what use these can have, but the gardener can visualise uses for all manner of materials. I have found many treasures on rubbish skips; pieces of wood to use as stakes, old carpets to cover the compost heap, and window frames for the construction of cold frames.

David Crouch and Colin Ward's allotment book is quite different. A fascinating slice of social history, it traces the cultural and practical significance of the British allotment through the last century and a half. *The Allotment* underlines the importance of access to the land to urban dwellers, especially for the poor; there have, for example, been many times when the allotment shed was the only shelter available to families turned out of tied housing.

The Allotment Book
Rob Bullock and
Gillie Gould
Optima, 1988
£4.95

The Allotment
Its Landscape
and Culture
David Crouch and
Colin Ward
Faber and Faber, 1989
£13.95

The Allotment Society

The National Society of Allotment and Leisure Gardeners can provide help and guidance on all aspects of allotment gardening, including legal advice, model lease and tenancy agreements, and a seed discount scheme. They also have a library, and run an allotment insurance scheme. If you belong to an allotment society membership will only cost you 35p a year; otherwise it's £5.

**The National Society of
Allotment and Leisure Gardeners Ltd**
O'Dell House
Hunters Road
Corby
Northamptonshire
NN17 1JE
0536 66576

Ashram Acres

Blooming in Birmingham's Sparkbrook is this project to reclaim inner city wasteland and use it to grow both European and traditional Asian vegetables. Ashram Acres members pay £2.70 a week each, work on the project, and receive fresh organic produce as their reward. Many neighbours of the project came to Britain from rural areas and have traditional farming skills from Pakistan, India, the West Indies and Ireland among others. Volunteers (welcome every Saturday 10-2) learn organic gardening and multi-cultural experience at the same time, and produce not needed by the project members is sold locally.

Ashram Acres
23-25 Grantham Road
Sparkbrook
Birmingham
B11 1LU
021 773 7061

Compost

If nature is left to itself, fertility increases. Organic remains of plants and animals accumulate and are decomposed on the surface by bacteria and fungi. With the movement of rainwater, the nutrients are taken deep into the soil to become food for micro-organisms, earthworms, and other small animals. Plant roots reach to the lower soil strata and draw the nutrients back up to the surface. If you want to get an idea of the natural fertility of the earth, take a walk to the wild mountainside sometime and look at the giant trees that grow without fertilizer and without cultivation. The fertility of nature, as it is, is beyond reach of the imagination.

Masanobu Fukuoka, *The One-Straw Revolution*, Rodale, 1978

Composting is as old as agriculture. There is some evidence that many of the ancient civilizations, when in their prime, based their cultivation on systems of composting and irrigation.

Eva Balfour, *The Living Soil*, Faber, 1975

On a Radio Four programme in 1985 called *Mr Small Is Beautiful*, Labour MP Tony Benn dismissed the ideas of Fritz Schumacher as 'the philosophy of the compost heap'. What a compliment that was, albeit an unwitting one. The biological processes that take place inside the compost heap — still not fully understood in all their complexity — are a unique way of recycling organic waste to continue the cycle of fruitful growth, a reinterpretation of economics which Schumacher would fully endorse, and which would bring Tony Benn immortal recognition if the same principles were applied to the national economy.

The compost heap turns organic 'rubbish' into a valuable nutrient-rich material which feeds and conditions the soil. Without a healthy soil, plants would not grow, and life on this planet would be unsustainable. Yet we continue to throw away thousands of tons of valuable organic material with the rest of our rubbish, much of it sealed inside plastic bags which explode when the resulting gasses cannot leak out, causing fires and stenches at landfill sites which are no fun at all for local residents.

Vegetable and fruit peelings, outer leaves of cabbages, weeds, and hedge and lawn clippings make up a fifth of all domestic 'rubbish', all of which could be pulverized and matured to make compost, the organic equivalent of the the nitrate and phosphate fertilizers currently being used by farmers which pollute crops, land and water indiscriminately.

Local authorities elsewhere in the world are organizing compost recycling schemes. In Germany and Holland prototype schemes produce compost for local farmers. To encourage local townships to establish composting programmes, the Broome County landfill in upstate New York banned leaves from its premises in 1986 and all organic waste in 1988. There have been small-scale schemes in Britain, but recycling organic waste has never received much official backing.

So what can you do? For a start, segregate. Keep a plastic bucket by the sink for organic waste, and if you have a garden, make compost. It doesn't matter how small your heap is, or even how tidy it is (within reason). If you don't have a garden or an allotment, find someone who does — urban gardeners can rarely get enough household organic waste. Ask your local authority what you can do with your segregated organic waste (and don't be put off when they shrug, or laugh).

There are many ways of making compost, and many different structures in which to make it. . . The best and most fine compost is achieved by providing lots of air for the hard-working bacteria, so if you can put energy into turning a heap two or three times you will get your reward in muscles and good compost. For heat retention and neatness, it is a good idea to make wooden compost bins, and most economic to build two or three next to each other, each forming a cube with a side of about a metre. You can also use special plastic bins or make free-standing heaps, covering them with an old carpet to keep the heat in.

Margaret Elphinstone and Julia Langley,
The Green Gardener's Handbook (see page 76)

The best book you can read on compost and compost making is Dick Kitto's *Composting* (Thorsons, 1984, £3.95). For small amounts of compost you can buy a reycled-plastic-barrel compost maker from Blackwall Products — it works very well, and is ideal for a small urban garden, though at £43.95 is expensive when the alternative is a home-made wooden bin.

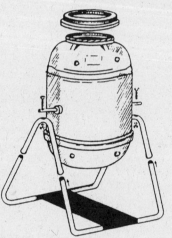

Blackwall Products
Unit 4, Riverside Industrial Estate
150 River Way
London
SE10 0BE
0(8)1-305 1431

And The Next Step

A feature of life in the poorer areas of many South-East Asian towns and cities is the nightsoil cart which circulates every morning, returning human excrement to the soil of the surrounding fields. Without this vital link in the nutrient chain, agriculture in many parts of that area would be unsustainable. What it is that makes us believe that our own excrement is beyond, below and outside the cycles of nature is unfathomable, but the law of ecology that says 'everything must go somewhere' applies with a vengeance where sewage is concerned. Stand at the end of the jetty in seaside towns as far apart as Lerwick and Porthleven, and see the untreated sewage being flushed into the sea (you get a good idea of what colour toilet paper is in vogue, too). Britain is now the only country discharging untreated sewage sludge into the North Sea, as the residents of Lowestoft will be only too glad to tell you.

What can you do about it? You could try a composting toilet (see page 100) but, because sewage disposal is a local authority responsibility in Britain, your best bet is to read up on the subject (you could start with *Green Britain or Industrial Wasteland?* (page 58), and *The Good Beach Guide* (page 291)) and then tackle your local district council. The Greenpeace book *Coastline* (page 70) puts sewage dumping within the wider context of dumping our nasties at sea in the vain hope that they'll go away for ever.

Gardening Tools

'Tools' in its widest sense means 'the best and most appropriate means to achieve life-enhancing ends'. We have become so used to thinking in terms of crafted bits of metal and wood, not to mention petrol and electricity driven machinery, that we often forget that nature has been gardening for a lot longer than human beings.

Here is Masanobu Fukuoka reminding us of this fact in his book *The One-Straw Revolution*:

For thirty years I lived only in my farming and had little contact with people outside my own community. During those years I was heading in a straight line toward a 'do-nothing' agricultural method. The usual way to go about developing a method is to ask 'How about trying this?' or 'How about trying that?' bringing in a variety of techniques one upon the other. This is modern agriculture and it only results in making the farmer busier. My way was opposite. I was aiming at a pleasant, natural way of farming which results in making the work easier instead of harder. 'How about not doing this? How about not doing that? — that was my way of thinking. I ultimately reached the conclusion that there was no need to plough, no need to apply fertilizer, no need to make compost, no need to use insecticide. When you get right down to it, there are few agricultural practices that are really necessary. The reason that man's improved techniques seem to be necessary is that the natural balance has been so badly upset beforehand by those same techniques that the land has become dependent on them.

At the Butser Hill experiment near Petersfield in Hampshire, where neolithic agricultural techniques have been used to grow neolithic crops on land untouched by modern agricultural practices, researchers have been amazed to discover that yields of grain are often as high as those achieved with modern chemical farming. Adventurous farmers are discovering that a massive input of worms can drain and fertilize marginal land far more efficiently than tractors and chemical fertilizers, and many gardeners are now beginning to find that no-dig techniques can produce rich harvests.

It has been shown repeatedly that the successful growing of plants requires the nurturing of the soil they grow in. Sometimes this involves digging nutrients into poor soil, but you can as often improve things by not disturbing the soil profile. Kenneth O'Brien's otherwise rather dull book, *Veganic Gardening* (Thorsons, 1986, £6.99), does explain both theory and practice of no-dig gardening rather well, with good chapters on the importance of good soil structure and the making of raised beds.

Hand Tools

It is generally acknowledged the world over that some of the best handtools in the world are made in Britain, and serious gardeners from New Zealand to California specify British if they want the real thing. The very best (and with handtools the best will always be worth the money) are Bulldog Tools, made in Wigan and claimed to be 'the strongest tools on Earth'. Close on Bulldog's heels are Spear and Jackson, founded in Sheffield in 1889 and still going strong as part of the Neill Tools Group. Both will send a detailed full-colour catalogue on request.

Bulldog Tools Ltd
Clarington Forge
Wigan
WN1 3DD
0942 44281

Neill Tools Ltd
Handsworth Road
Sheffield
S13 9BR
0742 449911

Worms

Charles Darwin had a thing about worms. His 1881 book *The Formation of Vegetable Mould through the Action of Worms with Observations on their Habits* was more revolutionary than its title might suggest. In it Darwin tells us that there are about 54,000 living worms in an acre of land, between them shifting sixteen tons of soil every year. They do all this without you plunging a single spade into the topsoil, or even dirtying your wellies. If conditions are right, worms provide a round the clock soil cleaning service without any supervision. If worms decided on an all-out strike we would quickly be forced to the negotiating table at any price they cared to name.

Before you rush out to spend money on tools, therefore, first consider whether your money wouldn't be better spent on worms. There are now several British firms promoting the use of worms for gardening and horticulture — send for the catalogues and settle down for a fascinating read.

Worm Firms

It is difficult to judge whether Catherine Morris and Margaret Burton Lingen's Turning Worms or Charlie Denham's Wonder Worms produce the best literature. Turning Worms' booklet and pricelist are excellent, with some memorable cartoons, but maybe Wonder Worms are as good with their 'turning muck into brass' slogan and the cartoon of the worm-mine. You'll have to get both and choose for yourself.

Turning Worms produce the only worm-worked compost to receive Soil Association approval. Wonder Worms concentrate on worm cultures, and coming as they do from a thousand feet up in the Pennines they are very hardy. Charlie Denham is convinced that worm-worked compost can make you lots of money as well as providing lots of good compost for your own land, and encourages you to visit his farm first to see how it all works. His worm kits, which are on a much larger scale than Turning Worms', start at just over £100, but you can buy his *Earthworm Manual* for £11.50, which gives you good idea of what is possible.

Turning Worms
Perthi Yard
Llanrhystud
Dyfed
SY23 5EH
09746 240

Wonder Worms UK
Pine Trees Farm
Hubberton
Sowerby Bridge
West Yorkshire
HX6 1NT
0422 831112/834696

Seeds

Plant seeds are in many ways like miniature filing cabinets in which the ecological experiences of the past are stored, added to as new information is received and used as a resource on a daily basis. Each type of seed contains irreplaceable information, and even though we as humans may find it unnecessary to open a particular drawer for a very long time, it is vitally important that we keep the cabinet intact, for when conditions and circumstances change who is to tell what information may be invaluable?

Yet all the time human beings are destroying whole sections of that genetic filing cabinet, which puts at risk both our own future as a species and the future of the global ecosystem. At the level of human subsistence it is vital to have replacement strains of seed when virus attacks a uniform crop of hybrid corn, as it did in the USA in 1970, or when potato blight strikes. A large part of the seed crisis is that we are depending more and more on an ever- smaller range of food crops. In pre-historic times over 1,500 species of wild plant were used as food. In classical times over 500 types of vegetable were grown. Today 95% of human food comes from just thirty species.

And these thirty species have been bred and bred until they will produce large crops, but often only with high inputs of fertilizer and pesticides. Moreover, these are usually hybrid seeds which, although they produce large and uniform crops, will only do it once before they revert to type, and we have to buy another batch of hybrid seed.

Legislation now enables the 'ownership' of seed in the form of patents; moreover, because traditional species may 'contaminate' these hybrid wonder crops it is now also illegal to buy and sell 'unlisted' varieties. What economic and moral nonsense this is. If it were not for the work of organizations like the HDRA (see page 70) we could lose these species altogether, and once a species is lost it is lost for ever. As it is we have lost over 800 vegetable varieties in the last twenty years.

The Socialist Countryside Group has published *The Seed Scandal* (75p from HDRA Sales), which tells how seed legislation plays straight into the hands of giant multinationals. Bees, Bush Johnson, Rothwell, and Webbs are not the proud independents your parents (if they were gardeners) swore by. They are all owned by the largest seed company in the world — Royal Dutch Shell. In one week of 1981 alone, 83 small seed firms were bought up by Ranks Hovis McDougal.

Henry Doubleday is your first point of call if you are looking for undressed seeds, especially of the rarer varieties. You can buy many varieties from their Heritage Seed range — ask for a catalogue — and by joining the Association you have access to the HDRA Seed Library too.

As well as Henry Doubleday, there are a few other independent organic seed companies:

Chase Organics

Chase have for many years been known as a reliable supplier of chemical-free seeds, and Mike Hedges is always happy to answer his customer's enquiries. The annual Chase catalogue, available from October onwards, lists a very wide range of vegetable and flower seeds, and Chase also sell organic extracts, feeds, stimulants and supplements.

Chase Organics (GB) Ltd
Coombelands House
Addlestone
Surrey
KT15 1HY
0932 858511

Suffolk Herbs

Caroline and John Stevens moved from London to deepest Suffolk in 1971 with the express purpose of growing herbs and wildflowers organically, to see if there was a demand for them. Their catalogue now goes all over the world, with Japan being their main export market, so they have certainly succeeded in demonstrating the demand. The catalogue (free for an A5 sae (150g postage)) is a mine of information for gardeners and botanists alike, listing herbs, herb seeds, conservation mixtures (for sowing large areas), vegetables (including many unusual species), green manure mixes, wildflower seeds and masses more. Suffolk Herbs are now being asked by local authorities to seed road verges with wildflower seed, and in 1985 seeded ten acres of the Great Cornard Country Park near Sudbury — go and see it for yourself next summer. They also produce a range of herb and wildflower seeds which you will find in places like Culpepers and National Trust shops.

Suffolk Herbs
Sawyers Farm
Little Cornyards
Sudbury
Suffolk CO10 0NY
0787 227247

Other Wildflower Seed Suppliers

Emorsgate Seeds in Norfolk supply a wide variety of wildflower seeds for different types of soils, and do quantities up to a kilo — you can buy 4,000,000 seeds of vervain for £54! Their catalogue is packed with good advice on sowing and maintenance, and their service is first-rate. Johnson's Seeds also sell a limited range of wildflower species in quantities up to a kilo. Martin Gould will send you a catalogue from his recently-established nursery in south-west Scotland on receipt of an sae — he does a wide range of wildflower seeds and also sells plants.

Emorsgate Seeds
Terrington Court
Terrington St Clement
Kings Lynn
Norfolk
PE34 4NT
0553 829028

Martin Gould
Stockerton Nursery
Kirkcudbright
DG6 4XS
0387 31266

Johnson's Seeds
London Road
Boston
Lincolnshire
PE21 8AD
0205 65051

Nurseries

To a very large extent garden centres have become to nurseries what industrial estates are to cottage industries and, like real cottage industries, real nurseries can be hard to find. By 'real' I mean places where plants are nurtured and cared for, and where you can get sound advice and wisdom from people who obviously know about their plants. Ideally the plants would be grown organically in the containers that you buy them in, and the containers would be big enough to prevent the plants from becoming rootbound. Such a nursery might well sell a range of good tools, organic sprays and biological controls, but it certainly wouldn't be stacked to the ceiling with chemicals and machinery.

And where will you find such nurseries? Ryton Gardens (page 78) is a good place to start if you live within a reasonable distance of Coventry; the HDRA or Soil Association (page 67) will probably be able to tell you what is available locally. Suffolk Herbs, Emorsgate Seeds and Stockerton Cottage Nursery (page 82) also sell plants.

The selection of nurseries that follows is only a small one, but each of them is run on the principles outlined above, and most of them do mail order.

Herbs in The North

There is a long tradition of growing herbs in Scotland, partly because more showy and less hardy plants can be difficult to grow. There are two advantages of buying your herb plants from the north of Britain — they will tend to be less polluted and, most importantly, they will be very hardy and will not wilt at the first mention of frost on the weather forecast.

High in the Grampians is the Old Semeil Herb Garden, established by Gillian and Philip Cook in 1981. They grow more than a hundred varieties of herb, and their clearly labelled display garden is a treat if you are ever in their part of the world — they actually encourage you to touch, smell and taste before you buy. They will also design you a herb garden and supply the plants to fill it. A catalogue costs 70p plus an A5 sae.

Duncan Ross's Poyntzfield Nursery on the Black Isle north of Inverness has been supplying herb plants and seeds since 1977. You can buy more than 300 varieties from Poyntzfield, and they have sent plants as far afield as Zimbabwe and New Zealand. The catalogue — a good read in itself — will be sent on receipt of three first class stamps. Both Poyntzfield and Old Semeil grow entirely organically.

The Local Herb Company in south-west Scotland stocks a wide range of organically-grown culinary, medicinal and aromatic herb plants — a full list is available on request. If you are ever in that part of Scotland they welcome visitors in the afternoon from Thursday to Sunday between April and September.

Old Semeil Herb Garden
Strathdon
Aberdeenshire
AB3 8XJ
097 56 51343

Poyntzfield Herb Nursery
Black Isle
by Dingwall
Ross-shire
IV7 8LX

The Local Herb Company
Stonehouse Cottage
and Culnoag Cottage
by Sorbie
Wigtownshire
DG8 8AN
098 885 249/303

Plants in The Midlands

Ruth Thompson started Oak Cottage twenty years ago at Nesscliffe in Shropshire. Recently taken over by Edward and Jane Bygott, it concentrates on growing culinary herbs and old fashioned garden plants in compost of their own making and without chemical sprays. Over 300 varieties are grown, and the catalogue (30p plus an A5 sae) is also a well laid out cultivation guide. Visitors are welcome if they ring first.

Fold Garden near Stoke on Trent is an organic herb and plant garden selling over 250 varieties of herbs and wildflowers. Patricia Machin also makes traditional jams and mustards. Visits are by appointment only, though she does encourage parties to visit, and gives them a talk, a catalogue and a selection of herb teas at £1.50 a head. The catalogue is 30p including postage.

Oak Cottage
Herb Farm
Nesscliffe
nr Shrewsbury
SY4 1DB
0743 81262

Fold Garden
26 Fold Lane
Biddulph
Staffordshire
ST8 7SG
0782 513028

Trees and More in Lincs and Yorks

Majorie Stein at Eden Nurseries in Lincolnshire specializes in traditional fruit tree varieties grown organically. For 'Pitmaston Pineapple' apple trees and 'Packham's Triumph' pears this is the place to go. Mail order; catalogue for an sae.

Lindy Williams and Danny Powell moved from London to Yorkshire three years ago to establish Limit's Field at Long Preston in North Yorkshire. Here they specialize in organically grown native trees and hedging (including Scots Pine, Britain's only native conifer — forget the ubiquitous *Leylandii*), and have established an ecological garden which you are welcome to visit by appointment. Three first class stamps for a catalogue.

Eden Nurseries
Rectory Lane
Old Bolingbroke
Spilsby
Lincolnshire
079 03 582

Limit's Field
The Prospect
Long Preston
nr Skipton
North Yorkshire
BD23 4QH
072 94 206

And Herbs Again in The South

Linda Laxton runs a half-acre garden of herbs and wildflowers in east Norfolk, open on weekend and bank holiday afternoons from Easter till October. Her stock includes a large number of scarce native plants which she grows from seed, and she takes a great deal of trouble to ensure that her customers receive both seed and plants in first-class condition. A catalogue is available if you send an A5 sae.

Since 1976 Hollington Nurseries have been growing and selling herb plants, and the Hollington Herb Garden has become an established part of the Chelsea Flower Show. Hollington (just south of Newbury on the Andover road) is well worth a visit — open most days at least 10-5 — for inspiration and ideas, and the catalogue (£1.50 including p&p) is an attractive reference book too, but Hollington is not entirely organic and is in danger of turning into a rather up-market garden centre.

Linda Laxton
23 Yarmouth Road
Ormesby St Margaret
Great Yarmouth
Norfolk
NR29 3QE

Hollington Nurseries Ltd
Woolton Hill
Newbury
Berkshire
RG15 9XT
0635 253908

Gardening Supplies

Ideally you would be able to buy a complete range of safe organic products — composts, manure, fertilizers, sprays and biological pesticides — at your local nursery or garden centre. Unless you are very lucky, however, this will prove difficult, so here is a selection of suppliers who will be able to sell you organic supplies backed up with sound advice.

HDRA Sales

If you can't easily get to Ryton Gardens (page 78), and they are well worth quite a journey, send to the Henry Doubleday Research Association for their Complete Organic Gardening Catalogue, which also includes a list of their 'Heritage Seeds'. The catalogue is a mine of information, covering composts and organic fertilizers, safe pesticides, HDRA developed biological controls, books about gardening and even videotapes.

HDRA Sales Ltd
National Centre for Organic Gardening
Ryton-on-Dunsmore
Coventry
CV8 3LG
0203 303517

Cowpact

'The compact cow pat' is how they describe it, and it's the raw material of a range of organic products including the original Cowpact, Cowpeet, Cowpost, and now Pure Goodness for houseplants. Cowpact is produced from cow slurry from farms holding the Soil Association symbol, which is passed through a separator to extract most of the moisture, then composted at a temperature high enough to kill pests and weed seeds. The end result has a slightly woody aroma, and you would never guess its origins. Cowpeet is the end result mixed with sphagnum, which with added perlite becomes Cowpost, an excellent growing medium, recently endorsed by the British Fuchsia Society as ideal for these sometimes fickle plants.

Cowpact Products
PO Box 595
Adstock
Buckinghamshire
MK18 2RE
029 671 3838

Seagold

A local Lancashire firm called Vitaseamin used to make this seaweed soil conditioner; production has now been taken over by the big Silvaperl company who do a wide range of products, many of which are not organic at all. But they do also produce a range of natural rock growing media including perlite and vermiculite, and each product has a useful fact-sheet to go with it. If you write to them for details, specifying that you are only interested in natural products, maybe they'll get the message in the end.

Silvaperl Products Ltd
PO Box 8
Harrogate
North Yorkshire
HG2 8JW
0423 870370

All Gain

All Gain Organics are suppliers of safe pesticides and biological controls and fertilizers. You'll find old favourites like Bordeaux mixture alongside newly developed soap concentrates for the control of aphids and other bugs — all safe to both humans and wildlife. They also offer advice over the phone on any organic matter.

All Gain Organics
8 Netherlands Road
New Barnet
Hertfordshire
EN5 1BN
0(8)1-449 1605

Stimgro

Stimgro produces a whole range of organic products, notably the first organic 'grow-bag', an organic planting mixture, a rose feed, and a mosskiller and lawn tonic which blackens moss and allows it to be raked out. An sae will bring you the name of your local stockist, or you can order directly from them.

Stimgro Ltd
Unit 2b
Longfield Road
Tunbridge Wells
Kent
TN2 3EY
0892 36731

Cumulus and Glenside

Cumulus in Gloucestershire and Glenside near Stirling market similar wide ranges of organic supplies — with either you should find it easy to fulfil all your needs in a single order. Cumulus also produces a useful series of booklets on organic gardening, and have put together an organic starter kit for £27, which would make a good present for a gardening friend you are trying to convert to organic. Glenside market what they call the 'real hoe', the head of which swivels to cut the weeds with both forward and back stroke — leaflet on request.

Cumulus Organics and Conservation Ltd
Timber Yard
Two Mile Lane
Highnam
Gloucestershire
GL2 8DW
0452 305814

Glenside Organics Ltd
Glenside Farm
Plean
Stirlingshire
FK7 8BA
0786 816655

HOME

*'Housing choice and responsibility for one's home should be decisions made not by
the bureaucrats but by the occupants. The future should be in their own hands.'*
Alice Coleman, *Utopia on Trial*

Almost everything begins at home — the conception (and increasingly the birth) of
new life, childhood, patterns of behaviour, attitudes, the working day. And home is the
haven where you retreat when it all gets too much. In many ways, home is what you
make it, though you always have to work within the constraints of your resources and
your circumstances. Yet much of what constitutes 'home' needs few resources beyond
your innate capacity for feeling that you have a right to enjoy being where you are. As
any zen priest will tell you, real home is what you carry round in your heart.

Oikology

When in the 1850s the German zoologist Ernst Haeckel was wondering what to call the
new science of the study of living things within their environmental context, he chose
the word *ökologie*, which was rapidly taken into English as 'ecology'. The term derives
from the Greek words *oikos* and *logos*, meaning 'the study of homes'. We may call the
homes of plants and animals 'habitats', but our own suburban semi, country cottage or
city flat is just as much our habitat as the wood is the fox's home or the mountaintop
the eagle's.

And our homes in turn provide habitats for many more living things than just the
human beings. An 'empty' house isn't empty at all. We may prefer not to think about
them all, but we live alongside bookworms, silverfish, earwigs, spiders, bluebottles,
little brown mice, fungi and moulds of astonishing variety, and millions of minute lice
and fleas.

Separate though 'our home' may appear to be from everybody else's, it is only the
human beings (and even then not always) who recognize the territories laid out by
estate developers. It makes it easy to think that the world you inhabit isn't necessarily
the same as the people's next door, but in reality we all inhabit the same home, and
there is only one of it.

Who Decides?

If you can afford it, you have a lot of say in where you decide to live and what sort of house you live in. If you own your own house or rent on a long-term lease you have almost complete freedom to do what you like with the inside of it, though the housing department will have something to say if you try to do anything dangerous or unhygienic.

With the outside and the garden you can do less outrageous things before the planning department starts making enquiries (and the neighbours concerned noises), but you can still make a wide variety of choices. 37% of households in Britain rent their accommodation, and they are far more restricted in what they can do, both inside and outside their homes. More than two thirds of these families rent from local authorities, and while some councils stand out like beacons of good management too many still maintain distant and insensitive housing bureaucracies, do not fulfil their maintenance obligations, and treat prospective tenants like scroungers. There is still a tendency to think of homeowners as automatically upright, decent and honest, while dwellers in council houses are lesser mortals, out to bankrupt the country by insisting on state handouts. And that's not to mention the 100,000 homeless in Britain today.

Everybody needs a home, but post-war housing policy decisions have combined to make it virtually impossible to move towards a more equitable distribution of the houses that are available. There is nothing more soul-destroying than having no control over the place you live in. Lack of individual control over the immediate environment has dominated the housing scene in Britain for decades, stunting imagination, breeding conformity, and persuading people that the design and building of structures they might enjoy inhabiting is a subject they could never hope to understand, let alone take part in.

But things are changing. Community design-and-build projects, community architecture, housing co-operatives, self-build — all these initiatives and more have flourished in the last ten years as people recognize that they can't wait for someone else to tell them what they need, and that they do have the resources (given the right sort of assistance) to create the sort of home they want to live in.

Household Consumption

Around 7p in every £1 spent by British consumers is spent on household goods and consumer durables — slightly less than is spent on alcohol or on clothes. Every household needs a basic range of equipment, and depending on the needs of the people living in it each household will also have its own specific range of facilities; as with so many aspects of living ecologically, appropriateness and imagination are the keys. What do you really *need* in the way of household equipment? Does it really mean buying a new version every so often? And with the little-used but very useful items, what are the options for sharing?

The members of the Findhorn Community in Morayshire (see page 183) have at their service (subject to the necessary supervision) a fully kitted-out pottery, a weaving studio, a 16-track recording studio, a darkroom, phototypesetting equipment, a bus, a lorry and a large library. Not to mention televisions, washing machines, dishwashers, food mixers and computers.

The difference is that these facilities are under the joint ownership and supervision of two hundred people, which also makes recycling, transport arrangements, community events, childcare and food-buying so much simpler. What are the lessons for the rest of us?

Our Architectural Heritage

To anyone reviewing today's environment, the most obvious and inescapable fact is change. Since the mid-fifties, when the stringent controls of the immediate post-war years were relaxed, we have been indulging in an orgy of urban change — little less than the transformation of our towns and cities. The change was not only in the towns. In the last thirty years we have been witnessing just as profound an agricultural revolution: 90 per cent of farm buildings, I am told, are strictly speaking redundant. The countryside is now more deserted than at any previous period in history.

We have in short experienced the most massive and comprehensive environmental changes. Such changes are often gradual and sometimes seem trivial. But small features in the end affect the character of the whole. And that change is something best described, not as a set of statistics, but as a change in the grain of town and country, something more profound than appearances, a change and movement in their underlying structure and social fabric.

Patrick Nuttgens, 'Postscript' to
Reviving Buildings and Communities (see page 93)

The Pattern of English Building

Alec Clifton-Taylor's classic book about the architecture of England, now in its fourth and again expanded edition, constantly reminds us of the enormous variety and intricate detail of the built heritage we have inherited. His style is immensely readable, the illustrations clear and relevant; even though there is a wealth of information about materials, building techniques and traditional crafts, nothing is out of place in this comprehensive yet most approachable study. It does only cover England; the closest equivalents for Wales and Scotland are Smith's *Houses of the Welsh Countryside* (HMSO, 1975), Naismith's *Buildings of the Scottish Countryside* (Gollancz, 1985) and McWilliam's *Scottish Townscapes* (Collins, 1985).

The Pattern of English Building
Alec Clifton-Taylor
Faber, 1987 (4th edn)
£12.95

British Vernacular Architecture

The whole range of domestic architecture in Britain is brought together in R.W. Brunskill's excellent *Illustrated Handbook of Vernacular Architecture*. More than two hundred pages are packed with information, drawings and photographs, introducing the reader to every aspect of traditional building down to the end of the nineteenth century — even in some cases beyond. This splendid reference book will change the whole way you look at the built environment.

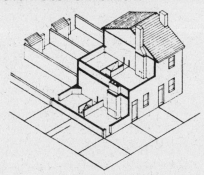

Illustrated Handbook of Vernacular Architecture
R W Brunskill
Faber, 1987 (3rd edition)
£7.50

It can almost always be made to show that demolishing a building and starting again is cheaper than recycling what can be saved of an existing building. With rare and notable exceptions, the new is rarely as attractive and as fitting as the old. In *The House Restorer's Guide* (David and Charles, 1986, £16.00) architect and builder Hugh Lander shows exactly what can be done in the way of recycling old buildings, making them cozy to live in, and even guaranteeing a financial return on your investment.

Housing By People, For People

Until relatively recently the future occupants of a house had a great deal of say in how the house would be designed and built; in most parts of the world this is still the case. No specialist firms of architects and builders were involved in creating the whitewashed villages of island Greece, the timber and turf houses of the Sami, or the adobe towns of Central America, and the millions of people living in Third World squatter settlements often succeed in building comfortable and even attractive surroundings with very few resources.

Only in the West has building been taken so completely out of the hands of the occupiers of buildings, especially when those occupants have little or no economic and political power. This often leaves them at the mercy of people who believe that they know best what people need (even though they would not dream of living in such buildings themselves).

In *Utopia on Trial* (Hilary Shipman, 1985, £6.95), Alice Coleman has examined over 100,000 houses and flats built in the 1950s and 60s, trying to find out why the vision of post-war planned housing has so often resulted in squalor, vandalism and social breakdown. Not all is gloom and doom, however, and she suggests very practical ways in which past mistakes can be rectified and similar mistakes avoided in future.

Architect and housing consultant John Turner has been advocating more community involvement in housing for decades. 'When dwellers control the major decisions and are free to make their own contribution to the design, construction or management of their housing,' he says, 'both the process and the environment produced stimulate individual and social well-being.' He has written several books on the subject, but his arguments are possibly most forcefully developed in *Housing by People: Towards Autonomy in Building Environments* (Marion Boyars, 1976, £3.95). The British community architecture movement is also very involved in looking at ways in which ordinary people can be involved in designing and building their own environments — see pages 92-94 for more details.

Building Basics

There are a number of very basic 'look after your house' DIY books, and if you're at all handy, or just interested in the structure that surrounds you, it's well worth having one of these handy. The Readers Digest booklet *Looking After Your House* (1986, £1.95) tells you a lot in a short space, and very clearly. Readers Digest do other books on DIY, right up to their massive *New DIY Manual* (1987) at £19.95, a volume which graces many a workshop shelf; it is very clear and detailed, and usually tells you far more than you need to know about things you're not currently interested in, but omits to tell you in enough detail about the specific job in hand.

A vital reference book for any serious DIY house-owner is the new edition of the Penguin *Dictionary of Building*, which has been revised and updated specifically with you in mind. It still suffers from the 'he' syndrome, but does acknowledge that it should also be read as 'she' since 'women are entering the field in increasing numbers'. This pocket-size volume will tell you everything you need to know about cross banding, gunstock stiles, horsed moulds, nosing lines and splayed skirting, and ensures that you'll always be able to hold your own in one-up-personship at Texas Homecare in future.

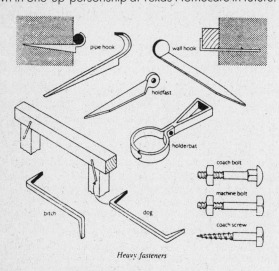

Heavy fasteners

Dictionary of Building
John S. Scott
Penguin, 1984 (3rd edn)
£4.95

Two organizations that any budding builder should know about are the Building Research Establishment, and the various Building Centres throughout the country.

The Building Research Establishment is a government body under the wing of the Department of the Environment. It operates an advisory service, but probably its most useful function to the individual householder is its very wide range of publications, which include useful and non-technical reports on subjects such as condensation, draughtproofing and insulation. Send for a current publications list.

In Store Street off Tottenham Court Road in London is the DIY buff's Mecca — The Building Centre. The bookshop carries more than a thousand books on every aspect of building, from the most general to the most detailed. Downstairs is a literature counter where you can collect an armful of free manufacturers' literature; there are always exhibitions and specialist advice services by people like the Energy Efficiency Centre and the Solid Fuel Advisory Service. The Building Centre has an extensive library, which can be consulted by prior arrangement. There are other Building Centres with bookshops in Bristol (35 King Street, BS1 4DZ; Tel: 0272 277002) and Manchester (115 Portland Street, M1 6FB; Tel: 061 236 9802); Centres without bookshops in Newcastle-upon-Tyne (6 Higham Place) and Glasgow (15 Fitzroy Place).

If you're really serious, however, do make an effort to get to Store Street at some point. The bookshop produces an extensive catalogue and will send books by post.

Building Research Establishment
Bucknalls Lane
Garston
Watford
Hertfordshire
WD2 7JR
0923 894040

The Building Centre
26 Store Street
London
WC1E 7BT
0(7)1-637 1022

Conserving What We've Got

Architectural conservation should be accorded the same consideration which is already being shown to the conservation of other resources, both natural and man-made [sic], and for the same reasons. Nowadays, we literally cannot afford to neglect the investment, the hard financial investment, stored in our built environment. Buildings — and not just historic ones — represent energy, labour and materials, which either cannot be replaced or can only be replaced at enormous cost. The fight to save particular buildings or groups of buildings is not the fancy of some impractical antiquarian. It is part of a battle for the sane use of all our resources. Architects Journal, December 1975

Conservation of the built environment in Britain is both good news and bad news. The good news is that nearly 300,000 buildings in Britain are now 'listed' — that is, they cannot be destroyed or altered without special planning consent — and the number of urban conservation areas continues to increase as local authorities recognize the need to retain the character of our towns and villages.

The bad news is that this protection offered by legislation is too often ignored or overruled when economic considerations come into play. Add bureaucratic delays, and you end up with beautiful historic houses ending up as sad and decaying shells when they could — at relatively little expense — be renovated and used for much-needed housing. Pell Wall Hall in Shropshire; Mavisbank near Edinburgh; Highcliffe Castle in Dorset; Revesby Hall in Lincolnshire — so the list goes on.

And these are just the big houses. Although many architects now recognize that both money and beauty can often be conserved by renovation rather than demolition and rebuilding, there are still too many with grandiose and destructive designs. All over Britain small yet serviceable houses are being needlessly destroyed because of lack of imagination and foresight.

Ecological Housing

Our forebears certainly knew better how to build in harmony with the local environment than we do. Modern homes may be warm, comfortable and convenient, but most modern houses are pretty boring to look at, and they certainly don't blend in with their surroundings like stonework, weathered brick, wattle and daub, thatch, and white-painted stone cottages.

When it comes to even more 'unconventional' houses, many of the experiments from the past that we now admire simply wouldn't get planning permission these days. It would seem that Britons are desperately unimaginative when it comes to building design. The Americans, Australians, Scandinavians, even the traditionalist Germans are way ahead of us in designing — and more importantly building — exciting new sorts of buildings to live and work in. Have a look at some of the American publications on sale at the Building Centre Bookshop — *Handmade Houses*, *The Underground House Book*, *Domebook* and *Shelter* — then ask yourself why we insist on right-angled corners, standard windows and bathrooms, boring rooflines and general monotony.

To give you a taste of what is possible, here are some pictures from a recent German book, *Angewandte Baubiologie: Beispiele aus der Praxis* (Applied Ecological Building: Some Practical Examples, Karl-Hermann Schwabe and Guntram Rother, Felicitas Hübner Verlag, 1985, about £14.50). The house is built entirely from recycled building materials, has four bedrooms and a large living/dining/kitchen space. It was built largely by the family who then occupied it, and cost around half of the price of a similar conventional house. Which would you rather live in?

SAVE, SPAB and Friends

Since 1975 Save Britain's Heritage has been playing a decisive role in saving a series of important buildings from demolition and decay by proposing alternative uses for them, showing how they can be converted rather than destroyed, and lobbying government and local government on conservation issues. As well as being involved in 'big house' projects like Mentmore, The Grange in Hampshire and Barlaston Hall in Staffordshire, SAVE has been involved in finding new uses for Billingsgate Fish Market and Battersea Power Station, and in formulating guidelines for shopfronts which have been adopted by many planning authorities. SAVE produces a wide range of literature — send an sae for a list.

The Society for the Protection of Ancient Buildings plays a leading part in the conservation of Britain's architectural heritage. They run an advisory service, courses for architects, surveyors and builders, and publish a range of material including a series of technical pamphlets and a quarterly *Journal*.

SAVE Britain's Heritage
68 Battersea High Street
London
SW11 3HX
0(7)1-228 3336

Society for the Protection of Ancient Buildings
37 Spital Square
London
E1 6DY
0(7)1-377 1644

A quarter of Britain's housing stock was built before the first world war, and less and less of these houses are now being demolished as architects and house-buyers begin to appreciate the craft and quality materials that went into their construction. Two societies which exist to encourage the appreciation and preservation of these buildings are the Georgian Group (eighteenth and early nineteenth century buildings), and the Victorian Society (nineteenth and early twentieth century). Both act as pressure groups for the conservation of period buildings, work with planning authorities on the designation of conservation areas, and advise owners and occupiers of period buildings on subjects like repairs and renovations. Each publishes a *Newsletter* three times a year and an annual report.

The Georgian Group
37 Spital Square
London
E1 6DY
0(7)1-377 1722

The Victorian Society
1 Priory Gardens
Bedford Park
London
W4 1TT
0(8)1-994 1019

Green Design

Building materials and the numerous chemicals used in the building industry are increasingly coming in for closer green scrutiny; Avril Fox and Robin Murrell's Green Design is an important new A-Z of building materials and their environmental impact. There are often knotty problems trying to weigh up greenness of materials: whilst stone and brick are indubitably natural, for example, their use often means the quarrying of vast areas of unspoilt landscape. Green Design is an important reference source, though there are some inconsistencies and omissions. Insulation foam is mentioned as a cavity wall filler but nothing is said about the potential dangers of poisonous foraldehyde vapours, while polystyrene blocks (which no longer contain CFCs) aren't included as a useful insulating material.

Green Design
Avril Fox and Robin Murrell
Longman, 1989
£10.95

Building Materials

Until a hundred and fifty years ago nearly all houses were of necessity built from the materials that were closest to hand; nowadays a building made of local materials is a rare event. It is the variety of building materials available in different parts of the country that give older buildings their character, and which tell you at a glance which part of the country you are in. The experienced eye can distinguish exact localities of building style as readily as Henry Higgins could tell the origins of different accents: Bath stone, Welsh slate, Pennine limestone; wattle, daub and thatch where stone was harder to come by.

Nowadays many new houses could be anywhere, an anonymous mixture of Barrett and Wimpy — perfectly satisfactory but entirely uninspiring, even when there is an effort to add a little class with 'real stone cladding' and 'Georgian windows'. The economics of building make it far more 'economic' to import bricks and concrete blocks from hundreds of miles away than to quarry (or even recycle) the local stone or explore the possibilities of rammed earth, thatch or turf roofs, and (they say) you always have to think about selling it at some point — the new occupants may not appreciate the hand-made bricks and goats grazing round the chimney.

It isn't that building in traditional materials is intrinsically better, and many modern buildings in concrete, brick and steel function efficiently and look good. But there are aesthetic and ecological reasons for using local materials where you can. Providing that the design is good, your building is far more likely to blend with its surroundings than is one made of imported materials, and you will have the satisfaction of knowing that your house is uniquely yours. You will almost certainly be using less energy than goes into the making of a mass-produced house, and you will be keeping alive traditional building skills that will in all probability be needed much more in the future than they are today.

Stone

Building dry stone walls is a good way to start working with stone, and you don't need to be a bodybuilder or have an 'A' level in mechanics to learn how to do it. A useful primer, Building and Repairing Dry Stone Walls, is available from the Dry Stone Walling Association at £1.25, and as you get more proficient you may well want their latest book, just published, called Building Special Features in Dry Stone; they have a mail order service for a whole range of books about walling. As well as producing information about walling techniques, the DSWA also organizes training and competitions. If you are thinking of building in stone, Asher Shadmon's Stone: An Introduction (IT Publications, 1987, £9.95) is a good clear description of the varieties and uses of stone in building.

Anybody seriously interested in traditional stonework should contact Men of the Stones in Stamford (there are quite a lot of women of the stones too): they can provide information about training, conservation architects, stone sculptors, masons and builders, quarries and specialist services in stone. They recommend Crawshaws in Surrey as the best suppliers of masonry tools, especially hand tools like box trammels and riffler files.

Dry Stone Walling Association
Young Farmers' Centre
National Agriculture
Centre
Kenilworth
Warwickshire
CV8 2LG
021 378 0493

B.I. Crawshaw and Co.
53 Willow Lane
Industrial Estate
Mitcham
Surrey
CR4 4NA
0(8)1-685 9860

Men of the Stones
The Rutlands
Tinwell
Stamford
PE9 3UD
0780 63372

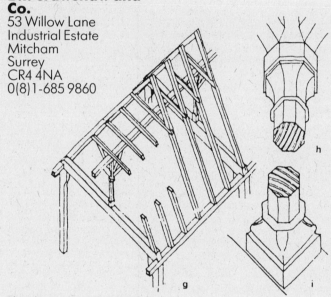

Wood

Wood is of course a renewable resource, but some woods are far more renewable than others because they grow much faster. If you buy tropical hardwoods (and many plywoods are veneered with tropical hardwoods) it can be very difficult to know whether the wood has been plantation-grown or whether it has been felled as part of the disastrous wholesale clearance of tropical forest. If you care about such things, then you will be interested to know that Friends of the Earth (see page 65) have produced a detailed regional Good Wood Guide, giving details of sources of 'certified' hardwoods — that is, hardwoods which come from well-managed and sustainable forestry activities. Buying only certified timber ensures that rainforests are not decimated on your behalf.

The reference books mentioned on page 88 give basic timber terminology and woodworking techniques. The Timber Research and Development Association in High Wycombe is happy to answer enquiries from the general public.

Timber Research and Development Association
Stocking Lane
Hughenden Valley
High Wycombe
Buckinghamshire
HP14 4ND
024 024 3091

Thatch

Bob West's book called *Thatch* (David and Charles, 1987, £14.95) is a very good introduction to the whole subject of thatching, whether you are interested in it as a houseowner or a prospective thatcher. Bob West also runs the Thatching Advisory Service, which can answer virtually any question to do with thatch and thatching. If you are looking for training, the organization to contact is the National Society of Master Thatchers.

Thatching Advisory Service
29 Nine Mile Ride
Finchampstead
nr Wokingham
Berkshire
0734 734203

National Society of Master Thatchers
30 Little Lane
Yardley Hastings
Northamptonshire
NN7 1EN
060 129 280

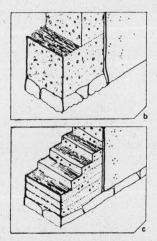

Rammed Earth and Earth Shelters

If used correctly, dried mud or soil can be used as building material. You can still see many wattle and daub houses in lowland Britain, and cob, a building technique using mud and small stones, was widely used in the West Country. Nowadays the most common form of earth building is rammed earth, where subsoil is compressed between moveable frames to make the walls (a wood or stone framework actually holds the house up). Probably the best source of information on earth building techniques is the IT Bookshop (see page 296), where you will find John Norton's handbook *Building with Earth* (1986, £4.95). Earth-sheltered housing (or underground housing) is much further advanced in the USA than in Britain, though there are some notable earth-sheltered buildings in this country, such as the Sir Joseph Banks Building at Kew Gardens. Stu Campbell (especially his *Underground House Book*, Garden Way, 1981, £6.95) is considered the guru of underground building, and there is a British Earth Sheltering Association which will give advice and information about this novel and energy-saving building technique.

British Earth Sheltering Association
Department of Architecture and Planning
Liverpool Polytechnic
98 Mount Pleasant
Liverpool
L3 5UZ
051 207 3581 ext. 3704

Recycled Building Materials

As new building materials become costlier, builders (and particularly self-builders) are increasingly looking at the potential for recycling materials. In up-market areas this often means just the period fittings (doors, fireplaces, bathtaps and the like), but most materials can be recycled given a little time and trouble — the fact that they have already lasted for a century or more suggests that they are well-seasoned and ready for the next century. The Architectural Salvage Index, a trade information service run from Surrey, has a database of materials available for recycling: it costs £10 to register with them, then when they know your requirements they will provide appropriate contact lists.

Architectural Salvage Index
Hutton and Rostron
Netley House
Gomshall
Guildford
Surrey
GU5 9QA
048 641 3221

And Recycled Tools

Good builders' tools will last a lifetime if they are looked after: the same British firms that make world-renowned garden tools (see page 81) also make excellent building tools. Yet tools are superseded, or broken and set aside, and caches of wood-working and metalworking tools lie rotting away in the corners of workshops. If you know of such unused resources, give a thought to Tools for Self-Reliance, who have a national network of tool restorers who will collect your old tools, refurbish them, and make up sets of tools to send to Third World countries. If you are interested in helping in the refurbishment process, even better — they produce an excellent *Handbook* showing how to do it.

Tools for Self-Reliance Ltd
Netley Marsh Workshops
Netley Marsh
Southampton
SO4 2GY
0703 869697

Self-Build

Most people — in the West at least — have come to believe that building is something completely beyond their skills and capabilities, requiring massive machinery, equally massive muscles, and a detailed knowledge of almost-incomprehensible planning and building regulations.

It's a convenient myth, and one that more and more people are shattering. You don't need superhuman strength or a superhuman brain to plan and build your own shelter, just imagination, access to resources and information, time, and determination.

Building Your Own Home

Murray Armor is a walking encyclopedia of wisdom and information about self-built housing, and you will find a lot of that experience in the two-hundred-odd pages of *Building Your Own Home*, a book which is updated every couple of years — the current edition is 1989-90. He takes you through all the practicalities — planning, finance, design, materials, consultants, and a very sensible chapter on energy saving — then describes two dozen projects in detail so you can see the range of projects that are possible.

Bob Matthews' *Talking about Self Build* consists of a series of wonderful, humourous, heart-rending interviews with a number of people who have built their own homes. There is, for example, the woman who spent three weeks in a downpour digging out trenches in clay, and the group of tradesmen who finished their houses in thirteen months. This is the book to read if you're toying with the idea of self-build and want some insight into what it's *really* like. Bob's second book, *Practical House Building*, is due in mid-1990 (Blackberry, £12.50), and will deal with the nitty-gritty information on how to actually do the building. He has built his own house, so he should know.

Building Your Own Home
Murray Armor
Prism Press, 1990
£9.95

Talking About Self Build
Bob Matthews
Blackberry Press, 1990
£7.50

Kita Slooman's bungalow - nearly finished !

Constructive Individuals

I felt that I had learnt to 'have a go' at many things that I was previously nervous about. I now have more confidence, more skills, more knowledge. It was an amazing and unique experience.
Silvia Ebert, a retired dancer
on one of Constructive Individuals' training courses

Phil Bixby started Creative Individuals in 1985 to help people who want to learn how to build their own homes. CI offers several training courses for people wanting to learn building skills; tailored training course for specific self-build schemes; and design and management courses for organizations like local authorities or housing associations. If you just want to learn building skills, then they do courses for that too.

Constructive Individuals
1 The Cottages
Chapel Street
Hambleton
Selby
YO8 9JE
0757 82562

CONSTRUCTIVE INDIVIDUALS

Cohousing

The cohousing movement started in Denmark in the mid-1960s when professional families, feeling the strains of raising children when both parents are working and feeling the isolation of the nuclear family, began to think that there had to be a better way of organizing their lifestyles. Now there are over 100 cohousing developments in Denmark, with pilot schemes in Sweden and the USA.

A recent American book called simply *Cohousing* shows how these communities work. A dozen or so private houses of varying sizes cluster together around a common larger house where daily communal evening meals are eaten, where there is space for childrens' play and communal supervision, and maybe a library, workshop or laundry. Individual houses face on to an unmotorized street, with private yards at the rear. Naturally most of the life goes on in the street, since the design encourages a sense of community and interaction amongst residents, who have after all been involved in designing the buildings themselves.

Cohousing
A Contemporary Approach to Housing Ourselves
Kathryn McCamant and Charles Durrant
Ten Speed Press, 1989 (distributed in the UK by Airlift)
£14.95

In Memoriam Walter Segal

The much loved and respected architect Walter Segal died in 1985, bequeathing us an approach to low-cost housing which is showing tangible results in many parts of Britain. In particular he showed that self-build housing was not just the preserve of the well-off. The Walter Segal Trust exists to give advice and support, especially to those people on low incomes and in housing need, to build decent homes for themselves and their families. Working with local authorities or private groups, and now in an exciting new development with housing associations, the Trust is showing that people can build their own housing. You will find the Trust and its newsletter, *You Build*, very helpful indeed.

Walter Segal Trust
Room 212
Panther House
38 Mount Pleasant
London
WC1X 0AP
0(7)1-833 4152

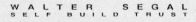
WALTER SEGAL
SELF BUILD TRUST

Some Professional Help

I'll end with two firms in the relative big-time of self-build, mostly of very conventional houses, but they are too important to be overlooked by any potential self-builder. Homesmith in West Yorkshire offer a complete consultancy and liaison service for self-builders, and even if you don't need their services it is well worth subscribing to their quarterly magazine *The Self-Builder*.

Design and Materials in Worksop organize package deals for self-builders, from looking at your site to preparing semi-customized plans and providing all the materials you will need in kit form — they are flexible and do pretty much what you ask for. A folder of plans is available, and while they are for the most part not very original they may give you some ideas.

Homesmith
The Spire
Leeds Road
Lightcliffe
Halifax
HA3 8NU
0422 204121

Design and Materials Ltd
Carlton-in-Lindrick
Industrial Estate
Worksop
Nottinghamshire
S81 9LB
0909 730333

Community Architecture

The aim of community architecture is to improve the quality of the environment by involving people in the design and management of the buildings or spaces they inhabit. Community architecture gets people directly involved in the design of the buildings or spaces they use with the result that they have more control over decisions affecting the buildings they want.

RIBA Community Architecture leaflet, 1986

Creating Your Own Environment

Community involvement in the creation and management of the built environment is here to stay, and award-winning journalists Charles Knevitt and Nick Wates (who also helped to edit the book on squatting reviewed on page 98) have produced an excellent survey of the many initiatives currently taking place all over Britain. The resource sections at the end are comprehensive, including organizations, further reading, and a concise glossary.

*

Community enterprise is a continuing process. There are no instant solutions. Communities change in their needs and aspirations, cities grow and shrink, and there is a continuous process of renewal which can be helped — or hindered — by experts. The real task for today is to create a partnership between those different sectors that have different resources to offer: the public sector, which can often assist with supply of land, the private sector, which has the finance, the professionals, who have the skills, and the voluntary movements — housing associations, cooperatives, self-build associations, etc., which know the immediate needs and have the commitment to resolve them. It is a task which must be addressed urgently.

Lord Scarman, from the Foreword

Community Architecture

How People are Creating Their Own Environment
Charles Knevitt and Nick Wates
Penguin, 1987
£4.95

Reviving Buildings and Communities

Charles Knevitt and Nick Wates' book concentrates on the social and political aspects of community architecture; Michael Talbot's *Reviving Buildings and Communities* emphasizes how community initiatives can bring about the regeneration of community spirit and recycle old buildings at the same time. Using case studies from both urban and rural settings, and concentrating on Wirksworth in Derbyshire where a whole town has been rejuvenated in this way, he shows how many other communities could join forces to help breathe new life into the built environment.

*

The difference in Wirksworth was that all the methods were used together in a short, sharp co-ordinated assault on the town's problems. The direct cost of setting up and staffing the project is estimated to be £25,000 a year at 1979 prices, about £4 per head of population, over a three-year period. For this comparatively small sum, the one-hundred-year decline of the market town was reversed.

Reviving Buildings and Communities

A Manual of Renewal
Michael Talbot
David and Charles, 1986
£16.95

The RIBA Community Architecture Group

With the controversial appointment of Rod Hackney to the Chairmanship of the Royal Institute of British Architects, the institute underlined its commitment to wider community participation in the design of the built environment. In fact the RIBA has had a Community Architecture Group since 1976, promoting the involvement of the public in the design of the buildings they inhabit. The group can advise community groups on ways of using architects' skills to the best advantage, and (for England only) has small grants scheme called the Community Projects Fund. To date the Fund has helped with slum renewal schemes, a drug rehabilitation project, rural community centres and community arts projects.

RIBA Community Architecture Group

66 Portland Place
London
W1N 4AD
0(7)1-580 5533 ext 4033

ACTAC

The Association of Community Technical Aid Centres was established in 1983 to co-ordinate the community-oriented work of architects, landscape architects, planners, surveyors, designers, ecologists and environmental educators. Membership currently stands at around 70, and ACTAC member organizations can offer a very wide range of services to community groups, from feasibility studies and educational courses to parliamentary lobbying and consultation with local and national government. If you tell them what you need, the Liverpool office will be able to put you in touch with appropriate professionals; a new membership list, giving full details of the services that each member organization offers, is currently being compiled. A Scottish ACTAC office has recently been opened in Glasgow.

ACTAC

Royal Institution
Colquitt Street
Liverpool
L1 4DE
051 708 7607

ACTAC Scotland

58 Fox Street
Glasgow
G1 4AU
041 221 6126

The Timeless Way

We have been taught that there is no objective difference between good buildings and bad, good towns and bad. The fact is that the difference between a good building and a bad building, between a good town and a bad town, is an objective matter. It is the difference between health and sickness, wholeness and dividedness, self-maintenance and self-destruction. In a world which is healthy, whole, alive, and self-maintaining, people themselves can be alive and self-creating. In a world which is unwhole and self-destroying, people cannot be alive: they will inevitably themselves be self-destroying, and miserable.

But it is easy to understand why people believe so firmly that there is no single, solid basis for the difference between good building and bad.

It happens because the single central quality which makes the difference cannot be named.

The Timeless Way of Building

How often have you thought about where you would ideally like to live; about what it would look like, sound like, feel like? And then thought 'But it could never really be like that'.

I recently visited the Alhambra in Granada (out of season, luckily), and spent hours exploring its magical intricacy — enclosed shady courtyards leading to arcaded balconies with breathtaking vistas, hand-painted ceilings and subtly coloured tiled walls, a bathroom with stars pierced in the roof and a circular underground chamber with the most wonderful acoustic resonance. The Alhambra, of course, could not have been built without enormous private wealth and privilege. But many of our own towns and villages, built over the centuries by people who knew what was both functional and fitting, possess that same quality of organic wholeness and purpose.

Today, it seems, we can't do it any more. With very rare exceptions we just can't create that feeling of welcoming rightness in our buildings and the spaces between them. Yet if all urban designers, architects and, above all, developers and builders, were to take heed of what California-based master-architect-and-guru-to-many Christopher Alexander had to say, things could be very different.

It was in 1966 that one of Christopher Alexander's first books, *Community and Privacy*, was published in Britain (a 7/6d Penguin which still turns up in secondhand bookshops), addressing the perennial problem that many urban-dwellers face: how can you provide people with the ease of interpersonal communication that pulls them to the city in the first place with sufficient privacy to maintain their sanity?

The Alexander 'bibles', however, are a pair of books called *The Timeless Way of Building* and *A Pattern Language*, published just over a decade ago. The American *Whole Earth Catalog* raves about these books: 'They should be in the hands of every citizen, city dweller, home builder, office worker,' writes Stewart Brand; yet they are still only available in expensive hardbacks and, being published by the New York end of Oxford University Press, are very hard to track down in Britain (EcoLogic Books in Devon, see page 340, is the only reliable source I know of).

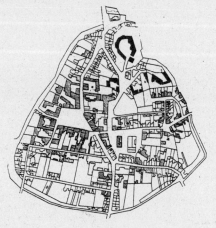

Of the two, *The Timeless Way* provides the theory and *Pattern Language* the practice of building in a truly satisfying way. The first book isn't afraid of exploring in compelling depth ideas like 'the quality that has no name' and 'living patterns'. *Pattern Language* is a thicker book of nearly 1,200 pages, containing the 'pattern language's' 253 guidelines for urban design that works, guidelines which range from large scale suggestions like number 14, 'Identifiable Neighbourhood', to the most domestic like number 242, 'Front Door Bench'.

Let's have these important books in widely-available paperback versions, and soon. Then let's make them required reading for every planner, engineer, architect and social scientist in the country. And then let's adjust our building and planning systems to encourage the timeless way, rather than to stultify and destroy it.

The Timeless Way of Building
Christopher Alexander
Oxford University Press, 1979
about £27.00

A Pattern Language
Christopher Alexander, Sara Ishikawa and Murray Silverstein
Oxford University Press, 1977
about £32.50

A Vision of Britain

When Prince Charles speaks out, many jump. And our green royal heir apparent now has his teeth firmly into those who want to replace our very own 'timeless way' with monstrosities like the 'unmitigated disaster' (his words) of the new convention centre in Birmingham. His critics have accused him of wanting to live in the past, but the weight of public opinion is clearly with his recent book *A Vision of Britain* as he wades in with his 'ten principles we can build on', from 'Don't rape the landscape' to 'Let the people who will have to live with what you build help guide your hand'. It sounds remarkably like Christopher Alexander, yet neither Prince Charles nor the author of the next book acknowledge his influence.

In response to *A Vision of Britain* the president of the Royal Institute for British Architects, Maxwell Hutchinson, has written *The Prince of Wales: Right or Wrong?* In fact they see eye-to-eye on a great many more issues than the media would like, and while Prince Charles's book is a pretty coffee table volume, Maxwell Hutchinson's book has far more substance. His primary aim is to reinstate the architect as visionary and facilitator, and to dispel the idea that architects just add the fancy bits when the developer and engineer have done their job. Most hideous architecture, he points out, has never seen an architect, and he derides the 'bimbo architecture' of the Gateshead Metro Centre just as vehemently as would the prince. 'Our task,' he concludes, 'is to create the spaces which define our towns and cities.' With which Christopher Alexander would wholeheartedly agree.

A Vision of Britain
Prince Charles
Doubleday, 1989
£16.95

The Prince of Wales Right or Wrong?
Maxwell Hutchinson
Faber and Faber, 1989
£4.99

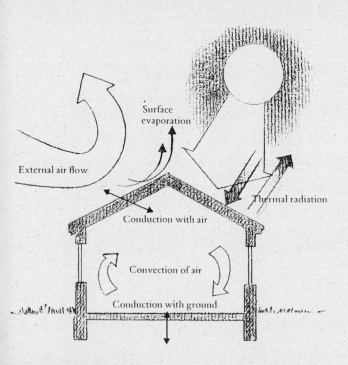

Surface evaporation

External air flow

Thermal radiation

Conduction with air

Convection of air

Conduction with ground

Natural Homes

Health for the body, peace for the spirit, harmony with the environment — these are the criteria of the natural house. All three have deep roots in the human experience and in the ethnic traditions of home building in cultures across the world — the 'timeless way'.
David Pearson, The Natural House Book

Whilst many of us are now beginning to do something about how we are polluting our environment outside the home, we are also discovering that 'home' is not always the snug, safe place that we fondly imagine. There is growing evidence, and attendant concern, that the materials and appliances we use inside our buildings are slowly and subtly poisoning us. Since most of us spend more than 90% of our time indoors, and more than two dozen groups of domestic toxins have been identified, it is hardly surprising that we go down en masse with ailments like conjunctivitis, nausea, lethargy, stuffy noses, puffy eyes and headaches. In the light of recent research and with the help of more natural products, however, you can do something about this alarming state of affairs.

Take a look round your home and you will be surprised to find sources of pollution everywhere. Starting at the top, roofing timbers may have been treated with toxic fluids . . . Cavity walls could be injected with insulating foam emitting formaldehyde vapour, while interior decoration will consist of petro-chemical based paints or vinyl papers, which emit more dangerous vapours . . . Furnishings are often filled with polyurethene foam and upholstered with synthetic fabrics . . . Fumes and gases come from poorly combusting fires and stoves . . .

Thus David Pearson describes the 'dangerous house'. But his book, *The Natural House*, concentrates on removing the load of pollutants from your home and replacing the offending materials with safe ones. This is a beautiful book with lovely photographs of perfect houses, mostly new ones; any part-time house renovator will be very conscious of the limitations of many existing houses (ceilings less than 2 metres high, small windows facing east . . .) and of many homeowners' limited income. In some ways this inspiring book doesn't address the problems of existing British housing, but it should be read by all planners, architects, builders and building materials manufacturers so that we can move towards natural houses instead of filling them with polluting tat. You may find the author's spiritual references hard to digest, but there is plenty

of practical information too, and the resource section at the end is very good.

Carol Venolia's *Healing Environments*, an American import, explores many of the things that builders and householders rarely think about: colour, light, temperature, air quality, symbols in the environment, sound and noise, and how all these things affect us. With gentle questions and exercises in visualization and fantasy she asks us to look at what *feels* best, and from this new-found awareness the practical steps you need to take will almost certainly seem easier than before.

Your Home, Your Health and Well Being is another American book rich in practical details about how to make every room in your home as safe and comfortable as possible, especially if you are particularly sensitive to chemical pollution. With a gruelling chapter at the end about a woman struggling to overcome her multiple allergies the book brings home just how badly polluted our environment is — the only really fresh air in the USA, say the authors, is on the top of mountains, along some coasts and in the middle of the deserts. What if you live in Croydon?

The Natural House Book
David Pearson
Conran Octopus, 1989
£14.99

Healing Environments
Your Guide to Indoor Well-Being
Carol Venolia
Celestial Arts, 1988
(distributed in the UK by Airlift)
£6.95

Your Home, Your Health and Well Being
David Rousseau, W.J. Rae and Jean Enwright
Ten Speed Press, 1988
(distributed in the UK by Airlift)
£10.95

Home Ecology

If you want to do something now without rebuilding the house or spending lots of money, then Karen Christensen's *Home Ecology* should take pride of place on your (untreated locally-grown) bookshelf — essential reading if you want to make your world a better place. It is absolutely crammed with advice, information and resources about everything: how to eat sensibly and cheaply; which sources of energy use least resources and how to use them economically and safely; how to improve the lighting in your home (wash the light bulbs for example . . . which, feeling guilty, I immediately did); how to have a non-toxic home (throw out all those horrible plastic bottles of synthetic chemicals and use borax, salt and vinegar instead).

There is so much in this book that it really is a good idea to follow Karen Christensen's advice early on in the book of making a list and prioritizing the things you plan to do, otherwise you'll end up ruining your health through sheer exhaustion!

Karen Christensen
Home Ecology
Arlington Books, 1989
£4.95

Housing Rights

'Tenants can stand up to a landlord's bully-boy tactics and win' says tenant Leslee Udwin. Leslee should know. Along with other tenants in Kensington and Chelsea she was on the receiving end of harassment by notorious landlord Nicholas van Hoogstraten. This included disconnection of essential services, verbal abuse, physical threats of violence and illegal eviction. Most of the tenants were single women. Joining forces in five of Hoog-straten's properties they turned to the Royal Borough Council for help. After six months of intensive campaigning the tenants finally persuaded the council to take action.

Bedsit Rights, Spring 1987

Unless they are very lucky or very rich, almost everyone will have a housing problem at some point in their lives. If you do not own your own property the chances of running into housing problems increase enormously since property owners are almost certain to know about loopholes in the law better than the tenants who occupy their property. In fact the 1988 Housing Act changed a great many rights for tenants and gave a good deal more power to landlords so in seeking information from books and pamphlets it is important to check that the publication has been updated.

Not having a home of your own can lead to insecurity in every other area of your life; eviction still too often means the splitting of families, discrimination at work, and the ultimate threat of homelessness.

Housing law in Britain is extremely complicated, and unless you want to make it your life's work you can never hope to understand all the ins and outs. This is where it is important to know where to go for help. Housing problems are amongst the main areas dealt with by Citizens' Advice Bureaux and community law centres (see page 333); in addition there are a growing number of housing aid and advice centres — you will find a complete list of them at the end of *The Housing Rights Guide* (see below). If you have a problem, or think you see one looming on the horizon, these advice services are the first place to go.

The Housing Rights Guide

It's difficult to imagine what people did before SHAC (see below) first published this invaluable handbook in 1985. This latest edition takes account of the 1988 Housing Act. The subtitle is 'The practical guide on how to find, pay for and keep your home', and in as readable a form as it's possible to make complicated procedures that's what it is. The first and longest section is about finding somewhere to live, and all types of housing are covered, from buying and private renting to council housing, hostels and squatting.

The section on housing benefit and rate rebate is the clearest explanation I have seen of this thorny area, and there is also a useful section on housing rights if your relationship breaks down. The last section, which is in many ways the key to the rest, explains how to find advice and representation, including details about legal aid.

Finally there is a comprehensive list of law and housing aid centres and other useful addresses, and suggestions for further reading. Anybody working in the caring professions should have a copy, and as an ordinary person about the house it could well be one of your most important investments.

Because housing law is different in Scotland, the *Guide* only applies to England and Wales; if you live in Scotland the Scottish Information Office produces a series of leaflets on housing rights which you can get from your local rent officer's office or citizen's advice bureau — as yet there isn't a Scottish equivalent of the SHAC guide.

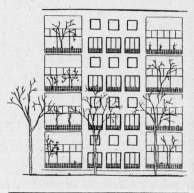

The Housing Rights Guide
Geoffrey Randall
SHAC, 1988
£5.95

SHAC

Originally a Shelter project called Shelter Housing Aid Centre (hence its acronym), SHAC is Britain's leading housing aid centre. Its main emphasis is on housing problems in the London area, though it conducts research which is applicable throughout the country (though with limited relevance to Scotland — see above). SHAC also produces the most comprehensive range of literature on housing rights available, including a *Rights Guide for Home Owners* (6th edn 1987, £4.50); *The Fuel Rights Handbook* (5th edn 1986, £5.95); and a pertinent and comprehensive *Guide to Housing Benefit and Community Charge Benefit* (1988, £6.50). Write with an sae for a publications list.

SHAC (The London Housing Aid Centre)
189a Old Brompton Road
London
SW5 0AR
0(7)1-373 7276

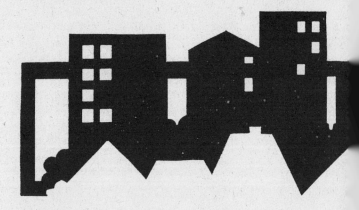

Bedsit Rights

The Campaign for Bedsit Rights works for the rights of tenants in multiple occupancy houses, people who are more at the whim of private (and some council) landlords than any other group and who comprise one in twenty of the British population. Bedsit Rights bimonthly *Bedsit Briefing* is newsy, hard-hitting; available on subscription (£6.50) to non-members and free to members. Their *Handbook of Bedsit Rights* is subtitled 'A Handbook for people who live in Bedsits, Flatlets, Share-houses, Lodgings, Hostels, Bed and Breakfast Hotels'. At £2.50 plus 30p p+p it is excellent value.

Campaign for Bedsit Rights
5/15 Cromer Street
London
WC1H 8LS
0(7)1-278 0598

Housing Associations

The first housing associations, started in the nineteenth century, were designed to provide low-cost but decent rented property. This is much the role that housing associations still have, though with the establishment of The Housing Corporation in 1964 to oversee and regulate the activities of housing associations, housing association building has become established alongside private ownership and local authority housing as the 'third arm' of British housing policy, and nearly ten per cent of new houses now being built are built by housing associations. They also renovate many old buildings. Housing associations vary enormously in size, sometimes owning one large subdivided house, sometimes several thousand houses. Many receive subsidy from central or local government. Some operate in much the same way as local authority housing, having a mix of accommodation types, while others cater for the needs of a particular group of people, such as the elderly or the disabled.

The best way to find out about housing association activity in your area is by contacting your local authority housing department. Then, because the way that housing associations operate varies so widely, it is best to contact each association directly. Look them up in *Yellow Pages*, or contact the Housing Corporation whose local office may also be in the *Yellow Pages*.

Housing Co-operatives

A housing co-operative is a form of housing association, but as with workers' co-operatives (see page 275) the idea is that a group of people come together to buy or rent and manage the property, rather than relying on an 'outside' agency to develop and manage the housing. If you decide to live in a housing co-op it means both greater control and greater responsibility (like attending co-op meetings or taking part in joint decorating projects), but you are much more likely to get what you want in the way of housing.

Housing co-operatives qualify for funding from the Housing Corporation, and as building societies and banks have become better informed private finance in the form of mortgages is now more readily available. Funding is also available from the Housing Corporation for short-life housing and, in a recent development, for self-build co-operatives.

If you are a tenant there are a growing number of tenant management co-operatives (TMCs), whereby tenants of a street or estate form a co-operative to take over the day-to-day management of their housing. Each member remains a tenant of the council (or in some cases of another landlord) but manage the property themselves, often employing their own housing manager. Council tenants can opt to change to another landlord under tenants' choice legislation, or become a housing association, housing co-operative or any other body approved by the Housing Corporation. Funding is available to assist in working out a proposal to set up a TMC or to investigate the various options available.

The Housing Corporation publishes a wide range of useful information leaflets about housing co-operatives, while the Tenants' Participation Advisory Service is a good source of independent advice to help tenants assess what is in their best interest.

There are now around 600 housing co-operatives in Britain, housing more than 20,000 people — minute compared with the contribution of the housing associations but growing steadily. Since 1981 the housing co-op movement has been represented by the National Federation of Housing Co-operatives, which acts as a liaison and campaigning body. The NFHC will give advice and information and has a range of publications for people interested in becoming part of a housing co-operative. They produce a magazine called *Around the Houses*, and two *Directories of Housing Co-operatives* — one for the London area and one for the rest of Britain; they cost £3 each. The *Directories* give excellent summaries of what housing co-operatives are, how they are developed, and the different types of co-operative.

In Scotland, information about both housing associations and housing co-operatives is available from Scottish Homes, the organization which took over the work of the Scottish Special Housing Association in 1989. They have a range of literature, including a comprehensive directory.

The Housing Corporation
149 Tottenham Court Road
London W1P 0BN
0(7)1-387 9466

National Federation of Housing Co-operatives
88 Old Street
London
EC1V 9AX
0(7)1-608 2494

Tenants' Participation Advisory Service
48 The Crescent
Salford
Manchester
061 745 7903

Scottish Homes
Rosebery House
Haymarket
Edinburgh
031 337 0044

Buying Your House With Other People

If you want to do it yourselves, Dave Treanor, a veteran of housing co-operatives and communal living and now working more than full time for housing co-operatives, has written a book comparing and explaining all the options that are currently available for the joint ownership of property. The book includes very practical chapters on understanding and establishing the most suitable legal framework for your shared ownership, the best sources of finance, responsibilities and rights, and how to be tenants rather than owners. The appendices at the end — legal agreements, a glossary, and names and address of useful organisations — make this first comprehensive guide to shared ownership of housing a vital resource for anybody considering shared housebuying.

Buying Your House with Other People
Dave Treanor
NFHC and Shelter, 1987
£5.95

Squatting

Squatting can be a solution to the housing problems of people who don't qualify for public housing and can't afford to buy a place or pay the extortionate rents asked by private landlords. It can also be the answer for people who have spent years on council waiting lists without a home of their own. Squatting is a way of using houses that would otherwise stay empty while the bureaucrats quibble over statistics and people stay homeless. With the present cuts in public spending, housing authorities are finding it hard to carry out many of their planned improvements, resulting in even more houses and flats being left empty — so it's up to us to beat the cuts by squatting houses that would other-wise be left to deteriorate or sold off to speculators.

Squatters Handbook (see below).

It's sad but not surprising that squatting has such a bad name. The same thing in pioneering days, when it was white Euro-peans taking aboriginal or native land, was called 'home-steading', and was heralded as the entirely ethical way to create a home for yourself. Most squatters want and are able to look after a home just as well as any house-owner, and are not at all averse to putting time and energy into houses that would otherwise be left to rot until they constituted the perfect excuse for redevelopment.

If you are squatting, or are thinking of squatting, do contact the Advisory Service for Squatters, who can offer advice and encouragement and who publish a clear and comprehensive guide to squatting, *Squatters Handbook*, now in its ninth edition (60p + 18p p+p). It really is an excellent resource, and shows that squatting is a vital (and still legal) part of the British hous-ing scene. Again, because of differences in the law much of the legal advice is not applicable to Scotland; for information about squatting in Scotland contact Edinburgh SHAC, 103 Morrison Street, Edinburgh EH3 8BS, Tel: 031 229 8771.

Advisory Service for Squatters
2 St Pauls Road
London
N1 2QN
0(7)1-359 8814

The story of squatting is eloquently and descriptively told in a large format illustrated paperback called *Squatting: The Real Story* (Bay Leaf Books, 1980, £4.90 — now sadly out of print). Read about Ruff, Tuff and Cream Puff, the only estate agency for squatters, the occupation of Lambeth Town Hall and much more.

Travellers' Rights

Just as there have always been squatters, there have always been travellers, and just as squatters have been marginalized and denigrated in our static property-owning society, so have travellers. Although local authorities are supposed by law to provide adequate site provision for them, most simply haven't bothered to discuss the issue.

A 1986 NCCL (see page 333) report about the Stonehenge festival clarifies the issue: 'The background to the convoy is a moral panic in which all travellers are identified as part of the unified whole, "the convoy", and characterised as medieval brigands, carriers of AIDS or hepatitis . . . Some travellers have seasonal work, although there are complaints that this is now in short supply. Some travellers claim social security, some do not. There is no evidence that a higher proportion of travellers with the convoy have criminal convictions than an equivalent cross-section of the settled community; as far as we know there have been no prosecutions for possession of hard drugs, nor have firearms been used.' This is not the picture presented by the popular press; no wonder travellers feel angry.

For a realistic and very human view of the life of present-day travellers read *Stonehenge '85* and *Stonehenge '86*, £1.50 each plus an sae from Unique Publications, PO Box 23, Glas-tonbury, Somerset. *New Anarchist Review* produces a very useful little handbook called *Ideal Home: Survival Edition* (1986, £2.40), crammed full of tips, hints and ideas to convert your bus, and where and when not to trespass ('On seeing a silver and green bus, approach the owner and say "You are Venusian and I claim my free cup of tea"; don't worry if you've got the wrong bus, you might get a free cup of tea anyway'). Good fun. Wolverhampton Social Services and The Travellers and Benefits Working Party have recently produced a *Guide to Benefits for Travellers*; for a copy write to TBWP c/o A. Viney, 4th Floor, Riverside House, Beresford Street, London SE18 6DF.

Tipis

In a valley near Llandeilo in south-west Wales is a tipi village of nearly two hundred people, established in 1976. Even though a DoE Inspector said in a 1985 report that 'in relation to the local ecology their presence seems to me, on balance, to be beneficial rather than harmful', the community is con-stantly under threat of eviction.

If you would like to join the growing number of people following the North American tradition of tipi dwelling, the expert is Patrick Whitefield, who makes tipis at the Dove Workshops near Glastonbury, and has written a seductive yet eminently practical little book called *Tipi Living* (£2 plus a sae from the address below). Patrick's tipis are 100% cotton and start at around £450 for a 14' diameter tipi, everything (cover, lining, poles, pegs, etc.) included, and each tipi comes with complete instructions.

Patrick and Co.
Dove Workshops
Butleigh
nr Glastonbury
Somerset
BA6 8TL
0458 50682

Planning

The planning system, as we know it today, will this year celebrate its 40th birthday. Yet the celebrations will be muted. The vision and idealism which lay behind the 1947 Town and Country Planning Act have almost gone. As the recently published Nuffield Report observed, 'the immediate postwar consensus on planning objectives — the consensus on which the planning system was founded — has largely disappeared.' Despite its successes — and they have been many — planning is generally seen as having lost its way. It is now under threat, as never before, both institutionally and philosophically. However, the need for effective planning is greater than it has ever been. There are major challenges facing this country — inner city decline, the north-south divide, the changing countryside, newly emerging patterns of employment — challenges which cannot and will not be solved by the simple operation of market forces.
John Blake, TCPA Annual Report 1987

In its most neutral sense, planning means deciding in advance how things should best be done in the future. When it involves the futures of a lot of people, as land use planning does, it presupposes that there is some basic level of agreement not only about how things should be done, but about what needs doing. The problem has always been that no such agreement ever existed.

Post-war planning got off to a good start, with regional and city plans showing clean-cut tower blocks and almost-empty dual carriageways, civic centres and landscaped parks. Everybody (who was asked) thought it was A Good Thing, and before long there was detailed planning legislation to Make It All Happen.

Right from the beginning, planning had to emphasize control and limitation rather than experiment and vision, since it rarely had the opportunity to do anything more than say yes or no to proposals from people who wanted the increase the value of their property. There have been exceptions, but there are very few examples of community-wide, community-based building projects in Britain.

As well as emphasizing the negative aspects of land use planning, planners also tend — often unwittingly — to have put barriers between themselves and the people they are employed to serve. To many people 'planning' means either faceless and insensitive 'expertize' or bungling bureaucracy — too often both.

There have always been people in planning and the related professions, however, who have retained the vision of grassroots social and environmental reform. In his influential 1972 book *After the Planners*, Robert Goodman outlined what he thought a good planner could be, given the will of the profession and the trust of its clientele: 'Instead of remaining the outside expert trying to resolve conflicting needs or simply "helping the poor", we can become participants in our own community's search for new family structures or other changing patterns of association, and participants in the process of creating physical settings which would foster these ways of life — in effect, we become a part of, rather than an expert for, cultural change.'

The Town and Country Planning Association

Founded in 1899 as the Garden City Association, the TCPA took its new name in 1941 at the beginning of the postwar boom in plan-making. Its aims are to work for the greening of towns and cities and the revitalization of the countryside. Having hit a rather staid patch in the 1970s, the TCPA has now turned into one of the most exciting professional organizations in Britain, paralleling the community architecture activities of the RIBA (see page 93) on a broader canvas.

On the practical side, the TCPA is sponsoring experiments in communal housing such as Lightmoor in Shropshire, where fourteen families are building their own energy-efficient village, complete with workshops and smallholdings. The Association also runs the Planning Bookshop at the Carlton House Terrace headquarters, widely thought to be one of the best bookshops on environmental issues in Britain.

Their monthly magazine, *Town and Country Planning*, is very good, while the recently established bi-monthly *Community Network* (published jointly with the RIBA Community Architecture Group and ACTAC — see page 93) is excellent if you are interested in self-help building, community participation in planning, and neighbourhood initiatives.

The TCPA also publishes a useful handbook called *Us Plus Them: How To Use The Experts To Get What People Really Want* (£2 plus 30p p+p from the TCPA). The title is self-explanatory; this explanation of how co-operation operates in practice shows that We and They can work together to produce results on the ground.

Membership of the TCPA is open to anyone, with reduced rates for students and OAPs.

Town and Country Planning Association
17 Carlton House Terrace
London
SW1Y 5AS
0(7)1-930 8903

Planning Aid for London

Since 1983 PAFL has been advising Londoners with planning problems how they can go about checking and upholding their rights. With three-full time staff and over a hundred volunteers, PAFL's successes are rarely spectacular, though it did help 25 Westway households to negotiate a change to plans for a motorway which would have run within a metre of their front doors. PAFL produce a helpful *Planning Problems?* leaflet in nine languages, and their services are free (though donations are gratefully accepted).

Planning Aid for London
100 Minories
London
EC3 1JY
0(7)1-702 0051

Practical Alternatives

David Stephens, who operates Practical Alternatives from Rhayader in Mid-Wales, is an alternative innovator. In the last five years PA has built up an extensive mail order catalogue of intriguing and energy-saving equipment, and fascinating explanatory literature to go with most of it. As well as a Green Accounts scheme and plans for a solar village, which is at the stage of beginning to be built. David can provide information, plans, advice and encouragement for a range of household options, including electric storage heaters, vertivent ducts and fans (for bringing near-ceiling heat down to floor level), eco-lavatories, clothes driers and pressure cookers.

The literature (send sae for a pricelist) includes an advice sheet called *Keeping Warm at Little Cost*, the *Catalogue and Guide to Home Energy Saving*, and the irregular but fascinating magazine called *Practical Alternatives*.

David Stephens' main concern is with energy (and thus cost) saving. He reckons that using a low level of continuous heating is by far the best way of dealing with draughts and dampness, and can reduce heating bills by around half; Bristol City Council among other clients have used his ideas with marked success. It will be interesting to see how the Rhayader solar village progresses.

*

The benefits of insulation are much overstated. Insulation is only of benefit if there is some heat to conserve, and most people who are genuinely trying to save fuel usually heat just one downstairs room, when roof insulation has negligible effect. Insulating the loft may keep bedrooms about 0.5°C warmer, which is of some significance in controlling condensation, but you'll hardly notice the difference in warmth, and won't save fuel unless you have heated and thermostatically controlled bedrooms.
Practical Alternatives 5, April 1987

Practical Alternatives
Victoria House
Bridge Street
Rhayader
Powys
LD6 5AG
0597 810929

For more information about heating, energy efficiency and energy saving, see the pages at the end of the 'Energy' section, pages 307-308.

Greenprints for a Healthier Life

One of the latest volumes from the proliferous John Seymour, this time in conjunction with Herbert Girardet, is *Blueprint for a Green Planet: How You Can Take Practical Action Today to Fight Pollution*. The battleground in question extends to the garden and the car, then spreads wider to embrace agriculture and water pollution, but the main emphasis is on the home. The information is good, the advice sound, though mostly of a fairly general nature. On the other hand, the authors have no illusions about the safety of nuclear power ('the risks are simply too great for us to place any faith in it') or the cleanliness of modern electricity generation ('there is no such thing as clean power').

Each chapter includes a 'Positive Action' guide, showing what you can do to reduce pollution in that sphere of your activities, and at the end is a small but adequate list of addresses and suggestions for further reading. Being a co-edition (published in several countries simultaneously) the drawings are all-purpose European, but clear and self-explanatory.

*

There is a law which applies to building roads, and it is this: no matter how much land you bury under tarmac to relieve traffic congestion, enough cars will be found to clutter it up. New roads destroy our natural heritage. Motorways are the worst example. These great stretches of concrete ravage the countryside, cutting across fields, knocking down woodland, bulldozing away hills and slicing in half villages and small towns. To the planner, the rights of people in the path of a new road are the lowest of priorities. In order to shave a few minutes off a journey they condemn households to live with the constant rush of traffic, or force people to leave areas where they were born and brought up.

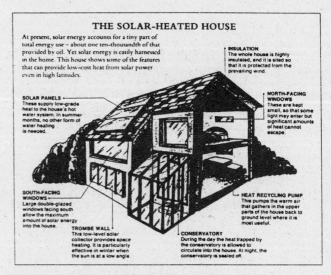

THE SOLAR-HEATED HOUSE

At present, solar energy accounts for a tiny part of total energy use – about one ten-thousandth of that provided by oil. Yet solar energy is easily harnessed in the home. This house shows some of the features that can provide low-cost heat from solar power even in high latitudes.

INSULATION The whole house is highly insulated, and it is sited so that it is protected from the prevailing wind.

SOLAR PANELS These supply low-grade heat to the house's hot water system. In summer months, no other form of water heating is needed.

NORTH-FACING WINDOWS These are kept small, so that some light may enter but significant amounts of heat cannot escape.

SOUTH-FACING WINDOWS Large double-glazed windows facing south allow the maximum amount of solar energy into the house.

TROMBE WALL This low-level solar collector provides space heating. It is particularly effective in winter when the sun is at a low angle.

CONSERVATORY During the day the heat trapped by the conservatory is allowed to circulate into the house. At night, the conservatory is sealed off.

HEAT RECYCLING PUMP This pumps the warm air that gathers in the upper parts of the house back to ground level where it is most useful.

Blueprint for a Green Planet
John Seymour and Herbert Girardet
Dorling Kindersley, 1988
£6.95

From Mangle To Microwave

Christina Hardyment's *From Mangle To Microwave* is a fascinating book about the history of domestic appliances. Did you know that in her *Household Management* Mrs Beeton devoted six pages to describing exactly how to do the weekly clothes wash? Or that the earliest vacuum cleaners looked like fire engines from which hoses were unfurled into the house? And whatever happened to the Vortex suction cleaner, where you just screwed the end of the hose into a hole in the wall and the dust ended up in a cylinder below stairs?

In this illuminating study of the hidden side of labour history, Christina Hardyment is very clear that manufacturers' profits depend upon the selling of ever more machinery, so standards of domestic cleanliness must always be slightly beyond the reach of the most dedicated housewife. Despite the plethora of supposed labour-saving devices, many women today spend more time on housework than their grandmothers did fifty years ago.

*

The old washday was as exhausting as swimming five miles of energetic breast stroke, arm movements and general dampness supplying an almost exact parallel.

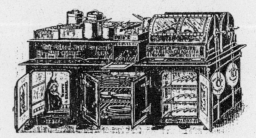

From Mangle to Microwave
Christina Hardyment
Polity Press, 1989
£15.00

Labour Savers or Millstones?

Having convinced yourself that you need a new washing machine or cooker, it is always worth checking the latest tests on that range of products in the Consumers' Association magazine *Which?* (see page 333). Do remember, however, that although the CA are thorough, there are important considerations they won't be testing (though even *Which?* is a good deal greener that it was). These are considerations which have a more or less direct impact on the environment and on your future, and you may like to keep them in mind as you go shopping for any new household appliance.

▶ How long will it last before you need to buy another new one?
▶ Can you do basic repairs to it yourself if necessary?
▶ Does the handbook cover minor repairs and basic maintenance as well as good operating instructions?
▶ Will you be able to get spares easily? For difficult-to-find spares for electrical appliances, the best suppliers are Rarespares in Banbury, who run an instant despatch service: St Johns Road, Banbury, Oxfordshire OX16 8NY; Tel: 0295 251568.
▶ Can later improvements be added without having to buy a new machine?
▶ Does it use energy as efficiently as possible?
▶ Is it adjustable if necessary to suit people of different heights and shapes?
▶ Is it made by people who receive a decent wage, or is it made by underpaid Third World women workers?
▶ Is any of it made from recycled materials?
▶ Will it be easy to sell or trade in when your needs change?

Some Common Household Appliances

Lighting
Though electric lights use relatively little energy, the average house contains twenty of them, so it does pay to switch off any that are not necessary. Long-life bulbs, especially the new low-energy bulbs you can now buy, are well worth looking out for, since even though they cost more to buy they use 20-30% of the electricity and can last up to eighty times as long as a conventional bulb. Wotan bulbs are available from many electrical wholesalers, but if you have problems finding them or want to see their technical information before you buy, write to Wotan Lamps, Wotan House, 1 Gresham Way, Durnsford Road, London SW19 8HU; Tel 0(8)1-947 1261. Full spectrum lighting (light which mimics daylight by incorporating more of the blue end of the spectrum) is now being recommended by many interior designers and health professionals. If you are one of the many people who feel 'the winter blues', it could be because you need more daylight. True-lite (Unit 5, Wye Industrial Estate, London Road, High Wycombe, Bucks HP11 1LH; Tel 0494 26051) specialize in this kind of lighting. Since True-lite lamps are fluorescent there will also be some energy saving.

Cookers
Whilst gas cookers are more energy efficient than electric ones, they produce carbon monoxide and nitrogen dioxide, both of which can cause breathing problems — make sure your cooker is well ventilated. Pilot lights often burn a substantial amount of gas; with most models (and if in doubt, check with the gas board) you can turn them off and use matches or an electrical 'sparker' instead.

Microwave cookers are very energy efficient, though many people don't like the idea of using a form of cooking which could harm them without their knowledge. Modern microwaves are very safe from this point of view, though the effect they have on our diet by encouraging processed ready-made dishes is causing concern to many nutritionists.

Most energy efficient (and healthiest) of all is a pressure cooker, preferably stainless steel since aluminium has been implicated in Alzheimer's disease.

Washing Machines
Automatic washing machines use a great deal of hot water, which is then simply pumped out into the sewage system. Hot fill machines are generally more efficient than cold fill, especially if your hot water is heated by gas or solid fuel. A twin-tub (or even a single tub with a wringer — you can still get them) is much more efficient. Most importantly (and even if this seems a silly question), do you actually need to wash your clothes as often as you do? (See also the section on washing powders on page 114).

Tumble Driers
Fresh air is the best place to dry clothes, and failing that an old-fashioned rack hanging from the kitchen ceiling or a clothes horse in front of a heater. It can be difficult if you live in a flat in a wet climate, but as Michael Allaby says in his book *Conservation at Home* (Unwin Hyman, 1988, £9.95), 'A tumble drier is an extremely efficient device for devouring money, with dry washing as a somewhat incidental by-product.'

Dishwashers
Apart from tumble driers, dishwashers are possibly the most inefficient machines you can buy, using vast amounts of hot water and hot air. If you have a very large household then perhaps a dishwasher is justifiable, but in a small household it is much easier, as well as cheaper, to wash up as you go along.

Refrigerators and Freezers
Before the days of refrigeration most houses had a good cool larder; being extremely energy efficient, larders are again being included in many new 'green' houses. The most important thing about a refrigerator as far as food storage is concerned is not so much that it is cold, as that it is airtight. In warm weather a fridge will certainly keep milk from turning and salads crisp, but in winter you would achieve the same effect by putting food in a cupboard at the same temperature as unheated air outside. Some foods, like eggs, gain nothing from being refrigerated. Think carefully about the size of the fridge you really need, and about keeping it somewhere that isn't centrally heated.

Freezers are great if you live miles from anywhere or grow your own fruit and vegetables in quantities, otherwise they will very rarely save you money (usually the opposite as you buy to keep the thing full), and food that has been frozen is never as nutritious as fresh food.

Televisions
Modern television tubes do not emit X-rays, though old and dirty ones may in small quantities. If you have a remote-control television, make sure (for the sake both of the planet and your purse) that you switch it off properly and don't just leave it on standby — this still uses considerable amounts of energy even though you might think the machine is 'off'. The biggest (technical) problem with television is that it can cause eye-strain; the other issues I won't even start to enumerate (though see page 218)!

Composting Toilets

In many parts of south-east and eastern Asia, the daily return of nightsoil to the land around the cities is an exercise in recycling which employs thousands of people and keeps millions of acres of farmland in good heart. In the civilized West we expect all our body wastes to disappear miraculously as though we had never produced them.

In fact the solid wastes from some of our domestic sewage does eventually find its way back to the land, though far more is dumped, untreated or partially treated, into Britain's rivers and coastal waters (see also page 80).

Seeing the products of our body as part of the constant cycling of nutrients within the biosphere is partly an issue of re-education, partly a question of developing appropriate technologies which combine an ecological understanding with general public acceptance. Ten or fifteen years ago adverts for composting ('dry') toilets could be found in the Sunday papers; now interest appears to have waned again. Techno-logies for producing useful organic fertilizer from sewage have improved, however. Several farms are now producing their own usable methane gas from quantities of animal manure, and on a much smaller scale, individual composting toilets are now very clean and acceptable (albeit expensive) affairs. For domestic use the best now available is an electrically-assisted aerobic toilet, such as those made in Sweden by Merus Milieu and distributed in Britain by Swedal. These ventilated and filtered toilets use very little electricity to produce chemical-free dry manure which you can use to great effect on your roses. They are not cheap at £600, but that's cheaper than a com-plete water and drainage system to provide the standard flush loo and it is UK approved. Swedal will send very comprehen-sive information.

Swedal Leisure (UK) Ltd
PO Box 10
Camberley
Surrey
GU17 7NX
0252 890427

Water Filters

Although the public water supply anywhere in Britain is not likely to give you any dread disease and is as germ free as any public supply in the world, an increasing number of people are concerned about the quality of the water that comes out of their taps (see page 42). Nitrate and lead pollution are but two subjects for growing concern.

Many turn to water filters to improve the quality by taking out the unwanted substances, but if these things were easy to filter out, rest assured that the water company would already have done it. Since water filters are flooding the market now, it's wise to be really check what is removed by the filter and what you have to replace, how often and how much it is. Look for reports from independent organizations like *Which?* maga-zine. You get what you pay for in this area!

Jug-type purifiers with an activated carbon cartridge absorb some of the organic detritus and improve the flavour of highly-treated tap-waters, but they don't remove nitrates, flourides, salts or heavy metals. Brita do a wide range, starting at about £10.

Plumbed-in filters include ceramic filtration, reverse osmosis or activated carbon filters. Starting at around £130 you can buy a water filter that you can have plumbed in under your kitchen sink and with varying degrees of efficiency they will remove chlorine, organic pollutants, fluoride, and some heavy metals, especially mercury (assuming that these pollutants are in your water supply). Most people do notice a considerable difference in the taste of their water when it is thus filtered, especially in urban areas where the water has been highly treated. Aquabrite, Researched Water Products and Everpure produce ranges for domestic and commercial users — all will gladly send information.

Many hi-tech industries enjoy telling us that their products are a spin-off of space technology; Bon Del water filters are one such. Starting at around £180 for a plumbed-in system, Bon Del is reckoned to be one of the best water filter systems currently available. General Ecology is another highly thought of filter manufacturer — you will pay over £300 for their Seagull IV filter, but they claim it removes every impurity you can think of from the water — including radioactive fallout.

Brita UK Ltd
Brita House
62-64 Bridge Street
Hersham
Walton-on-Thames
Surrey
KT12 1AT
0932 228348

Aquabrite
Philip Burrows, Agent
4 Chester Road
Winsford
Cheshire
CW7 2NQ
0606 554366

**Researched
Water Products**
Unit 2, Lancaster
Enterprise Workshops
White Cross
Lancaster
LA1 4XH
0524 843115

Everpure
Lympne Industrial Park
Hythe
Kent
CT21 4TL
0303 62211

Bon Del
11 Upper
Wimpole Street
London
W1M 7TD
0(7)1-486 1025

**General Ecology
UK Ltd**
64-70 High Street
Croydon
CR0 9XN
0(8)1-760 0522

Interior Decorating

With increasing awareness about environmental pollutants, 'natural' paints are now becoming available. Since more than 40,000 different chemicals are used in the manufacture of paints, varnishes and wood treatments, we are exposing ourselves to many toxins as we beautify our homes. As well as being toxic within the home, many products (such as acrylic paints, for example), are highly polluting during manufacture.

In Germany this has been an area of concern for some years, and products from that country are now becoming more widely available in Britain. Both Auro Organic Paints and Livos use natural ingredients like plant and tree oils, resins, minerals and earth pigments. The ranges include interior and exterior paints and wood finishes, furniture treatments, timber protection finishes and adhesives. You can even buy plant-based paints and crayons for artists.

When it comes to timber treatments for rot and infestation, the record on health and pollution risk is appalling. What's more, most of the treatments simply don't work. The London Hazards Centre (3rd Floor, Headland House, 308 Gray's Inn Road, London WC1X 8DS; Tel: 0(7)1-837 5605) has produced a frightening study of the effects of timber treatments on the people that work with them and the people whose homes are poisoned by them — if you are considering timber treatment for your home, don't do anything until you have read *Toxic Treatments* (1988, £5.95). Even Rentokil are now reviewing some of their products; they use 'ozone-friendly' insecticide aerosols, for example — but they still have a long way to go.

**Livos Natural
Paint Products**
27 Harvest Green
Newbury
Berkshire
RG14 6DW
0635 37988

**Auro Organic
Paints**
16 Church Street
Saffron Walden
Essex
CB10 1JW
0799 24744

The Environment Indoors

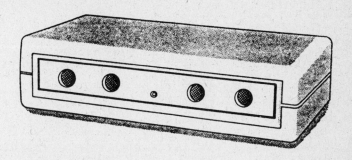

It's nice to be warm and cozy on a miserable winter's day, and we are told that efficient heating, insulation and draught-proofing (see pages 307-308) are the best ways to achieve this. As with almost everything, however, even this can be taken to extremes. A room which is fully insulated and draught-proofed, then heated, acts like a very slow oven, desiccating and threatening to suffocate its living occupants.

Ventilation
Luckily our draughtproofing efforts rarely succeed in blocking up all the holes in a room. If you got anywhere near to 100% success, you would eventually find it hard to breathe. In an old house, sufficient ventilation is rarely a problem (unless it is accompanied by a dampness problem); in an energy-efficient house it is important to leave some small spaces where air can leave and enter.

Humidifiers
With electric heating now being so popular, and particularly with the expansion of central heating, the chances are that your house will now be too dry to feel comfortable in. You can buy all sorts of fancy humidifiers to hang on your radiators, but jam jars filled with layers of absorbent material and kept topped up with water will do just as well.

Static Electricity and Ionizers
Much is currently being made of the advantages of negatively charged ions to the human system, and there are a score or more of different ionizers on the market, promising to make your indoor environment more invigorating and life-enhancing.

Again part of the problem is the design of modern indoor environments. An excessive build up of positive electrons — usually discharged straight to earth — builds up wherever we block their path by laying wall to wall carpeting, or insulating ourselves from the floor with rubber-soled shoes. With all the windows shut and in dry air, the positive ions have nowhere to go except to make our hair stand on end, and if you are sensitive to static electricity (as many people are) you may start to feel headachy.

If this happens, and before you decide to buy an ionizer to make negative ions to balance the excessive positive ones, try opening the window, keeping the air in the room a little moister, or taking your shoes and socks off to give you a better connection with the ground.

Should all this fail, or if your indoor environment cannot easily by adapted, then you could consider buying an ionizer.

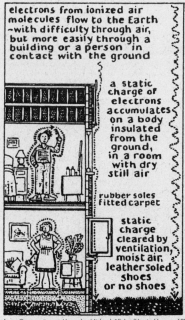

electrons from ionized air molecules flow to the Earth ~with difficulty through air, but more easily through a building or a person in contact with the ground

a static charge of electrons accumulates on a body insulated from the ground, in a room with dry still air

rubber soles fitted carpet

static charge cleared by ventilation, moist air, leather soled shoes or no shoes

Andy Martin, from Conservation at Home by Michael Allaby (Unwin Hyman, 1988, £9.95)

Air Ionizers

In our modern life we have created an environment that virtually eliminates negative ions from the atmosphere. Pollution from car exhausts, air conditioning, cigarette smoking, overcrowding and even breathing all contribute to this. In addition, fluorescent lighting, electrical and electronic equipment, air conditioning units and static-producing artificial fibres, clothes and curtains all reduce the level of negative ions and increase the positive.
John and Farida Davidson (see next page)

There is no doubt that air ionizers bring comfort and enormous relief to many people, especially sufferers from respiratory problems. Not only do ionizers create large numbers of negative ions; they also precipitate dust, smoke particles and fine pollen on nearby surfaces, thus taking them out of the air you breathe.

Ionizers usually cost between £30 and £40, unless you go for a combined ionizer and air purifier, which can cost up to £150 but is useful for a large modern office or shop with insufficient ventilation and fitted carpets.

You can either buy directly from a manufacturer (most ionizers sold in Britain are made in this country), or from a shop or mail order firm which stocks them (these days you can buy ionizers from almost any department store or furniture shop — though you won't find a very good selection). The best-known range is produced by Mountain Breeze in Lancashire, known to many as the firm where they all stop to meditate twice a day — whether or not this helps the ionizers, they are generally considered to be good value and reliable.

Two smallish but extremely helpful mail order firms, each carrying a good range of ionizers and providing advice and service, are Healthy Products in Derbyshire and Surplus Value in Stockport. Healthy Products especially promote the Mountain Breeze range, and are 'never knowingly undersold', so it's worth getting a quotation from them. They also sell ionizers with a 40-day money-back guarantee.

Joe Gorton at Surplus Value goes one better, with a 100-day trial period — less than one in every two hundred is returned. Surplus Value offer an excellent advice service, too, and are green-minded right down to recycling the packaging and using recycled paper for their stationery. If you are anywhere near Stockport, The Beehive at 40a High Street sometimes sells Surplus Value's returned and shop-soiled ionizers at bargain prices.

Mountain Breeze Air Ionisers
6 Priorswood Place
Skelmersdale
WN8 9QB
0695 21155

Healthy Products
3 Gordon Crescent
Broad Meadows
South Normanton
Derbyshire
DE55 3AG
0773 863034

Surplus Value
107 Lowndes Lane
Offerton
Stockport
Cheshire
SK2 6DD
061 483 9436

WHOLISTIC RESEARCH COMPANY

Wholistic Research (and Sales)

If Practical Alternatives (page 99) is an all purpose mail order firm for the appropriate technology end of the householder's needs, Wholistic Research Company fulfils the same function at the health and wellbeing end.

Five years ago John Davidson left his job at Cambridge University to set up a company marketing and promoting the best of what technology has to offer that is in harmony with the natural environment and its cycles. Many of the designs are John's own, for which he finds local manufacturers — one such is the Ovia natural fertility computer, into which a woman can feed information about her menstrual cycle and have instant feedback on the likelihood of being fertile on a given day.

Their range covers the things you would expect like ionizers and humidifiers, stainless steel cookware and juicers, together with many items which can be difficult to find. They sell full spectrum lighting units, VDU and television radiation screens, and water distilling units (an expensive alternative to water filters, but sometimes necessary if you are allergic to water pollutants).

The more specifically health oriented lines include pulsors ('to balance subtle energy fields'), herbal tablet makers, grain mills, bouncers (a mini-trampoline, not a nightclub attendant), iridology cameras, and a wide range of books on all the above subjects.

My favourite product from their catalogue is the humane Whole Live Mouse Trap ('catches one mouse at a time, but has enough space for food and bedding — mice are sensitive to cold. £5.55'), though all of Wholistic's literature provides stimulating reading.

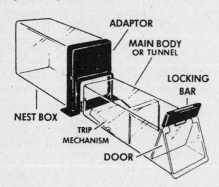

John and his naturopath wife Farida also write, and have published a fascinating handbook to the technologies they promote. Called *A Harmony of Science and Nature: Ways of Staying Healthy in a Modern World*, it costs £1.50 from WRC.

For your bundle of literature, send WRC an sae with two first class stamps on it.

Wholistic Research Company
Bright Haven
Robin's Lane
Lolworth
Cambridge
CB3 8HH
0954 781074

Household Equipment for the Disabled

Many people have difficulties with the way things are designed for household use — awkward handles and controls, parts you can't reach, attachments you can't understand — and some have more problems than others. Rather than design an environment where less agile people can feel at home, the tendency has been to deny more or less disabled people access to many of the gadgets and products that the able-bodied take for granted. But things have changed rapidly in recent years.

The Disabled Living Foundation (see also page 118) has a permanent display of aids on show at their Harrow Road headquarters in London. Here you can see an enormous range of furniture, equipment and living aids, including music for one-handed pianists, rotating car seats, grab rails and bath hoists, and much more.

Two friendly and comprehensive mail order services for aids for the disabled are Nottingham Rehab and Homecraft Supplies. A flip through the catalogues will convince you that any items designed specially for less agile people make very good sense for all people — plates with a slightly raised rim so you can get your fork under the peas, kitchen knives with L-shaped handles so you can get your full weight behind them, egg cups with a suction pad base.

Disabled Living Foundation
380-384 Harrow Road
London
W9 2HU
0(7)1-289 6111

Homecraft Supplies Ltd
Low Moor Estate
Kirkby-in-Ashfield
Nottinghamshire
NG17 7JZ
0623 754047

Nottingham Rehab Ltd
Ludlow Hill Road
West Bridgford
Nottingham
NG2 6HD
0602 234251

Freedom From Clutter

If you ever feel quite overwhelmed with all the stuff you have collected over the years, I can thoroughly recommend *Freedom From Clutter*. Don Aslett is hilarious and very practical; he hasn't earned his millions (well, thousands) as a professional de-junking consultant for nothing. If you can manage to ignore and excuse your unnecessary and unwanted clutter after reading this book then you are probably beyond help.

*

Getting the clutter out of our lives can and will rid us of more discouragement, tiredness and boredom than anything else we can do.

Freedom From Clutter
Don Aslett
Exley Publications, 1985
£5.95

Chairs

Did you know that you put half as much pressure again on your spine when you are sitting on an ordinary upright chair as when you are standing upright? Sitting puts more strain on the spine than standing or walking, and if you lean forwards while you are sitting, the strain increases very rapidly. Some of us spend a great deal of time sitting, so we might as well learn to do it as healthily and painlessly as possible.

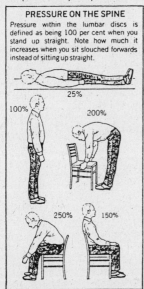

PRESSURE ON THE SPINE
Pressure within the lumbar discs is defined as being 100 per cent when you stand up straight. Note how much it increases when you sit slouched forwards instead of sitting up straight.

25%
100%
200%
250%
150%

Most tribal peoples very rarely sit on chairs as we do. They more often squat, with their spines unsupported. Westerners find it hard to balance without having something under their bottom, though the next best thing to the squatting posture is a 'balans'-type chair, of which more soon.

There is certainly nothing 'natural' about sitting on a horizontal seat, and thus no 'correct' way. The contortions we put our bodies into to sit on them are symptomatic of their inadequacy — a fixed back discourages you from turning your spine, prolonged knee crossing can encourage circulation problems, and the strain on your spine can do nasty things with your discs, especially if you already have back problems (see page 152).

So what is the alternative? The main thing is that the way you position your body should suit what you're doing. If you are relaxing, you may as well lie down — or the closest you can get to it (British Rail could learn a thing or two about this). Having big cushions around the place rather than fixed armchairs and sofas can help in this respect, as well as being much more flexible when it comes to room layout.

If you need to be sitting up to work, especially for long periods, think seriously about getting yourself a 'balans'-type chair — they're rapidly becoming so common that its unlikely that anyone in the office will laugh at you if you ask for one. At least get a comfortable version of the more conventional sort of office chair. For eating, the most comfortable position for your digestive system is standing up, so there's something to be said for informal stand-up buffets after all.

Cushions

It's getting easier to find big floor cushions and sag bags, but in general they are expensive, and you're much better off making them. Habitat do three-foot square cushions at around £13-17, as do some of the Habitat lookalikes, but you can make them for the cost of a couple of metres of decent upholstery material and a similar amount of fairly heavy sheeting for the inside layer. Stuff them with old clothes cut up fairly small. Some Third World craft shops (see page 288) have beautiful cushions from South America and South-East Asia — I have some appliquéd cushions from a Thai refugee camp which are almost too beautiful to sit on.

Back Supplies

The Back Shop in London stocks everything to do with the prevention and the alleviation of back pain. They have working chairs, home chairs, backrests, pillows — the list is endless. Send an sae for their mail order catalogue. Putnams produce a number of back aids to use with existing furniture, including attractive wooden beadmats to hang over your car seats which stimulate your circulation whilst driving and prevent those horrible sticky patches developing in hot weather. Putnam's inflatable cushions are great to carry when travelling, since you can stuff them in your bag uninflated, then blow them up when needed.

The Back Shop
24 New Cavendish
Street
London
W1M 7LH
0(7)1-935 9120

Putnams Back Care
333 Goswell Road
London
EC1V 7JT
0(7)1-278 9321/2

'Back Chairs'

This is the generic title for the backless chairs developed in Norway by a group of designers who collaborated with doctors and psychotherapists to design an alternative to the conventional chair which would be both comfortable and kind to the spine. Unfortunately, if you go for the Balans originals, they are not so comfortable to the purse. The cheapest of the Balans range is their metal-framed non-adjustable stool, which weighs in at around £60. By the time you get to the useful adjustable versions, the 'Wing' office chair and the neat and pleasing 'Multi', you're talking about £196, with prices going on up to over £500. Various people stock Balans chairs; the address below is one of the biggest importers.

Balans Chairs
Harmill
Grovebury Road
Leighton Buzzard
Bedfordshire
LU7 8RX
0525 383100

What To Do When You Feel The Strain

When you've been sitting up at the desk for hours on end the best thing you can do is get someone to give your back a massage. Failing that, try lying flat on your back on the floor for a few minutes with a book under your head, your knees up, and your arms spread out. Doing this regularly can help ease your back enormously.

Failing that, here are a few exercises from Michael Reed Gach's *Bum Back Book* (see page 152):

▶ Sit up straight on an ordinary upright chair. Put your arms behind you (and behind the chair back) and interlace the fingers. Breathe in and let your head drop back. Keeping them together and straight, lift your arms up behind your back. Breathe out, bring your head forward, and relax your arms. Do this twice more.
▶ Now slowly bend forward and grasp the sides of your heels with your hands. Gradually lower your body forward until your eyesockets meet your knees. Take five deep breaths in this position.
▶ Now sit up and interlace your fingers behind your neck. Slump forward and bring your elbows in towards each other. Breathe in, lift your elbows and sit up, then breathe out and slump forward again. Take three long deep breaths as you do this cycle of movements.

Kitchen Equipment

In many ways it is helpful to compare kitchen equipment with gardening or woodworking tools. A well designed and high quality knife or saucepan should, if looked after, last a lifetime. Since basic kitchen equipment has such a long life, it is good advice to buy the best that you can afford.

As in the garden or toolshed, moreover, the last twenty years has seen a massive increase in the variety of gadgetry you can buy for your kitchen, which makes it very hard to sort out what you really need from what the manufacturers would like you to buy. A great deal depends upon how often you will need to use a particular tool, and whether it does something which is difficult or excessively time-consuming to do any other way, though the chances are that if you can't decide whether or not you need something, then you don't.

This is particularly true of electrical equipment, where you can buy machines which do virtually all your food preparation for you. If you do need a food processor, again the best plan is to go for a reliable, sturdy, long-lasting machine which should last for many years with little maintenance. David Mellor (see below) recommends the Braun UK20 Multipractic food processor at around £65 and the Krups 4004 Mixer at around £40. No food processor, however, will ever chop a mixed salad like a professional cook with a sharp knife.

David Mellor

Before you buy any kitchen equipment at all it is well worth investing a pound in the two catalogues from David Mellor's specialist cook's shops. *Basic Cooking* provides a fully illustrated introduction to the commonest kitchen tools, with a heavy emphasis on the simple, efficient and good-looking; *Specialist Cooking* leads you on into the world of lattice pie makers, game pie moulds, alphabet cutters, yogurt thermometers and trout grillers.

The David Mellor shops are a delight to browse in. If you decide to buy, kitchen equipment bought here will almost certainly be more expensive than you'll pay elsewhere, but the quality is always of the best and the staff are very helpful. And you'll find some cheapish things too, like a birch twig beater for sauces or a wooden porridge spirtle. If you can't get to one of their shops they do a full mail order service.

David Mellor
4 Sloane Square,
London SW1W 8EE
(0(7)1-730 4259)

66 King Street,
Manchester M2 4NP
(061 834 7023)

Lakeland Plastics

Downmarket from David Mellor, but equally helpful and with an efficient mail order service, is Lakeland Plastics in Windermere. Although kitchen plastics are their speciality, their twin catalogues (*Everything for Home Cooking* and *Everything for the Fridge, Freezer and Microwave*) are indeed pretty comprehensive, and provide excellent value for money. Traditional farmhouse kettles (hard to find these days), jam pot covers, a petal folding steamer which fits inside any saucepan — very useful these — for £3.25. Their Spring 1990 catalogue has started stocking a Homekind range, 'tough on dirt, kind to the environment', including a Homekind sponge made from cotton fibres and 'regenerated cellulose'. All this and much more in a hundred pages of catalogue, either by mail order or from their shops at Windermere or Chester (11 Eastgate Row North; Tel: 0244 313758), or York (87a Low Petergate; Tel: 0904 627737).

Lakeland Plastics
Alexandra Buildings
Windermere
Cumbria
LA23 1BQ
09662 8100

Ladderback

Ladderback Co-operative

Basket-making is one of Britain's best-loved traditional crafts, and as it appears on more and more evening class programmes it seems that we might be moving back towards more ecological containers for our logs and houseplants. Rosemary Hawksford and the Ladderback Co-operative in York has been making and restoring willow baskets for eight years; they also specialize in restoring cane-seated chairs. What Rosemary especially likes is commissions for producing baskets and woven furniture to fit into existing spaces — from bottle containers to medallion-backed sofas.

Ladderback Co-operative
St Mary's Church
Bishophill Junior
York
YO1 1EN
0904 644788

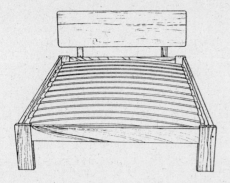

Beds

Chiropractors, osteopaths and others who have to deal with the back problems created by poor posture are generally agreed that the beds that most people sleep in do not let the body rest in a truly relaxed position.

If the mattress is too soft it will not support you properly, and every time you move you will have to climb out of the hollow your body has created. A good mattress is firm and should not sag at all. If your mattress does sag, it may well be the springs in the base rather than the mattress itself; this can be rectified by putting a board between the base and the mattress. Ideally the board should cover the whole area of the base.

Neck support pillows have been around for a long time for people with neck injuries; you can now buy these pillows, which have a hollowed out central portion, in many bedding and health shops.

One of the fastest shifts in household practice in the last decade has been that from sheets and blankets to the duvet or continental quilt. More than 40% of Britons now prefer sleeping under a downie, and quantities of un-needed blankets are finding their way to charity shops. A novel recent development is a three-in-one duvet — a lightweight summer duvet and a medium weight spring/autumn one which velcro together and keep you snug through the winter. You should be able to find this kind in any good bedding shop. Down duvets are best if you can afford them, though some artificial fillings are very good — with duvets you really do get what you pay for. Because you don't tuck duvets in it's a good idea to buy them a good three inches longer and wider than the mattress they are to go on.

Futons

Ten years ago futons were almost unheard of in Britain; today futon shops are opening in chic neighbourhoods all over Britain.

Futons are what the Japanese traditionally sleep on — layers of cotton wadding (usually three) held together by brightly coloured ties inside a closely woven cotton cover. During the day they are rolled up against the wall, where they can be used to sit on, or alternatively they can be laid over a wooden base to make a comfortable sofa.

The enormous advantages of a futon are its flexibility as a piece of furniture, and the support it gives to a resting body. Some futon manufacturers also make mattresses by doubling the layers of wadding — this also gives a firm bed but it cannot be rolled up.

In London, futon manufacture and selling is pretty big business, The Futon Company being the leaders with several branches — they do a catalogue and a mail order service. The Futon Factory in Balls Pond Road is a good place for original ideas, and you can see the futons being made (they also do a catalogue and mail order).

The Futon Company
654a Fulham Road
London
SW6 5RU
0(7)1-736 9190

The Futon Factory Ltd
192 Balls Pond Road
London N1 4AA
0(7)1-226 4477

For futons outside London, there is Electra Colios's Reading-based Full Moon Futons. She makes her own futons to order, offering personal and friendly advice as required. There is the well-established and reliable Pennine Futons in Huddersfield, while Mariko-San in Edinburgh makes and sells a wide range of futons and bases at very reasonable prices, including high beds and frames that you can walk/work/play under.

Full Moon Futons
20 Bulmershe Road
Reading
Berkshire
RG1 5RJ
0734 65648

Mariko-San
109 Restalrig Road
Leith
Edinburgh
EH1 1JY
031 553 3502

Pennine Futons
Cellars Clough Mill
Manchester Road
Marsden
Huddersfield
0484 846748

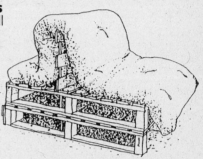

Alphabeds

Alphabeds (of the 'Beds for Greens' adverts) make solid pine bedframes of various sizes and styles, four different sorts of futon, mattresses using organic or recycled materials as stuffing, and unbleached cotton sheets. With the increasing demand for natural materials in bedding Limericks, the well-known linen-by-post people, have expanded their range to include several natural fibre lines including cotton-covered mattresses, fleecy cotton blankets and pure wool underblankets.

Alphabeds
16 Broadway Market
London
EC8 4QJ
0(7)1-249 6100

Limericks Linens
Limerick House
117 Victoria Ave
Southend-on-Sea
Essex
SS2 6EL
0702 343486

Ecological Furniture

Paul Griffiths' of Ecological Furniture makes tables, benches, cupboards, desks — anything you ask for — from native or recycled hardwoods, using only handtools and normally finishing the furniture with a natural product. He also aims to plant five times as many trees as he uses. A six seat dining table in oak will cost about £800. He doesn't have a list because he works on commission and likes to discuss both the article you want and his philosophy of working.

The three-drawer ash chest that was used in the Green Home Exhibition (page 103) was made by Treske, a company in North Yorkshire which makes all its furniture from home-grown hardwoods. From a stickback kitchen chair in beech at £44 to a four door Northallerton style dresser at £1,115, they make a huge range; send 50p for their excellent catalogue full of lovely drawings. Treske has a shop in London (5 Barmouth Road, Earlsfield, SW18 2DT; Tel 0(8)1-874 0050), and their workshop at Thirsk is also a retail outlet.

Ecological Furniture
Vailima
Broomhall
Nantwich
Cheshire
0270 780626 (evenings)

Treske Ltd
Station Works
Thirsk
North Yorkshire
YO7 4NY
0845 22770

Recycling

Recycling

Some throwaway facts:

▶ 60 million tonnes of waste are dumped or burned in the UK each year, half of it industrial, a third of it domestic and the rest commercial.
▶ It costs £800 million every year to deal with all this 'unwanted' material.
▶ 8.7 million tonnes of paper and board are consumed in the UK in a year, of which only 35% is recycled. Our consumption of paper involves the felling of 130 million trees each year. Wood and paper pulp imports currently run at 14 million tonnes a year, costing £5.5 billion.
▶ 89% of the waste from Greater London is taken by road, rail and barge to landfill sites in seven counties. Some London boroughs pay over £30 a tonne to get rid of their waste. Already there are trainloads of waste travelling 60 miles west to Didcot to bury waste, and they are passed by trains from Bristol carrying waste 100 miles east to a site in Buckinghamshire!
▶ If put one on top of another, the metal cans used in Britain in a year (80% of them drinks cans) would reach from the Earth to the Moon, back again, and half-way there again. If laid out flat, the metal would cover an area of sixty square kilometres.
▶ In Britain we produce 700 million aerosol cans each year, even though the cans are dangerous if burned or punctured, cannot be recycled, and often use a chemical propellant which may harm the protective ozone layer in the atmosphere.
▶ The average British family produces the equivalent of six trees' worth of waste, together with 600 cans, 90lb of plastic, 350lb of glass, 1,12lb of metal, 100lb of food and 21lb of clothing and textiles.

Happily, since the first edition of *Green Pages* was published there has been a marked change in public awareness about waste, and a desire to do something. In a survey carried out by the *Daily Telegraph* and Gallup in late 1989 io launch a county-by-county series of recycling directories (see next page), 74% of the public said they were dissatisfied with the government's policy on recycling. 47% said they currently recycle some of their household rubbish, but 81% said they would do it if they had facilities close by. Forty-three per cent of British housewives feel guilty about the amount of rubbish they throw away each day, a fact which emerged from an opinion poll by Addis, the rubbish-bin firm. They found that people would like more information on products than can be recycled, less packaging in general, and industry to use more recycled paper.

But though the public seems to be crying out for recycling, the provision of recycling facilities has a long way to go to catch up. Providing facilities costs money and needs careful organization. The waste then has to be reprocessed and in some regions there just aren't the factories prepared to take it, so waste has to be trucked a long way. It still appears to be 'cheaper' to produce many products from raw materials than to use reprocessed waste, and there is an unwillingness to

make tax and subsidy changes that would shift the balance. We end up with nonsenses like the collapse of the British waste paper market in 1989 because the compulsory recycling of paper in the USA flooded our pulp mills with cheap, subsidized waste.

And while there is a growing awareness of the importance of buying recycled goods, there is still a great deal of cultural inertia to overcome. You can now buy recycled toilet paper in almost every supermarket, but I still quite often hear people saying 'Recycled toilet paper? Ughhh'.

Modern technocracy . . . postulates infinite resources on one side and an infinite dump on the other. Of course, the technocrats know that resources eventually are used up but they say, 'Well once we use up petroleum, we will develop nuclear fission energy and then nuclear fusion energy. And when we have used up all our iron, copper, aluminium, selenium and so on, we can always find substitutes.' So in effect they believe in infinite resources. And when you do something like putting lead in gasoline or mercury in paints or copper and mercury in pesticides, then you believe in an infinite dump too. These very precious metals are being used in such a way that they become uniformly and atomically spread over the planet, with the result that they can never be recovered. This model is lunacy. It doesn't work. In the closed model system of nature there is no waste. The residues of one are the resources of another. When Indians defecate in the forest, they are fertilising the trees. But when we of industrialised society put dirt into the ground or a river, we are creating pollution, because we are putting it in the wrong place. Sanitary engineers see something fundamentally undesirable in garbage and industrial development, so they do things like build enormous dumps to bury it in, and then put trees over it. But it hasn't disappeared; it's just like sweeping dirt under the carpet.
José Lutzenberger, in *The New Economic Agenda*
(see page 245)

Though recycling is an important green concept, it is still best to produce as little waste as possible. The basic guidelines for a green approach to recycling are simple in outline, more complex in practice, though the next few pages should help you to explore practical ways in which you can help the recycling effort.

Simply put, the guidelines are:

▶ Use only what you really need; keep the amount of rubbish you produce to a minimum.
▶ Use things that come with as little packaging as possible.
▶ Avoid using things which cannot be recycled, and chemicals which harm the environment.
▶ Wherever possible use containers which can be used again without having to be recycled.
▶ Mend rather than throw away.
▶ When it comes to disposing of things, recycle as much as possible — organic matter as compost, paper and glass and metal to recycling schemes.

You don't have to be fanatical or purist to be a recycler — just someone who cares about the future.

Recycling Directories

The production of a nationwide series of recycling directories means that for the first time everyone in Britain will have at their fingertips information on recycling facilities available in their neighbourhood. Let us hope this will lead to a greater use of existing facilities and to greater pressure on local authorities and supermarkets to increase the the number of recycling facilities.

Thus writes Jonathon Porritt in the introduction to each of the 51 county-by-county *Recycling Directories*, published jointly by *The Daily Telegraph* and Friends of the Earth at the end of 1989 (yes, on recycled paper). Each directory lists details of the collection points or organizations where you can take glass, waste oil, paper, cans, other metals, batteries, plastics, textiles and furniture. Where there aren't facilities available the gaps are glaringly obvious, which gives you a chance to pressurize your local authority. Peppered throughout with frightening facts and ending up with a page of addresses for further information, the relevant local directory should be in every home.

Order the directory for your area by sending £1.35 (£1 plus p+p) to Recycling Directories, A3/4 Lanterns Court, Millharbour, London E14 9TU (cheques and postal orders payable to *The Daily Telegraph*, or you can order using Access or Visa on 0(7)1-538 8288).

Friends of the Earth produces a wide range of information about recycling — send a large sae to their recycling department.

Friends of the Earth
Recycling Department
26-28 Underwood Street
London
N1 7JQ
0(7)1-490 1555

Waste Watch

Waste Watch is a national initiative which supports and encourages community based recycling schemes and provides a channel for voluntary organizations to have a voice in waste management at a national level. Their *Recycling — a Practical Guide for Local Groups* includes masses of very useful information including a stack of *Recycling Fact Leaflets*, guidelines on how to start a group (with many examples of success stories), information about how to produce a local waste directory, contact and reading lists, and a variety of information booklets.

*

SWAP (Save Waste and Prosper, Leeds) began in 1977 with more than 70 small centres, manned by volunteers one day each month, collecting paper, textiles and foil. In 1978 bottle banks were introduced and by 1980 there were Save-A-Can skips and an experimental PET-A-Box collection for plastics. Now there are 13 permanent collection centres around the city of Leeds with containers for paper, glass and cans. Since August 1977 the SWAP scheme has collected over 32,000 tonnes of recyclable material, realising a profit of more than £200,000.

Waste Watch
c/o National Council for Voluntary Organisations
26 Bedford Square
London
WC1B 3HU
0(7)1-636 4066

Paper

Recycling paper makes sense in many ways.

It makes ecological sense, since less trees have to be felled and less of Scotland's hills and plateaux have to be planted with conifers which acidify the soil and silt lakes and rivers, or tropical rainforests felled and replaced with eucalyptus plantations.

It makes environmental sense, since less paper has to be burned or otherwise disposed of. This means less landfill and less 'waste' heat to add to the global atmospheric heat and pollution problem. Less chemicals are used in recycling than in the pulping process, thus easing the pressure on river animals and plants in paper-making areas.

It makes economic sense, since there is a 40% saving in energy if paper is made from waste paper rather than from pulp. Because it is cheaper to produce recycled paper, consumer pressure can bring prices down to a point where recycled paper for many applications is cheaper than non-recycled paper. Paper recycling also creates useful jobs, and can make money for the collectors — newsprint is worth up to £20 a tonne and high quality paper and cardboard waste is even more valuable, selling at up to £100 a tonne.

About a quarter of the 1.1 million copies of The Daily Telegraph read each day contain the re-pulped, de-inked fibres of wastepaper. But less than a fifth of all Britain's newspapers are recycled — most waste used by British newsprint mills comes straight from printing plants or is imported. Each tonne of recycled paper saves the felling of 17 trees.

Recycling Directory (see above)

In response to my request for information from the British Paper and Board Industry Federation, they said in their encouraging reply: 'The tissue mills are using an increasing amount of waste paper in their products, but are not necessarily anxious to tell the public so, since it conflicts with the "soft, clean, white image" they try to convey. That really leaves printing and writing papers, where public demand could really influence the mills' decisions to promote the sale of stationery etc. made from recycled fibre.'

You can buy recycled personal stationery whenever possible, but have you also thought of leaning on your local authority, employer, health board, school, college and bank? At a time when companies want to appear as green as possible there is really no need for any office not to stock up with recycled paper, since it is now available for practically every application and at prices which compare favourably with virgin paper (see page 251 for more about the 'green office'). Most paper and office sundries suppliers are now carrying recycled paper products, but if you have problems or need recycled paper in bulk, contact one of the suppliers on the next page.

The Main Suppliers

Conservation Papers

Conservation Papers started life as Conservation Books seventeen years ago in Reading. Others are now providing that service and Conservation Papers have become the marketing agents for a variety of recycled papers. They have samples available, can tell you where to get supplies, and have a list of stockists. In the same building is Forestsaver (with the same phone number, but ask to be put through to Forest-saver) who are CP's wholesale supply side. I'm glad to see that through all the changes they still sell the Conservation Society envelope re-use labels (they cost less than a penny each if you buy them in bulk) which say boldly: 're-use paper; save trees' — to date they've sold over 40 million of them.

Forestsaver also has a personal stationery mail order department based in Bristol; send for their full-colour catalogue containing details of all types of recycled paper products.

Conservation Papers/Forestsaver
228 London Road
Reading
Berkshire
RG6 1AH
0734 668611

Forestsaver
Freepost PO Box 1
Portishead
Bristol
BS20 9BR
0272 845559

Paperback

Founded in 1983, Paperback are the 'big time' of the paper recycling companies, though very human with it. This workers' co-operative supplies paper for copying, duplicating and printing, and a range of stationery items, and they are the people to go to if you have a big project (like this book) in mind and think that recycled paper can be used. Their regu-larly-updated price list is informative and helpful.

Paperback Ltd
Unit 2, Bow Triangle Business Centre
Eleanor Street
London
E5 4NP
0(8)1-980 2233

Greenscene

The main business of the Greenscene shop in Exeter's Fore Street is the sale of recycled paper, general stationery, office supplies like computer listing paper and Opti toxic-free correction fluid, though they also sell other 'green' lines like cruelty free cosmetics, books and recycled paper gifts. Green-scene supplies recycled paper to the RSPB, CND and the Devon Trust among others.

Greenscene Co-operative
123 Fore Street
Exeter
Devon
EX4 3JQ
0392 215969

Earthwrite

Earthwrite Co-operative was established early in 1987 to provide the same service in the north as Paperback does in the south — selling paper in bulk to organizations and businesses, but also selling copier and duplicator paper by the ream if that's all you need. They also sell notepads, card and boards, sugar paper, and bright art and play papers — all recycled.

Earthwrite Co-operative
Unit 1b
Carlisle House
Carlisle Street East
Sheffield
S4 7QN
0742 739123

The Smaller (But No Less Important) Suppliers

FoE Birmingham

Friends of the Earth in Birmingham have been selling recycled paper for twelve years, and now have an impressively efficient business operating from their Digbeth shop. They're not quite as cheap as Paperback and Earthwrite, especially if you're buying in bulk, but if you live in the West Midlands they have a good range and deliver orders (over £30) free.

Friends of the Earth (Birmingham) Ltd
54-57 Allison Street
Digbeth
Birmingham
B5 5TH
021 643 7336

FoE Sheffield

A smaller Friends of the Earth operation in Sheffield supplies personal stationery and paper for crafts and playgroups, and acts as an information centre for green activities in Sheffield. They also sell a delightful *Little Home Paper-making Book* which explains clearly how you can make your own paper.

Sheffield Friends of the Earth
Voluntary Action
69 Division Street
Sheffield
S1 4GE
0742 721896

PaperWorks

PaperWorks, recently established in a little shop off Totnes's High Street, carries a range of recycled paper products including coloured paper and board, kitchen rolls, notepads and greetings cards.

PaperWorks
10 High Street
Totnes
Devon
TQ9 5RY
0803 867009

Arboreta

Arboreta is associated with Avon Friends of The Earth, and will deliver within an 80 mile radius of Bristol. Like PaperWorks, Arboreta carries a good representative range of recycled papers and paper products.

Arboreta Papers
St John's Street
Bedminster
Bristol
BS3 4JF
0272 660478

Traidcraft

Traidcraft (see page 240) markets a wide range of recycled paper products, all of them oriented to the individual con-sumer rather than the commercial customer. They also sell recycled toilet rolls and kitchen roll, though these are becom-ing increasingly easy to find at your local wholefood shop or supermarket.

Printing on Recycled Paper

Conscious that only a quarter of Britain's waste paper is currently recycled, London-based printers Disc To Print (25 Liddell Road, off Maygrove Road, NW6 3EW; Tel: 0(7)1-625 5225) print only on recycled paper. They will take on any printing job, from books to letterheads, on a wide variety of paper weights and colours.

Metal Recycling

The recovery and recycling of some metals is well-established in Britain. Specialized scrap merchants buy ferrous metals (iron and steel), copper, tin, lead and zinc, and in any city you will find merchants with a list of today's buying prices per ton chalked up at the yard gate.

The same is not true, however, of cans, some of them tin-plated steel, some aluminium. Britons use nearly 13.4 billion cans each year, then throw them away — that's nearly 250 for every adult, child and baby in the country (I wonder who's using mine?). Three quarters of the beer cans are tin-plated steel; three quarters of the soft drinks cans aluminium.

Demand for aluminium as a lighter substitute for steel has grown considerably in recent decades. It is used for everything from beverage cans to household appliances and jet aircraft. Some analysts believe that up to 80 per cent of all aluminium could be recycled, but in 1981 the figure for recycled aluminium was closer to 30 per cent. This has meant more bauxite mining and greater demand for the coal needed in extracting aluminium from the bauxite. Producing raw aluminium uses up to 20 times as much electricity as does recycling the metal. As energy costs rise, so the case for increasing the amount of aluminium recycled gains ground.

John McCormick, *The User's Guide to the Environment*, Kogan Page, 1985, £7.95

The most obvious advice when it comes to cans is — don't use them save in exceptional circumstances. If you must buy things in cans, then do whatever you can to ensure that they are recycled. For a start, don't litter. Keep cans separate from other 'rubbish', and find out what you can do with them — get a copy of your local recycling directory (see page 109). The Save-a-Can scheme run by The Can Makers (see below) now has over 200 skips in 150 towns in England and Wales, so if there is a can skip near you, use it. The cans put into these skips (of all varieties except aerosols) are collected regularly and sorted for recycling, using technology which has developed rapidly in the last ten years.

Even if Save-a-Can doesn't operate in your area, you can still save aluminium for recycling. The Aluminium Can Recycling Association will provide an information pack, including a list of aluminium can recycling centres. They also produce a newsletter, and will send an initial supply of sacks and magnets to any group wanting to start a local aluminium recycling scheme. The magnets are to test the cans to see whether they're aluminium or steel — either you have to sort them or check that your local recycling centre has the facilities. If you've gone to all the trouble of collecting cans and paying a haulier to take them to an aluminium recycling centre, you won't want steel cans in with them. Aluminium cans are worth about 1p each.

Aluminium is the 100% recyclable drinks container material. After collection and baling it goes back to the aluminium rolling mill. It's remelted, rolled into coilstrip, made into cans, filled, then returned to the consumer. But why recycle aluminium ? It can save energy. Reclaimed aluminium is processed and melted at an 95% energy saving compared with making aluminium from ore. It can save natural resources. The more reclaimed aluminium we use, the less raw material we need. It can improve the environment. It keeps our country tidy and reduces domestic waste. It can help the economy. Recycling aluminium cans creates new business for the UK.

ACRA Information Pack, 1989

All very nice, but why use the wretched cans in the first place? British Steel Tinplate now has a very plush *Information Pack*, some of which is printed on recycled paper, a good example of the growing campaign by packaging companies in the face of arguments in favour of cutting down on packaging. 'Steel cans,' they say, 'are an extremely energy-efficient form of packaging'. Who are they kidding?
The Can Makers, a rather unholy alliance of all the manufacturers of cans in Britain, has to appear to be taking public concern into account yet at the same time ensure the continued growth of all its sponsors — not a job I would like to take on. Their literature includes an up-to-date Save-A-Can site list and a leaflet called *Are You Green About Recycling?*

Aluminium Can Recycling Association
Suite 308
I-Mex House
52 Blucher Street
Birmingham
B1 1QU
021 633 4656

British Steel Tinplate
PO Box 101
Velindre
Swansea
West Glamorgan
SA5 5AW
0792 310011

The Can Makers
36 Grosvenor Gardens
London
SW1 0EB
0(7)1-629 9621

Aluminium Foil

The Foil Container Bureau (representing the interests of the makers of milk bottle tops, kitchen foil and the trays you get your Chinese takeaway in), caught in the same double bind, has realized that if it doesn't do something soon it will get left behind in the recycling stakes. They say that they are about to launch a new recycling initiative soon, but that's what they were saying two years ago . . .

Foil Container Bureau
38 and 42 High Street
Bidford on Avon
Warwickshire
B50 4AA
0789 773347

Recycling Glass

So far, glass is Britain's best effort at recycling. This is partly because glass is fairly easy to recycle, partly because it's easier to keep separate from other rubbish, partly due to the efforts of the Glass Manufacturers' Confederation. There are now over 4,000 bottle banks in about 450 local authority areas, but still only 16% of our glass is being recycled compared to more than 50% in Holland. The Department of Industry and the glass manufacturers have made a commitment to double the number of bottle banks by 1991.

But recycling bottles still isn't the best solution. If you buy soft drinks in East Germany, Denmark, or some states of the USA, the glass bottles have by law to be re-usable. It's a stupid waste only to use bottles once before they are smashed and melted down, so as far as possible don't buy drinks which come in no-deposit-no-return bottles. We've been swayed into thinking it's for our convenience; it isn't, it's for their profit. Buy only bottles — like milk bottles — which are returnable. Give used wine bottles to your wine-making friends.

If there isn't a bottle bank in your area, contact the local authority Environmental Health Department and ask why not. The British Glass Manufacturers' Confederation are happy to provide information on glass recycling (not quite so happy to tell you about re-use!), and can tell you where your nearest bottle bank is. If you ask them they will also send you a copy of the useful *Expanding Glass Recycling* report compiled by the Local Authority Recycling Advisory Committee in January 1987. They also have a 20-minute video, 'Banking on Glass', which can be hired free of charge.

British Glass Manufacturers' Confederation
Northumberland Road
Sheffield
S10 2AU
0742 686201

And Plastics?

Plastics make up about 20% of the volume of domestic waste, and most of it goes straight to the dump. Whilst industrial plastic is often recycled on site, the wide variety of domestic plastics (about 50 different types) makes recycling more of a problem. As supermarkets increasingly stamp plastic containers with an identifying mark, the separation of plastics will make recycling a lot easier. Tesco has now started to provide plastic banks, the British Plastics Federation is involved in two pilot schemes, and the British Soft Drinks Industry is sponsoring a scheme for transparent recyclable drink bottles.

As with other forms of waste, you can do a lot to not create plastic waste in the first place. When you go shopping don't always automatically ask for a new plastic carrier bag — remember to take some with you to the shops. Don't buy overpackaged items, and don't buy 'individual portion' foods (the additional cost always comes back to the consumer). Re-use containers whenever possible. See page 27 for more about packaging.

P.D. Technical Mouldings, who make the Unibank bottle bank skips, now also produce a Multibank skip, which is segregated to take waste paper, cans, plastic and glass. These can either be bought or rented — if you are interested or want to draw the attention of your local authority to them, contact PDTM at Rotation House, 20 Mayday Road, Thornton Heath, Surrey CR4 7HL (0(8)1-689 4336).

Every so often one manufacturer or another comes up with a new 'biodegradable' plastic — the latest being a project from ICI to produce one based on sugar. So-called 'biodegradable' plastics actually only break into smaller pieces of plastic, although the starch in them does degrade in sunlight. But most domestic plastic waste is encased in yet more plastic (black sacks) and dumped in land fills where the sunlight never penetrates. Under these conditions your 'biodegradable' plastic degrades into toxic compounds which do great damage to the soil and the subsoil. There is (as yet) no such thing as a safely-disposable plastic.

A *Directory of UK Companies Involved in Recycling of Plastics* is available from The British Plastics Federation.

British Plastics Federation
5 Belgrave Square
London
SW1X 8PD
0(7)1-235 9483

Recycling Resources

Resource: The Quarterly Review of Reclamation, Re-use and Recycling is an excellent magazine put together by Avon Friends of the Earth. It isn't afraid to take on big industry, and will keep you informed and up-to-date on developments in this rapidly-expanding field.

Resource
Avon Friends of the Earth
Avon Environment Centre
Junction Road
Brislington
Bristol
BS4 3JP
0272 715446

Warmth from Waste

'Don't waste,' says the *Warmer Bulletin*, 'use it!'

Britons produce 30 million tonnes of household and commercial rubbish every year, most of which could be mass-burned or recycled as fuel. The Government itself has admitted that energy equal to 8,500,000 tonnes of coal would be available annually if we turned our waste into energy, or about £400 million worth at today's energy prices. Only 6% of Britain's waste is recycled, compared with 76% in Luxembourg and 75% in Denmark. There is change afoot in Britain — five local authorities now operate incinerators producing electricity or steam for district heating; there are eight plants producing fuel pellets from waste — but much more could be done. Recycling and economic sense come together on the warmth-from-waste issue in a way that your councillor or MP will find it hard to ignore.

The Golden Rule of recycling is that growth in the volumes handled is limited by demand for the product rather than its availability. Until a market is found, the recovered material can only be considered as waste. Do not be disappointed if the recycling project does not make a lot of money. Waste disposal is a social necessity and recycling is an integral part of a least-cost waste management strategy.

Warmer Bulletin, Autumn 1989

Warmer

Set up in 1984 as an independent information and campaigning body funded by the man who made his money from tetrapaks, Warmer is a very active organization committed to ensuring that if we do throw things away, we get as much use from our rubbish as possible. As its name suggests, Warmer's main concern is that the energy potential in rubbish is used to the full, either in district heating schemes, electricity generation, or refuse-derived fuel (RDF). In its quarterly magazine *Warmer Bulletin,* distributed free to interested individuals and organizations, Warmer waxes enthusiastically about actual and potential schemes and all manner of newsy items in the whole recycling/renewable energy field. The Database section of the *Bulletin* is devoted to abstracts of material available from Warmer's electronic data base.

The Warmer Campaign
83 Mount Ephraim
Tunbridge Wells
Kent
TN4 8BS
0892 24626

Recycling Cities

Co-operation between Friends of the Earth, UK 2000 and the government has resulted in the launch of the 'Recycling City' programme, a three-year project designed to help people recycle their waste more efficiently. There are to be four such cities — Sheffield is the first, Cardiff will be the second, the third will be in Scotland and the fourth is not yet decided. Most innovative is Sheffield's scheme for door-to-door collection, set up as a community enterprise, in which households have been provided with special containers to store materials separately; the collection vehicles also have separate bays. Sheffield now has 54 paper banks, 50 bottle banks and 25 plastic recycling containers, while oil recovery points are being provided at garages and civic amenity sites. The intention is that if it all works well, other cities will be able to take advantage of the experience of these pilot schemes. Sheffield's *Recycling City Waste Directory* and other information about the scheme can be obtained from Sheffield Community Recycling Action Programme (SCRAP).

SCRAP
140 Devonshire Street
Sheffield
S3 7SF
0742 721170

Wastesaving

OXFAM's pioneering Wastesaver Recycling Centre in Huddersfield was relaunched in January 1990, and is a model of what can be achieved given imagination and commitment. Forty people are employed sorting through ten tons of clothes a day, and every three weeks a container load is sent off to the Third World as part of OXFAM's relief work. Other clothes go for recycling into more clothes (see page 123) or are used for mattress flock or industrial wipers.

A smaller but no less important project is the Forest Recycling Project, a co-operative trading in the London Borough of Waltham Forest. Initially they are collecting waste business paper and selling a wide range of recycled paper products, but they hope soon to expand their business to other waste materials. Forest Recycling has produced *A Guide to Business Waste Paper Collection,* covering the reasons for doing it, what can be recycled, how to set it up and, very important, how to make it run smoothly.

OXFAM Wastesaver
Units 4, 5 and 6
Ringway Industrial Estate
Beck Road
Huddersfield
HD1 5DG
0484 542021

Forest Recycling Project
108 Palmerston Road
Walthamstow
London
E17 9PZ
0(8)1 509 3151

Chemicals In The Home

There is such a lot of confusion about the 'chemicals' we use daily in our homes and whether or not the health and environmental risks are worth the benefits we gain from their use. Michael Birkin and Brian Price's excellent *C For Chemicals* cuts through that uncertainty, and is a handbook that should be on every household's kitchen bookshelf where it can be referred to any time. Household, garden, DIY and motoring chemicals are explained in a very accessible style, both under general headings like 'bleaches' and 'disinfectants' and in an A-Z reference section under specific chemical names. It also includes practical advice on safe alternatives.

*

It is impossible to avoid chemicals in everyday life. Indeed we ourselves are made up of thousands of complex chemicals, which interact in subtle ways to keep our bodies working. When we use the term 'chemicals' however, we often mean artificial substances used in industry and the home to maintain the standard of living and lifestyle of the (usually) developed world.

C for Chemicals
Chemical Hazards and
How to Avoid Them
Michael Birkin and
Brian Price
Green Print, 1989
£4.99

Homes today contain a vast armoury of chemicals, most of them harmful to the environment even in small quantities, and many of them poisonous or harmful to human beings.

It's not that we shouldn't want to live in a relatively clean house, but there are many ways of keeping things clean and dirt-free without resorting to chemicals. Washing, dusting, brushing, beating and sweeping all work very well, and fresh air is the best air freshener ever invented — as well as being free.

For more information about chemicals in the home and what you can do to avoid them, chapters 6 and 8 of *Blueprint for a Green Planet* (page 99), Karen Christensen's *Home Ecology* (page 98), and the 'spring-greening' section of my *How to Be Green* (page 261) are good resources.

Doing The Washing

As long ago as 1962 Rachel Carson was warning us about the dangers of the overuse of detergents. As with so many chemicals, it is the quantity of detergents we use that causes the serious pollution, and as the chemical cocktails vary according to fashion water treatment plants find it hard to ensure a consistently clean end result. Some early problems that chemical manufacturers had with detergents have now been more or less solved — most surfactants, for example (the actual cleaning agents in detergents), are now biodegradable. The three main concerns about modern detergents are the phosphates added to soften the water, the enzymes designed to eat the bits of food on your clothes and dishes, and the chemical bleaches included to make everything whiter and shinier with every wash.

In fact you don't really need any of these additives, and it is easy to find cleaning products which contain no phosphates, enzymes or chemical bleaches. However, as the big guns of the cleaning industry mobilize, there is a lot of argument about the effectiveness and environmental friendliness of the various products available, and about what is or isn't harmful. For a discussion of these issues write to Ecover for a copy of their *Information Handbook*, which provides excellent and very readable background information about the whole subject.

At least fifteen companies now make 'safe' cleaning products, including the Green Force range made by a subsidiary of BP (it was only a matter of time . . .). The autumn 1989 issue of *New Consumer* magazine (see page 250) looks at all these companies, the ranges they sell and the environmental and social policies of the firms involved.

The best known of the 'green cleaners', also among the most widely available, is the Ecover range from Belgium, distributed in Britain by Full Moon and available in wholefood shops and a growing number of supermarkets including Asda, Sainsbury's and Tesco. As an example of the lengths that Ecover go to protect you and your environment from harmful chemicals, the washing powder contains a water softener made from sugar (instead of polluting phosphates) and a surfactant made from cotton and wood pulp. Even the nice smells come from natural oils — pine, eucalyptus, lemon, lavender and orange. With the exception of the washing up liquid, which contains milk whey, the whole range is 100% vegan, and none of the products is tested on animals.

One of ARK's aims (see also page 261) is 'to make individuals aware of their personal impact on the natural world and of the link between the well-being of the planet and human health.' Their cleaning products (including washing powder, washing-up liquid and window cleaner) are available in many supermarkets, including Gateway, Safeway and Tesco.

Honesty Cosmetics (see also page 166) is a Derbyshire-based workers' co-operative that has recently branched out into household cleaners; the Honesty range includes washing-up liquid, washing powder, a multi-purpose cleaner and a toilet cleaner. Another cruelty-free natural-products toiletries firm which has also moved into green cleaners is Faith (see also page 165), who manufacture the Clear Spring range.

Full Moon
Mouse Lane
Steyning
West Sussex
BN4 3DF
0903 815614

ARK Trust
498-500 Harrow Road
London
W9 3QA
0(8)1-968 6780

Honesty Cosmetics Ltd
33 Markham Road
Chesterfield
Derbyshire
S40 1TA
0246 211269

Faith Products
Unit 5
Bury Industrial Estate
Kay Street
Bury
BL9 6BU
061 764 2555

CLOTHES

*'Who said that clothes make a statement? What an understatement that was.
Clothes never shut up. They gabble on endlessly.'*
Susan Brownmiller, *Femininity*

Though we may like to think that we choose our clothes to suit ourselves, there are few areas where our choices are more affected by fashion, advertising, and ever-changing trends. Most of us enjoy buying clothes — when W.H. Smith conducted a survey to find what people most like shopping for, 70% of their respondents said clothes — but do we get what we want? The choice of styles in clothes has never been wider, yet as Lynda Nead pointed out in a letter to *The Guardian* in September 1987, 'Fashion today is clearly an extremely heterogeneous entity; nevertheless, across its various forms and manifestations it remains one of the most visible areas within contemporary society where definitions of class and gender are made and where images of masculinity and femininity are fought over.'

Creativity and Comfort

Luckily the days seem to have gone when the colours of clothes reflected the worst of British weather, and the use of bold colours, often in stark contrast, is something many of us can learn from current teenage fashion. It is easier now to dress comfortably *and* acceptably than at almost any time since the Renaissance, and the widespread availability of t-shirts and dresses, leggings, dungarees, loose jerseys and sneakers is an acknowledgement in part that people actually prefer to wear comfortable clothes if they can get them.

But too many clothes are still designed in ways that restrict the wearer, and this is particularly true of 'fashion clothes'. Women have traditionally suffered the most, toes crammed into high-heeled shoes which make it impossible to stand properly, tight skirts which hobble them at the knees, complicated tight underwear that leaves its imprint several hours later.

It's sometimes amazing what lengths of discomfort people will go to for fashion's sake, but unless we are extroverts and masochists more than we are intelligent human beings, we generally (within the bounds of what we feel is attractive) choose our clothes to keep us warm and dry without limiting our body movement too much.

Value for Money

I have a black t-shirt I'm very fond of, 100% cotton, made in Portugal. I bought it for £1.99 at a Poundstretcher sale. In a recent issue of *Vogue* a tanned model wears a 'black cotton jersey cuffed bandeau top with long skinny sleeves', £120 from Romeo Gigli. It looks suspiciously like my t-shirt.

Clothes can cost a lot; but they needn't. If you can afford to there's no reason not to buy whatever takes your fancy. Yet if you shop wisely in sales and end-of-line shops, or in one of an increasing number of nearly-new clothes shops, you can clothe yourself in basics fairly cheaply, and jumble sales and charity shops will eke out your and your household's wardrobe still further. Recycle the things you don't need any more, so that other people can find good things at the Oxfam shop too.

One of the ironies of clothes shopping is that the cheaper the garment, usually the more sweated labour has gone into it — you can't do much about this at the clothes shop level beyond glancing at the label, but you can educate yourself on the trade and labour aspects of the rag trade, and actively support suppliers who do work to break oppressive patterns of employment.

Natural Fibres

For most clothing, natural fibres — cotton, wool and silk — are the natural choice. Unless you are looking for stretch clothing, waterproofs, or extreme strength, natural fibres feel good to the touch, wear well, breathe better than synthetic fibres, and are made from renewable resources.

Cotton is hard-wearing, absorbent, machine-washable and dyeable, light, gets softer with every washing, non-allergenic, static resistant, and is wonderful to feel next to the skin, which makes it extremely popular for underwear and shirts. It is ideal for lightweight summer clothes, but when used in knitted garments it can retain warmth very well. As well as making light, open fabrics, cotton can also be woven into coarser, heavier fabrics which are very strong, including cotton drill and denim.

Wool is warm, long-lasting and, depending upon the amount of oil left in the wool, relatively waterproof, making it ideal for outer garments. The millions of coiled molecules that make up wool create air pockets which act as natural insulation to keep you warm, even when the wool is wet. They also make wool extremely crinkle-resistant, and a very durable fibre. Wool dyes extremely well, is static and flame resistant, and feels good against the skin, especially the finer and softer yarns.

Silk, although expensive, is exquisitely soft, smooth, strong and unrestricting, cool in summer and warm in winter. It cannot be bleached or exposed to high temperatures.

As far as the long-term future is concerned, anybody with an eye to the environment may want to choose to use renewable textile resources rather than non-renewable ones. This means not buying petroleum-based textiles (acrylics and polyesters) as far as possible, and adds to the many reasons why a natural fibres policy is a sound one.

The clothes section of *New Green Pages* also includes pieces on the rag trade in the UK and the Third World (where nearly 10% of our clothes and 30% of our textiles come from), South African imports, and the international fur trade, showing that even something as seemingly innocuous as buying clothes has global implications.

Clothes, Women and Men

The American author Susan Brownmiller has at least partially succeeded in doing what has so far been a stumbling block for fashion historians and feminists alike — managed to write a chapter about clothes, women and men which makes sense. She has been quite heavily criticized for false logic (by Elizabeth Wilson, see below), but she's only being candidly honest when she tells us why she doesn't wear dresses even though she misses them. The rest of the book is also thought-provoking and very readable.

*

Every wave of feminism has foundered on the question of dress reform. I suppose it is asking too much of women to give up their chief outward expression of the feminine difference, their continuing reassurance to men and to themselves that a male is a male because a female dresses and looks and acts like another sort of creature.

*

In corporate law and finance, two conservative fields where ambitious women have established a tenuous foothold, the conventional uniform for the new female executive is the dull-coloured jacket and matching knee-length skirt, suggesting a gentlemanly aspect on top and a ladylike aspect down below. Pants are not worn, except by an occasional secretary, for they lack the established tradition, and bright colours do not signify efficiency, responsibility and steadiness on the job. Calling attention to the breasts by wearing a sweater or silk shirt without a jacket is unprofessional on the executive level, especially since men persist in wearing regulation suit jackets to show their gentlemanly status. Few think it odd that the brave new careerist must obscure her breasts and display her legs in order to prove she can function in a masculine world and yet retain some familiar, comforting aspect of the feminine difference.

Femininity
Susan Brownmiller
Paladin, 1986
£2.95

Adorned in Dreams

Rather a heavy and heavily-written book, but worth reading because Elizabeth Wilson has taken the idea of 'fashion' to pieces to show just how fashion and its critics often tie themselves in knots in the attempt to justify their activities. If you're interested in the history of fashion, this is a welcome antidote to the 'straight' social histories. The chapters on eroticism, gender and identity, oppositional dress (cross-dressing), utopian dress, and the feminist debate about fashion are a welcome departure from most fashion writing.

*

In Britain the hippie style meant something different from its transatlantic counterpart. The British variant wore a message that was anti-capitalist in the sense that to create a unique appearance out of a bricolage of secondhand clothes, craft work and army surplus was to protest sartorially against the wastefulness of the consumer society. You rejected the mass-produced road, and simultaneously wasteful luxury, and produced your own completely original look. Yet although this was undertaken in a spirit of anti-consumerism it did involve the expenditure of much time if not money, and reintroduced the snobbery of uniqueness, since there was, necessarily, only one of the 'frock' you had found — just as much as if you'd bought a Dior original.

To the extent that a feminist style does exist, it has to be understood as a sub-theme of the general fashion discourse. Boiler suits and dungarees are after all fashion garments, not just a feminist uniform. They are commercially marketed items of casual chic; and the contortions necessary in the lavatory, and the discomfort in cold weather of having to undress completely in order to relieve oneself, should prove conclusively that this form of dress is not worn to promote rational apparel, but to announce the wearer's feminism in public.

Adorned in Dreams
Fashion and Modernity
Elizabeth Wilson
Virago, 1985
£5.95

And All Was Revealed

If you find it hard to believe the power that the fashion world holds over us, Doreen Caldwell's study of the way that fashion has dictated not only what women wear, but how that affects their body and their self-image, may well persuade you. From Edwardian corsets ('no hint must be given that the bosom is composed of two breasts') to 1980s worries about the VPL ('visible pantie line'), she uses hundreds of illustrations, period advertisements and a witty commentary to show the manufacturers of women's underclothes have sold their wares and their dreams of how well-dressed women should look.

And All Was Revealed
Ladies' Underwear 1907-1980
Doreen Caldwell
Arthur Barker, 1981
£4.95

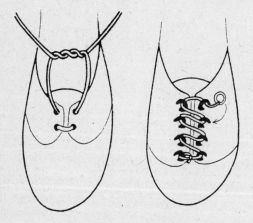

**Clothes for
Disabled People**
Maureen Goldsworthy
Batsford 1981
£8.95

Clothes and Disabled People

People who find it hard to cope with 'ordinary' clothes can have enormous problems finding attractive and comfortable garments. But in the last few years, especially since the establishment of the Disabled Living Foundation in 1971, things have become much easier. The Foundation produces a very comprehensive range of booklets, including *Dressing for Disabled People* and *Footwear and Footcare for Adults* (plus one for children). Write for their publications list, which includes books from other publishers. They also run a a General Advisory Service and a Clothing and Footwear Advisory Service. If you can get to London to see them, at the Harrow Road office they have a constantly changing exhibition of clothes which are currently available in multiple stores or from mail order suppliers. Their annual report and several free leaflets give full details of all these services.

Disabled Living Foundation
380-384 Harrow Road
London
W9 2HU
0(7)1-289 6111

Clothes for Disabled People

A bit on the expensive side for 118 pages, *Clothes for Disabled People*, approved by the Disabled Living Foundation, contains many innovative ideas for people who have problems getting into most clothes (ideas which could usefully be incorporated into the design of clothes in general). It includes sections on sewing and knitting, adapting bought clothes, dressing aids, and sewing and knitting aids, all with names and addresses of suppliers.

*

The two great difficulties with clothes are the planning of openings large enough, and in the right places, for easy dressing — and the choice of fastenings that are simple to manage and as few as possible.

*

A very efficient sewing frame is an ordinary drawer, pulled halfway out of a chest of drawers. It should be at a convenient working height for you. Stretch your work tightly across the open drawer, fastening it with thumb-tacks at each side. The wood of the side-rails is usually soft, so thumb-tacks will go in easily. You can even stick your needle into the top of the drawer rail, to thread it with one hand.

The Environmental Perspective

Wildlife is threatened by direct exploitation for luxury products. The skins of crocodiles, turtles, lizards and snakes are used for bags, belts and shoes. The skins of leopards and other cats are cut up and made into clothes, hats and rugs. In 1975 over 164 million wildlife products entered the United States alone. Europe and Japan are the other main markets. London is still a major centre for world trade in wild animal products.

Friends of the Earth pamphlet, 1985

Lynx

Lynx is the only national organization solely devoted to campaigning against the world fur trade. It puts out a quarterly newsletter and has mounted an extensive poster and cinema commercial campaign. Lynx organises an annual competition for fashion students to design sumptuous and extravagant alternatives to fur coats; during 1990 they aim to start campaigning in the rest of Europe. A mail order catalogue can be obtained from the Dunmow headquarters.

In 1989 Lynx opened a shop at 79 Long Acre, in London's Covent Garden, selling a range of cruelty-free clothing, plus cards, books, ceramics and jewellery; a similar shop has recently opened in Cambridge at Quayside, off Silver Street.

Lynx
PO Box 509
Dunmow
Essex
CM6 1UH
0371 872016

South Africa

British imports of South African textile fibres like raw wool are currently running at about £50 million a year, and total imports of yarns, fabrics and manufactured articles amount to about £10.3 million a year (South Africa is after Australia the second largest supplier of Merino wool and supplies nearly 30% of the mohair, second only to the USA). We also import more than 6% of our cotton thread and yarn from South Africa. The internationally-known Woolmark symbol was originally the trade mark of the South African Wool Board, though this does not necessarily mean that knitwear and other woollen items bearing the symbol come from South Africa.

The South African clothing industry employs 300,000 people, and is probably the largest employer of black women in the country. A qualified woman machinist in the Western Cape earns £27 a week, compared with an estimated subsistence level of £38, and an average wage for whites in the same industry of £156.

If boycotting South African products is part of your political practice there are several steps you can take. Shops regularly selling quantities of South African clothes include Lewis's, Country Casuals and Harrods, and Swakura Fur, François Villon, Rex Trueform, Miss Cassidy, Pat Shub and Jogger garments should be avoided. Some clothes are marked with their place of manufacture so it is possible to check. Both Next and Richard Shops have a policy of not buying South African.

The marketing system for wool means that it is not possible for the shopper to discern the country of origin of the wool from which a particular garment is made, though pressure is being put on the International Wool Secretariat to identify country of origin, as with foodstuffs.

AA Enterprises is a workers' co-operative which raises funds for the Anti-Apartheid Movement and is developing direct trade links with the Front Line States — Angola, Botswana, Mozambique, Tanzania, Zambia and Zimbabwe. Products they currently stock include honey, coffee, tea and wines. Also in their mail order catalogue are clothes — cotton t-shirts and sweatshirts printed with bright slogans and attractive designs, mugs, cards and books — or how about a pair of socks discreetly printed with the AA logo?

AA Enterprises
PO Box 533
London
NW1 9EW
0(7)1-281 7878

The Rag Trade in Britain

In few cases is homeworking a freely-chosen, life-enhancing option. On the contrary, in almost all cases it is a poor alternative to working outside the home, selected only because the homeworker's domestic commitments prevent her from going out to work.
Sweated Labour (see below)

Outworkers are treated as secondary labour force, with pay and conditions inferior to those given to people doing similar work on the premises when they are given work, but vulnerable to short-term fluctuations in the quantity of work and even to being laid off during the trough months. Outwork plants were more likely than others to employ a female workforce, and had relatively high proportions of ethnic minority and part-time workers.
Employment Gazette, April 1984

The clothing industry still has some of the worst working conditions and wage levels in Britain. Over 60% of clothing manufacturers employ less than twenty people, which makes figures difficult to obtain, but in a recent survey in South Yorkshire, 82% of women workers (and over 90% of clothing industry employees are women) were 'low paid' (earning less than two thirds of average male earnings). One third were earning less than £70 per week, or £2 per hour. The basic wage is so low that clothing workers rely heavily on bonus earnings to contribute to their take-home pay. There are probably more than 300,000 homeworkers in Britain today.

Liz Bissett and Ursula Huws' *Sweated Labour: Homeworking in Britain Today* (Low Pay Unit Pamphlet No. 33, available from the Low Pay Unit, 9 Poland Street, London W1V 3DG, £1.50) is a detailed and alarming picture of the women who work at home, mostly in the 'sweated trades' of clothing manufacture, button making, knitting and toy assembly. A more detailed picture of the situation in the West Midlands is given in *Below the Minimum* (available from the West Midlands Low Pay Unit, Wolverley House, 18 Digbeth, Birmingham B5 6BJ. In the growing garment industry of the West Midlands wages for many Asian women can be as low as 60p an hour and health and safety conditions dangerously poor. This pamphlet looks at working conditions in the trade, and makes strong recommendations for change.

If you get a chance, see the film produced by Women Now Films called 'The Hidden Worlds', which shows the working conditions of homeworkers in the rag trade, and includes several Asian women talking about their experiences.

Through The Looking-Glass

The crinoline, so often seen as the cage of the Victorian lady, replaced up to twelve layers of heavy full petticoats. The lightness of the hoops and the lack of constriction around the waist were seen as a positive liberation, at least to begin with.. When they reached about six feet in width, Princess Pauline Metternich wrote '. . . to be able to sit so as not to cause the rebellious springs to fly open required a miracle of precision. To ascend a carriage when the evening toilettes were made of tulle and lace required a great deal of time, much quietness on the part of the horses and much patience on the part of husbands and fathers.'
Through the Looking Glass

The mini-crini represents a consideration of the history of sexuality and of fashion's changing definition of the female body. If the crinoline stands for the mythology of restriction and encumbrance in women's dress, in the mini-crini that mythology is juxtaposed with an equally dubious mythology of liberation associated with the mini-skirt. In it two sets of ideas about female desirabilty are conflated: one about covering, the other about uncovering the female body.
Women and Fashion: a New Look

Two recent thought-provoking books about fashion show that the only way the industry can survive is to keep re-inventing the wheel. Elizabeth Wilson (see also page 117) and Lou Taylor's *Through the Looking Glass*, the book which accompanied a BBC television series of the same name, is a comprehensive yet intelligent look at the clothes that people have worn from the 1860s to the present day. It isn't just a *Vogue* parade; it looks at what ordinary folk were wearing and shows how political and technological change has shaped our clothes.

By contrast, Caroline Evans and Minna Thornton in *Women and Fashion: A New Look* provide a thoroughgoing critique of recent fashion. This is a fascinating if sometimes jargon-ridden exploration of how we use clothes to project our images of ourselves and what designers will do to pander to our fantasies. The book starts with the symbolic burning of the bra (if it ever happened) in the mid 1960s and progresses through the gender bending of the early 80s to the inevitable 'organic tailoring' of the green 90s.

Through The Looking Glass
Elizabeth Wilson and Lou Taylor
BBC Books, 1989
£9.99

Women and Fashion: A New Look
Caroline Evans and Minna Thornton
Quartet, 1989
£15.00

Conspicuous Thrift

Although now out of print, Carolyn Chapman's *Style on a Shoestring* is a mine of information for anyone who wants to experiment with interesting and exciting clothes but has very little money. It is true that money and time are often in a precarious balance, but Carolyn Chapman shows that buying in sales, markets and secondhand shops can be an entertainment in itself, and needn't take hours if you know what you're looking for.
*

Conspicuous thrift dressing clearly thrives in a climate of eclectic fashion. This kind of dressing cuts across age, class and sex because it is concerned with the wearer finding clothes to suit his or her identity — or to emulate a style he or she admires. It is about saving money, feeling comfortable and looking good in the context of one's own lifestyle.

Style on a Shoestring
A Guide to Conspicuous Thrift
Carolyn Chapman
Hutchinson, 1984
£4.95

For anyone living in London, *City Limits* quite often runs lists of second-hand clothes shops, and another good source of information is *Survivors London* (see page 343) which lists charity shops and very cheap non-charity shops.

Damart

A family firm which has been based in Bingley for the last twenty-one years, Damart now run one of the biggest direct mail operations in the country with over three million customers. While I wouldn't recommend some of the things they've got into recently, it's their practical and comfortable thermal underwear that wins them a place in *New Green Pages*. Like the nylon element of the Snickers range (see next page), the petroleum-based thermolactyl chlorofibre which is the basis of the garments' thermal properties is a justifiable exception to a natural-fibre policy.

If you're humping winter fuel, herding the goats, or merely enjoy wintertime clifftop walks, you won't regret your Damart vest and long johns. Unless you want a mountain of catalogues, tell them you only want the underwear catalogue. If you don't need the extra insulation of Double Force then don't bother with artificial thermolactyl — go for all-cotton vests, long johns and all-in-ones which are now available in many places.

Damart
Bowling Green Mills
Bingley
West Yorkshire
BD16 4BH
0274 568211

Clothes Recycling

Obvious places for finding recycled clothes are the charity shops, often conveniently sited in close proximity to one another in most towns. The clothing from OXFAM shops that doesn't sell goes to their Wastesaver depot in Huddersfield (see page 113), where it is sorted and sent on to specialist dealers for re-processing or sent out by the container load to Mozambique.

It's amazing what rags can be turned into: low grade rags can even be used to make roofing felt. Unwanted rags from jumble sales can be sent in any quantity to Perfected Waste, 10 Louisa Street, Birmingham B1 2RW (Tel 021 236 7195). There they are sorted into the different sorts of materials: woollens go to Levinson Fibre in Morley near Leeds where they are pulled into separated fibres and spun into yarns which are then woven into cloth by T.W. Thorpe in Huddersfield. Good quality cotton can make a high grade paper, and lower grade cotton or synthetic rags go for recycling into industrial cleaning clothes or stuffing for coach seats.

Jeans

The American *Whole Earth Access* catalogue informs its readers that drill, a tough diagonal-weave (twill weave) material which is the ancestor of the material that jeans are made of, was first used by the English cavalry in a battle near the River Tweed, and changed its name from 'tweed' to 'twill' to 'drill' through the vagaries of the language. In fact twill is an old Scottish word, first recorded in the thirteenth century, and 'drill' is short for 'drilling' (from the German 'dreilich', or 'threefold', indicating its twilled weave). The most interesting of the terms used to describe the material that jeans are made of is 'denim', which was first used in the seventeenth century to describe the coarse blue overall cloth used by the traders of Nîmes in France, hence 'de Nîmes'.

Easily recognizable by its white yarn weft and coloured (usually blue) warp, denim is very strong and hardwearing. Jeans have been the uniform of the North American farmer and labourer for more than a century. Levi's were first produced in 1850, and the first pair of Oshkosh overalls went to work in Oshkosh, Wisconsin, in 1895. Nearly always made of 100% cotton, denim is still the obvious choice for hardwearing and long-lasting work clothing.

There is a wide variation of quality and prices available. Since the price of seemingly identical jeans (down to the brand name) can vary by as much as £10, and the same brands can differ in quality, it is worth choosing very carefully. Levi's 501s are the closest you'll get to the original jeans — they're the ones you have to wash three times before they're fully shrunk, so make sure you buy them one size too large in the waist and 2" too long in length. Most people these days, however, buy pre-washed, pre-shrunk, and sometimes stone-washed (prematurely aged!) jeans.

About two-thirds of our jeans are made abroad, mainly in Hong Kong and the Far East. Look round for relative bargains, but because jeans are usually with their owners for a long time and are expected to wear hard, almost more than with any other item of clothing you will get pretty much what you pay for. A good pair of Levi's will cost around £20-25; a jacket around £30; a good pair of bib overalls around £30. Pay much less for a name you've never heard of and you'll probably have problems before long.

Snickers

It was Jennifer, an architect and builder friend, who introduced me to Snickers working clothes, so it's a bit ironic that all the faces smiling out of their catalogue are fresh-faced male workers. 'Snickers are wonderful;' she said, 'enough pockets for everything, straps to hang your hammer from, removable knee pads for when you're laying tiles. They drip dry. And they're not that expensive.'

Snickers trousers, jackets, toolcoats and one-pieces come from Sweden, where thirteen years ago an electrician called Matti Viio got so fed up with his overalls that he decided to design his own. Now more than a million people all over the world wear the workclothes he helped to design. Although the outside is 75% nylon, to resist water and dirt, the inside is 75% cotton, so you don't get too hot and sweaty while you work. The toolcoat has four extra holster pockets, and hammer loops to let you carry your toolkit round with you. A recent development is a toolcoat with an integral safety harness, so you can dangle from rooftops and trees in relative safety.

Trousers are around £26, jackets start at around £17, and the toolcoat is about £30. Most builder's and plumber's merchants sell them, and there is a permanent display at the Snickers Centre. If you have any problem finding them, they will gladly send a catalogue so you can order by post.

Snickers Original Ltd
Snickers Centre
1275 Stratford Road
Hall Green
Birmingham
B28 9AJ
021 778 5041

Other Outdoor Clothes Suppliers

If you're looking for tough outdoor trousers for hiking, gardening or climbing, you can't do much better than order made-to-measure trousers from Colne Valley Sports. They're not colourful, but the catalogue with its samples of Olive Drab and Dark Green shows that they are cheap (from £24 for a pair of wool trousers), hard-wearing, and made-to-measure. Their Derby Tweeds have been up Everest, so they must be good.

Functional Clothing in Warrington supply a large range of waterproof and windproof clothing, jackets, overtrousers, leggings and caps. Hawkshead Sportswear's range from Cumbria is a 'country casuals' style of clothing, some pure cotton corduroy trousers at £13, cotton needlecord shirts at £10, plain coloured pure shetland jumpers and comfortable, sensible sturdy shoes for the country or for hill walking.

Laurence Corner is well known for its hats — 'the best variety in London' says David Benedictus in *The Absolutely Essential Guide to London* — but they also have a wide range of government surplus clothing, boiler suits, gloves and gauntlets, and secondhand theatrical clothes too.

Colne Valley Sports
5 Albert Street
Mytholmroyd
nr Halifax
West Yorkshire
HX7 5NN
0422 883470

Hawkshead Sportswear
Rothay Holme
Rothay Road
Ambleside
Cumbria
LA22 0HQ
05394 34000

Functional Clothing Ltd
Unit 5
Palatine Trading Estate
Causeway Avenue
Wilderspool Causeway
Warrington
Lancashire
WA4 6QQ
0925 53111

Laurence Corner
126-130 Drummond Street
London
NW1 2NU
0(7)1-388 6811

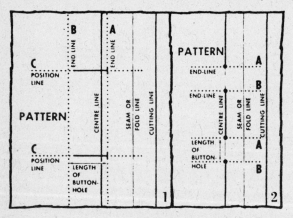

Making Your Own Clothes?

For anybody interested in making clothes and knowing about the fabrics they are made of, Ann Ladbury is a sort of seam-stress's guru. Apparently her great-great-grandmother worked as a tailor at the court of Emperor Franz Josef, and as the author of more than twenty books, the presenter of four television series, and a monthly columnist to *Pins and Needles* magazine she must eat, breathe and sleep clothes. But she knows what she's talking about, and whether you want to know the difference between barathea, bayadere and bord tire, or how to sew a yoke seam, Ann Ladbury is your woman.

Fabrics

From abbot cloth to zibeline, *Fabrics* will tell you more than you need to know about any fabric you will ever come across. Most libraries have a copy, but if you do a lot of sewing it's a very useful reference book to have at your elbow.

*

The disadvantage of prints is that they are nearly always off the straight grain of the fabric. It is perfectly possible to begin printing with the end of the fabric accurately placed with the weft threads exactly at right angles to the warp, or the wales of knitting straight, and it is possible to control and regulate the fabric so that the print remains on grain, but few manufacturers take the trouble to ensure this is so. Examine the fabric carefully before purchase to ensure that the print is not so badly off-grain that it will be impossible to make a satisfactory garment.

Fabrics
Ann Ladbury
Sidgwick and Jackson,
1985
£8.95

Short Cuts

'Invaluable,' said an ex-fashion-college friend of Ann Ladbury's *Short Cuts for Busy Dressmakers*. Every aspect of sewing is covered, and every so often there's a little box in the text headed 'Tip'; some very useful ones there are too, especially when it comes to things like zips and complicated hems.

*

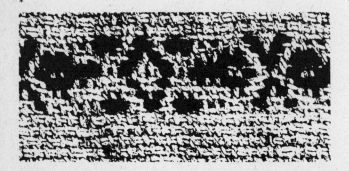

If zip teeth seem tough, run your beeswax along them to lubricate. Always stitch in the same direction on both sides of the zip. If the two edges of fabric have to be exactly level, as, for example, when matching stripes or where there is a crossing seam, stitch that part first for about 3cm, then start again and sew the entire zip. It is not easy to work a second row of parallel stitching using the zip foot because you have no guide. It helps to put a piece of Sellotape on the fabric with one edge marking the position of the stitching.

Short Cuts for Busy Dressmakers
Ann Ladbury
Batsford, 1980
£5.50

Batsford have long been the acknowledged specialist publisher in craft books, and every year they issue a useful free catalogue of their craft books each year. If you don't have a good bookshop nearby they will send you the books you want, adding only £1.50 postage regardless of how many you buy. You can return books you decide you don't want after all for a refund within ten days.

Batsford Books
4 Bakers Mews
London
W1M 1DD
0(7)1-486 8484

Magazines

If you really wanted to, you could swamp yourself with fashion, knitwear and sewing magazines in a matter of weeks. Buying the occasional copy, however, does keep you up to date with suppliers of yarns, materials and equipment. If you do want to see one of the magazines regularly, it's no more expensive, and usually cheaper, to have a subscription and wait for it to arrive through the post.

If you sew, the main magazines are *Burda* and *Vogue Patterns*; the latter is published six times a year and has an excellent classified section, especially for fabrics, plus the continuing offer of a free Vogue pattern with every pattern ordered.

Hand-knitting magazines are reflecting the down-turn in the market, with new slimmer magazines with names like *Annabel*. There is *World of Knitting*, a monthly with good advertisements, and *Hand Knitting News*, a more expensive and glossier monthly which tends to be more imaginative than *World of Knitting*. For machine knitters there are several magazines, but the best for tips as well as patterns and classifieds is *Machine Knitting*.

Vogue Knitting International is expensive and irregular (about three issues a year), but exciting — Kaffe Fassett, Calvin Klein and Adrienne Vittadini originals, for example, and when you want to find some really different yarns you can send off for sample swatches to Australia, New Zealand and the USA, like angora from the Cosmos Rabbit Factory in Silverdale, Washington, or alpaca direct from Peru.

The bible of the British clothing industry (worth buying if it's your livelihood, asking for from the reference section of your library if not) is *The British Clothing Industry Year Book*. Published by Kemps Publishing Group in February each year, it costs £30, and contains information about companies, trade names, manufacturers of textiles and fabrics, specialist ser-vices (like transparent tie wrappers), trade and professional organizations, and import and export houses.

Kemps Publishing Group
701-705 Warwick Road
Solihull
West Midlands
B91 3DA
021 711 4488

Natural Fibres

'The trouble with natural fibres,' said a recent writer to the consumer page of a women's magazine, 'is you can't get them. and if you can, they're always more expensive, and that's because most people aren't particularly bothered what their clothes are made of.'

It's true that if you don't look out for pure natural fibres, — wool, cotton, linen, silk — you can easily overlook them. Even when you find them, you may well discover that they are trimmed and decorated with artificial fibres. This may not bother you, but many people find that wearing artificial materials next to the skin irritates them.

Things are changing, though, and there are few clothes retailers who haven't recognized that a growing number of their customers are specifically asking for natural fibres. Until recently it looked as though artificial fibres were gradually going to take over the textiles scene, having risen from 13% of total world fibre consumption in 1951 to 40% in 1971, but this share has remained fairly constant for the last decade, and cotton with 52% and wool with 7% have both held their shares. Thus cotton is still the most important source of textiles in the world, so it shouldn't be that hard to find.

People do mind what their clothes are made of. A student at Manchester Polytechnic recently did a survey of women who were shopping in a high street chain store. When they were asked what they looked for when buying a blouse, 98% of them mentioned natural fibre, and 72% pure cotton (80% of the 20-25 year olds). They knew exactly why, too — more than half said they would only buy pure cotton because it was less sweaty, less smelly and more comfortable.

Although some artificial fibres like rayon are made from wood cellulose, most are oil by-products. Natural fibres on the other hand are renewable resources. They are generally kinder to your skin, non-allergenic, more adaptable in their uses, and longer wearing than artificial fibres. Yet even the growing of artificial fibres has an impact on our environment. While most of Britain's 25 million sheep graze moorland areas which cannot sustain other forms of agriculture, they also prevent rich, natural ecosystems from developing. All the cotton we use is grown chemically, often causing widespread soil degradation, and what is considered the best quality silk involves the asphyxiation of the silkworm moth in its cocoon (see page 126). Most natural fibres are routinely treated with moth-repelling insecticides before being made into clothes.

Many shops are beginning to take note of the increasing public demand for natural fibres. Marks and Spencer has always been particularly good for many cotton items, and so it should be when so many people buy their underwear at M&S —34% of all bras, 31% of all knickers and 52% of all slips bought in this country come from them.

Natural Fibres by Mail Order

Being aware of how difficult it is to buy natural fibre clothing, especially if you live in rural Britain, Janet Groome established Natural Fibres in 1986 to provide a mail order service for British-made pure natural fibre clothes. The range is basic — shirts, jumpers, socks and stockings, vests, pants and bras — but the purity and quality are guaranteed, and there is a discount if you buy more than one of any item. They specialize in large sizes too.

Natural Fibres
2 Springfield Lane
Smeeton Westerby
Leicester
LE8 0QW
0533 792280

The Smock Shop

'In a woollen gown which reached his knee,' was the way Geoffrey Chaucer described the shipman pilgrim in the Canterbury Tales. Not the most practical gear for work at sea — soggy round the hem and folds of cloth getting in the way. More often than not the sailor found it easier to strip off altogether, which must have been a bit parky in a bad summer. Life moved slowly then, and it took about 250 years to shorten the length and add sleeves and pockets. But then, anything worth having is worth waiting for.

From The Smock Shop leaflet

So begins the potted history that Pam Smith and her daughter Jennie Pearce give to customers of The Smock Shop, Britain's only shop specializing in this traditional garment. They do also sell dresses and t-shirts, and some synthetics, but 90% of their trade is in all-cotton smocks in a dozen colours of needlecord, denim, drill and canvas. Most of the fabric is woven and dyed in Britain, and they do not buy Taiwanese cloth because of the exploitation of textile workers there. Local women make the smocks in their own homes at guaranteed industrial rates. Besides smocks, they also have elastic waisted trousers, shorts and skirts. There is also a smock with lots of pockets.

The smocks are particularly useful for disabled people; stroke patients can often wear a smock when a jacket is impractical because of the buttons, and the big front pockets give easy access to whatever you need to carry with you.

The Smock Shop
The House That Jack Built
11 Southside Street
Plymouth
PL1 2LA
0752 220507

Denny Andrews

Denny Andrews used to work in a Covent Garden ethnic fashion shop, and when she moved to a village near Swindon she decided to start a mail order business to supply interesting and colourful clothes in pure fibres. As she says in her catalogue (which she sends out twice a year), she concentrates on 'casual, comfortable wearability and the somewhat unusual' — Indian hand-spun cotton, Welsh wool shirts and shawls, Irish flannelette shirts and nightshirts, 'the kind of clothes that other shops forget to buy' is what *The Sunday Telegraph* said of her range.

These clothes are not as cheap as Indian cotton clothes you can buy in Carnaby Street, but the quality is high, the service good, and Denny Andrews will give you your money back if the garment doesn't suit you. Many of the Indian clothes are handloomed and handspun, or hand-blocked: shirts start at £8, nighties at £25, cotton skirts with an elastic waist at £12 — the catalogue explains the details of Indian clothes: kurtas, chikan embroidery, lunghies and sarongs. Welsh wool shirts from £24, shawls from £27, and Irish shirts from £17, cotton twill navy bib and brace overalls for £17. She also has some of the fabrics by the yard.

Most of Denny's business is done by post, but visitors are welcome if they ring first.

Denny Andrews
Clock House Workshop
Coleshill
nr Swindon
SN6 7PT
0793 762476

Big Bird

Big Bird co-operative, established in London's East End in 1986, has recently moved to north London, but is still thriving. They make clothes specially for people who find it difficult to get attractive and comfortable clothes which are big enough. Send for a catalogue.

Big Bird Clothing Company Ltd
290a Amherst Rd
London
N16 7UE

Bolton Alternative Clothing Co-op

You'll have to go to their stall called 'Downbeat' at Afflecks Palace in Manchester to see the bright clothes of this enterprising workers' co-operative. Using mostly cottons and other natural fibres, they create comfortable cheap clothes for 15-35 year olds, and also sell secondhand clothes.

Bolton Alternative Clothing Co-op Ltd

Stall: Affleck's Palace
52 Church Street
off Oldham Street
Manchester

Work: 35 Alder Street
Great Lever
Bolton
BL3 2DR
0204 361862

Pink Fish

Pink Fish specializes in gorgeous hand-screen-printed 100% cotton or polycotton long- and short-sleeved t-shirts, shorts, shirts, skirts and wraps. Inspired by Third World themes and calling their designs Medicine Man, Infinite Wisdom, Night Whale, Woman Buddha and the like, the intricacy and colours of Pink Fish's range takes art on to simple basic clothes.

Pink Fish
The Arches Craft Arcade
Granary Wharf
Leeds
LS1 4BR

Cotton Shirts

Asdir markets what they call 'the comfortable businessman's shirt' — a completely natural cotton shirt from Germany, guaranteed to contain no formaldehyde or sythetic resins (the things manufacturers normally put in a '100% cotton' shirt — for 'easy care'). Allergy sufferers in particular will appreciate the availablity of a real 100% cotton shirt.

Asdir Ltd
192 Tyne Crescent
Bedford
MK41 7YI
0234 217478

A number of the mainstream clothing catalogues make a point of stocking clothes made from natural fibres. Next usually has quite a lot of cottons (though don't start getting their mail order catalogue; they'll never give up!); Nightingales (who do a mail order catalogue) also carry all-cotton clothing, especially summer dresses. It's now easy to get t-shirts and simple clothes like shorts and skirts from many of the catalogues of campaigning groups like CND, Greenpeace, Friends of the Earth and Anti-Apartheid. Friends of the Earth have recently introduced a range of unbleached cotton denim clothes designed by Basic English; these can be bought from Top Shop, Top Man and Miss Selfridge as well as through their catalogue.

Nightingales
23 Union Street
Barnet
Hertfordshire
EN5 4HY
0(7)1-435 4070/3179

Cloth by the Metre

Matching. We still have plentiful stocks of a 40" wide heavy cotton ribbed T shirting in cerise. Tremendous cloth and if cerise doesn't happen to be flavour of the month let's get together and make it so. A gift.

So runs one of the several hundred descriptions of material kept by Croft Mill, Britain's best-known textiles overstock warehouse. Not all the materials are natural fibres but a lot are, and the prices are incredibly low. Once you have read through the catalogue, for a small sum (refundable on sending in your first order) they will send a swatch of fabrics. They stock t-shirt material, sheeting, dress cloth, furnishing fabrics, notions (a wonderful word, that) and all sorts of other odds and ends.

Croft Mill
Lowther Lane
Foulridge
Colne
Lancashire
BB8 7NG
0282 869265

Ethnic Clothes

Fashion has not stood still since the 1960s, when colourful ethnic clothes started to appear in Britain in large quantities, but then neither have ethnic clothes. Manufacturers in the Third World keep a very close eye on Western fashions, and garments made in the Third World often succeed in combining quality and originality with a style that is perfectly acceptable for every occasion, even the most formal.

Here are a handful of the many shops which specialize in ethnic clothes, almost all of which also sell a wide range of craft goods, and make excellent browsing places for presents (see also page 260 for more Third World craft shops and page 127 for Traidcraft's ever-expanding range). Some of the issues raised by the trade in Third World fashions are discussed in more detail on the next page.

Anokhi

Anokhi imports brightly patterned clothes and fabrics from Rajasthan and other parts of India, including padded jackets, silk dresses, bags and scarves. They also have beautiful (though not cheap) bedspreads and clothes in their Covent Garden shop.

Anokhi
22 Wellington Street
London WC2
0(7)1-836 0663

Tumi

Moh Fini set up Tumi in 1977 to provide an outlet in Britain for high quality South American crafts. The idea was, and is, to give Britain a taste of South American culture and at the same time provide a stable livelihood for more than a thousand Andean families. The shops, in Bath, Brighton (here the shop, called Tucan, is on Bond Street), Oxford (1 and 2 Little Clarendon) and London (23-24 Chalk Farm Road) sell a wide range of clothes and crafts, including hand-knitted jumpers, hand-dyed cotton dresses, woollen socks and hats. The prices are very reasonable, but because Tumi buys directly the manufacturers are guaranteed a reasonable living too.

In many instances Tumi has managed to keep old skills alive, and even encouraged craftspeople to return to skills which they had given up as unprofitable. They also work closely with a Bolivian folk music group, whose tapes you can buy in the shops. In the Oxford shop there are frequent exhibitions on Latin American themes and the London shop has a permanent exhibition.

Moh Fini travels extensively in South America looking for crafts for the Tumi shops, and in 1987 he did a sponsored trail bike journey across the continent to raise money for Amnesty International.

A Tumi catalogue is produced each October; send an sae for a copy. June 1990 should see the first issue of a magazine which tells all about Tumi's activities; it will be available in the shops. Tumi also sells wholesale.

Tumi
8-9 New Bond Street Place
Bath
Avon
0225 462367

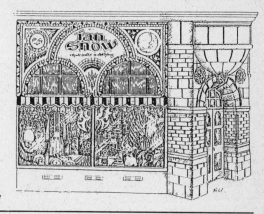

Ian Snow

Ian Snow started importing Indian clothes in 1977 following extensive travels in the sub-continent, and now runs two shops in the mid-Wales towns of Newtown (the main shop) and Llanidloes; anyone who has been to the Glastonbury Festival (see page 292) will almost certainly have seen Ian's colourful stall in the Green Field there.

He sells crafts, gifts, ceramics and jewellery, kelims from Afghanistan, rugs and durries, and colourful clothes from many parts of the Third World. There are tapes and records (including a wide range of Latin American music), and a selection of unusual cards. Being vegan, he tries to avoid selling leather items, and checks all his sources carefully for ecological sustainability and commercial justice. The Newtown shop will shortly incorporate a craft gallery. There is a mail order service — send for a catalogue; Ian also sells some items wholesale.

Ian Snow

1 The Cross	47 Longbridge Street
Newtown	Llanidloes
Powys	Powys
SY16 2LF	SY18 6EF
0686 622185	05512 3439

Schmocks and Phrocks

S&P is a small rural workshop in the heart of Devon which produces comfortable but stylish smocks and dresses. They use only good quality cotton with some interesting prints, including batik or Javanese. They cater for large sizes up to size 28, and produce a mail order catalogue.

Schmocks and Phrocks
Unit 2
Kingston Workshops
Staverton
Totnes
Devon
080 426 255

Original Breton Shirts

The eminently comfortable and typically French shirts made by the Breton Shirt Company come in stripes of cream and red, cream and green, cream and maroon, cream and navy — cream with everything. They are all 100% knitted cotton, and cost £12.50 each (plus £1 p+p).

The Breton Shirt Company
99 Watermoor Road
Cirencester
Gloucestershire
GL17 1LD
0285 652977

Clothes Imports

Since industrialized countries hold a near-monopoly over synthetics (80% of which are produced by the United States, Japan and Western European countries), cutting down on their use would allow for considerable savings in developing countries. Experts feel that the increased cost of synthetic fibres, the use of simple and efficient methods for extracting food products from cotton, and the product's multiplier effects in industrial development all lead to the conclusion that the task of expanding cotton production is both urgent and necessary.
                          Third World Guide (see page 239)

We are endlessly plagued by lung tuberculosis, athlete's foot, and various stomach diseases. Women workers have yellow, swollen faces from inadequate sunlight. We are harassed by the close supervision and pressing demands of the company. We are struggling to free ourselves from these miserable conditions which are too many to enumerate.
              Women from a Korean factory, quoted in
          Third World, Second Sex (Miranda Davies, Zed, 1983, £3.90)

Slightly more than a third of the clothes we buy are imported, and the UK exports 19% of the clothing produced in this country. Nearly 40% of our clothes imports come from developing countries, particularly Hong Kong, India, Korea and Turkey, and about the same proportion from the EEC, with £266m worth from Italy in 1984 and £136m from Portugal. A growing source of our clothing is Israel. It is always worthwhile to look at the label and see where your clothes are being made.

The Third World produces about a third of the world's cotton crop, and supplies about half of the world's exports. It is an important cash crop for many Third World countries, though erratic price fluctuations can be disastrous for countries like Sudan, where cotton provides 52% of export earnings.

If you are interested in the history of the cotton industry, its role in nineteenth century industrial development and world trade (including of course the slave trade), and its current status still as the world's most important source of textile fibre (52%, compared with synthetics at 40% and wool at 9%), then read *The Rise and Fall of King Cotton* by Anthony Burton (Andre Deutsch/BBC, 1984, £10.95).

Silk

A lot of what passes for silk these days isn't, and real silk tends to be very expensive. You can, however, still find bargains: the oriental basement at Liberty's central London shop (corner of Regent Street and Great Marlborough Street), for example, often has wonderful fabrics which aren't too expensive.

Why not get your silks directly from the Far East, though, bypassing a lot of the unnecessary middle people, and benefiting the Third World manufacturers in the process? The Angus International I/E Agency in Hong Kong may sound like an impersonal multinational, but in fact it's Angus Hardern, a handful of local helpers, and the cat, in a penthouse flat in Kowloon, who for the last eight years have been supplying a wide range of pure silks to a growing postal clientele in Europe. With 45" lining silk from £4.00 a yard, and an enormous range (over a hundred) different plain and patterned silks from around £6 a yard, you couldn't do much better for price. Their delivery times are faster than many deliveries from UK sources — when I sent out the questionnaires for *New Green Pages*, Angus Hardern's reply was one of the first, complete with detailed price lists and sample swatches.

*

Prices include air or surface mail delivery to your door, but not duty or sales tax, sometimes levied, sometimes not, depending on which side of bed your customs man has got out of that morning!

Angus International
Penthouse
6 Fok Loh Tsun Road
Kowloon
Hong Kong
(010 852) 3 7182748
Fax (010 852) 7184565

Pure Silks from
Angus International
Penthouse
6, Fok Loh Tsun Road,
Kowloon
Hong Kong
Tel: 3-7182748

Some people are concerned that the production of silk involves cruelty to the silkworms, and although some silk production does involve killing the silkworm moths, the majority does not. Most silk is taken from one species, *Bombyx mori*, a moth which has been domesticated for so many centuries that it now needs human intervention to help it complete its life cycle.

The silkworms are reared intensively, the larvae feeding on mulberry leaves and pupating in cocoons made from silk fibres they have spun themselves. Each cocoon is made from one long unbroken filament. Usually the adult moth leaves the cocoon by dissolving a small hole, and the cocoon can then be used to manufacture 'spun silk'; this, however, is often considered inferior to silk unreeled in one long thread from the unbroken cocoon. To obtain an unbroken cocoon the moth is killed before it emerges, usually by asphyxiation.

Avoid 'weighted silk', which is treated with salts of tin and lead to make it heavier, since even small amounts of lead can be toxic.

Traidcraft Clothes

Traidcraft (see page 240 for their main entry) produce what is possibly the most comprehensive mail order catalogue of natural fibre Third World fashions currently available. The clothes come from India and Bangladesh, where Traidcraft and the World Development Movement are jointly sponsoring manufacturing co-operatives.

The clothes are a clever mixture of tradition and stylishness, with the fashion tastes of the west being the basis for their products — big Madras cotton check shirts, batik summer dresses, elegant silk dresses, vegetable-dyed khadi trousers, matching chambray jacket and trousers, and bold hand-printed skirts. There is also a fashion accessories catalogue — bags, scarves, ties, jewellery, belts and hats which is handy to have with the clothes one.

*

Garments are made individually, often using handloom cloth. The maximum quantity of any garment is 600, and considerably fewer of the more intricate designs. This ensures that the production capacity of the producer isn't overstretched and that each garment is quite exclusive. Many of the techniques and designs used are an integral part of the craftspeoples' culture. Traditional techniques make economic sense for the poor communities with who we work. Block printing, batik, embroidery and handloom weaving are ideal for small scale and village-based industry. The equipment needed is relatively inexpensive and easily available. In addition many techniques cannot be imitated mechanically, so the local co-operative is able to compete in a world market.

*

'Working for the rights and dignity of women' is the slogan of the Ankur Kala group in Calcutta. About 30 women work in and run two centres in the city. Batik, tailoring and catering units provide jobs which are as important as the members are desereted, widows or migrants from the countryside in search of work. But the group is about more than work. It meets regularly to hear from women who are actively involved in areas like law, employment, family problems and health. And they supporteach other in times of difficulty, such as desertion by their husbands or threats by them. The business leads to a richer community life: a small work growing.

The prices are very reasonable — dresses from £25, skirts from £12.50 and trousers from £8.50, and everything is made of cotton. As with the products sold by Tumi (page 125), you can be sure that because the garments are bought directly from the producers, they are getting a decent wage for their work.

Traidcraft plc
Kingsway
Gateshead
Tyne and Wear
NE11 0NE
091 487 3191

Co-operative Clothes

The Co-operation Catalogue is a mail order marketing organization for garments and other products from workers' co-operatives in Britain. The current catalogue includes screenprinted t-shirts with interesting designs, trousers, shirts and skirts. Their clothes are not always made from natural fibres, but the prices aren't bad.

Co-operation
Freepost
London
SE15 6BR
0(7)1-703 7064

the co-operation catalogue

Clothkits

Clothkits, as the name suggests, started life in 1969 when Anne Kennedy designed the first dress with the pattern actually printed on the fabric, so the buyer bought the fabric length, cut it out, and made it up into the garment. Clothkits was sold three years ago and the number of kits went down drastically — the winter 1989 catalogue only has a couple of things for children, including a rainforest patterned jacket from the sale of which 50p goes to Friends of the Earth, and one complete outfit for women. The kits come complete with matching thread and fastenings, and very clear instructions. As well as the mail order catalogue, Clothkits have twelve shops — three in London, Lewes, Oxford, Bath, Guildford, Winchester, Cambridge, Cheltenham, Canterbury and Tunbridge Wells.

Clothkits are not particularly cheap (£29.95 for a pleated needlecord skirt, £34 for a printed, jersey dress), but they're well made, very good quality, colourful and original, and as they say themselves, they are designed 'to fill the gap between exciting but expensive boutique clothes and the cheaper but rather dull chainstore clothes'. The catalogue at least is free.

Clothkits
24 High Street
Lewes
East Sussex
BN7 1BR
0273 477111

clothkits

Sewing Machines

Like so many modern marvels, electronic sewing machines these days can do everything from buttonholes to embroidery, though you can of course still buy hand machines, and since hand sewing machines were made to last, secondhand machines can be very good value. Frank Godfrey's *An International History of the Sewing Machine* (Hale, 1982, £15.95) is a fascinating read for anyone particularly interested in sewing machines: a big book with lots of pictures and intriguing social history. *The Complete Book of Sewing Machine Repair* (by Howard Hutchison, Tab Books, 1980) is good if you want to know how to mend your machine when it goes wrong.

Two places in Britain which guarantee to mend almost any sewing machine are the Wimbledon Sewing Machine Company and Olympic Sewing Machines. Both claim to offer a 48-hour service and a very wide range of spare parts, and can also advise you about what sort of machine is best for you to buy (and of course supply it).

Wimbledon Sewing Machine Co. Ltd
Balham High Road
London
SW17 7AA
0(8)1-767 4724

Olympic Sewing Machines
1c and 1d Shepherds
Bush Road
London
W6 7NA
0(8)1-743 6683

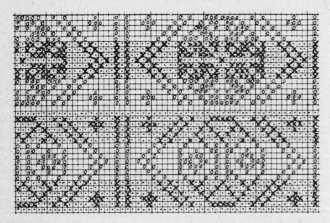

Knitting Books

For complete beginners a good buy is the Ladybird 'Learn-about' book called *Knitting* (75p). It starts from absolute basics, and though written for keen eight-year-olds, is clear and not at all patronizing.

The Ebury Press's *Good Housekeeping: Knitting* (1981, £4.95) is a small but beautifully-illustrated book which shows more than ninety different patterns in full colour. This is one of a series of five full-colour books, all worth looking at. The other titles in the series are: *Needlepoint; Embroidery; Crochet;* and *Patchwork and Appliqué.*

*

Many stitch patterns were created simultaneously in different parts of the world, while others, such as Arabian two-colour knitting, are indigenous to certain places. However, most of the single-coloured stitch patterns we use today developed largely from the distinctive patterns woven into the knitted Guernseys of the fishermen of Great Britain; from Sheringham and Whitby, to Aberdeen, Inishmore [when was Galway in Great Britain?] and Portmadoc. These densely knit regional patterns contrast strongly with the cobwebby effect of a Shetland shawl, Fair Isle patterns knitted in browns and fawns of natural- coloured fleece, and the deep-embossed cables and bobbles of Aran knitting.

Traditional and Glorious Knitting

Of all the books you can buy which tell the history of traditional knitting and give sample patterns, Rae Compton's *Complete Book of Traditional Knitting* is one of the best, combining history and practicality, and giving examples from all over Europe and as far afield as South America. The last chapter gives thirteen detailed patterns, including traditional Aran, Fair Isle, Norwegian and Icelandic garments.

For the last twenty years Kaffe Fassett has gradually been making a big mark on the knitting scene by throwing out many previously-held ideas about design and knitting technique. His designs, which are really imagination boosters rather than patterns, involve lots of different yarns and colours in one garment, looking at the natural world of rocks and flowers for inspiration, and seeing knitting as a sort of zen exercise.

*

What I would really like to do is invite you to paint with wool. Having been a painter for years, I can tell you that needlework is a much more enjoyable way of working with colour than painting and requires far less instruction to get satisfying results. I'm assuming that you already have your basic knitting skills, which are, amazingly, all you need to create these designs.

The Complete Book of Traditional Knitting
Rae Compton
Batsford, 1983
£9.95

Glorious Knitting
Kaffe Fassett
Century, 1985
£9.95

Spinning and Dyeing

For an excellent introduction to every aspect of spinning, read Eileen Chadwick's *The Craft of Hand Spinning* (Batsford, 1980, £5.95), which covers everything from a detailed pattern for a spinning wheel to the working characteristics of British regional wool types. She includes information about the sources and qualities of every sort of yarn you are likely to come across, even to Old English Sheepdog hair and nettles (an alternative to flax), and has a good glossary and list of suppliers.

If you are interested in experimenting with natural fabric dyes, Hetty Wickens' *Natural Dyes for Spinners and Weavers* (Batsford, 1983, £4.95) is another very practical book, with colour plates showing the results of different dyestuffs. For a more detailed approach, Ken Ponting's *A Dictionary of Dyes and Dyeing* (Bell and Hyman, 1981, £9.95) is truly encyclopedic, fully illustrated, and written with the practitioner in mind.

The British Wool Marketing Board

Set up in 1950, the British Wool Marketing Board is the central marketing agency for the entire British wool clip, and all but the smallest herds must be registered with them. They can also supply information about the types, qualities and characteristics of every sheep variety in the country, and also sell fleeces and 'matchings' (parts of a fleece of uniform colour and quality). The BWMB also produce a very useful annual list of suppliers of British-grown machine and hand knitting yarns, with complete details of the types of yarn spun by each mill. By contacting mills which manufacture the yarns you are interested in, a stamped addressed envelope will usually result in a set of sample cards, and you can then buy balls and cones of wool as you need them, though you will often need to buy in bulk, as mills are usually dealing with shops rather than individuals. If you ring up and check in advance, you can often buy very cheap cone ends and slightly substandard yarns at the mills themselves.

The BWMB publishes an annual mail order catalogue, with garments made in Britain from British-grown wool. Chunky oiled sweaters start at around £20, scarves in natural jacob wool at £4.50.

British Wool Marketing Board
Oak Mills
Clayton
Bradford
West Yorkshire
BD14 6JD
0274 882091

Wool-Producing Areas

There are about 25 million sheep in Britain today, little changed in numbers since the late nineteenth century. It was the monastic houses of the Middle Ages that first herded sheep in large numbers, and by the sixteenth century great stretches of the Pennines, the Lake District and Wales became vast sheep-walks. The invasion of the Scottish highlands by Blackface and Cheviot sheep started in about 1760, an invasion which cleared many areas of their human population. Not surprisingly, the woollen industry in Britain is still to be found in the areas where sheep are still an important part of the agricultural economy — Shetland, the Scottish Highlands, Wales and the Pennines.

Knitwear producers, especially small ones, seem particularly prone to market forces and personal circumstances, and since the first *Green Pages* was published many have moved on to other pastures. Some of the best places to find interesting knitwear at reasonable prices are craft workshops, or the many craft fairs that you will find throughout the summer wherever tourists congregate.

Scottish Knitwear

Scottish knitters have traditionally produced a diverse range of knitwear, from windproof ganseys to lace shawls that will go through a wedding ring. Finding firms that do mail order is not as easy as it once was, but *A Visitors Guide to Scottish Craft Shops* (available from the Scottish Tourist Board, local tourist offices or The Scottish Development Agency) gives details of workshops you can visit, while Craftpoint's *Buyers Guide* to retail products from Scotland contains information about some of the many producers of beautiful knitwear. This guide really exists to help promote the marketing and sales of Scottish craft industries, but you can contact suppliers, some of whom have shops or retail outlets, through its pages.

Scottish Tourist Board
23 Ravelston Terrace
Edinburgh
EH4 3EU
031 332 2433

Scottish Development Agency
Rosebery House
Haymarket Terrace
Edinburgh
EH12 5EZ
031 337 9595

Scottish
Development
Agency

Craftpoint
Beauly
Inverness-shire
IV4 7EH
0463 782578

Shetland Knitwear

have an allover Fair Isle sweater, hand-knitted from natural coloured wools on Papa Stour, one of the more remote of the Shetland islands — for softness, fit, natural oily smell, intricacy of knit and subtlety of colour I've never seen better. It's the fine, soft wool rooed (plucked rather than clipped) from the sheep introduced to the islands by the Vikings that makes Shetland knitwear unlike any other, and the patterns reputedly learned

from Spanish seamen that have made Fair Isle famous the world over. Until recently, however, it was difficult to tell whether a 'Shetland' garment came from Shetland at all. The Shetland Knitwear Trades Association has now registered a Certification Trade Mark which can only be used on garments knitted in the islands, so look out for the Shetland knitter on anything that calls itself real Shetland. The Association is happy to send anyone who is interested a list of manufacturers of Shetland knitwear and a manufacturer's resource guide.

Shetland Knitwear Trades Association
93 St Olaf Street
Lerwick
Shetland
ZE1 0ES
0595 5631

Of the fifty-odd members of the SKTA, a few are worth special mention.

Maggi Prytherch lives on Foula — sometimes called 'the island on the edge of the world' — and spins and dyes and knits her own wool; she is teaching the children on Foula to do the same. Fair Isle Crafts is a workers' co-operative set up in 1980 to promote the production of traditional Fair Isle knitwear in its original home. Allover Fair Isle sweaters start at around £50, scarves at £12, hats at £5.50. Victoria Gibson has a rich collection of knitwear including hand-knitted coats, jackets, waistcoats and jumpers. She sometimes uses fancy yarns and mohair to give interesting textures.

Maggi Prytherch
Breckans
Foula
Shetland
039 33 3224

Fair Isle Crafts Ltd
The Koolin
Fair Isle
Shetland
ZE2 9JU
035 12 225

Victoria Gibson Knitwear
Grieg's Pier
Esplanade
Lerwick
Shetland
ZE1 0LL
0595 4117

Pure Shetland yarns in lots of dyed and natural colours for hand and machine knitting can be obtained from Jamieson and Smith in Lerwick. They spin mostly 2-ply lace and jumper yarns, but also do a thick 4-ply Shetland yarn called Unst-fleece. Send an sae for yarn samples.

Jamieson and Smith (SWB) Ltd
90 North Road
Lerwick
Shetland
0595 3579

There are several good wool mills in Scotland, but the one that most people swear by is Hunters of Brora, which also provides much-needed employment in this northern county of Scotland. Hunters do a comprehensive range of yarns for both hand and machine knitting from British wools: the qualities are Embo, Aran, Unstfleece and Cheviot, which comes in a wonderful selection of colours.

T.M. Hunter Ltd
Sutherland Wool Mills
Brora
KW9 6NA
0408 21366

Zig Zag

Bright, colourful designer knitwear by Zig Zag in Ayrshire is made in wool, starting at about £29.00. They also make about 20% of their products in cotton. They have a colour brochure for mail order.

Zig Zag
Riverford Mill
Stewarton
Ayrshire
K43 5DH
0560 85187

Welsh Knitwear

Much the same situation exists here as in Scotland. The equivalent organization to the Scottish Development Agency is the Welsh Development Agency. They also produce a buyers guide, but it's mostly for retailers wanting to buy to stock their own shops; the Welsh Craft Council have had to abandon the various excellent craft guides that used to cover the whole of Wales because of lack of funding. For craftspeople themselves the Crafts Council now publishes a monthly *Information Bulletin* instead. Local craft guides are available for some areas; ask at tourist information offices.

Welsh Development Agency
Treforest Industrial Estate
Pontypridd
Mid Glamorgan
CF37 5BR
0443 841777

Welsh Craft Council (Cyngor Crefft Cymru Cyf)
20 Severn Street
Welshpool
Powys
SY21 7AD
0938 5313

Rhoscolyn Knitwear

Pam Webb at Rhoscolyn Knitwear in Anglesey specializes in undyed natural Welsh wool knitwear. The borders knitted into the patterned yokes feature celtic designs, mountain sheep and shepherds' crooks. A recent addition to the range is the Anglesey Pullover, a tough outdoor garment with a little raised relief picture of the Menai Bridge down by your waist to remind you where it came from.

Rhoscolyn Knitwear
Tyn Rhos
Rhoscolyn
nr Holyhead
Anglesey
LL65 2SJ
0407 860861

Louise Critchlow

Louise produces unique garments handknitted in top quality natural fibres. Her trademarks are beautiful colours and different textured yarns worked into intricate floral and geometric patterns based on ideas taken from flowers, embroideries and oriental carpets. Send for a brochure.

Louise Critchlow Exclusive Knitwear
The Old Station
Machynlleth
Powys
SY20 8NT
0654 3380

English Knitwear

The English craft knitwear industry seems to have hit hard times, though I'm sure there are still lots of handknitters supplying individual craft shops. But as a friend who runs a craft shop told me recently, 'For many people handmade knitwear is a fashion item and it's just not fashionable these days.' Strange — I'd never thought of the jumpers in my wardrobe as anything other than essential protection against the British climate.

Black Sheep

North Norfolk is hardly where you'd expect to find a large flock of black Welsh mountain sheep, but there they are, with a whole range of natural oiled wool products to prove it. Their shops and mail order catalogue include plain and patterned sweaters, socks, scarves, hats, skirts, waistcoats, and a range of sheepish gifts — all the garments made in the natural black, dark grey and light grey of the Welsh mountain wool. The Sloppy Joe at £39.00 is an excellent all-purpose garment, and you can see them being handframed if you visit Black Sheep's farm shop at Aylsham in Norfolk. They also supply yarns. There are also Black Sheep shops in Cambridge and Lincoln.

Black Sheep
9 Penfold Street
Aylsham
Norfolk
NR11 6ET
0263 733142/732006

Knitwitz

Manchester Craft Village is well worth a visit, with a wide range of craftspeople working in different materials. Among them is Jackie Needham, who did her degree in knitting at Manchester Poly and then wondered what to do with it. What she did was to start Knitwitz, which specializes in pure wool knitwear with a creative streak. Her latest venture is a sweater incorporating the wearer's name — on the expensive side at £40 a time, but certainly different and individual, and she will consider discounts for unwaged customers.

Knitwitz
Unit 9
Manchester Craft Village
Oak Street
Manchester
M4 1HS
061 835 1017

Dandelion

In Swindon, home of many green activities, is a little shop called Dandelion where you can see jumpers knitted up from the patterns and wools that the shop stocks. You can also order a jumper to a pattern you like and they will knit it up for you: the price depends on the pattern and the wool. The shop also sells tasteful gifts and hand-made jewellery.

Dandelion
10 Wood Street
Old Town
Swindon
SN11 4AB
0793 511099

Resources for Craft Textile Workers

Rowan Yarns
Wool spinning mills are thicker on the ground in West Yorkshire than anywhere else in Britain, and Rowan Yarns in Holmfirth have taken advantage of the recent upsurge in interest in handknitting to produce a wide and colourful range of handknitting yarns, all in 100% wool. Kaffe Fassett recommends Rowan yarns, and Rowan now do yarn packs specially made up for many of the Fassett designs. Since they don't do mail order send an sae for a list of stockists.

Rowan Yarns
Green Lane Mill
Holmfirth
West Yorkshire
HD7 1RW
0484 681881

Ries Wools
With more than 5,000 yarn shops in Britain to choose from, you should be able to find something very close to what you are looking for. By popular consent, however, the one shop that stands out above the others is Ries Wools in Holborn, which for 35 years has been selling a comprehensive range of knitting yarns, accessories, patterns and books. They offer a discount to bona fide charities and have special 'Zoo Check' knitting kits from which £1 goes to Zoo Check (see page 72). A 24-hour telephone ordering service and an efficient mail order organization ensure that your yarn arrives quickly if you can't get to the shop.

Ries Wools
242-243 High Holborn
London
WC1V 7DZ
0(7)1-242 7721

Striped, Speckled and Spotted

I remember sitting one winter evening in a friend's cottage talking, sipping homemade wine, and carding her jacob wool into 'roll-lags' — little sausages of wool with the fibres all aligned so she could then spin them. Anne and Martin Wray are spinners and suppliers of yarns, fleeces and spinning equipment. They have Jacob and other locally-grown wool supplies and stock a range of rare breed fleeces, including Shetland, North Ronaldsay, Hebridean and Manx. They have an excellent range of spinning wheels, some in kit form to assemble yourself, including Scottish Haldane, traditional Lewis and Orkney wheels, Louet wheels made in Holland, the Ashford range from New Zealand and Westbury English-made wheels. They also stock a full range of bobbins, flyers, lazy kates, niddy noddys, wool winders, skein winders and carders. Then there are yarns for knitters — Jacob, Dorset

Down, Clun, English Cross and mixes with names like 'Highland Tints' and 'Pinks', which is a mix of mohair and merino. Send for their fascinating brochure.

Striped, Speckled and Spotted
Studio 7
Warmington Craft Workshops
Warmingham
nr Sandbach
Cheshire
CW4 7LQ
0477 37085

Eve Spinning Centre

Besides stocking the usual range of supplies and equipment for spinning, felting and weaving, Mary Eve's Spinning Centre in Witham also runs workshops, demonstrations and lectures. The Spinning Centre's premises are shared with M&R Dyes, who produce the Spectrum range. Both companies offer a mail order service.

Mary Eve Handspinner and M&R Dyes
Carters
Station Yard
Wickham Bishops
Witham
Essex
CM8 3JB
0621 891405

Books for Textile Craftworkers

If you want books about textiles and textile crafts, Fibrecrafts stock nearly two hundred different titles. They also stock some thirty shades of natural dye and yarns for knitting — wool, cotton, linen and some mixed fibres. They also sell fleeces and a full range of spinning wheels. Send £1 and a large sae for a copy of their comprehensive catalogue.

Fibrecrafts
Style Cottage
Lower Eashing
Godalming
Surrey
GU7 2QD
04868 21853

Copp Design

For something completely green and creative on the borders between textile design and recycling, Gerry Copp who lives near Lincoln uses a combination of recycled paper and rags to create collages, hangings, rugs, papier maché pots and greetings cards. Often she uses handmade paper for a collage which will in turn become the basis for a rag rug or wall-hanging made from hand-dyed cotton strips. The handmade paper cards and collages often incorporate leaves and seeds, creating a pleasing evocation of her rural surroundings. Gerry is also happy to work with school and youth groups on creative environmental projects.

Copp Design
School Cottage
Aisthorpe
Lincoln
LN1 2SG
0522 730218

Making Your Own Shoes

Christine Clark's *Make-it-Yourself Shoe Book* is the only book that shows you clearly how to make your own shoes without needing masses of specialized equipment or previous experience. The large format allows for photographs and drawings of each stage, and rather than covering a lot of different styles, the author concentrates on just a few basic designs, including sandals, moccasins, slippers and hiking boots. At the end of the book there is a good list of suppliers of leather, thread and tools.
*

With care and attention to detail, and above all practice, you will be able to turn out a shoe, sandal or moccasin, a boot or a slipper, that will not only feel superb but will have none of the crude look of so many handmade items. It will be a proud day for you when in answer to an admiring question you will be able to say 'I made them'.

The Make-it-Yourself Shoe Book
Christine Lewis Clark
Routledge and Kegan Paul, 1979
£7.95

Footwear

Sturdy construction and good foot support are the qualities to look for in footwear. Comfortable shoes can make a big difference to the way you feel — the effect of good foot support extends to the legs and back, particularly if you stand or walk a lot. With the high cost of today's footwear — a sturdy pair of shoes will cost between £30 and £50 — it's important that they should last a long time, and if well-constructed so they do not sag, swell or fall apart, good shoes should last you for years and become ever more comfortable.

The last few years have seen enormous advances in shoe design and construction. An increasing interest in sport for all, especially jogging, has set off a booming market in trainers, and these shoes with their new and innovative designs have now become everyday wear for many people, especially the young. You will find more about running on page 149.

Most shoemakers will tell you that with the possible exception of some shoes made from synthetics, good shoes should always be made from full-grain leather. Because this is the part of the hide that originally protected the cow, it is the only leather that can be properly waterproofed. The inner layers of hide are suitable for shoes that need to breathe more and are used in dry conditions, like desert boots.

The use of natural materials in footwear — leather and natural crêpe rubber — is to be encouraged for the same reasons as natural fibres for clothes. They are renewable resources if harvested wisely, and mould easily to the shape of the foot. If your vegetarian principles extend to the use of animal-originated leather, then look for shoes made in Cordura, a lightweight nylon material, or stick to trainers, though these will inevitably contain artificial materials.

There are definite advantages to having shoes made specially for you. With the boom in small individual shoemaking businesses in recent years, you will almost certainly find a good shoemaker reasonably close to you, and the chances are that you will pay no more than you would for a good pair of readymade shoes.

Good shoes will last longer and maintain their looks if you clean and oil them regularly. Leather contains natural oils which leach out when exposed to weather, dirt and long use. Once you have brushed away the dirt, especially what has collected in the seams, saddle soap is an excellent cleaner and lubricator — your local saddlers or equestrian shop will stock it. Shoe polishes usually contain wax, which clogs the pores of the leather and stops shoes 'breathing' properly, so it's best to avoid them.

Simple Way

If you don't want to start making shoes from scratch, an excellent middle way between making your own shoes and buying them from a shoe shop is kit from Simple Way in Somerset. They provide everything you need to sew your own shoes together — the pieces are cut out and the holes are all punched, so there is no glue needed and no mess involved. The kits even come with a finger protector so the needle doesn't go where it shouldn't. The kits start at around £22, saving of some £15 on shop prices for a similar style and quality, and many people have founded a small-scale shoemaking business on Simple Way kits.

All the leather used is from British tanneries, and is only accepted if it is accompanied by a certificate stating that it is free from whale-based products.

The business started in the small town of Street five years ago, and Simple Way now has over 15,000 regular customers. Director David Price believes that popularity of Simple Way kits comes from a unique combination of the need for comfortable footwear, the therapy provided by the simple yet satisfying work involved, and the possibilities for making a modest income.

They also sell foot care products and footwear accessories. Write for a current catalogue.

Simple Way
5 The Tanyard
Leigh Road
Street
Somerset
BA16 0HE
0458 47275

The Natural Shoe Store

In 1977 an American shoemaker called Robert Lusk introduced 'alternative shoes' to Britain, in particular the negative heel, which for the first time in centuries put the heel where it should be — near the ground. From these small beginnings developed The Natural Shoe Store, which now sends its mail order catalogue all over the world.

If you want to see the full range of footwear stocked by The Natural Shoe Store you will need to visit one of their London shops (in Neal Street and the Kings Road, Chelsea) or their recently-opened shop in Glasgow, but they also produce a good mail order catalogue, which includes Birkenstock sandals from Germany (both cork soles and the increasingly popular 'noppies' — lots of little rubber knobbles which massage your feet as you walk), the original negative heel shoe from Roots in Canada, foot-shaped Danish Naturforms and traditional birchwood clogs. Sandals cost from £20 and shoes from £32. They have an annual sale, so maybe buy then.

The Natural Shoe Store

York House
Avonmore Place
London W14 8RW
0(7)1-602 2866/2085

Princes Square
Buchanan Street
Glasgow
G1 3TX
041 226 3356

Ward and Wright

used to have terrible problems with sandals coming apart at the stitching on the back strap until I found Ward and Wright. Now I have just two pairs of sandals, both from W&W — I've had them for seven years, and every other year I send them back to be reheeled.

Ward and Wright started making sandals in 1979, and their reputation has grown to the point where they send their colour catalogue all over the country, a catalogue which contains more than twenty designs of sandal plus traditional clogs. They will always repair their own sandals, and even if they drop a design you like, they will be happy to do a repeat order for you. Sandals start at £25 and clogs at £16; their friendly shop in Norwich sells well-made boots and shoes from Scandinavia as well as the full range of sandals.

Ward and Wright

7 Timberhill
Norwich
NR1 3JZ
0603 610636

Adams and Jones

Without paying over the odds as you do with some of the London hand-made shoemakers, Adams and Jones are the BMW of the small shoemakers. Using leather which is often dyed with vegetable dyes (always avoiding whale oils) and Malaysian natural plantation crepe, each shoe is made to measure. Based in Glastonbury in Somerset, a traditional leatherworking area, A&J employ a number of local outworkers to do the final stitching and handwork, paying good hourly rates rather than the kind of piece rates that have given outworking such a bad name. Nearly all their business is mail order, and they specialize in making shoes for people with problem feet. Reckon to pay £38 for a pair of shoes, £50 for a three-quarter pair of boots, but they'll last for ever.

Adams and Jones Ltd

The White Cottage Courtyard
Magdalene Street
Glastonbury
Somerset
BA6 9EH
0458 34356

The Devon Shoemakers

In South Devon there is a thriving hand-made footwear industry, where Green Shoes and Conker Shoes in Totnes both make their shoes to their customer's individual specifications. Prices are similar: sandals start at around £15, shoes at £32 and boots at £38. They each do a mail order catalogue.

Green Shoes is a women's collective; they have a flexible work structure which encourages the employment of women with children, and one of their aims is to show how well women can work together and be financially successful. They make adults and childrens shoes, do mail order and have a catalogue. Conker Shoes operates in a similar way, but as a mixed group — ecologically-minded down to the paper bags and Ecover washing-up liquid behind the sink.

Green Shoes
10 High Street
Totnes
Devon
TQ9 5RY
0803 864997

Conker Shoe Company
83 High Street
Totnes
Devon
TQ9 5PB
0803 862490

Marged

Marged have expanded a lot since they were established as a women's co-operative in 1981, and now produce shoes for children as well as a wide range for women. The children's shoes are available in size seven upwards, in one good simple natural shape and various widths. There are some thirty different styles of shoe — lace-up, slip-on and buckled — and ten different boots from walking to knee-length lace-up. They make roomy shoulder bags and a leather duffle bag too. They use leather for the uppers and crêpe for the soles, and the shoes come in a range of colours from neutral to bright red.

Marged Shoes
Stable Cottage
Derry Ormond Park
Betwys Bledrws
Lampeter
Dyfed
SA48 8PA
057 045 557

The Rest of Britain

Recommended makers of handmade shoes in other parts of Britain include the following.

Elfin Shoes, Shrewsbury

Elfin will only make shoes once they have actually measured your feet, so you will need to visit them for a fitting — they are happy, however, to send your shoes to you when they are ready. The Elfin workshop is in the St Julian's Craft Centre in Shrewsbury (well worth a visit if you are in the area); the address below is their trading address.

Elfin Shoes
Bumpy Lane
Stanton upon Hine Heath
Shropshire
SY4 4LH
0939 250954

Charles MacWatt, Bristol

Charles MacWatt, well known in the Bristol area for the quality of his workmanship, makes a very wide range of handmade shoes. He also produces a helpful catalogue.

Charles MacWatt
7 Christmas Steps
Bristol
BS1 5BS
0272 214247

Charles MacWatt

Made to Last, Leeds

Made to Last is a women's co-operative, making shoes for adults and children in a pleasing range of styles. They can deal with specific foot problems. Send an sae for their mail order catalogue. They are striking out into a new line too — ready made cotton clothes made from Indonesian cloth.

Made to Last
77 Raglan Road
Leeds
LS2 9DZ
0532 426079

Guat Shoes, Sheffield

Guat makes a wide range of shoes in a variety of exciting colours, including rainbow shoes and sandals, button boots, and stylish men's brogues. They offer a choice of Vibram non-slip or natural crêpe soles. There is no extra charge for made-to-measure shoes.

Guat Shoes
221 School Road
Sheffield
S10 1GN
0742 686364

Cordwainer, Gloucestershire

Sarah Juniper specializes in seventeenth century footwear for green-minded actors, but she does also make modern footwear. She has a catalogue for the 1640s styles, so if you want to set a new trend then send for it. She likes to measure customers personally, but she does have a form for postal enquiries.

Cordwainer
109 Woodmancote
Dursley
Gloucestershire
GL11 4AH

Galloway Footwear Co-operative, South-West Scotland

The members of The Galloway Footwear Co-operative make six styles of good brightly coloured shoes, and sturdy lace-up boots. They also do a whole range of clogs, including low-lace clogs, clasp clogs, one-bar clogs and wellington clogs. There is a mail order service, so send for a catalogue.

The Galloway Footwear Co-operative
Balmaclellan
Castle Douglas
Kirkcudbrightshire
DG7 3QE
064 42 465

Clogs

Clogs used to be worn to work by farm labourers and factory workers all over the country, but clog-making now is limited to clogs for traditional dancing and the few people who prefer wearing clogs to shoes. If you would like to know about the history of clogs and clogmaking, then read Jeremy Atkinson's *Clogs and Clogmaking* (Shire Publications, 1984, £1.50), which is a clear and concise history of the subject, with some fascinating illustrations.

Kite Clogs

The author of *Clogs and Clogmaking* runs his own clog workshop, Kite Clogs, in Hereford. If you would like him to make a pair of clogs for you he prefers to see you and measure your feet first, though he will do postal orders. A lot of his leather is water buffalo hide from India, and he is the last clogmaker to carve his own wooden soles. He also makes shoes and Jesus sandals, for which there is a catalogue.

Kite Clogs
Unit 1
Capuchin Yard
Church Street
Hereford
HR1 2LR
0432 274269

Dandy Clogs

John the Fish of Dandy Clogs in Cornwall specializes in decorated clogs for clog dancing.

Dandy Clogs
2 Tarrandean Bungalows
Perranwell Station
Truro
Cornwall
TR3 7NP
0872 863825

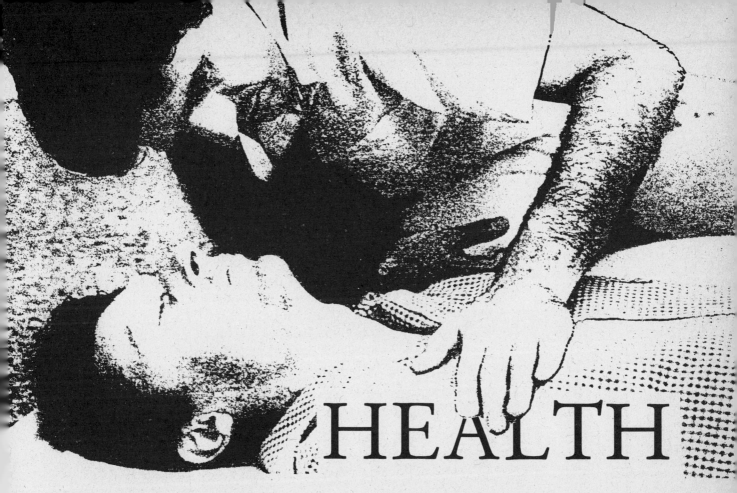

HEALTH

'There has been a conflict at the heart of medical practice since Roman times at least. This is the question as to whether the physician should concentrate on actively intervening in disease or whether the primary emphasis should be on helping the patient's self-healing systems to work more effectively. . . We are now reaching for a new synthesis of the two viewpoints, an understanding of the strengths and weaknesses of both. We are beginning to learn where each is useful and how best to combine them.'
Lawrence LeShan, *Holistic Health*

Whatever you might be led to believe in this age of tablets and supplements, good health is not an impossible dream, something that you might aim for but never actually attain. Being healthy is the natural state of a living organism, and health is both a privilege and a right, for we reach our full potential only when we are fulfilled and active.

Though it is tempting to believe that somebody else, in this case a 'health professional', will always be able to tell you what to do if you feel unwell, it is up to each of us to take responsibility for our health. When it comes to your body, *you* are the expert. If you hurt, nobody has the right to tell you that you must be imagining it. And when you feel good, you have to ignore the people with vested interests who want to persuade you that there's something wrong. Revel in your health.

As Ivan Illich says in *Limits to Medicine*, 'To be in good health means not only to feel alive in pleasure and in pain; it means to cherish but also to risk survival. . . A world of optimal and widespread health is obviously a world of minimal and only occasional medical intervention. Healthy people are those who live in healthy homes on a healthy diet in an environment equally fit for birth, growth, work, healing and dying; they are sustained by a culture that enhances the conscious acceptance of limits to population, or ageing, of incomplete recovery and ever-imminent death. Healthy people need minimal bureaucratic intervention to mate, give birth, share the human condition, and die.'

An Unhealthy Environment

Despite all the evidence that certain food additives can cause hyperactivity in children, that acid rain is implicated in Alzheimer's disease, and that excessive lead in water pipes can cause brain damage, it is surprising how slow we are to accept such findings and, when the evidence is irrefutable, to accept that it is the human environment which needs changing, not the speed at which more medications are introduced.

'Environmental illness' is still seen only as a small category of disease even by those who acknowledge it at all, even though some environmental factors in health are obvious — cigarette smoke, toxic chemicals, nuclear radiation, carbon monoxide from vehicle exhausts; others are conveniently overlooked — food additives, ozone, pesticide and hormone residues; and others are mentioned but largely ignored because they cannot easily be measured — stress, overcrowding, poverty.

Meanwhile pharmaceutical companies make ever-increasing profits, NHS waiting times grow inexorably, and more than one in ten British women takes tranquillizers on a regular basis. Britons consume over two billion pounds' worth of medicines every year — £30 worth each, 80% of them prescribed (the Americans are way ahead, however, taking nearly three times as many pills each as we do).

The Whole Person — and the Positive Approach

If you go to see a doctor, probably the first thing they will say is: 'And what's wrong with you?'. Here is the first clue to the shift that we need to make in our understanding of health. We don't have a National Health Service in Britain, we have a National Illness Service. The alternative to an illness service is to provide ourselves with a *real* health service — a good diet, pollution-free surroundings, fulfilling work, enough support and acknowledgement and attention. We may still need medical help when we hurt ourselves or feel under the weather and don't know why, and we shall still need to be checked for cancers and be vaccinated against tetanus and tuberculosis, but we shall *not* need to drug ourselves stupid and become overly dependent on high-tech medicine.

After the initial question, your doctor might ask you how you feel, but they rarely want to know how you *feel* — what they want to hear about is the pain in your chest, the lumps on your arm, or the blood you coughed up this morning. Here is the second clue to what's wrong. The National Illness Service is mostly interested in your body, not in you. A healthy body is important, but is only one aspect of good health. Dividing physical health from overall health — as our present medical system does — will never lead to real health. Holistic health practitioners are fond of reminding us that human beings are mind, body *and* spirit, all enfolding and influencing each other all the time.

Alternatives — not Either/Or but Both/And

Mainstream and alternative medicine sometimes find it hard to acknowledge and admire each other's strengths, but you as the consumer can choose for yourself, and you can try different approaches; none of them has a monopoly. There is at last some indication that the different disciplines within the healing professions are beginning to talk to each other (see page 144 for details of the British Holistic Medical Association, for example). Yet even though many doctors are beginning to see the sense of taking a broader view of healing, most of the impetus for such change will have to come from us, the public, because we have a much larger interest in being truly healthy than they do.

Some Basic Books

Ever since books were invented there have been single volume 'home doctors' which claimed to tell you everything from how to deal with chilblains to the symptoms of bubonic plague. Such volumes are still around, with authoritative titles like *Family Medical Encyclopedia* and *The Family Doctor Home Adviser*. They make interesting reading if you like to frighten yourself and bore your doctor, and you can check whether you have gynecomastia, molluscum contagiosum or systemic lupus erythematosus, but all you really need is a good first aid manual and access to a phone for anything more urgent. On the other hand, we are interested in our health, and so we should be in this unhealthy world. There are now a number of 'alternative' reference books in the field of holistic medicine and health care.

First Aid

There are a number of first aid manuals available, and even though some are cheaper than the 'official' Red Cross/St Johns/St Andrews one, this is still the best value for money. Six hundred full-colour illustrations show you exactly what to do in emergencies and many other circumstances where medical knowledge is needed, from splinters to splints, sunburn to sunstroke. This is really the only 'home doctor' you need.

SNAKE BITES

The only poisonous snake native to the United Kingdom is the adder. However, there are many poisonous snakes kept as pets, some of which may escape or attack their owners. In addition to the injuries produced by a bite, fright resulting in severe shock may also be evident. Contrary to popular belief, snake bites are only rarely fatal.

In countries where there are numerous dangerous snakes, it is important to identify the snake so that appropriate anti-venom serum can be administered. Therefore, record its description (colour and markings are the best guide) or if it has been captured or killed, keep it.

SYMPTOMS & SIGNS
- Casualty may experience disturbed vision.
- Casualty may feel nauseated or already be vomiting.
- One or two small puncture wounds with sharp pain and local swelling.
- Breathing may become difficult or fail altogether.
- Symptoms and signs of shock (see p.86).
- Salivation and sweating may appear in advanced stages of venom reaction.

AIM
Reassure the casualty, prevent absorption of venom, and arrange urgent removal to hospital.

TREATMENT

1 Lay the casualty down and advise her not to move.

2 Immobilize the affected part and keep it below the level of the heart.

3 Wash the wound thoroughly with soap and water, if available.

4 If the casualty becomes unconscious, open her airway and check breathing. Complete the ABC of Resuscitation if required and place her in the Recovery Postion (see pp.14–25).

5 Arrange removal to hospital. If possible take the snake in a safe container.

First Aid Manual
Dorling Kindersley, 1987
(5th edn, fully revised)
£4.95

The Handbook of Complementary Medicine

Stephen Fulder writes with clarity and insight about areas of medicine which are often rendered fogbound and mirey. In 1980-81 he and Robin Monro were funded to explore the state of complementary medicine (techniques which complement mainstream medicine and each other), and the *Handbook* is based on and updated from that research. Part 1 describes the current healthy state of complementary medicine, with chapters on background, the patient, the therapist, legal aspects and the international scene, then Part 2 describes the different therapies in as clear and common-sense way as I have seen anywhere. Part 3 consists of nearly a hundred pages of annotated address lists of organizations and training centres, which in the new edition have been completely revised and updated. Stephen Fulder's *Handbook* is by quite a long lead the best introduction to the state of complementary medicine in Britain today.

*

In 1981 10 per cent of the patients of lay therapists arrived through a recommendation of their GP despite a British Medical Association ruling discouraging connections with complementary practitioners which was in force at the time. Today the situation is quite different. The majority of GPs refer patients to complementary medicine, no longer making a secret of the fact that they are relieved to have somewhere to send their difficult cases. A survey of GPs in the county of Avon found that no less than three-quarters referred patients to therapists. Above half of the 145 doctors wanted complementary medicine on the NHS and more than half felt that acupuncture and hypnosis were useful or very useful. Why are GPs en masse doing something that would have been unthinkable fifteen years ago? What made them change their minds? The answer, according to the Avon study, is simple: the doctors themselves are receiving treatment from complementary practitioners, and they like it.

The Handbook of Complementary Medicine
Stephen Fulder
Coronet, 1989
£5.99

Natural Healing

Mark Bricklin is the editor of the American magazine *Prevention*, and in this big book has brought together titbits about health from many different natural therapies. It's an American book and not that easy to get hold of over here, but it's well worth the effort as to my mind it's the most practical of the alternative healing handbooks. This is partly because it doesn't pretend to be comprehensive, simply to provide information in easy-to-read articles on subjects as diverse as psoriasis and music therapy. On the other hand, you will find common sense things you can do about an enormous range of problems in a no-nonsense and very readable style. The author makes it very clear when self-treatment is and is not appropriate: 'The therapies discussed in this book are strictly adjunctive or complementary to medical treatment. Self- treatment can be hazardous with a serious ailment. I therefore urge you to seek out the best medical assistance you can find whenever it is needed.'

*

To the extent that you learn to accept more responsibility for your own health, your health should improve. . . Besides avoiding unnecessary expense or risk, there is, in the words of Stanford University psychiatrist Dr. Stewart Agras, 'an extra dividend, a philosophical advantage.' Speaking specifically about people who turn to natural solutions like relaxation training for simple tension headaches, Dr. Agras explains that 'People feel so much better when they're not dependent on drugs.' And, he adds, 'There is a growing feeling that people should take control of their own health care. What better way than to shift from drugs — a passive solution — to self- management.

The Practical Encyclopedia of Natural Healing
Mark Bricklin
Rodale Press, 1983 (distributed in the UK by Thorsons)
£12.95

High Level Wellness

Wellness Programs are big in the USA: corporations have them, hospitals have them, even summer camps have them. 'Wellness' is author Don Ardell's synonym for 'real health', 'an alternative to doctors, drugs and disease which centers around self-responsibility for rip-roaring good health'. That also gives a good idea of the Californian think-yourself-well style of this pioneering book but, even if at times it makes you want to throw up, *High-Level Wellness* covers a lot of interesting health-related topics and includes practical suggestions for looking after yourself properly in a high-speed, high-tension world. First published in 1977, the new edition has been completely revised and updated.

*

I recall a story a young woman told of an encounter in a Los Angeles bar. While on vacation from Stevens Point, Wisconsin, she was visiting relatives in a suburb of Los Angeles. During a visit to one of the local night spots, a young man approached and asked if he could buy her a beer. She indicated to him that she did not drink alcohol. He then offered her, in succession, marijuana, Quaaludes and cocaine. After she declined all these offers, he said 'What do you do, anyway?' She proceeded to tell him that she was into wellness. The young man said 'Walnuts! What in the hell do you do with walnuts?'

High Level Wellness
Donald Ardell
Ten Speed Press, 1986 (distributed in the UK by Airlift)
£7.95

The Natural Family Doctor

The Natural Family Doctor is the best attempt so far to provide a comprehensive reference book to natural healing therapies. There's a lot of information that it would be difficult to amass without reference to a large pile of other books, some interesting (though not very original) reading, and a collection of practical advice which makes a welcome change from that in a more conventional 'family doctor'. But somehow the book is bitty and doesn't really hang together — it can't decide whether to arrange itself by symptom, therapy or issue, and the attempt to integrate medical information and traditional philosophy likewise seems to fail on both counts. Some of the illustrations are crude and the dark green print rather bilious. But there's nothing better in the way of a natural family health guide — yet.

Relaxed breathing

The Natural Family Doctor
edited by Andrew Stanway
Century, 1987
£12.95

Alternative Medicine

This book, also by the mightily-prolific Dr Stanway, is the cheapest of the alternative therapy handbooks. First published in 1982, it has recently been reissued with a long new introduction, bringing the natural therapy scene up to date. It has thirty-two chapters, simply laid out and simply written, which provide an introduction to a range of the therapies you are likely to come across — all the commoner ones and some of the less-common. An up-to-date and comprehensive reading list in this rapidly developing area is inserted after the new introduction.

*

Recent research on feverfew has shown that it is just as powerful as modern anti-inflammatory, non-steroidal drugs, yet no one knows what the active ingredient is, so it can't be synthesized. A writer in The Lancet suggested that western doctors should use whole plants if they could be shown to work, rather than waiting for scientists to isolate the active ingredients and then make them into medicines.

*

The turning point will only come when alternative medical therapies are considered as first line treatments in their own right and not as they are today in the West — the final resting place of the 'garbage' untreatable by the medical profession. As western medicine is accepted by the developing world, more of the world's population gets the best of both traditional and western medical systems. Why shouldn't we in the West have the same privilege?

Alternative Medicine
Andrew Stanway
Penguin, 1986 (revised edition)
£3.95

Disease and Mainstream Medicine

Don't overestimate the 'sophisticated' approach to medicine. Please don't underestimate the importance of an awareness of what lies beneath the surface of the visible and of those ancient, unconscious forces which still help to shape the psychological attitudes of modern man [sic]. Sophistication is only skin deep and when it comes to healing people it seems to me that account has to be taken of those sometimes long neglected complementary methods of medicine which, in the right hands, can bring considerable relief if not hope to an increasing number of people. I hope that, while maintaining and improving the standards with which the [British Medical] Association is so rightly concerned, the medical profession will at the same time keep a corner of its mind open enough to admit those shafts of light which can preserve a sense of paradox so vital to our sense of unity with nature.

Prince Charles' address to the BMA, 29th July 1983

In spite of the great advances of modern medical science we are now witnessing a profound crisis in health care in Europe and North America. . . Despite a staggering increase in health costs over the past three decades, and amid continuing claims of scientific and technological excellence by the medical profession, the health of the population does not seem to have increased significantly. The causes of our health crisis are manifold and can be found both within or without medical science. Nevertheless, increasing numbers of people, both within and outside the medical field, perceive the shortcomings of the current health care system as being rooted in the conceptual framework that supports medical theory and practice, and have come to believe that the crisis will persist unless this framework is modified.

Fritjof Capra, Foreword to
Space, Time and Medicine (see below)

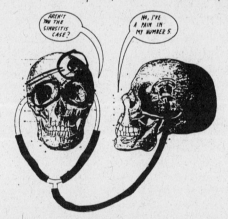

At the most basic level the problem with modern medicine is that it still sees human beings as machines — complex machines for sure, but still machines. Whether or not the idea bothers scientists and medical researchers, life is not only far more complex than can ever be imagined, but every time we find out more about it there will always be more to amaze us.

And complexity is only one of life's attributes. Another is synergy: life works as a whole, which is far more than the sum of its bits. Despite the use of computer modelling and complex systems analysis, nobody ever knows for sure why a person gets better after being ill — or, for that matter, exactly why they don't. One of the qualities that holistic medicine learns to live with is paradox, and most technicians hate paradox. Just because a certain treatment has 'worked' for a hundred patients, there is no guarantee at all that it will work for the hundred-and-first.

This is certainly not to deny that 'mainstream' medicine has come up with some extremely useful technologies; simply that one important aspect of real healing skills must be humility in the face of uncertainty — an uncertainty that will always remain and which is what makes life so exciting. Is it better to die of excitement, or of boredom?

The Holistic Revolution

As with many things, thinking in the area of a holistic approach to healing in North America is about ten years ahead of Britain, and two of the best books on the subject are by American doctors. Both should be required reading by anyone involved in the healing arts — they are not frightening; they are very approachable and extremely thought-provoking. Larry Dossey's *Space, Time and Medicine* takes you through recent developments in science and philosophy to present a vision of health in its widest context, showing how the mechanistic model of health still so widely held is doomed to failure, and what can be done to bring about the radical change that is needed. He fills out the argument with many specific examples, and is even witty.

*

But maybe, just maybe, our skin does think — and our muscle cells and sweat glands and ear drums, too. . . Our concept of our brain as the centre of thought may be utterly spurious, a kind of chauvinistic cerebralism which will not bear the scrutiny of our new knowledge. Far better, perhaps, to regard the entire body as a brain — if by brain we mean the site of human thought.

Patrick Pietroni paints the same subject on a smaller and more domestic canvas, but is no less convinced of the need to change to a view of health which is far larger than the current definition of 'lack of disease'. He looks beyond physical health to the mental, emotional and spiritual realms, but is always eminently practical: *Holistic Living* includes a wide variety of self-help exercises and a good resource section. I particularly like the chapter called 'About Time', which suggests that our attitudes towards time cause us a great deal more stress than we generally admit.

*

It is only fairly recently that we have begun to study more carefully the influence of time on health and more specifically on the body's physiological processes. We now know for instance that blood pressure, pulse rate, hormone levels, sleep patterns and several other physiological activities have their own 'inner clock' which does not always follow the outer clocks on our wrists or mantelpieces. Physicians now feel that some of the illnesses present in our civilisation today are the direct result of the disturbance in relation to 'time' that has occurred in the last fifty years.

Space, Time and Medicine
Larry Dossey
Shambala, 1982
(distributed in the UK
by Element)
£7.95

Holistic Living
Patrick Pietroni
Dent, 1986
£3.95

The Whole Truth

I like Rosalind Coward's writing very much. With few exceptions she is fluent, challenging and perceptive, a breath of fresh air finding its way into dusty corners of the human psyche. Having dealt in her last book with the thorny subject of *Female Desire* (Paladin, 1984, £2.95), in *The Whole Truth* (a pun, get it?) she has turned her attention to the selfish individualism of much contemporary therapy and alternative medicine.

Few people have been prepared to ask why the holistic health movement has been so anti-political, anti-intelligence even, preferring to mouth ill-considered incantations like 'true wholeness' and 'finding the real self' instead of protesting about inhuman conditions in the real world. Rosalind Coward is perfectly prepared to admit that not everyone in the alternative health movement is like that, and that she has gained real benefits from alternative treatment, but she is also clear that current woolly head-in-the-sand beliefs and attitudes simply won't do unless they are matched by an equally fervent political rigour. I don't agree with everything she says, but almost every paragraph of *The Whole Truth* would make a good starting point for an evening's productive debate.

*

It is clear that the emphasis on personal responsibility rarely generates political empowerment. It may generate a sense of being able to accomplish things within the existing status quo, but it rarely promises the ability to transform social structures. Very often the aims are almost explicitly conservative. They are aims of harmony, order, balance, the end of struggle, strife, and 'unproductive' conflict. The possibility that there are very real objective interests governing the form of society in which we live is erased in these aims. The healed individual is one who can have and be everything in the existing society. Small wonder then that the 'type' I met most often while researching this book was the wholesome entrepreneur, the perfect resolution of a personal politics of the body with a peaceful co-existence within the existing economic structure.

The Whole Truth: The Myth of Alternative Health
Rosalind Coward
Faber, 1989
£12.99

The Limits to Medicine

Probably Ivan Illich's most important and influential book, *Limits to Medicine* is still in print and still as vitally relevant as it was when it was written more than ten years ago. Giving shocking examples from all over the 'civilized' world, he shows how modern medicine is hurting far more people than it cures, and how both the medical establishment and contemporary beliefs about health and disease combine to maintain this sorry state of affairs. Newcomers to Illich may find his style overbearing and unnecessarily verbose, the encyclopedic footnotes daunting, but the message is clear —as with so much of our consuming, the first question to ask of medicine is: 'do you really need it?'

*

Medicines have always been potentially poisonous, but their unwanted side-effects have increased with their power and widespread use. Every twenty-four to thirty-six hours, from 50 to 80 per cent of adults in the United States and the United Kingdom swallow a medically prescribed chemical. Some take the wrong drug; others get an old or a contaminated batch, and others a counterfeit; others take several drugs in dangerous combinations; and still others receive injections with improperly sterilized syringes. . . Unnecessary surgery is a standard procedure. Disabling non-diseases result from the medical treatment of non-existent diseases and are on the increase: the number of children disabled in Massachusetts through the treatment of cardiac non-disease exceeds the number of children under effective treatment for real cardiac disease.

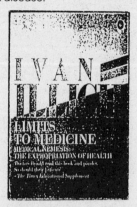

Limits to Medicine
Ivan Illich
Penguin, 1977
£4.95

How to Survive Medical Treatment

Another memorable book by the author of *The Handbook of Complementary Medicine* (page 137), this time a practical and common-sense guide to handling the mainstream medical establishment. His main message is: only call on help when you really need it, go in with your eyes open, keep them open, and take responsibility for your own health regardless of the pressures to be taken over by the system. The small resource section, entirely without explanatory notes, is a disappointment — what is the point of saying 'holistic dentists can be found these days' if he doesn't tell you where? If you do have to have mainstream medical treatment, however, and especially if you need to go into hospital, this book is essential bedside reading — and make sure the doctor sees that you're reading it!

*

Keep minor symptoms to yourself. Unless symptoms are serious, unusual for you, persistent or possibly related to some serious disease in the history of your family, don't run straight off to get a diagnosis. Treat a headache which you feel is a tension headache with a hot bath, a rest, a massage; treat a sore throat with lemon and honey; treat insomnia with herb teas of chamomile, lemon balm or valerian; treat an autumnal fever with fluids, rest and cold water compresses. Don't be continually diagnosed because you are worried about having a disease but there are no signs of it. Doctors can easily give you much more to worry about.

How to Survive Medical Treatment
Stephen Fulder
Century, 1987
£5.95

from Medicine for Beginners (Writers and Readers, 1984)

The Health Scandal

In his most recent book prolific doctor-turned-popular-journalist Vernon Coleman has managed to criticize virtually everything about the way health services in Britain are provided, from the excessive use of rubber gloves to the what he sees as the nonsense of many alternative therapies. 'The sickest thing about Britain today,' he writes, 'is its health service,' and in spraying the anti-establishment bullets every which way he scores a great many direct hits. His holier-than-thou style can be infuriating, but a great many home truths are exposed in this important book which doctors love to hate but keep on their bookshelves nonetheless.

*

In November 1986 Mr Philip Hunt, Director of the National Association of Health Authorities, told a seminar on security that crime could be costing the NHS £36 million a year. From my own experiences I suspect that the total amount of money lost to the NHS through dishonesty is far more than £36 million. More and more doctors are cheating the NHS by claiming money for work they have not done and in hospitals consultants (particularly surgeons) turn a blind eye to porters stealing linen because they are themselves busy stealing instruments and drugs for use on their private patients.

*

The vast majority of doctors are committed interventionists. They treat their patients as battlegrounds, the illness as an enemy and their own armoury of drugs or techniques as weapons with which to fight illness. The interventionist philosophy is so strong that many patients hesitate to deal even with mild symptoms without first asking for professional advice. The interventionists have gained total control of our health.

The Health Scandal
Your Health in Crisis
Vernon Coleman
Mandarin, 1989
£4.99

Or Is It A Conspiracy?

If Vernon Coleman goes for the health service as a whole, Joe Collier, a clinical pharmacologist in one of London's leading teaching hospitals, reserves most of his fire for the drug companies who have bribed, lied, threatened and cajoled their way into becoming one of the quickest ways of making profits in the Western world. While the multinationals receive the largest dose of criticism, Joe Collier also has many pertinent points to make about doctors who think they know everything but won't tell their patients anything. Better written than *The Health Scandal*, but then Joe Collier doesn't make his living from writing a weekly column for *The Star*.

*

In December 1986 three senior cardiologists at St Thomas's, one of London's leading teaching hospitals, openly accused the US drug company, Sterling Winthrop, of attempting to harass and discredit them when, during clinical trials, they decided that Sterling's experimental heart drug, amrinone, was neither safe nor effective. They were threatened with legal action and in a final, high-handed act, the Sterling company even arranged to have its drug removed from the hospital pharmacy in the middle of the trial so that the doctors were prevented from concluding their damaging survey. Even though the doctors were so incensed that they made their allegations to a national newspaper, the drug company, which denied the allegations, neither sued for defamation nor complained to the Press Council.

*

In the advertisements the French drug company Labaz claimed that its new heart drug amiodarone 'enjoys a wide safety margin; the side effects and contraindications seem minimal'. Yet in the smallest print of the same advertisement the following side effects were listed: nerve damage, tremor, photosensitization, skin discoloration, diffuse scarring in the lungs and hepatitis. These can hardly be described as trivial.

The Health Conspiracy
Joe Collier
Century, 1989
£4.95

Whose Health Is It Anyway?

In this in-depth study Judith Cook, an experienced medical journalist, has attempted to find out why we now have a health service which is struggling from crisis to crisis trying to stay afloat. She also looks at the sort of service we deserve *and* can afford — more concerned with preventive medicine, real community care and better health education. The chapter on the pioneering and very successful Peckham experiment, closed down after the war with its lessons not taken to heart, is particularly interesting.

*

We are now at the bottom of the heap. We are the smallest health spender among the Western developed nations. The proportion of gross national product the UK devotes to health has lagged behind the Organization of Economic Co-operation and Development average by 25 per cent per year. In 1960 the UK was one of the nine largest health spenders in the developed world. Now we are right at the bottom.

*

The National Health Service was set up in such a way that it has a built-in patriarchal structure. This was almost inevitable. It was devised by politicians who decided what was best for people, run by civil servants trained to carry out the orders they were given, funded by the Treasury to whom all Health Ministers have to go every year, cap in hand, when the amount of public expenditure has to be decided. At senior level, naturally, it is staffed by doctors who, with a handful of rare exceptions, tend to be among the most conservative of professionals, possibly only lawyers being more rigidly set in their established views.

Whose Health Is It Anyway?
The Consumer and the National Health Service
Judith Cook
New English Library, 1988
£3.50

Self-Help Health Magazines

Of the many 'new health' magazines you can now buy, the oldest established is still the best and the best value — the monthly *Here's Health*, usually prominently displayed in health food shops as well as in newsagents. It does tend to be heavy on the vitamin supplement ads, but there is always something well worth reading. The Consumers' Association publishes the bi-monthly *Which? Way to Health* magazine, available on subscription only (for £23 a year). It is well thought-out and contains articles on a wide variety of subjects, from the side-effects of drugs through alternative therapies to recipes and how our food will change when trade barriers come down in 1992. As you would expect from the publishers of *Which?* it is packed full of information, and lists support organizations and 'where to go for more information' sections with every article.

Here's Health
Argus Health
Publications Ltd
Victory House
Leicester Place
London
WC2H 7QP
0(7)1 437 9011

Which? Way to Health
Consumers' Association
Subscriptions Department
Castlemead
Gascoyne Way
Hertford
SG14 1LH
0992 589031

Health Directories

When I first heard about the *National Directory of Alternative Aid* I thought that at last we were going to have a truly comprehensive and easy-to-use resource for healing and therapy in Britain; sadly it belies its promise. The *Directory* is difficult to use, being cross-referenced in several equally confusing ways, and some of the information is several years out of date; on the other hand it is packed full of detailed information, and is worth looking at if you're having trouble tracking something down.

The annual *Alternative and Complementary Medicine Practitioners' Yearbook* from the publishers of *Here's Health* is designed primarily for practitioners, and contains listings of organizations, information centres, publishers, book suppliers, training bodies, research organizations, testing and analysis centres, suppliers and practice support services. While the information is not comprehensive (though the 1990 edition promises to be better than its predecessor), it is clear and straightforward to use.

The National Directory of Alternative Aid
Michael Williams
Health Farm Publishing,
1989
£9.95

Alternative and Complementary Medicine Practitioners' Yearbook 1988/1989
Christianne Knight
Argus Health
Publications, 1988
£3.50

The Patients Association

The Patients Association was set up in 1963 to provide a collective and independent voice for medical patients. The Association provides help and advice, and works hard to

ensure that the medical establishment remembers that it is there primarily to help its patients. If you need to complain about your treatment at the hands of mainstream medics, the PA is there to help you. It produces a quarterly newsletter called *Patient Voice* and has recently, together with the College of Health and Thames TV, helped to compile the Bedford Square Press publication called simply *The Health Directory*, which costs £7.70 including p+p.

The Patients Association
18 Victoria Park Square
London
E2 9PF
0(8)1 981 5676

The College of Health

The College of Health was set up in 1983 by Michael Young, founder of the Consumers' Association and the Open University, and Marianne Rigge. Its aims are to give the public information about self-care, disease prevention, making effective use of the Health Service, and self-help groups. Their work also includes campaigning on health issues and working with the NHS to improve the quality of information to patients. They publish several booklets, including the useful *Guide to Going into Hospital*, and a number of reading and resource lists.

The College also runs a 24-hour phone advice service called Healthline. Tapes on specific subjects give advice and where to go for more information. Write to the College of Health for a copy of their directory listing more than 280 tapes you can ask them to play for you.

The College of Health
18 Victoria Park Square
London
E2 9PF
0(8)1 980 6363
0482 29933/0392 59191 (Healthline)

Health Promotion

The Health Promotion Information Centre, run by the Health Education Authority, has available a range of support materials for teachers and health personnel, teaching kits, and a library and information service which is open to anyone interested in the promotion of better health. They can provide booklists and source lists on a wide range of topics.

Health Promotion Information Centre
Hamilton House
Mabledon Place
London
WC1H 9TX
0(7)1 631 0930

The Scientific and Medical Network

If you are a medical professional interested in learning more about recent developments in holistic medicine, The Scientific and Medical Network, founded in 1973, exists to promote discussion and sharing of ideas between qualified scientists and doctors. The Network now has more than 600 members in 34 countries, who keep in touch through a substantial *Newsletter* full of reviews and articles with titles like 'The Pyramid of Philosophy' and 'Semantic Space'.

The Scientific and Medical Network
The Old School House
Hampnett
Northleach
Gloucestershire
GL54 3NN
0451 60869

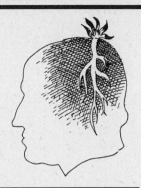

A Healthy Mind

'Mental illness' is a difficult concept for most of us. If we have known someone who has been 'out of their mind' we will know that people can certainly be ill without having any obvious physical symptoms; on the other hand more and more people are coming to agree with Dr Thomas Szasz, author of the far-reaching *Myth of Mental Illness* in 1972, that 'mental illness' more often indicates something very wrong with the world the 'ill' person is living in rather than something wrong with the 'patient'. Thomas Szasz's book is still basic reading for anyone concerned with the issue of 'mental illness', as is the prize-winning *Politics of Mental Handicap* by Joanna Ryan, first published in 1980, which shows very clearly how the mentally handicapped have become scapegoats for all of our culture's worst fears about itself.

Robin Blake's *Mind Over Medicine* puts the role of the mind in healing to the forefront in a detailed look at that innocent phrase 'it's all in the mind'. He links together the emotional, mental and physical strands of our existence in a journalistic yet very readable account of how medicine must start to see human beings in the round.

A new handbook by Elaine Farrell called *Choices in Health Care* has a useful chapter on 'Mental Health Choices', including four pages of listings of useful organisations, information centres, etc. A further chapter does the same for people with mental handicap.

**The Myth of
Mental Illness**
Thomas Szasz
Paladin, 1972
£2.95

Mind over Medicine
Can the Mind Kill or
Cure?
Robin Blake
Pan, 1987
£3.95

**The Politics of
Mental Handicap**
Joanna Ryan with Frank
Thomas
Penguin, 1980
(out of print)

**Choices in
Health Care**
Elaine Farrell
Optima, 1989
£5.99

MENCAP and MIND

MENCAP (The Royal Society for Mentally Handicapped Children and Adults) is the largest national parent organization for people with a mental handicap and their families. It runs residential services, training and employment services, legal and information services, and leisure facilities and holidays. A monthly magazine called *Mencap News*, a booklist, and an information pack bursting with leaflets are all available. MIND is the United Kingdom's leading mental health charity, and aims to support people in mental distress. Through a network of 200 local groups it campaigns tirelessly on issues such as housing and legal rights, transport facilities and tranquillizer addiction.

MENCAP
Mencap National
Centre
123 Golden Lane
London
EC1Y 0RT
0(7)1 253 9433

MIND
National Association
for Mental Health
22 Harley Street
London
W1N 2ED
0(7)1 637 0741

On Ageing and Dying

I know that I'm covering both this subject and the previous one very perfunctorily, but as with the 'myth' of mental illness the 'myth' that being old is very different to being young has been turned by our strange society into a rationale for the treatment of old people as second-rate, and the fear of death into our last great taboo. Without death and decay the cycle of renewal is incomplete — ageing and death are as crucial to our own and our collective health as birth and growth.

There are four books I particularly like in this area. The first is Mary Stott's eminently common-sense *Ageing for Beginners*, essential reading for everyone who is ageing — and that means everyone. When it comes to dying, or even thinking about death, everyone should read Elisabeth Kübler-Ross, whose *On Death and Dying* is a classic. 'I think,' she says, 'there are many reasons for this flight from facing death calmly. One of the most important facts is that dying nowadays is in many ways more gruesome, more lonely, mechanical and dehumanized.' In an attempt to bring dignity and humanity back to the process of dying, she has established the organization Friends of Shanti Nilaya (10 Archery Fields House, Wharton Street, London WC1X 9PN; Tel: 0(7)1 837 9796) to run workshops on different aspects of death. Books, cassettes and videos are also available.

A recent Thorsons book, *Living While Dying*, is a practical, commonsense account of the time leading up to the death of one of the authors: her feelings, her experiences, and the changes she goes through. It explores some of the reasons why our society is so embarrassed and afraid to talk about death, and the problems this creates for those going through the experience. A very personal book, but a good place to start. It contains a good selection of further reading and useful organizations.

Cruse (Cruse Bereavement Care, Cruse House, 126 Sheen Road, Richmond, Surrey TW9 1UR; Tel: 0(8)1 940 7638) has over 150 branches in Britain, and offers help to all bereaved people by providing counselling for the individual and in groups, advice and information. Their publications include the monthly *Cruse Chronicle* for members and *Bereavement Care*, a journal for all those who help the bereaved.

The hospice movement in Britain, though young, is thriving, providing dying people with a dignified alternative to loneliness or an impersonal hospital ward — Denise Winn's new guide is a comprehensive guide to 'the hospice way' with a full resource section. The Hospice Information Service (St Christopher's Hospice, Lawrie Park Road, Sydenham, London SE26 6DZ; Tel: 0(8)1 778 9252) can provide a *Directory of Services* including in-patient units, home care and hospital support teams. They also publish fact sheets on all aspects of hospice care and can give information and advice over the phone.

**Ageing for
Beginners**
Mary Stott
Blackwell, 1981
£3.95

The Hospice Way
Denise Winn
Optima, 1987
£3.95

On Death and Dying
Elisabeth Kübler-Ross
Tavistock, 1973
£4.50

Living While Dying
R.G. Owens and
F. Naylor
Thorsons, 1989
£4.99

The Holistic Health Network in Britain

There are two main organizations in Britain whose primary aim is to expand interest in and awareness of the benefits of a holistic approach to healing. The BHMA, formed in 1982, is primarily for healthcare professionals — mostly qualified doctors and nurses but also qualified practitioners from other healing disciplines; the BHMA has also instituted an 'open' membership for interested members of the public. The Institute for Complementary Medicine, founded a year later (though it likes to trace its roots back to a Trust started in 1967) exists primarily to increase public awareness of the range of healing techniques currently available, and to provide an information and referral service.

British Holistic Medical Association

Of the two organizations the BHMA, maybe surprisingly, seems the more human, from the honest description of its membership structure in its introductory leaflet to the lively discussion about its role and function in the quarterly news-letter *Holistic Health*. The BHMA, unlike its giant establishment soundalike the BMA, isn't afraid to espouse the benefits of a wide range of healing techniques, though it is quick to point out that by no means all alternative therapies are holistic. The spring of 1987 saw a major reorganization of the BHMA, which has now set itself the goal of becoming Britain's first multidisciplinary health care organization. The BHMA has an expanding network of local groups, and in Scotland is represented by a lively group called Whole Person Care. I would recommend all healing practitioners interested in the evolving holistic view of medicine to join the BHMA, even if only to keep up to date with new developments.

British Holistic Medical Association
179 Gloucester Place
London
NW1 6DX
0(7)1-262 5299

Whole Person Care
78 Polwarth Terrace
Edinburgh
EH11 1NJ
031 337 8474

The Institute for Complementary Medicine

The ICM, though it may seem little glossy and impersonal from its literature when compared with the BHMA, nevertheless does a very important job and is very approachable. The Institute is Britain's biggest and most comprehensive referral service for practitioners of healing techniques outside the mainstream medical establishment. During 1990 they plan to move from Portland Place to Harley Street, a building which they will use while their own purpose-built premises are being built. 1990 will also see the start of courses in complementary medicine for nurses.

The London office can either put you directly in touch with the appropriate organization or centre, or they can give you the number of one of seventy-two local volunteer public information points all over the country. The London office holds computer records of the memberships of all the largest professional organizations in acupuncture, chiropractic, homeopathy, herbalism and osteopathy, together with information about hundreds of other organizations and centres. The ICM prefers people to write with an sae for information about particular therapies and local practitioners, though you can ring them. They also have a large library which is available to anyone wanting to research particular aspects of complementary medicine.

The Institute for Complementary Medicine
21 Portland Place
London
W1N 3AF
0(7)1-636 9543

The Natural Medicines Society

Many natural medicines are currently under threat of being banned by law, and the NMS exists to protect our freedom to choose and use natural medicines by ensuring that we continue to have open access to them and by encouraging the development and testing of such remedies. The quarterly *NMS News* will keep you up to date with their progress.

Natural Medicines Society
Edith Lewis House
Back Lane
Ilkeston
Derbyshire
DE7 8EJ
0602 329454

Health and Nutrition

You may think that having given more than thirty pages to wholefoods at the beginning of *New Green Pages* was enough, but since nutrition and health are so vital to our wellbeing and so vitally connected I shall not apologize for giving the subject another airing here.

Another reason for including this page in the health section is that many people are confused about the difference between drugs and dietary supplements. This is hardly surprising, since the drug companies want us to believe that all medications are good for us, so they put them all in the same clean packaging and ensure that we can buy them all in the same friendly chemists' shop. On the other hand, the 'healthy' supplement manufacturers rely on us spending our money on their products, so how on earth can we possibly find out what we really need?

This is a tricky one. The health magazines are full of adverts for Cantassium B and Mega H40, Multivite and Seatone, Melbrosia and Lactaid — all these wonderful natural alternatives to the chemicals prescribed by most doctors. You want to be healthy, you want your children to be healthy, and our world is in general a pretty unhealthy place, polluted by heavy metals, radiation, nitrates, ozone and the rest; surely you need to do something to combat the symptoms which you know are brought on by photochemical smog, crop spraying and vehicle exhausts. So who do you trust?

Before you spend a penny on dietary supplements — minerals, vitamins and the rest — think about the following considerations:

▶ See things in their context. Diet supplements can never be anything more than supplements; if your diet is right, you don't need supplements.
▶ Even then, diet is only part of the health equation. What about fulfilment, relaxation, exercise? Minerals and vitamins can never make up (except very marginally in the short term) for lack of the other prerequisites for health.
▶ Think about the money — are you really better off spending £10 on a 28-day pack of vitamins, or would it be better spent on fresh fruit, saved up for a holiday, or sent to OXFAM or Greenpeace?
▶ Think about the packaging, the advertising hype, the 'rush me without obligation' — do you really want to be part of this sort of consumerism?

Diet supplements and dietary therapies are very important when kept in perspective, but Britons do not need £60 million worth of supplements every year. Don't stop buying vitamin C tablets when you have flu (and do if you don't already!), or vitamin E cream for burns and scalds, or iron tablets for anemia, but do think very carefully before you start swallowing indiscriminate amounts of multivitamins — you almost certainly don't need them.

Optimum Nutrition

I have misgivings about Patrick Holford and his Institute of Optimum Nutrition, mostly to do with money, prestige and glossiness, but I would much rather have the ION than any and all of the promises of the pharmaceutical industry. Despite its glossiness, the ION has its heart in the right place. Founded five years ago to educate and enlighten people about the role of nutrition in health, it receives over 10,000 enquiries a year. The quarterly ION magazine, *Optimum Nutrition*, is well worth subscribing to if you are interested in the subject, containing news of recent research findings that you won't easily find elsewhere. ION also do individual nutritional counselling and workshops, but you don't need to spend £39 for a day's instruction on how to look after yourself — treat yourself to a day in the country and a good healthy meal instead. Patrick Holford has written several books on his 'optimum nutrition' ideas, including *Vitamin Vitality* (Collins, 1985, £4.20).

Green Farm Nutrition Centre in Sussex offers a similar service to the ION: nutritional advice via its 'Health Hot Line'; a detailed computer-aided nutritional analysis service (costing £15 a time), and a quarterly *Green Farm Magazine*. Green Farm is probably best known for its ever-growing mail order catalogue, covering everything from clothes to cosmetics but concentrating on the ubiquitous supplements.

The Institute for Optimum Nutrition
5 Jerdan Place
London
SW6 1BE
0(7)1-385 7984

Green Farm Nutrition Centre
Burwash Common
East Sussex
TN19 7LX
0435 882180

The Help Society

Many years ago a young woman was sitting on a bus travelling to work, but wishing the bus would crash so she could die. She had neither the energy nor the will to do anything about killing herself, but all her enthusiasm for life had gone... Looking back now find it difficult to believe that poor creature was me! For eventually I found a chink of light at the end of the tunnel. I managed to escape from that life sentence of almost constant pain and depression and although I can never be fit enough again to take a proper job or dance, or do many of the things I would like to, some days I have virtually no pain and I am so happy it is like being at a party.

*

This is Patricia Byrivers' story of how she overcame the pain and incapacity of arthritis with a strict dietary regime that has allowed her to live a relatively normal life after twenty years of cortisone treatment (*Goodbye to Arthritis*, Century, 1985, £2.95). As a result of her experiences, and together with allergy specialist Erick Manners, Patricia set up in 1975 an organization to pass on vital information about the links between what we eat and how our bodies respond — write to them with an sae for more information.

Help Yourself to Less Pain Society
PO Box 31
Riverside
Martham
Great Yarmouth
Norfolk
NR29 4RG
0493 653597

Helping Your Body to Help Itself

The next few pages are concerned with diseases which result from a breakdown in the immune system of the human body. This group of diseases includes cancer, AIDS, rheumatoid arthritis, diabetes, rheumatic fever, asthma, migraine — in fact any disease which you would normally be able to throw off very quickly as your natural defences came into action, but which for some reason your body seems unable to cope with.

Most doctors would be loathe to acknowledge the causal links between such a wide range of diseases, and would find it even harder to accept the seemingly simplistic scenario I am about to offer, but more and more people — including many medical practitioners — are coming to believe that even though the solutions may be problematic, the reasons for our current malaise are all too obvious.

First consider some international comparisons: 20% of Americans die of cancer; 7% of Peruvians — among tribal peoples cancer is almost unknown. Then consider that the atmosphere over Britain is estimated to contain around 500 times as much lead as it did two hundred years ago. Human bodies have developed over millions of years, but it is only in the last hundred or so that we have bombarded them with a growing range of chemicals and pollutants, and only in the last thirty that stress has become such a widespread feature of 'developed' society.

The human body is built to be resilient, to bounce back pretty quickly when thrown off balance. Yet we are now asking our bodies to cope with constant attacks from things it hasn't much of a chance to deal with in the quantities and combinations we throw at it. The immune system can deal with small indiscretions — our bodies are doing it all the time — but in the end we tip the balance and the system says 'Help, I can't cope any more — and here are some symptoms to try and make you listen.' The more we ignore the minor symptoms — the headache, the sneezing, the sweating — the louder our body has to shout. And sometimes, in the end, it gives up.

Medics are very fond of looking for specific causes so they can administer specific remedies. It's never as simple as that, at least with immune deficiency diseases. Hay fever is never just to do with pollen. If it were, agricultural societies would starve. It's almost always to do with one thing piled on top of another — pesticide residues, plus hormone residues, plus atmospheric pollution, plus water pollution, plus stress . . . plus pollen.

And it's even worse than that, because the drugs that are supposed to help us often upset our natural defences even further, and when they work it's usually because they just halt everything in its tracks, including the healing process.

It's a terrible problem knowing what to do in such a polluted environment, but the answer cannot be to add to the pollution. The solution to chemical weapons isn't to issue the whole population with gas masks and antidote pills, it's to stop using chemical weapons. The parallels with real life pollution are obvious.

But there is a great deal you can do to help your body to heal itself and, once healthy, to keep it healthy. Most of it is common sense — eat well, rest well, exercise well, get what support and love and acknowledgement you need. Simpler said . . .

Maximum Immunity

I'm surprised that there aren't more books which cover the whole spectrum of what can be done to help your natural defences to cope with immune-deficiency disease; most deal with a specific disease such as cancer, arthritis or allergy. One important book does, however, make the connections between all the immune-deficiency diseases, and offers very practical suggestions about what you can do to help yourself. Writing very readably and carefully, Michael Weiner suggests how you can build up and look after your immune system, which will almost certainly lower your chances of succumbing to diseases like cancer and AIDS, and other common and less serious problems like candidiasis. He does, however, place a great deal of emphasis on vitamin and mineral supplements, without making it clear that a healthy person in a healthy environment needs little or no dietary supplement.

*

That nature heals cannot be questioned. That she heals best when augmented by sound stimuli is the thrust of this book. We are not passive animals when it comes to illness and healing. Yes, some of our synthetic drugs are truly lifesaving, and they must be seen as part of the overall healing picture. The immune-enhancing nutrients, and other components described for maximizing immunity, are best when incorporated as preventive measures — before illness appears. Instead of looking outside of our bodies for healing properties, we should conceptualize the pharmacy within and clearly see that by providing the shelves with the necessary starter compounds in the form of required nutrients, we can use our mind to make the inner drugs.

Maximum Immunity
Michael Weiner
Gateway, 1986
£5.95

Allergy

I am one of the 'lucky' people whose allergy — in my case 'hay fever' — is acknowledged by the medical establishment. If by 'allergy' is meant the incapacity of the immune system to cope with particular ingested substances, my guess is that at one time or another most people suffer the symptoms of allergy.

Scientists and doctors still tend to think of allergy sufferers as a very small and unfortunate portion of the population who cannot cope with the realities of modern life. Now that I've changed my lifestyle and diet and am looking after myself much better I rarely suffer even at the height of summer, but in my teens examination time was a nightmare: I could hardly see, and sometimes sneezed myself semi-conscious. All around me I see people with symptoms that are at least worth checking to see if they're allergic, but they are too often given a sedative or an antihistamine, and told that everything should be fine now.

Luckily you can do a great deal for yourself where possible allergy is concerned, and working with your body to find out what it reacts against can be a fascinating voyage of discovery. You don't need to kill the symptoms, and you don't need to suffer them either. The first thing to do is find — and eliminate — the cause. Take the splinter out before kissing yourself better.

Allergy Societies

There are several voluntary associations whose purpose is to offer support and information for allergy sufferers and their friends. Two that are particularly active are Action Against Allergy and the National Society for Research into Allergy. AAA produces a newsletter three times a year, and its founder Amelia Nathan Hill has written a useful booklet called Against the Unsuspected Enemy which can be bought from AAA. Both AAA and the National Society have local groups, and can put you in touch with one near you. The National Society produces an occasional chatty magazine called Reaction. The National Association seems to be concerned mostly with food allergy whereas AAA's interests cover agrochemicals, lead in petrol and fluoride in water — both organizations will answer specific enquiries if you enclose an sae.

Action Against Allergy
Greyhound House
23-24 George Street
Richmond
Surrey
TW9 1JY
0(8)1-948 5771

National Society for Research into Allergy
PO Box 45
Hinckley
Leicestershire
LE10 1JY
0455 635212

Food Allergy and Intolerance

Clinical immunologist Jonathan Brostoff and medical journalist Linda Gamlin have joined forces to produce what for the time being must be *the* book on allergy and intolerance. Well-written, comprehensive and up-to-date, it manages to be almost compulsively readable as well as providing a great deal of detailed information. Lots of personal accounts of patients' experiences are included, together with clear, scientifically-sound explanations of the body's complex biochemical processes. Excellent appendices cover drugs, organizations, suppliers of allergen-free foods and nutritional supplements, alternatives to common foods, and even cross-reactions between plant products.

The Complete Guide to Food Allergy and Intolerance
Jonathan Bristoff and Linda Gamlin
Bloomsbury, 1990
£4.99

The Allergy Connection

To produce this important book Barbara Paterson has brought together a large number of case histories and interviewed most of the doctors in Britain who currently practice 'clinical ecology' or environmental medicine. It opened my eyes to the extent of the misery caused by wrongly-diagnosed allergy, and to the additional suffering caused by the routine administration of drugs which frequently make the problem a great deal worse if not intractable, as the last case study in her book shows: the story of four-year-old Alex who died because hospital staff refused to listen to his mother and gave him aspirin when he choked on a piece of bread. The resource lists at the end of Barbara Paterson's book are excellent, even if already somewhat out of date.

If you or somebody close to you is suffering from symptoms that you don't understand, read *The Allergy Connection* and see if it helps you decide what to do next.

The Allergy Connection
Barbara Paterson
Thorsons, 1985
£5.95

There are several cookery books now available which give you recipes which leave out certain ingredients such as flour, sugar or milk which are known to give rise to allergic reactions in some people. In general, if you simply eat more healthily and pay attention to your emotional needs it is unlikely that you will need to keep to a strict exclusion diet; if such a course of action is necessary, however, I would recommend two books from Ashgrove Press in Bath — Stephanie Lashford's *The Allergy Cookbook* (1986, £4.95) and Honor Campbell's *The Foodwatch Alternative Cookbook* (1987, £5.95).

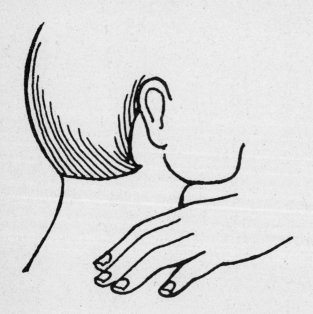

Cancer

*'How do you feel when someone tells you you have cancer?'
I've been asked this question so many times that it must be an
area of considerable interest to a lot of people. I have some
difficulty in answering it because the first thought that overwhelmed me at the time was that, regardless of whatever
emotional response was welling up inside me, I must not let my
feelings show. In true British style, I braced myself. Eaves-
dropping later on a conversation between my informant and the
ward sister, I heard that 'I had taken it very well'. I had not, in
fact, taken it at all well. I hadn't raged or cried. His management
of my crisis consisted of a pat on the head and an assurance that
he was very sorry. I was glad he was sorry. I was pretty sorry
myself.'*
Penny Brohn, Gentle Giants (see next page)

One in five people is likely to be diagnosed as having cancer
at some point in their life, and it is generally accepted that
although some people are more susceptible than others,
cancer has a great deal to do with lifestyle, diet, pollution and
stress. Despite this understanding, many mainstream medics
are still convinced that drugs, surgery and radiotherapy are
the best way to 'fight' cancer, and that changes in environment and attitude only have limited benefits.

Laser surgery, cancer drugs and x-rays all have their place,
but more and more people are becoming aware that changes
in diet and lifestyle, together with a range of techniques from
'alternative' medicine, can almost always aid healing, and in
some cases can slow down and halt the growth of tumorous
tissue.

There are so many suggestions as to what can be done
about cancer that it can be hard to know where to start,
especially if you are still recovering from the shock of being
diagnosed as having cancer. The books and organizations
mentioned in this section provide an excellent resource for
anybody wanting to work with their own cancer or with their
feelings about a close friend or relative with the disease. It
may, however, be worth listing briefly the more obvious steps
you can take to improve your health and your chances of not
being taken over by unwanted cell growth.

▶ Try to stop smoking if you do (see page 151).
▶ Look carefully at your diet (see pages 11 to 18).
▶ Think about getting more regular exercise (see page 161).
▶ Look at the role of stress in your life, and what you can do to
reduce it (see page 155).
▶ Explore ways of looking at your feelings about disease and
death. This can often be done in individual or group therapy
with an experienced counsellor or group leader (see pages
172-173).

▶ Explore the possibilities provided by meditation and
visualization (see page 178).
▶ If you have been diagnosed as having cancer, find and join
your nearest cancer support group (see the Cancerlink
directory mentioned on the next page); sharing what is going
on for you gives you permission not to be brave all the time.

As Shirley Harrison points out (see next column): 'Bob
Champion rode in the Grand National after being told he had
cancer. Sir Francis Chichester sailed solo round the world with
lung cancer. Solzhenitzyn, who wrote Cancer Ward, was
diagnosed in his mid-fifties and then went on to marry and
have two children. Sigmund Freud had mouth cancer when 60
and died in his eighties' (I expect a few women have done
equally notable things). How about you?

New Approaches to Cancer

Subtitled 'What everyone needs to know about orthodox and
complementary methods for prevention, treatment and cure',
Shirley Harrison has brought together a vast range of approaches and resources which should be required reading for
anybody who is even vaguely concerned about cancer. The
style sometimes borders on the journalistic and slightly
condescending ('Meditation is not the hobby of hippies,
maharishis or Beatles. It is not a pagan ritual . . .'), but it is
readable and reassuring, and the glossary, bibliography and
resource list are excellent.

*

*Today, once cancer is diagnosed, you can choose to hit the thing
head on with the benefits of science through chemotherapy,
radiotherapy, surgery, or you may take such gentler complementary routes as acupuncture, psychotherapy or diet. Or — so
important — you may use both. That is your right and there is a
better chance of reaching this ideal than at any time this century.
Neither traditional nor complementary approaches has a
monopoly over your health. They should be pulling together, with
the aim of making you well. The choice on offer should not be
'either/or', always 'both/and' — and because they are so much
in the public mind those working with cancer could carry the flag
of cooperation for the medical world as a whole.*

*

*Norman Cousins, former writer and senior lecturer in medicine at
the University of California, discovered just how important
laughter is and wrote a best-seller on his discoveries — The
Anatomy of an Illness. It is about his own 'terminal' illness and
his belief that the human mind can mobilise the body's own
ability to combat disease — and if not always to conquer it, at
the very least to improve the quality of life remaining. Working as
a team with his doctor, he devised a programme which included
massive doses of vitamin C and equal doses of laughter. . .
Carefully logging his progress, Norman Cousins went through a
week. At the end of the eighth day, he was moving his thumbs
without pain and the granular nodules on his neck and the backs
of his hands were beginning to shrink. Some months later he
returned to work, was riding and playing the piano and his
mobility has improved yearly.*

**New Approaches
to Cancer**
Shirley Harrison
Century, 1987
£6.95

Gentle Giants

Penny Brohn's account of her life with breast cancer and what she did to fight it is honest, witty and deeply moving — an inspiration to anyone who actively wants to work with their cancer. As a result of her experiences she co-founded the Bristol Cancer Help Centre (see below), which pioneers research and counselling on the mental and spiritual aspects of cancer as well as the medical.

*

My retreat leader returned after breakfast the next day and gave me my exercise. I revamped my tragedienne 'I might be dying' number, and he said softly, 'We're all dying.' Now this was not news to me, it was something I had said many times to myself, and even to other people, in an attempt to keep things in perspective, but nobody had ever said it to me before. Nobody had ever shown a detached lack of interest in my suffering, made me feel that it wasn't particularly important, almost brushed the details aside. He acknowledged it of course, he accepted that I was suffering, and that as a result I was wrestling with fear and anxieties, but saw this as part of the human condition. Part of the way things are. Nobody could corner the market. Suffering is suffering is suffering. No particular suffering is more special, or more worthy of attention than any other. My having cancer was not significant, although how I felt about having it — that might be significant, he was interested in that.

*

With every bookstall shouting out the various merits of a plethora of self-help therapies, the problem for the cancer patient is no longer whether he [or she] can do anything for [themselves], but where on earth to start. (As time goes by, this evolves into the question of where to stop. But that comes later.) The place to start is with something that you think is important. Before buying a single book, arranging any appointments with 'highly-recommended' practitioners, before allowing any decisions to be made on your behalf, settle down and think about what is happening to you and how you want to see the problem solved. However impotent your surroundings may make you feel, nobody can stop you doing this. Allow yourself the luxury of exploiting your own reactions and responses to your crisis.

Gentle Giants
Penny Brohn
Century, 1987
£4.95

Penny Brohn has also compiled *The Bristol Programme*, an introduction to the holistic therapies practised by the Bristol Cancer Help Centre. She does tend to talk at length about 'models of man', but as an introduction to the benefits of a healthy diet, relaxation, meditation, visualization and self-empowerment this is an excellent resource. A good bibliography would have improved the book. A companion volume, *The Bristol Recipe Book* by Sadhya Rippon, is useful if you can face a vegan diet and are new to dietary therapy — but the diet section in *The Bristol Programme* is all you really need.

The Bristol Programme
Penny Brohn
Century, 1987
£4.95

The Bristol Recipe Book
Sadhya Rippon
Century, 1987
£3.95

Penny Brohn
THE BRISTOL PROGRAMME
An introduction to the holistic therapies practised by the Bristol Cancer Help Centre

by the co-founder of the Bristol Cancer Help Centre

Alternative Approaches

In the first nine years of its operation, the staff at the Bristol Cancer Help Centre have seen hundreds of patients overcome their cancer against great odds. They provide counselling, residential and day courses, stress recognition classes, guided meditation and spiritual healing, and organize a seminar and lecture programme for carers working with cancer sufferers. Charges for treatment and advice are kept as low as possible, and there is a bursary fund. A series of leaflets is available, and they also sell books, cassettes and a video. An exciting development is that the Centre has recently started working with the National Health Service at Hammersmith Hospital in the first ever link-up between complementary and conventional approaches to cancer treatment and education.

New Approaches To Cancer has similar aims, but offer advice and information only, rather than operating an alternative treatment centre. They have recently produced a video of their work which can be hired or bought from them.

Bristol Cancer Help Centre
Grove House
Cornwallis Grove
Clifton
Bristol
BS8 4PG
0272 743216

New Approaches to Cancer
c/o Seekers Trust
Addington Park
Maidstone
Kent
ME19 5BL
0732 848336

Information about Cancer

For many people, the realization that they have cancer is extremely traumatic, and instant and accurate information is what is most needed. Cancerlink was formed in 1982 to provide a detailed and accurate information service for cancer sufferers and their families and friends. They produce some excellent resource booklets including a *Directory of Useful Organisations* (£1) and a *Directory of Cancer Support and Self-Help Groups* (£1.75), both of which are kept up-to-date. Cancerlink have recently opened an office in Edinburgh.

BACUP provides an information service with experienced cancer nurses available on five telephone lines throughout the day — they also produce a wide range of literature. They have recently established a Freefone line, available 10am- 7pm Monday-Thursday and 10am-5.30pm on Friday.

Cancerlink
17 Britannia Street
London
WC1X 5JN
0(7)1-833 2451

BACUP
121/123 Charterhouse Street
London
EC1M 6AA
0(7)1-608 1661 (6 lines)
Freefone 0800 181199

Cancerlink (Scotland)
9 Castle Terrace
Edinburgh
EH1 2DP
031 228 5557
(Monday-Thursday 1-5pm)

After Cancer

Cancer Aftercare provide support and comfort to cancer patients and their relatives and friends, with a 'phone link' service to put people in touch with local groups and other cancer sufferers, a network of more than forty local support groups, and a monthly newsletter full of practical information.

Cancer Aftercare and Rehabilitation Society
21 Zetland Road
Bristol
BS6 7AH
0272 427419 (evenings 0272 691868)

AIDS

AIDS certainly is a serious and debilitating illness. Indeed, it is often fatal. But it is also a rare disease which is difficult to catch.
Peter Tatchell, *AIDS* (see below)

For such a rare disease, AIDS has caught the popular imagination in a unique way. This is partly because it is so tied up with no less than four of the biggest taboos in our culture: sex, death, drugs and homosexuality; partly because it has mainstream medicine foxed. Here is something that can kill us and we can't stop it; the ultimate failure of a technology which promised complete salvation.

As with so many worries, it is ignorance and prejudice which fan our fears, so the first thing to do about AIDS is to find out more about it. Read one or two of the many books now available. Then if you are worried on your own account, get yourself some good counselling — often not so much advice as a space to talk about your fears and concerns. Then think about what you are actually going to do about it.

Instant Advice

Headlines like 'AIDS Panic Scare' are calculated to have people scurrying for their phones, and HM Government haven't helped matters much. If you read about AIDS, discuss it, and decide what you are going to do, the chances are that you won't panic if you feel a bit under the weather or have an itch in your nether regions.

If you do need instant advice, however, the DHSS have a national no-cost 24-hour advice service called AIDS Helpline on 0800 567123 (freefone information is also available on Tuesday evenings 6-10pm in Cantonese and Mandarin on 0800 282446, and Wednesday evenings in Hindi, Punjabi, Gujarati, Urdu and Bengali on 0800 282445).

For more detailed advice, especially if you have been confirmed HIV positive, the Terrence Higgins Trust exists to give help and support. They also produce a range of literature on AIDS and related conditions. Their AIDS Helpline is available between 3 and 10pm each day; their legal line 7-10pm on Wednesdays.

The Terrence Higgins Trust Ltd
52-54 Greys Inn Road
London
WC1X 8JV
0(7)1-831 0330 (general)
0(7)1-242 1010 (helpline)
0(7)1-405 2381 (legal line)

Some Common-Sense Thoughts on AIDS

Of the many books on AIDS now available, the most practical, straightforward, yet compassionate is Peter Tatchell's *AIDS: A Guide to Survival*. He takes you through all that is currently known about AIDS, and the different ways you can look after yourself, from hygiene and diet to positive attitude. Most of what he has to say applies equally to anyone worried about contracting AIDS. As is to be expected from Peter Tatchell, he is very clear about the parallel need to see AIDS in a medical and a political context, but this is also a very humane book. For more thoughts about women and AIDS see page 194 of *Green Pages*.

AIDS: A Guide to Survival
Peter Tatchell
Heretic, 1986
£3.50

Why On Earth Didn't They . . .

'Heartbreaking, provocative . . .' said *Newsweek* of this 630-page blockbuster, and that's an understatement. Written after years of research by the only journalist to cover the 'AIDS story' full-time since it broke in 1982, *And The Band Played On* uses first-hand histories, official documents and contemporary news reports to weave together an unfolding story of confusion and fear, passion and determination, which is all the more immediate for being true. If this doesn't move you to think long and hard about how you are responding to AIDS and its implications, nothing will.

*

The next morning, Dr. Michael Lange peered into Nick's room at St. Luke's-Roosevelt Hospital. A neurologist had found three massive lesions on the young man's brain during a CAT scan. Lange had been called in as an infectious disease specialist. Nick was slumped to one side of the bed. His gray eyes were covered with a milky white film and the left side of his face seemed to sag. His fever was escalating. Nick had been dying in slow motion for a year, the doctors told Lange, and nobody could say why.

*

The bitter truth was that AIDS did not happen to America — it was allowed to happen by an array of institutions, all of which failed to perform their appropriate tasks to safeguard the public health. This failure of the system leaves a legacy of unnecessary suffering that will haunt the Western world for decades to come

And The Band Played On
People, Politics and The AIDS Epidemic
Randy Shilts
Penguin, 1988
£8.95

Heart Problems

It was so sudden. I was just getting a meal ready and my husband went out into the garden to pick some vegetables. The next thing I knew he had collapsed and died. Nobody expected it — he always seemed so fit and healthy.

from *Beating Heart Disease* (see below)

Heart disease in Britain has reached epidemic proportions, and more than a quarter of deaths are now due to this one cause alone. When you realize that heart disease is preventable (Austrians, for example, are half as likely to die of it than are the British; Japanese less than a quarter as likely) it's surprising that more people don't take steps to protect themselves from this sudden and agonizing form of self-inflicted torture.

The causes of heart disease are now widely known — too much saturated fat which clogs up the arteries; too little exercise which results in sluggish circulation and heartbeat; smoking which raises blood pressure and reduces the oxygen in the blood.

Smoking is dealt with at the bottom of the page; here we'll look at the other two — diet and exercise. On the diet front it's not difficult to look after your heart: cut down on meat; eat less fried food; drink skimmed milk (or none at all) rather than full-fat; eat low-fat cheese and margarines; eat much more fibre in the form of grains, fruit and vegetables.

One of the first obvious signs that your heart is in trouble is when you can't get up stairs without feeling uncomfortably breathless — this is almost certainly because your poor old body has forgotten what exercise is. Regular running, swimming or cycling is the best you can do for your body in the way of opening up the arteries and making your heart really work, but you don't have to be fanatical and buy lots of body-building equipment. Leave yourself time to walk to work for a change; see what the world looks like from the top of the nearest hill; put on your favourite tape and dance for twenty minutes.

If the worst should happen, it is useful to know what a heart attack looks and feels like. The main symptom is a sudden crushing pain in the chest, accompanied by giddiness, faintness and a cold clamminess. The sufferer's skin will go pale and waxy as the blood supply is cut off. Get medical help as quickly as possible — dial 999, and when you are through to the ambulance service simply say 'Suspected heart attack' and give the address — the few minutes before help arrives are crucial. If the sufferer is conscious, gently sit them against a few cushions — this is the most economic position for the heart; if they stop breathing or the heart has stopped breathing you will need to apply the resuscitation techniques given in any good first aid manual (see page 137).

The Health Education Council has produced some excellent booklets as part of their 'Look After Your Heart' campaign; they should be available free at your local health centre.

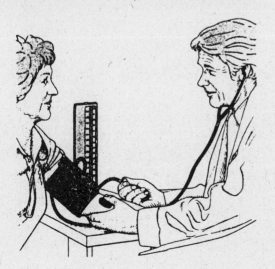

Fighting Heart Disease

Fighting Heart Disease is a wise and gentle book by one of the council members of the British Holistic Medical Association. Having spent sixteen years as a GP working particularly with heart patients who want to help themselves rather than being totally dependent on drugs, Chandra Patel writes knowledgeably about all the medical aspects of heart disease, and also points her reader in the direction of a variety of alternative approaches to stress reduction, including yoga, meditation, massage and biofeedback. An excellent book even if you're not worried about your heart, this book is a lifeline if you are.

Fighting Heart Disease
Chandra Patel
Dorling Kindersley, 1987
£5.95

Smoking And Your Lungs

Fourteen million smokers in Britain get through nearly a quarter of a billion cigarettes every day. There is irrefutable evidence that smoking kills, which explains why the proportion of smokers in the population has fallen from 47 per cent in 1972 to 33 per cent now. Smoking — even light smoking or living with a smoker — can cause lung cancer, duodenal ulcers, bronchitis and emphysema. More than 100,000 deaths each year are caused directly by smoking, and the annual cost to the National Health Service of smoking-related illness is about £500 million.

How To Be Green (see page 259)

Most non-smokers have little patience for anyone who tells them that they have a right to smoke anywhere nearby; more for someone who consciously has the occasional cigarette and goes outside to smoke it; most for someone who stops and takes the time to look at why they did it in the first place.

There is now so much evidence that smoking ruins not only your own health but that of anyone close to you that any extension of smoking bans in public places is to be applauded. The more that people don't smoke (and non-smokers are now a large majority) the more they become aware of how disgusting it is for other people to 'exercise their right to pollute', and the more smoke-free spaces we acquire.

There has recently been a spate of books on giving up smoking; one of the best (despite its appearance) is Judy Perlmutter's *Kick it! Stop Smoking in 5 Days* (Thorsons, 1987, £1.99), which even guarantees your money back if it doesn't work. The Health Education Authority produces a useful leaflet called *A Smoker's Guide to Giving Up*, which you should be able to get from your local health centre.

ASH (Action on Smoking and Health) has a nationwide network of supporters, and will put you in touch with other people working for a smoke-free environment; they organise seminars and produce literature about the benefits of stopping smoking and about how to set up smoke-free zones in buildings and public spaces. Smokestop works with local authorities and employers to co-ordinate activities promoting non-smoking and the advantages of a smoke-free environment; if you are in a position to affect company or organization policy on smoking, write to them.

ASH
5-11 Mortimer Street
London
W1N 7RH
0(7)1-637 9843

Smokestop
Department of
Psychology
The University
Southampton
SO9 5NH
0703 583741

Back Problems

Your spine has to be firm enough to support the body weight in standing erect, but at the same time it must be strong and flexible enough to provide a firm anchorage and the source of movement of the upper and lower limbs. In addition it must provide a safe, cushioned channel for nerves. In order to achieve this, all the separate parts of the spine — bones and joints, discs, ligaments, muscles and nervous system — must be working in unison, each one making its contribution of stability, power, movement, strength or flexibility.

John Tanner, *Beating Back Pain* (see below)

It has been estimated that around 80% of Britons suffer from significant back pain at some point in their lives, and only half of those that do do anything about it. This figure is probably an underestimate. Nearly a third of workers' compensation claims are for back injuries, and there must be an enormous amount of back pain that sufferers simply endure, not to mention the aches that never quite turn into pain.

We are not very good at looking after our backs, and most of the problems that arise are because we ask our backs to do things they were never designed for. Tribal peoples usually squat rather than sit, giving some indication of the position your spine would prefer to be in. Human spines certainly weren't made for sitting behind steering wheels, desks and word-processor keyboards. For more thoughts about chairs and sitting see page 105.

One of the worst things you can do to your back is attempt to lift things in such a way that puts enormous strain on your spine — lifting heavy weights with your back bent is the easiest way to cripple yourself. If you have to lift something heavy on your own, use your legs to get down to it rather than your back; if you need help, make sure you get it. If you start to feel twinges of pain in your back, stop at once.

The two most important things you can do for your back are: exercise it properly and often, but without putting unnecessary strain on it; and give it some physical attention like massage or shiatsu (see *The Bum Back Book* below).

Swimming is one excellent way of keeping your spine in trim; another is yoga (see page 161). If you are really interested in keeping your back healthy you might look into autogenic training or the Alexander technique (also on page 161). You don't need a specific regime of exercises, however. A first step is to stop working (or driving, or whatever) for a few minutes whenever you feel the tension in your back, and gently stretch your spine. Here are some very basic exercises:

▶ Stand up, stretch your arms out sideways at shoulder height, then move them slowly back and down until you can clasp your fingers together — don't worry about the occasional crack, but do stop if it begins to hurt.
▶ Now put your arms by your sides, your chin on your chest, and very slowly lean forward, keeping your head tucked in, your centre of gravity over your feet, and letting your arms dangle. When you have reached the bottom, stop, take a deep breath, then gradually come up again. See if you can feel each vertebra unfolding one at a time.
▶ Now try the same only backwards — but stop if it hurts or if you begin to feel dizzy.
▶ Finally, reach back over your right shoulder with your right hand and back round your waist with your left hand. See if you can clasp both hands together in this position (don't strain anything!). Then try the same the other way round.

This series of exercises takes about five minutes — much less than a tea break.

The Back Pain Association

The Back Pain Association was founded in 1968 to alleviate the suffering of people with back pain and educate people in how to prevent such pain. The Association has branches throughout the country and produces an excellent range of literature (send an sae for more details). Their quarterly magazine *TalkBack* includes advice, news about local branch activities and adverts for gadgets to relieve back pain; they also produce a useful little leaflet called 'Think Back' which you could pin to your notice board as a constant reminder.

Back Pain Association
Grundy House
31-33 Park Road
Teddington
Middlesex
TW11 0AB
0(8)1-977 5474/5

Back Books

A very good back book is John Tanner's *Beating Back Pain* in the series edited by the British Holistic Medical Association. There are few areas of medicine where the names of the ailments sound more frightening — brachyalgia, coccydinia, spondylolisthesis — and John Tanner takes you through them in such a way that you understand what it is that's wrong, what they're suggesting you do about it, and some alternative treatments you might consider. The many illustrations are extremely clear, the suggestions common sense, and the resource section useful. Self-diagnosis charts help you work out for yourself what might be the problem.

Another useful book if you are interested in seeing what you can do for yourself and are not put off by an unconventional approach is Michael Reed Gach's *The Bum Back Book*, a Californian import that will introduce you to self-help acupressure. The book is designed to be very practical, and the photographs make it clear that this is a technique for everyone. If exploring your back pain is part of a wider exercise in self-discovery, this is a book for you.

Beating Back Pain
John Tanner
Dorling Kindersley, 1987
£5.95

The Bum Back Book
Michael Reed Gach
Celestial Arts, 1983
(distributed in the UK
by Airlift)
£5.95

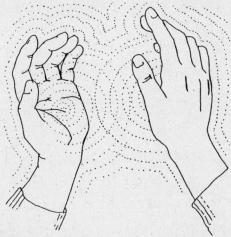

Healing

Until very recently healers had little contact with the practitioners of other forms of natural medicine, and even less with the medical profession. There is now, however, a greater (though still grudging) readiness on the part of scientists to admit the possibility of paranormal forces. As Britain's Healing Research Trust recently pointed out, the discoveries of the quantum physicists have made it possible to award healing a measure of scientific responsibility. The hypothesis is that healers have something in their 'energy fields' which is cap-able of interacting with, and replenishing, the 'energy fields' of patients. How this happens remains a mystery, but the admission that it does happen begins to make sense of therapies which have been reported in every era of history.

Brian Inglis and Ruth West,
The Alternative Health Guide (Mermaid, 1985)

'Healing' is a an ambiguous word, yet a very necessary one. On one hand it has come for many people to be synonymous with faith healing, which makes those who are unsympathetic to the 'paranormal' shy away. On the other it has recently come to be used as an alternative to 'medicine' by many practitioners who prefer not to be associated with the drugs-and-surgery scene which modern medicine now implies. We might think of healing simply as 'helping people to be healthy in a holistic way', but I am also aware that for many people the 'faith' aspect in healing is vitally important.

Spiritual Healing

It is pretty obvious that most people in the West are in need of some sort of spiritual healing alongside the healing of their bodies and minds, but 'spiritual healing' tends to have a very unfortunate Victorian-drawing-room-table-tapping image, which healers themselves are not always particularly concerned to replace. Although most spiritual healers are at pains to point out that they are not spiritualists (whatever that means), spiritual healing still appears to be rather old-fashioned, and still tends to attract older people, mostly women.

The main organization for spiritual healing in Britain is the National Federation of Spiritual Healers, which represents the more contemporary aspect of the art (despite its insistence on calling people 'Man' and spirit 'the Divine'). With a nationwide membership of over 4,500, the Federation can refer you to a local healer and answer questions you may have about spiritual healing; they also publish *Healing Review* four times a year and run a book and tape service.

National Federation of Spiritual Healers
Old Manor Farm Studio
Church Street
Sunbury-on-Thames
Middlesex
TW16 6RG
0932 783164/5

The Churches and Healing

Faith healing has always been associated with organized religion. Even though shrines like Lourdes and the worst excesses of fundamentalist Christianity may seem to have commercialized spiritual healing out of all recognition, many people are certain that their religious faith helps them both in their own healing and in their ability to help other people towards healing. For very many people it provides spiritual solace and inspiration, especially at times when the going is hard.

The churches in Britain are involved in some very important haling work, especially among people who are ill and in need. Most churches have some sort of organization which deals specifically with the role of that church in the healing ministry; some are more active than others. The most important of these organizations, largely Anglican though its membership is much wider than that, is the Churches' Council for Health and Healing.

The CCHH dates back to 1944, though with reports on issues like AIDS and complementary medicine could never be accused of being behind the times. The CCHH produces a very good bi-monthly magazine, *Health and Healing*, three times a year, publishes a wide range of material, and runs a book service. CCHH will put you in touch with healers, courses, local groups and congregations, and reading the magazine will keep you up to date with the role of Christianity in this rapidly developing field.

The Methodist Church has a Division of Social Responsibility (Healing) which offers educational material on various aspects of healing; the Quakers have the Friends Fellowship of Healing, which runs two guest/retreat houses (at Lingfield in Surrey and Greystoke in Cumbria). There is a Jewish Association of Spiritual Healers which can refer you to a suitable healer, and The United Reformed Church have a Committee for Health and Healing. I'm sure I have missed some, but your local church should be able to tell you more.

The Churches' Council for Health and Healing
St Marylebone
Parish Church
Marylebone Road
London
NW1 5LT
0(7)1-486 9644

Methodist Church Division of Social Responsibility (Healing)
1 Central Buildings
Westminster
London
SW1H 9NH
0(7)1-222 8589

Friends Fellowship of Healing
5 Old Manor Close
Ifield
Crawley
RH11 0HQ
0293 21267

Jewish Association of Spiritual Healers
33 Grendon Gardens
Wembley Park
Middlesex
HA9 9NE
0(8)1-904 6021

The United Reformed Church Committee on Health and Healing
86 Tavistock Place
London
WC1H 9RT
0(7)1-837 7661

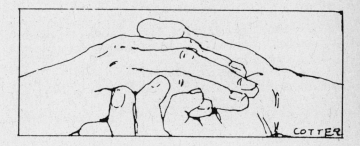

How To Find the Right Treatment for Yourself

There has been a veritable boom in interest in and information about 'alternative' therapies in recent years, so that knowing exactly what to read and where to get useful and non-partizan advice can be daunting. You will hear about things that have helped your friends, things they wouldn't touch with a barge-pole, practitioners who have overcharged them and left them worse than they were before. You will hear claims and counter-claims, high praise and horror stories. Here are some thoughts about first steps, and things to watch out for. Much of what follows applies both to healing techniques and disci-plines (the next six pages) and to psychotherapeutic tech-niques (covered on pages 172-173); the distinction is often fairly arbitrary.

Where To Find Out

Books are a good start, and Stephen Fulder's *The Handbook of Complementary Medicine* (see page 137) probably the best: this will give you some idea of what the different therapies are so you will at least recognize their names. If you have a natural health centre near you, ask what therapies they offer and (very important) how much they charge. Wholefood shops, radical bookshops and community centres often have noticeboards on which local practitioners advertise, though the more 'prof-essional' practitioners might look down on such a practice, and the best (and therefore the busiest) might well have a large enough clientele without advertising.

What To Spend

There are people who spend fortunes on their health, going from practitioner to practitioner, therapy to therapy. There are a lot more people who are desperate for help who believe that any sort of treatment beyond the NHS is completely beyond their reach. It is true that, with some exceptions, any sort of treatment outside the NHS (and an increasing number within it) will cost something, but if you make a little effort to explore the different options you may be surprised to find how much you can afford.

For a start there are some therapies you can get within the NHS if you make it clear that this is what you want. They include homeopathy, massage (they call it physiotherapy) and, less commonly, osteopathy and chiropractic. Outside the NHS, many practitioners have different rates for high and low earners and for unwaged people. Don't promise to pay what you can't afford, but don't be mean either. If you are reason-ably rich you will be helping to subsidize people who need the treatment just as much but have fewer resources. Some practitioners are open to payment with things other than cash — home-grown vegetables, perhaps, or a couple of hours of baby sitting; you will need to play this one by ear.

Rates vary enormously from practitioner to practitioner, and from area to area. An hour's massage in London can easily cost £18-20, while in rural Scotland it still costs less than £10; treatments like acupuncture and osteopathy will usually be more expensive. Beyond a certain level, however, you will not be getting any better value for your money however well known the practitioner.

Is It The Right Practitioner?

Any half-decent practitioner will give you the chance to meet him or her for a short chat without any obligation — but this does mean short. You cannot expect a half-hour session for nothing. A short meeting should give you enough to go on to decide whether you want a full first consultation with this person. Always remember that you don't have to go to the first herbalist you're referred to, or the nearest acupuncturist; nor do you have to go back after the preliminary consultation, though it's polite to tell them.

Many practitioners will advise you to take a course of treatment, and once you've started it's a good idea to finish. Alternative practitioners are usually, but by no means always, happy to talk about any problems that might arise, even when they are problems you may be having with them as practition-er. If you have an intractable problem with an alternative practitioner, you should go to their professional organization and see what they can do; beyond that the BHMA (page 144) may be able to help.

Keeping Everybody Informed

When you need specialist help within the mainstream medical system there is an established system of referral, and your medical notes should automatically be available to the new specialist. If your GP knows about your 'alternative' treatment (they may have referred you) they may write to the comple-mentary practitioner with a brief case history. The chances are, however, that they won't, so you will be working with two systems which find it very hard to communicate with each other.

Whether you choose to tell your GP about your alternative treatment is up to you — if you think they can hear it, it is a good idea. On the other hand, for your own good you should tell your complementary practitioner about any medication or other mainstream treatment you are undergoing, and when-ever there is any change in this regime. You should also tell them if you are having any other sort of complementary treatment, since although some techniques combine well, others (herbalism and homeopathy for example) may mask each other or even be harmful in combination.

Whatever healing discipline or regime you decide to follow, always remember that you are in charge, and that nobody knows about your body and your needs better than you do.

Relaxation and Stress Reduction

Nothing is more healing than rest and relaxation, and though this usually means being physically still, there are many ways in which you can become more relaxed in your daily life. It is possible to learn to be efficient and relaxed, even busy and relaxed.

First, though, you need to learn to stop completely from time to time — not crashing out exhaustedly or wandering round aimlessly trying very hard to do nothing, simply stopping. Part of the problem is that there are very few places apart from the privacy of your own home where you can lie down comfortably, though any cleanish floor or stretch of grass will do. Put cushions or pillows under your head, the small of your back and your knees if you need them. Then relax.

Easily said, and once you know what to do it isn't difficult. Take a moment or two to really feel the ground holding you up, and relax on to it. Then start at the top of your body, with your face; first tighten all the muscles and then let the tightness go. Repeat this all the way down your body, concentrating especially on the places where people tend to 'carry' their tension — shoulders, hands, stomach, bottom, knees, ankles. When you're as comfortable as you can be, take a couple of long deep breaths, then relax into even breathing and watch your breath. Being aware of your breathing is one of the oldest forms of yoga, and an excellent way of being in touch with your body.

Fifteen minutes of relaxed breathing like this, done regularly, will help your body to heal itself more than many expensive and time-consuming treatments.

This sort of relaxation is the first step towards meditation (page 178) or yoga (page 161), and you might like to look at these techniques while you are thinking about relaxation.

Stress Reduction

'Stress management' is now very big business, especially within big business. Large corporations, aware that some of their best people are suffering from 'burnout', are investing hefty sums in teaching jet-set executives how to cope with stress. But stress affects most people who live in the fast lane of our urbanized, rapid-transit, noisy, smelly and frustrating culture. There are now several good books on dealing with stress, but one of the best is L. John Mason's *Guide to Stress Reduction*, a Californian import now in its second edition. What I like about this book is its no-nonsense no-hype approach to relaxation, and the way it integrates techniques like meditation and biofeedback without making any of them the answer. He sees 'stress' in its widest sense, and is very clear that the aim isn't to rid life of all excitement: 'Stress is, always has been, and always will be, a part of being alive.'

**Guide to
Stress Reduction**
L. John Mason
Celestial Arts, 1985
(distributed in the UK by Airlift)
£6.95

Autogenic Training

A technique which originated in the 1930s in Germany, autogenic training helps you to relax with the use of a series of exercises, taught and checked by an experienced health professional. It isn't cheap — currently up to £150 for an eight-session course — but they have helped pilots deal with jet-lag and many people to come off tranquillizers. Try something cheaper first, autogenics if you need professional help.

**Centre for Autogenic Training
Positive Health Centre**
101 Harley Street
London
W1N 1DF
0(7)1-935 1811

Relaxation for Living

Since 1972 Relaxation for Living has been co-ordinating courses all over Britain which help people to heal themselves through relaxation. They will refer you to a local group, produce a range of useful literature, and train both professionals and interested amateurs in relaxation techniques. Relaxation for Living prefers interested enquirers to write, enclosing an A5 sae, rather than ringing.

Relaxation for Living
29 Burwood Park Road
Walton-on-Thames
Surrey
KT12 5LH
0932 227826

Biofeedback

Listening to your body takes skill and practice, and in the last twenty years several simple electronic gadgets have been produced which can help you to hear what your body is saying to you, giving you immediate information about things like your heartbeat, blood pressure and skin temperature. This is called biofeedback, and has been developed into a fine art by some practitioners. It really does produce results, since you can see how much effect you can have on your body (not surprisingly really, since the two are the same). You can spend thousands on biofeedback equipment, but you can also try it out at or hire it from a company in Hammersmith called Audio Ltd. This is also the centre for biofeedback workshops in Britain, and they will be pleased to send you details of forthcoming events — at £20 for a day workshop, including use of biofeedback instruments, this is well worth a try.

Jacyntha Crawley of the London Biorhythm Company is a tireless campaigner for the technique, and the organization offers a wide range of services, including computer-printed charts, research and lectures.

Audio Ltd
26-28 Wendell Road
London
W12 9RT
0(8)1-743 1518/4352

**London Biorhythm
Company Ltd**
PO Box 413
London
SW7 2PT
0(8)1-877 0834

Many people use tapes — often in personal stereos — to help them relax. The BHMA (page 144) produces such tapes, as does the Matthew Manning Centre (39 Abbeygate Street, Bury St Edmunds, Suffolk IP33 1LW; Tel: 0284 769502). See also 'spiritual music' on page 179.

Herbs and Herbalism

Herbalism is one of the alternative therapies I have no doubts about at all. Many modern drugs are derived either directly from herbs, or from chemical counterfeits: a herbalist friend made me a tincture of ephedra for my hay fever; when I looked at the pills my doctor had been prescribing for years I found they contained artificial ephedrines. Fresh mint tea in the morning wakes me up and chamomile tea at night helps me sleep: there's no magic involved, the chemical constituents of the relevant essential oils can be isolated and measured.

What's more, with a little knowledge and experience you can easily become your own herbalist, and it will be a relatively cheap way of boosting your health. A qualified herbalist will be able to provide diagnosis and prescribe herbal mixtures to suit your precise circumstances, but if you take a few precautions it is hard to do any damage to yourself using commonly-available herbs.

The Holistic Herbal

As well as being sound, clear and well-illustrated, *The Holistic Herbal* enables its reader to approach any specific question from several different angles. There is a section on each of the systems of the human body — nervous, respiratory, digestive and so on; an alphabetical list of herbs; a repertory of herbs suitable for different ailments; and chapters on herb gathering and preparation, the chemistry and actions of herbs, and an excellent bibliography.

EYEBRIGHT
Euphrasia officinalis
Scrophulariaceae
Part used: Dried aerial parts.
Collection: Gather the whole plant whilst in bloom in late summer or autumn and dry it in an airy place.
Constituents: Glycosides including aucubin, tannins, resins, volatile oil.
Actions: Anti-catarrhal, astringent, anti-inflammatory.
Indications: Eyebright is an excellent remedy for the problems of mucous membranes. The combination of anti-inflammatory and astringent properties make it relevant in many conditions. Used internally it is a powerful anti-catarrhal and thus may be used in *nasal catarrh, sinusitis* and other congestive states. It is best known for its use in conditions of the eye, where it is helpful in acute or chronic inflammations, stinging and weeping eyes as well as over-sensitivity to light. Used as a compress and taken internally it is used in *conjunctivitis* and *blepharitis*.
Combinations: In catarrhal conditions it combines well with Golden Rod, Elder Flower or Golden Seal. In allergic conditions where the eyes are effected it may be combined with Ephedra. As an eye lotion it mixes with Golden Seal and distilled Witch Hazel.
Preparation and dosage: Infusion: pour a cup of boiling water onto 1 teaspoonful of the dried herb and leave to infuse for 5-10 minutes. This should be drunk three times a day.
Compress: place a teaspoonful of the dried herb in half a litre (1 pint) of water and boil for 10 minutes, let cool slightly. Moisten a compress (cotton wool, gauze or muslin) in the lukewarm liquid, wring out slightly and place over the eyes. Leave the compress in place for 15 minutes. Repeat several times a day.
Tincture: take 1-4ml of the tincture three times a day.

Eyebright

The Holistic Herbal
David Hoffmann
Element, 1988
£8.95

For most medicinal purposes it is best to use the fresh herb whenever possible, and this is where a small herb garden of your own, which can be grown in pots on the windowsill if you have no garden, is useful. A number of important herbal remedies have to be imported, however, and most herbs are difficult to obtain fresh during the winter and spring, so this is where supplies of dried herbs are needed. You can dry your own herbs very simply by hanging or laying them in a dry place out of the sun until they are brittle enough to crumble, or speed things up by putting them in the microwave for a few seconds.

Some herb gardens also sell dried herbs (Fold Garden in Staffordshire and Poyntzfield Herb Nursery in Ross-shire for example: see page 83), but for a full range of dried herbs, plus essential oils, herbal fluid extracts and tinctures, and other sweet-smelling and health-giving herbal products you will need a specialist herb supplier.

Herbalists

Named after the celebrated English herbalist Nicholas Culpeper, The Culpeper Company was started in 1927 by Hilda Leyel, who also founded The Herb Society (see below). From their eighteen shops — and by mail order — they sell a full range of organically-grown herbs grown on the company's own farm at Wixoe in Suffolk, herbal pills and cosmetics, soaps and smelly bathroom gifts, and wild flower seeds. Ian Thomas from Culpepers has written an extremely useful guide to the cultivation and use of all the herb varieties they sell called *The Culpeper Herb Collection* (£1.75). Prices are on the high side (packet herbs 50p-£6.50; bath soap £1.50), but the specially-made pesto sauce from Italy, made with virgin olive oil and fresh basil, is superb (albeit costing £2.95 a jar!).

Trading from a small old-fashioned shop near the Elephant and Castle, Baldwins probably stocks the largest range of herbs and herbal products in Britain. Dried herbs are sold in 1oz packs, at around 40p for the commoner herbs up to a pound or so for Golden Rod and Dittany of Crete, and they also carry a full range of oils, tablets, bottles, and bases for home-made cosmetics. Baldwins run an extremely efficient mail order service, and offer good discounts on bulk purchases.

At Neal's Yard Apothecary a wide range of herbs is dispensed at the counter, and oils and a cosmetic range are sold in distinctive blue glass bottles. They do a mail order service; send an sae for a catalogue.

Potter's supply dried herbs and herbal tinctures, together with a wide range of herbal medicines. Write for their booklet, *Herbal Remedies: The Treatment of Common Ailments*.

Culpeper Ltd
Hadstock Road
Linton
Cambridge
CB1 6NJ
0223 891196

Neal's Yard Apothecary
2 Neal's Yard
London
WC2H 9DP
0(7)1-379 7222

G. Baldwin and Co.
171-173 Walworth Road
London
SE17 1RW
0(7)1-703 5550

Potter's (Herbal Supplies) Ltd
Leyland Mill Lane
Wigan
Lancashire
WN1 2SB
0942 34761

Organizations

The most important of the professional bodies concerned with herbalism is the National Institute of Medical Herbalists, which produces an annual list of qualified members. They will gladly put you in touch with your nearest herbalist.

The Herb Society organizes lectures and garden visits all over the country; write for further details.

National Institute of Medical Herbalists
41 Hatherley Road
Winchester
SO22 6RR
0962 68776

The Herb Society
PO Box 415
London
SW1P 2HE
0803 867823

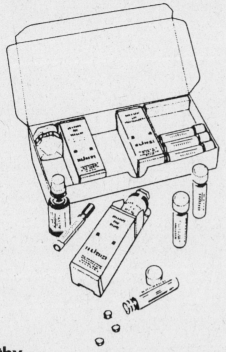

Homeopathy

The basic ideas behind homeopathy (homoeopathy if you're classically-minded) are that you should take the minimum amount of a remedy that will restore your balance of health, and that 'like cures like'. Thus hot spices can help flu, and a very small dose of smallpox can protect a person against a large dose of the disease later in life.

Your introduction to homeopathy may well be via a row of pill bottles in your chemist or health food shop with strange names like *6xRhus toxicodendron*. This can be off-putting, as can some of the simplistic guides which suggest that a specific symptom or ailment will automatically succumb to a particular homeopathic remedy. A good homeopath will take into account all the circumstances of your needs, and will explain what each remedy is being prescribed for.

Many homeopaths use homeopathy very much as part of a treatment for the whole patient, and it is alongside good counselling and a physical therapy like massage or shiatsu that homeopathy works best — healing for the whole body. Homeopathic remedies seem to work better for some people than for others. Homeopathy certainly can't do you any harm, and is well worth a try.

If you want to read about homeopathy, a clear and value-for-money account is Stephen Cummings and Dana Ullman's *Everybody's Guide to Homeopathic Medicine* (Gollancz, 1984, £4.95). Both of the organizations listed below will send you introductory leaflets in return for an sae.

Homeopaths differ as to which brand of remedies is best — some (like Katie Boyle) swear by Nelsons, others by Weleda. I don't suppose there's much difference.

The two main professional organizations in Britain concerned with homeopathy, both of which will put you in touch with a local practitioner, are the British Homeopathic Association, an organization for medically-qualified doctors who are also qualified homeopaths, and The Society of Homeopaths, which recognizes homeopaths who are not qualified in mainstream medicine.

**British
Homeopathic
Association**
27a Devonshire Street
London
W1N 1RJ
0(7)1-935 2163

**The Society of
Homeopaths**
47 Canada Grove
Bognor Regis
West Sussex
PO21 1DW
0243 860678

Bach Flower Remedies

There is no true healing unless there is a change in outlook, peace of mind, and inner happiness.
Edward Bach

The 38 Bach flower remedies are prescribed by many alternative practitioners (and some mainstream ones) to help a person experiencing 'negative' states of mind to move into a more positive attitude and thus towards healing. Why they work nobody seems to know; there is much talk of 'vibrational states' and 'personality types', but it is enough for me that they relate beautiful plants with human conditions, that they serve as reminders of the ability of the human mind and body to heal themselves, and that many people have benefited from taking the remedies (though I have to admit that I have never experienced any noticeable, immediate and direct benefit from the couple of times I have taken the Bach 'rescue remedy'). The standard books on the Bach flower remedies are published by C.W. Daniel (1 Church Path, Saffron Walden, Essex CB10 1JP; Tel: 0799 21909 — ask for their very informative *Health and Healing* list): *Introduction to the Benefits of the Bach Flower Remedies* by Jane Evans (70p) is a primer pamphlet; *Illustrated Handbook of the Bach Flower Remedies* by Philip Chancellor (£5.25) the complete works. The remedies themselves (£43 for a set of 38 10ml dropper bottles), together with further information, can be requested from the Edward Bach Centre in Wallingford.

The Dr Edward Bach Centre
Mount Vernon
Sotwell
Wallingford
Oxfordshire
OX10 0PZ
0491 39489

Harebell Remedies

Some people who have used the Bach Flower Remedies have extended the use of essences as healing remedies, and make their own essences from a wider range of flowers and plants. You can make your own essences very easily, though if you live in a city remote from the countryside a wide range of more than fifty flower essences is obtainable from Ellie Web of Harebell Remedies. St John's Wort for protection and guidance; Red Clover for shock; Daisy to help true understanding — each remedy comes in a dropper bottle (20ml of remedy for £1.75; a 10ml stock bottle for £2.25). Ellie has also written a helpful leaflet which she will send on receipt of an sae.

Harebell Remedies
Monybuie
Corsock
Castle Douglas
DG7 3DY
064 44 202

Alternative Diagnostic Techniques

Most mainstream medicine operates on the diagnostic principle that if you feel a pain in a particular place, that's the place which needs treatment. This is a gross oversimplification, but it is a major distinction between mainstream medicine and holistic medicine, insofar as the holistic practitioner will rarely only look at the most obvious symptoms before attempting a diagnosis. Good mainstream doctors will take into account your lifestyle, medical history, overall energy level and so on, but many have neither the time, nor apparently the interest — at least, not unless you have something really interestingly wrong with you.

Knowing that the human body works as a whole, and that what is happening in one part reflects what is happening everywhere else, you will probably find that your alternative practitioner will be interested in much more than your GP. Having asked quite a lot of questions, she or he may then use one of a range of diagnostic techniques.

One such technique is muscle testing, part of a massage technique called Touch for Health. All you have to do is hold each part of your body against the gentle pressure of the practitioner while they check the relative strength of your muscles — this gives a good idea of where you lack energy, and the imbalance can then be adjusted using touch or massage. Another technique, often used in conjunction with muscle testing, is iridology, based on the belief that the various parts of the body are reflected in the iris of the eye. I first had my iris read as a complete skeptic — and was amazed at how accurate the diagnosis was. Reflexology (also known as Metamorphic Technique or Zone Therapy) sees the whole body mirrored in the soles of your feet, and the ensuing treatment involves having your feet massaged, which is extremely pleasant even if you don't believe in the diagnosis at all.

Many alternative practitioners use these diagnostic techniques in combination and in conjunction with other therapies, but the relevant national associations should be able to put you in touch with a local member.

British Touch for Health Association
8 Railey Mews
Kentish Town
London
NW5 2PA
0(7)1-482 0698

British Register of Iridologists
Dolphin House
6 Gold Street
Saffron Walden
Essex
CB10 1EJ
0799 26138

Metamorphic Association
67 Ritherdon Road
London
SW17 8QE
0(8)1-672 5951

All the other therapies listed on these two pages, while considered to be important within the overall framework of complementary medicine, are outside my personal experience. Where osteopathy and chiropractic are concerned, I have been lucky enough never to have suffered severe back pain — if I did I wouldn't hesitate to try a recommended practitioner rather than submit to drugs and surgery. I have always been too much of a coward to try having acupuncture needles stuck in me, though I'm told that you often don't feel a thing. Given a friendly acupuncturist and a problem that didn't respond to anything else, I'd certainly give it a try. I do know people who swear by acupuncture, and who have found it extremely good at dealing with acute pain.

Another thing that acupuncture, osteopathy and chiropractic have in common is that they should never be practiced by somebody who is unqualified. While you might accept herbal advice from anybody who knows what they are talking about, or a massage from an untrained friend, being treated by an amateur in any of these disciplines is not a good idea.

Acupuncture

Simply put, acupuncture is based on the ancient Chinese model of the human body, which sees the various parts of the body being linked by energy channels or 'meridians'. When an energy imbalance is diagnosed, very fine needles are inserted into the skin on the lines of the meridians with the purpose of influencing these energy channels.

A related form of treatment which does not involve needles is called acupressure. Here the fingers are used on the surface of the skin at the same points as are used in acupuncture. If it is the needles that concern you, you might try acupressure first. A good introduction to acupressure is Michael Reed Gach's *The Bum Back Book* (see page 152). Another related therapy is shiatsu (see page 160).

Acupuncture should only ever be practiced by a qualified acupuncturist, since serious damage and infection can result from unskilled use of the needles. There are a number of professional organizations for acupuncturists — every school seems to have its own professional organization, and they all sound very similar. In an attempt to circumvent the confusion for the layperson, and to ensure that it is relatively easy to find a local practitioner (of any persuasion), the four main British acupuncture organizations have together created a list of practitioners called *The Register of Acupuncturists*, which can be obtained from any of the four participating bodies:

British Acupuncture Association
34 Alderney Street
London
SW1V 4EU
0(7)1-834 1012

Register of Traditional Chinese Medicine
7a Thorndean Street
London
SW18 4HE
0(8)1-947 1879

Traditional Acupuncture Society
1 The Ridgeway
Stratford upon Avon
Warwickshire
CV37 9JL
0789 292507

International College of Oriental Medicine
Green Hedges House
Green Hedges Avenue
East Grinstead
West Sussex
RH19 1DZ
0342 313106/7

A very good introduction to acupuncture and its context within Chinese medicine is Ted Kapchuk's book, *The Web That Has No Weaver: Understanding Chinese Medicine* (Hutchinson, 1984, £4.95). The British Acupuncture Society produces a useful little handbook with four pages of basic questions and answers about acupuncture — send them an A5 sae for a copy.

Osteopathy and Chiropractic

It is very easy to be unclear when describing what osteopathy and chiropractic are, even more so when you try to distinguish between them. They both claim ancient roots, but in fact were both only named in the late nineteenth century, and are only now coming into their own. They both concern themselves with the correct alignment and functioning of the bones of the body, more particularly with the spine and (in cranial osteopathy) the skull; thus they are most often called upon to deal with back problems. While manipulative and deep massage techniques are used in mainstream medicine, these more holistic techniques shun the drugs and surgery so often resorted to by hospitals, and always take the patient's whole medical history into account, seeing problems in the joints and muscles as indicative of wider issues.

And the difference between them? An osteopath is more likely to use soft muscle manipulation, though the most effective treatment is often a sudden, but controlled and painless, thrust which puts your bones back into alignment. An osteopath is less likely to use X-rays, relying more on your posture and his or her hands to check your spine. A chiropractor tends to concentrate on joints and their effects on your nervous system, an osteopath on exercises for the joints and associated muscles. A more practical point is that there are currently about three times as many qualified osteopaths as qualified chiropractors, though the British Chiropractic Association is doing its best to train more chiropractors and has recently launched an impressive literature drive. Their new series of leaflets (send an sae for a set) explains chiropractic as well as any book.

As with acupuncture, never use an unqualified practitioner in either of these disciplines. The main national organizations, both of which will be glad to put you in touch with a local practitioner, are the:

General Council and Register of Osteopaths
1-4 Suffolk Street
London
SW1Y 4HG
0(7)1-839 2060

British Chiropractic Association
5 First Avenue
Chelmsford
Essex
CM1 1RX
0245 358487

Alexander at work

Movement and Posture Techniques

Two ways of restoring the full physical efficiency of your body are named after the men who worked out the systems of exercise and movement upon which the present-day techniques are based. The Australian actor F. Matthias Alexander originated the exercises for balanced posture and fluid movement that are now called the Alexander Technique; Russian-born Israeli Moshe Feldenkrais developed the system of gentle repetitive movements called the Feldenkrais Method. Neither is cheap, but both will put you in touch with your body, and help you to use your body freely and awarely without putting undue tension on it. Dancing and reciprocal massage will do the same job more cheaply, but if you are rich enough and need the discipline, one of these techniques may be the one for you.

Movement is life. Without Movement life is unthinkable

Moshe Feldenkrais

Society of Teachers of the Alexander Technique
10 London House
266 Fulham Road
London
SW10 9EL
0(7)1-351 0828

Feldenkrais Information Centre
188 Old Street
London
EC1V 9BP
0273 27406 (yes, that is a Brighton number!)

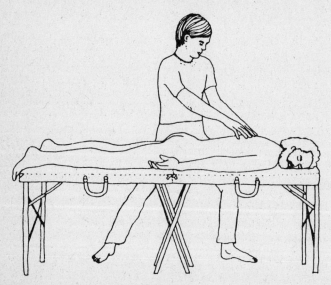

The Touching Therapies

Touch is a vital yet much-abused human need. We all need to touch and be touched; being 'in touch' with ourselves and other people is a crucial part of seeing how we fit into the overall scheme of things.

But many of us have been hurt by being touched in ways we didn't want, and are now so frightened of being touched that the idea of spending an hour, half naked on a couch, being stroked by a relative stranger, sends shivers down the spine.

Massage is an ancient form of therapy, widespread in Asia from medieval times; massaging a traveller's feet is still part of the welcome received at some Japanese inns. In recent years massage and its close relatives have been revived as a much needed, health-promoting and extremely therapeutic form of treatment. Sadly it has often been subverted, and the word 'massage' will almost invariably produce winks and nudges at the pub bar.

The link between massage and sexuality is a close one and should never be denied, but the key is that the contract between masseur and client should always be clear, and respect the needs and express wishes of both parties. There is never a case for abusing the trust implicit in a close relationship between client and practitioner.

Having sounded the warning, it must be said that good massage is wonderful, and will do things for you that no other therapy can achieve. The other good thing about massage is that anybody can learn how to do it — you can't easily hurt yourself or anybody else in massage, and if you can find a friend or friends who will exchange massages with you, you can get a regular massage without it costing anything. Sometimes, though, it is nice just to receive with no obligation. Money spent on good massage is about the best investment you can make in alternative healing.

Unfortunately there is no national register of qualified masseurs, but then, unlike some techniques, qualification or lack of it seems to make little difference to the quality of the massage. The best school of massage in Britain, however, is the Northern Institute in Blackpool, and they will be glad to put you in touch with a local graduate. Beyond that the personal columns of Spare Rib (page 197) or the Women's Therapy Centre (page 198) should be able to put any woman in touch with a woman masseur; men — I'm afraid — may find it harder to find a massage without sexual connotations (though sort out your motives before you look for a good massage — clarity is essential).

Northern Institute of Massage
100 Waterloo Road
Blackpool
Lancashire
FY4 1AW
0253 403548

Books on Massage

Massage is easily learned, but there is no doubt that it is best learned with a teacher. Some teachers charge a great deal, but if you ask at your local community centre or community bookshop, you may well find that there are low-cost self-help massage groups in your area:

As far as books go the best is still George Downing's Massage Book, first published in 1973 but wearing very well alongside the newcomers. The style and the line drawings are very clear, the instructions very easy to follow, and the book has none of the prudishness of some of the more purely health oriented books — it makes it clear that massage should be enjoyable! Penguin are planning to publish a new edition early in 1990.

Lucinda Lidell's more recent The Book of Massage is also very approachable. The book actually teaches you shiatsu and reflexology (see below) as well as massage, using clear colour illustrations and step-by-step instructions. Lucinda Lidell is also good on anatomy and on the emotions that are aroused during massage; altogether a sensitively-written and practical introduction.

George Downing
The Massage Book
Penguin, 1981
£2.25

The Book of Massage
Lucinda Lidell
Ebury, 1989
£7.95

Variations on a Theme

Shiatsu is a cross between massage and acupuncture, using the fingers and hands (and even the feet) to stretch and stimulate the meridians; it has a long tradition in oriental healing. There is a national society which can put you in touch with a local practitioner; they also run a book service. Elaine Liechti, the Secretary, has written a useful guide called Beginning Shiatsu, available for £2.50 from the society.

Aromatherapy is massage with natural scented oils — a real treat. Some people make the choice of oil into quite a science; others work more intuitively. The two main organizations for aromatherapy are the International Federation of Aromatherapists, and the rather elitist Tisserand aromatherapists, who all have to have trained with the great man for at least three months. This tends to make them rather expensive!

Rolfing is a cross between massage and osteopathy, concentrating on the deep tissues and thus working with structural imbalances in the body. Working deeply but gently, the trained Rolfer can work wonders with deep-seated pain and fatigue. Rolfing is a specialized form of massage, and should only be done with a qualified practitioner, but if you feel that ordinary massage never quite reaches deep enough to reach the tension, Rolfing may well be the therapy for you.

Reichian Bodywork (see page 172) is very close to massage in some respects, though I have chosen to include it under psychotherapy rather than alternative medicine.

Shiatsu Society
19 Langside Park
Kilbarchan
Strathclyde
PA10 2EP
05057 4657

International Federation of Aromatherapists
46 Dalkeith Road
West Dulwich
London
SE21 8LS
0(8)1-670 5011

The Association of Tisserand Aromatherapists
PO Box 746
Brighton
East Sussex
BN1 3BN

Rolfing Network
80 Clifton Hill
London
NW8 0JT
0(7)1-328 9026

Yoga

'Yoga' means so many things to so many people that it is difficult to say what it is, let alone categorize it. Is it a healing technique, a therapy, a spiritual discipline, or a way of exercising? In Sanskrit the word means 'union', and invokes the connection between the individual and the universe. For many people, yoga is a series of exercises rather like slow aerobics that you do in a class once a week.

The connection is self-realization or self-knowledge, and as you study yoga it will probably become all of the above things to you. A good teacher — and it is best to start with a teacher — will stress the therapeutic and spiritual aspects of yoga, and will almost certainly advise you do spend some time each day doing your yoga, just as you might meditate regularly.

There are several yoga organizations in Britain, and which you approach will depend to some extent on your understanding of what yoga means to you. Perhaps the most approachable is the Yoga For Health Foundation, which organizes events all over the country and publishes a very good quarterly magazine called *Yoga and Life*. They have their own residential centre near Biggleswade in Bedfordshire, and work a lot with disabled people, for whom yoga can be a lifesaver.

A more purist approach to yoga as a spiritual tradition is provided by the British Wheel of Yoga, which has an active membership nationwide and publishes a quarterly magazine called *Spectrum*.

There are very many books on yoga, but I would still advise anyone to start with B.K.S. Iyengar's classic *Concise Light on Yoga* (Unwin, 1977, £2.50).

Yoga For Health Foundation
Ickwell Bury
Biggleswade
Bedfordshire
SG18 9EF
076 727 271

British Wheel of Yoga
1 Hamilton Place
Boston Road
Sleaford
Lincolnshire
NG34 7ES
0529 306851

T'ai Chi

T'ai chi is what you see Chinese and Japanese workers and students doing before they start work every day — and what an excellent way to start. T'ai chi chuan (to give it its full name) has ancient oriental roots, and is best thought of as a moving yoga. There are many different 'forms' — 'yang', 'lee' and 'wu'; 'short' and 'long' — but don't worry about the content. Find a teacher you feel comfortable with, then enjoy moving and discovering the grace and balance in your body.

Quite a rivalry (usually friendly) has arisen between the various schools of t'ai chi in Britain, so rather than list the half dozen or so different schools, I would advise you to find the name of a teacher near to you regardless of what particular school they belong to, and see how you get on. Ask at your community centre or wholefood shop — they will usually know of a local teacher.

Running and Jogging

Venture on some parts of Hampstead Heath of a summer Sunday morning and you'll be trampled underfoot by the joggers; there's so many of them in New York's Central Park that they have their own one-way system and traffic lights.

There's no mystique to running: half-marathons and fun runs now take place all over the country all through the year, and anyone can take part. And that's just the organized running; hundreds of thousands of people now regularly don tracksuits and running shoes and do a regular circuit round the local park.

The one item you'll need to buy is a pair of running shoes, and good ones aren't cheap — you can pay over £70 for a pair of state-of-the-art air-wedge heel-counter-support ZX5001 specials. But don't unless you really know what you're doing. Expect to pay around £20 for a decent pair of running shoes that won't fall apart; you'll probably find them so comfortable that you won't want to take them off again.

Everything else about running is common sense. Don't ever overdo it, especially at the beginning, and stop if it hurts. Unfortunately, women who run alone can become the subject of abuse or attack; the Reebock Running Sisters Network will put you in touch with other women who run, so you can run together — send them an sae at 57-61 Mortimer Street, London W1N 7TD.

There are running clubs throughout Britain, and most of them welcome beginners — your local Recreation and Leisure Department will be able to give you names and addresses.

Alternative Healing Centres

Practically everybody knows what a health centre looks like. It has a reception area with people and records on the other side of a counter, a lot of chairs for people to sit on and wait, piles of dog-eared magazines, and perhaps a tankful of bored fish. The doctors and specialists each have their own room, and an announcement system penetrates the tension every few minutes: 'Mr McEwan to Dr Smithers please'.

Many health centres try to make things as pleasant as possible while you wait, but it's difficult to imagine anything less conducive to healing than the average health centre waiting room — noisy, cramped, perfect for exchanging airborne infections, a system designed to raise fears, frustrations and tensions.

Then if you are lucky you have five minutes to explain what's wrong, be diagnosed, and be prescribed a treatment. Doctors don't like this way of working any more than you do, but they simply don't have more time. So off you go with your prescription, often not sure that the doctor really understood what you were trying to say.

But what is the alternative? Private medicine? Paying health professionals to come and see you at home? To a very large extent the solution is a much more holistic approach to health in general, and this includes changing the ways in which the client, the healer, and the organization which brings the two together envisage the process of healing.

In places in the USA they have been looking at this process for a couple of decades, and experimenting with alternatives. Perhaps the best-known of the American pioneers in this field is the Berkeley Holistic Health Centre, which ten years ago initiated a LEARN (Lifestyle Education and Referral Network) programme. Here's how it works:

A person calls up and makes an appointment to see an educator. We mail them an extensive holistic-health questionnaire to fill out and bring to the session. The questionnaire is most of all a teaching tool for the client. Often, before filling it out, the person has never seen the prominent patterns in his or her life. Once people can see them, they can start to decide which patterns are causing problems, and perhaps try to change them. For example, if person has trouble expressing feelings, that will show up in the questionnaire. Another person may be under great stress: perhaps they have a sedentary job, don't get any exercise, and also have an ulcer. We'd recommend they see a doctor about the ulcer, but at the same time we'd help them to see what in their life is contributing to these problems. Then they can begin to look at the patterns that are causing problems and try to change them, fundamentally to change their lifestyle, but something realistic, not more than they can handle at one time. We explain what holistic health is, review the questionnaire, provide information about available alternatives, such as who the local practitioners are. What comes out of the session will be an informal contract, one that the client makes with himself or herself, about choosing an area to work on, and setting a few realistic goals.
The Holistic Health Handbook, And/Or Press, 1978

It could happen here — indeed as you'll see on the next page it already is in small corners of the country, but it will take a major shift in awareness before the medical establishment makes any real move. So much is at stake if the present system were to crumble — jobs, the earnings of pharmaceutical companies, control over a large proportion of the population. But change will come as more and people become dissatisfied with the way in which their health has become a pawn in somebody else's power game. People are beginning to say 'Enough is enough'.

So what of the 'alternative health centres' that are springing up all over Britain, the Other Clinics and Wellness Centres and Community Health Foundations? What do you need to know about them before you commit yourself to a first visit?

For a start, there are as yet no truly comprehensive 'holistic health centres' in Britain, in the sense of a community-based service able to advise, counsel, diagnose and refer across the whole spectrum of health issues. The nearest to this sort of service is run by some of the more enlightened NHS group practices — there is a pioneer scheme in Leyton Green in East London, for example.

Most 'holistic health centres' are in fact a group of alternative practitioners who share the same premises, and sometimes the same receptionist. You may well find that your local 'centre' is really only a rather grand name for one or two types of treatment, and while the treatment may be more holistic than your GP would provide, it won't give you any idea of the full range of alternative treatments. The lack of any sort of referral service such as that operated by the Berkeley Centre is probably the greatest current setback to the growth of holistic health services in Britain.

Some alternative health centres do stand out from the pack, however, and here is a selection that warrant particular attention. Remember though that this is only a very small selection of the two hundred or so 'centres' operating throughout Britain; you will have to make enquiries about the others. Talk to other people that have used the services offered by such centres, read and evaluate their literature, ask for a short chat before you commit yourself to anything.

Community Health Foundation

The CHF is really more of a workshop centre than a community health centre, though they do also provide individual consultations in macrobiotics and shiatsu, and individual sessions in tai-chi and yoga. There is an annual membership fee (currently £15) which gives you a reduction on all course fees and keeps you informed of activities. There are also reductions in course fees for the unwaged. The emphasis is very much on eastern approaches to health and healing, though Swedish Massage also features in the current brochure. Course prices are on the cheap side for London, and everything happens in the East West Centre in Old Street which also has a very good restaurant, a good wholefood shop, and quite a good bookshop, so you're likely to meet quantities of like-minded people. Folk sometimes get hooked on the East West Centre and are found wandering the corridors in a trance-like daze; you can be fairly sure though that the staff there will be friendly and helpful. The quarterly programmes produced by CHF are very informative, and will give you other leads and contacts in the field.

Community Health Foundation
East West Centre
188 Old Street
London
EC1V 9BP
0(7)1-251 4076

Middle Piccadilly

Jo and Gerry Harvey started Middle Piccadilly Natural Healing Centre in 1985 as a residential centre which also provides an outpatient service to the population of central Dorset. A wide range of therapies is offered, from aromatherapy and allergy testing to counselling and visualization, with a particular emphasis on the Chinese healing art of shen tao, a form of acupressure. As healing centres go Middle Piccadilly is not too expensive, and they are planning to start a bursary scheme soon. They will provide full board in the sixteenth century thatched farmhouse which accommodates the centre, an excellent way of treating yourself to a holiday and a health treatment at the same time, and are currently developing a weekend retreat centre. They have also installed a jacuzzi and sauna to help provide what they call a 'total sensory healing environment'.

Middle Piccadilly Natural Healing Centre
Holwell
Sherborne
Dorset
DT9 5LW
096 323 468

The Isis Centre

The Isis Centre in north London provides a service which is probably as close as any in Britain to a comprehensive community-based programme. The practitioners who work from the centre offer a wide range of therapies both physical and psychotherapeutic, and they offer a general consultation (currently £22) which looks at your individual needs and which treatment(s) might be appropriate. Some of the practitioners are open to negotiating reductions for the unwaged; in general the rates are about average for London. Above all, they say, they are there 'to celebrate the part played by fun, imagination, creativity and deeper spiritual meanings in our orientation towards health and vitality'.

The Isis Centre for Holistic Health
5 Clonmell Road
South Tottenham
London
N17 6JY
0(8)1-808 6401

Wellspring

At the bottom of Leith Walk in Edinburgh is Scotland's answer to Isis, a comprehensive holistic counselling and treatment centre called Wellspring. Founded in 1978, it has outgrown its premises twice since then, and eleven practitioners now offer a range of techniques, with an emphasis on the links between the body and the unconscious. Wellspring has a conscious policy of ensuring that nobody is turned away simply because they cannot afford their services, and charges are made in proportion to each client's resources and earnings. The therapists who work at Wellspring meet regularly as a support group, and to refer clients to those techniques which are felt to be most appropriate to their needs.

Wellspring
13 Smith's Place
Edinburgh
EH6 8NT
031 553 6660

Swindon Health Hydro

In the old railway workers' baths in Swindon the local council own and run a unique health centre, housing a well women clinic, wholefood vegetarian café, and the original Turkish baths and swimming pool. Milton Road also offers various therapies including Alexander technique, shiatsu, massage, acupuncture, chiropractic, Bach flower remedies, hypnotherapy and counselling. They even offer 'gold card' facilities for the unemployed. Prices are about average for out of London.

The Health Hydro
Milton Road
Swindon
SN1 5JH
0793 511060

The Body Shop

I have mixed feelings about The Body Shop. There is so much about it that is right: the refusal to overpackage anything, the use of natural ingredients that have not been tested on animals, their staff policy, their support for Friends of the Earth, Greenpeace and Third World projects.

So what's the problem? Is it the prices? Body Shop products are in general no more expensive than the cruelty-free natural-ingredient alternatives. Is it the 'branches all over the world' with its 'multinational' feel? Is it the question of whether people (meaning mostly women) really need all this stuff at all, regardless of who sells it to them? Is it the emphasis on profit and competition and success? Is it that I find gung-ho save-the-world-through-spending a bit creepy? Or is it just that I'm jealous?

Opposite a picture of Anita Roddick (who started it all), a glossy brochure about The Body Shop quotes Elizabeth Arden as saying 'The cosmetics business is the nastiest business in the world', and we must be very grateful to The Body Shop for humanizing that 'nasty business' and questioning its most dearly-held beliefs, including the importance of testing on animals and the imperative use of whale oil and musk.

If you need to buy cosmetics and fancy toiletries, then The Body Shop is far and away one of the better choices. If money is to be raised for environmental issues by successful businesses, then it is better that it comes from The Body Shop than from Ford or Tonka Toys. But can we entirely trust the managing director of an international company quoted on the stock exchange who says 'we will be the most honest cosmetics company around', or who makes militaristic comparisons between green economics and the SAS such as Anita likes to point out to her staff (see pages 60-63 in *The Body Shop*, below)?

Having said all that, with 451 shops in every corner of the Western world The Body Shop is likely to be the nearest place where you can buy a full range of toiletries and cosmetics made from natural ingredients. Do remember that they will refill your bottle for you if you take it back, and that they do take account of what you put in their suggestion boxes.

I'm glad that The Body Shop is there, and extremely pleased that at least one high street chain has an environmental and social conscience.

The Body Shop International plc
Hawthorn Road
Wick
Littlehampton
West Sussex
BN17 7LR
0903 717107

The Body Shop Books

There are two Body Shop books. The first is a slim paperback in Pan's 'Business Profile' series, a history of The Body Shop which sees everything in the garden as being rosier than rosy. There's an awful lot that business — the big sort — can learn from The Body Shop, and the world would be a very different place if all business was run the way Anita Roddick runs it. But the simple fact that the companion volume in the series is about British Airways must alert us to the possibility that The Body Shop might be the currently acceptable face of an economic system that is ultimately unacceptable. Read it and see what you think.

The other Body Shop book is *The Body Shop Book*, a big glossy pop-art volume with lots of metallic gold and silver. If you need 216 pages to tell you how to look after your hair, face and skin, then this is probably the best book you can buy, full as it is of tips, advice and information about how to look after yourself. It is particularly good at warning of the dangers and implications of using 'mainstream' toiletries and cosmetics. Sections of *The Body Shop Book* have also been published as slim paperbacks on specific issues such as face care and looking after yourself in the sun.

*

Many of the anti-dandruff shampoos on the market are harsh in themselves. One common ingredient in these products is zinc pyrithione which tends to make the hair look dull and should not be used regularly. Selenium sulphide, another common ingredient, has caused concern among experts in the heavy-metal poison field. It is a highly toxic anti-bacterial agent which can be absorbed through the skin. Continued use of products containing this substance may cause a harmful buildup of levels of minerals which can lead to premature aging.

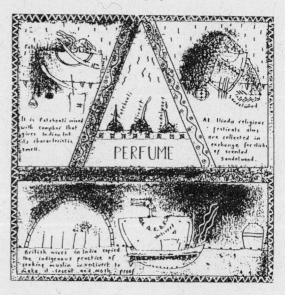

The Body Shop	**The Body**
Franchising a Philosophy	**Shop Book**
Gilly McKay and	Anita Roddick *et al*
Alison Corke	Macdonald, 1987
Pan, 1986	£7.95
£2.95	

Bathroom Basics

Toothpaste

Many toothpastes contain sugars, known to cause tooth decay, and the addition of fluoride to toothpaste is a questionable activity. There are now several toothpastes available which are made with pure products, will clean your teeth effectively and make you nice to be near, and contain herbs and minerals known to have healing properties. Weleda produce a range of toothpastes from a plant gel toothpaste for young teeth to a herbal toothpaste for older ones, and will send samples if you write to them.

Mandala market a herbal toothpaste 'containing the extracts of 18 valuable herbs and barks every one of which has been esteemed for centuries in India'; send for a leaflet about it. Kingfisher produce cruelty-free toothpaste in either fennel or mint with lemon, at around 94p a tube, suitable for vegans and homeopathic users and packaged in 100% recycled cardboard boxes.

The tops in toothpaste, however, has to be Tom's of Maine, which comes in fennel, spearmint, and cinnamint (cinnamon and peppermint). Tom and Kate Chappell started making Tom's toothpaste in Kennebunk, Maine in 1970, and it is an American institution, now widely available in Britain.

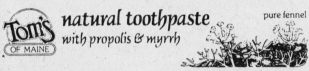

Weleda (UK) Ltd
Heanor Road
Ilkeston
Derbyshire
DE7 8DR
0602 309319

Kingfisher
12 St Mary's Works
Duke Street
Norwich
NR3 1QA
0603 630484

**Mandala
Ayurvedic Imports**
7 Zetland Road
Redland
Bristol
BS6 7AG
0272 427124

Soap

As *The Body Shop Book* points out, 'soap' is for many women a four-letter word: they would rather use lotions, creams, exfoliating tools, cleansing bars, toners and moisturizers. Yet soap made from natural ingredients can do very little to harm your skin, and there are plenty of natural-product cruelty-free soaps around. For value for money together with nice smells, my choice is the pure vegetable soap from Faith Products — the lavender and the orange are particularly nice, and if you buy them unwrapped a 90g bar only costs around 75p. Caurnie Soaperies produce a completely natural nothing-added white soap, and a scented range which includes honey-and-almond.

Faith Products
Unit 5
Bury Industrial Estate
Kay Street
Bury
BL9 6BU
061 764 2555

**Caurnie
Soap Company**
The Soaperie
Canal Street
Kirkintilloch
Glasgow
G66 1QZ
041 776 1218

Don't forget to buy recycled toilet paper — it doesn't have to be nasty, hard and grey, and is now available in most supermarkets.

Home-Made Cosmetics

People today might make a big fuss about cosmetics made with natural ingredients, but as with herbalism they often overlook the fact that many of those natural ingredients are growing all round them. In fact it is this link between herbalism, body care, diet, local environment and health that make it clear that you can't pursue natural health in one area without considering them all, and in all of them you can do a great deal for yourself without having to believe, or pay, a professional expert.

This is as true of what you put on your skin as of what you put inside you, and while the books you can buy on do-it-yourself cosmetics are still packaged around the inconstant idea of 'beauty', you will learn a lot about your body and what you put on it if you make your own preparations.

Jeanne Rose's book is very American-pretending-to-be-Olde-Englishe, but it does have some tempting suggestions, such as what to put in your bathwater to make you smell nice (ginseng, mint, lavender, rose and rosemary in equal parts, followed by a very large terry towel . . .). Camilla Hepper, proud proprietor of a Knightsbridge shop which sells some of her own products, has written a more straightforward and practical (and cheaper) book of herbal recipes, with a useful list of suppliers at the end.

Kitchen Cosmetics
Jeanne Rose
Thorsons, 1986
£3.99

Herbal Cosmetics
Camilla Hepper
Thorsons, 1987
£2.50

Natural Looks and Natural Smells

Natural toiletries and cosmetics are at last coming into their own. The chain stores, especially Boots, have not surprisingly jumped on the bandwagon, and you can now buy natural cruelty-free cosmetics in most chemists' shops, which is definitely a Good Thing. A few green and ecological thoughts, however, before you rush out to see what's available.

The first consideration must always be: do you really need it? Whether you think of cosmetics as a take-it-or-leave-it whim, an occasional treat or a grim necessity, it's important to at least consider who it is that you're *really* doing it for: for you, for him/her, or to boost someone else's profits?

The second thought is, given the range of natural cosmetics available would you rather give your money to the shareholders of a chain store or to a small home-based manufacturer? The suppliers mentioned on this page are all fairly small, are all using natural ingredients, and are all doing their best only to use products that have never been tested on animals. Prices vary from manufacturer to manufacturer, but not by much — they obviously keep a close eye on each other! Fuller lists are available from the British Union for the Abolition of Vivisection (see page 72) and in Lis Howlett's *Cruelty Free Shopper* (see page 47).

Norfolk Lavender

On the coast of north-west Norfolk is Britain's last remaining lavender farm, growing a hundred acres of assorted lavenders without pesticides and producing a wide range of perfumes, cosmetics and toiletries. Visitors are always welcome, and they will send a fascinating brochure if you send them an A5 sae. I'm not so sure about the 'Men of England' range for the US market . . .

Norfolk Lavender Ltd
Caley Mill
Heacham
King's Lynn
Norfolk
PE31 7JE
0485 70384

Simply Simple

There are so many small skincare/haircare/bodycare product manufacturers these days that there can't be many suitable names left — 'Pure Simple Natural Honest Wholecare Plant Products' perhaps?

Beauty Without Cruelty has been going longer than most and produce an enormous range of cruelty-free cosmetics, right down to lipliners and eye crayons. My misgivings about The Body Shop also apply largely to BWC; if you're going to buy cosmetics then make sure you buy cruelty-free ones, but do you really need such a vast range and so much full-colour advertising?

Honesty in Chesterfield is a workers' co-operative, and sometimes work with Third World co-operatives to import toiletries like Pacific Isle soap from Sri Lanka (a slight case of geographical licence). They do a wide range of products, including some very pleasant shampoos — try the lime blossom for example.

Nick Webley of Kittywake Perfumes trained as a perfume maker in France and Egypt and produces up-market perfumes using only pure plant extracts. They are handmade and packed in classy glass bottles, though their prices compare favourably with mass-produced perfumes: £8.50 for 8ml of Eau de Parfum; £12.75 for 60ml of Eau de Toilette.

Cosmetics To Go produce a zany, colourful catalogue packed full of bath products, make-up, men's toiletries, baby products, gift ideas, sun and ski products and perfumes, all with names like Red Hot Soaker, Strandlooper, Abu Razi's Hand Cream and Zanzara Mosquito Zapp, all cruelty-free and based on natural plant extracts.

Neal's Yard does a range of natural skin, hair and bath products, using organically grown herbs and pure essential oils wherever possible. All their products are cruelty-free and packed in beautiful glass bottles with labels giving information about every ingredient they use. They also sell individual essential oils.

Beauty Without Cruelty Ltd
Avebury Avenue
Tonbridge
Kent
TN9 1TL
0732 365291

Honesty Cosmetics Ltd
33 Markham Road
Chesterfield
Derbyshire
S40 1TA
0246 211269

Kittywake Perfumes
Cae Kitty
Taliaris
Llandeilo
SA19 7DP
0558 3619

Cosmetics To Go
29 High Street
Poole
Dorset
BH15 1AB
0800 373366

Neal's Yard Remedies
2 Neal's Yard
London
WC2H 9DP
0(7)1-379 7222

The Soap Shop

Most chemists' shops and department stores now stock cruelty-free natural products, but one shop in Exeter sets an example for others in selling only such products, plus a range of biodegradable detergents and washing up liquid and a refill service to encourage the re-use of containers and keep prices down. Pretty flannels, soaps and bathtowels make it a one-stop bathroom shop. Dot Milton's Soap Shop is an initiative that could usefully be repeated all over the country.

The Soap Shop
44 Sidwell Street
Exeter
Devon
EX4 6NS
0392 215682

THERAPY AND SPIRITUALITY

'It is a time of searching and a time of vision.'
Brian Tokar, *The Green Alternative*

Therapy and spirituality are in many ways very close to each other. The word 'therapy' comes from a Greek word meaning 'attendance', and good therapy is first and foremost good attention. As psychotherapist John Rowan says in his book *The Reality Game* (see page 170), therapy is 'a kind of compassionate skill, a kind of love work'. Given this sort of attention, it is incredible how quickly healing can take place, how quickly a person can find themselves, and how quickly they can discover how powerful and effective they can be.

Love and power link therapy with spirituality, 'spirituality' being the acknowledgement and direct experience of something beyond the material and the immediately tangible, something which is all-powerful and all-loving. 'The love and power of God' is how many people express it; others see 'divinity' in every aspect of the universe, making no distinction between personal love and power and those same qualities as they permeate everything, one reflecting and being enfolded in the other.

Describing the Indescribable

'I don't know what happened, but it was wonderful!'

This is a fairly common reaction following moments of insight in both therapy and spirituality, and it shows that not everything that works has to be explained, a notion with which our scientifically-based culture often has great problems. The *Tao Te Ching*, a classic of ancient Chinese literature, opens with the unforgettable line: 'The way that can be spoken of is not the constant way', a lesson that could usefully be taken to heart by almost every Westerner. Everybody knows what it is like to be bowled over by the beauty of a sunset or by a particular passage of music — and trying to describe what has moved us is certain to detract from the experience.

Sadly, however, such moments of self-discovery are generally considered to be secondary to the real business of living, earning, doing and being busy. There isn't time for inner exploration, for simply being still. Thus to many people spirituality — beyond going to church at pre-ordained times — is otherworldly and escapist; therapy is self-indulgent navel-gazing.

People who are interested in becoming more green know better. They don't always need to know why something helped them to feel wonderful before trying again.

The Manipulation of Personal Experience

Fundamental to the green way of thinking is the belief that each of us knows best what we need, and that although we may well agree on many issues, each of us has to come to our own understanding of our place in the overall order of things. This doesn't fit very well with the world views of those who think they know us better than we know ourselves, and so we end up with manipulation and oppression in the name of other people's Great Universal Truths.

It's not that you can't learn a great deal from good and experienced teachers, simply that in the end you have to decide for yourself. Searching for outside answers will never get you very far in the search for who you really are and how you relate to the rest of the world. There is a wonderful children's book by Michael Foreman called *Panda's Puzzle*. Panda is desperately worried because he can't decide whether he's a black bear with white bits or a white bear with black bits. He travels the world in his search for an answer, asking everyone from ancient Chinese sages to the Egyptian sphinx — he learns all sorts of things on the way, but in the end he has to sort things out for himself. And what does he find out about himself? That the important thing is that he is a traveller who makes music.

The small-scale guru Stephen Gaskin, who founded the well-known American community of The Farm in Tennessee, once said that you should be able to tell a decent guru from a manipulative one (and the same goes for therapists and priests too) by asking three questions:
— Are they prepared to offer their services for nothing?
— Are they compassionate and caring in the way they work?
— Are they clearly helping people in the here and now?

If you can honestly answer all three in the affirmative, you're probably on to a good thing.

Getting Hooked

Everyone has heard of 'therapy junkies', people who have been in analysis for fifteen years and are still sorting things out with their dead mother. Religion can easily do the same thing — Karl Marx knew what he was talking about when he called religion the opiate of the people.

But the purpose of therapy isn't to be training for yet more therapy, and the purpose of spirituality isn't to learn how to meditate for hours at a time. The purpose of therapy is to find your own inner strength so that you can be more effective in the world and live life to the full; spirituality is about experiencing directly the unity and flow of the universe.

Whatever path you choose, keep your eyes wide open, question everything, and always have faith in yourself. As with Panda's journey, all sorts of things may happen on the way, and some of them will probably be frightening and threatening, perhaps even terrifying. Like life itself, however, the only way on is through, and given the attention, support and love that you deserve, eventually you will end up with the power you need to change both yourself and the world you live in.

Therapy

Psychotherapy

I am ambivalent about psychotherapy — a great deal of what calls itself psychotherapy is very suspect, and at the same time I believe that there are ideas and techniques central to most techniques in psychotherapy which are very exciting and which are crucial to any real change in the world — both for people individually and for the planet in general.

So why is it that so much of what calls itself therapy is at best mediocre and at worst destructive? And how do you go about exploring the difference and finding out what is right for you? The key is *empowerment*. 'Power' is a two-edged word, used (often in the same breath) to mean something both positive and potentially destructive, but if we distinguish between 'power from within' and 'power over', then some of my ambivalence about therapy immediately becomes clearer.

Every human being has enormous potential — 'power from within' — to do or be any number of things, but from a very early age we are unnecessarily limited by circumstances and by other people, so much so that we start disbelieving in ourselves. This process of disempowerment, often called oppression, is continuous and painful, and the system which ensures its continuation is held in place by the people who seem to benefit from it, reaping status and financial reward. They maintain control — 'power over' — through institutions, laws and cultural assumptions. The task of therapy is to help us break out of the personal cages that we have built up to protect ourselves within this oppressive system, and having dealt with at least some of the fear, pain and frustration of that imprisonment, to go on to change the world in such a way that eventually there will be no prisons.

Though most psychotherapists know this in principle, many seem to have forgotten it in practice. They forget that a good therapist seeks to do him or herself out of business as quickly as possible by helping people out of prison and then waving goodbye; they forget that they need to deal with their own problems, or that other people's solutions are not necessarily the same as theirs. They forget that being a therapist doesn't necessarily mean having lots of letters after your name, being known both sides of the Atlantic, or having people think you're wonderful all the time (nice though that is).

Unless you have heard glowing reports about a therapist, it is not a good idea to go straight into individual therapy without doing some research. If you are new to therapy, do some reading first, and then find out whether there are any self-help therapy groups in your area (your health centre, community centre or citizen's advice bureau might be able to help). Following this — and with both your time and your precious money in mind — see if there is a co-counselling teacher in your area, since co-counselling (see page 172) is an excellent way into psychotherapy, is easy on your purse, and will almost certainly put you in touch with the therapy network in your area.

Having voiced all my misgivings, I must stress that the right sort of therapy — therapy which truly empowers you — will be well worth searching out, even if the search is a lengthy one.

In Our Own Hands

Though written particularly for women, Sheila Ernst and Lucy Goodison's book is by far the best introduction to psychotherapy that you can buy, whether you are female or male. It starts gently, not assuming that you know anything about therapy, and with a combination of theory, examples and exercises you can do yourself or in groups, leads you through the whole range of therapies you may come across. It pulls together many different strands of therapy, and puts therapy firmly into the framework of social and political change. Not that *In Our Own Hands* is a heavy political tome, far from it, but it does make it very clear that the best therapy is by its very nature a subversive activity. The authors also include very practical advice on how to find a self-help therapy group or choose a therapist. I would have liked a decent index — it's very frustrating trying to find a specific reference that you know is there somewhere . . .

*

Therapy can either appear to be a painful or terrifying process, or people may have unreal expectations as to how it will change their lives. We are sure that the extent of our capacity to change is limited by the nature of the society we live in. The inner changes we make through therapy need to be combined with taking action to change our material situation outside the therapy group. Nevertheless, the gains to be made through therapy are real and quite distinct from what can be gained by the 'discussion' of problems within friendship or an intimate relationship.

In Our Own Hands
A Book of Self-Help Therapy
Sheila Ernst and
Lucy Goodison
The Women's Press, 1981
£5.95

Another useful book if you are completely new to therapy is Lindsay Knight's *Talking to a Stranger: A Consumer's Guide to Therapy* (Fontana, 1986, £2.95); she writes very clearly with plenty of illuminating case histories and comments from people who have benefited from therapy. One book to avoid, on the other hand, is Joel Kovel's *Complete Guide to Therapy* (Penguin, 1978, £4.50). This is a misleading title, since although it does cover a wide range of psychotherapies, it gives a rather staid account of where therapy was some twenty years ago, and is very top-heavy on the jargon and 'professional' psychoanalysis.

Humanistic Psychology

A world-wide movement started in the 1940s, grew slowly in the 1950s, grew much faster in the 1960s and finally reached its full flowering in the 1970s. Today it is consolidating itself, and becoming much more widely accepted. It is now part of the main stream, rather than being something new and unfamiliar. In the process of change and development, it has changed its name several times. Sometimes it has been called 'third force psychology' (the other two being psychoanalysis and the behavioural-cognitive approach); sometimes the 'self-awareness movement'; sometimes the 'human potential movement'; and sometimes just 'personal growth'. Today it is less of a movement and more of a tendency or approach within the whole field of psychology.

John Rowan, *A Guide to Humanistic Psychology* (see below)

There are as many interpretations of humanistic psychology as there are practitioners of it; in this section of *New Green Pages* I have used the terms 'humanistic psychology' and 'therapy' virtually synonymously. The basic beliefs of humanistic psychology are easily stated:

▶ Every human being is fundamentally perfectly okay. We may have learned to think of ourselves and/or other people as no good, evil or beyond the pale, but this is something we have learned and which we can unlearn again.
▶ Every human being must be seen as a whole; there's no point dividing mind from body and body from spirit. If you don't see someone as a whole person you don't really see them at all.
▶ Every human being ultimately knows what is best for them; better than their parents, better than their teachers, and better than their therapist. Hence the emphasis in humanistic psychology is on 'client-centred' therapy — a constant reminder to both therapist and client of who it's all for.

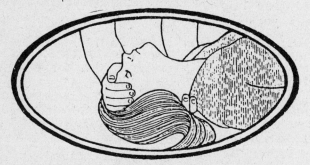

Humanistic Psychology in Britain

The Association for Humanistic Psychology in Britain is the offspring of the American association of the same name, and was born in 1969. It has a wide membership of practitioners and people who are just interested, and is the liveliest and most reliable of the therapeutic networks in Britain. The AHP runs a lecture and workshop programme (mostly in London), has an annual conference which is open to anyone interested in the subject, a regular events listing and newsletter, and a magazine called *Self and Society* which appears four times a year. The AHP also has a practitioners' group called AHPP (P for Practitioners) to maintain the standards of practice within humanistic psychology; the AHPP offers a referral service which will put you in touch with an appropriate counsellor or therapist (they prefer you to write in the first instance rather than ring).

Association for Humanistic Psychology
26 Huddlestone Road
London
E7 0AN
0(8)1-555 3077

AHPP
45 Litchfield Way
London
NW11 6NU
0(8)1-455 8737

British Association for Counselling

The British Association for Counselling is the country's leading organization for the administration and regulation of counselling. Its excellent information pack includes information sheets and the recently-updated (1989) *Counselling and Psychotherapy Resources Directory*. BAC has also set up a working party on counselling and peace which runs a training programme in Surrey, Edinburgh and Bristol.

British Association for Counselling
37a Sheep Street
Rugby
Warwickshire
CV21 3BX
0788 78328/9

Books About Humanistic Psychology

The clearest explanations of the sometimes tortuous meanderings of humanistic psychology are those by John Rowan. For an introduction try his *Guide to Humanistic Psychology*, published by the Association for Humanistic Psychology. This gives a brief overview of sixteen different approaches to therapy, together with a reading list. A list of centres and organizations would have been even more useful, but apparently this is still being prepared.

John Rowan's *Ordinary Ecstasy* is a good guide to the theory and practice of humanistic psychology, bringing together many different ideas and tying them all up neatly. I sometimes find this book very mechanistic and wordy (what does the average layperson make of terms like 'paleo-logic', 'mythic thinking' and 'syntaxical membership'?), but if you are prepared to do a bit of brain-work it is on the whole quite approachable. The books concludes with a very comprehensive bibliography and a very short resource guide. John Rowan's earlier book, *The Reality Game* (Routledge, 1983, £5.95) is also worth looking out for.

A Guide to Humanistic Psychology
John Rowan
AHP, 1987
£1.00

Ordinary Ecstasy
John Rowan
Routledge, 1988
£7.95

Beyond Therapy?

David Smail, who looks after Nottingham's clinical psychology services, has already written two excellent books about psychotherapy, but his latest, *Taking Care*, is brilliant — a real indictment of most of the therapy practised in Britain today. He sees therapy being administered to 'sick' people in the same way that drugs are used to 'cure' physically ill people, with the same results — constant failure. Only when we collectively take responsibility for each other and start truly caring for each other, he says, will things really change. This attention to each other's real needs — this *therapeia* — is the only sort of therapy that will really work.

Taking Care
An Alternative To Therapy
David Smail
Dent, 1987
£5.95

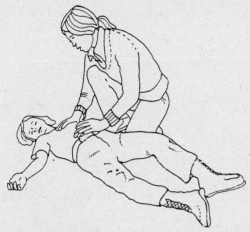

Human Potential

Maureen Yeomans started the quarterly magazine *Human Potential Resources* in 1977 to provide regularly updated information about activities within the human potential movement. In 1987 the magazine changed its name to *Human Potential* and streamlined its design, but it continues to be the most comprehensive guide to the latest developments in therapy in Britain. Each issue contains articles and reviews, together with an extensive resource directory and calendar for the coming three months. *Human Potential* covers a very wide range of activities within healing, therapy and spirituality, but although some of the activities mentioned within its pages are as far afield as Dorset and Gloucestershire, Spain and Greece, it is inevitably very South-East oriented.

Human Potential

5 Layton Road
London
N1 0PX
0(7)1-354 5792

Regional Directories

'Comprehensive and easy to use listings of psychotherapy, alternative health and spiritual centres in the capital' it says on the front cover of *The London Guide to Mind/Body/Spirit*, an excellent guide to everything human-growth-oriented in the city from the same authors as *Survivors London* (see page 343). Succinct introductions to a wide range of techniques and details of hundreds of practitioners, centres, courses and suppliers make up this important handbook.

If you live anywhere other than the South-East the range of available workshops and courses is not quite as extensive, but there is still plenty going on. South-West England has its own guide to the human potential movement called *South West Connection. Connection* appears three times a year (mid-April, mid-August and mid-December), and 4,000 copies are distributed free of charge throughout the region.

The London Guide to Mind/Body/Spirit

Kate Brady and
Mike Considine
Brainwave, 1988
£4.95

South West Connection

Greystones
Church Street
Yetminster
nr Sherbourne
Dorset
DT9 6LG
0935 872257

Training in Therapy

Many people who find that psychotherapy helps them to change their life for the better think about training in therapy so that they can in turn help other people.

Two of the main centres for training and research in counselling and psychotherapy are the Human Potential Research Project based at the University of Surrey in Guildford, and the Bath Counselling and Psychotherapy Courses. HPRP was established in 1970, and is the longest established centre for humanistic and transpersonal education in Europe. The Project offers an enormous range of courses, programmes and one-off events — the whole range fills forty closely-printed pages. The subjects covered include assertiveness training, stress management, group facilitation skills, healing touch, co-counselling, gestalt, relaxation and holistic education. A similar programme is offered in Leeds, Bath, Cornwall (at CAER, see page 174), and London. These courses are co-ordinated by the Institute for the Development of Human Potential, a loose network of therapy educators who have been running training courses since 1982. IDHP can be contacted c/o CAER. The Bath BCPC courses are based on several years' experience in the training of counsellors and psychotherapists; they are designed to train people to work as one-to-one therapists at the same time paying a great deal of attention to the student's own development.

The Serpent Institute in west London offers training and sessions in counselling and psychotherapy 'recognizing the sacredness in life and the spirit within matter'. They offer a 2-year course in counselling and a 3-year course in psychotherapy. Humanistic psychology is also offered at the London School of Economics as a course of evening classes: a one year course costs £495, a 12-week course in counselling £145 and a 10-week course in meditation £55. Free open evenings are held in July and September before term starts.

HPRP
University of Surrey
Guildford
Surrey
GU2 5XH
0483 509191

BCPC
Openings
Bluecoat House
Saw Close
Bath
BA1 1EY
0225 445013

The Serpent Institute
18 Mark Mansions
Westville Road
London
W12 9PS
0(8)1-743 8124

Department of Psychology
The London School
of Economics
Houghton Street
London
WC2A 2AE
1(7)1-405 7686 ext 3313

Beechwood

It's difficult to know where in *New Green Pages* to list Beechwood College Conference Centre in Leeds. Established in 1977, it offers a meeting place for any group interested in personal and cultural change; its lengthy list of users includes over fifty groups from the Royal College of Nursing and NALGO to Postural Integration and the Group Relations Training Association. With space to accommodate over forty people, conference rooms, a bar, massage room and sauna, Beechwood is an excellent venue for group activities based in the North. Another of Beechwood's current activities is the compilation of a computer database of trainers offering a variety of skills of interest to the College's client groups.

Beechwood Conference Centre Ltd
Elmete Lane
Leeds
LS8 2LQ
0532 650229

Some Varieties of Therapy

Many pages could be filled describing specific therapeutic techniques which you might find suited you — what I have done, however, is describe five approaches which I have found particularly helpful, together with the resources you will need to follow them up. Some people will think it unforgivable that I haven't included gestalt or transactional analysis, encounter or primal, but if you want to find out about a wider range of therapies, then read the books by Sheila Ernst and Lucy Goodison, or by John Rowan, mentioned on pages 169 and 170.

Co-Counselling

I had this difficulty of explaining what co-counselling is when I had only ten seconds at my disposal. Instead of a long discussion right then or making an appointment for later, I just cryptically say 'Initially, listening; finally taking charge of the world,' and I dash off.

Ramakrishna Iyer, Bombay, *Present Time*, July 1987

To my mind co-counselling is almost the perfect therapy, in that it has a well-thought-out theoretical basis, is easily taught, has almost no hierarchical structure, and costs almost nothing. Simply put, co-counselling allows you the space to look at what is going on in your life, and the feelings that brings up, in a session where you receive minimal intervention and no heavy advice from your counsellor. In return, you provide that attention for them while they look at their own issues. For half of each co-counselling session you are the client; for the other half you are the counsellor; thus there is no 'expert therapist' (we are all experts!) and nobody who needs to be paid.

To prepare you for this sort of therapy and to teach you the theory and practice of giving attention and letting go of unneeded emotional blocks, you first attend a short course or series of weekly meetings — this usually costs about £1 a session, or £20-30 for a residential weekend. Then you learn by doing.

The idea of responsibility is central to co-counselling — ultimately each of us is responsible for everything, including all of our own decisions. Responsibility comes from personal power — 'power from within' rather than 'power over' — and co-counselling is about empowerment. Hence 'taking charge of the world'.

Started in California in the 1950s, there are now co-counsellors all over the world. It may be confusing to discover that there appear to be two 'brands' of co-counselling in Britain — RC (Re-evaluation Counselling), which is the 'old original' and to my mind the soundest, having a firm theoretical base and a real commitment to working with oppressed groups like women and blacks; and CCI (Co-Counselling International), originally a breakaway organization but now well-established in parts of Britain, which has a looser structure. Co-counselling, however, depends more on your teacher and your counselling partner(s) than on the brand you find locally available. As with all techniques, there are good teachers and

not-so-good ones; with co-counselling almost more than any other technique I would urge you to persevere until you find a teacher and a counselling partner who will truly help to you look at the challenges in your life.

For reading matter you can either try Harvey Jackins' *The Human Side of Human Beings* (£2.70 from Changes Bookshop in London — see page 338 — or your local RC teacher), or Rose Evison and Richard Horobin's *How To Change Yourself and the World* (£2.95 from the same place). John Southgate and Rosemary Randall's *The Barefoot Psychoanalyst* (recently republished by Gale Centre Publications, 1989, £6.95), a very approachable cartoon-style introduction to self-help therapy, makes use of many co-counselling techniques. I use co-counselling techniques a lot in groupwork, and you might like to read my own *Making Love Work* (Turnstone, 1985, £4.95) which includes what I intended to be a very approachable account of co-counselling theory and practice.

Re-Evaluation Counselling
Sue Edwards
7 Kemble Road
London
SE23 1DH
(write to the above address putting your address on the back of the letter so it can be forwarded unopened to your nearest RC contact)

Co-Counselling International
Westerly
Prestwick Lane
Chiddingfold
Surrey
GU8 4XW
042 879 2882

Reichian Bodywork

The best way is just to breathe and relax, and let it come naturally. Never force anything. Just let it be natural and it will always be okay.

Wilhelm Reich

Most approaches to bodywork which include a complete appreciation of the way that emotions and their physical expression are linked owe a large debt to Wilhelm Reich. Reich believed that energy flows naturally through a healthy body, but that most people (especially Westerners) are blocking that energy, usually at specific points in their body — their stomach, their throat or their mouth, for example. By exploring where the blocks are experienced, and working with your body — sometimes gently, sometimes quite forcefully — a good Reichian therapist can assist you to find out what is stopping you from being really effective in your life, and help you to find ways to keep those 'channels' unblocked in the future.

Reichian bodywork provides an excellent physical counterpart to the language-and-feeling strengths of co-counselling, though both disciplines stress the importance of being very clear exactly which techniques you are using when, and of the differences between them.

A good introduction to Reichian therapy is Nick Totton and Em Edmondson's *Reichian Growth Work: Melting the Blocks to Life and Love* (Prism, 1988, £5.95), a practical and at the same time very personal account of energy work. In Britain, the best way into Reichian therapy is to contact Energy Stream (The Post-Reichian Therapy Association) in Leeds, who will be able to tell you about therapists, courses and training in different parts of the country.

Energy Stream
12 St Ann's Avenue
Leeds
LS4 2PB
0532 785601

Psychodrama

'All the world's a stage,' wrote Shakespeare, and psycho-drama uses that idea to the full. Roleplay is now used a great deal in groupwork to try out different ways of approaching a situation, but the technique was first developed by a Viennese psychiatrist called Jacob Moreno in the 1920s. Psychodrama has very little to do with acting, so it doesn't matter at all whether or not you think you can act; it isn't a performance, it's acting out your feelings in a safe setting along with other people. While co-counselling is my ideal one-to-one technique, psychodrama is an excellent approach to group therapy.

Many different sorts of roleplay have been called 'psycho-drama'; but the real thing is quite organized and has its own terminology — borrowed from the theatre — with 'protago-nists' and 'auxiliaries', 'doubles' and 'soliloquies'. Psycho-drama can go very deep very quickly, but both fears and exhilarations can be shared with a like-minded group, and given good leadership psychodrama can be extremely rewarding. Unfortunately there is no readable introduction to psychodrama, though chapter seven of Sheila Ernst and Lucy Goodison's book (page 169) gives you a good idea. The main centre in Britain for psychodrama training is the Holwell Centre in Devon — send an sae for more information.

The Holwell Centre
East Down
Barnstaple
Devon
EX31 4NZ
027 182 267/597

Psychosynthesis

Psychosynthesis was developed by Roberto Assagioli, a pupil of Jung's who wanted to develop the spiritual aspect of psychotherapy — what has come to be called the 'transper-sonal'. Psychosynthesis reaches out to embrace both indivi-dual experience and the universal; though some of the theory is rather daunting, psychosynthesis seems to links counselling and meditation in a very powerful and creative combination. Psychosynthesis uses a great deal of guided fantasy; a fine balance between free association and a gentle dredging of the client's unconscious in order to find the 'inner teacher'.

The best books about psychosynthesis come from Turnstone Press — Piero Ferrucci's *What We May Be: The Visions and Techniques of Psychosynthesis* (1982, £4.95), and Diana Whitmore's *Psychosynthesis in Education: A Guide to the Joy of Learning* (1986, £6.99). The best place to learn psychosyn-thesis is the Psychosynthesis and Education Trust in Stockwell; they have now been approved by the BAC as a recognized training centre for counsellors, run short courses and a coun-selling service, and special courses for men and for children. Slightly upmarket from the Trust is The Institute of Psycho-synthesis, offering workshops like 'Creativity, Play and the Inner Child' and 'Bridge to the Outer Courtyards'.

Psychosynthesis and Education Trust
48 Guildford Road
Stockwell
London
SW8 2BV
0(7)1-622 8295

Institute of Psychosynthesis
3 The Barn
Nan Clarke's Lane
London
NW7 4HH
0(8)1-959 2330

Assertiveness Training

How many times have you been in an embarrassing situation and wished you could say exactly what you wanted clearly and concisely, without mumbling, apologizing, backing down or getting angry? If you would like to be powerful without being aggressive or manipulative, then assertiveness training is what you need.

Some therapists see assertiveness training as a skill rather than a therapy, since it doesn't emphasize the need to express your feelings in ways other than using words. Assertiveness is probably best learned alongside something like co-counsel-ling or Reichian work, but it is well worth learning for its own insights, and can be an excellent way into therapy.

The best introduction to assertiveness is Anne Dickson's books, *A Woman in Your Own Right* and *The Mirror Within: A New Look at Sexuality* (Quartet, 1982 and 1985, £2.95 and £3.95). Though written specifically for women, men can learn a great deal from Anne Dickson too. In 1980 Anne established Redwood, a national network of assertiveness trainers and trainings: send an sae for further information.

Redwood
Invergarry
Kitlings Lane
Walton on the Hill
Stafford
ST17 0LE
0785 662823

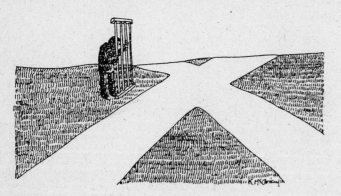

Therapy Centres

One of the biggest problems when it comes to finding out what sorts of therapy are available in your area is that nothing seems to stay put for any length of time. I wonder if it's any indication of what therapy does for people that therapists probably move round the country faster than any other group of people!

You would think that therapy centres might stay put for slightly longer, but with a few exceptions they too come and go with alarming regularity. In fact, many 'centres' aren't really centres at all — names like 'The McTavish Centre for Human Potential Research' or 'The Radical Therapy Centre' are very often covers for one or two therapists with lofty ideas and insufficient funds.

But there are a few exceptions . . .

The Open Centre

The Open Centre, which occupies the same Old Street premises as the Community Health Foundation (page 163), was established twelve years ago. A group of seven practitioners works together to organize a continuous programme of introductory meetings, weekend courses and individual sessions — the techniques offered include body therapies, transactional analysis, encounter, psychodrama, dance and gestalt. They recently renovated their premises to make them even more inviting, and the centre is a good first place to look for a suitable psychotherapy if you live in London. Their quarterly brochure is friendly and informative — send an A5 sae for a copy.

The Open Centre
188 Old Street
London
EC1V 9BP
0(8)1-549 9583

CAER

CAER, too, has been around a long time — nearly twelve years — and looks set to be there for a while yet. The Centre for Alternative Education and Research (though 'caer' is also a Cornish word meaning 'fort') is housed in a beautiful Cornish manor house near the sea just south of Penzance. Throughout the year they offer a wide range of residential workshops, mostly weekends but some 5-days, on techniques varying from yoga and the Alexander Technique to counselling and voicework. CAER always has three rates for their courses (waged, low-waged and unwaged), which makes their courses very good value; the food is excellent and the setting hard to beat. CAER also works very closely with the Institute for the Development of Human Potential (see page 171), and together they offer residential workshops and a two-year part-time course in humanistic psychology, particularly designed for people in the caring professions.

Centre for Alternative Education and Research
Rosemerryn
Lamorna
Penzance
Cornwall
TR19 6BN
0736 810530

See also the communities-cum-workshop centres listed on page 291.

Therapy Networks

There are several networks of therapists in Britain and they often overlap and duplicate both information and resources, which makes it difficult to track down anything you are specifically interested in. It also frustrates therapists and group leaders, who often find that information about events has been badly circulated, that similar events clash in their timing, and that many never take place because of lack of bookings. The most consistent national networks of therapists are listed on page 171, but there are also some regional networks worth knowing about if you live within their area.

People in Sheffield (12 Rupert Road, Sheffield S7 1RP; Tel: 0246 581528) co-ordinates events in and around the Sheffield area including residential weekends, massage and yoga groups, and many special day events.

Midlands Interpersonal Skills Training (54 Frederick Street, Loughborough LE11 3BJ; Tel: 0509 237992) co-ordinates a programme of group skills workshops in the East Midlands, concentrating on interpersonal and counselling skills for anyone involved in pastoral or residential care, youthwork and social work.

Books for Therapists and Therapees

Derek and Elsien Gale run The Gale Centre in north-east London (Whitakers Way, Loughton, Essex IG10 1SQ; Tel: 0(8)1-508 9344), which organizes a programme of workshops mostly on psychodrama and voicework (see also page 285). They also read a great deal, which is reflected in the book service they operate (more than 500 titles on therapeutic and green issues) and their excellent *Therapist's Bibliography*. If you are interested in personal and planetary development but haven't got time to read all those books, you will probably find that the Gales have, and the three volumes of the *Bibliography* (the original 1987 volume plus two annual updates) contains pocket-sized reviews of everything from *Taoist Ways to Transform Stress into Vitality* to *Green Pages* (thanks, Elsien!).

Whether you are what is euphemistically called 'a professional carer' or just an interested bystander, *A Therapist's Bibliography* will provide a fascinating browse and a way of ensuring psychological one-up-personship.

A Therapist's Bibliography
Derek and Elsien Gale
Gale Centre Publications, 1987, 1988 and 1989
£4.50 (updates £2 each)

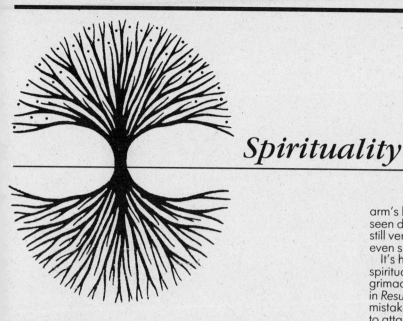

Spirituality

Spirituality

Kit Pedler, a life-long ecologist, wrote this just before he died: 'It has taken me all my life so far to realise that the single greatest obstacle in the way of survival and an extended human vision is the industrial society itself, and its suppression of the most sensitive and creative qualities of the mind.'

That spiritual vacuum has a lot to do with politics today. Politicians talk about people's needs as if material things were all that matter. And then, when the poison of cynicism is hard at work, they profess astonishment that we seem to have lost a sense of purpose, a sense of our own identity. We bow down before materialistic and 'rational' values, and correspondingly devalue the natural, the spiritual and the emotional.

Such values do not serve us well. Most of us need some spiritual dimension to our lives just as much as we need food to eat and friends to love. Be we Christians or Buddhists, existentialists or agnostics, pagans or mystics, a vital part of our green politics, of our love and respect for the Earth and for each other, is to establish a spiritual democracy for all people.

Politics for Life, Ecology Party (Green Party) Manifesto, 1983

There can be few things that divide people more than spiritual outlook; not just religious or sectarian fanaticism — it runs much deeper than that. It goes to the heart of the way people perceive the world, the way that education — and everything that our teachers learned too — assumed and continues to assume that spiritual experience is fundamentally different from practical day-to-day experience. Church is for Sundays; meditation (if it means anything) means finding a quiet place apart; even the overt expression of joy or sadness is something to be saved for the comfort and privacy of our own homes.

People from most traditional cultures would find this very hard to understand, and deep down in all Westerners, fluttering somewhere in each of our subconscious minds, is the knowledge that the distinction between the material and the spiritual is a false one. Perhaps this is why all of the great names in nuclear physics — Heisenberg, Schrödinger, Einstein, Planck and Pauli — were deeply interested in mysticism.

It seems hard enough to for most Westerners to accept that a green lifestyle means embracing the material, the political and the spiritual, constantly seeing them as different viewpoints from which to see the same reality. That objects and events could actually be all three *at the same time* (a concept that a Hopi or an Amazon forest dweller would have no problem with) seems incomprehensible, but we are probably the only culture of the only species that ever wanted everything to be explained to us.

The political/spiritual divide still runs deep even within that section of society which accepts broadly green principles, with the mystics and I Ching readers hardly talking to the windmill builders, the pastoral counsellors keeping the white witches at arm's length, and the bicycle campaigners who wouldn't be seen dead at the Festival of Mind, Body and Spirit. There are still very few people who are able to bridge the divide, who even speak both languages.

It's hardly surprising that many people take refuge in the spiritual dimension, using the word 'political' only with an inner grimace, but it must change. As Gitta Mallasz says in an article in *Resurgence* magazine (see page 346), 'I realize that it is as mistaken to take refuge in the spirit and despise matter as it is to attach oneself to matter and deny the spirit. To live the life of the body as fully as that of the spirit now seems essential.'

Spirit and matter, body and soul, politics and the inner life — they are not separate, or opposites, or mutually exclusive. The full acknowledgement and joyful celebration of every aspect of life on earth is essential to real fulfilment.

The Spiritual Dimension

One day there will be a really good book on the spiritual aspects of a green lifestyle. In the meantime there are two books which begin to explore the subject — both are American, so lack a perspective which is in some ways unique to Britain.

Deep Ecology is a well-presented anthology of thoughts and writings which questions the deepest roots of the current crisis. Thought- provoking and disturbing, it still seems to have a certain elitism about it — all the 'right' people are in it, few grass-roots voices, few women, no children. Gandhi, Buddhism, metaphysics, feminism all find their way into the extensive appendices. It not always easy reading, but amply rewards the effort. An index would help enormously.

Thinking Like A Mountain is what Americans call an 'inspirational book', full of meditations, poems and guided fantasies — good if you like that sort of thing but (with some justification) easily demolishable by your average person-in-the-street. 'When one thinks like a mountain,' writes John Seed, 'one thinks also like the black bear, so that honey dribbles down your fur as you catch the bus to work.' Yes, well . . . On the other hand, there is some moving writing: the book includes the full text of the well-known 1854 speech of Chief Seattle which includes the memorable line: 'Where is the thicket? Gone. Where is the eagle? Gone. The end of living and the beginning of survival.'

Deep Ecology
Living As If
Nature Mattered
edited by Bill Devall
and George Sessions
Peregrine Smith, 1987
£8.95

Thinking Like A Mountain
Towards a Council
of All Beings
John Seed, Joanna
Macy, Pat Fleming
and Arne Naess
Heretic, 1988
£3.95

Western Traditions

But ask the beasts, and they will teach you;
the birds of the air, and they will tell you;
or the plants of the earth, and they will teach you;
and the fish of the sea will declare to you.

The Bible, Job 12: 7-8

Judging from the number of books currently being put out by the religious publishing houses with titles like *Theology for an Ecological Nuclear Age* (a contradiction in terms?), *A Time For Peace, Animals and Christianity* and *Christianity and the Rights of Animals*, there's some hard thinking going on in Judeo-Christian circles. It's certainly true that the religious establishment has had a rather bad press from green-tinted commentators. Starting with a damning late-1960s ecological critique from the American Professor Lynn White, through Mary Daly's 1973 feminist classic *Beyond God the Father*, to the renewed papal refusal to allow gay people to celebrate mass, the church has had some serious explaining to do. Does being a little lower than the angels (Psalm 8) really mean that we have the right to do what we like with the planet and to each other?

But change is coming, and here are some of the recent initiatives of the churches in Britain. You will find church healing organizations on page 153 and other religious activities scattered elsewhere through *New Green Pages*; here are some more broadly-based initiatives.

The Christian Ecology Group

Founded in 1982, the Christian Ecology Group exists to create links between Christian and ecological insights. Members come from various Christian traditions — Anglican, Roman Catholic, Free Church and Quaker. There are several local groups, but no formal membership structure, though you can be on the CEG mailing list and receive the quarterly *Green Christian* and information about day and weekend conferences organized by the group.

Christian Ecology Group
17 Burns Gardens
Lincoln
LN2 4LJ
0522 29643

Christian Rural Centre

Set in the picturesque Peak District valley of Dovedale, the Christian Rural Centre runs courses looking at a wide range of environmental issues. Their 16-week 'certificate' courses cost £320 and accommodation is available at £45 per week. This isn't just a talking shop — lots of practical conservation work is undertaken too.

Christian Rural Centre
Dovedale House
Ilam
Ashbourne
Derbyshire
DE6 2AZ
033 529 365

Clinical Theology

The Clinical Theology Association was started in 1962 to provide a framework for the integration of counselling and groupwork skills into the Christian faith. Its main clientele is Anglican though it welcomes Christians from all denominations. Though the emphasis is on psychotherapy and personal growth within the framework of Christianity, this invariably brings the church in touch with related issues from the nuclear threat to domestic violence, and the CTA provides a supportive setting in which to air these important issues. The association publishes a useful journal three times a year called *Contact*. If you are looking for a specifically Christian approach to things greenish, write to the CTA and ask for details of their seminars.

Clinical Theology Association
St Mary's House
Church Westcote
Oxford
OX7 6SF
0993 830209

Quaker Peace and Service

Nonviolence is central to the everyday practice of the Friends, and they have been pioneers in finding new ways of bringing about reconciliation and communication between the different 'sides' in important issues. QPS came together in 1979, and now provides Friends and their friends with news, information, practical ideas, and above all the faith that change can come about through individual and group action. *QPS Reporter* is their free quarterly journal; they also publish posters and pamphlets. A recent publication called *Poverty and Peace* reviews nearly 150 important books; many of them can be bought at the Friends House Book Centre, where there is also an extensive library and small bookshop.

Quaker Peace and Service
Friends House
Euston Road
London
NW1 2BJ
0(7)1-387 3601

St James's, Piccadilly

St James's, Piccadilly is always moving in new directions, many of which are noticeably green-tinted. Recent developments include the expansion of St James's as an internationally known centre for creation-centred spirituality and as a venue for the Green College lecture series (see also page 223). The Alternatives Project draws large audiences to talks and workshops on a wide range of spiritual topics, and also serves as an information network. Much more than just a church, St James's also provides a venue for concerts and has a café, a healing and advice centre, women's groups, men's groups, ecology discussion groups — given half a chance there's not much that St James's wouldn't do. If you live within twenty miles of central London and don't mind setting foot inside a church, send for their current programme immediately.

St James's Piccadilly
197 Piccadilly
London
W1V 9LF
0(7)1-734 4511

Eastern Traditions

The immediate environs of the Valley Spirit Hermitage [a Taoist retreat in western China] gave the impression of a series of rocks and caverns, overhung by ferns and luxurious plants, which just happened to emerge from the undergrowth in this vicinity, adding enormously to its picturesqueness. What aroused my suspicion was that no other section of the mountain, apart from the chasms and waterfall, looked so exactly like the original of a Taoist painting. There was, of course, no obvious symmetry, but yet sense of underlying harmony that was just a shade too pronounced to be altogether natural. Whoever had been responsible for making the 'guided wildness' of the approach to the hermitage had surely been a master of subtlety, for there was not an object within sight of the stairway of which one could confidently affirm that it had been tampered with.

John Blofeld, *The Secret and Sublime*, Allen and Unwin, 1973

The 'Eastern tradition' is of course many traditions, but in relation to *New Green Pages* I shall concentrate on Taoism and Buddhism, and particularly the latter, since these teachings and practice contain a great deal of wisdom which those exploring a green lifestyle are beginning to rediscover.

The teachings vary in detail, but all believe in the importance of change, of compassion, of the relative unimportance of the individual, and of the harmony of the universe. They also, especially Zen Buddhism, embrace the creativity of paradox — in the garden described above it is impossible to tell what is natural and what artificial, and it matters not at all. Most Buddhists also believe passionately in a doctrine of nonviolence — 'Not to do evil; to cultivate good; to purify one's heart.'

The Buddhist Society

Since 1924 the Buddhist Society, founded by the great protagonist of Western Buddhism, Christmas Humphreys, has been encouraging the study and practice of Buddhism in Britain. It claims to embrace no one school of Buddhism, but provides an important meeting place for British Buddhists, together with wide range of supporting services. The society's library contains a wealth of information, and members can apply to use it. The society also runs a mail order book service, meetings, classes and courses; a series of eight free introductory talks is held at the society's London premises — ring to find out when the next series starts. Then there is the *Buddhist Society Diary* (£3.00), which includes an abbreviated directory of centres in the UK, and the comprehensive *Buddhist Directory* (£2.95), now in its fourth edition, which contains well over two hundred Buddhist organizations in Britain and Ireland, together with libraries, bookshops, and local contacts. The quarterly journal *The Middle Way* has been published continuously since 1926.

The Buddhist Society
58 Eccleston Square
London
SW1V 1PH
0(7)1-834 5858

The Western Buddhist Order

Friends of the Western Buddhist Order (FWBO) was founded in 1967 to establish a movement which would reflect the response of Buddhism to the circumstances of the modern West. There are now seventeen FWBO centres in Britain, all of which run courses, events and retreats; the FWBO also runs the London Buddhist Centre Bookshop at its London headquarters, which offers a wide range of books on Buddhism, including a mail order service. Of the many books on Buddhism, the Buddhist Centre Bookshop recommends Dharmacari Subhuti's *The Buddhist Vision: An Introduction to the Theory and Practice of Buddhism* (Rider, 1985, £7.95) as a comprehensive and balanced introduction to the subject. FWBO also publishes an attractive quarterly magazine called *Golden Drum*.

Friends of the Western Buddhist Order
51 Roman Road
London
E2 0HU
0(8)1-981 1225

The Buddhist Peace Fellowship

Established in the USA in 1978 and in Britain in 1984, the Buddhist Peace Fellowship exists to promote both inner and outer peace. Open to Buddhists and friends of Buddhism, it is a network of people concerned to reduce suffering from all kinds of violence. It organizes workshops and retreats, and has local groups in Devon, Dorset, London and Yorkshire. The fellowship produces a quarterly newsletter called *Indra's Net*, has produced a booklet called *Buddhism and the Bombs* by Ken Jones (£1.10) which looks at Buddhist approaches to social action and activism, and has a small but very relevant selection of books for mail order.

Buddhist Peace Fellowship
Plas Plwca
Cwmrheidol
Aberystwyth
SY23 3NB
097 084 603

Meditation

While meditating once, I saw myself as a drop of water in a stream. The stream was flowing from the mountains to the sea. I experienced the stream as a symbol of life; all the other drops of water were people and objects moving through life. I felt that I was everywhere in the stream at once. I saw the fast currents, the slow currents, and the eddies of the stream, as stream grew into river and swirled towards the ocean. I was one with all the drops of water in the stream; I was one with all the people and things in the world. I felt great joy. All of this happened in an instant, and yet I can recall this powerful experience, see it again, and describe it at any time. The impact of the symbols etched the vision indelibly into my mind.
    L. John Mason, *Guide to Stress Reduction* (see page 155)

For many people for whom meditation means anything at all, it is very closely related to relaxation (see page 155) and used as a way of counteracting the stress they experience in their lives. For many others, while meditation is relaxation of a kind, it is also a spiritual discipline, focusing the attention in order to experience in a very direct way the connections between the meditator and the cosmos that she or he inhabits.

Taking time out of the business of life on a regular basis to sit quietly and take stock may seem a fairly obvious way to go about things, but while meditation is part of everyday life for most Buddhists, Westerners often have to relearn the skills involved in meditation.

You can learn meditation out of a book, but the best way is to become part of a meditation group until you have the technique established and can take it out into the wide world with you. You might choose to learn with a meditation organizations like Transcendental Meditation; while TM did a great deal to demystify meditation in the early 1970s, the cost (£150 or so for an introductory course) and the things that go with the meditation technique (adoration of a gold-rimmed portrait of Maharishi, for example) are highly questionable.

The Meditation Group for the New Age in Tunbridge Wells has contact with local meditation groups, and also provides instruction in meditation, including a correspondence course. Gaia House in Devon runs a programme of residential workshops, mostly on insight (Buddhist vipassana) meditation, but they also do retreats and t'ai chi — prices are reasonable and some bursaries are available. A good place to look for a local group is either *Link Up* magazine or the Open Centre newsletter (see page 182).

Transcendental Meditation
Roydon Hall
East Peckham
nr Tonbridge
Kent
TN12 5NH
0622 812121/813243

Gaia House
Woodland Road
Denbury
nr Newton Abbot
Devon
TQ12 6DY
0803 813188

Meditation Group for the New Age
Sundial House
Nevill Court
Tunbridge Wells
Kent
TN4 8NJ

To The Elements
Diane Mariechild

Creature of fire
let me unite with you
that I may have passion and power.
Creature of water
let me unite with you
that I may have fluid movement.
Creature of air
let me unite with you
that I may have wisdom and intuition.
Creature of earth
let me unite with you
that I may have stability and steadfastness.

from *Meditation in a Changing World*
by William Bloom (Gothic Image, 1987, £5.95)

Books on Meditation

There are many books about meditation, many of them erudite and specialized. The point about meditation is to experience it, not to read learned books about it, but you will need some basic instruction. Lawrence LeShan's *How To Meditate* (Thorsons, 1984, £3.99) is a good and respected primer, and a book by Erica Smith and Nicholas Wilks called simply *Meditation* a very readable all-round introduction to a complex subject. They explain the paradoxes implicit in meditation clearly yet without being simplistic, and are not afraid to tell you what to avoid when looking for a teacher. They also provide a comprehensive resource list.

*

The kind of meditation which is the subject of this book is a state of pure awareness in which the mind is completely free of thoughts. It is a psychological state that you can slip into in much the same way that you drift into sleep from the waking state. What meditation really is can only be grasped by experiencing it, but an understanding and recognition of the experiences we have been talking about will help give some idea of what it is like. However, whereas in the broader sense of meditation there is an absorption in an outer subject, in the kind of meditation we shall be concerned with here the mind is merged within, and there is total inner stillness.

Meditation
Erica Smith and Nicholas Wilks
Optima, 1988
£4.95

Spiritual Supplies

Traditional religion wouldn't be the same without music, vestments, incense, candles and kneelers. Even new age ritual needs certain props which go to make your healing or meditation space feel, look, sound and smell appropriately sacred.

Candles

Candles provide a focus for meditation, a symbol of the light that shines inside each of us, a soft light to see your loved one(s) by. You can now buy beautiful candles in many craft shops, and there are even some specialist candle shops. The Candle Shop in Covent Garden sells a wide and ever-changing range of candles, including natural beeswax, dip-dyed and landscape candles. The Edinburgh Candles Shop in — of course — Candlemaker Row does much the same from a lovely old-fashioned shop. Of very many rural candle-makers I must mention Inger John's Cilgwyn Candles in South Wales, where you can see her dipping her candles in the traditional way — she also does mail order. If you want to try making your own candles don't buy an expensive kit; buy a booklet called *Simple Methods of Candle Manufacture* (£2.95) from the Intermediate Technology Bookshop (page 296) and buy your candle-making supplies from Carberry Candles in Edinburgh, who sell powdered paraffin wax at 65p the pound and a wide range of everything else you'll need — they also produce a wide range of decorative candles including some fabulous carved ones.

The Candle Shop
30 The Market
Covent Garden
London
WC2E 8RE
0(7)1-836 9815

The Edinburgh Candles Shop
42 Candlemaker Row
Edinburgh
EH1 2QE
031 225 9646

Cilgwyn Candles
Trefelin
Cilgwyn
Newport
Dyfed
S42 0QN
0239 820470

Carberry Candles
Carberry
Musselburgh
EH21 8PZ
031 665 5656

Crystals and Music

Having a crystal hanging in your window can send rainbows shimmering through the room whenever the sun shines. Many people believe that crystals have healing properties too; I know one person who hangs a crystal in front of her word-processor screen and swears that it prevents her from getting headaches. Aurora Crystals markets a wide range of Austrian-made crystals, from little frosted hearts to your genuine gypsy crystal ball (nearly £100). The Crystal Research Foundation, alias Geoffrey Keyte, produces a *Crystal Healing* newsletter — fascinating reading — and runs a healing centre in Lancashire which offers a range of therapies including crystal massage and electro-crystal therapy.

Earthworks are importers, distributors and retailers of precious stones, crystals and minerals, and gemstone jewellery; they have established a fascinating gem and fossil museum at their craft centre in Dorset. They deal directly with the producing nations, and support charities like Friends of the Earth and Greenpeace (there is a 10% discount for members of the Vegetarian and Vegan Societies). Crystal House in Bristol offer a mail order service, and also run certificated courses approved by the British School of Crystal Healing.

I'm not a good judge of 'new age music': a great deal of it seems monotonous and unoriginal, and even the names of the tapes are uninspiring — 'Images', 'Emergence' (at least three of this name), 'Crystal Dancer', 'Serenity'. But a lot of people do like it, so if I haven't put you right off I suggest that you write to Colin Willcox at New World Cassettes, which has recently

joined forces with Aurora Crystals, and ask him to send their amazing full-colour catalogue (which includes both tapes and crystals). They often do special offers, so watch out for them (there is even some real music — the Gregorian Chant from St Cecilia's Abbey on the Isle of Wight is excellent). Glastonbury-based Starchild has now taken over Heartstrings (my recommendation in the first edition of *Green Pages*), and distributes a range of tapes (similar to New World but more diverse) which are also available from local shops. This is a small local enterprise compared with the glossiness of New World.

Aurora Crystals/ New World Cassettes
16a Neal's Yard
Covent Garden
London
WC2H 9DP
0(7)1-379 0818

The Crystal Research Foundation
37 Bromley Road
St Annes-on-Sea
Lancashire
FY8 1PQ
0253 723735

Earthworks
Broadwindsor
Craft Centre
Broadwindsor
Dorset
DT8 3PX
0308 68911

Crystal House
24a Princess Street
Clifton
Bristol
BS8 4BU
0272 737414

Starchild
The Courtyard
2-4 High Street
Glastonbury
Somerset
BA6 9DU
0458 34131

Spiritual Paraphernalia

Incense sticks (joss sticks) provide instant ambience to any indoor ritual. You can buy them in most oriental, craft or esoteric bookshops in a range of exotic fragrances. A renewable alternative to joss sticks is a small burner which evaporates oil placed in a dish over the flame. Id Aromatics in Leeds make these 'fragrancers' and can also supply a wide range of natural oils and instructions to go with them. At just over £7 for a kit complete with oils this makes a very nice present for someone you love.

The Unicorn Place in Brighton is a treasure trove for everything spiritual, esoteric, psychic and wonderful: pendulums, pyramids, pentacles, and more books and tapes than you ever imagined existed. The shop ('Britain's Largest Holistic and New Age Store') covers 2,000 square feet, and the bulky mail order catalogues (£1 each) are fascinating resources in themselves. Mysteries in London's Covent Garden fulfils a similar function, an Aladdin's cave of candles, oils, tarot cards, incense burners, books, 'paranormal research equipment' and much more. Send £1.50 for their weighty mail order catalogue.

Id Aromatics
12 New Station Road
Leeds
LS1 5DL
0532 424983

Mysteries
9-11 Monmouth Street
London
WC2H 9DA
0(7)1-240 3688

The Unicorn Place
39 Duke Street
Brighton
Sussex
BN1 1AG
0273 725276/725298

The Links with the Earth

There is a circle. The people hold hands; they chant together to the Goddess, the Gods. Now one is inspired to begin a chant; now another. They move together in a dance. The power moves through them, uniting them in a common bond with each other, with the land that supports them and the spirit that enters into them... Rituals create a strong group bond. They help build community, creating a meeting-ground where people can share deep feelings, positive and negative — a place where they can sing or scream, howl ecstatically or furiously, play, or keep a solemn silence.

Starhawk, *Dreaming the Dark* (see page 198)

For many Westerners 'pagan' has become a dirty word, synonymous with savagery and dark forces. It just shows how far we are from our roots, for the 'paganes' were originally the country-dwellers, the folk who lived outside the city walls.

Today more and more people are recognizing how important it is to reclaim our links with the natural world — not the 'natural' of deodorant adverts and scrubbed pine kitchens, but the natural of places where human influence has been minimal, the natural of the cycles of the seasons and the stars. This is the world that the country-dwellers — the pagans — inhabited, and which many of us still do.

Rather than continue to sublimate their longing for real connections with the earth, the reclaimers of those links are organizing themselves. What follows is just a handful of pagan and earthwise goings-on, but through them you will undoubtedly encounter others.

The Pagan Network

The pagan network in Britain has two main foci — one in South Wales, where Nicola Miles and Philip Cozens co-ordinate PAN (Pagans Against Nukes) and the Pagan Parenting Network, and one in London, where Shan Jayran runs The House of the Goddess and its affiliated operations. PAN was established in 1980, produces a quarterly newsletter called *The Pipes of PAN*, and welcomes correspondence about paganism and earth magic — they have also written a helpful little introduction to paganism called *What is the Pagan Faith?* — send an sae for a copy.

The House of The Goddess 'exists to provide contact, support, training and celebration for pagans and like-minded folk'; it puts together an occasional mailing full of events, information, reviews, suppliers and adverts, and organizes fortnightly 'Pagan At Home' evenings and monthly full-day Pagan Moon festivals to which anyone is welcome.

Moonshine Magazine, the quarterly review of everything going on in pagan Britain, has sadly recently become defunct,

probably not to resurface. Pagan Animal Rights is a Merseyside-based network providing advice and information in the campaign for animal rights; it has eight branches throughout the country.

PAN
Blaenberem
Mynyddcerrig
Llanelli
Dyfed SA15 5BL

House of The Goddess,
33 Oldridge Road
London
SW12 8PN
0(8)1-673 6370

Pagan Animal Rights
23 Highfield South
Rock Ferry
Birkenhead
Merseyside
L42 4NA
051 645 0485

Oak Dragon

It's difficult in one paragraph to say exactly what the Oak Dragon Project is. The way most people will experience it is through one of the Oak Dragon Camps, up to a hundred or more grownups and children gathered together for a week of activities focusing on healing, or ancient landscapes, ordance and creativity. The Oak Dragon organization is friendly and informal, yet generally well thought out and organized — the detailed literature they produce gives you both background and detailed information on each of the half dozen or so events organized each year. The camps cost around £70 per adult and £15 for a child — you bring your tent or camper and Oak Dragon do all the rest.

Beyond the camps, Oak Dragon have dreams of creating a permanent network of 'spiritual landscapes' in rural Britain to provide the basis for a real alternative to urbanized materialism. Pie in the sky or the beginnings of Ecotopia?

At the end of 1987 a breakaway group of Oak Dragonites, at first named the Oakdragon Clan and later the Rainbow Circle Camps, set up their own network. Rainbow Circle feels that Oak Dragon is too hierarchical and structured, and after the summers of 1988 and 1989 when it attempted to reproduce the Oak Dragon camp format but with lower rates to attract poorer people, it has now set its sights slightly lower and for 1990 is organizing a number of smaller gatherings where people can get to know each other better.

Oak Dragon Project
Elfane
Mynyddcerrig
Llanelli
Dyfed
SA15 5BL
0269 870959

Rainbow Circle Camps
18c Frognal Lane
London
NW3 7DT
0(7)1-794 7093

Oracles

Ask someone in the Britain of 1990 what an oracle is and they'll most likely tell you that its the teletext pages on ITV. Independent Television carefully chose the acronym (Optional Reception of Announcements by Coded Line Electronics) to make the connection with the main meaning of the word, which is 'a message or prophecy revealed through a person or a method of divination'.

Maybe today it's a way of divining what tonight's film is, but divination used to be much more widespread and important than it now is. There are many people who still have enormous faith in methods of divination, however, and more and more Westerners are having a little dabble now and again.

Oracles can be thought of as 'fortune telling', but there is another important and linked aspect of oracles. Many users of the tarot, or the ancient Chinese I Ching (or astrologers for that matter), are clear that they are not using these oracles to 'tell the future'. They would say that each and every one of us is part of the wider cosmos, and that we all 'know' much more than we think we do — thus when you 'tune in' to the oracle it can work with you to give important clues as to things that you already know but haven't yet brought into the full light of day. Thus using an oracle will never tell you anything utterly surprising, but it can confirm, question, give hints, give you something to think about. As with 'teachers' and 'gurus', it's important never to be taken over by an oracle — it will never know better than you. When you are rendered helpless by indecision and doubt, however, the tarot or the I Ching — used wisely — can be a real stimulus to thought and action.

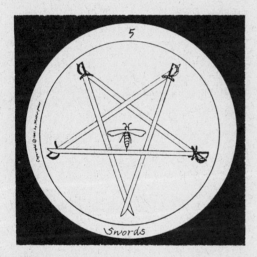

The Tarot

The church and the likes of Aleister Crowley have combined to give the tarot a bad name. Nobody knows where the tarot originated, probably between the twelfth and early fourteenth centuries and somewhere in the western Mediterranean region — but its strength is that the symbolism of the tarot is universal and ageless. Tarot scholars and mystics have come to blows over the real meanings of the cards, their esoteric significance, their relation to the kabbala, numerology, hermeticism — unless you are really interested you can ignore all that. If you want to experiment with the tarot I would recommend that you approach it via one of the several recent interpretations of both the cards themselves and their context. For a good range of packs and books try Watkins in London or the Inner Bookshop in Oxford (page 338), or Thorsons do a good mail order service, but only of their own publications. I like the Motherpeace Round Tarot Pack (around £16) from America; the book that goes with it, called *Motherpeace* by Vicki Noble (Harper and Row, 1983, £8.95) is an excellent interpretation of the tarot which constantly reminds you of the universality of a good oracle. Prepare yourself to deal with your thoughts and feelings associated with 'the goddess', however.

The I Ching

The I Ching is said to be the oldest book in the world, dating from about 1400BC. It is an oracle traditionally approached by throwing 49 yarrow stalks, though most people nowadays use three coins — these are used to generate a pattern of lines called a hexagram, and each of the 64 hexagrams has a symbol and a 'commentary'. In detail there is much more than this, but as you can imagine, the I Ching operates on the same basic principle as the tarot in providing a series of universal images upon which you can ponder or meditate. As with the tarot, there are people who seek to impose their own detailed order upon the I Ching, but resist doing it yourself. A book that has been around for three thousand years deserves respect.

There are two well-known translations of the I Ching. The most popular is the Richard Wilhelm version (Routledge and Kegan Paul, 1984, £3.95); it's certainly thick and looks authoritative, but I don't think it's the best. The main problem is that it's a translation of a translation (from Chinese via German), and an important secondary problem is that it's very dated (1951). I much prefer John Blofeld's translation (Unwin, 1976, £2.25) which is a translation directly from the Chinese by a scholar of taoism — the introductory chapters are good, too. More recent I Ching interpreters include Rowena Pattee, who has produced in *Moving With Change* (Arkana, 1987, £5.95) a feminist I Ching equivalent of the Motherpeace tarot.

For years I've been on the lookout for a supplier of real yarrow stalks in a beautiful container, but so far I've failed and I think you'll have to do it yourself: buy a beautiful carved box from Traidcraft (page 240), line it with purple silk (page 126), and dry your own yarrow — less effort than you might imagine.

Angel Cards

A very simple and easy-to-use oracle is provided by the 52 'angel cards', created in 1981 to accompany The Game of Life, a workshop established at the Findhorn Foundation. Each beautifully-illustrated little card carries the name of a 'positive quality' such as 'harmony' or 'trust'; a simple meditation (outlined on the accompanying instruction sheet) leads you to one of the cards for you to ponder on and integrate into your life. For what they are they are expensive (£5.50 a pack plus 60p p+p), but they are a good introduction to the world of oracles. Buy them from the Findhorn Foundation Trading Centre (see page 183).

In recent years many other publishers have attempted to cash in on the oracle market with plastic runes, nasty little 'I Ching Cards', Star+Gate Cards — you name it. Remember that the ancients used (and many tribal peoples still use) the natural world as an oracle — you'll probably get more insight from a walk through a beechwood than an evening with an overpackaged board game.

The Spiritual Network

'Networking' is one of the buzzwords of the late 1980s. The champions of networking would like to see us all networking like mad, and have turned it into a fine and extremely time-consuming art.

But what is networking? Jessica Lipnack and Jeffrey Stamps (*The Networking Book*, Routledge and Kegan Paul, 1986, £5.95) broadly define networking as 'people linking with people', then go on to say in good networking jargon:

In the end it is the sense of co-operation among self-reliant decision-making peers that vitalizes a network. Networking swallows up buck passing and renders each of us more responsible, self-respecting and creative. The process of networking itself changes those who are networked, by expanding each person's matrix of consciousness.

Any the wiser? Well, I very much see *New Green Pages* being a tool for networking, providing you with the resources to make connections with like-minded people. But like therapy, do remember that the point of networking is not to network — it's to help ourselves and the planet we live on to be a healthier and happier place. Networking is a means, not an end in itself. Therefore treat all 'professional networkers' with caution until you can see what they're actually doing with their lives. If they're just using other people's money to travel the globe telling people how to network, it really isn't on. If, like many people who are good networkers, they are actually doing things to make the world a better place, they deserve attention.

You will find networkers in every area of human activity, but they are probably thicker on the ground within the overtly spiritual section of the community than anywhere else. This — it has to be said — is partly because of the proselytizing nature of many religious groups, 'new age' no less than established, but it is also because many such networkers recognize the urgent need for people to get together and communicate rather than stand by and watch our world become ever more inhuman.

Kindred Spirit

Kindred Spirit, born early in 1988, shows that you can produce an attractive, readable and informative alternative magazine and expect it to survive more than a couple of issues. 'In tune with the holistic vision', it says on the front cover, and to give you an idea of the contents the Winter 1989/90 edition of this eclectic quarterly carried a beautifully sensitive interview with Elisabeth Kübler-Ross (see page 143) together with articles on complementary medicine, the Dalai Lama, money, astrology and dolphins. It has a good resource directory, a mail order section for books and crystals, and a fascinating range of advertisements large and small (could you be the possible soulmate for a Leo lady with the looks and maturity of a goddess and the joy of a child?). Send £1.95 for a sample copy.

Kindred Spirit
PO Box 29
Warminster
Wiltshire
BA12 9YD
09853 775/6 or 0985 217772

Link Up

Founded in 1980 'to connect with others concerned with creative change', *Link Up* magazine has survived its infancy to become a fully-fledged and very attractively-presented guide and discussion forum concerned with a wide range of spiritually-inclined activities. Each quarterly issue takes a theme — 'Healing', 'Meditation', 'The Feminine' — and includes a detailed diary and directory of 'holistic events in Britain'. A recent and most welcome innovation is *Link Up*'s 'Green Pages', a special environmental centre section printed on green recycled paper (now where could they have got that idea?).

Link Up
51 Northwick Business Centre
Blockley
Gloucestershire
GL56 9RF
0386 701091

Open Centres

OPEN CENTRES
Meditation~Movement~Healing
~Interfaith work~

Open Centres has been appearing twice a year since 1977, and is the newsletter that links spiritual centres and groups concerned with meditation, healing and interfaith work. It gives an excellent overview of the developing network in Britain, containing articles, reviews, news from different centres, and — most importantly — a comprehensive and constantly updated list of centres and meditation groups, complete with addresses and telephone numbers. The list of 'Friends of the Open Centres' also includes some very useful resources. Send 75p and an A5 sae for a sample copy. See also page 292 for more on retreats and centres for spiritual renewal.

Open Centres
Avils Farm
Lower Stanton
Chippenham
Wiltshire
SN14 6DA
0249 720202

The Findhorn Foundation

Whatever you feel about it (and most people who know about it do tend to have strong feelings towards it), the Findhorn Foundation has played a decisive part in the 'new age' movement in Britain, those millennial people who believe that we have now reached a turning point in human development.

The Foundation is Britain's largest intentional community, with more than 200 permanent members. Founded 27 years ago, and wedged between a Scottish seaside village and an RAF base, its purpose is to experiment with and learn and teach about more co-operative and harmonious ways of living and working. The 'how' varies from person to person involved in this enormous project, but invariably includes the idea of working 'with spirit'. The spirit sometimes gets in the way of the practice (as in 'I don't feel moved to do the washing up today'), but most members meditate regularly, there is a lot of holding hands in circles, and what has been achieved shows that much hard work does get done.

An early claim to fame was giant cabbages helped along by friendly nature spirits, and a few people still see fairies in the impressive organic gardens. Another impressive aspect of the community is the practical way in which everyday communal life has been thought out over the years, and the techniques for ensuring that members have an say in community decision making, especially decisions that affect them. Less impressive is the sometimes unaware affluence and attitude to money. The community's main source of income is its 'guest programme', which will cost you £180 (some bursaries available) for an 'experience week', £300 for a conference week with big 'names', and £1450 for a twelve-week course called 'The Essence of Findhorn'.

If you are rich then by all means spend it on a Findhorn workshop; if you are poor and would like to visit the community, you can arrange to stay for a couple of nights at Newbold House in Forres, which is affiliated to the Foundation and which offers bed and breakfast (and some good workshops) at a rate which you will be able to afford — there isn't a set rate; you are asked to give what you can, so the rich subsidize the poor. While you are there, you can take the day tour of the Foundation, which will give you the services of a community member to show you all the different places and activities, plus lunch — if you use your day wisely to ask questions of your guide and the other members you meet, you will see and discover a great deal. There are also short tours every summer afternoon and three days a week in the winter. These are free but tend to attract quite large groups, so don't expect to see very much of the real community.

The community produces an illustrated brochure about its workshops and other activities, and they will be glad to send you a copy.

Findhorn Foundation
The Park
Findhorn
Forres
Morayshire
IV36 0TZ
0309 72288
0309 30311

Newbold House
St Leonards Road
Forres
IV36 0RE
0309 72659

The main 'campus' of the Findhorn Foundation is divided between the site at Findhorn itself and two large houses five miles away in Forres (a regular community bus service links the two). The Findhorn sites incorporates the Universal Hall, used for public concerts and events as well as Foundation activities, the Moray Steiner School, the Apothecary (which sells herbal remedies and delicious cakes and herb teas), and the Trading Centre — an excellent craft shop and the best alternative bookshop in the region (send for a catalogue). Minton House is a nearby affiliate specializing in healing workshops and activities. The community also publishes a bi-monthly magazine called *One Earth* — send £1 to Findhorn Publications at the above address for a sample copy.

Opposite Iona on Scotland's west coast is the island of Erraid — the community which now inhabits the island is affiliated to the Findhorn Foundation. You can arrange to stay there for a few days or a week, and join in work projects and the life of the island. The rates are not cheap, but more flexible that those at the Foundation — Erraid is ideal if you like wild scenery and a rural setting, and want a fairly gentle way into everyday spirituality.

The Trading Centre
The Park
Findhorn
Forres
IV36 0TZ
0309 31074

Isle of Erraid
Fionnphort
Isle of Mull
Argyll
PA66 6BN
068 17 384

The Dance of Change

Unfortunately the best book about the Findhorn community, *Faces of Findhorn*, is now out of print; a new edition of *The Findhorn Garden*, an earlier book telling how the community began, has recently been published by The Findhorn Press (1988, £9.95), but this doesn't tell you much about what Findhorn is like today. To give you some idea of the philosophy and practice underpinning the community and its work, community member Michael Lindfield has written *The Dance of Change*, which calls itself 'an eco-spiritual approach to transformation'. That sets the tone of the book, which is rather too cliché-ridden for my liking, but other people whose opinions I respect think it's wonderful, so if you want to explore the ecological fringes of spirituality this is your book.

*

Crises, be they of a global or personal nature, can either be seen as times of extreme danger and even destruction of life, or they can herald the birth of new beginnings. A time of crisis can be an opportunity to learn from our past mistakes and make the move into a more mature relationship with life.

MICHAEL LINDFIELD
THE
DANCE OF CHANGE
AN ECO-SPIRITUAL APPROACH
TO TRANSFORMATION

The Dance of Change
Michael Lindfield
Arkana, 1986
£5.95

Centres for Spiritual Education

As well as the established churches there are several foundations and networks in Britain whose purpose is spiritual exploration and education which is not specifically aligned with any particular faith or denomination.

The White Eagle Lodge was founded in 1936, and is the most overtly Christian of the centres, though 'Christ' and 'God' are used as much to indicate the divinity of each of us as they are to describe an external influence. The Lodge (which has centres in Hampshire and London) emphasises the importance of prayer and hope in personal and planetary healing; organizes events; publishes books about yoga, meditation and healing; and produces a bi-monthly magazine called *Stella Polaris*.

The Wrekin Trust was established by new-age-guru-to-some Sir George Trevelyan in 1971 to explore the borderlands of spiritual experience and new discoveries in psychology and science. It has recently moved to larger premises under the Wrekin Hills near Malvern, and offers a very wide range of courses at manageable rates both at Runnings Park and in London and other cities. It is gradually overcoming its tweeds and pink rinse image with exciting ventures like an exploration into the power of music with Van Morrison. They also do a very comprehensive book and tape mail order service.

Since 1973 The Bridge Trust has been co-ordinating and promoting links between individuals and groups working for spiritual change. To some extent it has outgrown some of the earlier need for spiritual outreach and has become a network of friends interested in the wider aspects of meditation and holistic education, linked by a quarterly newsletter and involvement in the Bridge Trust Country Centre at Donhead St Mary in Dorset. The Bridge Trust is currently involved in setting up a computer database of holistic educational resources.

The Salisbury Centre in Edinburgh is home to a range of spiritual, therapeutic and creative activities. There are regular meditation and yoga groups, and weekend workshops at very reasonable rates. The Sempervivum Trust, an Edinburgh-based network of spiritually-oriented people which organizes events including a popular Easter School, can be contacted at the Centre. The Salisbury Centre is also the home of *4D* ('the fourth dimension') magazine, providing information on events and courses throughout Scotland, together with articles, reviews and listings. The magazine is produced by a co-operative, and costs £5 for 3 issues (£3 unwaged).

The White Eagle Lodge
New Lands
Rake
Liss
Hampshire
GU33 7HY
0730 893300

Wrekin Trust
Runnings Park
Croft Bank
West Malvern
Worcestershire
WR14 4BP
06845 60099

The Bridge Trust
Wychwood
20 The Chase
Reigate
Surrey
RH2 7DH
0737 762261

The Salisbury Centre
2 Salisbury Road
Edinburgh
EH16 5AB
031 667 5438

The Graigians

Early in the 1970s a group of young people in North London called themselves The Positive Movement and organized several successful community events. Though TPM contracted after about 1973, a core of those involved went on to establish centres in London and North Wales, which go under a range of titles depending upon whether your main interest is spiritual, artistic or environmental — the umbrella title, The Graigian Society, comes from the Welsh word for 'rock'. TPM produced a 'Green Manifesto' as long ago as 1965 (not many Greens know that), beautifully handwritten copies of which can be bought from the Graigians at £1 each. The hippy feel may put you off, but the warmth and gentle humour of the Graigians will almost certainly turn you back on again (unless your heart has truly turned to stone!) — send an sae for their immensely practical and inspiring literature.

*

These, then, are the aims of The Positive Movement: Less production instead of more; Communities instead of masses; Quality before quantity; Use instead of abuse; Nurturing instead of exploitation; Value before money; Need not greed.

The Graigian Society
10 Lady Somerset Road
Kentish Town
London
NW5 1UP
0(7)1-485 1646

The Festival for Mind, Body and Spirit

It's hard to believe that there was ever a year without the Festival of M, B & S, this annual focal point for everything meaningful, wonderful and weird that could even vaguely be called 'holistic'. One visit every few years is probably enough, since the same 'names' turn up time and time again — but it does draw the crowds. £10 is too much to charge for a 2-hour workshop, and there's still an awful lot of guru-worshipping, but the Festival serves an important function and is an excellent way of seeing the whole range of possibilities on display all at the same time.

Festival for Mind/Body/Spirit
New Life Designs Ltd
Arnica House
170 Campden Hill Road
London
W8 7AS
0(7)1-938 3788

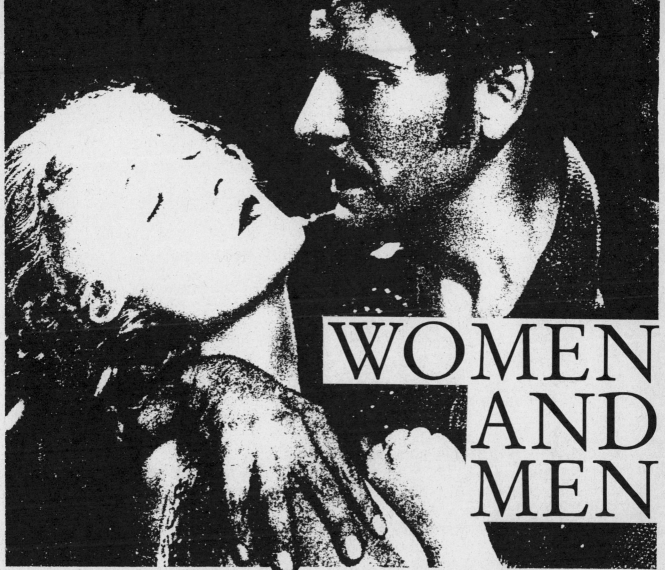

WOMEN AND MEN

'I think the remedy lies in our own hands, and it will be found in social change, not on the analyst's couch. . . Now and in the future patriarchal attitudes will benefit no one, least of all the men.'
Eva Figes, *Patriarchal Attitudes*

I won't bore you with the misgivings I had when I thought about this section; how I thought I might ask one of my women friends to work on it with me and agree on my selection. As it is, the women who helped most with *New Green Pages* were involved in other sections, leaving me to sort this one out for myself. I hope I have at least given you food for thought in this man's selection of books and resources by women, mostly for women.

After twelve pages of 'women' come three for 'men'. I'm aware of the discrepancy, but when it comes to books and resources in the field of sexual politics for and by men in contemporary Britain, three pages is more than ample.

The section finishes with a short section on 'relationships'. Relationship is a much-maligned and narrow concept in current usage, overlain as it is with thick layers of beliefs and assumptions about coupledom, heterosexuality and a strict moral code. In a society where only 45% of households are nuclear families (and in some inner city areas the figure is around 30%), the idea of relationship must be extended beyond the concept of one exclusive lifelong partnership; these pages look at some of the different ways of relating to other people.

Second-Rate Citizens
The facts speak for themselves. In 1989 full-time women employees earned 64% of men's gross weekly earnings, a proportion little changed and if anything worsened

since 1975. 40% of female pensioners are on or below supplementary benefit level, compared with 25% of men. Women constitute 52% of the population of Britain, 4% of MPs, 19% of councillors, 7% of industrial tribunal chairs, and 4% of crown court judges.

As a result of government spending cutbacks, many women's projects have been hard hit, often just at the point when they were beginning to provide a real benefit and showed signs of being able to break even financially. Such cuts have often been arbitrary and sudden, leaving single working women without playgroup facilities and a wide range of women's projects from theatre groups and advice centres without funds.

Feminism Today

Most of the women I talk to about sexual politics — the vast area of mixed social life where issues of power must be aired if we are to meet each other as equals — are worried about contemporary feminism. It isn't that they have any doubts about the importance of feminism and feminist ideas, nor that they want to deny their deeply-held feminist beliefs — at root the certainty that the world will be a better place when women and men have the same rights and the same opportunities to be fully human.

What appears to concern them most is that feminism is in constant danger of being hi-jacked by women with a single-minded preoccupation with a particular issue. The issues in themselves are important — sexual violence, lesbian discrimination, racism — but what seems to happen is that just one of these issues becomes 'what feminism is really all about', often to the extent of berating other women with a wider (though not intrinsically better) understanding as unsisterly and unsupportive.

Feminism grew up around the twin beliefs of inclusivity and solidarity, and most feminist women believe that while it is vitally important to acknowledge and respect the strengths and varied experiences of women in a world fashioned to a large extent by men, the ultimate aim is a world in which everybody's strengths and experiences are recognized and respected, whatever their sex, colour, beliefs or life experiences. As Lynne Segal says at the beginning of *Is The Future Female?* (see page 187), 'I wanted to write this book because I was disturbed by what has been emerging as the public face of feminism in the eighties. The most accessible feminist writing today is one in which we are likely to read of the separate and special knowledge, emotion, sexuality, thought and morality of women, indeed of a type of separate "female world", which exists in opposition to the world of men. The central theme of this book, in contrast, is the inadequacy of such polarized thinking about women and men.'

Towards a New Equality

A green world is a world of shared responsibility, in which both work and its rewards are distributed equitably to all of its inhabitants, and in which everybody's real needs are met. We are still a long way from such a world, yet feminism, for all its inconsistencies, has provided us with a vision for the future and some important pointers on the route.

One important concept that the women's movement has given us is 'Different, therefore equal'. An egalitarian world is not one of boring monotony, in which we all try very hard to be the same. It is one in which individual creativity is nurtured and used to humane and life-enhancing ends. Many women and a small but increasing number of men *are* working hard to understand — and put into practice — this new awareness of equal responsibilities and equal rewards.

Feminism, Women (and Men)

There are now so many books in this whole area, most of them more theoretical than practical, that it really is hard to know where to start, especially if as a man you have problems being seen perusing the 'Women's Issues' shelves of your local bookshop. It is worth it, though, since women are currently doing much more than their share of the really useful thinking in the practical areas of social, political and economic reform.

What do Women Want?

Is it just a coincidence that the titles of all the books on this page are couched in the form of a question? Absolutely not: as the veteran American anarchist Su Negrin said in her classic *Begin at Start*: 'I feel myself clearly bigger than I used to. The difference is question everything'. Luise Eichenbaum and Susie Orbach make it very clear that whatever women really want — and it isn't so very different from what everybody needs — they're not getting it. What women need is support, love and acknowledgement without strings, and men are pretty useless at giving it to anyone because they are so dependent themselves. Simple really, though *What do Women Want?* gives plenty of examples of where this basic imbalance rears its head — in the home, in bed, in relation to children, in relation to friendship between women — and has a practical and positive chapter at the end about how things could be different.

*

Being raised as a boy in our society hampers men in their emotional relationships. Responding to another's emotional needs, giving nurture, is a potential which all human being possess. But this potential, just like so many others, must be developed. It is not formed at birth, it is not natural and inevitable because of one's biology as male or female. In our culture nurturing becomes woven with gender and femininity. 'Mothering' is something girls are continually given the opportunity to develop in themselves. Girls are given dolls to practise on, girls are given tea sets in order to rehearse feeding and serving others, girls are told to 'be nice', which for a girl means not fighting, letting others have their way, being selfless. We know that this training in a rigid sex-role society is extremely oppressive to girls, but there is no doubt that at the same time girls are developing that part of themselves, a human potential of nurturing and giving and thinking about others. Boys are discouraged from developing that part of themselves. In the same way that girls' outward, active, achieving, daring and energetic aspects of their personalities are hampered and restrained, so on the other side of the coin are boys' emotional, caring, gentle, nurturing, relational aspects of their personalities denied growth and development.

What do Women Want?
Luise Eichenbaum and
Susie Orbach
Fontana, 1984
£1.75

Is the Future Female?

As a single-stop analysis and appraisal of current feminism in a readable and provocative style you will find a great deal in Lynne Segal's book. Her main concern is that many feminist writers have been sidetracked into fighting patriarchy in its own terms — in terms of an innate biological difference between women and men. She argues that with this belief as a starting point things can never change, an untenable position for any feminist who sees there being any future at all. She points out how power relationships between women and men are changing and will continue to change, bringing benefits for women and men alike.

*

It is not so much the social realities of women's mothering which are stressed in today's popular feminism as the links between women's lives, women's bodies, and the natural order of things. The eco-feminism of the eighties, which overlaps with 'cultural' feminism and has been called a 'new wave' in feminism, suggests that women must and will liberate the earth because they live more in harmony with 'nature'. Susan Griffin, introducing the British feminist ecology anthology Reclaim the Earth, argued that 'those of us who are born female are often less severely alienated from nature than are most men.' It is woman's capacity for motherhood which is presented as connecting her with what Adrienne Rich calls the 'cosmic essence of womanhood', keeping women in touch with the essentially creative, nurturing and benign blueprint of nature. It is a strange projection on to nature, of course, that nature is female; that it can be seen as gentle, sensual and nurturing rather than as brutal, ravaging and indifferent to individual life and survival. We have here an inversion of the sociobiology which is so popular on the right, where nature is 'male'. And bloody.

Is the Future Female?
Troubled Thoughts on Contemporary Feminism
Lynne Segal
Virago, 1987
£4.95

What is Feminism?

What is Feminism? is a surprisingly even collection of essays on different aspects of the contemporary women's movement. Rosalind Delmar's piece, 'What is Feminism?', makes it clear that feminism must be an inclusive rather than an exclusive set of beliefs; Ann Oakley on motherhood and medicine is good, as is Judith Stacey's 'Are Feminists Afraid to Leave Home?'.

*

The fragmentation of contemporary feminism bears ample witness to the impossibility of constructing modern feminism as a simple unity in the present or of arriving at a shared feminist definition of feminism. Such differing explanations, such a variety of emphases in practical campaigns, such widely varying interpretations of their results have emerged, that it now makes more sense to speak of a plurality of feminisms than of one.

What is Feminism?
edited by Juliet Mitchell
and Ann Oakley
Blackwell, 1986
£6.95

Patriarchal Attitudes

Eva Figes' book was first published in 1970, and of all the early seventies feminist primers it is the one which remains almost as fresh and relevant now as it was then. In a style reminiscent of Virginia Woolf (whose *Three Guineas* is also required reading) she looks at the roots of patriarchy — religious, economic, political, sexual and psychological — to show how and why things are the way they are, with women losing out at every level. She is cautiously optimistic when looking at recent changes, but at the end of her introduction to the new edition she warns that 'We may have won the first battle, but we are still a long way from winning the war.'

*

Our present difficulties with regard to marriage are largely due to the fact that we perpetuate a legal partnership based on finances, but allow people to contract in and out of it for reasons which have nothing to do with money. This anomaly means that a lot of people are entering into legal contracts with no real understanding of what is involved. When, as most people do, they get married because they are in love, they become involved in a legal contract which, unless it is dissolved by a complicated process, is intended to be binding for life. A parson may enumerate your moral obligations during the wedding service, but a registrar does nothing to make you aware of your civic obligations. There is no printed contract to be signed, only a skimpy marriage certificate. When you consider the care with which people go over a five-year lease for a flat . . .

Patriarchal Attitudes
Eva Figes
Virago, 1977
£2.75

Right-Wing Women

Andrea Dworkin has a reputation for being a demanding woman who is difficult to read. I admire the clarity and precision of her non-fiction writing, nowhere more so than in this collection of essays. In 'The Promise of the Ultra-Right' she takes on the women of the American 'moral majority', Phyllis Schlafly and Anita Bryant, and wins hands down, showing

what women can gain (and what they can't) from being everything their reactionary menfolk want them to be. 'The Politics of Intelligence' is a brilliant plea for the supremacy of personal choice and moral intelligence, making it clear that whatever happens in the world, each of us is responsible for it all the time. Andrea Dworkin is not always easy reading, and certainly not always comfortable reading, but passages stick with you years after the first reading.

*

Moralism is passive: it accepts the version of the world it has been taught and shudders at the threat of direct experience. Moral intelligence is characterized by activity, movement through ideas and history: it takes on the world and insists on participating in the great and terrifying issues of right and wrong, tenderness and cruelty. . . Moral intelligence must act in a public world, not a private, refined, rarefied relationship with one other person to the exclusion of the rest of the world. Moral intelligence demands a nearly endless exercise of the ability to make decisions: significant decisions; decisions inside history, not peripheral to it; decisions that arise from an acute awareness of one's own mortality; decisions on which one can honestly and wilfully stake one's life.

Right-Wing Women
Andrea Dworkin
Women's Press, 1983
£4.95

Magic Mommas, Trembling Sisters *et al*

Joanna Russ's latest collection of essays about sex and pornography (the categories of the title are the gamut of feminist reactions to pornography) is like a breath of fresh air in the discussion of a very heavy issue. As it says on the back: 'feisty, opinionated, and a joy to read'.

*

The best cure for pornography is sex — I mean autonomously chosen activity, freely engaged in for the sake of real pleasure, intense, and unmistakably the real thing. The more we have experiences like this, the less we will be taken in by the confusions and lies and messes all around us.

**Magic Mommas,
Trembling Sisters,
Puritans and Perverts**
Joanna Russ
Crossing Press, 1985 (distributed in the UK by Airlift)
£5.95

Once A Feminist

On a chilly Friday in late February, 1970, I dressed carefully in a mini-sweater dress, long black leather boots and an ankle-length black and white herring-bone coat. I was preparing to go to my first ever political conference — the 'Women's Weekend' being held at Ruskin College, Oxford.

Thus writes Michelene Wandor at the beginning of this collective biography of some of the best-known names in the British women's movement, published to celebrate twenty years of new-wave feminism in these islands. The organizers of the Oxford conference expected maybe a hundred women; more than 400 came, along with 60 children and 40 men. For many of those who attended it was both exciting and awe-inspiring. 'I found I was no longer alone in my bewilderment,' writes Michelene Wandor, speaking for many.

And what have those women done since? As can be seen from the pages of *Once A Feminist* they have achieved a great deal, and the excellent editing of these seventeen interviews allows their subjects to speak very immediately about those achievements as well as the setbacks. For the generation of feminists many of whom have recently been celebrating their fortieth birthdays, this volume will be read with grateful nostalgia.

*

Our group still meets. During the late 1970s we withdrew very much more into the personal, away from the political. You could moan, and you could talk about relationships, about feelings, worries. In a sense it became a kind of group therapy. I think it's had its doldrums now for several years, but out of sheer loyalty and friendship we continue to meet.

Juliet Mitchell

*

I was going to write a book about the history of the women's movement, years ago. But now I no longer have this burning sense of the righteousness of my own position, or the wrongness of everybody else. I'd like to be rooted. We 1960s people have had a prolonged adolescence.

Amanda Sebestyen

Once A Feminist
Stories Of A Generation
Michelene Wandor
Virago, 1990
£4.99

The Politics of Reality

Marilyn Frye, it says at the end of this important collection of essays, was born in Oklahoma in 1941 and now teaches philosophy, writes, and engages in housework and home maintenance. I can't vouch for her housework and DIY, but her philosophy is coherent and her writing fluent and powerful. In less than 200 pages she treats us to her insights on virtually every important concept within the ambit of sexual politics:

oppression, sexism, power, anger, racism and separatism. Rarely have these important ideas been discussed so clearly and with such integrity.

*

That we are trained to behave so differently as women and as men, and to behave so differently toward women and toward men, itself contributes mightily to the appearance of extreme natural dimorphism, but also, the ways we act as women and as men, and the ways we act toward women and toward men, mold our bodies and our minds to the shapes of subordination and dominance. We do become what we practice being.

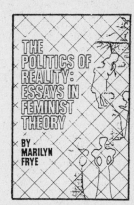

The Politics of Reality
Essays in Feminist Theory
Marilyn Frye
Crossing Press, 1983
(distributed in the UK
by Airlift)
£6.95

Too Much Loving?

Though my heart usually sinks when I see yet another mass-market paperback full of accounts of American women's relationship experiences, I feel I must include Robin Norwood's *Women Who Love Too Much* if only because of the immense following it now commands on both sides of the Atlantic. Its theme is not so much love as an overdependence on a particular concept of 'love' which seems always to involve pain and disappointment, and it's very clear why so many women can relate to that experience. Myself, I suspect that it isn't loving too much that causes the pain so much as demanding that the other person loves you in a particular way and responds to your love in an equally particular way. Whatever you think, *Women Who Love Too Much* will give you plenty to ponder on as you wish yet again that if only you could get it right next time . . .

*

If you have ever found yourself obsessed with a man, you may have suspected that the root of that obsession was not love but fear. we who love obsessively are full of fear — fear of being alone, fear of being unlovable and unworthy, fear of being ignored or abandoned or destroyed. We give our love in the desperate hope that the man with whom we're obsessed will take care of our fears. Instead, the fears — and our obsessions — deepen until giving love in order to get it back becomes a driving force in our lives. And because the strategy doesn't work we try, we love even harder. We love too much.

**Women Who Love
Too Much**
Robin Norwood
Arrow, 1986
£2.99

Women and the Environment

In December 1987, two prizes were awarded in Stockholm: the Nobel prize for economics was given to Robert Solow of MIT for his theory of growth based on the dispensability of nature. In Solow's words, 'The world can, in effect, get along without natural resources, so exhaustion is just an event, not a catastrophe.' At the same time, the Alternative Nobel Prize (the popular name for the Right Livelihood Award [see page 334]), instituted 'for vision and work contributing to making life more whole, healing our planet and uplifting humanity', honoured the women of the Chipko movement who, as leaders and activists, had stated that nature is indispensable to survival.

Vandana Shiva, *Staying Alive* (see below)

*

The tragedy is that programmes of environmental rehabilitation often ignore women's needs and fail to build upon their capacity to conserve. Yet women are the ones who could make a major contribution to environmental rehabilitation. First, they have the knowledge and the skills of natural resource management that can be built upon. Secondly, women have a remarkable ability to work together. Many women are experienced in co-operative working, something that male-dominated governments and multinational companies have yet to learn. Thirdly, in caring for children, women have a powerful influence over changing attitudes to the environment. They can turn the short-term expediency of remedial action into a lasting habit of environmental protection.

Finally, perhaps most important of all, it is likely that restoring women's capacity to care for the environment will be associated with improvements in their independence and their status.

Irene Dankelman and Joan Davidson,
Women and Environment in the Third World (see below)

*

All that I know, I know in this earth, the body of the bird, this pen, this paper, this tongue speaking, all that I know speaks to me through this earth and I long to tell you, you who are earth too, and listen as we speak to each other of what we know: the light is in us.

Susan Griffin, *Woman and Nature* (see below)

In recent years there has been a growing understanding among many feminists and green-thinkers that the cause of a just, sustainable nonviolent world order is very much their common goal. The recognition of the importance of feminist principles within the (still largely male-led) green movement is gaining ground and, at the same time, more and more women are seeing that although there are dangers in equating women's struggle to be seen and heard with the struggle of the earth itself, there is clearly a common purpose. This cause requires a very radical reassessment of much that the 'developed world' currently holds dear — ideas which range from 'growth' and 'development' to 'life' itself.

There is no essential difference between the rape of a woman, the conquest of a country, and the destruction of the earth. the his/story of the world records the gender of the rapists, conquerors and destroyers.

Petra Kelly, quoted in Marilyn Waring's
If Women Counted (see page 191)

Woman and Nature

Writing about our ecological predicament in personal terms is always caught on the horns of the 'scientific/anti-scientific' dilemma. If you write within the conventions of 'real science' you are almost certain to take the pseudo-objective 'male' view of nature which creates many of the problems we now face; if you write passionately and with total personal involvement (particularly if you write as a woman) you can too easily be written off as over-emotional and thus be ignored by serious scientists.

In *Woman and Nature* Susan Griffin has created a remarkable dialogue between the two voices, the voice of cold 'reason' and the voice of passionate concern. This is a vitally important book, not to be hurried over; read it slowly, out loud if possible. I doubt if you will feel the same afterwards about the earth and the rich panoply of life it supports.

*

We are the rocks, we are soil, we are trees, rivers, we are wind, we carry the birds, the birds, we are cows, mules, we are horses, we are Solid elements, cause and effect, determinism and objectivity, it is said, are lost. matter. We are flesh, we breathe, we are her body: we speak.

Woman and Nature: The Roaring Within Her
Susan Griffin
The Women's Press, 1984
£4.95

Women's Environmental Network

Ecological concerns have appeared late on the feminist scene. The 1990 *Spare Rib Diary* lists many organizations concerned with women and the arts, women's history, black women and disabled women, but only one under 'women and the environment': The Women's Environmental Network. Launched in 1988, WEN's aims are to inform, educate and empower women on environmental issues, and the newly-formed organization went straight for the jugular of the women's-product marketplace by launching an attack on tampons, sanitary towels and disposable nappies bleached with dioxin-contaminated chlorine bleaches. Though the industry did its best to stand its holier-and-more-scientific-than-thou ground, the campaign and associated book, *The Sanitary Protection Scandal* (WEN, 1989, £5.95), were an outstanding success. WEN has since gone on to mount the Green Home travelling exhibition, and current plans include a growing network of local groups, and links with similar organizations in other countries. WEN has already sent out more than 50,000 information packs, and is constantly in need of practical and financial support to continue its important work. Membership costs just £10 (unwaged £7), a small price to pay to know that WEN is fighting for your green rights.

Women's Environmental Network
287 City Road
London
EC1V 1LA
0(7)1-490 2511

Women in the World

It can be misleading to talk about women as a whole without ignoring the vast economic and cultural differences between them. Yet some generalizations are useful, since they demonstrate how women in every corner of the globe tend to become a second-rate underclass in an economic and development system imposed largely by men. Among the things women share are their relative poverty, which in many parts of the Third World descends into abject destitution, and the long hours of unrewarded labour which go to caring for the people around them. A 1985 Tanzanian study showed women working an average of 3,069 hours a year while men worked an average of 1,829 hours. A Chase Manhattan Bank survey showed that if the average American housewife were paid the going rate for each of the 99 hours a week spent on cooking, food buying, childminding and the rest, she should rightfully earn $258 a week.

Three recent important books look at how this process works in Third World countries, and how Third World women are increasingly taking matters into their own hands. Vandana Shiva's *Staying Alive* is at the same time the most difficult (less-than-good proofreading doesn't help) and the most rewarding of the three, insofar as she adds a thoroughgoing critique of science and technology to her exploration of what needs to change.

Women's Role in Economic Development is a welcome reprint of Ester Boserup's ground-breaking classic of 1970 which led among other things to the United Nations' Decade for Women of 1975-85. *Women and Environment in the Third World* shows very clearly how women in many Third World countries are spearheading the grassroots campaign to conserve the land and crops which alone can provide them with the basis for a sustainable livelihood; the book includes many case studies and first-hand interviews.

Staying Alive: Women, Ecology and Development
Vandana Shiva
Zed, 1989
£8.95

Women's Role in Economic Development
Ester Boserup
Earthscan, 1989
£6.95

Women and Environment in The Third World
Irene Dankelman and
Joan Davidson
Earthscan, 1988
£5.95

If Women Counted

Marilyn Waring — experienced New Zealand politician, able economist and goat farmer — has in her new book *If Women Counted* produced a stout and irrefutable critique of economics as currently defined by academics and politicians alike. She shows blindingly clearly what a nonsense is an accounting system which gives no value to trees and hills until they are ravaged, bulldozed and mined to provide marketable product, and how women's work is denied and devalued using the same blinkered arguments.

If Women Counted is a fluent, often witty, exploration of patriarchal economics and of the humane economics that must prevail if we are to understand and find a way out of our present impasse. Marilyn Waring is largely successful in her stated aim of demystifying conventional economics; I wish she had spent a little longer demystifying the models — that of the Finnish economist Hilkka Pietilä in particular — which might take its place. But this is a tiny niggle: *If Women Counted* should be very high on any green-thinker's reading list.

*

We frequently hear from politicians, theologians and military leaders that the wealth of a nation is its children. But, apparently, the creators of that wealth deserve no economic visibility for their work. As a means of reproduction, woman is irreplaceable wealth. Reproducing the system depends on her. Control derives ultimately not from the possession of wealth, but the control of reproduction. In terms of value, reproduction of the human species is either the whore, debased, of no worth, or the virgin on the pedestal, valued beyond wealth.

*

The US Department of Defense is the largest centrally planned economy outside the Soviet Union. In the capitalist, free market United States, the department's property — plant and equipment, land, inventories of war and other commodities — amounts to over $200 billion. This is equal to about 7 per cent of the assets of the entire American economy. It owns 39 million acres of land, roughly an area the size of Hawaii; it rules over a population of more than 3 million — direct employees or soldiers — and spends an official budget of close to $100 billion, a budget three-quarters as large as the entire Gross National Product of Great Britain.

*

I have a little dream that in 1990-91, which is the next period designated by the United Nations for a census to be held in every country, all women claim unpaid worker as their designation. Since housework is nowhere defined, it would seem totally legitimate, and they should insist on such a designation in all labour force and household surveys as well. if any government were to contest such a strategy through the civil courts, we can rely on the Bella Abzugs of the world as legal counsel. But if millions of women everywhere behaved in this way, the government could not afford to block up their legal system with contested suits.

We women are visible and valuable to each other, and we must, now in our billions, proclaim that visibility and that worth. Our anger must be creatively directed for change. We must remember that true freedom is a world without fear. And if there is still confusion about who will achieve that, then we must each of us walk to a clear pool of water. Look at the water. It has value. Now look into the water. the woman we see there counts for something. She can help to change the world.

If Women Counted
A New Feminist Economics
Marilyn Waring
Macmillan, 1989
£14.95

Women and Food

Women hold a unique position in relation to food. Though their part in farming and the food processing industry is largely invisible in Britain, their position as consumers is virtually unchallenged. Not only do they work extensively in the retail trade, but virtually all advertising is directed at them — and their images are used to sell food. . . The images of women and food are inseparable. It is seen as part of women's nurturing role to be the providers. Who asks whether a woman can cook, or why a man is not at the cooker? The medium of advertising reinforces stereotypes, be it woman as mother or woman as sexual being. The Bisto Mum and the Black Magic Lady have more in common than at first appears —neither of them relate to the reality of women's lives; both impose standards which no woman should be expected to conform to. Yet, paradoxically, women must not eat. They must be thin, attractive, inviting. This has created a whole section of the food industry that caters for women alone — the so- called 'diet aids' market. Though women must always be available to provide food for others they must conform to an image imposed externally.

The Green Party, *Our Borrowed Land*, 1987

Fat is a Feminist Issue

FFI1 was published in the spring of 1978 and rapidly went through printing after printing as thousands of women realized upon reading it that they weren't alone in having problems with their food, their weight, and their body image. Illustrating her argument with stories of women with histories of compulsive eating and equally compulsive dieting, Susie Orbach, one of the founders of the Women's Therapy Centre (see page 198), showed how many women are trying to live two mutually contradictory images, inevitably failing at both, and becoming ill as a result. Six years later came *FFI2*, covering much of the same ground (and still assuming that thin is what women ought to be), but with less theory and more practical suggestions — food awareness exercises, self-help groups, bringing your body and your image of your body into synch with each other. These two books are still probably the best introduction to the sexual politics of food if the theoretical issues are fairly new to you.

*

Questions to ask yourself (if you feel too fat) after trying a guided fantasy on the subject of fatness and thinness: What positive aspects of fatness emerged that you hadn't realized you felt? What emerged about aspects of your personality that you express through your fat? How might you express that part of you if you were your ideal size? What emerged about you at your imagined 'ideal' size? What fears came up for you about being slim? What aspects of your personality are you currently suppressing that you imagine go with slimness? How might you express those aspects now?

Fat is a Feminist Issue
and
Fat is a Feminist Issue 2
Susie Orbach
Hamlyn, 1978 and 1984
£1.75 each

The Hungry Self

This is Kim Chernin's second book about food — the first was *Womansize: Reflections on the Tyranny of Slenderness*, a title which speaks for itself. *The Hungry Self* looks at the links between women's relationships with food and daughter's relationships with mothers, which she sees as being part of the key to many women's eating problems. Starting from the belief that at some level most women want to be at least as good as, if not better than, their mothers, she looks at the fear, the guilt and the anger that many women carry with them, feelings which if unacknowledged and unexplored too often result in a morbid preoccupation with food. Much of the book is written in the form of dialogues between the author as counsellor and her imaginary clients, which makes it very readable.

*

Close your eyes, I say to women who sit opposite me in my consultation room. Can you remember the kitchen in the house where you lived when you were a child? Women of all ages, women who have not been able to remember their childhood, women who have, as they tell me, not cried for many years, sit with their eyes closed describing the plastic cloth on the kitchen table, the bright color of the knobs on the cabinets in a room they have not seen since they were three or four years old. They see their mother young again or for the first time acknowledge an absent mother or recall a mother whose back was always turned, bent over the hot stove, ignoring them.

The Hungry Self
Kim Chernin
Virago, 1986
£3.95

The Anorexic Experience

A practical handbook from the Women's Press for women concerned that they or a close friend are not in control of their dieting. Marilyn Lawrence, a therapist with a great deal of experience of counselling young women on so-called 'eating disorders', covers the theoretical and practical issues, linking them together in a very direct way without ever talking down to her reader. A good bibliography, but a not very helpful resource list.

The Anorexic Experience
Marilyn Lawrence
The Women's Press, 1988
£4.95

In the years since Fat is a Feminist Issue was published, compulsive eating groups and regular workshops have been set up in many parts of Britain. The Women's Therapy Centre (see page 198) acts as a liaison centre for these groups and workshops; if you send an sae to The Compulsive Eating Programme c/o The Women's Therapy Centre they will send you further information.

Turning the Tables

Given the importance of food in women's lives and the knots it can tie them up in, it's great to see a feminist cookery book in celebration of food. Under headings such as 'Memory', 'Ambivalence' and 'Changing' many well-known writers in the women's movement say some pertinent words about food in their own lives before sharing their favourite recipes. There's nothing preachy or puritanical — just a really enjoyable and informative book.

Turning The Tables
edited by Sue O'Sullivan
Sheba, 1987
£5.50

Women and Health

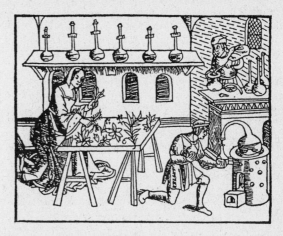

Two ideas in particular seem to be basic to contemporary medical definitions of women and can be found in medical textbooks and in the attitudes and pronouncements of individual doctors. The first is that men are normal whereas women are abnormal. The second is the belief that this abnormality stems from the fact that a woman's natural role is motherhood. Little attention is paid in the medical curriculum to problems suffered by women unless they relate directly to childbearing, so that common problems such as thrush, cystitis and other vaginal infections are not taken seriously either by researchers or by most doctors. Textbooks almost always emphasize the inevitable superiority of the doctor's clinical experience over a woman's subjective experience, even when it is the woman's own experiences that are under discussion.

Angela Phillips, in *Our Bodies, Ourselves* (see below)

While the ideology of health and fitness has clearly affected men and women of all ages, it has nevertheless been directed at women in a particular way, enmeshing with other very definite attitudes towards the body and appearance. The new emphasis on overall health is also a new kind of obsession, which has the effect of making the female body a particular site of concern for Western culture. This new obsession makes women the bearers of a whole series of preoccupations about sex and health.

Rosalind Coward, *Female Desire*, Paladin, 1984, £2.95

Access to information, and to correct information, is one of the vital prerequisites for women's physical and emotional health. One only has to think of the pill and thrombosis, the Dalkon shield and severe gynaecological disorders, thalidomide, and unnecessary caesarian sections, to see how crucial is the dissemination of medical knowledge. Health is an intensely political issue. Feminist concern with health aims both to free women from notions of biological determinism and to turn upside-down accepted definitions of women's bodies, minds and emotions. We attempt to seize knowledge and under- standing of these in order to have more control over our lives.

Sue O'Sullivan, *Women's Health* (see below)

entirely new chapters on body image, alcohol and other mood-altering drugs, alternatives to medical care, mental health, occupational and environmental health, older women and international perspectives.

*

Some women's centres and women's health groups provide pregnancy tests very cheaply (look on noticeboards and in your local paper), otherwise try a chemist (they advertise in the window), or a pregnancy advisory service (listed under 'Pregnancy Testing' in the Yellow Pages). Beware of agencies offering free tests which are only trying to promote something else. Lifeline, for example, offers free testing and counselling but will actually try to persuade you not to have an abortion and will use frightening propaganda to push you into rejecting the option that they disapprove of.

The New Our Bodies Ourselves
A Health Book
By and For Women
Angela Phillips and
Jill Rakusen
Penguin, 1989
£12.99

(The New) Our Bodies Ourselves

If you thought the first British edition of *Our Bodies Ourselves* was comprehensive, brace yourself for the new version, possibly the largest paperback Penguin has ever published. There is so much information crammed into the 700-odd large-format pages (the print isn't that large either) that if you invest in *The New Our Bodies Ourselves* you should never need another health book — nor will you need to buy weights for weight-training nor steps to reach the top shelves.

The new British edition has been a long time coming. Three pages of acknowledgements attest to the army of women (and a few men) who have contributed to the mammoth task, an undertaking which gives new meaning to the word 'thorough'. Massive resource sections at the end of each chapter list every book and organization you could ever need, while the footnotes ensure that every quotation and every idea is faithfully acknowledged. As well as all the practical information and advice you would expect, there is hardly a social and political innuendo within contemporary health practice that isn't looked at and analyzed.

Yet, like earlier editions, *The New Our Bodies Ourselves* remains supportive and compassionate. Poems, stories and photographs add variety and immediacy, and the clear layout makes it an easy book to dip into. As well as all the sections included in the earlier version, the new British edition contains

WHRRIC

Founded in 1982, the Women's Health and Reproductive Rights Information Centre is the only independent feminist resource centre in Britain covering every kind of women's health issue, with an emphasis on reproductive rights. It has an extensive library which women are welcome to visit (currently on Tuesdays and Thursdays from 10 till 4), and comprehensive and up-to-date lists of health resources both local and national. They don't have the resources to deal with individual advice or counselling, nor do they keep comprehensive lists of practitioners. They can, though, tell you where to go for the right information, or the best literature to read. They also produce a regular newsletter which you can receive by becoming a subscriber, and a wide range of literature — send an sae for full details.

Women's Health and Reproductive Rights Information Centre
52-54 Featherstone Street
London
EC1Y 8RT
0(7)1-251 6332

For Her Own Good

During the early 1970s Barbara Ehrenreich and Deirdre English taught a course in 'Women and Health' at New York State University, out of which came a couple of influential booklets looking at why women got such raw deal out of attitudes and practices in health care. *Witches, Midwives and Nurses* is a history of women in healing, showing how their traditional healing skills have been systematically belittled and ignored; *Complaints and Disorders* looks at current beliefs about 'women's ailments' and how their 'treatment' often renders women powerless, as for example in the treatment of depression with tranquillizers.

For Her Own Good brings together all their original and stimulating thoughts about women and health, the title underlining the fact that for the last century and a half male medical professionals (not to mention male experts on everything else to do with women) have stopped listening to what women really think is wrong with their lot. Male doctors define what is wrong, work out the treatments, and then wonder why their women patients keep coming back with yet more symptoms.

*

There are clues to the answer in the distant past, in a gynocentric era that linked woman's nurturance to a tradition of skill, caring to craft. There are the outlines of a solution in the contours of the industrial era, with its promise of a collective strength and knowledge surpassing all past human efforts to provide for human needs. And there are impulses toward the truth in each one of us. In our very confusion, in our legacy of repressed energy and half-forgotten wisdom, lies the understanding that it is not we who must change but the social order which marginalized women in the first place, and with us all 'human values'.

For Her Own Good
150 Years of the Experts' Advice to Women
Barbara Ehrenreich and Deirdre English
Pluto, 1979
£7.95

A Health Reader

For seventeen years *Spare Rib* has been carrying articles about women's health issues, and Sue O'Sullivan has brought nearly a hundred of the best together in a volume called *Women's Health: A Spare Rib Reader*. The pieces are grouped by subject, and cover many aspects of women's health, from the use of the suspect injected contraceptive Depo Provera in the Third World to how to deal with acne.

Women's Health
A Spare Rib Reader
edited by Sue O'Sullivan
Pandora, 1987
£5.95

Women and Alternative Medicine

When you have read *For Her Own Good* (see page 193) you may well come to the conclusion that it is frequently women's traditional healing skills, recently resurrected as aspects of 'alternative medicine', that are the real mainstream in health care, and the last few decades of drugs and surgery the aberration. As you will soon find out, however, it is in general the men who have hogged the market in alternative medical texts too.

There are some exceptions, however. One of the first off the mark was medical journalist Liz Grist, with her *Woman's Guide to Alternative Medicine*, a rather pedestrian yet comprehensive guide to many of the treatments available. The approach is problem by problem, with a couple of introductory chapters on the range of therapies and on nutrition; no pictures but pretty good resource lists at the end.

More attractive and readable, with some useful illustrations and resources but less information, is Patsy Westcott's *Alternative Health Care for Women*. At the end is a clever diagram showing which therapies might well be effective in the treatment of specific problems. Patsy Westcott's book gives a useful overview of what is available together with sufficient information to follow up her leads, and is probably the best book on alternative health care for women currently available, though the chapter on alternative and complementary approaches to health and healing in *The New Our Bodies Ourselves* (see page 193) is very good.

A Woman's Guide to Alternative Medicine
Liz Grist
Fontana, 1986
£3.95

Alternative Health Care for Women
Patsy Westcott
Thorsons, 1987
£5.99

Abortion

There can surely be no issue involving conflicting rights which rouses such passion and such intransigence as does abortion. In *A Difficult Decision* Joy Gardner, an experienced Canadian healer and grief counsellor, acknowledges the trauma of abortion, at the same time setting out clearly the necessary practical information and helping the reader to look at the wider implications of their decision. You may find the sections on creative visualization a little offputting, but this is indeed a compassionate and insightful little book that anyone thinking about abortion will get a lot out of. The book includes sections written especially for men.

*

The act of having a baby is far more binding than marriage. You cannot get a divorce from your child. Children are such a blessing when they are truly wanted. I believe we should have fewer children, and take better care of the ones we have.

A Difficult Decision
A Compassionate Book About Abortion
Joy Gardner
Crossing Press, 1986 (distributed in the UK by Airlift)
£4.95

Women and Cancer

This is an expanded and updated version of Carolyn Faulder's earlier book on breast cancer; breast cancer is still her main subject, but the new book includes an exploration of cervical and ovarian cancer, melanoma and smoking-related cancers. A clear, honest, reassuring book with an excellent resource section.

*

The smallest tumour a mammogram can pick up is about half a centimetre in size; the smallest tumour a woman or her doctor can feel is about two centimetres. Given that a centimetre of tumour represents one gram of tissue — which is about a billion cells, or thirty doubling times — and could have taken anything from three to eight years to grow in what is known as the 'silent interval', the nature of the problem becomes evident. It suggests that some seemingly 'early' breast cancers could have been present for many years.

*

Every year around 2,000 women in this country die of cervical cancer. Almost every one of these deaths is a special tragedy, because it should never have happened.

The Women's Cancer Book
Carolyn Faulder
Virago, 1989
£5.99

Women and AIDS

'AIDS,' point out Cindy Patton and Janis Kelly, 'is an equal opportunity disease.' It was convenient to think for a while that AIDS only affected gay men, or blacks, or intravenous drug users. Many still believe this to be the case, but there is no doubt that AIDS has changed the way that many women think about their lives and their relationships. Two recent books will provide the background you need for an aware and mature approach to this controversial subject.

Matters of Life and Death is an extraordinary collection of first-hand pieces by nearly fifty women from all over the world. Some have AIDS or have tested HIV positive, some have cared for husbands or lovers with AIDS, some work as prostitutes and some are AIDS activists. As with that classic of AIDS reportage, *And The Band Played On* (see page 150), this book will not leave you unmoved.

Making It is a down-to-earth practical guide of no more than a couple of dozen pages (though you get it in Spanish as well as English), explaining with both clarity and humour exactly what safe sex is really all about. 'Mutual oral sex with a condom and a dental dam in a hot tub?' wonders one cartoon character when the subject turns to AIDS prevention. 'I dunno,' says another. 'Sounds kinda risky to me.'

Matters of Life and Death
Women Speak about AIDS
edited by Ines Rieder and Patricia Ruppelt
Virago, 1989
£6.50

Making It
A Woman's Guide to Sex in the Age of AIDS
Cindy Patton and Janis Kelly
Firebrand, 1988
(distributed in the UK by Airlift)
£2.50

Depression

One day I couldn't get up at all; my body wouldn't allow it. I was immobilized, muddled, scared. I couldn't understand what was happening. I'd had glandular fever two years before. This was different, more intense, if that's possible. I fought the great lethargy and stood up. The wail that rumbled out of me shook my whole body.

Val Johnson, in *Through the Break* (see below)

Though both women and men suffer from depression, many more women suffer than men, turning life into a meaningless monotony of despair. Because you are not considered to be 'properly ill', the depression often isn't taken seriously, which makes things even worse. And nobody wants to spend time with anyone who moans all the time, so friends are hard to come by. . .

It is only recently that depression has been analyzed as a widespread yet unnecessary aspect of many people's experience. Two good recent books present a very good account of depression, and what you can do to pull yourself out of it.

Kathy Nairne and Gerrilyn Smith are both practising clinical psychologists who work with women suffering from depression. Using many quotations from women they have worked with, and working very clearly within a feminist framework, they present a forceful account of the roots of depression and a variety of options which anyone who suffers from depression can try.

Much of the same ground, with helpful diagrams and explanations but not, of course, from a feminist perspective, is covered by Richard Gillett in his book in the British Holistic Medical Association series published by Dorling Kindersley. A novel inclusion is the twenty page section of flow charts to help you find possible answers. This is the book for men suffering from depression, though men will get a lot from Dealing with Depression too.

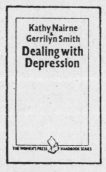 

Dealing with Depression
Kathy Nairne and Gerrilyn Smith
Women's Press, 1984
£3.95

Overcoming Depression
Richard Gillett
Dorling Kindersley, 1987
£5.95

Through the Break

This moving collection of women's experiences of personal upheaval breaks new ground in sharing what is usually kept hidden. Breakdown, alcoholism, disability, hypochondria, rape, domestic violence — but ultimately breakthrough and empowerment — are the subject of these twenty-odd pieces, the reading of which will do you more good than any amount of Valium.

Through the Break
Women in Personal Struggle
edited by Pearlie McNeill, Marie McShea and Pratibha Parmar
Sheba, 1986
£6.95

Women's Rights

The best guide to women's rights currently available is Maggie Rae's *Women and the Law: You and Your Rights*. This practical handbook covers most aspects of law that you are likely to need, and the resources section at the end is very good. It doesn't provide much background and analysis, but it does give a very clear description of the current state of the law.

An updated and revised edition of Eveline Hunter's invaluable *Scottish Women's Handbook* is now available, containing an enormous range of information for women living in Scotland, from social security and discrimination to cohabitation and divorce. It includes a comprehensive list of Scottish organizations, and explains clearly the important instances where Scottish law in relation to women's issues differs from the law south of the border.

Women and the Law
You and Your Rights
Maggie Rae
Longman, 1986
£3.95

The Scottish Women's Handbook
Eveline Hunter
Stramullion, 1988
£8.50

Rights of Women

Rights of Women was started in 1975 by a group of feminists who strongly support the fifth demand of the women's liberation movemnt — that women should have legal and financial independence. Composed of solicitors, law teachers, social scientists and many other women, RoW monitors law and legal practices and their impact, advises government bodies and officials, and demystifies the law so that it is more understandable. They also offer advice and assistance, provide a forum and support network for women working in the legal profession, undertake research and disseminate information. They run a free legal advice line some evenings of the week, and have produced a number of leaflets. In 1986 the RoW Lesbian Custody Group produced the *Lesbian Mother's Legal Handbook* (Women's Press, 1986, £3.95), which any lesbian mother having to fight for child custody will find invaluable. The book describes the legal process so clearly that it would be valuable for any women having to go to court.

Rights of Women
52-54 Featherstone Street
London
EC1Y 8RT
0(7)1-251 6577

Learning to Lose

Though many teachers are now aware of the effects of differentiating between girls and boys at school, a discrimination which leads to an overwhelming imbalance of opportunity in adult life, there is still a very great deal to be done if girls are not to continue to lose out in education. This collection of essays shows clearly how sexism operates in schools to the detriment of girls' opportunities, and looks at what can be done to tip the balance in their favour.

*
I got two per cent for my O-level mathematics paper, and I had come top of the class in mathematics at primary school. I had more knowledge of maths when I was ten than I have had in all my adult years. I have to ask myself what happened in the interim. How does this make sense? I had the same maths teacher for all of my secondary schooling and he certainly didn't think too highly of females wishing to do mathematics. Whenever I asked a question of him the reply was generally 'Oh, you don't need to know that.
Pippa Brewster, 'School Days, School Days'

Learning to Lose
Sexism and Education
Dale Spender
Women's Press, 1989 (2nd edn)
£5.95

The Open University (see page 226) organizes a very good ten-month long course called 'The Changing Experience of Women', focusing mainly on women in Britain. You don't need any academic qualifications to do it, and it forms a half credit in any OU degree course.

Women, Planning, Architecture and Housing

In the same way that education maintains very male-oriented standards and goals, the built environment is almost exclusively a male-planned and male-built version of what 'people' are thought to need. In recent years women have started to point out that the clients of the professionals involved in the built environment may have different — and better — ideas about what is needed and how it might be provided.

Founded in 1981, the Matrix Feminist Design Co-operative works with women's groups in London to provide advice and training in architecture and encourage women's participation in the design process, as well as providing straightforward architectural services. They have also produced some interesting literature, such as *Building for Childcare: Making Better Buildings for the Under-5s, Jobs Designing Buildings*, and *Making Space*. The Women's Design Service is a technical aid agency providing a resource centre, library and consultancy service on issues related to women and the built environment. They publish a quarterly journal called *WEB* and a range of booklets and leaflets.

In some inner city areas there are now housing associations which exist to provide adequate and secure housing for single women with special needs. An umbrella organization for two such associations is Housing for Women in Westminster, which exists to provide decent housing for women in central London. Homeless Action provide accommodation for homeless women in London, and have more than twenty houses, each of which is run as a housing association. Homeless Action also works with local authorities to find long term housing for as many women as possible, and also acts as an advisory service, especially for young homeless women.

Matrix Feminist Design Co-operative
8 Bradbury Street
London
N16 8JN
0(7)1-249 7603

Women's Design Service
62 Beechwood Road
London
E8 3DY
0(7)1-241 6910

Housing for Women
8th Floor, Artillery House
Artillery Row
London SW1
0(7)1-799 2050

Homeless Action
52-54 Featherstone Street
London
EC1Y 8RT
0(7)1-251 6783

Women's Magazines

The quality of information and debate in many of Britain's 'women's interest' magazines has improved enormously in recent years, and it's rarely that *Cosmopolitan* or *Company* doesn't carry an article or two both well-written and well-reasoned. But I don't think either of these with their hundreds-of-thousands circulations needs a special plug in *New Green Pages*.

EVERYWOMAN

For a combination of readability, no-nonsense interviews and articles, lively style and plain engagement, I have been impressed with *Everywoman* since its first issue early in 1985. *Everywoman* appears monthly, published by a women's co-operative and available either by subscription or from your newsagents. The magazine is very approachable, and can be extremely witty.

SPARE Rib

Spare Rib is now nearly eighteen years old, completely confounding the detractors who said it would never make it beyond the first few issues. Subtitled 'A Women's Liberation Magazine', it unashamedly takes on each and every issue the women's movement finds itself tackling, which can lead to harsh words and recriminations, almost nothing of which (for better or worse) is censored. Whether it is the debate about lesbianism and heterosexism, or racism and anti-semitism, *Spare Rib* is rarely boring, even if at times it can be very frustrating, but there is still no better way of keeping up to date with the nitty gritty of what the women's movement is currently up to. While it is available in many newsagents (usually sandwiched between *Slimming* and *Vogue*), a subscription will guarantee your monthly copy.

Everywoman Ltd
34a Islington Green
London
N1 8DU
0(7)1-359 5496

Spare Rib
27 Clerkenwell Close
London
EC1R 0AT
0(7)1-253 9792

For a full list of feminist publications, see the 'Publications' listings at the end of the *Spare Rib Diary* (below).

The Spare Rib Diary

The annual *Spare Rib Diary* is to many feminists what *Housmans Peace Diary* (see page 268) is to pacifists, a diary to fill with activist appointments and meetings with friends, together with a detailed resource list of everything within the movement you might ever need to know. Like Housmans it has a different theme every year — the 1990 theme is 'Women of the World'. Forty pages of resources, a menstrual calendar, blank pages at the end for addresses — all for £4.99 from Spare Rib at the above address. Each year's new diary is available from mid-October onwards.

An Encyclopedia of Feminism

Lisa Tuttle has put together a fascinating collection of potted biographies, mini-histories of feminist organizations, and discussions of basic feminist ideas in this recently published reference book. The *Encyclopedia* is particularly strong on contemporary novelists, artists and activists, and on international women's organizations, though the entries on things like gender, motherhood and violence provide good introductions to these topics.

Piercy, Marge, 1936–
American poet and novelist. A political activist, she came to the women's liberation movement via the civil rights movement, and anti-war activities. Her poetry and novels reflect her politics and are concerned with the realities of women's lives today. Among her novels are WOMAN ON THE EDGE OF TIME (1976), in which she created a non-sexist UTOPIA, and *Vida* (1979) about the experiences of a political radical and fugitive in the America of the 1960s and 1970s. Her many collections of poetry include *To Be of Use* (1973), *The Moon is Always Female* (1980), and *Circles on the Water: Selected Poems* (1982). A collection of her essays, reviews and interviews, many of them concerned with women's writing, women's lives, and connections between feminist politics and culture, was published in 1982 as *Parti-Colored Blocks for a Quilt*.

Pilgrimage
Long novel by Dorothy RICHARDSON, published in thirteen volumes over the course of fifty-two years. It reveals, in stream-of-consciousness fashion, the experiences of the autobiographical Miriam Henderson as she comes to maturity between the 1890s and 1915. Most of the characters are based on people Richardson knew, including H. G. Wells who appears as 'Hypo Wilson', but the chief interest of the book is less in the people and events than in the viewpoint character's changing perceptions of reality. Writing contemporaneously with Proust and Joyce (a French critic later described the work as '*proustienne avant Proust*'), yet from a thoroughly female consciousness, Richardson found few readers sympathetic to her new and apparently difficult technique. The idea expressed in the book, that women perceive and live more deeply and truly than men, alienated some male critics, but Virginia Woolf, May Sinclair and others hailed the early volumes as evidence of a welcome development in the art of the novel. A rediscovery, and re-evaluation, of *Pilgrimage* began in the mid-1970s, and no one in search of a female aesthetic can afford to ignore it.

Encyclopedia of Feminism
Lisa Tuttle
Arrow, 1987
£6.95

Womanspirit

Women's spirituality has always taken many forms, from the selfless service of women like Mother Theresa in the slums of Calcutta to the wisdom and joyful sisterhood of white witch-craft and the daily witness of Quaker women at the gates of Greenham Common air base. Yet even (and often especially) in the spiritual realm, men have frequently told women how they should be, and it is men who have dominated the hierarchies of organized religion. Even in the early 1990s there is sufficient opposition to women in the Anglican priesthood for it to be considered by some an issue worth splitting the church for.

A fundamental tenet of green thinking is that each of us should be free to choose our own ways of expressing and sharing our spiritual lives. After centuries of domination by 'men's religion', many women are rejecting the models of religion and spirituality they grew up with and are exploring new ways.

A great deal of the debate has taken place in the USA, though it rapidly filters across the Atlantic. Hence the books mentioned here are American. In Britain, women's spirituality is intimately tied in with the women's peace movement (see page 266) and with women's therapy — but then, spirit permeates everything we do.

Spirituality and Politics

In the States more than anywhere else, the spirituality/politics dialogue has become an artform. Most women that I talk to about it have no problem in stressing the importance of both spirituality and politics, yet at the same time see the balance frequently tipping into 'sloppy' spirituality or hard-line political positioning. Many of the issues — from matriarchy to mythology — are aired in this thick collection of essays edited by Charlene Spretnak, a leading light in the emerging US green movement.

*

At the moments when I have acted assertively, or downright aggressively when faced with physical violence, I did not feel 'masculine' in any fiber of my being; I simply felt like a strong woman. Likewise, I imagine that when men give nurturing and affection, they do not feel 'feminine'; they are simply being loving men. Moreover, the New Age rallying cry of 'Balance the masculine and feminine parts of your mind in order to be whole' has actually accomplished very little.

The Politics of Women's Spirituality
edited by Charlene Spretnak
Harper and Row, 1982
around £10.50

Dreaming the Dark

Starhawk is a therapist, a political activist and a witch. She is also an extremely good writer. *Dreaming the Dark* uses insights from all three strands of her experience to put together an exploration of personal power and magic which makes complete sense without being condescending, pedantic, jargonistic or spiritually wishy-washy. For me the two most practical aspects of *Dreaming the Dark* are Starhawk's thoughts about the importance of personal power, and her suggestions about creating powerful harmony within groups. She is also excellent on sexual liberation and on the importance of ritual. Primarily a book by a woman for women, *Dreaming the Dark* is in no way anti-men, though Starhawk will plough ruthlessly through any sexist assumptions you may have about the power of women. Not easy to get hold of, being an American book (it's distributed in Britain by Harper and Row), but definitely an ovular work.

Dreaming the Dark
Magic, Sex and Politics
Starhawk
Beacon Press, 1982
around £5.50

Women and Therapy

While there are issues relating to sexism which are best looked at in mixed groupwork, when it comes to therapy many women prefer to work with a woman therapist or in women-only groups. Sheila Ernst and Lucy Goodison's book *In Our Own Hands* (see page 170) is the key book here, full of sound and very practical advice; Anne Dickson's books on assertiveness for women (see page 173) are excellent too. The main centre for women's therapy in Britain is The Women's Therapy Centre, who will probably be able to suggest a woman therapist if you tell them what you need. For a very readable account of the role of feminist psychoanalysis by two women who helped to start the Centre, try Luise Eichenbaum and Susie Orbach's *Understanding Women* (Penguin, 1985, £4.50). Also in London is the London Women's Therapy Network — in neither the Centre nor the Network is heterosexuality assumed.

The Women's Therapy Centre
6 Manor Gardens
London
N7 6LA
0(7)1-263 6200

London Women's Therapy Network
3 Carysfort Road
London
N16 9AA
0(7)1-249 7846
(contact number for North London)
0(8)1-855 2510
(contact number for South London)

Women and Work

Women's domestic work is closely bound in with discrimination against women in paid work. Careers, training, promotion and pay are still centred on full-time continuous working lives which allow nothing for the changing demands of responsibilities at home. As a result London's women workers are cut off from better jobs and better pay. Of all London's skilled, professional and managerial jobs, women account for only 11%, but make up 59% of the so-called semi-skilled and unskilled labour force. . . It is one of the paradoxes of our present society that while private companies and states grow ever larger and more centralised in their planning of labour, domestic work and consumption are becoming ever more isolated. For an economics centred around finance these issues are marginal. For an economics centred round need they should be our starting point.

London Industrial Strategy, GLC, 1985

Finding Work

In her book *Job Hunting for Women*, Margaret Wallis quotes an American author who says: 'If you don't know where you're going you'll probably end up somewhere else.' Deciding what you want to do which will fulfil your ambitions and make enough money to fulfil your basic needs can often seem well nigh impossible, but there are some places to turn to for help. The Training Agency (which used to be the Manpower Services Commission) produces a wide variety of helpful literature for women looking for work, particularly women who have trained in a profession and are looking for ways back in after raising a family.

Training Agency
Moorfoot
Sheffield
S1 4PQ
0742 753275

Most of the ideas you will find in the 'Work' section of *New Green Pages* are well-suited to flexible ways of working — flexitime, co- operatives, and job sharing for instance. The book I mentioned above, Margaret Wallis's *Job Hunting for Women*, is straight and straightforward, concentrating on full-time work in conventional careers, but it doesn't ignore discrimination in education and in the workplace. The lengthy and fascinating statistical survey at the end of the book shows how the proportion of women is increasing in most professions, but at the same time how very far there is still to go in reaching real equality.

Job Hunting for Women
Margaret Wallis
Kogan Page, 1987
£4.95

Women's Businesses

In the 1986 edition of *What do Graduates Do?* by Margaret Dane, a graph shows that in the last twelve years there has been a very significant increase in the proportion of women graduates going into business, an increase which is particularly marked in certain areas of activity like private practice, commerce, manufacturing and building. Together with a renewed (and very necessary) emphasis on co-operative working and community businesses, which actively encourage women to organize work in flexible ways conducive to their needs, there has been a flowering of women's businesses in recent years.

Once women's businesses are visible women can encourage each other by putting work their way, and networks can be established so that these new businesses are not isolated. To this end, *Everywoman* magazine (see page 197) has produced *Women Mean Business*, a directory of women's co-operatives and other enterprises (£3.95 plus 55p p+p).

There are also several networks of women working in particular trades. One particularly active group is the Women In Construction Advisory Group, which aims to open up women's access to jobs and training in the trades associated with the construction industry.

Women In Construction Advisory Group
South Bank House
Black Prince Road
London
SE1 7SJ
0(7)1-587 1802

Women and Computing

Computers are designed specifically to do repetitive jobs without complaining, and the cynical might point out that women have been fulfilling this role for centuries. It is women who assemble most of the computers in the world — a very repetitive job — but at the same time traditional 'female' skills like typing have been given a new lease of life as the keyboard can now provide access to vast amounts of information and communications possibilities.

Microsyster is a six-woman consultancy set up to provide computer training, advice and support for women's groups in London. Microsyster provides a home address for the excellent quarterly *Women and Computing Newsletter*, which is always full of very practical and pertinent news and information; a subscription currently costs £6 a year. They also administer the London Women's Mailing List, a database of active women's groups in the capital, and the National Women in Computing Register, which helps women in computing to stay in touch with each other.

At the same address the Women's Computer Centre organizes computer training, both for beginners and for more experienced operators. They can also provide advice on careers, and the Centre houses a library and a drop-in centre where you can go if you'd like a quick hands-on to see what a computer feels like. Write for a copy of their booklet, *Working with Computers*.

Women Into Computing was initiated by a group of university and polytechnic teachers concerned at the falling numbers of women entering computing courses at every level of education. As well as providing encouragement and support, WIC sees the involvement of more women in computing as being vital when it comes to decisions about the uses to which computers are put. There are six regional contacts; your initial contact should be with Barbara Segal on 0(7)1-380 7212.

Microsyster
Wesley House
4 Wild Court
Holborn
London
WC2B 5AU
0(7)1-430 0655

Women's Computer Centre Ltd
Third Floor
Wesley House
4 Wild Court
Holborn
London
WC2B 5AU
0(7)1-430 0112

The Other Half

Most of the knowledge produced in our society has been produced by men; they have usually generated the explanations and the schemata and have then checked with each other and vouched for the accuracy and adequacy of their view of the world. They have created men's studies, for, by not acknowledging that they are presenting only the explanations of men, they have 'passed off' this knowledge as human knowledge. Women have been excluded as the producers of knowledge and as the subjects of knowledge.

Dale Spender, *Men's Studies Modified*, Pergamon, 1981

Balancing the Language

'Only recently have we become aware that conventional English usage, including the generic use of masculine-gender words, often obscures the actions, the contributions and sometimes the very presence of women', say Casey Miller and Kate Swift near the beginning of *The Handbook of Non-Sexist Writing*. 'Turning our backs on that insight is an option, of course, but it is an option like teaching children the world is flat.'

Writers brought up on the Victorian rules which insist that 'man' embraces 'woman' find endless mirth in new words like 'spokesperson', yet apparently without seeing the illogic in a title like 'Development of the Uterus in Rats, Guinea Pigs, and Men'. *The Handbook of Non-Sexist Writing* looks at this and much more as it shows how non-sexist language is not a clumsy way of rectifying balance in the Ennglish language; it involves recognizing where our language is male-dominated, and neatly and elegantly using alternative constructions which make the meaning clear without making sexist assumptions.

The Handbook of Non-Sexist Writing for Writers, Editors and Speakers
Casey Miller and Kate Swift
Women's Press, 1988 (2nd edn)
£4.95

Balancing History

Rosalind Miles has, in less than 350 pages, largely succeeded in rewriting history. In *The Women's History Of The World* she shows again and again how women and women's concerns have been instrumental in bringing about change and reform in a world which, even two and a half millennia ago, was overwhelmingly controlled by what she calls the 'phallusy' of patriarchal power. She writes fluently, passionately, and with both wit and wisdom, so you will hardly notice the drawbacks of squeezing 300,000 years into a medium-sized paperback. Generalizations are kept to a minimum, and it is the specifics that stay with you — the American missionary Anna Shaw's escape from a fellow traveller and would-be rapist, Queen Olga of Russia's born-again Christianity and the resulting reign of terror ('the more sophisticated of the women under the early monotheisms speedily grasped that her God in fact offered a post-dated cheque, and no one had ever come back to claim that it had bounced').

*

Not infrequently women's resistance to masculine control was expressed directly, even violently, as the Roman senators found to their cost in 215 BC, when to curb inflation they passed a law forbidding women to own more than half an ounce of gold, wear multi-coloured dresses or ride in a two-horse carriage. As the word spread, crowds of rioting women filled the Capitol and raged through every street of the city, and neither the rebukes of the magistrates nor the threats of their husbands could make them return quietly to their homes. Despite the fierce opposition of the notorious anti-feminist Cato, the law was repealed in what must have been one of the earliest victories for sisterhood and solidarity.

*

For the earth still has to be won. The removal of most of the more blatant of the injustices against women has served to concentrate. After the euphoria of the first handful of spectacular triumphs, late twentieth-century feminism has come to terms with the fact that, with every battle won, the enemy regroups elsewhere; new oppressions emerge, which like their predecessors are only symptoms and expressions of more fundamental inequalities whose roots are hard enough to identify, let alone remove. With a sense of history sharpened by repeated disappointment, women are coming to see the essentially repetitive nature of their struggle; to understand, too, that the circumstances under which they win rights and freedoms in themselves can undermine those very rights and freedoms so painfully won.

The Women's History Of The World
Rosalind Miles
Paladin, 1989
£4.99

Taking Back Our Space

The text can be daunting, but the 2,000 photographs in Marianne Wex's monumental study of male and female body postures will on their own ensure that you never again take for granted the way you sit on a park bench or lie on the beach. If you hadn't already noticed, you will learn how men all too often expand to fill the available space, while women daintily make themselves as small and as inconsequential as possible — unless they are being posed by men, when sexual invitation is the name of the game. Marianne Wex's book will almost certainly be the one your visitors pick up from the coffee table pile, and is excellent value too.

"Masculine"

"Feminine"

Let's Take Back Our Space
Marianne Wex
Frauenliteraturverlag Hermine Fees, 1979
(distributed in Britain by Element)
£5.50

Women, Men and Violence

Women are trained to be rape victims. To simply learn the word 'rape' is to take instruction in the power relationship between males and females. To talk about rape, even with nervous laughter, is to acknowledge woman's special victim status. We hear the whispers when we are children: girls get raped. Not boys. The message becomes clear. Rape has something to do with our sex. Rape is something awful that happens to females: it is the dark at the top of the stairs, the indefinable abyss that is just around the corner, and unless we watch our step it might become our destiny.

Susan Brownmiller, Against Our Will (see below)

Violence is a complex issue, but more and more people are recognizing that violence is not simply a given in society, an unfortunate but occasional occurrence that has always been with us and always will.

People — including men — are not violent 'by nature'. They are taught to be violent, and given the will and the resources, can learn nonviolent ways of behaving. Neither are women by nature 'victims', having every bit as much right to feel at home in their environment as men.

Following Susan Brownmiller's 1975 study of rape, many women and some men have looked at the issue of violence in an attempt to understand it and see what can be done to rid society of its excesses. Here is a selection of their conclusions.

Against Our Will

The main theme of Susan Brownmiller's study of rape is that in a society where violence against women is encouraged and even romanticized, violence against women is a pervasive undercurrent in all relationships between the sexes. All women are at risk and all men are potential rapists. Her approach is historical and thematic, discussing war ('you know, it makes the boys feel good'), racism ('rape was an insurrectionary act'), and — central to her thesis — the myth of the heroic rapist. *Against Our Will* is passionate and horrible, but ultimately optimistic. As she says at the end: 'My purpose in this book has been to give rape its history. Now we must deny it a future.'

Against Our Will
Men, Women and Rape
Susan Brownmiller
Penguin, 1986
£4.95

What Is To Be Done About Violence Against Women?

In the last ten years a great deal has been done to raise general awareness about the linked issues of rape, incest, sexual harassment, domestic violence, pornography and prostitution. There are now few places in Britain beyond the reach of a rape crisis centre, and there are far more refuges than there were for the survivors of violence. There has been some progress in campaigning for better legal and official handling of cases involving violence; some men's groups (see page 189) now offer counselling and rehabilitation for men who want to change their violent behaviour. But there is far more still to be done.

Elizabeth Wilson's book on violence against women is a good overview of the present scene in Britain, describing many of the initiatives of the past few years. It doesn't, however, tell you how you as a woman can deal with violence when you come up against it, and doesn't include addresses and phone numbers. For more detailed information the handbook put together by the women of the London Rape Crisis Centre called *Sexual Violence: The Reality for Women* is an excellent source, covering every aspect of sexual violence against women, from the legal jargon to advice about sexually transmitted diseases.

What Is To Be Done About Violence Against Women?
Elizabeth Wilson
Penguin, 1983
£2.50

Sexual Violence: The Reality for Women
London Rape Crisis Centre
Women's Press, 1988
£4.95

Rape Crisis Centres in Britain

Most crisis centres are not supervised all the time, though most have a 24-hour answering service. The London centre is open 24 hours a day. For more detailed information ring the London Rape Crisis Centre on 0(7)1-837 1600, though remember that each centre is run independently.

Birmingham	021 233 2122	Inverness	0463 233089
Bradford	0274 308270	Leeds	0532 440058
Brighton	0273 203773	Liverpool	051 727 7599
Cambridge	0223 358314	Luton	0582 33426
Carlisle	0228 36500	Manchester	061 228 3602
Central Scotland	0786 71771	Norwich	0603 667687
Cleveland	0642 225787	Nottingham	0602 410440
Coventry	0203 677229	Oxford	0865 726295
Dorset	0305 772295	Portsmouth	0705 669511
Dundee	0382 201291	Sheffield	0742 755255
Edinburgh	031 556 9437	South Wales	0222 373181
Glasgow	041 221 8448	Tyneside	0632 329858

The Women's Aid Federation has a network of refuges throughout Britain offering support or temporary safety for women and children who have suffered domestic abuse of any kind. The three many ones are listed here — they will be able to put you in contact with more local refuges.

England	0272 428368
Scotland	031 225 8011
Wales	0222 390874

Men and Violence

See page 205 for more information about men and violence. A useful handbook for men who want to look at their violent behaviour (and women who want to know if it's really possible for men to change), is Daniel Sonkin and Michael Durphy's *Learning to Live Without Violence*. Though it is American and a bit chatty in its style, it does give some insight into how violence might be tackled at root — within the male psyche, and within male behaviour.

Learning to Live Without Violence
Daniel Jay Sonkin and Michael Durphy
Volcano, 1982 (distributed in Britain by Airlift)
£8.95

WELL SUE...

The Mothers of Men

In *All That . . .*, a tongue-in-cheek feminist view of history written by Kate Charlesworth and Marsaili Cameron (Pandora, 1986, £5.95), there is a cartoon of two women looking at a 1917 vintage school essay. One reads aloud to the other '"Little boys grow up to be soldiers and little girls to be mothers who have little boys who grow up to be soldiers . . ."— it's neat,' she says, 'I'll grant you that.'

This dilemma is examined in detail by Judith Arcana in her book *Every Mother's Son*, where she asks whether it will ever be possible to bring up boys in a non-sexist way. Prompted by her experiences with her twelve-year-old son Daniel, this is a beautifully written and thought-provoking account of the dilemmas faced by any mother who wants her son to grow up respecting himself and the women he relates with — his mother among them.

*

If sons can recognize that there is no danger to them inherent in the mother, discarding the layers of masculinity that cover their humanity, and if mothers will undertake the painful struggle to restore our integrity as women, then mothers and sons can begin to break the constraints of fear and anger between us. We cannot live the lives the great-grandmothers lived, long times ago; women know this. And we know that men have gone far away from us; they have replaced their ancient respect for the mother with a desperate and abusive need of women. They have become aliens, strangers to their past and to our present. But when we learn that it has not always been so, we know that it need not always be so.

Every Mother's Son
The Role of Mothers
in the Making of Men
Judith Arcana
Women's Press, 1983
£4.95

A couple of years before *Every Mother's Son*, Judith Arcana wrote *Our Mother's Daughters* (Women's Press, 1981, £4.95), a collection of interviews with a linking narrative, showing the amazing variety of women's earliest and often most formative relationship. As in *Every Mother's Son*, she stresses the importance of learning from the relationship, and not blaming our parents for what we have become.

The Problems of Men

On the cover of this unique collection is a little man in a grey raincoat saying 'We'll sue . . .', though I find it hard to imagine a man who isn't secretly interested in finding out what women really think about the whole subject of Men. Though mixed in style, approach and readability, there will certainly be something in the two dozen pieces in *On the Problem of Men* which will interest any reader, female or male. Jill Lewis's 'Politics of Monogamy' addresses a rarely discussed issue, Diana Leonard's 'Male Feminists and Divided Women' warns us to beware of he who is righter-on-than-thou, and my favourite, Jan Bradshaw's 'What Are They Up To Now?', provides an honest and searching women's angle on the activities of anti-sexist men's groups.

*

Anyway, most men aren't in any political group and lots of women want them to stay that way. A set of agreed demands on men in general would be a way of getting ourselves together too. I'll give an example of the kind of dilemma that comes up in my life — how do I express my own personal feminism in an uncompromised way to men, without in practice putting other women down? The problem comes at me several ways:
— Do I admit criticisms of Margaret Thatcher when a man is around?
— Do I admit to any disagreement with any feminist position that differs from mine in a pro-male direction?
— Do I confront a woman whose stated position I totally agree with, but who cancels out her words by flirting or dressing in ways I have stopped doing for political reasons?
Amanda Sebestyen,
'Sexual Assumptions in the Women's Movement'

On the Problem of Men
edited by Scarlet Friedman and Elizabeth Sarah
Women's Press, 1982
£4.95

The Fathers of Children

A few years ago a West German men's collective produced an excellent little book called *Das Vaterbuch* (*The Fathers' Book*), a collection of pieces both practical and personal, some of them very moving. I have watched in vain for a British book along the same lines, only to be rewarded with a handbook for fathers called *Shared Parenthood* — by a woman.

It's very good as far as it goes, paralleling Sheila Kitzinger's *Pregnancy and Childbirth* (see page 211) very closely but keeping the father in mind all the time. It's certainly a comforting, reassuring book, which makes the whole thing approachable for fathers who might have been too embarrassed to be seen reading 'women's books', but the title is misleading (it's about childbirth and babyhood rather than parenthood in general), and the other book still needs to be written.

Shared Parenthood
A Handbook for Fathers
Johanna Roeber
Century, 1987
£5.95

Men, by Women

The last few years have seen the publication of several books on men by women. It is frequently suggested that men speak more freely to women about the things that bother them than they will to other men, which provides something of a rationale for these books. On the other hand, answering questions into a microphone then being transcribed rarely gives men the chance either to communicate clearly and in depth about their thoughts and feelings, or to expand little snippets of their lives into a coherent and gripping story.

Thus these books rarely give any real depth to the male characters they portray; what comes across is a mess of attitudes and experiences cut together by the editor to make a narrative which makes some sort of sense. But there is a value to each of these books, and enough difference between them to make them all worth dipping into.

Mary Ingham's *Men* was first on the scene, and is still one of the best. The interviews are kept to a minimum, so the book is largely Mary Ingham's own observations on the role and position of men in contemporary Britain.

*

Yet men actually seem to know very few women, aside from women to whom they are related, or women with whom they are involved, women in a particular kind of role relationship towards them — mother, sister, wife. Few men had ever worked with women as colleagues, on a level with them, and most men regarded the suggestion that they might have 'female friends' as an attempt to discover whether they had ever been unfaithful to their wives. Perhaps because the male is always supposed to be on the look-out for sex, most men regarded the idea of close friendship with a woman as unthinkable, almost an infidelity in itself.

Men
Mary Ingham
Century, 1985
£2.95

Apparently only Dennis Thatcher and the Archbishop of Canterbury declined to be interviewed by Anna Ford for her survey of men. Well over half of the text is transcribed interviews, though the book is rather predictable: I leave it to you to judge whether this is the result of the author's predictable questions or her respondents' predictable replies.

Deidre Sanders' *Men* is a collation of the answers received from five thousand men who responded to a questionnaire in *Woman* magazine — ' A book about ordinary blokes' says the cover blurb. It's shallow in places, but it's the nearest that anyone in Britain has come to the mammoth American *Hite Report* (see below), and very readable if taken in small doses and with a pinch of salt.

Men
Anna Ford
Corgi, 1986
£2.95

**The Woman
Report on Men**
Deirdre Sanders
Sphere, 1987
£2.95

Slow Motion

If Lynne Segal's last book, *Is The Future Female?* (see page 187), helped women to think clearly about the achievements of twenty years of feminism, *Slow Motion* brings the same spotlight to bear on men. Subtitled 'Changing Masculinities, Changing Men', it examines the complex and often contradictory web of roles that men feel they have to play in a changed world, where many of the old rules simply don't apply any more. While Lynne Segal is always worth reading, her 'men' book is less fluent, less coherent and less sure of itself than her 'women' one, and I suspect the difference isn't just in the editing. Even her insight finds it hard to reconcile the fact that men do seem to want to change, yet when it comes to the practicalities — either of domestic or public life — almost every survey shows that it's business very much as usual.

Slow Motion
Changing Masculinities, Changing Men
Lynne Segal
Virago, 1990
£6.99

The Hite Report

In 1977 the American sociologist Shere Hite published the book about women's attitudes to sex and intimacy which riveted millions of readers with its clear and revealing answers to a carefully thought out questionnaire. Four years later came the 'male' volume, *The Hite Report on Male Sexuality*, a brick of a volume with over 1,100 pages, which looked at men's experiences and attitudes in response to an even more detailed questionnaire.

Male Sexuality takes 'sexuality' wider than the original report, to look at relationships, marriage, feelings towards women, and men's thoughts about women's liberation. The responses are quoted at length, and the impression is that the men are really being allowed to speak from their hearts, rather than having the odd juicy sentence picked out for the reader's delectation as in Deirdre Sanders' book (above).

A new and much expanded version of the Hite report on female sexuality, *Women and Love*, was published early in 1988 (Viking, £14.95) — it's fascinating to see the changes that have taken place in the last ten years.

The Hite Report on Male Sexuality
Shere Hite
Optima, 1990 (new edn)
£7.99

Men, by Men

There is a great temptation to leave this page blank, such a dearth is there of well-written, compelling, witty, human, heartfelt writing by men about the experience of being a man. There is almost nothing that can be recommended whole-heartedly, and it isn't for want of looking. In many respects an autobiography like Bob Geldof's *Is That It?* (Penguin, 1986, £3.95) comes closest — more honest, funny, unpretentious autobiography would go a long way to balancing the heavy academic soul-searching which constitutes so much of 'men's studies'.

The Sexuality of Men

This is the one collection which comes close to being readable and engaging all the way through. Andy Metcalf and Martin Humphries have brought together nine pieces about men's experiences of manhood, and the still of a determined and pensive bound Clint Eastwood on the cover neatly sums up the approach — no-nonsense but not quite sure what to do next.

Particularly good is Richard Dyer's 'Male sexuality in the media' (Dr Who will never be the same again), and Vic Seidler's 'Fear and Intimacy' is the closest I know in men's writing to the passion and poetry of the best feminist writing.

*

I can hear the cry of anger and frustration as it is directed at me. It is all too familiar, and even though I pretend to understand it intellectually, I am always surprised and shocked when this happens. I recognize that something is terribly wrong but I don't really know what to do about it. I'm shaken by the fury and the bitterness. I find it hard to accept that things can be that bad, though I know at some level they are. Part of me just wants to flee or withdraw. It is as if all long-term heterosexual relationships in our time are doomed. For all my efforts at a more equal relationship I have to recognize how blind and insensitive I am. It is harder to know what to do about it.

Vic Seidler

"thoroughly engaging" Susie Orbach

The sexuality of men
edited by
Andy Metcalf and Martin Humphries

Pluto Press

The Sexuality of Men
edited by Andy Metcalf and Martin Humphries
Pluto, 1985
£4.50

Men Against Sexism

One of the few authors to inspire me when it comes to exploring how men can rise creatively and joyfully to the challenge of picking up the ravelled ends of masculinity is the American John Stoltenberg. Several of his pieces, including the classic 'Refusing to be a Man', appear in a late 1970s collection from the Californian publishing house Times Change. Though not now in print, it is well worth searching out a copy of this little book (and any other Times Change titles you may come across, like *Unbecoming Men* and Su Negrin's fluent and heartwarming *Begin at Start*).

*

The truth of my body and the sexual ethics of my life have nothing in common with the lies of the culture in which I live. I am male, but I endeavor with my heart to rid my life of male sexual behavior programming. My body never accepted that programming in the first place. I used to think there was something wrong with me. Now I'm dead certain there's something wrong with the program. My body doesn't lie.

For Men Against Sexism
A Book of Readings
edited by Jon Snodgrass
Times Change, 1977
(out of print)

The Heartsearching of the New Man

A male friend, an academic, recently told me how delighted he was that so many men's books had appeared recently. Like which, I asked, so he gave me a list. After a great deal of effort I managed to get hold of several and, after a great deal more effort, managed to plough through some of them. And that's the problem. How many men are going to struggle with 'the distinction between precapitalist and capitalist patriarchy', or a 'constitutive conception of language'?

I can't pretend that any of them grabbed me, at least not in any more than very small doses. The same Vic Seidler that wrote the moving piece in *The Sexuality of Men* (above) has written *Rediscovering Masculinity*, but though there are some telling passages he uses too many words and forgets that most other people aren't, unlike him, trained sociologists. Then there is a recent collection of American writing called *New Men, New Minds*. Some of the contributors, like my hero John Stoltenberg, are up to scratch, but there are a lot of hangers-on (and the proofreading's pretty appalling). So I'm still searching . . .

*

We are no less men because we have learnt to identify our needs to be held and touched.

Victor Seidler

*

Some of us are the other men that some of us are very wary of. Some of us are the other men that some of us don't trust. Yet some of us are the other men that some of us want to be close to and hang out with. Some of us are the other men that some of us long to embrace. The world of other men is a world in which we live behind a barrier — because we need to for safety, because we understand there is something about other men that we know we have to protect ourselves from.

John Stoltenberg

Rediscovering Masculinity
Reason, Language and Sexuality
Victor Seidler
Routledge, 1989
£9.95

New Men, New Minds
Breaking Male Tradition
edited by Franklin Abbott
Crossing Press, 1987
(distributed in the UK by Airlift)
£6.95

Men for Change

Brotherly hugs are not enough! I've now been involved in the men's movement for three years, and it seems to me that Men Against Sexism has reached the stage where its ideas and concepts are . . . becoming part of a new trendyism. . . In general its ideas are becoming something to be seen and presented, rather than lived. . . One particular example is the showing of brotherly affection: this is something that's almost expected nowadays in anti-sexist circles. It's . . . my impression that it's one thing we do because we feel we're supposed to rather than because it's what we want to do. It isn't necessarily very radical in itself . . . it can be just a reconfirmation of hetero-sexual maleness. . . This affection has to be real, not just a pose in the credibility game of the trendy left. . . The only answer to this watering down and distortion is to keep on increasing the radicality and relevance of our ideas out of our rather cliquey groups into the general awareness. . . It's a question of not being afraid of being extreme, of really confronting people with the sickness of the world and the harm that certain attitudes cause.

KCL, letter to *Men's Antisexist Newsletter*, Spring 1985

Men's Antisexist Newsletter

The longest-running, and best, of the occasional magazines and newsletters put together by men which addresses the issues of men and sexism. It appears every six months or so, and each issue is produced by men in a different area — it has recently been produced in Leamington and Leicester, though the contact point is in Cardiff. It's very hard to get the tone of a magazine like this right, and *MAN* doesn't have the confidence of the feminist magazines (see page 197), but it isn't afraid of taking on difficult issues, including hard-hitting criticism. The news items and list of men's groups in Britain are the most comprehensive available, and *MAN* will put you in touch with your local contact if you write to them.

*

I didn't notice him at first sitting across the gangway from me. He was by the window, late forties I'd say, fairly ordinary really, trying to talk to a woman across the table. I half turned away but was quite shocked as I heard him speak '. . . my wife and children are dead . . .' dropping four rail tickets onto the table as he said it. . . Quite impulsively I got up and changed seats to sit next to him not really knowing what I was going to say. The embarrassed young woman opposite was clearly relieved and

disappeared behind her book. 'What happened?' . . . (it sounded so inane). 'My wife and sons were killed yesterday in a car crash.' There it was, as clear and as stark as that. The railway tickets taken from his wallet were for them . . . I asked him their names. Very slowly little bits started to come out, names, what they did together, how well the children were doing at school. I reached out to take his hand . . .

Men's Antisexist Newsletter
60 Rhymney Street
Cathays
Cardiff
CF2 4DG

Achilles Heel

Achilles Heel has recently re-emerged after a period of dormancy, put together by a Sheffield-based men's collective. In the past I have found *AH* hard going and a bit humourless, and some of the same features (me and my new baby, how I like wearing frocks) keep turning up time and time again. The latest issue, however, included some fascinating comparison photographs of a man and a woman of similar height and build wearing a range of clothes both very gender-specific and unisex — a graphic and thought-provoking exercise. I hope the next long-awaited issue will maintain the improvement.

Achilles Heel
34 Rivelin Street
Sheffield
S6 5DL
0742 311548

Men for Change

Another newsletter that has recently been relaunched, designed to put like-minded men in touch with each other and with activities, information and events throughout the country. The newsletter, which comes out quarterly, contains some worthwhile articles and reviews.

Men for Change
15 Milverton Terrace
Leamington Spa
Warwickshire
CV32 5BE
0926 334155

There are more or less active men's groups all over the country, varying enormously in format, organization and practicality. MOVE (Men Overcoming Violence) groups deal specifically with domestic violence and provide a help telephone line and one-to-one or group counselling for men who are being violent towards women. MOVE is currently most active in West Yorkshire, where the contact phone number is 0204 364550. The Men's Centre in London (0(7)1-267 8713) offers the same service.

A Scottish men's network has recently been established under the aegis of the Scottish Health Education Group's 'Better Health for Men' campaign. A recent 'Men Together' day in Edinburgh brought together more than sixty men to look at personal growth and relationship issues.

Men Together
c/o Jim Griffin
9 Brunswick Street
Edinburgh
EH7 5JB
031 557 2448

Sex

Sex is a problem. But this is neither because men are by nature sexually aggressive and coercive, nor because women have lost touch with their own natural sexuality which, rediscovered, would be wonderful. Sex is still a problem because whatever the current sexological steps to orgasmic happiness, at a more fundamental level many of the ideologies surrounding 'sex' have remained unchanged over the last hundred years. What we call sexual behaviour is still concealed from children, confined to a very special area of life, cut off from other activities, and acceptable only in certain kinds of relationship. It is still surrounded by taboos, shame, disgust and fear. Above all, sex remains the endorsement of gender. Language creates sex as the symbol of the male and the female. And whatever the questioning which is going on, and whatever the tolerance for 'deviance', sexuality is still seen in terms of its reproductive functioning, symbolised by a genital heterosexuality which men initiate and control.
Lynne Segal, in Sex and Love (see below)

Male (and Female) Sexuality

There aren't many books about sex which are both profound and funny. Surveyors of the radical therapy scene will almost certainly have come across Jenny James' outspoken books on the importance of crashing straight through painful inhibitions, and her latest volume on *Male Sexuality* is no exception. The book is in three parts. The first consists of thumbnail sketches of the main 'male character patterns': The Married Romeo, The Armdangler, The Philosophy Lecturer . . . Part Two lets seven men give their extended thoughts on their own sexuality and how it affects their relationships with women, while the last section is a relationship alphabet, from 'antics' to 'zen'. A mix of a book that may annoy you but won't leave you unmoved.

*

A while ago I developed the idea that rather than look for love relationships, I should be glad to find hate relationships. Because when we can hate each other hotly and energetically, the love and sex that flow are much better than the rather tense, insecure feeling of maybe losing a love relationship. With love, you stand to lose everything. With hate, you stand to lose only your temper.

Male Sexuality: The Atlantis Position
Jenny James
Caliban, 1988
£4.95

Sex and Love

'This is the book for which generations of women have been waiting', says the back cover, and it isn't just women who will find a great deal of wisdom and stimulation in this collection of fourteen essays by women on the dual themes of sex and love. Tricia Bickerton's 'Women Alone' is the best discussion I have read on the issues facing women who choose to live on their own in a society where 'the choice to live alone' is seen as a contradiction in terms, but my favourite is Lucy Goodison's 'Really Being in Love means Wanting to Live in a Different World', which makes it clear how contradictory versions of 'love' have confused an area of our lives which we know is crucial but never seem able to get right.

*

We use the term 'falling' in love which disguises the fact that we have chosen to leap and have abdicated responsibility for our experience. The feelings, fantasies and sensations that possess us are in fact our own. We say that another 'makes' us feel unbelievable excitement, but actually the excitement is ours. If we feel it in one situation, we can feel it in another.

Sex and Love
New Thoughts On Old Contradictions
edited by Sue Cartledge and Joanna Ryan
Women's Press, 1985
£5.95

The Sexual Fix

'The intravenous injection of a drug' is the most recently-coined meaning of 'fix', and Stephen Heath's witty and passionate book makes it clear that the popular association of sex and drugs is by no means coincidental. We live in a society which is supposed to be grateful to the sexologists for having liberated sex, yet which is riddled with contradictions about sexuality. Books, films, televisions and advice columns all tell us that there is no reason why we shouldn't be getting our fix at the prescribed dosage and frequency, without daring to look at the shaky historical and cultural scaffolding holding up the assumptions. Not a book for the fainthearted or squeamish.

*

And inevitably the 'oh, horror!' stories [in sex manuals] are accompanied by 'well done!' ones in which, as though from some interminable American family TV series, model adults and model children do model things, like reading sexology books: 'Walter intimated that Michael was spending several hours each afternoon reading Everything You Always Wanted to Know About Sex. His mother, with a twinkle in her eye, confronted Michael, who readily admitted to his research. He giggled and said, It's not going to be any of that three-minute stuff for me.' Mother was convulsed with laughter. Michael was an unlikely candidate for sex therapy.' Well done, Mother! Well done, Michael! Twinkle, giggle, super lover.

The Sexual Fix
Stephen Heath
Macmillan, 1982
£4.95

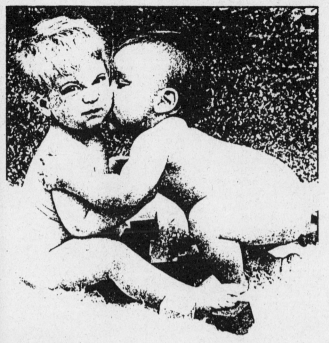

Relating

The complexity of human relationships hasn't deterred commentators on the human situation from writing about them, but there is little that can be recommended. The literature tends either towards a shallow 'think yourself attractive' approach, or follows Desmond Morris's pseudo-scientific 'manwatching'.

If you are looking for something that might actually help you sort your life out, the practical help is likely to come from looking into therapy (see pages 169-174), or from reading the accounts of people who have met life head on and dealt with what came up for them — three outstanding books are the subject of the reviews below. As well as autobiography, novels are often an excellent way of exploring issues; far from merely being escapist, a story like Keri Hulme's *The Bone People*, Marge Piercy's *Braided Lives* or David Storey's *Pasmore* says far more about the complexities of real relationships than any amount of generalized advice.

Combat

I would very much like to see Ingrid Bengis 1973 classic *Combat in the Erogenous Zone* reissued before long. It has lost nothing of the fire that caused Susan Brownmiller to start her review of it: 'So goddam brilliant!'. And it has lost none of its relevance either, as many women continue to admit that the first word that comes to mind in their dealings with men is 'frustration'. Ingrid Bengis's book is a painfully honest account of her experiences in relationships with men and women.

*

Hands, mouths and genitals speak as loudly as voices. There is in them the articulation of everything that otherwise remains mute within us. They describe every arc of feeling of which we are capable. But within each relationship they describe something singular and personalized, something that can be translated only within the context of so many other aspects of being close to another human being. I cannot be free sexually with a man I don't know well or feel deeply for, partly because of simple reserve and partly because everything I have to say with my body takes a while to decipher. It takes unanticipated phone calls, made not out of duty (so many men seem to require a 'reason' for phoning, never realizing that the gesture contains its own reason). It takes the accretion of experiences shared, whether that's the experience of sitting alone together in a room

and doing very different things, or the experience of spending three days together in concentrated intensity, or the experience of seeing all of your defenses and affectations split off from you in a moment of unexpected closeness.

When all that is ignored, the effect is like dry ice tearing off a layer of skin.

Combat in the Erogenous Zone
Ingrid Bengis
Wildwood House, 1973
(out of print)

The Shame is Over

None of these three accounts is by a man, and none is British —had I found either I would have mentioned them. It would be heartening to think that British authors (maybe even male British authors) could write honest and compelling books about the other people in their lives.

Anja Meulenbelt's *The Shame is Over* is a classic autobiography of a committed life, by turns beautiful and harrowing, always open and honest and often very funny. The failures are here as well as the successes, but as the author says, we must allow ourselves to fail without shame. We must learn to fail proudly and start again equally proudly.

*

And I see, slowly, how unequal our relationship was. Anna, who was for me a warm place, someone who was always there even though I might not see her for a week. A fixed point in my life which is otherwise such a turmoil, with so many uncertainties and changes. She was almost a mother to me. I trusted her because she was a woman, because I didn't think that women would be able to hurt each other as men hurt women. Because I trusted her so much, the pain was so much worse.

The Shame is Over
Anja Meulenbelt
Women's Press, 1980
£2.95

On Loving Men

Like Ingrid Bengis, Jane Lazarre is American. In this personal account of intimacy and sexual development, she argues forcefully for relationships which are less damaging to everybody involved, and which take account of the real needs of the participants. She is also one of the few writers to acknowledge that one of our needs in relating may well be plain novelty.

*

I am a woman trying to understand love. I am trying to understand how the uprooting exhilaration of the first months of expressed passion can become, in a short period of time, the source of pain, of loss of self.

On Loving Men
Jane Lazarre
Virago, 1984
£4.50

Getting to Yes

Clear communication and sensitive negotiation are two key features in the best relationships, whether personal or commercial, internal or international. There is of course a lot more to successful relating than that, but you can do a lot worse than read Roger Fisher and William Ury's best-selling *Getting to Yes*.

The authors work with the Harvard Negotiation Project, a group working with all levels of conflict resolution from domestic disagreements to international disputes, and they present a simple strategy for reaching conclusions which benefit all concerned.

It is sometimes oversimplistic: it requires at least a basic agreement to want to work something out, and tends to ignore the emotional elements which get in the way of reasoned solutions. It contains many important insights, however, like not confusing the people with the problem, focusing on common interests, and learning to co-operate. And it suggests a number of useful techniques for reaching agreement even when the 'other side' won't play.

*

From time to time you may want to remind yourself that the first thing you are trying to win is a better way to negotiate — a way that avoids your having to choose between the satisfactions of getting what you deserve and of being decent. You can have both.

The National Bestseller

GETTING TO YES

Negotiating Agreement
Without Giving In

Roger Fisher and William Ury
Of the Harvard Negotiation Project

Getting to Yes
Roger Fisher and William Ury
Penguin, 1983
£2.95

Dealing with No

Given the legal, financial and material responsibilities that come (often with little recognition) with the institution of marriage, it is unsurprising that separation and divorce create such upheaval and havoc in people's lives. This is a time when you will need good and timely advice, and Jeremy Leland's *Breaking Up* sets out the current situation clearly and approachably. Scotland, where the law is somewhat different, has a chapter of its own.

OPTIMA

BREAKING UP
SEPARATION AND DIVORCE
JEREMY LELAND

**A CITIZEN'S
ADVICE GUIDE**

Breaking Up
Separation and Divorce
Jeremy Leland
Optima, 1987
£3.95

Living Communally

Though you don't hear as much about them these days as you did ten years ago, there are more than a hundred groups of people in Britain living in groups with the intention of exploring ways of living and working together beyond the confines of the nuclear family. The best available guide to living communally is *Diggers and Dreamers: A Guide to Communal Living*, recently published by the Communes Network (1989, £4.95). It is an excellent distillation of the last twenty years of communal experience and covers the some of the pains and joys of trying to get a group going, how to organize work, income pooling and childcare. There is some good practical advice on finance, property and insurance, but the bulk of the book is a directory of over fifty British communities which are still thriving. Many other good books about community living (see the bibliography in *Diggers and Dreamers*) are now out of print, though John Mercer's *Communes* (Prism, 1984, £3.95) gives a reasonable historical overview.

The Communes Network links about a dozen of the older-established communes on a regular basis, and for £7.50 you can subscribe to their quarterly newsletter. The Network is currently being run from Lifespan Community in Yorkshire, where visitors are welcome (though ring in advance!).

The Alternative Communities Movement is run from The Teachers community in north Wales. The ACM produces an occasional magazine and has the most comprehensive mail order booklist of communal living that you'll find. An important aim is to put people in touch with projects and like-minded potential initiators of communal projects. Their idiosyncratic hand-printed publications are works of art in themselves.

**Communes
Network**
Lifespan Community
Townhead
Dunford Bridge
Sheffield
S30 6TG
0226 762359

**Alternative
Communities
Movement**
18 Garth Road
Bangor
Gwynedd
LL57 1ED

Natural Friends

Easy-going, peace-loving, broad and open minded male vegetarian seeks new friends and ventures . . .

I am a natural living 27 year old artist . . .

Natural Friends was established in 1985, and Barbara Bradshaw who runs it from a Suffolk village takes great pride in offering a confidential, caring and efficient service. There are hundreds of people on the lists who are interested in alternative therapies, holistic philosophies, personal development, peace, rambling and gardening, all looking for another person or people to share their lives or make friends with. Currently you pay £15 for a year's subscription, for which you have your advert included in Natural Friends' files, receive a hundred (more at £5 a hundred) adverts from other people, and the bi-monthly newsletter *Natural Interests*. For £2 extra you can have a box number to retain anonymity.

A similar service is offered by Vegetarian Matchmakers, who offer a friendship network for people who are vegetarian or vegan. They can arrange introductions, and will also organize parties and gatherings if that's what you'd like. If you write to them they will send an information pack.

Natural Friends
15 Benyon Gardens
Culford
Bury St Edmunds
Suffolk
IP28 6EA
028 484 315

**Vegetarian
Matchmakers**
Johnson House
Coronation Road
London
NW10 7QE
0(8)1-348 5229

STOP ACID RAIN

CHILDREN

'A child stands, taking a first meaningful look at her world . . .
She is like a dreamer; for she dreams of a world where there's unity and love . . .
Where she would be able to enjoy life to its fullest,
Or walk on clean sandy beaches feeling satisfied, feeling free
She dreams of a 'forever world'.
Althea Perry (aged 15, from Antigua), from *Cry For Our Beautiful World*

Anyone reading this is or has been a child, and it is important that childhood be as positive as possible, yet we need to accept with the realism of the 1990s that children don't have an easy or effortless time of it. Being a child can be tough. Deciding what should be on offer to children, what sort of food, drink, toys or stimulus infants should have, what sort of holidays seven-year-olds might enjoy, what kind of education should be available to teenagers — these can all be difficult decisions for children and those who care for them.

But the decisions we make are not just for 'them' — the children. We each have our own child, the one who longs to play, to be imaginative and intuitive. Many of us involve ourselves with children precisely in order to feed that child within ourselves. Remembering what it is like to be a child will always be one of the best guides to imagining what a child most needs.

Childbirth
A green approach to bringing children into the world must ask questions like how many, how often, with whom, where and why? Conception by choice is a presumption of the early 1990s, at least in the 'developed' world, but most of us will continue to have children at some point in our lives. We may limit the number of children we wish to parent, we may fulfil ourselves through the nurturing of children conceived by others — but the human race shows no sign of discontinuing procreation, even in the face of the increasing overpopulation of our planet.

Many people today seem relatively unencumbered by notions of a 'right time, right place' attitude to children. Women are having babies with the support of husbands, lovers, friends of either sex, or on their own. People are evolving their own childbirth patterns, having babies in hospitals or at home, and the medical service is finally responding to these pressures, making it easier for parents to choose the conditions of childbirth.

Babies

'Birth feels like the climax to long months of waiting,' writes Penelope Leach (see page 213), 'but it is not really a climax at all. You were not waiting to give birth, you were waiting to have a baby. Your labour has produced that baby and there is no rest-pause between the amazing business of becoming parents and the job of being them.'

Babies, especially first babies, make enormous demands for change in the lives of those who parent them. There are suddenly 'experts' to be held at bay, firmly insisting that they know what is best for baby. Local support groups, both formal and informal, come into their own when you have a baby to look after, and you may be able to help create a network of support for parents like yourselves, like-minded people to share books, baby-minding, problems and pleasures.

From your first visit to the antenatal clinic you will be aware that there is a whole industry out there just yearning for you to send off one of their Freepost coupons for samples of baby porridge, talcum powder, and nappies with special moisture indicators. Babies are big business — and big money. After all, few of us would want to wrap our infants' bottoms in disposable green leaves, and most of us welcome mother's milk substitutes if for some reason breast-feeding is not possible. In general, however, the do-it-yourself approach to baby products goes a long, long way. It's astonishing to discover how little babies need - and how much of that can be handed on or made at home.

Children and Their Needs

'Our first memories are tied to eating, and for many of us certain foods have the power to evoke feelings of security. Therefore, it is really unfair to allow, much less encourage, the distribution of questionable food to children who are too young to make a reasoned judgment about what they do or do not want to risk ingesting into their bodies.'

This statement, from the (now sadly out of print) book *Ourselves and Our Children* (Penguin, 1981), is still very relevant at the beginning of the 1990s. There has been a good deal more response from the food manufacturing industries to adults' demands for healthier food than there has been to children's need for healthy food, even though it is children who suffer as much or more than the rest of us from the additives in food.

In a different climate the choice of clothes for our children might be less of a problem for us all. We can at least be grateful that children's clothes today give them the chance to express themselves without having to cover their bodies (or our kitchen walls) with paint. In general, good clothes for us and for our children have a lot in common — natural fibres, clothes made for moving in with a sense of individuality and fun, make us all feel better.

When in doubt about toys, do without, or look at what other people's children actually play with. Some beautifully-made toys may please the collector in your child, but may have the play value of a Van Gogh.

Education is not just something that happens to children, job-training, learning by rote, or preparation for a lifetime in a niche in an economic structure. 'Education policy must be decided by each community to match its individual needs and priorities,' says the Green Party's 1987 General Election Manifesto. 'Learning is part of living, and the community is where we live. Such an important part of our lives cannot be left to the whims of party politics. Education is about life — for life.'

Childbirth

Exciting things are happening in childbirth today. Instead of suffering birth passively and leaving decisions to the professionals who help them, women are assuming much more of an active, decision-making role for themselves.

Sheila Kitzinger, *The Experience of Childbirth* (see below)

'Active' is the keyword for the eighties' attitude to childbirth. Women and men are getting involved in support networks and pressure groups pushing for changes in the standard NHS attitude to birth, and active, natural and informed childbirth is being sought after and experienced by more and more women.

One of the most important figures in this revolution is Sheila Kitzinger. A copious and versatile author, she has raised the consciousness of millions of women in relation to childbirth since the first publication of *The Experience of Childbirth* in 1962.

The Experience of Childbirth

This is the book to get your hands on if you are thinking of becoming pregnant (or of being a father) — it is as easy to understand and as complete as one book can be. Perhaps because she is an anthropologist rather than a doctor, Sheila Kitzinger is as clear when discussing the psychology of pregnancy, relaxation techniques and the issue of home versus hospital birth as she is when considering the use of drugs in labour (and how to avoid them if you wish). Her style is straightforward and direct, but not condescending. A cheering and inspiring book, packed with information, diagrams and practical ideas.

Also worth consulting as you plan for childbirth is Sheila Kitzinger's *The New Good Birth Guide*. Here are the results of her survey of hospital birthing practices throughout Britain, with the emphasis on how parents-to-be can make an informed choice. She praises good medical practice where she finds it, and describes in detail the variety of medical policies they may meet and what options they have. She shows how to construct a 'birth plan' so that the mother, her birth partner and her medical attendants know what is wanted. The second half of the book is a maternity hospital directory to Britain — although not all hospitals are covered, the information is detailed and precise, and is constructed from women's own accounts together with feedback from hospital staff.

The Experience of Childbirth
Sheila Kitzinger
Penguin, 1981
£3.95

The New Good Birth Guide
Sheila Kitzinger
Penguin, 1983
£3.95

Birthrights

Sally Inch, an experienced midwife and an advanced National Childbirth Trust teacher (see below), has written two clear and sensitive books about birth which give all the facts you will need without ignoring either the personal or the political. *Approaching Birth* takes you up to the first signs of labour, while *Birthrights* is the complete works. Both books have recently been republished in updated editions, and *Approaching Birth* contains an up-to-date and comprehensive resource section.

Approaching Birth
Sally Inch
Green Print, 1989
£4.99

Birthrights
Sally Inch
Green Print, 1989
£7.99

There are so many other books about preparing for childbirth, exercises, diet, breathing, infertility and birth management that you could easily fill a pram with them. Many of them are derivative, vague, or offer you a system with little attempt to compare and assess its merits in relation to other people's ideas. They often assume that prospective mothers never compare notes and amalgamate different ideas — if this is true for you, then find some like-minded souls and get talking (and book-swapping). There are, however, one or two American books that are outstanding in their clarity and insight.

Rahima Baldwin's *Special Delivery: The Complete Guide to Informed Birth* (Celestial Arts (distributed in Britain by Airlift), 1979, £9.95) is a very practical illustrated guide for parents who want to take greater responsibility in their baby's birth. Rahima Baldwin's clear empathetic approach to the subject is most refreshing.

If you want more medical detail but with no less sensitivity, Celestial Arts also publish Elizabeth Davis's *Heart and Hands: A Midwife's Guide to Pregnancy and Birth* (2nd edn, 1987, £10.95), a large-format illustrated book of which Sheila Kitzinger — the pro's pro — has written 'An impressive and deeply caring book'.

The National Childbirth Trust

The NCT is one of the most helpful — and truly national — organizations for getting mothers together to share wisdom and experience. They have lots of local groups and will put you in touch with one near to you. They organize antenatal classes (encouraging the attendance of fathers or other birth partners), provide postnatal and infant feeding support, and market maternity wear, breast pumps, etc (none of it cheap, but excellent quality — particularly the Mava feeding bras). The NCT has been going a long time, and is criticized in some quarters for being too supportive of established medical practice. But each local group sets its own tone, and the NCT is definitely moving with current trends towards greater participation.

The National Childbirth Trust
Alexandra House
Oldham Terrace
London
W3 6NH
0(8)1-992 8637

Birth Options

If you are interested in finding out more about the possibilities of birth at home, your first step is to advise your GP of your interest and intentions. They may be willing to take you on and make the necessary arrangements.

The International Centre for Active Birth, who sponsored the first international conference on home birthing in October 1987 (the speakers included Sheila Kitzinger, Michel Odent and Ina Mae Gaskin), offers a comprehensive information service, including a sales list of books, pamphlets and videos. They also run seminars and training courses, but only in London.

The bottom line for arranging a home delivery if none of your local GPs will co-operate is to find a qualified midwife who will attend. Here the Association of Radical Midwives will be able to help you; the Association also provides information and publishes a quarterly magazine called *Midwifery Matters*.

There are also independent Birth Centres in some towns and cities which provide resources, advice and information about childbirth. One such centre — and probably one of the best — is the Reading Birth Centre, which provides support for women in the Reading area wanting to explore childbirth alternatives. It publishes an information booklet, advises and encourages women in relation to home birth, and works 'to improve women's experiences of childbirth and help them feel in control of their own bodies'.

The Association for Improvements in the Maternity Services (AIMS) has groups of parents and professionals throughout the country which campaign on both national and local issues. AIMS publishes a variety of useful information booklets and a quarterly journal. A similar function is provided by the longer-established but smaller group The Maternity Alliance which will, if you send an sae, send you a series of free leaflets on pre-conceptual care, rights at work, and money for mothers and babies.

International Centre for Active Birth
55 Dartmouth Park Road
London
NW5 1SL
0(7)1-267 3006

The Association of Radical Midwives
62 Greetby Hill
Ormskirk
Lancashire
L39 2DT
0695 572776

The Reading Birth Centre
20 Bulmershe Road
Reading
Berkshire
RG1 5RJ
0734 65648

AIMS
163 Liverpool Road
London
N1 0RF
0(7)1-278 5628

Maternity Alliance
15 Britannia Street
London
WC1X 9JP
0(7)1-837 1265

Naturebirth

A book which some love and some love to hate, *Naturebirth* is passionate and personal, and doesn't pretend to be even-handed in its evaluation of current medical practice. Danae Brook had her own three children in hospital, but she strongly believes that the method and location of a woman's childbirth experience should be her own choice. What makes this book particularly interesting is that mixed with the strong individual feelings is a very well researched account of what modern medical practice is: what all the medical terms mean, an excellent booklist, an appendix of useful organizations and suppliers, and some clearly explained exercises and diet and health advice. I didn't expect to like this book, but in fact it's both a good read and excellent value.

Naturebirth
Danae Brook
Penguin, 1986
£4.95

Maternity Clothes

Gone are the days when women felt obliged to dress like overweight milkmaids from the day they got their pregnancy test results. Lots of women manage to wear the type of clothes they're used to, in a size or two larger, for most of their pregnancy. Depending on the swings of fashion it may be possible to find chain store 'baggies' that will suit you at a reasonable price, and more and more of the big chain stores are including a maternity range. Mothercare have always prided themselves on their maternity range, and they do a mail order catalogue too.

The National Childbirth Trust (previous page) sell the best maternity bras. At £10-11 they're not cheap, but I'm told they last for ever. They also sell attractive nightdresses suitable for breastfeeding. Ask for their mail order brochure. Among other high street chains Marks and Spencer, Chelsea Girl and C&A now stock maternity clothes.

Blooming Marvellous was set up eight years ago by two women who couldn't find attractive maternity clothes that they were willing to wear. They now employ fourteen women, and produce some of the nicest maternity wear around. Dresses cost £25-35, but as they point out in their full-colour mail order catalogue, most women need slightly less fitted clothes for some time after having the baby, so you can carry on wearing their clothes through the post-natal period without feeling frumpy — and with most of their designs you'll be able to breastfeed your baby as discretely as anyone could wish for. They have a Blooming Kids section too.

Blooming Marvellous Ltd
PO Box 12F
Chessington
Surrey
KT9 2LS
0(8)1-391 0338

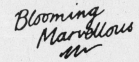

Infant Feeding — Breast is Best (But It Shouldn't Be Rammed Down Anyone's Throat)

One of the first and unavoidable areas of concern for parents faced with a newborn baby is feeding it. Most babies make it very clear that they want to be fed — and frequently; but the method of feeding is an issue for some parents. Medical opinion is now well agreed on the value of breast-feeding, unless for some reason (and there aren't many) it isn't possible. For many women breastfeeding is neither a practical nor a psychological problem, but both — when they arise — need detailed and sympathetic advice and support. The National Childbirth Trust (see the previous page) also encourages breastfeeding, and besides offering friendly and helpful support they can also supply things like breast pumps (so you can express a feed in order to leave the baby with someone else for a while) and nipple shields (to avoid having milk all down your front when you dribble).

It's important to recognize to what extent infant feeding is controlled by political and commercial interests. Who is it that *actually* benefits from the mountains of formula fed to babies every hour of every day? Gabrielle Palmer's rivetting and heart-wrenching book *The Politics of Breastfeeding* (Pandora, 1988, £6.95) shows how women the world over, but particularly those who can afford it least, have been conned into a dependence on an expensive manufactured substitute for a life-giving resource that is one of the few still under women's control. This should be required reading for all doctors, women thinking about motherhood, teenagers thinking about their future . . .

Gabrielle Palmer is also the national co-ordinator of the Baby Milk Action Coalition, which works to halt the commercial promotion of bottle feeding and to protect and promote good and appropriate infant nutrition. BMAC is a member of the International Baby Food Action Network, which has over 100 groups in more than 60 countries. Write for information about how you can help their work.

Baby Milk Action Campaign
6 Regent Terrace
Cambridge
CB2 1AA
0223 464420

La Leche

'Leche' is French for 'sucking', and the LLL was founded by a group of American women in 1957 to promote the advantages of breastfeeding over the then overwhelmingly dominant formula bottle, in a culture where breastfeeding was considered as indecent as glimpses of ladies' legs were to the Victorians. The League progressed from its early emphasis on making breastfeeding socially acceptable to a concern for the nutrition of older children too, advocating a diet based on natural wholefoods and organic produce. The LLL came to Britain in 1972, and there are now over 120 regional groups, providing counselling, advice about breastfeeding problems, and general support with infant care. Though the support of birth partners is encouraged, the emphasis is on providing women with a space where they can discuss and demonstrate feeding problems in the company of other women with young children. The League also produces an extensive range of books and pamphlets, many of them only available through the LLL.

Despite its dated title and even more dated illustrations, the best practical book on breastfeeding is still the LLL's *The Womanly Art of Breastfeeding*. It is an excellent source of information for women who choose to breastfeed, full of first-time accounts, photographs of bonny bouncing (American) babies and the results of scientific research into the benefits of breastfeeding.

Membership of the League is currently £9, with a generous £4.50 rate for the unwaged — send an sae for more details.

La Leche League
BM 3424
London
WC1N 3XX
0(7)1-242 1278 or 0(7)1-404 5011

Taking Population Seriously

The planet's five billionth human being was born in 1986; demographers believe that the six billionth will be born in 2001 and the seven billionth in 2012. Even the most optimistic don't see the graph beginning to level out until the middle of the next century, when world population will be approaching ten billion. The reasons for wanting and having children are many and complex, but what is clear is that we must consider carefully our personal responsibility not to add to the mouths and hands being supported by the earth's limited resources.

Taking Population Seriously (Frances Moore Lappé and Rachel Schurman, Earthscan, 1989, £4.95) is the title of a recent and vital study of the so-called 'population explosion' which examines the social, economic and political influences affecting choices in fertility and reproduction, both in the Third World and here at home. It's a short book, easily read and digested, but carries a very important message: only when poorer people can control their own destinies will population growth slow down.

Population Concern is Britain's foremost campaigning group on these important issues. Their aim is to promote planned parenthood as a universal right and to raise awareness about the issues involved in uncontrolled population growth. As well as detailed factsheets about every aspect of the population question, Population Concern has produced an attractive and useful *World Population Data Sheet* which you can pin on the wall (£1.20 including p+p), and computer-based population statistics software and a secondary level education pack for use in schools. Send for their publications list.

Population Concern
231 Tottenham Court Road
London
W1P 9AE
0(7)1-631 1546/637 9582

Babies and Toddlers

Each newborn infant carries within itself life's greatest promise: a new hope for the world.
　　　　Helen Arnstein, *The Roots of Love*, Unwin, 1980

When you start looking after this small, new human being, you lack that first essential for watchful care: baselines. The baby is brand new. However much you know about babies in general, neither you nor anyone else knows anything about this one in particular.
　　　　Penelope Leach, *Baby and Child* (see below)

Looking after babies and young children is not an easy task. Most people in our society feel a sense of isolation and lack of support from other adults beyond their immediate family groups during the infant and pre-school years. Much of the fun of parenting a baby can be lost in wondering whether or not you're doing it the 'right' way.

For many people, however, the chance to involve yourself in the care of a baby is a time of great joy. Some have very clear ideas about how the baby should be treated from the moment it is born. Others may have vague notions about childcare but want the support of more experienced parents, doctors, and child psychologists.

There are plenty of books to guide parents through the early years, but like most how-to-do-it books on aspects of human psychology they can often produce far more anxiety than practical and positive help. By far the most important thing to remember about childcare is that every child is different, every adult is different, and the circumstances in which childcare takes place vary so enormously, so there cannot possibly be a 'right' way to do it. On the other hand, we have all been told so many nonsenses about what young children do and don't need (indeed, all been brought up by parents using such guidelines) that we can no longer entirely trust ourselves to 'do what comes naturally'.

Rather than list a lot of books on the subject, I have chosen two, one of which should help you with any practical question you might have about your under-five, the other looking at the emotional and psychological experiences of being a young child. Much more important than books are other people with whom to share the experience, the work and the pleasure (see for example *Shared Parenthood* on page 204), support and acknowledgement (and adequate reward) for the important work you are doing, and the confidence that you are doing your best even when circumstances are trying.

Much of the support and sharing you need can be found locally. Your local health centre, community centre, women's centre or library will all have noticeboards with details of day care schemes, playgroups, parent and toddler groups and the like (see page 221 for more on playgroups).

Baby and Child

The publisher's blurb on Penelope Leach's book says 'At last, the baby book that is written from the baby's point of view'. Mercifully their claim is not substantiated by the contents. However, it is fair to say that Penelope Leach does try to incorporate as much helpful understanding of infant psychology as she does medical advice. The book is as complete as any on the market, covering the first five years of a child's life thoroughly and competently. It is an eminently practical book, with lots of charts and illustrations. Some of the outstanding sections in the book are those dealing with toys and activities appropriate for different ages and stages. The encyclopedia/index which occupies the last fifty pages is invaluable, providing not only the usual page references but also pieces of vital information which can in this way be found very quickly. For example you can look up 'birth — formalities after', 'penis — caught in zip fastener' and 'whooping cough' — among many others. Penelope Leach is at her best when reconciling the ideal with the everyday. Herself a working mother, she never ignores the conflicts that parents experience between what they want to do for their child and what they want to do for themselves — a mistress of the pragmatic solution (even when it involves a rapidly prepared non-whole-food meal). The editors have obviously had problems with pronouns — your child is a 'he' throughout the text, a 'she' in most of the illustrations, and a 'he or she' in a few headings — a minor niggle in an otherwise very good book.

Baby and Child
From Birth to Age Five
Penelope Leach
Penguin, 1979
£8.95

The Drama of Being a Child

This, internationally-known German psychoanalyst Alice Miller's most approachable book, has rapidly become the classic it deserves to be. It is an impassioned and perceptive plea for parents to allow their children to be who they are, rather than forcing them to be how they think children should be. She points out that children cannot afford to lose their parents' love, and so often suppress their real needs and feelings in order to be who their parents want. Then we wonder why adults are so screwed up, especially in relation to *their* children.

This is also a very personal book, in which Alice Miller acknowledges that her years of work as an analyst actually prevented her from recognizing this important truth. She now uses her newfound understanding in her work, and has helped countless people to stop repeating endlessly the distorted ways of relating which are but echoes of their unhappy childhoods.

*

Surprisingly, it was the child in me — condemned to silence long ago, abused, exploited, and turned to stone — who finally found her feelings and along with them her speech and told me, in pain, her story.

The Drama of Being a Child
Alice Miller
Virago, 1987
£4.50

Baby Products

You will hardly need to be told that babies are very big business indeed. As soon as you know the baby's on the way — and have let the mainstream medical profession know — you will be inundated with information, free gifts, money-off tokens, guides (sponsored by baby food companies) and handbooks (sponsored by nappy companies). They know that your life will never be the same again, that having a baby — especially a first baby — is a big event. They want to make sure that theirs is the name on the tip of your tongue every time you go out shopping with baby in mind, and in the guise of loving and caring advisers lead you gently by the hand to the payout desk, where you just happen to have bought more of what they gave you a free sample of.

I'm certainly not advising you to throw away your chances of some free gifts, simply to stop and think — and since there's a great deal to think about where babies are concerned it's a good idea to do some of the thinking well ahead of the event.

There are two main things you have to remember when it comes to buying things for your baby. The first, and most obvious, is that you will constantly be under pressure to buy more than you need. The second is that since babies can't spend money themselves, the companies who make baby products have to resort to the ploy of making you believe that what they make is absolutely vital to you baby's health, wellbeing and safety.

What has to be set against these pressures is the simple fact that babies actually need very little of anything, except love and affection.

Clothes

Babies grow very quickly, so whatever they wear will only fit them for a very short period of time, and the clothes will far outlast the need for them. Thus you almost never need to buy new clothes. If you already have children at playgroup or are going to ante-natal classes, you will almost certainly be part of a circle within which babygros and woolly hats will be circulating — just make sure you get as much as you give! If you do need new clothes (and even if you don't) you will find it hard to stay out of Mothercare, who sell a good range of fairly inexpensive cotton babygros — Boots are now doing all-cotton baby clothes too from first size upwards. Small Change at 25 Carnegie House, Junction Well Road, London NW3 (0(7)1 794 7043) sell good quality second-hand children's clothes.

Disposable nappies are specially designed to be as unecological as possible; if I was being purist I'd say only use them when you have to and use terry nappies otherwise (or none at all whenever it's warm enough). But disposable nappies also give a lot of people — meaning of course mostly women — more disposable time. Among the 'greener' disposables now available, Peaudouce Ultra Plus are trying hardest. A specially imported Danish nappy system — a combination of muslin nappies and oiled waterproof knitted overpants which are simply aired between uses — is available from Firstbørn, 28 Claremont Avenue, Bristol BS7 8JE (0272 240808) — write for details.

If secondhand baby clothes don't come your way on the grapevine, the local charity shop will almost certainly fulfil your needs, always remembering that your baby will be a lot less fussy than you about what it wears.

For a special present, Alan Carver's Leeds-based Tiny Boot Company (6 Roundhay Mount, Leeds LS8 4DW; 0532 405344) makes supple sheepskin footwear for babies from birth to crawling stage. These beautifully made boots keep baby's feet warm without limiting their movement. They cost £7.95 a pair plus 50p p+p, and there's a guaranteed money-back refund if you don't like them after all.

Equipment

You could spend a fortune on cots, prams, bouncers — you name it — but again you don't need to. Most of what you will need can be found secondhand, though look out for things that simply aren't safe. Most main items of baby equipment have a relevant British Safety Standard, so look out for the kitemark when you're buying. There are several toy/clothes/equipment exchange schemes in operation, mostly in inner city areas.

Food

If a mother is bottle feeding her baby and not in receipt of milk tokens and drinking a pint of milk a day then she is spending £314.53 a year to feed the baby. By breast feeding there is a net saving of approximately £250.
Tightening Belts, London Food Commission (see page 28)

Not only money but health too is at stake if you choose to bottle feed your baby. The choice must be yours, of course, and breastfeeding can be demanding of both your energy and your time. There are a few women who cannot breast-feed, but the longer you can breastfeed your baby, the longer you are providing a filter between the baby and the polluted world, the longer you provide an intimate physical link between you and the baby — and the longer you save money.

There is no need whatsoever to give your baby anything other than breast milk for the first five months, and there is no need to stop breastfeeding until the baby stops showing interest in it, though the food-industry feeding guides will say you should start with their special preparations at around three months.

There can be few more expensive — and resource-wasting — way of buying baby food than in individual tins and bottles. You don't need them. It's true that almost all commercial baby foods are now additive and sugar free, but so are the baby foods you make yourself. A liquidizer is a useful thing to have to mash up bananas, tomatoes, carrots, apples and so on, but not essential — a nylon sieve is adequate.

Don't, however, miss out on any free samples that are going. Boots put together a free 'bounty box' for new babies — one for first babies and another for subsequent ones. If you don't come across the coupon during the course of your 'confinement' — and it's hard to miss — get in touch with the people who act as intermediaries in the baby business: Bounty Giftpacks Ltd, Owen Road, Diss, Norfolk (Tel: 0379 651081). Read the attractive literature, eat and drink whatever you fancy yourself, then keep the rest for baby's first birthday party — by which time you should have saved enough money to take the whole family on a really good holiday.

Children And Food

A few decades ago, cancer among children was unknown; it is now a major cause of their deaths. The increase in deaths parallels the use of refined and processed foods, chemical fertilizers, poison sprays, food additives, and preservatives. Only the naive could believe the two are unrelated. As long as mothers complacently feed their children this type of food, they should expect the incidence of cancer to remain high or to increase, and often to take the lives of their youngsters. Junk foods will disappear from the market as soon as women refuse to buy them; and wholesome foods grown without chemical fertilizers or poison sprays can become available whenever the homemakers demand them.
Adelle Davis, *Let's Have Healthy Children* (Unwin, 1974, £2.95)

Plaques and fatty streaks which can develop into the early stages of heart disease can be found in the arteries of children as young as one year old. It would be several years before the artery might show signs of deterioration, but whereas the first set of teeth will be replaced, a deteriorating artery will never recover. When it comes to young children's teeth, over half of British children have tooth decay before their second set of teeth arrive.
Food and Drink for Under-Fives (see below)

Sainsbury's must be sailing very close to the legal limit of what is permitted in a product 'specially prepared for babies and young children' with their own brand of Blackcurrant Drink. Giving details of how the drink should be diluted for babies, the label admits that the product not only contains several added colourings (which other companies have voluntarily banned from baby foods) but also the artificial sweetener Saccharin, banned from baby foods by law. London Food News, Summer 1987

It's bad enough harming ourselves with the food we eat, but who would voluntarily hurt their children? This suggestion is not intended to make anybody feel guilty; merely to point out that a great deal of what children eat is doing them very little good, and not a little harm. Children's metabolisms are not as resilient as adults', and growing tissues and bones accumulate poisons more readily than fully-grown ones. Yet children's foods, particularly snack foods, are often laced with a cocktail of additives. It is estimated, for example, that the average child has eaten half a pound of toxic azo dyes by the time she or he is twelve years old.

When it comes to their children's diets many parents simply shrug and say 'Well, what can you do? If I tell them not to eat unhealthy foods they just go to friend's houses or buy them anyway.' This really is defeatist. You have almost complete control over what your child eats when it is very young, and it is right at the beginning that it matters the most. Later on you don't have to be strict, but you do need to be clear with children about what their diet is doing to them. My experience is that by the mid teenage years young people are often very aware of the health issues surrounding food, and as long as they are not addicted — and being hooked on sugar, for example, is every bit as difficult to kick as alcohol or smoking — they are perfectly capable of looking after their own food intake.

Children's Food

If part of your life is spent feeding children and you are concerned about what is going into their bodies, Tim Lobstein's *Children's Food* should be on your shelves. Well (even grippingly) written, full of illustrations and useful diagrams, the book takes you through all the things that are currently wrong with our children's diets, and what can be done to put them right. Tim Lobstein shows convincingly how the interests of producers and distributors almost always take precedence over those of consumers, and highlights the risks we run when we buy food for our children without first questioning whether or not we are helping them to remain fit and healthy. The action and resource sections are excellent, and he doesn't even duck the issue of customer resistance to real food as we follow Moll ('Ugh! What is it? I'm not eating THAT!!') through her early years.

*

The trouble is that present food regulations allow all manner of odd labelling practices and strange food processing techniques that raise serious questions about the possible damage to our children's health. Many of the products we buy in the stores today have never been eaten before. Young, growing children may be particularly vulnerable to these unusual, inappropriate foods and untested chemicals. They could be heading into a whole lot of trouble.

Children's Food
Tim Lobstein
Unwin Hyman, 1988
£3.95

Institutional Food

Tim Lobstein and the The London Food Commission (see page 28) have also produced an excellent short handbook about nutrition for playgroup leaders and caterers in Greater London; though it is primarily intended for people in the caring professions, it is very clearly written and provides excellent guidelines for a balanced and healthy diet for under-fives (and with little modification for all schoolchildren). It gives sample menus and a good bibliography — good value too.

Food and Drink for the Under-Fives
Tim Lobstein
London Food Commission, 1985
£1.00

Hyperactivity

In February 1987 Ellen Rothera of the Food and Chemical Allergy Association wrote to Edwina Currie for her views about environmental pollutants and allergic reactions, including hyperactivity. Part of the reply runs: 'While accepting that there is a need for further research in the area the view of the medical staff in this Department and of my other expert medical advisers is that relatively small numbers of people suffer significant ill-health due to allergic or other intolerant reactions. They also believe there is no evidence that food additives or synthetic chemicals in the environment are a more potent cause of allergic reactions than the naturally occurring chemicals in food and other products. Indeed, in the case of foods, there is good evidence that intolerant reactions to natural components of foods are much commoner than reactions to food additives.'

Michael Jopling, Minister for Agriculture, Fish and Food, wasn't so sure when interviewed on TV-AM a year earlier — 'The evidence is very strong,' he said, 'and it's all very distressing.' Luckily most people agree with Mr Jopling, which is why food manufacturers are falling over each other in the rush to market themselves as being more additive free than all the others.

HACSG

On that same television programme was Sally Bunday, who with her mother Vicky Colquhoun founded the Hyperactive Children's Support Group in 1977. At that time Sally's five-year-old son Miles was showing the classic symptoms of hyperactivity — ceaseless crying and screaming, head-banging and unresponsiveness. When her GP and the NHS could do nothing more than diagnose 'behavioural problems' she came across an American cutting about the Feingold Diet, a natural food regime pioneered by a Californian paediatrician. She immediately dropped all processed food from the family's diet, and within four days Miles was miles better.

The HACSG has now become a national network of groups, dealing with as many as a thousand enquiries a week. Given mounting evidence which implicates food additives in children's behavioural problems, more and more parents are willing to at least try a wholefood diet. As the correspondence received by the Group shows, in very many cases children are showing a marked improvement as a result.

Membership of the Group currently costs £8.00 (reduced rates for unwaged and single parents); you receive a *Journal* three times a year, have access to a local group, and advice and help as you need it. Useful lists of additive-free products are updated regularly in their *Handbook* (£3.50). Even if your child is not hyperactive it is well worth joining this vitally important campaigning group, since the advice and support it provides benefit all children and their parents.

Hyperactive Children's Support Group
71 Whyke Lane
Chichester
Sussex
PO19 2LD
0903 725182

Cooking For And With Children

In general there is no need to cook specifically with children in mind; as soon as they can manage solid food and as long as your creations are not too rich or spicy, children enjoy a wide range of healthy food. Not surprisingly, however, there are now a number of children's healthy cookery books around. If you can handle the 'utterly scrumptious recipes' style, Peggy Brusseau's *Let's Cook it Together* is great for young children. In its all-American way it gives detailed instructions for recipes where the grown-up and the child can work on a dish alongside each other. A well-thought-out book, illustrated in colour all the way through.

Stephanie Lashford's *The Kitchen Crew* is almost too clever, but despite the strange androgynous characters who fill the pages as the bus takes its journey through the digestive system, I am told by a knowledgeable and forthright ten-year-old that it's a really good book with some scrummy things in. I enjoyed eating the spicy samosas that appeared two hours later more than I did doing the washing up.

Rosamond Richardson's *Vegetarian Cooking For Children* is much straighter and more straightforward, though even she uses the obligatory 'scrumptious' from time to time. This book has some clever simple recipes in it that many grown-ups will enjoy too — like her 'vegetables in parcels' ('once discovered I couldn't leave it alone'), 'Charlie Brown's peanut flan', and felafels (or what to do when you've made too much hummus).

Let's Cook it Together!
Peggy Brusseau
Thorsons, 1985
£4.99

The Kitchen Crew
Stephanie Lashford
Ashgrove, 1987
£4.95

Vegetarian Cooking For Children
Rosamond Richardson
Piatkus, 1986
£5.95

H.A.C.S.G. 'SAFE FOOD' LIST. CORRECT AT TIME OF GOING TO PRINT, MAY, 1987

FLOURS/BREAD
White bread and white flours for home cooking are treated with certain bleaching and improving chemicals — so try to use 81% and 100% stoneground flours and wholemeal bread.

Jordan's stoneground 85%-100%
Allinson's   do (now contains malt vinegar
Marriage's   do
Prewett's wholemeal & 81% flour
Hofels organically grown flour.
Allinson's wholemeal bread. Some local bakeries also make wholemeal bread.

SUGARS
(keep sugar to absolute minimum)
Whitworth's demerara/muscavado/golden gran.
Billington's   natural demerara
                  golden granulated
                  molasses sugar
                  light & dark
                  natural muscavado
Whitworth's   white/yellow marzipan
                  soft rich brown sugar
                  brown light golden sugar
Sainsbury's   demerara/muscavado
Prewett's   demerara/light muscavado
                  muscavado & molasses
Tate & Lyle   icing sugar

CEREALS
All Kellogg's (except Honey Smacks) Shreddies, Shredded Wheat, Cubs, Bran Flakes, Bran Crunchies, Bran Fare, Grape-nuts.
There is malt flavouring in Kellogg's Corn-flakes, Frosties, Rice...Bran Flakes...

BISCUITS
It is very difficult to be precise about biscuits, but the ones listed are without colour/flavouring (unless natural)

Jordan's Coconut and honey
Paterson Bronte Coconut finger; Viennese finger; Shortcake oat finger; Golden crunch finger; Muesli; Oatflake; Ginger finger; Oatcake; Girdle oatcake; Rough oatcake; Oatcake Farl; Farmhouse oatcake; Bran oatcake; All butter shortbread fingers; All butter shortbread petticoat tails; All butter shortie; All butter shortbread.

Fox's biscuits Almond finger cookie; All butter shortbread; Apple crisp; Flaked almond square; Malt crunch creams; Orange triples.

Prewett's 'No added sugar' biscuits — Sesame and sunflower; Stem ginger; Rich fig, Carob chip cookies.
Allinson's Muesli wholemeal biscuits.

The following products meet the claim of no artificial colour, flavouring or preservatives and are split into two groups:
a) *No chemical aeration*
Crawford's Tartan shortbread; Balmoral shortbread; Butter puffs.
Carr's table water.
Ry King Crispbread, brown and light rye.
b) *Chemical aeration. These contain sodium bicarbonate or ammonium bicarbonate and the wholemeal contains both these and tartaric acid. All these are shown on the relevant label on the packaging.*
McVitie's Abbey crunch; Abbey crunch creams; Digestive; Fruit shortcake; Oat cakes (Forbes-Simmers); Royal scot; Natural choice (Fruit and nut crunch; Yoghurt creams; Blackcurrant yoghurt creams... ...muesli cookies.)

Children's Clothes

Children's clothes have undergone a revolution in the last twenty years. Gone are most of the grey courtelle pullovers, grey pleated skirts and grey shorts. In their place you can now get a wide selection of comfortable clothes in bright colours and natural fibres which wear well and wash well.

The arguments for choosing natural fibres for children's clothes are rehearsed on page 116; since children tend to have more sensitive skin than adults those arguments carry even more conviction. Most children's clothes shops, and the big multiples, have a reasonable range of natural fibre children's clothes — Marks and Spencer's, Boots and Mothercare (who also do a mail order service: Mothercare UK Ltd, Cherry Tree Road, Watford, Hertfordshire WD2 5SH; Tel: 0923 33577) are good places to look first. Do be careful though if you are wanting strictly all-cotton clothes, because many clothes which are sold as all-natural-fibre simply aren't; trimmings, thread and ornaments are usually made from artificial materials. This may not matter in your case, but if a child suffers from allergic skin reactions, even the dyes in an iron-on transfer can be very irritating.

Cotton On

Dorothy Pearson started Cotton On in 1981 when she found it almost impossible to buy pure cotton clothing for her daughter who suffered with severe eczema. Many of the clothes which were labelled 'all cotton' had nylon trimmings, chemical finishes, or were coloured with irritating dyestuffs.

All of Cotton On's growing range is made from pure cotton with no added irritants, and you could if you wanted buy your child's entire outfit from them — underwear, t-shirts, jumpers, padded jackets, the lot. They also sell school-uniform-style clothes including trousers, shorts and even a grey school cardigan. A limited adult range, mostly for women, is also available. Phone for a catalogue.

Cotton On
29 North Clifton Street
Lytham
FY8 5HW
0253 736611

Apart from these suggestions, many of the suppliers listed in the 'Clothes' section also produce and market children's clothes. In particular it is well worth getting the Clothkits catalogue (see page 123).

Children and Smoking

Three quarters of adult smokers pick up the habit before they are 18. 22% of 15-year-old girls and 17% of fifteen-year-old boys smoke regularly and, though it is theoretically illegal for them to buy cigarettes, it is estimated that children spend £70 million a year on them. Despite the overwhelming evidence that smoking maims and kills, the tobacco industry continues to spend more than £100 million a year to promote its products, and the government, recipients of £7 billion a year in tax, does almost nothing to curb it. The recently-formed campaigning group Parents Against Tobacco aims to change this lackadaisical attitude. It produces a campaign kit filled with action plans, survey sheets, posters and the PaT newspaper, telling you how you can support their efforts.

Parents Against Tobacco
2 Endsleigh Street
London
WC1H 0DD
0(7)1-278 9686

Children and Television

Greens are understandably ambivalent about television. It is certainly thanks to television that information about current green concerns have reached a wide audience, yet in its indoor passivity it can easily isolate and cajole an increasingly soporific audience for whom even getting up to change channels is a chore to be circumvented with the use of a handy little black box. So how bad is television, especially for children (who, incidentally, watch on average a whole hour a day less than adults)? Máire Messenger Davies thinks that given the way we live our lives today, television in general does more good than harm. I tend to disagree, acknowledging that while she makes some thought-provoking points she misses out some important educational, economic and political considerations. Whatever your views on the great television debate, however, this important book will give you plenty to think and argue about.

*

If we feel that in watching television, children are neglecting other more interesting activities, more thought needs to be given as to what these activities are supposed to be. In a world in which small children have to live in high-rise flats, and in which every available public space, including the streets, is dominated by traffic, it could be argued that it is not television that has restricted the lives of children, but the town planner and the motor car. We need to be honest with ourselves and admit that, without television, we would not necessarily be spending our entire time playing the recorder, making collages and reading one another poems out loud.

For the other side of the story, look out for Juliet Solomon's *Programmed For Life*, due from Optima in February 1991.

**Television is Good
For Your Kids**
Máire Messenger Davies
Hilary Shipman, 1989
£5.95

Toys

Play is for everyone. It's a way in which children learn about themselves and the world. Through play, all children make discoveries about their bodies, their abilities and their surroundings...Toys aid play, and this is especially so where children find it difficult to make discoveries for themselves. Toys can readily extend play, reinforce concepts, widen experiences, and give a reward which makes the effort of learning a new skill worthwhile.
    Helen Dawe, in *What Toy?* (see below)

Every child needs stimulation: things to touch, taste, smell, look at, manipulate, explore. Toys can often provide such stimulus which is exciting, manageable and safe, and they thus have an important place in a child's world. Good though toys may be, however, they are only a small part of the real world; though toy manufacturers would like to to be different you can't expect any child to reach its full potential in a world comprised entirely of child-size replicas of the stuff of the material world. Many of the things that most fascinate children can't be manufactured anyway — snails and worms, flowers and grass, the world close to the ground that grown-ups usually miss completely.

And good though some toys are, most toys simply add to the mountain of consumer goods which are overpackaged, use large amounts of energy and non-renewable resources in their manufacture, and rapidly become so much non-recycled rubbish. Add to this the mounting concern that many toys encourage children to behave in anti-social and stereotyped ways, and you can see that choosing toys for your children is not as innocent a play as you might have imagined.

Shared Toys

Like so many consumer durables, most toys are not used every day, and some are used only once every few weeks. Why then does each family need its own building kit, racing car set, dolls' house and paddling pool? Wouldn't it be better for everyone concerned to share their resources and buy a wide range of good toys between them?

In a way this is what toy libraries do, lending toys and giving advice so that a child has access to the toys best suited to its needs at each stage in the learning process. The first toy library in Britain was established in 1967, and the Toy Libraries Association was formed in 1972 to co-ordinate the activities of toy libraries throughout the country, of which there are now nearly 700. In 1983 the Association joined forces with ACTIVE, an organization concerned with the provision of play facilities for disabled children, to form Play Matters.

Toy libraries take many forms: some are run by voluntary organizations like the Red Cross or Save the Children; some are associated with a book library; most are run by parents on a voluntary basis. Some are mobile, serving remote communities; others are in children's units of hospitals. Play Matters also produce a magazine called *Ark* four times a year, the annual *What Toy?* (see below), and a wide range of other booklets and information packs. Send an sae to Play Matters and ask them for a publications list and details of toy libraries in your area.

Play Matters
68 Churchway
London
NW1 1LT
0(7)1-387 9592

Recycled Toys

'Scrapstores' or 'Play Resource Centres' are springing up in many areas in acknowledgement of the realization that a great deal of what firms and businesses throw out as rubbish can be used as toys and materials by children's groups. In this way children receive the materials they need, and a first-hand lesson in the vital art of recycling. There are now well-established scrapstores in Bristol (Bristol Children's Scrapstore: 0272 710061), London (South London Children's Scrap Scheme: 0(8)1-698 9280; Kids' Scrap Bank: 0(8)1-965 5718), Birmingham (Rubbish Ltd: 021 523 6538), Leicester (Leicester Waste: 0533 688591), Manchester (Greater Manchester Play Resource Unit: 061 223 9730), Milton Keynes (Milton Keynes Scrapstore: 0908 562466), Belfast (Belfast Scrapstore: 0232 230738), Cardiff (Cardiff Scrapstore: 0222 578100) and Newcastle-upon-Tyne (The Children's Warehouse: 091 232 1606), with other schemes planned or recently started. If you have useful things to donate or run a playgroup and would appreciate some offcuts, rejects and surplus, give your local scrapstore a ring.

Nonviolent Toys

In 1987 Finland became the first country to ban the sale of toys which resembled offensive military weaponry; how long will it be before Britain follows suit? 'Think before you buy war toys' is a campaign run by a group of people in Cheltenham, particularly during the Christmas shopping period; they would welcome similar initiatives in other areas of Britain. The Peace Pledge Union (see page 237) also produces 'No War Toys' material.

War Toy Campaign
50 Union Street
Fairview
Cheltenham
Gloucestershire
0242 574795

What Toy?

1986 saw the first publication of the authoritative *What Toy?* consumer's guide to playthings, published by Play Matters (see above). More than 600 toys are tested by children, and the results listed in this full-colour magazine. *What Toy?* concentrates on the period from 0-12 years, with special emphasis on the pre-school years — though articles even cover board games and grown-up toys like dish aerials and geiger counters. *What Toy?* does take into account quality and safety, but there are many things it doesn't. You'll find the Tomytronic 3-D Sky Attack, Rock Lords, Modifiers and Zoids (given a star for excellence) — it certainly isn't designed to deter you from unnecessary consumerism! It does, however, include very many worthwhile toys, especially for younger children, and at £1.95 must be good value.

What Toy?
CT Publications/Play Matters (annual)
£1.95

Tridias

¡tridias!

Tridias is one of the very few toyshops not to have succumbed entirely to being a display window for mass-produced expensive plastic rubbish, and they do very efficient mail order service too. From the main shop in Bath (there are others in Richmond, South Kensington, and Dartington in Devon) they will send you a delightful 50-page catalogue full of imaginative and original toys, most of which are also cheap. A speciality is their stocking fillers like neon lace at 40p for five feet or a submarine bath toy for 55p — yes, you can still get things like that. At the other end of the range their dollshouses are very tasteful and not too expensive, and they also sell a carefully selected list of children's books. 10% discount on bulk orders for playgroups and chazrities.

Tridias
The Ice House
124 Walcot Street
Bath
BA1 5BG
0225 469455.

Suffolk Playworks

While he was working as a community playleader, Mick Farrell found there were several things that would be useful but didn't yet exist. When he wanted to start his own engineering workshop in deepest Suffolk, therefore, he set about creating them. The best known is the folding wooden playbox, an 18″ cube that folds out to reveal pegs, ropes, ratchets, gearwheels and more boxes — it really is all your children's other toys rolled into one, and at just over £200 is a real must for any playgroup. Suffolk Playworks also produces a power kit for disabled childrens' tricycles, and has built an inflatable softroom which can be used by playgroups in East Anglia.

Suffolk Playworks
Box Farm
Allwood Green
Rickinghall
Suffolk
ID22 1LU
0359 258844

Wooden Toys

At Totland Bay on the Isle of Wight, the Toy and Furniture Workshop has been making wooden toys for more than twenty years. These toys are not cheap, but they will last several generations, which is partly why the designs are mostly all-time favourites — a beautiful dolls' house, a pullalong waggon, a car ferry, and stes of simple but ingenious 'ply roads' including a bridge and a dual carriageway.

Michael Mole (in reality Mike and Mo Flood) in Goudhurst, Kent, makes beautiful brightly painted nursery furniture and toys, including self-assembly rocking horses which have won design awards. The duck dressing table mirror is my favourite. Hand-made and sturdily constructed, these could be collectors' pieces in a hundred years' time. Again not cheap, but you'll only ever buy such things once.

Toy and Furniture Workshop
Church Hill
Totland Bay
Isle of Wight
PO39 0ET
0983 752596

Michael Mole
Allways
Goudhurst
Kent
TN17 1BU
0580 211231

Wooden Puzzles and Pictures

The Design Centre has said that George Luck wooden puzzles set the standard by which others must be judged. They really are beautiful, yet surprisingly, they are not all that expensive considering that you'll still have them for your children's children when they come to visit. They start at just over £3.25, rising to £12.75 for some lovely widlife designs and £35 for a large landscape complete with rainbow. The catalogue alone is a delight.

Dave Beetlestone in Palmers Green, North London, does similar things with wood, making jigsaws, wooden pictures to your specification, and a puzzle from your own name at 40p a letter plus 60p p&p. Dave made me a carved 'Green Pages' logo which sits on my windowsill and attracts many a compliment.

George Luck
12 Gastons Lane
Bower Hinton
Martock
Somerset
TA12 6LN
0935 822743

Dave Beetlestone
5 Fairbrook Close
Palmers Green
London
N13 6EZ
0(8)1-888 9089

Mail Order Catalogues

The mail order Co-operation Catalogue contains hand-made wooden toys from three workers' co-operatives: Picaroon of Norwich, No-Nail of Southampton, and Wood'n'Toys of Nottingham. You can buy a World Map Jigsaw at £6.95, a Rocking Welsh Dragon at £49.95, or a Noah's Ark at £39.95.

From the Early Learning Centre's mail order catalogue you can buy books, games and toys designed with a view to safety and durability as well as play value. They have a 'no tanks, no guns' policy, avoiding toys which blatantly express violence. The shops have play areas where children can try out the toys, and they also arrange activity mornings.

The Co-operation Catalogue
Freepost
London
SE15 6BR
0(7)1-703 7064

Early Learning Centre
South Marston
Swindon
SN3 4TJ
0793 831300

Education — the Pre-school Years

Educationally speaking, self-help is the mark of the pre-school years in most parts of Britain. Few and far between are the places which can boast sufficient day-care facilities even for that small proportion of single parents who are full-time workers, never mind the many part-time employed and those who would simply appreciate a full day's break now and again.

Even if nursery classes or schools are available in your area you may not be enthusiastic about their methods, their staffing — or their charges. Your local education authority should be able to tell you what is available in your area, and you may just be lucky enough to find a friendly and flexible nursery nearby which will provide your child with the sort of attention and education you would want for them.

The chances are, however, that you won't, and this is where the self-help comes in. Most pre-school playgroups are organized and run by parents — usually mothers, though fathers are beginning to take an active role in some playgroups. The playgroup movement was begun in the early 1960s by parents who were disappointed by the formality of the 'educational' experiences offered to their offspring in some nurseries, or who were simply trying to fill the gap where there were no nursery facilities of any kind.

The Pre-School Playgroups Association was formed in 1961 to develop and support the playgroup movement, and now has over 14,000 member groups — it can also advise you on the setting up of a playgroup and produces a wide range of useful publications. The PPA should be able to tell you which playgroups are operating in your area, though it is probably easier to ask at your library or community centre. Many playgroups also have mother and toddler groups (parent and toddler groups in enlightened areas), where you can take any child of pre-school age.

Parents with disabled children will be interested in the growing idea of 'opportunity groups'. These are playgroups for children with special needs, and the PPA will be able to tell you about groups in your area. Opportunity groups accept all types of disability from birth onwards, rather than the three-year-old limit generally set by playgroups. Opportunity groups also provide support for parents and the chance for them to talk to professionals on an informal basis.

Pre-School Playgroups Association
61-63 Kings Cross Road
London
WC1X 9LL
0(7)1-833 0991

Information for Scots

Fair Play is an organization devoted to promoting every aspect of play and pre-school education in Scotland. Membership brings you an imaginative quarterly newsletter and access to their extensive library. The Scottish Pre-School Play Association (14 Elliot Place, Glasgow G3 8EP; Tel: 041 221 4148) is the sister organization to the PPA. The lively and independent magazine *Scottish Child* deals with subjects ranging from school boards to womens' magazines, youth homelessness to the politics of food. A year's subscription costs £6 for 6 issues.

Fair Play for Children in Scotland
Unit 29
6 Harmony Row
Glasgow
G51 3BA
041 425 1140

Scottish Child
347a Pitton Avenue
Edinburgh
EH5 2LE

National Children's Bureau

The NCB is probably the best source for information about all aspects of children and childhood, combining as it does the roles of pressure group and research organization. Their resource sheets, of which there are over sixty covering subjects from adoption to solvent abuse, preschool provision to parental involvement in education, are comprehensive and relatively cheap (currently 75p each) — write for a current list.

National Children's Bureau
8 Wakley Street
London
EC1V 7QE
0(7)1-278 9441/7

Parent Support

Parents Anonymous is an emergency service for parents who have problems concerning children of any age. It operates rather like The Samaritans, and you can ask for advice or counselling. A similar organization is Parentline OPUS (Organization for Parents Under Stress); an important function of Parentline OPUS is to prevent child abuse by providing a telephone counselling service for adults who may be involved. On a longer term basis, The Parent Network provides a series of counselling sessions for groups of parents who can then provide support for each other.

Gingerbread has been providing assistance to single parents since 1970. A network of groups covers the country, offering friendship and group activities to lone parents.

Parents' Anonymous
6 Manor Gardens
London
N7 6LA
0(7)1-263 8918

Gingerbread England and Wales
35 Wellington Street
London
WC2E 7BN
0(7)1-240 0953

Parentline OPUS
106 Godstone Road
Whyteleaf
Surrey
CR3 0EB
0(8)1-645 0469 (admin)
0(8)1-645 0505 (help)

Gingerbread Scotland
39 Hope Street
Glasgow
G3 7DN
041 248 6840

The Parent Network
44-46 Caversham Road
London
NW5 2DS
0(7)1-485 8535

Education — A Lifelong Process

It has been suggested that the present crisis in education consti-
tutes a 'national emergency', to be dealt with by increased state
control and the provision of ever more cannon-fodder for a
'technologically sophisticated, internationally competitive, highly
skilled economy'. The politicians who advocate such policies
appear to be blind to the fact that such measures have already
achieved record unemployment and truancy. . . The mistake has
been to limit the concept of education. For too long it has meant
'training for a job'. Our lives cannot be chopped into three neat
portions — learning, working and retirement. . . Learning is
lifelong process, and undertaken at any age and at any level it
should explore and fulfil the potential of the learner.
Green Party General Election Manifesto, 1987

Few would disagree with the Green Party's call for education
to be seen as a continuous process, integrated into our lives
whenever there is a need to expand our understanding or
learn a new skill. This changing attitude to education, however, is not necessarily reflected in the educational opportunities open to us. Many primary children find themselves being
dulled rather than expanded by the curriculum on offer at the
local school, while older children may well find the promises of
freer choice of options limited by local authority budgets or
lack of skilled teaching staff. Despite the riches promised in
continuing education, adults may lack the resources needed to
pay for further learning, or be unable to spare the time
because all their efforts go into supporting themselves and
their families.

There is currently a great deal of dissatisfaction with education, but parallel to this (and not unconnected with it) there is
also a lot of change and innovation, both within the mainstream of state-funded education and in the independent
sector. Never has there been more opportunity to open out the
concept of education to meet newly perceived needs — in
theory at least.

State-funded education is now under so much pressure from
all sides to get its act together that many new ideas are being
tried out. Some will inevitably set off down blind alleys; others
will be the same old thing packaged in a new way. Yet there is
currently more debate and attention being focussed on the
education system than we have seen for a long time — and
that can't be a bad thing.

Some Basic Information

There are 104 local education authorities (LEAs) in England
and Wales and twelve in Scotland. Each LEA is run by a Chief
Education Officer, who is responsible to the local authority's
education committee. The minutes of the education committee
will be in your local library and you are usually allowed to
observe education committee meetings — if you are concerned about education policy in your area this is a good way
of keeping abreast of developments.

LEAs, however, are not directly involved in the running of
schools — this is left to the board of governors and the head
teacher. Almost all schools have parent-teacher associations,
and in most schools each child has either a form teacher or a
guidance teacher who you should have easy access to if you
need to ask about or discuss anything.

If you need basic information about educational establishments in Britain, your library will have copies of two very
boring but very comprehensive volumes called *The Education*
Authorities Directory and Annual — one covers primary education, the other secondary and post-school education. The
secondary volume includes special schools, careers centres,
specialist colleges and so on.

Every parent (and any child that finds basic questions about
education not being addressed) should know about ACE —
the Advisory Centre for Education. Founded in 1960 in an
attempt to emulate the style and success of the Consumers'
Association (see page 333), ACE has played an important
part in many educational initiatives of the last thirty years,
including the Open University (see page 226) and the
National Extension College. They produce a mass of useful
literature, and have an advisory service which can give
information on almost any aspect of education, detailed or
general. ACE has the same glossiness and well-to-do air as
the Consumers' Association and you may question whether it
really stands for change, but they do have a very great deal of
knowledge and experience, so you may as well use it.

Advisory Centre for Education
18 Victoria Park Square
London
E2 9PB
0(8)1-980 4596

And Now For Something Completely Different

Nature gives to each child the potential for immense intelligence an d creativity — and we do our level best to make sure
that they never fulfil it. This is the basic message of author,
parent and child psychologist Joseph Chilton Pearce in two
books that people either tend to adore or abhor. In *Magical*
Child and *Magical Child Matures* he gives a fascinating
account of the intellectual and emotional development of a
child, taking the concept of education right back to basics,
and showing that we don't have to educate intuition and
creativity out of children. Just because we have problems with
the idea of magic it doesn't mean that they do. Magical Child
Matures is the more ambitious of the two volumes, linking his
theories of child development with zen, psychic phenomena
and modern physics — not everyone's cup of tea, but it will
certainly start you thinking about what education really is. Or
what it could be.

Magical Child
Joseph Chilton Pearce
Bantam, 1980
£3.95

Magical Child
Matures
Joseph Chilton Pearce
Bantam, 1985
£3.95

Earthrights and Greenprints

Earthrights is one of the most imaginative and encouraging books I have seen for a long time. It provides in less than a hundred boldly illustrated pages a wealth of ideas and information for teachers concerned with environmental issues, taking 'environment' very widely to include subjects like Third World development and nuclear disarmament as well as the more obvious subjects like pollution and conservation. But *Earthrights* goes to the heart of education itself to look at why it is so important to teach peace and harmony, understanding and compassion. Games, poems, quotable quotes and a comprehensive resource section complete this remarkable book.

And now there is a companion volume to *Earthrights*. Called *Greenprints for Changing Schools*, it looks in depth at the process of greening that is currently going on throughout education. As with 'environment' in the earlier book, it takes a broad view of 'green'; thus it starts by looking at personal change and development, and isn't afraid to use concepts which reactionary elements within education might well pooh-pooh, such as the importance of feelings and 'the tao of headship'. These two books taken together cannot fail to inspire any thinking teacher.

Earthrights
Education As If The Planet Really Mattered
Sue Greig, Graham Pike and David Selby
WWF/Kogan Page, 1987
£5.50

Greenprints for Changing Schools
Sue Greig, Graham Pike and David Selby
WWF/Kogan Page, 1989
£7.50

Education Now

The first issue of *Education Now* appeared in the summer of 1988, an extension of the work of the Human Scale Education Movement (see page 224). The bi-monthly magazine is aimed at people interested in the wider concept of education rather than just at teachers, and the emphasis is on open learning, flexible schooling and wholeness in education. This is an attractive and well-conceived publication which fills an important niche. A subscription costs £15 for a year's issues.

Education Now
PO Box 186
Ticknall
Derbyshire
DE7 1WF
03316 4285

EDUCATiON NOW

Libertarian Education

Now in its twenty-second year of publication, *LibEd* is as radical as *Education Now* but in a different way. Here is the forthright — yet very human — voice of practical and political concern about the changes currently taking place within Britain's educational system. The main message of the magazine, encapsulated in its title, is that teachers must work to counter the stultifying centralist ideology that has given us such things as the national curriculum and impossible financial constraints in education. Thought-provoking reading and very attractively presented, *LibEd* appears quarterly and a subscription costs £2 for 3 issues.

Libertarian Education
The Cottage
The Green
Leire
Leicestershire
LE17 5HL
0455 209029

Green Teacher

Founded by teacher Damian Randle in 1986, *Green Teacher* magazine is a treasure trove of ideas for anyone working in the field of environmental education; anyone, indeed, interested in green ideas. The latest issue concentrates on Global Futures, and has other articles on racism, peace education and poetry — really a regular mini-update of *New Green Pages*. Forty information-packed pages per issue, six issues a year — all for £10.

Green Teacher
Llys Awel
22 Heol Pentrerhedyn
Machynlleth
Powys
SY20 8DN
0654 2141

Green Teacher

Teaching Green

Damian Randle's long-awaited book, *Teaching Green*, appeared late in 1989. Part One, 'The System and How to Change It', is a bit on the heavy side, reading more like a college textbook than a popular call to action, but it does contain many provocative ideas. Part Two consists of practical suggestions for the greening of our children's education. Damian Randle shows how green awareness can be brought into every aspect of the school curriculum, from music to maths; lots of projects culled from the pages of *Green Teacher* show how, for example, you can create puppets from recycled cans or use meditation in art classes. The resource section is very good, but why oh why isn't there an index??

Teaching Green
A Parent's Guide to Education for Life on Earth
Damian Randle
Green Print, 1989
£7.99

School and Its Alternatives

Whether it's putting your three-month-old down for Eton or choosing which of two primary schools your five-year-old should go to, deciding which school will best suit your child's needs can be a daunting task.

The first thing to do is find out what alternatives — if any — you have, then exercise your right to visit any school you have in mind (with the child if you think it's appropriate). Most schools welcome such exploratory visits, and if they don't it's a fairly sure sign that you can do better for your child. Such visits are not reserved for new schools, or even for parents' evenings; a good school will welcome the active interest — and even sometimes the involvement — of parents. You are not there as a schools inspector, however, only to find out how and whether the school is suiting your child!

If you cannot find what you want among the schools available to you, there are several courses open. You may want to investigate 'alternative' schools in your area, or perhaps further afield, where the educational ideas might be more congenial to your own. Always remember, however, that any child gains a great deal from going to school with other children from the same neighbourhood; there has to be a great deal going for a school some distance from home before the benefits start to outweigh the disadvantages.

There is no central register of alternative schools, though they will be listed in *The Education Authorities Directory and Annual* (see page 222). You should be able to find out about such schools by word of mouth, and Education Otherwise (see below) may be able to help. The fees payable are extremely variable; your local authority may be willing to find some of the fees if your child has special needs, and most independent schools have some sort of scholarship or bursary scheme.

Opting Out

Though few people know it, you don't have to send your child to school as long as it receives an education comparable to (not necessarily the same as) that provided by the mainstream system. Deschooling as a conscious choice probably reached its peak ten years ago; mainstream schooling has now become more adventurous and many parents who might once have thought of deschooling are now finding suitable schools for their children's needs.

If this is an avenue you would like to explore, Education Otherwise was formed twelve years ago by parents who were educating their children at home and wanted to support each other. They publish a useful booklet called *School is Not Compulsory* (£1 from them) which explains the legal situation and gives helpful advice about planning your child's learning. They also produce a contact list of members, and will put you in touch with like-minded people in your area.

Jean Bendell's book *School's Out: Educating Your Child at Home* (Ashgrove, 1987, £4.95) is an enthusiastic and practical account of the author's achievements in educating her two children at home. She describes in detail how the curriculum was organized, how she arranged it with her local education authority, and what she feels are the advantages and drawbacks.

Education Otherwise
25 Common Lane
Hemingford Abbots
Cambridgeshire
PE18 9AN
0480 63130

education otherwise

Flexischooling

The Human Scale Education Movement exists to encourage the development of small community-based schools, especially in rural areas. The movement is represented in practice by two 'alternative' primary schools, the Dame Catherine School in Ticknall, south Derbyshire, and the Small School at Hartland in Devon. The basic belief is that small is beautiful where children's education is concerned, and the encouragement of small community schools allows schools to play a far more real and flexible role within the community. The Movement produces a newsletter, and welcomes enquiries.

One of the protagonists of the small schools movement, Richard North, has written *Schools of Tomorrow: Education as if People Matter* (Green Books, 1987, £6.50), in which he sets out clearly the arguments for greater variety and more independence in schools. The book looks at several of the experiments currently taking place, especially the Hartland Small School.

Human Scale Education Movement
Ford House
Hartland
Devon
EX39 6EE
0237 441293

How Children Learn (and How They Fail)

John Holt is the leading spokesperson for the home schooling movement in the USA, but he is also a keen researcher who was one of the first to shine a practical and critical eye on teaching attitudes in state schools. Though *How Children Fail* was first published over twenty years ago it is still in print and still basic reading for all teacher training courses — because the lessons still haven't been learned and integrated. He has the courage to point the finger at teachers and the rigid attitudes they often enforce in classrooms, leaving children with the idea that whatever they do they're not good enough. The companion volume, *How Children Learn*, is based on his own work with children, putting into practice his theories about child-centred learning. Both books are highly readable, and no matter what your educational ideas are you will find much to stimulate you.

How Children Fail
John Holt
Penguin, 1969
£2.95

How Children Learn
John Holt
Penguin, 1970
£4.50

Girls, Boys and Sexism

One of the big issues for parents — and the children who live with it — is sexist attitudes in education and childraising. June Statham's *Daughters and Sons* is the first British book to look in detail at the experiences of parents who are consciously working at avoiding sexism in the rearing of their children. The families she has interviewed come from a wide range of backgrounds and living situations; she doesn't oversimplify the problems and looks at different ways of countering youthful sexism in all its forms.

Daughters and Sons
Experiences of
Non-Sexist
Childraising
June Statham
Blackwell, 1986
£5.95

Power to the Children

Where education and childraising are concerned, it's often assumed that parents and the people who care for children will know what they need better than the children do themselves. Care and support are one thing, however, and control and manipulation quite another.

This page is designed to be of particular interest and importance to young people themselves. Some of the information is to do with education, some to the way young people relate to their community, and some to do with finding out about things that adults often have an unwillingness to answer clearly and fairly.

First Rights

This important and helpful book has been compiled by the National Council for Civil Liberties (see page 333) to explain and clarify the law as it relates to young people under eighteen. It should certainly be in your school library, and everyone should know of its existence. It is very clearly written, and describes in useful detail the rights and responsibilities you have as a child. The sections cover 'home' (what rights do your parents have over you? for example), 'school' (what is the legal situation covering truancy?), 'being in care' (do you have the right to see your parents?), 'employment' (and unemployment), 'sex', 'alcohol', 'the police' and 'the court system'. First Rights is very accessible, and the cartoons are actually funny. At the end is a useful list of addresses and suggestions for further reading.

First Rights
A Guide to Legal Rights for Young People
Maggie Rae, Patricia Hewitt and Barry Hugill
NCCL, 1986 (3rd edn)
£2.95

Sex

There are lots of books about sex and sex education on the market. Some of them are slanted towards the younger school-age child; many are long on ideas about sex but are short on vital information. Jane Cousins' Make It Happy is packed with sensible information about sex for the teenager who is about to become sexually active. It was revised in 1986 and includes up-to-date information about birth control, AIDS, and the legal context of sexual behaviour. It goes into real detail and uses lots of illustrations and diagrams to ensure that everything is understood. It deals with some of the topics that other books tend to be a bit shy about, like masturbation, incest and genital infections, and talks a lot about feelings about sex and the different attitudes that boys and girls are likely to have. It is very strong on emphasizing the fact that we are all different and that there's no such thing as 'normal'. There is a very good reference section at the end. An important book that all teenagers will learn a lot from.

Loving Encounters is a much more straightforward information book covering the same ground as Make It Happy. It's nothing like as thought-provoking or contentious as Jane Cousin's book, but it does tell you a great deal about the facts surrounding sexual relating and the resource section is both comprehensive and up to date.

Make It Happy: What Sex is All About
Jane Cousins
Penguin, 1986 (2nd revised edn)
£2.95

Loving Encounters A Young Person's Guide to Sex
Rosemary Stones
Lions, 1989
£2.25

Child Abuse

Sarah Nelson's Incest is not written specifically for young people, but it deals sensitively and sensibly with an issue that all children — and certainly all girls — should be aware of. She clears away many of the myths surrounding incest, seeing it very clearly as a form of child abuse, rape within the family — indeed, the most common form of rape. The author is a former social worker who bases her ideas on extensive experience, often using the words of incest survivors themselves. This is a hard-hitting book which dismisses many 'liberal' attitudes towards incest, seeing it as part of a constant and society-wide threat to children, mostly girls, from older men. The book ends with a very useful appendix of organizations to help those who are of have been affected directly by incest, including support groups for men who want to face the issue.

No Is Not Enough is written in a more chatty style, obviously considered to be more accessible to a young audience. It includes many first-hand accounts of the sorts of situations in which assault arises, and will make you think again about the sexist violence inherent in many everyday activities. It costs less than Sarah Nelson's book, but the information section of this adaptation from an American original is not as good. Another book by the same authors, still in its American version, is No More Secrets, a sensitive and thought-provoking look at how the parents of young children can encourage a safe and supportive setting in which to discuss this important issue.

Incest: Fact and Myth
Sarah Nelson
Stramullion, 1987
(2nd edn)
£4.95

No Is Not Enough
Helping Teenagers
To Avoid Assault
Caren Adams, Jennifer
Fay and Jan
Loreen-Martin
Lions, 1989
£2.50

No More Secrets
Protecting Your Child
From Sexual Assault
Caren Adams and
Jennifer Fay
Impact, 1981
(distributed in the UK
by Airlift)
£3.95

If you are in trouble or danger, there is a nationwide helpline service: you can ring (free) for advice, information, or someone to talk to. Childline accepts calls from children of any age in any sort of trouble, though its primary aim is to help children who are suffering from emotional and physical abuse. If practical help is needed, they can alert the right organizations to your needs. In the first four months alone Childline helped over twelve thousand children, so don't be afraid to ring them.

Childline
Freepost 1111
London
EC4B 4BB
0800 1111 (24-hour freefone helpline)

Education After School

For many people, real education is what starts when compulsory education is completed. The problem with continuing education is that it isn't always easy to find what you want, and when you find it you may not be able to afford it. You will usually be able to get some sort of financial assistance for some kind of full-time further education if that's what you want; informal and part-time education may be subsidized but you will almost certainly have to pay something.

Formal Further Education

I'm not going to say very much about this, because the resources are fairly easy to find. There are any number of books telling you what sort of courses are available and how to go about choosing — as good as any are the Consumer Association guides called *Which Subject? Which Career?* (a guide to subjects and courses with careers in mind; Which Books, 1987, £7.95) and *Making the Most of Higher Education* (a more general guide to being a student; Which Books, 1987, £5.95). The Advisory Centre for Education (see page 206) can help with enquiries, and the National Union of Students (Nelson Mandela House, 461 Holloway Road, London N7 6LJ; Tel: 01-272 8900) is a useful resource for specific advice and information, especially if you have problems as a student.

Open Education

Part-time educational opportunities are currently experiencing a growth rate that can only be explained by increasing unemployment. The Open University continues to hog the glamour end of the market, constantly expanding its courses and modifying them to suit demand. Open University courses have the obvious advantage that they can be added together to produce a degree at the end; they also provide a good local tutor services, often much-needed breaks at summer schools, and produce some excellent teaching materials. They are currently planning a second level course specifically on the environment, spanning scientific, technological, social scientific and philosophical approaches: it will start in January 1991. When you write for information, tell them in as much detail what you would like to try your hand at, so they can send the most relevant information.

The Open College started in September 1987, using the media in a way very similar to the Open University, but depending much more on the perceived training needs of industry and business. The Open College plans to sell its training programmes to companies as well as to individuals, receives a lot of government support, and aims to provide career training and personally tailored educational opportunities — pretty strictly in that order. As yet it's difficult to see how much value the OC courses will have for the general public.

The Open University
Milton Hall
Milton Keynes
MK7 6AA
0908 653231

The Open College
St Mary's House
London Road
Sheffield
S2 4LA
0742 753275

Evening Classes and Educational Courses

Most education authorities run programmes of evening classes, details of which you will find at your local library. These are an excellent way of expanding your knowledge of learning a new skill, and large authorities like the Inner London Education Authority organize evening classes in almost every subject you can think of. At a slightly more academic level (though there are some very practical courses too), most universities have an extra-mural department which runs courses — sometimes at some distance from the university itself. Glasgow University, for instance, runs courses all over south-west Scotland on subjects ranging from local history to ornithology. Write to the extra-mural department of your nearest university and ask for a prospectus.

The Workers' Educational Association (WEA) has been running courses since 1903, so they should know what they're doing by now! The WEA has over 900 affiliated branches, which run an enormous variety of evening classes and courses. The WEA prides itself on its democratic structure, and makes a particular effort to bring educational opportunities to disadvantaged people. The WEA central office will be glad to give you the name of your local contact, who will then let you know about courses in your area. WEA courses are often run in association with local authority or university programmes.

The National Institute of Adult Continuing Education (NIACE) is the co-ordinating body for information about residential courses and summer schools throughout the country. They produce a fat booklet twice a year (£1.50 from them) detailing a vast range of courses which are open to anybody — over 3,000 every year.

WEA
Temple House
9 Upper Berkeley Street
London
W1H 8BY
0(7)1-402 5608

NIACE
19b De Montfort Street
Leicester
LE1 7GE
0533 551451

The Green College

Every few years somebody decides that it would be a good idea to have a truly green-tinted further education establishment, where people shared their skills and everybody could learn what they needed without it costing the earth. To this end 1987 saw the birth of The New University in Birmingham; sadly but perhaps inevitably 1989 saw its virtual demise.

Now there is The Green College, the brainchild of an Oxford lecturer Peter de la Cour. Established just over a year, more than a thousand people have already enrolled for the various courses and workshops being offered by the College, and many more attend the lecture series being offered at St James's, Piccadilly (see page 176). At present an 'internship programme' is being offered, combining academic work, small group seminars and practical experience. The main academic programme is planned to start in September 1991, with courses including green politics, environmental policy, sustainable development, the politics of agriculture, applied ethics and many others. It remains to be seen whether the reality matches the promise, but there is no shortage either of need or of vision. Write for their programme of courses and lectures.

The Green College
17 Western Road
Oxford
OX1 4LF
0865 249020

Books and Children

In the Children's Book Centre in Kensington, an expensive area of London, I often watch a father or mother looking at books with a child. The adult and the child together will look through a dozen or twenty easily, read the stories, talk about the pictures; and the child will run about, lift down other books, and bring them back to the parent to be read and looked at. No-one will complain. That is what the shop is for. The staff are trained for this, and are delighted the child is taking such an interest in the books. Two hours and twenty books later, the child and the parent may go out of the shop without even buying a book, because the child did not see one, or rather experience one, that was its own book. No-one will mind. They will come back another day, because they will both have enjoyed themselves, spend another two hours looking and reading and discussing, and perhaps this time the child will chose a book it feels is its own.

Leila Berg, *Reading and Loving* (see below)

Learning to read is an enormous achievement for any child, providing them with a passport to experiences and traditions that they can relate to first through story telling, and then directly with the book itself.

Books written and designed especially for children went through a very bleak period in the 1950s and 60's, with pre-dictable plots about stereotyped characters of the sort that would put any child off wanting to read about them. In the late 1970s, however, a few bold publishers began to publish a few bold books — it was in this period that Macmillan started publishing their *Nippers* series, and that authors like Shirley Hughes and Helen Oxenbury became popular.

Today there are many excellent children's books, and more appearing every week. Imported titles from Scandinavia and North America have brought British publishing up to scratch, and British originals are now some of the best children's books in the world. But there is still a lot of rubbish, particularly at the cheaper end of the market, the books that end up in remainder boxes in Woolworths'.

Many libraries, too, have woken up to childrens' books, with children's libraries adjacent to the grownup one where there are regular story-tellings and other activities, and the books are displayed at child height.

Bookshops have in general been slower to respond. The Kensington Road Children's Book Centre is no longer, and although shops like the Puffin Bookshop in Covent Garden have a good range of books, you couldn't honestly say that browsing was actively encouraged. Tony Bradman gives a good list of children's bookshops throughout the country at the end of *Will You Read Me a Story* (see below); The Book House at the Centre for Children's Books in Wandsworth, south London (45 East Hill, SW18 2QZ; Tel: 0(8)1-870 9055), is worth a visit if you're particularly interested in children's books — they have a copy of almost every children's book published in recent years, and are very good at giving help and advice.

Reading and Loving

It is ten years since Leila Berg's book about reading appeared, but it just as relevant now as it was then. She argues gently but persuasively for the integration of reading into the loving relationship between young children and the adults who care for them, with the help of books that a child can identify with and come to love. Her arguments for real books for real children have borne beautiful fruit, yet there is a great deal more to be learned about providing relevant resources for lively minds — much of what Leila Berg prescribes is important within the whole process of education. Reading and Loving is an easy and compelling book, required reading for all teachers and interested parents.

Reading and Loving
Leila Berg
Routledge, 1977
£5.25

What to Read?

Tony Bradman, who is the deputy editor of *Parents* magazine, has written two very good books about children's books. His first, *Will You Read Me a Story*, is a guide to books for the very young; his second, *I Need a Book*, is full of useful and sensitive suggestions about books which help children to understand what is going on in their lives. From fear to physical disability, dentists to divorce, I Need a Book suggests easily-obtainable titles which you can read with children and then talk about. The guide is modest and straightforward, and consciously espouses anti-sexism and anti-racism — its price and readability are added bonuses.

*

Another excellent point which was put to me recently is that sometimes a book can actually be more trouble than it's worth. The example I was given involved a parent reading a book designed to help children cope with a fear of the dark, to a child who had never had such a fear. In fact, this particular child never even realized that people could be afraid of the dark . . . until she had come into contact with this book. The result was that within a few days, her fertile imagination had begun to work on the material provided by the book and she began to become frightened of the dark.

Will You Read Me a Story?
Tony Bradman
Thorsons, 1986
£2.50

I Need a Book!
Tony Bradman
Thorsons, 1987
£2.50

Letterbox Library

Since 1983 the Letterbox Library has played an important part in making widely available books which present positive and powerful images of women and people other than nice white nuclear families. They do a mail order service (you can visit them if you're in London) of books from first readers to teen reads, with a quarterly catalogue (around twenty new books each issue) and a newsletter. It costs £5 to join, then you get discounts of up to 25% on club books — you only get what you order. They have recently initiated an inspection copy service for schools. Letterbox is an excellent initiative, well worth supporting.

Letterbox Library
8 Bradbury Street
London
N16 8JN
0(7)1-254 1640

Children's Action

Whether it's planting oak trees to replace the dying oaks in Sherwood Forest, setting up mini monitoring stations to measure acid rain, or taking part in a multicultural drama event, there are many initiatives being taken by children all over Britain which are both inspiring and important.

Many schools are undertaking their own environmental and social projects, projects which are not only designed to involve and excite the children, but which also benefit the local community and natural environment. The significance of the opinions and activities of young people should never be underestimated — they are both inheritors and inhabitants of the world we have helped to create, and it is to our profound loss that we overlook their contribution to the understanding and alleviation of the world's problems.

The next few pages look at some of the resources available to children and young people in Britain today. Whether you want to become involved in nature conservation or archaeology, find a good activity holiday or just go off youth hostelling, you should find something here to whet your appetite.

Earth Action

Earth Action is the recently-established youth section of Friends of the Earth, designed to 'give you the chance to do something about the issues that concern us all'. As a member (it costs £5 a year) you receive the Earth Action Pack, a quarterly newsletter, and you can join a local group to get even more actively involved.

Earth Action
26-28 Underwood Street
London
N1 7JQ
0(7)1-490 1555

Free Stuff

Not that many people know that there are lots of things you can find out about without spending any money at all (except for the cost of a stamp), and a lot more that is very cheap. You just have to know where to look and where to ask. The first *Free Stuff for Kids* appeared in the USA in 1976, and the first British version in 1981. Everything mentioned in *Free Stuff* is either free or costs under £2, and it's updated every couple of years so you can be pretty sure that most of the things it mentions are still going strong. Each page of *Free Stuff* covers a different topic, tells you where to write to, what to ask for, and what to send — the subjects range from ponies to cardboard cutout dolls, coffee (a really good value pack from Nescafé for free, but don't believe everything they say) to apples (a free variety chart from the Apple and Pear Development Council).

what is it like to be blind?

No sighted person can *really* know, but RNIB's Schools' leaflet describes some of the things that are different for a blind person – ordinary things like pouring out a cup of tea or telling the time or playing football.

directions:	Use paper and an envelope. Please enclose a 9½"x 6½" s.a.e.
ask for:	Schools leaflet
write to:	Royal National Institute for the Blind 224 Great Portland Street London W1N 6AA

Free Stuff for Kids
The Free Stuff Editors
Exley, 1985
£2.50

Kids' Britain

I'm well aware that all these books call you 'kids'; some of you don't mind at all, others really don't like it. I really don't know what the answer is.

Back to business. There have been several good guides to things that children can do and see in Britain. Several years ago the *Young Observer* people did a guide; perhaps one day they'll do another. The weekly page at the end of the *Observer* colour magazine is still usually a good read, though I prefer the Wednesday *Young Guardian*, a page which shows that the skills of young writers shouldn't be sneezed at either.

The two best guides currently available are the twin Pan books, *Kids' Britain* by Betty Jerman and *Kids' London* by Elizabeth Holt and Molly Perham. They are laid out in a similar format to each other, and are crammed full of places to visit, things to see and do, sports, camps, films, music — they really are about the best book value going.

The London volume starts with a calendar of events, from the cutting of the Baddeley Cake at Drury Lane Theatre on Twelfth Night to the New Years' Eve celebrations in Trafalgar Square. The rest of the book is then set out alphabetically by subject, including a suitably spooky 'Ghosts, gibbets, graveyards and gruesome places'. At the end are some clear maps and an excellent index.

The British volume works by region, and although the coverage is pretty good it is a bit sparse in some outlying areas. The 'Round Up' section at the end is particularly good, giving national organizations in all sorts of fields; so is the 'Going It Alone' chapter about activity holidays. Again the index is very helpful.

*

At Muncaster Castle in the Lakelands the family are the guides. Waving towards his bedroom Patrick Duff-Pennington explained: 'I have to shove pyjamas and shoes out of sight. Some chap complained he could see my shoes and that they needed cleaning.' In the drawing room he translated generations of family portraits by famous painters into who got chopped at Tower Hill and who damaged the family fortunes. Two schoolgirls with parents, accepting his informal style, asked about various small articles displayed around the room. He brought them over for a closer look at games, a sewing-box and one decorative box which he opened with surprise to find it empty. The elder girl, obviously experienced in the stately home segregation system, told him anxiously, 'You're behind the rope.' Hopping over it he assured her, 'That's all right, I live here.'

Kids' London
Elizabeth Holt and
Molly Perham
Pan, 1985
£2.95

Kids' Britain
Betty Jerman
Pan, 1986
£2.95

Saving The Planet

Given the amount of interest there is among young people in ensuring themselves and their planet a future, it was only a matter of time before the 'young green guides' started to appear. In fact the better magazines for young people have been pretty green for some time. A special mention must go to *Company* magazine, which regularly includes features on green themes. My favourite was the picture story 'Anne of Green Labels' in the September 1989 issue.

*

Our heroine, Anne, is woken by her alarm, powered by Varta batteries, and leaps out of her rainforest-friendly Futon Company bed to be greeted by Molly, her spaniel. For breakfast Molly feasts on Happidog vegan pet food.

*

Never mind that it's incredibly ungreen to use batteries at all and that the Happidog comes out of one of the 2 billion unrecycled petfood cans that Britons open every year; the magazines are doing a very important job, so keep it up.

The next book off the Gollancz Elkington-Hailes production line is a *Young Green Consumer Guide*, due in April 1990. It will be interesting to see if it's less consumerist and more radical than their previous guides, because young people who are thinking about these things most certainly are. Which is why it's refreshing to see Debbie Silver and Bernadette Vallely's *The Young Person's Guide to Saving the Planet*.

This is a slim, cheap volume (on recycled paper, of course) which explores the practical things you can do about everything from saving elephants to reducing demand for nuclear power. The book is arranged alphabetically under nearly ninety headings, including some not-so-obvious ones like 'green people', 'keeping sane' and 'you'. At the end are further reading and useful addresses (these would have been more useful if they were annotated to say which were most important), and at the beginning is one of those 'how green are you' quizzes which are appearing everywhere these days. Though it made me think, I had problems with this quiz. Question 4 in part 1, for example:

Recycling means:
(a) buying second-hand things
(b) putting waste back into service
(c) making gas from landfill sites

It says that (b) is the right answer, but surely all three are. But really this is a tiny quibble, and I would imagine that the majority of today's teenagers will score quite highly in terms of green awareness. Whether they are doing anything about it is another matter, but *Saving the Planet* will certainly help.

*

So now it's over to you. If everybody does something, by the year 2000 the planet will be cleaner, healthier and better set up for the future. It is time to get moving!

The Young Person's Guide to Saving the Planet
Debbie Silver and Bernadette Vallely
Virago, 1990
£2.99

Green Parenting

How to bring up your children in a green way was another obvious candidate for a handful of practical books. The first off the mark is Juliet Solomon's *Green Parenting*. This is a very practical and digestible mixture of ideas and examples of ways that you and your children can live more lightly and awarely on the planet. It's a very positive book, with lots of creative and inspiring ideas about how to celebrate the earth and bring real meaning into children's lives. The fourteen chapters follow a child's growth from conception to teenage, concluding with a useful 'Ideas To Get You Started' and a peek into a green future. The resources are a bit thin, but the joy and experience that have gone into *Green Parenting* make up for any amount of theory.

*

Advent not only allows time for preparation, but also allows time for Christmas fairs and bazaars run in aid of charity, at which it is usually possible for you and your children to find good presents without breaking the bank. Presented in decorated boxes, quite small items acquire some magic. Home-made fudge, coconut ice, marzipan fruits, marzipan stuffed dates, or small biscuits are gifts which children will enjoy making and which the recipients will enjoy eating. Pomanders (oranges stuck with cloves) are lovely scented gifts to hang in wardrobes. Small cloth bags of home-made pot-pourri (dried scented flower petals) are useful for underwear drawers. Growing flowers which can be dried and given as bunches doubles the rewards of the gardening involved. Or you and the children can have prepared bulbs in pots which will be ready to flower now.

Green Parenting
Juliet Solomon
Optima, 1990
£4.99

Children and Nature

Children respond to observations much more freely than they respond to textbook explanations. Take the case of a hemlock tree that grew near a camp where I worked. This particular hemlock sits between two huge boulders, so it has had to send its roots down twenty-five feet to reach the stony soil below. At the time, it was at least two hundred years old, and only eight feet tall. The children would frequently make a detour on their walks just to empty their water bottles at its roots. Several of them returned to the camp year after year, watching the tree's stubborn struggle for life in its harsh environment. In fact, as soon as they arrived at camp they would run out to see how it had fared through the dry autumn and cold winter. Their loving concern awakened in me an even deeper respect for the mountain hemlock.   Joseph Bharat Cornell (see page 232)

Getting Involved

There are many nature-oriented activities in Britain that children can get involved in, and many of the national conservation organizations have a junior membership. One or two merit special attention, however. Watch is the junior wing of the Royal Society for Nature Conservation: membership only costs £4 a year, for which you get three Watchword magazines, details of local projects, and various tidbits of information about all sorts of things from bats to trees. Watch activities are organized on a county basis by local Nature Conservation Trusts (see page 68).

The Young People's Trust for the Environment and Nature Conservation exists to inform children about the importance of the conservation of wilderness areas and the rare species which inhabit them. They run field study courses, produce a beautiful booklet called *Britain's Rare and Vanishing Species*, and a series of factsheets about particular species which are under threat — send an sae for more details.

The Woodcraft Folk have a wider interest than nature conservation. Seven hundred local groups provide a place for children to meet regularly for nature-based activities, singing, dancing and so on, with the noble aim of teaching children ways of living in co-operation and harmony with nature and with each other — a sort of mixed cubs-and-brownies without the forced discipline.

Watch
22 The Green
Nettleham
Lincoln
LN2 2NR
0522 752326

Woodcraft Folk
13 Ritherdon Road
London
SW17 8QE
0(8)1-672 6031 or
0(8)1-767 2457

Young People's Trust for the Environment and Nature Conservation
95 Woodbridge Road
Guildford
Surrey
GU1 4PY
0483 39600

Children's Books on Green Themes

The last ten years have seen a number of excellent children's books on environmental issues, but in the couple of years since the first edition of *Green Pages* appeared the flow of green titles from educational publishers has become a veritable surge, if not a tidal wave. Some are excellent, a few are bad. The majority are more or less mediocre. Here is a selection of some of the best I have come across.

Story Books for Younger Children

The TV people got very excited. The camera crew took lots of shots of the children in the tree. And the woman called Vanessa even interviewed Lizzie.

'How long are you prepared to stay in the tree?' she asked.

'I'll stay up here forever!' said Lizzie fiercely. 'If it'll save the tree from being cut down.'

'So will we!' chorused her friends.

'What about your parents?' asked the interviewer. 'Aren't they worried about you?'

'My mum's right behind me!' said Lizzie. 'She says trees are our friends. I expect she'll even bring me cheese sandwiches and stuff if I get hungry.'

'My mum will too,' added Michael Stubbs. 'And egg and chips.'

Sue Limb, *Trees Rule OK!* (see next page)

*

Every living creature is our brother and sister, dearer than the jewels at the centre of the earth. So let us be like tiny grains of sand, and protect all life from fear and suffering! Then, when the stars shine, we can sleep in peace, with the moon as our quiet night-light,

M.B. Goffstein, *Our Planet* (see next page)

Chris Baines is well known as a presenter of television programmes on environmental issues. Less well known is the series of 'ecology story books' he has written, lovingly illustrated by Penny Ives. The four short stories, *The Flower*, *The Nest*, *The Picnic* and *The Old Boot* are all set on a small piece of urban wasteland. They tell graphically and with humour how nature — in the form of smily slugs and beady-eyed blackbirds — constantly adjusts itself to the activities of human beings. At £2.95 these picture books for 4-8 year olds are very good value as well as getting across important concepts in a most approachable way.

Helen Cowcher's striking paintings in *Rainforest*, together with a simple but poignant text about the fate of the wildlife of this endangered habitat, have attracted the attention of the judges for both the Mother Goose Children's Book Award and Friends of the Earth's Earthworm Award. Another picture-book called *Antarctica* will be published in the spring of 1990.

For slightly older children I would highly recommend Sue Limb's two 'green stories', *Meet The Greens* and *Trees Rule OK!*. Lizzie Green is a clear-thinking and determined ten-year-old (I imagine her living in Sue's home town of Stroud in Gloucestershire where, like Lizzie, local green activists recently helped save trees in a local park from being felled). She knows what she wants, and whether she has to stay in a threatened tree all night or steal the chickens from a battery henhouse she'll do it (almost) regardless of the consequences.

The American artist M.B. Goffstein is well known for her simple, delicate, telling watercolours. In *Our Planet*, revised for the British market by Edinburgh-based Canongate Publishing, she captures both the variety of life on earth and the sadness we would feel if we were to lose it. The text is simple enough to be read to a four-year-old, but will move many of your adult friends too.

The Flower
The Nest
The Picnic
The Old Boot
Chris Baines
Frances Lincoln, 1989
£2.95 each

Rainforest
Helen Cowcher
Andre Deutsch, 1988
£5.95

Meet The Greens
Trees Rule OK!
Sue Limb
Orchard Books, 1988
£3.95 each

Our Planet
M.B. Goffstein
Canongate, 1988
£5.95

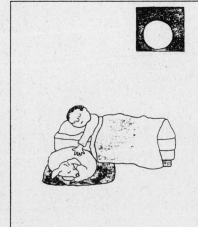

Facts for Juniors

Ladybird Books produce an excellent series of books about conservation for eight-to-ten-year-olds (Series 727; £1.20 each): *What on Earth are We Doing?* is a good introduction to conservation issues, while *Nature's Roundabout* deals with basic concepts in ecology. Another Ladybird series (Series S864; £1.20 each) is published in conjunction with the World Wildlife Fund; the topics covered include *Birds*, *Plants* and *Animals*.

Another very good introduction to ecological ideas for primary school children is Cambridge University Press's *Natural Links* — it says 9–13 but I have read it with an eager seven-year-old. It includes suggestions for activities, and encourages children to participate actively in conservation and living more lightly: 'Be a save-it shopper' it says in big letters on the last page.

Natural Links
Anne Clarke, Stephen Pollock and Phillip Wells
Cambridge University Press, 1985
£2.50

Green Books for Teenagers

This is where the bulk of recent environmental education publishing has been targeted. Despite cutbacks in educational expenditure, publishers obviously feel that middle and secondary schools will continue to dig into their budgets for books on important topics like conservation and recycling. It's interesting to note that not one of these books is printed on recycled paper: don't they take account of teenagers' eagle-eyed discrimination?

healthy foliage

affected foliage

Most are based on single issues, and though some are both well-written and attractive I have the distinct feeling that education-by-project-area can easily become yet another divide-and-rule exercise. Green awareness is about connections, which is why my absolute favourite in this category of books — essential for all school libraries and a worthy addition to any green home's bookshelf — is Nick Middleton's all-embracing *Atlas of Environmental Issues*. He sometimes gets it wrong, as on page 40 where he states categorically that 'Nuclear power stations produce cheaper energy than coal-fired stations': the next edition will have to take account of more realistic accounting within the energy industry! Yet with the proviso that the issues aired by the *Atlas* should ideally be discussed in more depth in both home and classroom, this is a stimulating and absorbing survey of the global environment. Nick Middleton's companion *Atlas of World Issues* (Oxford University Press, 1988, £6.95) is also very good.

The two educational publishers who have made something of a speciality of green issues are Franklin Watts (12a Golden Square, London W1R 4BA) and Wayland (61 Western Road, Hove, East Sussex BN3 1JD), who will gladly send catalogues to interested readers. At a fairly basic level are Wayland's 'Project Ecology' and 'World Issues' series. 'Project Ecology' consists of six titles, each with eighteen or so topic chapters. Most topics have an associated (and well-thought-out) activity, and each book ends with a helpful 'What Can We Do?' section, glossary, bibliography and contact address list. The 'World Issues' series, with environmental titles like *The Energy Crisis* and *The Environment*, is designed for older teenagers, looking at the choices we must make now to create the sort of world we want to live in.

More in-depth and specific are Wayland's 'Conserving Our World' series and Watts' 'Issues'. The six titles in the Wayland series are beautifully illustrated, pretty uncompromising, and refreshingly positive about what the reader can do to help things to change. The 'Issues' titles, which include *Toxic Waste and Recycling* and *The Climate Crisis*, are slightly more graphic and sensationalist, but this is no bad thing where these vital topics are concerned.

Atlas of Environmental Issues
Nick Middleton
Oxford University Press, 1988
£6.95

Air Ecology
Animal Ecology
Land Ecology
Plant Ecology
Urban Ecology
Water Ecology
Jennifer Cochrane
Wayland, 1987
£6.95 each

The Energy Crisis
Michael Gibson
The Environment
Adam Markham
Wayland, 1988
£6.50 each

Acid Rain
John Baines
Conserving Rainforests
Martin Banks
Waste and Recycling
Barbara James
Conserving the Atmosphere
John Baines
The Spread of Deserts
Ewan McLeish
Protecting Wildlife
Malcolm Penny
Wayland, 1989
£7.50 each

Toxic Waste and Recycling
Nigel Hawkes
The Climate Crisis
John Becklake
Franklin Watts, 1989
£6.50 each

Sharing Nature with Children
(and Listening to Their Reactions)

Now for two important books from Exley Publishers in Hertfordshire. Joseph Bharat Cornell's *Sharing Nature with Children* is originally an American book (hence the hemlock tree example on page 230), but it has been published in Britain in an edition completely revised to fit the British environment. It is a unique exploration of what can be done with children to share with them (and they with you) the magic of nature. It is arranged as a linked series of games, mostly for use with groups (though some are suitable for one or two children); games like 'Microhike' ('a very short hike guided by a string three to five feet long. The hikers cover the trail inch by inch on their bellies, viewing such natural wonders as grass blades bent by rainbow dewdrops, colourful beetles sprinkled with flower pollen, and powerful-jawed eight-eyed spiders'). A gem of a book.

Cry for our Beautiful World should be on every school bookshelf, despite costing a hefty £11.95. Helen Exley has brought together children's writings and paintings on environmental themes from every corner of the world. Here are the hopes, fears and feelings of the world's children in a beautifully-produced book which will help anyone to feel a little less isolated in their worries about the future of the planet.

*

I don't want the trees to be felled because I get a feeling here in my heart.
Maria José Barcos (aged 6), Uruguay

Sharing Nature
With Children
Joseph Bharat Cornell
Exley, 1979
£2.95

Cry For Our
Beautiful World
edited by Helen Exley
Exley, 1985
£11.95

Once Upon A Planet

But the children knew that small wild things did live in their neat garden, hiding out of sight. The two toads, for instance, who lurked in the rockery near the bird-bath. On the hot day the ants had swarmed, they had ventured out on to the lawn in the middle of the afternoon, crawling about and darting out their long tongues to feast on the winged ants that fell to the ground after their nuptial flight was over. Dicky and Sue had put down a shallow dish of water and watched them sprawl in it, with great grins of pleasure at the coolness. And on a small clump of nettles, in the tiny corner the children had for their own, there were a few Small Tortoiseshell caterpillars.
Elizabeth Berridge, from 'Loner'

Here's a useful stocking filler from Penguin and Friends of the Earth, in the form of a collection of stories and extracts on the theme of caring for the earth. From Jonathon Porritt's introduction onwards it tends to assume that all modern children live in nice suburban houses, but I suppose that the majority of children who read stories like this do. My favourite is Jan Mark's lively story 'Hide-and-Seek', specially written for *Once Upon A Planet*, about the natural history of the Great Crested Vandal.

Once Upon A Planet
Selected and introduced
by Christina Martinez
Puffin, 1989
£2.25

Resources for Teachers

A 1986 survey found that 78% of primary and secondary school teachers in Britain think that development and environmental education are central to achieving an understanding of, and active participation in, the world. This page is to help the 78% (many of whom will already know what I have to suggest); and gently to persuade the minority who still have not accepted that children need to understand the world in order to participate fully in its rich variety.

Teacher's Resources from National and International Organizations

Most of the organizations listed in *New Green Pages* are only too glad to hear from teachers who need ideas and resources for use with children; indeed many produce special material for teachers. The World Wildlife Fund (WWF Education Department, Panda House, Weyside Park, Catteshall Lane, Godalming, Surrey GU7 1XR; Tel: 0483 426444), for instance, produces a wide range of material; a boldly designed index in a neat wallet shows you exactly what is available. OXFAM (OXFAM Youth and Education Department, 274 Banbury Road, Oxford OX2 7DZ; Tel: 0865 56777) has several education workers who will come and discuss your needs with you.

The Council for Environmental Education provides a central co-ordinating role for national and international organizations involved in environmental education. Their resource library in Reading is probably the largest in Britain, and they handle more than 5,000 enquiries from teachers and educators every year. Their monthly *Newssheet* is an invaluable source of information on publications, resources and services, and they produce a wide range of *Environmental Education Resource Sheets* on subjects ranging from urban wildlife to nuclear energy.

Similarly, the Conservation Trust plays a co-ordinating role to other conservation organisations, runs an information service, produces displays to promote environmental awareness, and has a range of publications designed to keep subscribers informed about environmental topics. Membership is £7 a year, which gives you access to their conferences, projects and discussion forums. They also publish a magazine called *Conservation*.

Council for Environmental Education
School of Education
University of Reading
London Road
Reading
RG1 5AQ
0734 875234
extension 218

The Conservation Trust
National Environmental
Education Centre
George Palmer Site
Northumberland
Avenue
Reading
RG2 7PW
0734 868442/869464

Educational Resource Networks

'Development education' is a recent buzzword in educational circles, meaning helping children to relate to, understand and empathize with the world they live in, thus allowing everybody to benefit from the justice and freedom which follow. Fundamental to this sort of education is access to comprehensive and up-to-date resources, and from the early 1970s onwards resource centres have sprung up all over Britain, co-ordinated and represented by NADEC (National Association of Development Education Centres). Although each of the fifty or more centres is autonomous, NADEC will be able to put you in touch with your local centre, and also produces a useful quarterly called *Newsdec*.

The Centre for Global Education in York exists to promote a global perspective in school curriculums. They have produced a teachers' handbook and run a course for teachers in global and multicultural education; their lively *World Studies Journal* appears twice a year. The Council for Education in World Citizenship has been in existence since 1939, promoting peace, co-operation and understanding through education. CEWC can provide a wide range of resources on world issues, and encourages schools to become full members, giving them access to well-known speakers, a large resource library, advice and help, and regular authoritative broadsheets on important issues.

The National Educational Resources Information Service in Milton Keynes gives every school in the country the opportunity to gain access to hundreds of data files held in the NERIS database, which makes use of the Open University's computer. It provides a range of useful environmental material — recent resource files include ones on Australian aborigines, the desertification of Mali and the wildlife of river banks. NERIS also co-ordinates CAMPUS 2000, a computer information network linking secondary schools and further education establishments — write for their information pack.

NADEC
6 Endsleigh Street
London
WC1H 0DX
0(7)1-388 2670

Centre for Global Education
University of York
Heslington
York
YO1 5DD
0904 415157

Council for Education in World Citizenship
Seymour Mews House
Seymour Mews
London
W1H 9PE
0(7)1-935 1752

National Educational Resources Information Service
Maryland College
Leighton Street
Woburn
Milton Keynes
MK17 9JD
0525 290364

CAMPUS 2000
PO Box 7
214 Grays Inn Road
London
WC1X 8EZ
0(8)1-782 7104/7401

CAMPUS 2000

Adventure Holidays

Some people seem to like chalets by the seaside, noisy 'leisure centres' where everything is provided for your entertainment (and costs a packet), beaches where you can hardly find space to lie down, let alone build a sandcastle. It's not my idea of fun at all, and if it's not yours then here are some ideas for young people's holidays that will stretch and stimulate.

Youth Hostelling

The Youth Hostels Association started in 1930, designed to provide a network of accommodation where young people can stay cheaply and relatively comfortably as they walk and cycle round the countryside. There are now more than 300 youth hostels in Britain, and though a few things have changed since I started hostelling nearly twenty-five years ago (you can take your car now, and it costs a bit more than six shillings a night), youth hostels still provide that very necessary function of somewhere to arrive at after a hard day's walk and which won't cost the earth.

Membership of the YHA (the SYHA in Scotland) gives you access to more than 5,000 hostels worldwide, a colourful quarterly magazine, and information about a varied programme of events organized by the YHA. Two recent developments are the growth of family accommodation so you can take very young children, and a comprehensive programme of activity and special interest holidays, from sand-yachting in Wales to snooker in Norwich — weekend breaks start at £39 full board, which is excellent value.

Youth Hostels Association
Trevelyan House
8 St Stephen's Hill
St Albans
Hertfordshire
AL1 2DY
0727 55215

Scottish Youth Hostels Association
7 Glebe Crescent
Stirling
FK8 2JA
0786 51181

Forest School

The Forest School Camps started in 1947, and each year more than a thousand young people between seven and seventeen go camping with Forest School. Most camps last for a fortnight, and a whole range of activities are on offer, usually including swimming, exploring, night walks, dancing, games and campfires. Most camps are static, though there are some mobile ones; most happen in beautiful parts of Britain, though the programme usually includes at least one camp abroad. Prices start at around £100 for the fortnight. Disabled children are welcome at many of the camps — write for more details.

Forest School Camps
110 Burbage Road
London
SE24 9HD
0(7)1-274 7566

Expedition Centres

A number of reputable and well-organized expedition centres for children have been established in the last twenty years, together, unfortunately, with some less reputable ones. The activity holiday literature produced by the national tourist boards (see page 291) is fairly reliable, though before you send your young teenager away for a fortnight's adventure it is best to have the assurance of somebody who has already been there, or at least a good feel about a centre's literature and correspondence. My general advice is that the glossier the literature, the more you should be concerned.

One excellent centre is John Earle's Dartmoor Expedition Centre, the fruit of seventeen years' experience, run by a well known explorer, outward bound instructor and television personality (though still human!). Weeks of climbing, canoeing, caving, walking and sailing start at around £195 all found, each small group being individually supervised. They deliberately don't go for BMX bikes and similar 'gimmicks', sticking to outdoor education of the traditional kind.

Dartmoor Expedition Centre
Rowden
Widecombe-in-the-Moor
Newton Abbot
Devon
TQ13 7TX
(map reference 699764!)
036 42 249

Field Studies

The Field Studies Council co-ordinates the activities and offerings of eleven field studies centres throughout Britain. The many courses they offer are open to all, adults and young people, though some are obviously more appropriate for children than others; most children will experience field centres as a member of an organized school group, though it is useful to know that the services they offer are more widely available. Weekend courses (full board) start at around £67; weeks at £145. Write to them for a comprehensive information pack.

Field Studies Council (Central Services)
Preston Montford
Montford Bridge
Shrewsbury
SY4 1HW
0743 850674

And Finally

If history is a love in your life, membership of the Young Archaeologists' Club only costs £3.00 a year, for which you get a badge, a quarterly magazine, and information about local activities, including archaeological holidays. The Club is particularly active in places where the archaeology is thick on the ground like Cambridge, Lincoln, Oxford and York. Write for more details.

Young Archaeologists' Club
37 Micklegate
York
YO1 1JH
0904 611944

THE WORLD

*'Never have so many systems vital to the earth's habitability
been out of equilibrium simultaneously.'*
Lester Brown and Sandra Postel, *State of the World 1987*

In some ways we know far too much about our world, and knowing too much often shows us how little we understand. It's hard enough to keep track of what is going on in our immediate environment; how can we be expected to grasp the immensity of the whole planet?

International Peace and Justice

In *The New State of the World Atlas* (see page 330) Michael Kidron and Ronald Segal write: 'All along, the rich states have eloquently demanded the liberation of world trade from protectionist devices, so that lagging economies can grow faster, and the poor states can grow enough from expanding exports to repay their debts. But the same rich states have increasingly resorted to protectionist devices that restrain the expansion of exports from the poor, so as to secure the domestic market for their own products. Malnutrition and even famine have spread and strengthened their hold over much of the world poor, while the financial cost of storing enormous surplus stocks in the rich world constitute such an embarrassment that butter is being fed to power stations.'

While the Third World and a growing proportion of our own population are caught in a poverty trap, even those who have more than enough are forced to worry about money the whole time, knowing that it does not automatically bring happiness. Affluence can only continue at the expense of the poor of the world, and in the end at the expense of the planet itself. As Warren Johnson says in *Muddling Toward Frugality* (Shambala, 1979), 'If we are to enjoy this planet for a long time, we may as well face the fact that trying to perpetuate the affluent society is going to be an uphill struggle. Affluence will grow less comfortable, and there will be less peace and security in it.'

And what of peace and security? At the beginning of the 1990s it would appear that at last the superpowers have taken account of the majority of people in their nations who want a world free of the nuclear threat, but as peace campaigners constantly point out,

235

peace is far more than the cessation of hostilities. In our society 'peace' is usually equated with 'defence', and anyone who speaks seriously of peace is branded a 'wet'. 'Thinking peace' means letting go of — or at least questioning — concepts like 'standing firm' and 'the values of the free world'.

Power

'We all live in the world of business. And the world of business, in its structures, functioning and values, affects all our lives. It is a world which has much in common with the playing of games. The overwhelming objective is to win, and it is an objective that dominates all other considerations. While some people want to be players, most are merely counters, to be shifted or discarded altogether as the progress of the game requires.' Thus opens *The Book of Business, Money and Power* (see page 244).

The players want to keep playing, blind to the fact that what they are playing with is not plastic counters and Monopoly money but people, poisons, and the land that keeps the whole system alive. There is nothing that those in power like better than an obedient and quiescent following, but free will and personal choice are much more important than obeying somebody else's economic and political rules.

The key to justice is knowing who holds the power in the world, for then we can do something about creating a more equitable balance of power. Sixty-one million West Germans, for example, enjoy a larger collective income than all of the 2.4 billion people who inhabit the world's 41 poorest countries — including India and China. If it were not for state benefits, the income of the richest fifth of British households would be 150 times that of the poorest fifth. The average income of a single parent household in Britain is less than half that of a 'nuclear family' — after benefits. And the chairman of the British Oxygen Company earned £883,100 in 1985.

There are alternatives to inequality and competition and greed — we are right to explore them and right to put them into practice whenever we can.

Real Politics

Simply put, politics is the exploration of the ways in which power is exerted in society; without looking at that balance of power, politics is little more than a charade. Just before the 1987 general election Peter Ashley wrote in *The Guardian*: 'Politics appears to attract just the sort of person I would rather not vote for.' For the title of his autobiography, Ken Livingstone chose *If Voting Changed Anything They'd Abolish It*. Between them these opinions encapsulate the problems that face us when we try to understand what most politicians mean by 'politics'.

But in many respects we don't really need to understand: we need to start again with the basic principle that every time a human being does something that affects another, there is a power relationship which should ideally be a conscious one — the personal *is* political. Far from being something which happens on the green benches of Westminster, politics happens all the time, everywhere. This realization gives each of us the power of being agents for change in every aspect of our interactions with other people.

Brian Tokar sums it up in his book *The Green Alternative* (Miles, 1987): 'In a world where politics, for most people, means the proclamations of politicians and the petty squabbles among government officials, Greens promise to give the world a new meaning. Green politics embodies a new understanding of the public sphere as a forum for enhancing the living interrelationships among people and communities, not just a different way of administering the institutions of the state.'

Worldwatch

One of the biggest challenges facing anybody who promotes alternative ideas and projects to those supported by the mainstream power structure is that those in power have all the resources and all the information. But not quite all. Though government and industry sponsor the bulk of the world's research, there are now several independent organizations whose systems for gathering and disseminating important information are very impressive.

One of the most impressive is Worldwatch, and it is indicative of Worldwatch's influence that its annual report, published in book form, is now produced in nearly a dozen languages with a combined print run in excess of 200,000 copies. Worldwatch was established in Washington DC in 1975 to research and focus attention on global problems, and its strength is that it interprets 'global problems' very widely, being unafraid of tackling issues as diverse as Chernobyl, Third World urbanization, and the stranglehold of the multi-nationals.

As well as the annual report, called *State of the World* and published by Norton (though the 1990 edition will probably be published in the UK by Unwin Hyman at around £9.95), Worldwatch publishes a series of occasional papers at the rate of eight to ten a year — you can subscribe to the series in advance, though many of the papers are included in a shorter form in the annual report. *State of the World* gives an excellent overview of the issues covered, and is about the best book value around, which explains why it is now used as a standard text in more than 200 colleges and universities in the USA. I would love to see a similar British publication which looked at the same issues on a more local scale.

Worldwatch
1776 Massachusetts Avenue NW
Washington DC 20036
USA
(010 1) 202 452 1999

Only One Earth

There are actually two *Only One Earth*s. The original is a very influential though now rather dated (but still in print) book by Barbara Ward and René Dubos. First published in 1972 for the UN Conference on the Human Environment, *Only One Earth* was quite revolutionary as mainstream documents go. It's interesting reading for students of green history, and cheap.

The more recent *Only One Earth* is a brilliant and beautifully illustrated paperback by Lloyd Timberlake, an author I very much admire both for his clarity and his wisdom. The theme of this book (which was also the basis for a television series) is 'sustainable development' — development which is stable, resilient, appropriate, productive and self-reliant. Using nine areas from both 'developed' and 'developing' regions as case studies, the book looks at a wide range of environmental issues from desertification to water pollution, and what is being done about them. This could be a doom-laden book, but the overall message is one of hope — if we can learn from our mistakes.

Only One Earth
The Care and Maintenance of a Small Planet
Barbara Ward and René Dubos
Penguin, 1972
£2.95

Only One Earth
Living for the Future
Lloyd Timberlake
BBC/Earthscan, 1987
£6.95

The Real Cost

In *The Real Cost* Richard North covers some of the same ground as Lloyd Timberlake, but instead of looking at things area by area he guides us through the global trade and environmental degradation maze product by product. Thirty-one chapters examine the real cost of tea and coffee, eggs and milk, jeans and fridges, gold and aluminium, wildlife protection and modern warfare — among many others. This is a very intelligent book, well researched, eminently quotable, attractively designed; between them Lloyd Timberlake and Richard North will give you a lot to think about.

*

The junked batteries of the UK represent about 12,000 tonnes of lead, about the same amount of zinc, and about 300 tonnes of nickel, cadmium and mercury dumped into the environment. Almost all the zinc, mercury, cadmium, nickel and silver which gets wasted in the UK is wasted through having been made into batteries and then dispersed through the country in cells whose scrap value is nil.

The Real Cost
Richard North
Chatto and Windus, 1986
£7.95

Human Rights

'All human beings are born free and equal in dignity and rights.' So begins the Universal Declaration of Human Rights adopted by the UN General Assembly in 1948 without a single dissenting vote. Charles Humana compiled the first *Human Rights Guide* in 1983, and the latest enlarged and updated edition (Pan, 1987, £4.95) makes grim reading in a world where most people live in countries whose governments fail to honour the majority of their earlier promises. The guide devotes four pages to each of 120 countries, giving detailed information about which rights are respected and which denied — Denmark heads the list and Ethiopia comes in last. The United Kingdom, ranked fifteenth, comes up with a 'tries hard but could do better' rating: the guide cites police powers to ban public assembly, Northern Ireland abuses, telephone tapping, sexism and racism, and police detention without charges being brought.

The foremost campaigning group working for the rights and freedoms of political and cultural prisoners is Amnesty International, founded in 1961 and now a very active global network which has over the years intervened on behalf of more than 30,000 prisoners in more than 150 countries. In 1977 Amnesty's work was acknowledged with a Nobel Peace Prize, and in 1978 with the UN Human Rights Prize. One of Amnesty's most recent fundraising initiatives links them with concern about environmental issues, for they are currently in the process of buying a 29-acre storm-damaged wood in East Sussex — donations help both to conserve the woodland, to be called Amnesty Wood as a living memorial to prisoners of conscience, and to further the work of this vitally important organization.

Amnesty International
99-119 Rosebery Avenue
London
EC1R 4RE
0(7)1-278 6000

The Third World

Our Global Responsibility

If the world were a global village of a hundred people, seventy of them would be unable to read and only one would have a college education. Over fifty would be suffering from malnutrition, and over eighty would live in what we would call sub-standard housing. If the world were a global village of a hundred residents, six of them would be Americans. These six would have half of the village's income, leaving half for the other ninety-four residents. How could the two groups possibly live harmoniously with each other? Could they survive without enmity and conflict? In some Indian villages the so-called 'untouchables' have risen against the landlords, moneylenders and police, only to be crushed by armed force. Is this the kind of future we want? The conflict in rural India is about the control of land and resources; it is about the right to produce enough food to survive. As the resource crisis deepens, who can say that such conflict will not erupt on the global scale.

It can be hard — and painful — to remind ourselves constantly that we can only sustain the lifestyle we do as the result of a worldwide trading system in which the developed countries have the power, and the Third World is always the loser. It's painful enough to take in that 20% of the population of Britain own more than half of the disposable assets (the lowest 20% less than a thousandth) — but two-thirds of Bangladeshis earn less than a hundred pounds a year.

Once the knowledge has sunk in, however, it becomes clear that unfair trading operates in every area of our lives, from our breakfast cup of tea, through the sweated labour toys and kitchen equipment imported from South-East Asia and the metals in our motor cars, to the sugar in our teatime cakes and the electronic components in the television set made in piece-rate factories in Taiwan.

We can ignore it, or we can be paralysed by guilt, or we can do something to change our perceptions and our practices.

The Third World And The New Economic Order

Ever since the Bandung Conference of 1955, Third World countries have been discussing the need for a radical reshaping of the world's trading strategies — a 'new economic order'. Despite regular international meetings, the much-publicized Brandt Report of 1980, famine in Africa, food mountains in Europe and a growing Third World debt crisis, very little has changed in recent years. The industrialised West, especially the USA, refuses to endorse a code of conduct for multinational companies, which continue remorselessly to milk the Third World to ensure the continued and growing wealth of their shareholders. International organizations like the World Bank and the International Monetary Fund, which supposedly exist to even out inequalities in the world trading system, are controlled almost exclusively from the West — employees who are serious about their commitment to fair trade often have to be underhand or have to leave.

Lobbying and campaigning, taking part in aid events and collecting relief money locally — all have their part to play in changing things. The most important thing you can do, however, is to change your patterns of consumption. The only pressure that will make the multinationals listen is concerted consumer pressure. If enough people say they won't buy South African fruit, supermarket chains will ensure that alternatives are always available. Better still, avoid buying from multinationals as far as possible — until you've done a great deal of homework you can never tell who owns whom. Did you know, for instance, that the health food chain Holland and Barrett is owned by the Booker Corporation, which is heavily involved in genetic engineering and the buying up of small seed companies (see page 82)? Or that HMV record shops are owned by Thorn-EMI, one of Britain's largest defence contractors?

Buying and using things as little and as awarely as possible is the real key to change. Political and economic pressure is vitally important, but never underestimate the influence of millions of individual consumers.

If things carry on as they are, the prospects for a new international economic order are nil. A genuinely new order can only be created out of the destruction of the old one. This the First World will never allow, because it owes its dominant wealth and power to the present structure of international relations. And this the Third World will never achieve, for the present order renders the poor countries too weak and vulnerable to destroy it.
Michael Smith, in What's What in the 1980s
Europa, 1982, £8.50

Can we give up some of our privilege, or will this prediction inexorably move towards its inevitable and tragic conclusion?

Aid, Trade or Self-Reliance?

Over the last four centuries a situation of massive world inequality has become established. A few countries, mainly in Europe and North America, appropriate a proportion of the world's wealth which is totally unrelated to the size of their population. They have achieved this situation not just by using their own resources, productive skills and efforts, but by appropriating those of the rest of the world on a massive and unprecedented scale, and by methods which have little to do with fair exchange and more to do with plunder, loot and military might. . . Meanwhile, the governments of the rich countries of the West and their ruling class claim, with considerable hypocrisy, that they are providing 'aid' to help the Third World to escape from the underdevelopment and poverty which they and their predecessors created and continue to create. But much of this aid fails to alleviate poverty even in the immediate context in which it is provided; and its overall purpose is the preservation of a system which damages the interests of the poor in the Third World.

Teresa Hayter and Catharine Watson,
Aid: Rhetoric and Reality, Pluto, 1985, £4.95

What an indictment! But it's true. Official Western aid to the Third World consists mostly of stuff we don't need or want because we've worn out our land producing crops that nobody in Britain needs, and in real terms the amount of money paid as aid has steadily fallen over the last ten years. When you add to this the realisation that most aid is 'tied' anyway — we'll give you aid if you use British companies to build your roads and electricity supply systems — you begin to see just how corrupt the whole system is.

But, you'll say (I hope), I ran for Africa, I sent money to Ethiopia, I buy my gifts from OXFAM. Don't stop — to the extent that things can be done these charitable organizations are doing their very best, not only to provide emergency relief when it's needed but also to provide resources and training so that projects can be established which permanently support communities in the Third World. This is one of the best ways of using your money to help the Third World towards a sustainable future. 81p out of every pound you send to OXFAM is used in the field, half to provide emergency aid, but also half to train health workers, support producer co-operatives and provide credit to poor urban families wanting to build their own houses.

Yet it is important to see the links between giving and taking. What is the point of giving agricultural aid to Central America at the same time as importing vast amounts of coffee, tea, tobacco and sugar which are bad for us, bad for the land, and use land which could grow food for the local population? What is the point of famine relief to Mozambique while we continue to supply weaponry which extends a war which makes both the distribution of aid and the establishment of permanent projects a near impossibility?

Any real shift involves the deep-seated recognition and conviction that all people, the world over, must have access to their basic needs, and that in order for this to happen they must have power to make decisions about their own future.

Poor people in the Third World are not stupid — they know what they need and are prepared to work hard to get it. What we need to do is let them get on with it, providing advice when it is asked for and resources without strings, refusing to support economic and political systems which oppress them, listening to what they have to tell us (much of which we could learn from) — in short, supporting them in their own self-reliance.

This doesn't mean an end to trade, but it does mean reducing and refining trade so that we only use what we really need, and doing our best to ensure that what we use harms the planet, including its human population, as little as possible. To put it very succinctly: we must learn to live simply so that others may simply live.

Some Aid/Trade Reading

The books on aid and trade that I recommended in the first edition of *Green Pages* are all still worth reading, but since there has recently been a spate of excellent and provocative books about 'Third World development' I will skip very quickly through some of my previous suggestions. These included Paul Harrison's *Inside the Third World* (Penguin, reprinted 1982, £3.95), *The Guardian Third World Review: Voices from the South* (Hodder and Stoughton, 1987, £5.95), and *The Third World Guide*, a good and detailed reference book published annually in Brazil by Third World researchers and journalists (the 1989 edition, available from Third World Publications — see page 340 — costs £15.95).

Susan George's *A Fate Worse Than Debt* (Penguin, 1988, £4.50) shows how debt-induced poverty is destroying the lives of countless Third World families and creating environmental havoc on a massive scale. In *Developed To Death* (Green Print, 1989, £6.99) Ted Trainer explains how warped western concepts of 'development' have led to disastrous global and regional inequalities; he makes it clear that the rich are getting richer *because* the poor are getting poorer, and that the only way out of the impending impasse is for the rich to consume less.

Since its rebirth in 1988, Earthscan Publications (see also page 242) has published many important titles on aid, trade and the Third World; send an A5 sae to Earthscan at 3 Endsleigh Street, London WC1H 0DD for a catalogue. The new edition (1988, £5.95) of Lloyd Timberlake's *Africa in Crisis* offers real insight into that continent's plight, including the tragic nonsense of more than half of the West's £8 billion a year aid going to pay the salaries of the 80,000 European 'experts' working in the field, sometimes earning more than £80,000 each per year for the privilege. As well as creating widespread human poverty, it is becoming increasingly clear that badly-planned and mismanaged 'aid' projects have played a large part in the environmental degradation of many parts of the world. How this happens is well-documented in Teresa Hayter's *Exploited Earth: Britain's Aid and the Environment* (1989, £7.95), while the positive side of the coin is presented in *The Greening of Aid* (1988, £8.95), a collection of 33 case studies of sustainable development in the Third World, most of them written by Third World people themselves.

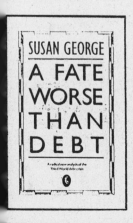

TRAIDCRAFT

Paul Johns, Traidcraft's Managing Director, calls Traidcraft 'big business on a small scale', even though the scale of this vitally important project grows every day. Traidcraft was set up in 1979 to provide an alternative way of trading with the Third World by setting up direct links with producer and marketing co-operatives in the places where the goods are grown and made. I first heard about Traidcraft in 1983 when I started buying Campaign Coffee from them, which comes from co-operatives in Tanzania; then a year or so later I started hearing about the network of Traidcraft outlets all over the country. Traidcraft now distribute 700 different lines through six hundred retail outlets and 1,200 voluntary representatives; their catalogues have print runs of up to half a million.

Their main objective is international justice — 'trading for a fairer world' — and to this end Traidcraft work with voluntary aid organizations like Christian Aid, Catholic Aid for Overseas Development, and the World Development Movement to identify and import products which are useful to the buyer, provide a decent living for the producer, and do as little environmental harm as possible.

Their main catalogue includes furniture, textiles, tea and coffee, crafts and jewellery. They also market a wide range of recycled stationery products, and books and posters. There is also a clothing catalogue, a separate stationery catalogue, and a catalogue of items which are available only in limited quantities because their supply is more erratic (though some of the nicest things are to be found there).

As well as buying what you need directly from the catalogue or from a local craft or wholefood shop, you can also help Traidcraft to expand its activities yourself, either by getting together with a group of friends to put together a bigger order, or by contacting your local representative and seeing if they need any help running Traidcraft stalls at fairs and fêtes, or talking about Traidcraft and world trade. There are also four Traidcraft shops called 'Tradefair Alternatives': these are in Newcastle-upon-Tyne (Carliol Square), Sheffield (142 Devonshire Street), Leeds (3 King Edward Street) and Liverpool (64 Bold Street).

In the financial year 1988-89 more than £2.75m worth of Traidcraft's sales were of craft goods, textiles, foods, tea and coffee imported from the Third World. Traidcraft gives a percentage of its sales income — over £50,000 a year — to charities, and helps to fund the work of the Traidcraft Exchange, Traidcraft's parent charity (Traidcraft plc, however, is a public limited company). With sales of goods from Third World sources expected to exceed £3 million in 1990, Traidcraft's orders to its overseas partners probably represent sufficient income to sustain more than 4,000 families for a year.

Deliberately setting up its operation in an area of high unemployment, Traidcraft has brought more than 150 jobs to Tyneside. Its policy of 'better jobs' applies equally to the Third World producers of the things that Traidcraft sells and to the people employed by Traidcraft in this country. In an *Objectives* leaflet (which you can ask for when you order your catalogue), Traidcraft say very clearly what they mean by 'better jobs', an initiative which could usefully be followed by other organizations:

▶ Fair wages.
▶ Recognition of each person's worth and of the need for the job each person does.
▶ A good match to each person's skills and capabilities but ones which will encourage personal development.
▶ Adequate facilities and equipment to do the job to the standard required.
▶ Adequate safety precautions.
▶ Opportunity to participate in decisions; to associate in free trade unions where appropriate, and to share in the responsibilities and benefits of ownership.
▶ A caring and friendly atmosphere and pleasant work environment wherever possible.
▶ Recognition of work-load and the flexibility to cope with this.
▶ Opportunities to take advantage of the skills gained or pay received o r saved to go on to other forms of training or employment or self-employment.

I came to Traidcraft on a YOP scheme two weeks after leaving school when I was sixteen. That was six years ago. I was offered a permanent job after 4 months and have had jobs in accounts, order processing and customer services. My present job draws on all this experience and I really feel I have something to contribute. Pete and I got married in 1986, he had joined Traidcraft exactly a year after me, and my Dad also now works in the maintenance section! The social side of work is very important to us. I've also had the chance to use my training in make-up in photographic and modelling work for several catalogues.

Janet Julsing, Trade Sales Co-ordinator

Traidcraft plc
Kingsway
Gateshead
Tyne and Wear
NE11 0NE
091 491 0591

Who Profits?

Richard Adams' book is partly autobiography, partly the history of the project which became Traidcraft. It is a well-told and remarkable story, proving that if you have enough integrity and patience you can have both your principles and your profit — any budding post-Thatcherite green entrepreneur can learn a great deal from reading about Traidcraft's struggles and successes.

*

Traidcraft's work depends on offering an alternative approach whereby the rich can recognise and respond to the needs of the poor. The structures and the systems must be different, but the finest 'people sensitive' organization counts for nothing unless it genuinely is setting out a way for the vast majority of the world, who cluster around the margins of our affluence, to be drawn in.

Who Profits?
Richard Adams
Lion, 1989
£4.99

TWIN/Twin Trading

The Third World Information Network (TWIN) and Twin Trading are sister companies, one concentrating on research and information, the other on practical marketing, set up in 1985 with funding from the Greater London Council. TWIN's activities started with an important conference which looked at practical ways of setting up international trading networks which would benefit producers and provide ongoing advice and information about finance and marketing. Twin Trading is still very much in its infancy, though it is marketing a range of Third World products from furniture and textiles to coffee and foodstuffs. TWIN offers some very useful services to producers and suppliers, including finding Third World sources of useful and worthwhile products, producing literature on the implications of trade and technology for the Third World, and assisting UK-based groups working on Third World issues with information and first-hand advice. TWIN is currently developing a database on the marketing needs of Third World producers, and on appropriate tools and equipment produced in this country which is of use in the Third World. TWIN publishes a quarterly journal, *The Network*.

TWIN/Twin Trading
345 Goswell Road
London
EC1V 7JT
0(7)1-837 8222/3/4

Anti-Apartheid Movement/ AA Enterprises

Consumer boycotts are of growing importance. The most successful has been a 17-year-long campaign against Barclays Bank in Britain, which partly withdrew from South Africa in late 1986. It had been a target because its subsidiary, Barclays National, was until 1985 South Africa's largest bank. Barclays was also one of the biggest lenders to South Africa. And, as the Guardian commented, there was 'no British company more closely identified with South Africa than Barclays Bank'. Barclays was seen as a strong backer of the South African government, and it had publicly adopted a policy of 'constructive engagement' with the government. But an intensive campaign by the Anti-Apartheid Movement, End Loans to South Africa, and the National Union of Students was so successful that Barclay's share of the student market fell from 27 per cent in 1983 to 17 per cent in 1985. Local councils, charities, Oxford colleges and other organizations and individuals closed accounts with an annual turnover of £7 billion. During the first 10 months of 1986 Barclay's shares fell 15 per cent in comparison with British bank shares as a whole, in large part because of its involvement in South Africa, with all the attendant bad publicity and disinvestment pressure, plus the increased risk. The day the withdrawal was announced, Barclay's share price soared.
Joseph Hanlon and Roger Omond,
The Sanctions Handbook, Penguin, 1987, £4.95

The Anti-Apartheid Movement is Britain's foremost campaigning group in the effort to bring the plight of black South Africans to the attention of people in Britain. *Anti-Apartheid News*, published ten times a year, will keep you up to date with all of its many activities, together with current news from South Africa and the front-line states.

AA Enterprises was established in 1986 to support and raise funds for the Anti-Apartheid Movement, selling products from the front-line states of Angola, Botswana, Mozambique, Tanzania, Zambia and Zimbabwe, and the usual range of mugs, t-shirts and so on. Bags of Mozambique cashews labelled 'Nuts to Botha' are a tasty reminder of the struggle; one of their t-shirts is based on a design by a Mozambique artist who was formerly a domestic servant, and money from the 'Release Mandela' mugs goes to help release Mandela.

Anti-Apartheid Movement
13 Mandela Street
London
NW1 0DW
0(7)1-387 7966

AA Enterprises
PO Box 533
London
N19 4BR
0(7)1-482 3883

Biashara

The idea of Biashara arose at the end of 1985 among the members of a Bristol-based education resource centre. They decided that a shop was the answer, which would sell Third World products, plus campaign merchandise, world music and recycled paper products. An important phrase they use is 'value for people before value for money', though not as a replacement, since most of the items that Biashara sell are very reasonably priced. Biashara's stock includes crafts, jewellery and carvings, most of which come from Third World co-operatives and family businesses who receive a decent return for their work. Biashara has close links with BREAD, Bristol Education for Action in Development, which helps young people to recognize their potential to act for real change in the world.

Biashara
47-49 Colston Street
Bristol
BS1 5AX
0272 260902

Tracing the Links

One of the biggest hurdles to using your intelligence, awareness and consumer power to change the pattern of economic activity in the world is knowing how and where the tentacle-like operations of multinational companies and chains of companies dip their toes, or more usually whole limbs, into the international market-place. You may buy something from your local builder, for example, only to discover that what was once a local firm — even though the name hasn't changed — is now part of a national company, which in turn has a majority of its shares held by an international corporation, which also has interests in armaments, pesticides and tobacco.

How on earth can you make sure that you're not supporting the things you don't believe in?

The Transnational Information Centre exists to research transnationals (another name for multinationals) and make the information available and accessible for people who need to know. They have produced many excellent reports, including recent ones on the Bhopal massacre, and the operations of GEC, which as well as manufacturing washing machines are also major armaments contractors. EIRIS (the Ethical Investment Research and Information Service — see page 249) holds stock- and shareholding information on a vast number of companies, including all the multinationals — detailed information can often be found about a particular company, but check with EIRIS what you can afford before you ask for such information; time is money even for ethically-sound organizations.

One of the biggest and most heavily-tentacled multinationals is Rio Tinto Zinc, among other things Britain's biggest mining corporation and one of the world's most unscrupulous operators. PARTIZANS (People Against Rio Tinto Zinc and Subsidiaries) was founded in 1978 at the request of Queensland's aborigines who were being threatened with illegal prospecting, and is now an international network. Following a massive campaign in 1981 many local authorities and public bodies disinvested in RTZ shares, but many still own them — PARTIZANS will give you all the information you need.

ELTSA (End Loans to South Africa) use the same kind of information to check which multinationals have South African connections, and to campaign for the ending of British financial links with an oppressive regime. They have produced a useful set of 'Company Cards' which put the facts about the SA connection at your fingertips — so far they cover ICI, RTZ, Consolidated Gold Fields, Standard Chartered and Shell.

Transnational Information Centre
9 Poland Street
London
W1V 2DG
0(7)1-734 5902

ELTSA
PO Box 686
London
NW5 2NW
0(7)1-485 8793

PARTIZANS
218 Liverpool Road
London
N1 1LE
0(7)1-609 1852

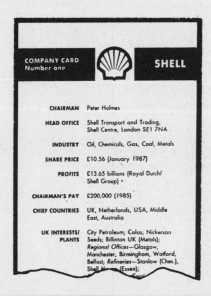

COMPANY CARD Number one	SHELL
CHAIRMAN	Peter Holmes
HEAD OFFICE	Shell Transport and Trading, Shell Centre, London SE1 7NA
INDUSTRY	Oil, Chemicals, Gas, Coal, Metals
SHARE PRICE	£10.56 (January 1987)
PROFITS	£13.65 billions (Royal Dutch/ Shell Group)
CHAIRMAN'S PAY	£200,000 (1985)
CHIEF COUNTRIES	UK, Netherlands, USA, Middle East, Australia
UK INTERESTS/ PLANTS	City Petroleum; Colas; Nickerson Seeds; Billinton UK (Metals); Regional Offices—Glasgow, Manchester, Birmingham, Watford, Belfast; Refineries—Stanlow (Ches.), Shell M___(Essex), ___

IIED/Earthscan

IIED (the International Institute for Environment and Development) works to demonstrate the links between the environment, economic development and the needs of the world's poor. With an annual budget of around £1.3 million it works on a number of projects around the world, particularly in developing countries, providing policy advice, information and technical help to leaders in governments, aid agencies, international organisations and grass- roots development organisations. IIED publishes an informative six-monthly newsletter called *Perspectives*.

IIED has its own publishing house, Earthscan, which is closely linked with IIED's work but editorially independent. Since it was founded in 1988, Earthscan has produced many important titles on such issues as desertification, economic development and Third World urbanization, and has recently established an arrangement with WWF to produce a series of books for the Fund's new adult education programme.

IIED/Earthscan
3 Endsleigh Street
London
WC1H 0DD
0(7)1-388 2117

Greening the Deserts

The campaigning group Green Deserts is currently putting most of its effort into a practical project called Sunseed Desert Technology. This provides people with the opportunity of undertaking a little practical reclamation work in the Spanish Sierra Nevada, where Sunseed runs a research project to examine ways of combatting desertification and soil erosion. It costs only £40 a week to take part, though you must be prepared to put up with fairly basic living conditions.

Green Deserts Ltd
Rougham
Bury St Edmonds
Suffolk
IP30 9LY
0359 70265

Sunseed Desert Technology
PO Box 2000
Cambridge
CB5 8HR

Survival

Part of the West's global domination strategy has been to destroy the habitats, livelihoods, and too often the lives of tribal populations. Survival International exists to alert us to the ongoing threat, and to enlist our help in supporting tribal peoples in their struggle for self-determination. More than 200 million tribal people are threatened by 'development projects', forced resettlement schemes, and military manoeuvres — they can fight in the ways they know how to, but are often ignored by governments and developers who see them as 'primitive'.

Membership brings a newsletter full of important information you won't find elsewhere, and the group also provides people with the opportunity to get involved through their Urgent Action Scheme. Participants of the scheme are sent an occasional bulletin informing them of a specific threat to a tribal group, together with the addresses of appropriate government bodies to write to in defence of the native people's rights. It has proved very effective.

Survival International
310 Edgware Road
London
W2 1DY
0(7)1-723 5535

Responsive Travel

In 1988 Britons took 20 million overseas holidays, 90% of them within Europe and 10% further afield. No doubt many of them learned a lot about lifestyles and conditions in places where much of what we take for granted in the West is simply not available; too often, however, people bring not only themselves to these countries but also their cultural prejudices, often unconsciously held. The need for responsive, sensitive travel is now needed more than ever before if we are not to experience the subtle annihilation of some of the world's most varied and valuable expressions of human life.

One important organisation which strives to propagate this kind of sensitivity is the Centre for the Advancement of Responsive Travel. A £5 annual subscription fee to CART will bring you a useful *Responsive Traveller's Handbook* (with regular free updates) which comes in three parts. Part 1 covers general guidelines relating to aware travelling; Part 2 includes resources such as guidebooks, travel clubs and exchange schemes. Part 3 covers an enormous range of alternative foreign holidays — tour organisers, centres and firms offering everything from Spain on horseback and Bavaria on bikes to rural development study tours in Sri Lanka and 'behind the scenes' tours of Nairobi. The *Handbook* is tremendous value for any budding green traveller.

Tourism Concern is a recently-formed organization for people who care about the quality of tourism, both as an experience for the tourist and for the places and people they visit. Membership (currently £10) brings a contacts list, a quarterly newsletter, and the chance to attend relevant seminars and meetings.

Centre for the Advancement of Responsive Travel
70 Dry Hill Park Road
Tonbridge
Kent
TN10 3BX
0732 352757

Tourism Concern
8 St Mary's Terrace
Ryton
Tyne and Wear
NE40 3AL
091 413 5393

SERVAS

'Servas' is Esperanto for 'serve', and is an international network of people working for peace who open their homes to travellers on a reciprocal basis. In 1950 a group of people worked out a system whereby approved travellers could receive lists of hosts in different countries. They would carry their own bed linen, stay no more than two nights unless expressly invited, and would always write before visiting. They would pay no money, but would be expected to join in with the activities of the host's family. The idea has grown until there are now 12,000 hosts in more than 112 countries. It costs £5 to become a host; to become a SERVAS traveller currently costs £20 for registration plus the hire of host lists for the countries you plan to visit.

SERVAS
Bankside Cottage
Welton le Wold
nr Louth
Lincolnshire
LN11 OQT
0507 602512

Voluntary Work Abroad

It was thirty years ago that Voluntary Service Overseas sent its first teams out to Ghana and Sarawak, and today there are over 1,200 VSOs working in 43 countries, with over 600 people a year setting out on two-year contracts taking with them skills which can help people in the Third World to stand on their own feet. If you think that voluntary service overseas may be something that you would like to look into, VSO produces a range of leaflets on different types of work. If you become supporting member of VSO you can make contact with one of the many regional groups, and receive their very good quarterly magazine, *Orbit*.

For those that may not have the necessary skills or be prepared to commit so much time to voluntary endeavour, International Voluntary Service organises workcamps throughout Europe, usually lasting between two to four weeks, which are open to everyone regardless of skills or abilities. Projects involve practical conservation work, construction, and activities with the handicapped and with children.

Voluntary Service Overseas
317 Putney Bridge Road
London
SW15 2PN
0(8)1-780 2266

International Voluntary Service
162 Upper New Walk
Leicester
LE1 7QA
0533 549430

Progressive Tours

At a time when travel firms are vying with each other to package and advertise exciting tours to far corners of the world, Progressive Tours offers only packages with a difference. They are certainly popular — as Managing Director Loudon Temple says: 'We haven't time to record things, only to do them!' Progressive specializes in tours to Russia, the Eastern Bloc and Latin America, places it can be hard to get to if you don't go with a party. Being experts in this field, Progressive will do their very best to help you deal with any bureaucratic delays, and their tours are all fully bonded.

Progressive Tours Ltd
12 Porchester Place
London
W2 2BS
0(7)1-262 1676

Rough Guides

The *Rough Guides* were only launched in 1982, but already they have become established as the guide books which really tell you what a country is like. For some countries, like Kenya, the *Rough Guide* is the only independent guide book. So far 25 guides have been published, with another seventeen titles promised by mid-1991 including volumes for disabled travellers and women travellers. A leaflet is available from the Rough Guide people at 149 Kennington Lane, London SE11 4EZ; they are published by Harrap Columbus.

Roger Lascelles Publishing (47 York Road, Brentford, Middlesex TW8 0QP) publishes the Lonely Planet Handbooks, another important series of 'real travel guides'; Lascelles also publishes a number of useful reference guides such as *A Directory of Jobs and Careers Abroad* (1989, £7.95) and *A Directory of Work and Study in Developing Countries* (1989, £6.95), aimed primarily at a younger readership. Finally, *The Independent* newspaper has produced Frank Barrett's *A Guide to Real Holidays Abroad* (1989, £5.95) which includes details of many green-tinted tour operators and country-by-country checklists of things which are really worth knowing before you visit.

Money

Money

In many ways money is a very useful invention. It enables us to obtain the things we need using symbols of value which are acknowledged all over the world; it can give us some idea of the relative value of things; if used wisely it can be seen as a creative way of channelling some of our energy.

Yet most of the money in the world is an abstraction from reality, given power as though it were reality. Money leaves out most of the qualitative differences between things, concentrating almost exclusively on quantity. Gross national product adds up every kind of money transaction, making no distinction between a tree and a car, a life-support system and a funeral.

The costs of 'knowing the price of everything, but the value of nothing' have become abundantly clear in a place like Tokyo, where the air is sometimes so polluted that oxygen cans are sold to people on the street. Here it has become all too obvious that money cannot ultimately replace the nourishment of the natural world. Marco Polo thought it hilarious that the thirteenth century Mongols accepted paper money in place of things that had real value, and wouldn't have dreamt of accepting a few bits of paper for his horses, however large the numbers on the paper.

If our culture seems to have lost sight of the distinctions between money and value, worth and wealth, we need new definitions of profitability. What is it, for instance, that is really being created when you exchange large sums of money for another currency when the exchange rate is in your favour, then change it back when the balance shifts to make a 'quick killing'? You may have increased your purchasing power, but you haven't actually created anything tangible. On the other hand, there is clearly value in the enormous amount of unpaid domestic work done by women, which is conveniently overlooked when it comes to reckoning the costs of production, and there is real value in the waste that we cannot be bothered to recycle.

Finally, if 'free market theory' has little to say about the real material needs of people and their environment, it cannot even acknowledge the non-material needs. What is the cash value of a walk in the forest? Is it really the amount that you are willing to pay at the turnstile entrance?

The Money-Fixers

There's a joke that runs:

'What's the golden rule?'
'I don't know, what is the golden rule?'
'Whoever's got the gold, rules.'

It would be even funnier if it weren't so true. Money value is constantly being adjusted by banks, businesses and governments to make the sums look good, yet wherever we look, it is becoming clearer and clearer that money value is not the be-all and end-all of human health and happiness. It has been remarked that people today are not noticeably any healthier as the result of a tenfold increase in NHS spending in the last twenty years.

Ex-civil servant and author James Robertson is very clear and forthright when it comes to the role of money in modern Britain. 'The argument is that money being the calculus we use to measure value, it is vital that the money system should operate fairly and objectively. Money values should reflect the actual values and preferences that people have; for example, people's pay should reflect the value of the work they do. As things are, however, everyone knows that the money system does not operate this way. Some people get highly paid for work of little value, while others get paid much less for work of much greater value. The people who run the money system — bankers, stockbrokers and so on — do not run it professionally, with the aim that it should operate fairly and efficiently in the interests of society as a whole. They operate it in such a way as to cream off above-average incomes and capital gains for themselves and their clients. In this sense, the present money system is fundamentally corrupt.'

Cashing in on Debt

Consumer credit in the UK is growing at a staggering 48% each year; the average Briton is £670 in debt — not counting mortgages. I remember once having a heated argument with my bank manager. He was telling me that if I couldn't reduce my overdraft he might have to repossess some of my belongings. I was telling him that if banks didn't lend money to people like me at extortionate rates, he would be out of a job.

This basic dynamic is at work all over the globe, with rich bankers and go-betweens making enormous sums out of other people's debts — to all intents and purposes holding the poor of the world to ransom. The debt crisis is fundamental to the current global environmental crisis, since having extracted all the wealth from Third World economies for our own benefit, we have gone on to shackle the people for whom those resources were their only livelihood with massive interest repayments. Their only apparent method of keeping up the ransom payments is to impoverish their resource base yet further.

The same is true for many Westerners, too. We often use all the means at our disposal simply to keep up the debt repayments — conveniently renamed 'credit facilities'. And what do the money managers do about it beyond encouraging us to spend more in order to boost industry in order to increase earnings in order to spend even more?

Who will be the first lemmings to turn tail?

Business, Money and Power

Renowned American economist Robert Heilbroner says of *The Book o f Business, Money and Power*: 'This will teach you more about modern day capitalism than you would learn by reading all the books of its Nobel Prizewinners.'

I'm sure that most people feel that the world of big business is so complex that they could never understand it. If this applies to you, yet you are concerned about the hold of multinational enterprise on the world market, this is an excellent introduction to loans, mergers, buy-outs, protectionism, banking, shares and commodity futures. It is detailed and authoritative, yet everything is explained with the help of dozens of potted histories, illustrations, diagrams, games and quotations — a book which is easy to dip into and hard to put down.

*

Not even religion, supposedly concerned above all else with the spiritual, has escaped the approaches and attitudes of the business system. Indeed, in many of its organized manifestations, religion is itself big business. The Mormon Church is the dominant economic force in the state of Utah, USA, and has considerable investments beyond. The Church of England has vast holdings in property, stocks and bonds. At the beginning of 1985, it had a portfolio worth some £1.8 billion; some £707 million of it in stock exchange investments. Richest of all is the Roman Catholic Church. [The story of the Vatican-Calvi-Masonic links follows . . .]

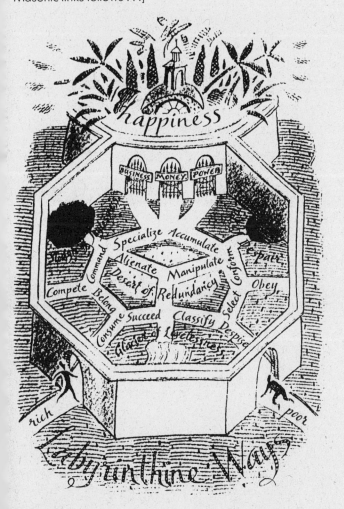

The Book of Business, Money and Power
Michael Kidron and Ronald Segal
Pan, 1987
£7.95

Affluence and Need; Poverty and Denial

Every human being has a number of basic needs, so basic that they ar e enshrined in most charters of human rights. They include food, shelter, warmth, clean water and clean air. The facts are, however, that a fifth of the world's population goes to bed hungry every night; that the number of homeless in Britain continues to rise; that many people in Britain (mainly inner city children and their mothers) are malnourished. Whatever we believe in theory, the affluent continue to take and use more than they need at the expense of the poor, who become relatively poorer with each passing year.

What you think about the redistribution of wealth is almost certain to depend upon whether or not you have any. As available resources begin to run out (especially land, which is very evidently finite), the gap inevitably widens between those who have and are afraid of losing it, and those who haven't and stand very little chance of ever having.

It is hard to imagine how anybody can believe that capitalism on its own can ever ensure that basic human rights are fulfilled. Without a parallel insistence on a person's right to their basic needs, there is no mechanism by which wealth can be redistributed in society. Nobody wants to be destitute or to have to worry constantly about where the next meal is coming from.

The Green Party shares with other observers of the economic scene the belief that until everybody's basic needs are met the situation can only get worse, and therefore calls for a complete reappraisal of the way the tax and benefits system works in this country. The details of such schemes may vary, but the basis is an idea which was suggested many decades ago — the 'social wage' or 'basic income', a cash sum paid to each person regardless of status, which would guarantee everybody the basic necessities and which would to a large extent replace the present complex systems of social security. Many writers have expanded on the idea in recent years — Charles Handy in The *Future of Work* (see page 245) sums up the arguments by saying: 'While a full national income scheme seems too big a step to take, the principle behind it is important — that a citizen is entitled to a livelihood as much as to education and health care, that the state is not a provider of last resort to those that cannot help themselves but a guarantor of basic rights.'

The Race for Riches

In this, his most recent book, Jeremy Seabrook writes knowledgeably and eloquently about issues of wealth and poverty, deftly weaving together reportage and commentary in a full-frontal attack on the capitalist ethic. He makes it crystal clear that money alone cannot cure the ills that an overdependence upon wealth has created, taking the reader *en route* via the housing estates and Third World ghettoes where oppression and impending rebellion have their seedbeds. Essential reading.

*

As faith in money grows, faith in ourselves and in each other decays. With time, even the memory of non-monetized ways of answering human need fades and dies, and money becomes the sole enabling agent of increasing areas of human activity. If the creation of wealth itself destroys and wastes humanity, that wealth, however vast, will never suffice to repair the ravages it has wrought. Money cannot cure what money has caused.

*

Poverty cannot be 'cured', for it is not a symptom of the disease of capitalism. Quite the reverse: it is evidence of its robust good health, its spur to even greater accumulation and effort.

The Race for Riches
The Human Cost of Wealth
Jeremy Seabrook
Green Print, 1988
£4.99

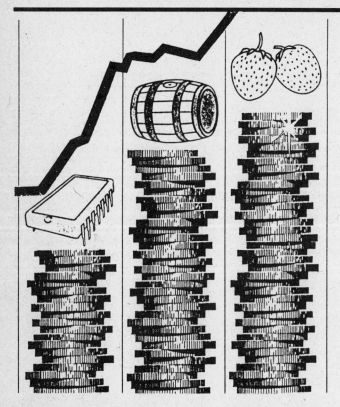

Who's In Charge?

Central banking is a phenomenon only of the last few decades: a hundred years ago there could never have been such widespread fluctuations as we have seen recently in the world markets. Until the growth of central banks in the early twentieth century, local banking put local money to use in local business, and the money it used was directly related to tangible assets. Notes of credit and deposit referred to real, actual goods.

Before the creation of central banks, reserve currencies were only created by those people who created the products which were used to back paper money. Thus it was only those who created wealth who had the ability to create money. Today the situation is back-to-front, with governments which absorb the wealth of nations having the exclusive power to increase the volume of money irrespective to the volume of wealth being created in the country. It is of course very much in the best interest of governments not to have their currency related to any specific product as this allows them the freedom to create as much money as they wish. However, the benefit of this facility would be lost if governments allowed other people to create a better type of money which did not lose its value from inflation.
Shann Turnbull, *Resurgence*, 1984

A growing number of people are beginning to reclaim control over the way they use money. Of course money is useful — it is a medium of exchange which is accepted by almost everyone, and which makes it unnecessary to have exactly what someone else wants before you can enter into a bargain with them.

The problem with money is not the idea of a universal medium of exchange, but that the medium is outside the control of ordinary people, and that the medium itself has become a 'commodity'. All of this increases the ease with which wealth can be drained from those areas where real wealth lies (food growing areas, for example), into areas where wealth comes from the manipulation of money.

As money has become separate from value, it has become increasingly easy to stockpile it ad infinitum. It can be bought and sold speculatively, and apparent wealth gained from charging interest. Little wonder that ordinary people feel completely out of control when it comes to money, and tend to see city bankers as an upmarket breed of con merchants.

Taking the Reins

So what can you do to have more control over the way that money flow s through your life? What can you do to bring an economics of reality into your daily dealings?

Informed Personal Choice

Conscious consumerism is probably the most effective way of restoring money to its proper role as a fair medium of exchange. This is really what the whole of *New Green Pages* is about — using what money you have in a careful and informed way, avoiding as far as you can supporting products and processes that damage the environment and disempower human beings. There are many signs that people do want to spend where their conscience dictates. Nine out of ten *Which?* readers are worried about pollution; 98% of housewives interviewed by the Addis company feel guilty about the amount of rubbish they throw away. In a recent Marplan survey, two in five respondents said they would go out of their way to buy 'environment friendly' products', and well over half said they would be prepared to pay more for products that didn't harm the environment. 62% of the UK population have been classified as 'potential green consumers'. For more on 'green consumerism' see pages 250-251.

Ethical Investment

Conscious saving is another way of affecting the use of resources. Ethical investment is looked at on page 249.

Local Economic Regeneration

The generation of local projects which create wealth within and for the community is of vital importance. It is all very well for an American company to provide jobs, thus enabling the workers to buy Japanese televisions, but unless wealth is generated within the community and stays there, there is little chance of long-term economic stability. The section on work (pages 273-279) looks at ways of generating real local employment; ways of raising resources for local investment are outlined on the next two pages.

Local Currencies

Though the law in Britain prohibits the setting up of alternative money systems, there are many opportunities for organizing systems of exchange which do not involve 'real money'. The simplest is a token scheme, used for example by many baby-sitting circles. Chapter 8 of *The Living Economy* (see page 252) describes several successful experiments in community currencies, including the continuing Guernsey scheme which involves the issuing of zero or low-interest banknotes.

Local exchange trading systems (sometimes called LETSystems) are probably the most successful community-based currency system so far developed. Such a system enables members of a community to exchange goods and services, even when 'real money' is scarce. No cash is used; members price their goods and services in notional 'green pounds', and advertise in a regular newsletter. Transactions are recorded by ansafone and computer; there is no interest and no repayment schedule. A negative balance simply means that for the time being you are wealthier and have issued currency to the community. A final important consideration is that local currency cannot leave the community.

Local money systems are more advanced in Canada than in Britain (see Guy Dauncey's *The Rainbow Economy*, next page, for detailed information), but there are one or two schemes operating here. Practical Alternatives (see page 100) operates a nationwide 'green pound' scheme, but probably the most advanced alternative money scheme currently in operation is the Dart Valley Exchange Network, where more than fifty members have access to the DVEN accounting facilities, paying and receiving any transaction they wish to (or any part of a transaction) in green pounds.

Dart Valley Exchange Network

8 Hunters Moon
Dartington
Totnes
Devon
TQ9 6JT
0803 867546

Money, People and the Environment

As is becoming increasingly self-evident, one of the main reasons we have got ourselves into such a mess is that our main method of reckoning the value of something — money — is so limited. It appears to be cheap to use processes which pollute because the environment simply doesn't feature in our accounting system. Food, raw materials, clothes and manu-factured goods from the Third World seem to be cheap because the health and living conditions of the workers are given almost no value.

Currently there are three ways of dealing with this dilemma. Either you ignore the problems, as politicians and industrialists have done for decades. Or you try to put a money value to what you consider to be important social and environmental qualities, as economists are increasingly trying to do. Or you say that the present ways of valuing the important things in life are so far from the mark that we might as well start again and think what we *really* mean by 'value'.

Several recent books have addressed this vital issue, with a varying degree of success.

Blueprint For A Green Economy

In this report, originally prepared as a discussion document for the Department of the Environment, David Pearce and his colleagues have unashamedly taken the middle road. In so doing they have been able to attract the attention of many powerful economic leaders, and to muster general agreement for the premise that the environment is important enough to be given a high value.

Much of the book is devoted to economic technicalities such as methods for discounting costs and benefits to fit future scenarios, but there is much that the non-economist reader can gain from reading it. To my mind too much of the thinking is little more than the re-invention of the wheel of cost-benefit analysis, a technique which has now been with us these last twenty years and which has trundled over a good many unique habitats and communities in the name of enlightened progress. But, like so many green-tinted ideas, you have to wait for the world to catch up with new-fangled economic concepts, be grateful for belated high-level interest, and keep asking difficult questions. Read it and see what you think.

*

Why is it important to place monetary measures on environ-mental gains and losses? At its simplest, what we seek is some expression of how much people are willing to pay to preserve or improve the environment. Some measures automatically express not just the fact of a preference for the environment, but also the intensity of that preference. Instead of 'one man one vote', then, monetization quite explicitly reflects the depth of feeling contained in each vote.

Blueprint for a Green Economy
David Pearce, Anil Markandya and Edward Barbier
Earthscan, 1989
£6.95

A Rainbow Economy?

I do admire Guy Dauncey's fearlessness in combining his critique of modern society and economy with an almost naïve new age symbolism. In *After The Crash* we are treated to a whistlestop excursion through an enormous number of green-tinted economic initiatives from all over the world, showing that — as in nature — diversity is the precondition for econo-mic stability and fulfilment. He likens this to a rainbow of values — purple for spiritual, dark blue for planetary, pale blue for economic, green (of course) for ecological, yellow for creative, orange for community and red for social — and the symbolism taken beyond what it can realistically convey sometimes threatens to pervert the course of the argument. Nonetheless, this is an important and thought-provoking study which does much of the questioning that Pearce doesn't. The references and resource lists at the end are very useful.

*

The world of economics can be a bewildering place, full of long words and mathematical equations. This book is not like that. Its major thesis is very easy to grasp. It proposes that as we think, see, love and do, so our economies are; and as we change the way we think, see, love and do, so our economies change. Our economies are only reflections of ourselves, expressing the ways we live and the values we live by.

After The Crash
The Emergence of the Rainbow Economy
Guy Dauncey
Green Print, 1988
£6.99

Green Capitalism

Can you realistically sup with and be on the payroll of big business *and* maintain your integrity as an asker of difficult green questions? John Elkington of SustainAbility (see page 250) and Francis Kinsman evidently believe that you can. I have my doubts, but that didn't prevent me from getting a great deal from their recently-published books — a post-*Green Consumer Guide* update of John Elkington and Tom Burke's *The Green Capitalists* and Francis Kinsman's momen-tous-sounding *Millennium*.

If you want to know how the market leaders, both compan-ies and individuals, are responding to the rapidly changing social and environmental demands of their customers and clients, these are the books that will tell you, since both authors are consultants (that word of many meanings) to some of the country's most influential businesses. While important seeds are being set in important places by books like this, however, *Millennium* and *The Green Capitalists* display a certain smug-ness and complacency that will make the darker green reader squirm uncomfortably from time to time. My suspicion is that this is to do with that important quality — integrity.

The Green Capitalists
John Elkington and
Tom Burke
Gollancz, 1989
£5.95

Millennium
Towards Tomorrow's
Society
Francis Kinsman
W H Allen, 1990
£12.95

Credit Unions

The biggest financial problem faced by most people is debt, made worse by crippling rates of interest charged by people and institutions who make their money from other people's debts. Most people think that if they need to borrow money, the best they can do in terms of interest is a bank loan, but by forming a credit union, loans cannot cost more than 1% per month (compared with around 1.5% for a bank loan and 1.75% for a credit card), savings are kept within easy reach as well as being safeguarded, and money is kept within the local economy.

The first credit unions took the form of 'people's banks' in Germany in the 1860s, though it was in the 1920s and 30s that credit unions became vitally important, especially in North America during the depression years. In was only in 1979 that credit unions received specific legal status in Britain, though many already existed under Friendly Society legislation.

Credit unions must have at least 21 members who have something in common — where they live, for instance, or where they work. This ensures the common interest of the members, who in joining become part owners of the union, and ensures that everybody knows where the money is coming from and where it is going.

The Association Of British Credit Unions will be happy to give you further information, and tell you about unions already in operation in your area.

The Association Of British Credit Unions
48 Maddox Street
London
W1R 9BB
0(7)1-408 1699

Mercury Provident

If you are involved in an experimental project designed to make the world a better place for its inhabitants, it is worth considering Mercury when it comes to finance. To date they have helped schools, shops, housing for students, old people, and the disabled, employment initiatives and farm projects. Mercury was founded in 1974 as a non-profit-making provident society, becoming a non-profit public company in 1986, and acts as an intermediary between worthwhile projects and concerned investors.

The borrowing side involves giving potential investors full details about current schemes, so that they can choose both what to invest in *and* the rate of return that they want taking into account the nature of the project. Although Mercury is the first enterprise of its kind in Britain, it has close links with similar organizations in Germany, Switzerland and The Netherlands. They produce a fascinating journal three times a year which they will send free to anybody interested in new ways of funding worthwhile projects.

Mercury Provident plc
Orlingbury House
Lewes Road
Forest Row
East Sussex
RH18 5AA
034 282 3739

Green Portfolios

In 1983 Giles Chitty founded Financial Initiative, Britain's first ethical venture capital company. Now he runs a division of Barchester Insurance and Investment which specializes in finding appropriate places to invest funds looking for a green-tinted home. He offers comprehensive, independent personal financial advice which takes into account your green, social and ethical values as well as your financial ones. It is now possible to base a mortgage, life assurance policy, pension plan, investment bond or savings plan on an ethical investment fund which performs as well as the best of the boringly conventional funds.

Barchester Green Investor
Phoenix Buildings
32 Market Place
Salisbury
SP1 1TL
0722 331241

A Green Building Society

Invest in the Alternative

Since 1981 The Ecology Building Society has offered an alternative to the big societies, guaranteeing investors (who receive all the usual services of a building society) that their money is put into energy-efficient community-enhancing projects, and providing funds for people to buy properties which encourage rural and inner city regeneration and promote a more ecological way of life. Thus the EBS has recently assisted a wholefood shop in Aberystwyth to buy the premises it was renting, lent money to the Lees Stables projects in the Scottish borders (the home of *New Cyclist* magazine — see page 312), and helped revive community spirit in the Alston area of Cumbria by lending to several households involved in an wholefood business. They don't usually lend on semis in Pinner.

The Ecology Building Society
18 Station Road
Crosshills
Keighley
West Yorkshire
BD20 8TB
0535 35933

Ethical Investment

Ethical investment is booming. Between 10 and 15% of all new private investment in the USA is now made subject to the conditions that it shall not be invested in companies whose policies are socially and environmentally damaging. Quite suddenly, it seems, the newspapers in Britain are full of adverts for 'conscience funds', 'ethical funds' and 'stewardship funds' — more than a dozen new ethical trusts and two specifically 'environmental' unit trusts have appeared in the last couple of years. What are they, and how do you choose between them?

On the surface they may all seem to offer similar services. They take your money and invest it, just like any other trust fund, but they guarantee (so they say) not to invest it in companies with an interest in militaria, alcohol, smoking, South Africa, the use of live animals in research, polluting the environment and so on. Most have some mechanism for checking the interests of companies they invest in (some use EIRIS — see below). Few give the positive side — what they will invest in — and most spend a lot more time telling you what return you will get rather than how you will help the world economy to be fairer and more humane.

A Guide to Socially Responsible Investment

Because the situation is changing so rapidly, it is difficult to find out exactly what the options are at a particular time. On all of the issues involved, however, Sue Ward's *Socially Responsible Investment* tells you exactly what to look out for as you chart the course of your investments — what to ask your broker, what to ask of trust funds, different investment strategies, and ways of checking that your money is being used as you would want it to be.

Socially Responsible Investment
A guide for those concerned with the ethical and social implications of their investments
Sue Ward
Directory of Social Change/EIRIS, 1986
£5.95

Research and Advice

Since 1983 the Ethical Investment Research Service has provided a unique and independent service to British investors, checking around 750 quoted companies to see how 'clean' they (and their connections) really are. They produce factsheets (which can be bought at £5 each) for the top 50 companies, plus a variety of reports, services and package deals for private and corporate investors. EIRIS have recently updated their handy guide called *Choosing an Ethical Fund* (£5), and their quarterly newsletter, to which you can subscribe separately (send an sae for a sample copy), is very good.

EIRIS Services Ltd
401 Bondway Business Centre
71 Bondway
London
SW8 1SQ
0(7)1-735 1351

Where to Invest

As you start looking at the ethical investment options available, you will find two well-established companies and a host of new ones which have appeared since mid-1987, usually managed by an established brokerage or building society.

Friends' Provident (as you might expect, since the Quakers have long been interested in ethical investment) operate a Stewardship Unit Trust, which was established in 1984. The Trust has strict investment criteria, with an independent 'committee of refernce' which uses information from EIRIS as a basis for their decisions. More than £200 million have now been invested in the fund, and it regularly surpasses the *FT* ordinary share index in performance, which suggests where real growth potential lies.

You might be unhappy that the Stewardship Fund is not independent of Friends' Providents' other (and non-ethical) activities, in which case you could look at the independent Ethical Investment Fund, which also has an excellent performance record, again doing better than the ordinary share index. 'Building for a Better Future' is their slogan, and they see money as a tool for positive social change. Their investment criteria are very wide-ranging —they will not invest in armaments, South Africa, nuclear power, companies giving large political donations, experiments on animals, advertising, gambling, alcohol, tobacco or banks; they also use EIRIS to monitor all investments.

The Stewardship Unit Trust
Friends' Provident
72-122 Castle Street
Salisbury
SP1 3SH
0722 411622

The Ethical Investment Fund
10 Queen Street
London
W1X 7PD
0(7)1-491 0558

The Merlin Ecology Fund is a unit trust which invests in companies which are either directly engaged in pollution control or which demonstrate a positive commitment to the long-term protection and sustainable use of the natural environment. If you are attracted by this specifically environmental, pro-active approach, Merlin could be the one for you.

Merlin Ecology Fund
197 Knightsbridge
London
SW7 1RB
0(7)1-581 8015

There are a number of other funds which call themselves 'ethical', but you need to check carefully their criteria and methods of assuring compliance with them. Two funds with good reports are the NM Conscience Fund and Buckmaster and Moore's Fellowship Trust. The Conscience Fund is a unit trust which is designed both to avoid 'the bad and the ugly' (though only those for whom these criteria are their 'main business') and to encourage employee welfare, environmental awareness, community involvement and charitable donation; the Fellowship Trust is similarly a unit trust which concentrates on the positive aspects of the performance of companies it invests in.

For a regular update of options in ethical investment it is well worth reading Jill Papworth's monthly 'Money' column in *Environment Now* magazine; among other information she monitors the performance of all currently available ethical funds. *New Consumer* also carries a regular 'Clean Money' feature.

N M Financial Management
York Mount Suite
Dudley House
Upper Albion Street
Leeds
LS2 8PN
0532 434837

Buckmaster and Moore Ltd
80 Cannon Street
London
EC4N 6HH
0(7)1-588 2868

THE GOOD   THE BAD   THE UGLY

Of course, in the light of stock market performance over the last couple of years you could always invest in something that would be certain to grow whatever happens to world markets — like trees, for instance, or organic vegetables, or healthy children.

Consuming — New, Ethical and Purest Green?

In 1989 British consumers spent more than £300 billion on personal goods and services. Of this sum only £30 billion was spent in areas where there was no effective consumer choice or where, through near monopoly, it was severely limited. Thus the average consumer more or less consciously directed at least £6,000 towards particular suppliers' goods and services.

New Consumer, *Good Business* (see below)

In the USA ethical consumerism, like ethical investment, is on the increase. Spearheaded by the work of the Council on Economic Priorities and aided enormously by American freedom of information legislation, it is now possible for Americans to find out very easily whether the things they are buying are supplied by companies which are supporting or destroying people and the environment.

Research and publications along the same lines have recently been established in Britain. New Consumer is a Newcastle-based organization which examines the ethical basis of economic decision-making over a wide range of social, justice and environmental issues. By becoming a subscriber you can receive their bi-monthly publication *New Consumer*, each issue of which looks in depth at a particular area such as alcohol or clothes. A series of New Consumer books is under way, starting with *Good Business*, an in-depth survey of the ethics of Britain's top 130 companies. This will be followed by a popular (and cheaper) version, *Shopping for a Better World*, covering the same ground, and an employment guide so that you can choose who to work for as much on ethical grounds as financial ones.

Also worth looking out for is the magazine *The Ethical Consumer*, a sort of 'green *Which?*' that looks at a range of products and services in each bi-monthly issue — a useful and timely publication.

New Consumer
52 Elswick Road
Newcastle upon Tyne
NE4 6JH
091 272 1148

The Ethical Consumer
100 Gretney Walk
Moss Side
Manchester
M15 5ND
061 226 6683

Green Consumerism

Our decisions to buy or not to buy give us enormous potential power. It is not simply a question of cutting the environmental impact of the products we purchase, but also of creating, through the choices we make, a commercial climate in which manufacturers and retailers see new market opportunities in 'green' goods and are encouraged to invest in new products and services. The Green Consumer has already triggered a major shift in the way that the business community views environmental issues.

John Elkington and Julia Hailes, *The Green Consumer's Supermarket Shopping Guide* (see below)

It is, of course, true that many big corporations are now selling chemicals and new technologies to clean up the environment. Yet much of the mess is down to them in the first place! The grey clouds of pollution have silver linings for the sellers of catalytic converters, desulphurisation equipment and other 'environmental repair kits'. The head of the Confederation of British Industry's Environmental Health and Safety Group was quoted in The Guardian as estimating a potential worldwide market of £100-150 billion for 'environment-friendly products and services'.

Sandy Irvine, *Beyond Green Consumerism* (see below)

It's amazing to think that when the first edition of *Green Pages* was published nobody beyond the team working with John Elkington and Julia Hailes had heard the term 'green consumer'. Yet now more than a quarter of a million of us have bought *The Green Consumer Guide*, and apparently getting on for half of us are such animals.

The concept has developed so rapidly that it has become something of a race to see whose version of 'green consumerism' will win. Will it be that of the supermarkets and multinationals, spurred by the promise of new profit horizons and cheered on by the new breed of highly-paid 'environmental consultants'? Or will it be that of the deeper greens, concerned that a great deal of 'green consumerism' is little more than tokenism and hype, insisting that it will only get us to where we want to be if we take on the thorny question of reducing what we consume?

Well, to some extent the two perspectives are gradually being reconciled. The *Green Consumer Guide* people are saying — though not very loudly — that no product can be 100% environment-friendly, and *The Green Consumer's Supermarket Shopping Guide* does look (briefly) at whether supermarkets are an acceptably green way of fulfilling our needs.

From the other side, there has been some useful thinking done about how far green consumerism can lead to change. Sandy Irvine's *Beyond Green Consumerism*, a Friends of the Earth discussion paper, presents a mass of useful background information, accepting both the potential and the limitations of the phenomenon and pointing the finger quite fearlessly in the direction of those companies and organisations that think they can get away with the minimum of action and the maximum of self-congratulation.

The Green Consumer Guide
John Elkington and
Julia Hailes
Gollancz, 1988
£4.99

Beyond Green Consumerism
Sandy Irvine
Friends of the Earth,
1989
£1.00

The Green Consumer's Supermarket Shopping Guide
John Elkington and
Julia Hailes
Gollancz, 1989
£4.99

Green Cons

'The Metro Surf is capable of running on unleaded petrol,' said the ads in the summer of 1989, 'which means it's as ozone-friendly as it's economical.' Your average ten-year-old would be able to tell you these days that lead has nothing to do with the thinning of the ozone layer, so it's only to be expected that Austin Rover were hauled before the Advertizing Standards Association on that one.

In September 1989 Friends of the Earth instituted their annual 'Green Con of the Year Award', the results being announced at the end of December. The 1989 winners were British Nuclear Fuels, for their incredible 'How green are you about nuclear power' ad, and an Essex furriers who claim their wares are 'completely environment friendly'.

Or how about Procter and Gamble's New Bold, the plastic bottle of which is 100% fully disposable. Wow.

Junk Mail

She tossed the junk mail into the bin, unopened. And in doing so, Chrissy unwittingly made a joke and a mockery of the lives, loves and endeavours of countless people whom she would never know. In that casual gesture she trampled upon an awesome human achievement and upon great sacrifices contributed by the natural world.

Ben Elton, *Stark*, Sphere, 1989, £3.50

The average British household receives more than 40 unsolicited direct mailings a year — 40% up on the number two years ago and rising rapidly — and this doesn't include the bumf that comes with your bank statements, leaflets pushed through the door, or 'free' newspapers. If you want to reduce the amount of instant waste that comes through your letterbox, what can you do?

In the early 1980s it became clear that a mechanism was needed by which customers could have some say about what came through their letterbox in the post, and the Mailing Preference Service was set up. By filling in a Freepost card (which should be available in all post offices but isn't), you can ask to receive only certain categories of literature, or none at all. The MPS covers all the main direct mail companies, and telling them that you don't want direct mail should stop at least 80% of the average household's haul.

The Mailing Preference Service
Freepost 22
London
W1E 7EZ

The 'Green Office'

Another potent source of waste is the mountain of office products consumed by Britain's businesses each year, currently running at more than £2 billion. Just think how much could be achieved if all those buying decisions were angled towards less environmentally destructive alternatives. This was obviously once of the motives, undoubtedly supported by the attendant considerations of financial advantage and kudos, behind Universal Office Supplies' decision to launch a 'green range' of office supplies and a *Green Office Guide*. Universal, Britain's largest office equipment supplier and a branch of the mighty John Menzies Group, asked the indomitable Elkington-Hailes consortium to look at what the commercial world can do to reduce waste and pollution, and as a first step down the green road it should be required reading for any company buyer that doesn't want to get left behind his or her more green-minded competitors. It doesn't, of course, ask whether 'the green office' isn't a contradiction in terms, and certainly doesn't discuss heated economic and political potatoes, but it will make a lot of influential people do some very useful thinking.

The Universal Green Office Guide
compiled by John Elkington and Julia Hailes
Universal Office Supplies, 1989 (Universal House, Trident Way, Southall, Middlesex UB2 5LF) £1.95

The New Economics Foundation

If the key words of the old economics are economic growth, full employment, and free trade, those of the new are human well-being, sustainability, good work and economic self-reliance.
From the NEF leaflet

In 1984 and 1985 The Other Economic Summit (usually known as TOES) held conferences which paralleled the London and Bonn Economic Summits, but which had the key words of the new economics firmly in mind. Speakers from around the world delivered more than fifty papers, the best of which have been brought together and edited by Paul Ekins in an important book for anybody interested in alternatives to the present economic system.

The Living Economy (Routledge and Kegan Paul, 1986, £8.95) is sometimes unnecessarily academic and wordy, and it has been criticized for playing along too far with the status quo, but it does give a very good idea of many of the exciting economic ideas currently being discussed in green circles, such as local currencies, basic income schemes and ethical investment.

The New Economics Foundation, which developed from TOES, seems on the way up. Founded in 1986, it exists to explore a new interpretation of economics which emphasizes the welfare of people and the planet both now and in the future. The NEF's quarterly, *New Economics*, is very good. Among NEF's future plans is a large-scale 'Living Economy' exhibition and events programme to run alongside the next major Economic Summit Meeting in London in the summer of 1991.

The New Economics Foundation
27 Thames House
South Bank Business Centre
140 Battersea Park Road
London
SW11 4NB
0(7)1-720 8674

The Next Economy

Here are two books which provide some stimulating insights into economics without your needing a PhD in economics. *The New Economic Agenda* is a collection of talks from a conference held at the Findhorn Foundation (see page 183) in 1984. The subjects range from the story of the Easterhouse Festival Society, an inner city revitalization project in Glasgow, to the fate of the forest dwellers of Brazil. That may not sound like the stuff of economics, but it most certainly is.

Paul Hawken is an American businessman and economist, and *The Next Economy* is a brilliant analysis of the shortcomings of our present economic system, and of what can (and can't) be salvaged — it makes interesting reading in the light of recent financial events: 'If the United States was a business, it would have difficulty getting a loan.' And that was in 1983.

The End Of Economics?

André Gorz is not an easy author to read. Like Illich and Bahro, he is an academic who doesn't understand the importance of saying things in a way which ordinary mortals can easily grasp, but like them he has some vitally important things to say. His new book, *Critique of Economic Reason*, is a carefully-thought-out, well-documented (and well-translated) survey of the impasse we have reached because of an over-dependence on capitalist versions of 'economics'. 'The central problem of capitalist society,' he writes, 'has been that of the limits inside which economic rationality is to operate.' He shows this very clearly by looking at a host of absurd mismatches between mainstream economics and what he calls 'the lifeworld' — have we a right to payment if we brush our teeth more often and the health service makes savings, and is sexual activity work if it stimulates creativity in our jobs?

The answer, says André Gorz, is to rethink many of our fundamental concepts, from 'right' and 'privilege' to 'value' and 'work'. He's still overdependent — as are so many socialists — on a tired framework of right-left politics, can (though he obviously tries hard not to) be blatantly sexist, and uses far too many words. My advice is to start half way through, at page 107, which will bring you to some of the most interesting ideas without first having to wade through an ocean of long-winded historical analysis. *Critique of Economic Reason* repays the investment, however, since it will make you think hard about what we are doing to ourselves and our surroundings in the name of economics.

*

Economic rationality is not only wrongly extended to cover actions to which it is not applicable; it 'colonizes', reifies and mutilates the very relational fabric on which social integration, education and individual socialization depend.

The New Economic Agenda
edited by Mary Inglis and Sandra Kramer
Findhorn Press, 1985
£4.95

The Next Economy
Paul Hawken
Angus and Robertson, 1984
£7.95

Critique of Economic Reason
André Gorz
Verso, 1989
£8.95

Politics

Chris Winn, from *Friends of the Earth Handbook* (see page 65)

Green Politics

Not only have we reached the end of our economic system, but also we and our whole industrial civilization have reached a state of crisis which will prove terminal if we are not prepared to change our total course. . . If in future we want to live lives at all fit for human beings, or even if we just want to survive, we must fundamentally change our way of life. We must design civilization anew. Everyone who has already reached these conclusions should vote for the Greens.

> Rudolf Bahro, *Building the Green Movement* (see below)

Albert Einstein, writing about the discovery of the ability to split the atom, wrote: 'From that moment, everything changed except the way we think.' Green politics, requiring a fundamental shift in thinking away from growth and competition and towards sustainability and co-operation, offers the chance for our thinking to catch up with our technology, a new way of thinking and behaving.

This is as fundamental a shift as the discovery of sedentary agriculture, or the dawn of the industrial revolution, but it is also a return to a deep wisdom and understanding about our place in the order of things which we have set aside at our peril. Green politics is not the rantings of a fanatical millennial cult, though it is convenient for some to present it in that light. It is a way of ensuring a future for us, our children, our neighbours both near and distant, and for our planet, based on ecological principles, social responsibility, grassroots democracy, equality and nonviolence.

Green Reading

From our side of the divide it's clear that all industrial nations are pursuing an unsustainable path. Every time we opt for the 'conventional' solution, we merely create new problems, new threats. Every time we count on some new technological miracle, we merely put off the day of reckoning. Sheer common sense suggests alternative remedies, yet vested economic interests and traditional political responses ensure that the necessary steps are never taken.

> Jonathon Porritt, *Seeing Green*

The starting point of Green politics is the dependence of human beings on the ecological well-being of the Earth. Its policies reassert this vital relationship respecting the rights both of future generations and other species. In doing so, it seeks to create the conditions for peace, social justice, and a flowering of rich diversity of lifestyles and environments. A Green political manifesto is for all forms of life on Earth.

> Sandy Irvine and Alec Ponton, *A Green Manifesto*

When you read of this destruction or that human misery, don't let it sap your spirit or make you turn away and think, 'There's nothing we can do, so why bother?' It's not true. I can't imagine a better way to sum up Green politics than in the line: It doesn't have to be like this. It really doesn't. Yes, the problems are many and serious, and yes, we don't have limitless time to sort them out, but it can be done, and it will be done if the Greens are given the chance. Green politics is about hope and vision. Not despair.

> David Icke, *It Doesn't Have To Be Like This*

Though the roots of the green movement go deep into history, the last five years have seen an abundant flowering of the tree. After promising to bud for a decade or more, the mid-70s saw die Grünen gaining substantial influence in the West German parliament, and other green parties springing up and consolidating their efforts from Japan to Brazil, Australia to the USA. With a massive 15% vote in the 1989 European elections, the British Green Party surprised even its most vocal detractors, and for every Green voter there are several others who are sympathetic but not quite convinced. With this burgeoning of activity has come, of course, the books. They all have 'green' in the title; they all have green on their covers.

Jonathon Porritt's *Seeing Green* is still by far the best introductory book to green politics in Britain, and it surely can't be long before we see a new and updated edition. He is clear, fluent, honest, witty, and pretty fearless. He challenges without ever being patronizing. He is particularly good at explaining the green perspective on economics and industrialization, the sticking point for many green-tinted socialists.

In 1988, and with a considerable degree of accurate foresight, Jonathon Porritt joined forces with journalist David Winner to produce *The Coming Of The Greens*, which traces the recent growth of interest in all things green. What this book does well is to show the wide range of green concerns, from the arts to commerce and mainstream politics, and the book includes interviews with many well-known greenies and almost-greenies.

Rudolf Bahro is the thorn in the side of German politics both red and green, an intelligent and provocative writer who sometimes says far too much at a time and thus becomes indigestible; well worth reading, though, especially on the relationship between socialism and green politics. Several of his books are available in English, though the quality of the translation varies enormously — *Building The Green Movement* is not well translated, but does show best the variety of Rudolf Bahro's concerns.

Sandy Irvine and Alec Ponton's aim in *A Green Manifesto* is to explore how green thinking might translate into practical policies. It isn't always easy reading, but it is broken down into digestible chunks which makes it easy to find specific policy areas. Sandy Irvine is a voracious reader of green literature, as is shown by the excellent and voluminous bibliography.

Finally, for an impassioned green plea to the person in the street David Icke's *It Doesn't Have To Be Like This* fits the bill admirably. As a television journalist he has clearly learned the effectiveness of the short sentence, the pithy example and the hard-hitting last line. Read it. Be inspired.

Seeing Green
Jonathon Porritt
Blackwell, 1984
£3.95

**The Coming Of
The Greens**
Jonathon Porritt and
David Winner
Fontana, 1988
£4.95

**Building The
Green Movement**
Rudolf Bahro
Heretic, 1986
£5.95

A Green Manifesto
Policies for a
Green Future
Sandy Irvine and Alec
Ponton
Optima, 1988
£6.99

**It Doesn't Have To
Be Like This**
Green Politics Explained
David Icke
Green Print, 1990
£4.99

The Green Party

Our policies — all of them — acknowledge the vital importance of our whole environment. That environment — its health, its safety, its wholeness — affects our lives, our politics, and our future, and whenever we damage the environment, we damage ourselves. Like all other forms of life, we depend for our survival and wellbeing upon a fragile network of physical, social and spiritual links with the rest of creation. Green politics is an acknowledgement of the complexity of that web of life.

Human beings are just part of that web, but we have become the dominant strand in it. Over the years we have set ourselves up to control, dominate and exploit the planet. The signs pointing to the need for a greater awareness of the results of human domination have become increasingly obvious. Now we can ignore the signs no longer. The Earth has been served by the wisdom of ecology for millions of years. We can use that wisdom to make us whole again.

*Green Politics: The Green Party
General Election Manifesto, 1987*

At much the same time as the German Green Party was beginning to appear on the news with increasing regularity, the British equivalent — The Ecology Party — was born in 1973, changing is name to The Green Party in line with other European and North American organizations in 1985. Having spent several years organizing and waiting, the Party leapt into prominence in May 1989 when it received a massive 14.9% of the vote in the elections to the European Parliament. The Greens beat the Liberal Democrats in every seat but one and beat Labour in six. The result sent shock waves through the political system. Had it not been for a patently unfair first-past-the-post system which in European Parliamentary terms is technically illegal, there would now be fourteen British Green MEPs sitting in Strasbourg.

While other political parties are now routinely including green issues in their policy statements (and increasingly in their policies), The Green Party is unique in having at the core of all its policies the recognition that people must learn to live within the limitations of the Earth's finite supply of resources. This understanding has been incorporated into a wide-ranging survey of requirements in every area of policy making, and put together in a document called *Manifesto for a Sustainable Society* (obtainable for £3.50 from Ecotrade, see below), an updated version of which appears each year incorporating new policy decisions made at the Party's annual conference. The Party's election manifestos from the 1987 General Election and 1989 European Election (£2 and £1.50 from the same address) present a shortened but nonetheless comprehensive picture of Green policies, which make fascinating reading and can hardly fail to give you new insights into areas where conventional thinking often obscures the many creative initiatives which could be developed.

The Green Party believes firmly that it is much more than just a pressure group, but it also sees itself as more than a conventional political party. Greens seek election to public office but are also working to educate the public about the real causes of the severe social and environmental problems now facing us. They see themselves neither as right- nor left-wing: their policies include encouraging home ownership and small businesses, self-responsibility and a basic income for all, protection of the environment and the breakdown of the power of transnational corporations.

There are now more than 250 local Green Party groups, five Green district councillors, and over a hundred Green parish and community councillors. Green candidates stood in 140 seats in the 1987 General Election, and contested every seat in the 1989 European election. Frustratingly, the present British electoral system makes it virtually impossible for any relatively small party to gain a foothold in national politics, and unlike the German system (where the electoral method is proportional representation, with each party being given funds in line with its proportion of the vote), Green politics in Britain is still too often bogged down in tactics and fund-raising. Nevertheless, the British Green Party is here to stay and will continue to be a very effective force in local and national politics.

The Green Party
10 Station Parade
Balham High Road
London
SW12 9AZ
0(8)1-673 0045

Wales Green Party
Trewylan
Brynymor Road
Aberystwyth
Dyfed
SY23 2HX
0979 611474

**The Scottish
Green Party**
11 Forth Street
Edinburgh
EH1 3LE
031 556 5160

Econews is The Green Party's newspaper, always full of interesting articles and news of forthcoming events; for a sample copy send a large sae to *Econews*, 10 Peploe Road, London NW6 6EB; Tel: 0(8)1 960 2662. Different policy working groups within the party also produce their own newsletters, including *Artworks* on the arts, *Growing Concerns* on agriculture, *Education Newsletter, Green International,* and *Ecomotion* on transport. You will find current details of all of these in the latest issue of *Econews.*

Ecotrade

Ecotrade started life as the Green Party's publications distribution network, but these days has grown like — well, like everything else truly green. Alongside the badges and policy briefing documents you would expect a political party to be selling to its members, Ecotrade now runs a large-scale mail order service from a full-colour catalogue, and the as-environment-friendly-as-possible products they sell include toys and clothes, paint and recycled paper products. All this is achieved from a small warehouse in Nottinghamshire, though there are active plans to open an Ecotrade shop in London before long. Send now for your Ecotrade catalogue (an A4 sae is appreciated); you don't have to be a member to buy things from it!

Ecotrade
Unit 22
Enterprise Workshop
Bowbridge Road
Newark-on-Trent
NG24 4EQ
0636 700232

The Green Political Bandwagon

Politicians of all hues have not been slow to adopt what they believe to be an acceptable package of green policies, often falling over each other to be greener than the opposition. Traditional parliamentary rhetoric has occasionally sunk to spectacular lows in the process. 'The truth is,' said William Waldegrave during one debate, 'that the only green in the Labour Party is the colour of its own putrefying political flesh.'

To read the green credentials of the major parties in manifestos, leaflets and speeches is at first sight very impressive. Rarely do they stand up to serious analysis, however, and often contain serious inconsistencies. The PR people have obviously read the right books (passages from 'standard texts' like Jonathon Porritt's *Seeing Green* are sometimes lifted verbatim), and there is no doubt that there are people in each of the political parties who are very concerned about the environment. The question is, however, how far is it possible to reconcile ecological principles with many of the other stated aims of the major parties such as economic growth, military expenditure, employment policies, fiscal programmes and plans for central government control?

Green politics represents such a very different view of the world from that of current mainstream politics that it is very hard to see how party politics as it is currently organized can ever make the break with a system which is inherently unsustainable. The Greens in the German Bundestag are frequently accused of wasting government time on irrelevant issues when they raise fundamental questions like land ownership, the distribution of wealth, and the need for defence. It is too easy to knock in a time when creative thinking and radical policy making are the only way out of the current political impasse.

The Conservative Party

Environmental concern is not an add-on optional extra like a sunroof on a new car. It has to be part of a basic philosophy of a party or it is nothing. So let us not forget that without vision the people will perish. This great party for hundreds of years has provided the vision of nationhood to which our people have warmed. Much of it is about our affection for our past, our built heritage, our countryside. So I do not have to say that we are the green party. I have a grander boast to make. I can boast that we are the Conservative Party of Great Britain.
William Waldegrave, Conservative Party Conference, October 1985

It is we Conservatives who are the true friends of the earth.
Margaret Thatcher, Royal Society speech, September 1988

There is an overwhelming ethical argument for prudent management of the environment. The same is true of prudent management of the economy. In the 1980s we had to win the argument that we should not impoverish our children tomorrow because of our own self-indulgence today. That is what cutting borrowing and over-spending is all about. Our job in the 1990s is a close parallel. What we need is not 'no' growth but 'green' growth. We need growth which doesn't sacrifice tomorrow in order to consume mindlessly today. Good economic practice is good environmental practice. It's for government to regulate on behalf of the community, to set the standards and the environmental goals. We must then harness market forces and the market place to prevent pollution, to change the sort of conduct that degrades the nation's resources, and to find the most efficient and effective ways of delivering environmental quality.
Christopher Patten, Conservative Party Conference, October 1989

It's prosperity which creates the technology that can keep the earth healthy. As Voyager 2, on its remarkable twelve-year flight, raced through the solar system to Neptune and beyond, we were awe-struck by the pictures it sent back of arid, lifeless planets and moons. They were a solemn reminder that our planet has the unique privilege of life. How much more that makes us aware of our duty to safeguard the world. The more we master our environment, the more we must learn to serve it. That is the Conservative approach.
Margaret Thatcher, Conservative Party Conference, October 1989

Conservative Central Office, 32 Smith Square, London SW1P 3HH (0(7)1-222 9000)

The Tory Green Initiative for 'keeping the Conservative agenda green' is at 1 St Michaels Street, London W2 1QT (0(7)1-724 4887); it publishes a newsletter called *Turquoise Times*. The Bow Group, a Conservative 'think tank', has published a detailed analysis of Tory thinking on environmental issues called *The Green Conservative: A Manifesto for the Environment* (Tony Paterson, Bow Publications, 1989, £6.00).

The Labour Party

The environment in which we live is an irreplaceable asset. We cannot afford to squander this asset, or allow a selfish few to destroy it for the rest. Labour will change direction for Britain, towards policies that give sustainable growth. We want to be sure that our children grow up enjoying good health, a clean environment and attractive surroundings in which to live.
This Green and Present Land, 1987

Protecting our environment is the greatest challenge we face. It can't be left to the 'free market'. Protecting the environment isn't a matter of clearing up the damage after it has been done. Concern for the environment has to be integrated into economic, industrial, energy, transport and social policy, so that individuals, industry and government all work together. Most people feel that their quality of life is a communal process, not a by-product of personal wealth. They also recognize that the degradation of our environment must be tackled. They recognize that if we do not begin to do that now our children may face insurmountable problems in the future.

Meet The Challenge, Make The Change, Policy Review, 1989

It is obvious that people want tougher environmental regulation — locally, nationally and internationally. In proclaiming Labour's policies for the environment as the most bold, comprehensive, radical and realistic programme on offer to the British people, we can draw on a proud record of achievement in central and local government. Our approach is integrated, precautionary and interventionist. This is Labour's ground, and none of the current political posturing on the environment by government ministers should convince people otherwise.

John Cunningham, Labour Party Conference, October 1989

We need to change fundamentally our attitudes about protection to the environment. A government's role must be to impose tough standards and effective enforcement coupled with long-term research into energy use and planning. We live in a world of finite resources. By working together we can use them responsibly and share them fairly now and in the future.

A Clean Start, 1989

The Labour Party, 150 Walworth Road, London SE17 1JT (0(7)1-703 0833)

SERA, the Socialist Environment and Resources Group (11 Goodwin Street, London N4 3HQ; Tel: 0(7)1-263 7424), exists to formulate socialist policies for the environment. SERA's influential Parliamentary Group comprises nearly sixty Labour MPs; it produces an impressive publications list and a quarterly journal called *New Ground*. Several books have been written about the relationship between 'red' and 'green' politics; one of the best and most recent is Martin Ryle's *Ecology and Socialism* (Radius, 1988, £5.95), in which he envisages the development of an 'eco-socialist society'.

Plaid Cymru

The earth is not ours to abuse. What we do today will affect our children and our children's children for generations to come.

Building the Future, 1987

The environmental threat is now acknowledged by all parties, but the London parties underestimate the changes necessary to avoid catastrophe. Policies to preserve the environment must be given the highest priority. Our environment is the result of a balance between the natural world and the activities of mankind. With uncontrolled growth of the world economy and the introduction of modern technology huge and irreversible alterations are occurring whose effects are uncertain but include the possibility of world-wide catastrophe.

Wales in Europe, 1989

Plaid Cymru, 51 Cathedral Road, Cardiff CF1 9HD (0222 31944)

Scottish National Party

The condition of any country can be measured by the strength of its economy and its industrial base. The SNP believe that the fundamental development of our society depends on the balance between people and resources. Effective measures must be taken to safeguard our environment and ensure our people live in a safe atmosphere.

Play the Scottish Card, General Election Manifesto, 1987

Conventional economic wisdom tends to be based on the assumption that the earth's resources are inexhaustible and can therefore be treated as income, and that human progress can be identified with never ending economic growth, industrial expansion dependent on overseas markets, and constantly increasing consumption of material goods. The SNP places a high priority on the concept of quality of life, on the desirability of national self-sufficiency, and on the belief that Scotland's future prosperity depends on avoiding overpopulation. These convictions are associated with a belief in the value of small communities with which individuals can identify, and in the principle of decentralisation of government.

Environment Policy Document, 1989

Scottish National Party, 6 North Charlotte Street, Edinburgh EH2 4JH (031 226 3661)

Social And Liberal Democrats

Our approach to the environment is based on the fundamental insight that the environment and the economy are inter-dependent and that it is necessary to balance economic and ecological imperatives in order to achieve sustainable development. Environmental considerations must be integrated into other policies. This will allow us to anticipate environmental problems and prevent them arising before they require expensive 'post facto' clean ups. Our aim is sustainable growth which will create jobs and wealth and build a better environment. This 'green growth' approach integrates our environment policy closely with our economic policy. The success of these proposals would not only put the economy back on its feet and create jobs, it would also improve the environment.

The Time has Come: Partnership for Progress, 1987

The Green approach is most immediately about individual people, their relationships with each other and the environment. It says that politics should not just be about the management of crises in our affairs either by huge bureaucracies or by the whip of the free market. It is an approach which puts the quality of life first. This should come naturally to Social and Liberal Democrats. It is part of the mainstream of our thinking.

Paddy Ashdown, Towards a Green Democracy, February 1989

We alone amongst political parties in Britain have turned green rhetoric into a reality.

Campaign Earth, 1989

Social and Liberal Democrats, 4 Cowley Street, London SW1P 3NB (0(7)1-222 7999)

Green Democrats (Canmore, 3 Chessington Road, Ewell, Surrey KT17 1TS; Tel: 0(8)1-394 0644) is a pressure group within the SLD, working 'to place the green perspective at the centre of the party's agenda'; it publishes a quarterly news-letter called *Challenge*. Several leading Liberals, including Simon Hebditch and Simon Hughes, have contributed to a recent thought-provoking volume of eco-essays called *Into the 21st Century: An Agenda for Political Realignment* (Green Print, 1988, £4.99).

The Social Democratic Party was contacted several times and asked if they would send material for this section, but nothing has been received from them. The SDP is at 25-28 Buckingham Gate, London SW1E 6LD (0(7)1-821 9661).

Cargo of 'market forces' stuff for a Mr. Patten...

Europe.

We European Greens ultimately envisage a new concept for Europe: a Europe of autonomous regions without any borders. Our Europe would have a decentralised structure and a democratic and social organisation in line with green principles — regions with self-determination, local production for local needs using energy-saving, non-polluting methods of production. We seek international co-operation on a large scale to solve our common problems.

Common Statement of the European Greens, March 1989

1992 — the year when the multinationals succeed in their dream of identical supermarket shelves throughout Europe or the year when the continent becomes a true community of interest and concern?

A great deal depends upon what is meant by 'community'. A European future driven by blind capitalism could easily create a 'Fortress Europe' in which wealth drains inexorably towards the already-rich regions and the periphery becomes even more marginalized. On the other hand, a Europe-wide community in which a sensitive legislature provided guidelines for human and environmental wellbeing, decentralizing decision-making and ensuring that economic and political power could not be used in oppressive and destructive ways, would transform the continent and promise it a future.

Blueprints for a Green Europe

The 1989 European Elections provided an excellent opportunity for green campaigning throughout the continent, and the high green vote shows the growing realization that environmental concern must be matched with political will. Two documents which provided much of the background for the debate — and are still well worth reading — are a discussion paper called *Blueprint for a Green Europe*, put together by a coalition of environmental organizations (obtainable free from Friends of the Earth — see page 65), and the Green Party's European Election manifesto *Don't Let Your World Turn Grey*. *Blueprint* includes a comprehensive programme of Europe-wide green action, while the Green Party manifesto is a very accessible introduction to the potential for a truly green Europe.

Green MPs now sit in the parliaments of nine EC countries as well as in the European Parliament, and it is only because of our archaic electoral system that a 15% share of the European vote did not result in twelve British Green MEPs. Sara Parkin's *Green Parties: An International Guide* shows how the political dimension of the green movement has gained momentum over recent years. She suggests at the end of the United Kingdom section that our Green Party is not yet prepared for power, an opinion much dwelt upon by the media — but that was before May 1989.

**Blueprint for a
Green Europe**
An Environmental
Agenda for the 1989
European Elections
FoE, CPRE, Green
Alliance and WWF, 1989

**Don't Let Your
World Turn Grey**
The Green Party
European Election
Manifesto
The Green Party, 1989
£1.50

Green Parties
An International Guide
Sara Parkin
Heretic, 1989
£5.95

European Information

Like any bureaucracy worth the name, the European administrative machine ploughs its way through mountains of paper every day, most of it to remain unread and unrecycled. The Commission's *European Documentation* service alone has distributed more than twelve million booklets since it was established in 1975, while the publications catalogues you can request from the addresses below provide several hours' reading. If you want detailed information, then Brussels and Luxembourg are the places to write to. The London Information Office, however, carries a wide range of literature, and is the place to contact if you would like to be put on the mailing list of the free monthly newspaper *European Parliament News*.

**European
Commission**
Division for the Co-ord-
ination and Preparation
of Publications
Office JECL 7/66
200 rue de la Loi
1049 Brussels
Belgium

**European
Parliament
Information Office**
2 Queen Anne's Gate
London
SW1H 9AA
0(7)1-222 0411

**Office for Official
Publications of the
European
Communities**
2 rue Mercier
L-2985 Luxembourg
(010 352) 499281

Europe-wide Environmental Information

1987 was European Year of the Environment, and in order to provide a context for the debate the EC produced a comprehensive survey called *The State of the Environment in the European Community*. Though now nearly four years out of date this attractive volume, with its full-colour maps and diagrams, shows more clearly than any number of technical typewritten EC reports the sort of problems we are up against, from water pollution to loss of wildlife.

Also in 1987 the Italian-based environmental information service DocTer produced an English-language version of their *European Environmental Handbook*. At £45 it is not cheap, but its 800 pages contain a wealth of information on environmental issues, initiatives and legislation throughout Europe, including much that is not readily available elsewhere, such as a complete list of international environmental treaties and when they were ratified by each state. A new edition is planned for the summer of 1990.

The only comprehensive analysis of all EC Environmental Directives is Nigel Haigh's *EEC Environmental Policy and Britain*, another expensive volume now beginning to date a little.

**The State of the
Environment in the
European
Community**
European Community,
1987 (distributed in the
UK by HMSO)
£11.60

**European
Environmental
Handbook 1987**
DocTer International
(27 Kensington Court,
London W8 5DN; Tel:
0(7)1-937 3535)
£45.00

**EEC Environmental
Policy and Britain**
Nigel Haigh
Longman, 1987
£25.00

Campaigning

The purpose of any campaign is to win. The first question, therefore, is: what do you want to win? Pin down your campaign aim to one sentence so you can tell the press not that 'we are campaigning to preserve the natural beauty of our unique and threatened environment', but that 'we are campaigning to prevent the destruction of Hundred Acre Wood by MegaBuck Developers Ltd.' That statement tells people what you are worried about and the name of your 'opponent'. The other important word in that sentence is 'we'. You can't do it on your own.

Friends of the Earth Handbook (see page 65)

The popular image of a campaign is of people lying down in front of bulldozers, contractors' lorries, or the gates of a military base, then being led — or preferably carried — into waiting police vans. Sometimes this is the only sort of action that has any chance of achieving what is needed, but it is only the most newsworthy aspect of the constant questioning of the activities of those with power in our society.

Paradoxically the term was originally a military one, meaning a co-ordinated plan of action on the battlefield (Latin 'campus'); now it has come to mean any programme of activities and events designed to achieve a particular goal. Many of the activities may be pretty mundane — public meetings, collecting signatures for a petition, local and parliamentary lobbying, letters to the editor, interviews for the local radio.

As you'll see from the pages of this book, there are thousands of issues worth campaigning for, and more than enough 'opponents'. The proliferation of public campaigns in recent years is an indication of just how unresponsive our democratic structures are to threats to the welfare of both our environment and the people who inhabit it.

We must always remember, however, that the ultimate aim of any campaign is to achieve its goals, then to pack up and go home. When there is so much that needs to be done it can feel as though campaigning will never end, but it is important to know when you have achieved what you set out to — and equally when there is no further point fighting a campaign you have clearly lost.

The Campaign for Lead-Free Air is the first contemporary green campaigning group to have achieved most of its aims; what a wonderful day it will be when CND can close its doors for ever, or when Greenpeace can stop fighting for the rights of whales.

Pressure

Des Wilson is widely regarded as one of the finest campaigners in the business. Be warned, however: he gets up every day at 6, and by 9 has read all the day's papers, dictated his correspondence, and is ready for his first meeting. And the meetings go on all day, and sometimes well into the night. In spite of this punishing lifestyle, Des Wilson has continued to organize a string of successful campaigns, including Shelter, Friends of the Earth, the Campaign for Lead-Free Air, the Campaign for Freedom of Information, and now Parents Against Tobacco. This is the book that tells you how to do it — an essential purchase for any budding pressure group.

*

Pressure groups write a lot of letters. There is no point what soever in writing these letters unless you do it well. A bad letter will have the opposite effect to that intended. A good letter should be brief; be clear; grab the reader's attention in the opening paragraph and encourage them to read on; be precise about what it wants from the reader; be neat and clean and without error.

Pressure
The A-Z of Campaigning in Britain
Des Wilson
Heinemann, 1984
£4.95

Getting Yourselves Organized

Many campaigns underestimate both the influence of the mass media and their ability to influence what it carries; this is all part of the great divide created by those in power to separate the media 'professionals' from the masses who are supposed to sit back and accept what they're given. Two useful books which cover this subject are Polly Bird's *How To Run a Local Campaign*, a step-by-step manual for anyone wanting to harness community action to ensure that people and environment are not trampled over, and Jane Butterworth's *Don't Just Sit There*. This short, punchy handbook is full of ideas and resources, and gets a special greenie point for calling *Green Pages* 'the ultimate guide' for anyone interested in environmental issues. You scratch our back . . . !

Before you start campaigning it is very useful to know how the 'opposition' works — there is nothing more frustrating than talking to a junior under-secretary for half an hour and then being told you've got the wrong department; or submitting a detailed statement about a planning proposal and being told you've missed the deadline by three days. For detailed but readable accounts of how Westminster operates, Paul Silk's *How Parliament Works* and Ian Greer's *Right to be Heard* are very good; *Playing the Public Enquiry Game* does a similar job for planning enquiries.

Holding Your Ground (see page 54) is another good source of campaigning ideas, and if all else fails you can get hold of a recent American book called *Ecodefense*. One American friend called it brilliant, another a handbook for terrorists — it tells you how to do very un-British things like put spikes in trees to stop them being cut down and immobilize motorway excavators. As it says at the front, you'd never actually want to use any of these suggestions — would you?

How To Run a Local Campaign
Polly Bird
Northcote House, 1989
£6.95

Right to be Heard
Ian Greer
Ian Greer Associates, 1985
£10.95

Don't Just Sit There
The Action Handbook
Jane Butterworth
Purnell, 1989
£6.99

Playing the Public Enquiry Game
Wendy Le-Las
Osmosis, 1987
£5.50

How Parliament Works
Paul Silk
Longman, 1989
(2nd edn)
£6.95

Ecodefense
edited by Dave Foreman and Bill Haywood
Ned Ludd Books, 1987
about £7.50

Some Successful Campaigns

We must do what we conceive to be the right thing and not bother our heads or burden our souls with whether we're going to be successful. Because if we don't do the right thing, we'll be doing the wrong thing, and we'll just be part of the disease instead of being a part of the cure.

E.F. Schumacher

It's so easy to sit watching the news, wondering how on earth they get away with it, feeling guilty that we're not doing anything about it, convincing ourselves that even if we did try to do anything about it, it wouldn't work.
Or would it?

Luxulyan

In 1978 the Central Electricity Generating Board began searching Cornwall for possible sites for a new nuclear power station; by 1981 three possible sites had been determined. By this time the Cornish Anti-Nuclear Alliance had its campaign plans drawn up. At Nancekuke members of CANA threatened to put their lives at risk, protecting colonies of Atlantic seals from the effects of seismic surveys by putting to sea in small boats, encircling the survey vessels, and entering the explosion zones. The CEGB withdrew their plans and moved on to Luxulyan.

Here CANA members barricaded a farm commandeered by the CEGB as a drilling site. Women chained themselves to the drilling rigs, and protestors maintained a 24-hour vigil for 172 days, refusing to react in any way violently. Their peaceful persistence won them the respect of the local police and the subcontractors. The CEGB was granted 32 writs of injunction against individual protestors, who immediately disbanded were replaced by another 32 — there were many more willing to be called upon.

In a local poll it was found that 92% of the population was opposed to the siting of the proposed plant; local MPs and dignitaries publicly voiced the fears and implacable opposition of the local community, and a strong case was made that the plant was beneficial neither to the local nor to the wider community. Even the Chief Constable of Cornwall was called before the full bench of the Court of Appeal to explain why he had repeatedly refused to identify any breach of the peace. After all, he said, the protestors were acting peacefully, on private land with the permission of the landowner.

The Court of Appeal promptly redefined 'breach of the peace', and after six months of blockade the protestors withdrew. Within months the CEGB announced that there was no site in Cornwall suitable for the construction of a nuclear power station. The prize would go elsewhere.

Otmoor

Otmoor in eastern Oxfordshire is a unique part of Britain. Low-lying land important to birds and wildlife is still divided into small square fields which more than a hundred years ago provided Lewis Carroll with the inspiration for the chessboard in *Alice Through The Looking Glass*. Having already run the M40 motorway over the Chiltern escarpment through an important nature reserve near High Wycombe, the Ministry of Transport in 1983 announced plans to extend the motorway north towards Birmingham at a cost of £250 million — straight through the middle of Otmoor. The destruction would also involve the felling of Bernwood, which was found to have the largest recorded number of butterfly species of any habitat in Britain.

The campaign against the M40 extension took many forms. Friends of the Earth produced an alternative plan showing that the improvement of existing roads and the building of bypasses could produce the same result for £100 million less than the proposed motorway. Local and national conservation groups showed how the motorway would damage a unique habitat.

Oxford Friends of the Earth thought up a novel and newsworthy scheme — they bought a two-and-a-half acre field on the proposed route, christened it 'Alice's Meadow', and proceeded to sell the field in 3,000 small plots to buyers from all over the world. If the MoT planned to purchase it compulsorily, they would have the tremendous task of dealing with thousands of private landowners.

Following a lengthy public enquiry the MoT abandoned the Otmoor route, though Friends of the Earth's proposal that the motorway not be built at all was overruled.

Greenham Common

Eight gruelling yet exhilarating years after the establishment of the women's peace camp at Greenham Common, the main objective of their campaign — the removal of the missiles — is on the verge of being achieved. Though detractors of their cause will inevitably say that it had little to do with the Greenham women, it is only their raised voices and the voices of millions of concerned people like them that brought about the political pressure for Gorbachev and the Americans to work out a way of dismantling weapons like the 96 Cruise missiles at Greenham Common.

Living through long months of abuse, assault, slander, imprisonment, cold and wet, the Greenham women have shown how powerful a peaceful protest can be. The symbolism of flowers and baby clothes woven into the wire surrounding the base, the dancing and singing in the face of officially-sanctioned violence, has moved people the world over to work actively for peace, proclaiming with them that 'Together we can help create the climate for peace that the warmongers won't be able to ignore'.

Personal Responsibility

Each of us has had the experience of responding to emergency. We may have rushed to douse a fire, or pulled a friend from in front of a moving truck, or raced to a child fallen into deep water. Each of us has the capacity to drop everything and act. That power to act is ours in the present situation of peril, all the more so since we are not alone. No outside authority is silencing us; no external force is keeping us from responding with all our might and courage to the present danger to life on Earth. It is something inside of us that stifles our responses. What leads us to repress our awareness of danger, miring so many of us in disbelief, denial and a double life?

Joanna Macy, *Despair and Personal Power in the Nuclear Age*
(see page 267)

As our politicians are fond of telling us, we live in a democratic country, but we don't — or at least not in the real sense of democracy, which means literally 'government by the people'. When pressed, the same politicians will admit that ours is a 'representative democracy'. This doesn't mean that individual people's views are represented in government, however, or at least not unless a politician decides to air such views. It means that each of us is free every four years or so to choose a politician to 'represent' us.

How can one politician, however good, represent the views of more than 50,000 very different people? Even at its best, Western democracy has become little more than a charade of true representation, a passive acceptance of a broad package of policies which may very generally benefit you, and the 'freedom' to complain if you feel hard done by. And that's if you choose to vote — more than a third of the population don't bother.

In *Diet for a Small Planet* Frances Moore Lappé is very clear about the need for real freedom and real democracy: 'Freedom to complain about what's wrong in our society without the power to do anything about the problems is virtually meaningless. Thus freedom from interference is only part of what democracy means. We must also have freedom to achieve what makes life worth living — the freedom to have safe and satisfying work; the freedom to enjoy security in the form of food, housing and health care; the freedom to share in decisions affecting our workplace, community and nation.'

The freedom to share in decisions which affect us — this is what true democracy means. But as Joanna Macy's thoughts on the subject make clear, you don't have to sit back and wait for the disasters engendered by 'democratic government' to engulf you. You can do something. It doesn't have to be momentous or newsworthy; in Britain you can (still) do a great deal without risking imprisonment — ridicule and threat are more important weapons here.

You may think that you can only vote every four years. This is nonsense. You vote every time you buy food for a meal, turn the cooker on, go to work or sign on, book a holiday, get in the car or on a bus. Given knowledge about the implications of the way you live, you can choose with every decision you make to work for life on earth rather than against it.

Fighting for Hope

'The system is bankrupt and nothing is certain.' This is Petra Kelly's starting point for a book about hope. Strange, you may think, that uncertainty can engender hope, but this collection of essays by West Germany's best known green politician shows how the breakdown of a bankrupt (in every sense) system can lead to fundamental questioning and fundamental and very necessary change. She is very clear that policy-making must move out of parliament and into the street, and is not afraid to tackle the challenges of power and leadership this will involve. She is also clear that true democracy cannot arise from the polarization of interests inherent in a party political system — you can read here her ideas about 'anti-party parties'. All this plus nuclear power, jealousy, poison gas and eroticism. A bitty book, as collections of essays tend to be, and all the poorer for not having an index. Well worth reading though.

*

We are living in a time when authoritarian ruling elites are devoting more and more attention to their own prospects and less and less to the future of humanity. We have no option but to take a plunge into greater democracy. This does not mean relieving the established parties, parliament and the law courts of their responsibilities, nor forcing them out of office. Information reaches society via the political parties; and the reverse process is important too: the parties and the trade unions also act as sounding-boards for ideas which first arise within society. But the formation of political opinion within the parliamentary system is undoubtedly a process that needs extending further. It needs to be revitalized by a non-violent and creative ecology and peace movement and an uncompromising anti-party party. In a period of crisis, a conveyor-belt system between society and the remote established parties is required. Otherwise the real problems are evaded in the endless game of power tactics, until eventually they become quite unmanageable.

Fighting for Hope
Petra Kelly
Chatto and Windus, 1984
£2.95

ARK

ARK burst on the environmental scene late in 1988 with a fanfare of celebrity endorsements, explaining that it had been created to provide everyone with the means to help restore the health of the earth by offering information, environmentally safe products, and a framework for positive community action. With a name like ARK, the organization has inevitably been prey to simplistic headlines about 'being afloat' and 'sinking' — the latter much to the fore when one of its prominent founders, Bryn Jones, moved on to fresh pastures before the first year was out.

It's not always easy to tell exactly what ARK is about, and what role it can play which is different from existing campaigning organizations like Greenpeace and Friends of the Earth. However, ARK's range of household products (see page 114) has become almost as well known as Ecover's, its lively presentation of green issues (the brilliant ARK video starring Dawn French as Mother Earth, for example) keeps it in the media limelight, and its emphasis on practical personal commitment is both vital and timely. ARK's latest up-beat quarterly newsletter suggests that the organization has now emerged from its early teething troubles to become an energetic and purposeful support network for a wide range of green activists.

The Ark Trust
498-500 Harrow Road
London
W9 3QA
0(8)1-968 6780

Being Green

An important part of the green message is that it is neither morally nor practically possible to separate our own actions from what happens elsewhere in the world; everything we do has consequences right down the line. A common response to the ills of our times is to say 'I'm sorry, but I just can't be responsible for that' — 'that' being anything from the burning of the rainforest to the homeless on the Thames Embankment. I'm afraid that none of us can make that choice — we are responsible whether we like it or not. Yet being responsible doesn't mean feeling so guilty and so overwhelmed that we do nothing. We can acknowledge the extent of our responsibility, both individual and collective, and then make clear decisions about the steps that we can realistically take to improve the situation.

As I point out again and again when it comes to the inevitable 'But doesn't green mean less?' question, a greenward shift doesn't mean deprivation. It certainly means using resources more carefully, but the potential gains are enormous — health, peace, sanity, fulfilment and sustainability.

A number of recent 'green lifestyle handbooks' make it very clear what is at stake, what we can do to improve things, and what we gain by taking these apparently small steps. Hugh and Margaret Brown's *Doing Our Bit*, a slim but very practical booklet, is a good starting point (if you have problems getting hold of it you can order copies directly from the Browns at Keeper's Cottage, Westward, Wigton, Cumbria CA7 8NQ; they also do a companion *Workbook* for 80p). A similar but rather more extensive and discursive treatment of the same material is provided by Marianne Frances in *Small Change*, which has been produced in conjunction with the Edinburgh-based Institute for Human Ecology and comes in a handy spiral binding.

Just when I had told myself I wasn't going to write any more green books Century asked me if I'd do 'the definitive book' on being green, so *How To Be Green* rolled off the production line towards the end of 1989. The idea behind *How To Be Green* is to make each issue, and what a concerned individual can do about it, so clear that nobody can say 'But I didn't know about that.' I would expect the average reader of *New Green Pages* to know most of what's in *How To Be Green*

already, but it's quite heartening to go through it thinking 'Ah yes, I already do that. And that. And that . . .' It's handy and pocket-sized (which you can hardly say about *New Green Pages*), and Friends of the Earth gets 5p every time someone buys a copy.

As I write, Bernadette Vallely of the Women's Environmental Network (see page 190) is putting the finishing touches to *1001 Ways to Save the Planet*, a handy A-Z of all the practical things you can do to help make the world a greener place. Like *How To Be Green*, it's on recycled paper (of course), and it promises to play an important part in Britain's rapidly rising green consciousness.

Doing Our Bit
A Practical Guide to the Environment and What We Can Do About It
Hugh and Margaret Brown
Brown and Brown, 1988
£1.65

Small Change
A Pocketful of Practical Actions to Help the Environment
Marianne Frances
Edinburgh Centre for Human Ecology, 1989
£4.50

How To Be Green
John Button
Century, 1990 (2nd edn)
£4.99

1001 Ways to Save the Planet
Bernadette Vallely
Penguin, 1990
£3.99

Is It Too Late?

In this important book, Bill McKibben tackles head on the possibility that we may have left it too late to save the planet as we have known and loved it. 'Wilderness' is no longer wilderness, 'summer' is no longer summer; we have denied the existence of nature as an independent entity and thus for all practical purposes nature is dead.

We must allow ourselves, he writes hauntingly, 'to feel the sadness of losing something we've begun to fight for, and the added sadness, or shame, of realising how much more we could have done.' Yet he also recognises that we must act on nature's behalf even if it is too late; the likelihood of defeat is not an excuse for inaction. Bill McKibben writes fluently and tellingly (though uses too many commas for my liking) and, like me, you'll probably find yourself repeating some of his more powerful sentences for weeks afterwards.

*

I've spent my whole life wanting more, so it's hard for me to imagine 'less' in any but a negative way. But imagination is what counts. If we decided against huge wardrobes (which is to say, against a whole way of looking at ourselves) and against every family having its own washer (which is to say, against a pervasive individual consumerism) then taking your clothes down the street to wash them would be the most obvious idea in the world. Our current ways of life might soon seem as bizarre as the six thousand shoes of Imelda Marcos.

*

A child born now will never know a natural summer, a natural autumn, winter or spring. Summer is becoming extinct, replaced by something else which will be called 'summer'. This new summer will retain some of its relative characteristics — it will be hotter than the rest of the year, for instance, and will be the time of year when crops grow — but it will not be summer, just as even the best prosthesis is not a leg.

The End Of Nature
Bill McKibben
Penguin, 1990
£4.99

Peace

Peace

And I shall have some peace there, for peace
  comes dropping slow,
Dropping from the veils of the morning to where
  the cricket sings;
There midnight's all a glimmer, and noon a purple glow,
And evening full of the linnet's wings.

  William Butler Yeats, from *The Lake Isle of Innisfree*

I often tell audiences about my dawning realization that the U.S.
and Soviet governments are out to kill me. They are building
more and more nuclear weapons, developing first-strike
weapons, stationing them all over the world — and the result of
all this is going to be my death . And as if that isn't bad enough,
the U.S. government wants me to pay them for this — through
federal income taxes. That seems like a cost overrun of vast
proportions. If I wanted to commit suicide, I could buy a gun for
$45 and shoot myself, or I could jump off the Golden Gate
Bridge for free.

  Fran Peavey (see page 265)

For the arms race is not an inevitable blight of nature, but a
humanly contrived disablement. And as such it ought to inspire
not resignation, but fury. Why, after all, should our chances of
survival and happiness be constantly sacrificed to something
within our powers to alter? Supposing we were to reverse this
process, reinstate the moment of 'pre-nuclear innocence' and
throw off this unremitting restraint on human well-being?

  Kate Soper, 'Rethinking Ourselves', in
  Prospectus for a Habitable Planet (see below)

I asked Reagan if he thought all Russians were evil, but he
declined to answer. I also asked him if he had ever met a
Russian, and he said 'No, but we hear from their emigrés.'

  Helen Caldicott, *Missile Envy* (see below)

Human beings have in general become so brainwashed by
currently prevailing ideas about 'peace' that we no longer
seem able to think about it in any way other than as an
absence.

  Peace has come to mean nonviolence, non-war, non-agg-
ression, antinuclear, disarmament. Co-operation, harmony
and joy seem to have little place in our world. The fact that we
have very little positive vocabulary based on peace itself
explains why when people talk about peace — real peace —
they are thought to be mad, soppy, or unpatriotic. When
politicians and policy-makers talk about peace, they usually
mean defence, readiness for war. George Orwell recognized
this way back in 1949 when in *Nineteen Eighty-Four* he made
the Party's slogan 'War is Peace'. And when the women who
stand in the way of Cruise missile carriers are charged and
imprisoned for 'breaching the peace' the deliberate miscon-
ception has come full circle. (Did you know that the American
air force's elite nuclear strike force, the Strategic Air
Command, has as its motto 'Peace is our Profession'?)

  Now — more than ever — is the time to add your voice to
those raised in Eastern Europe and elsewhere for a just, green,
peace.

Prospectus for a Habitable Planet

In 1980 the British government produced an illustrated 30-
page booklet called *Protect and Survive*, about how you could
build yourself a neat little nuclear shelter in your basement and
come out a few days later to set the world to rights. Films and
books like *The War Game* and *Where The Wind Blows* have
completely blown that myth, but the first sane, detailed and
considered response to the government's plans was E.P.
Thompson and Dan Smith's powerful collection of essays
called, most appropriately, *Protest and Survive*, still well worth
reading ten years on. The same editors have produced a
second volume of essays, arguing that protest alone is no
longer sufficient: the time for national and international action
has arrived. I found the articles by Mary Kaldor ('The Imaginary War') and Kate Soper ('Rethinking Ourselves') the most
stimulating of a thought and action provoking collection.

*

We have protested and we have survived. But non-stop protest
becomes exhausting, and mere survival is a poor fruit for
'advanced' civilization to bear — a passing on of the present
time's crisis unresolved to the next generation. The planet
remains divided into two armed camps and the true business of
civilization is to search for solutions which might bring this
condition to an end. If this is not done, then it is possible that —
at some moment in the twenty-first century — the planet will
become uninhabitable. We offer a prospectus which could lead
to an alternative future.

**Prospectus for a
Habitable Planet**
edited by Dan Smith
and E.P. Thompson
Penguin, 1987
£3.95

Missile Envy

Helen Caldicott, an Australian paediatrician, has become
known as 'the mother of the nuclear freeze programme',
arguing clearly, yet not without humour, for an end to nuclear
madness. *Missile Envy* is a brilliant book which looks in detail at
both American and Russian 'defence programmes', and the
psychology of the people who run the war machine. One
highlight of the book is her highly revealing interview with
Ronald Reagan, former US president.

Missile Envy
The Arms Race and
Nuclear War
Helen Caldicott
Bantam, 1985
£3.95

CND

Throughout its near 30-year history, the Campaign for Nuclear Disarmament has maintained a consistent, non-aligned, principled stand against all nuclear weapons. Now, in the 1980s, it has finally broken the political consensus that existed around British nuclear weapons policy for 40 years. Nuclear disarmament today is not only a party political debate, it involves many facets of society. It has drawn substantial support from doctors, nurses, the clergy, scientists, teachers, artists, musicians, and even retired military officers. Journalists, film-makers and civil servants have all exposed and explicitly condemned the secrecy of nuclear war-planning, and over the past six years more than 10,000 people have been arrested for acts of civil disobedience.

CND Scrapbook (see below)

Founded in 1958 as a result of public outrage at the manufacture and testing of nuclear weapons in a so-called time of peace, CND has always been a favourite target of reactionary politicians and media, yet its achievements are enormous. Campaigning against all weapons of mass destruction is an essential step towards a peaceful world, and through its campaigns and publications CND has amply demonstrated the links between the arms race, poverty and hunger, nuclear power and environmental issues.

Local and national membership stands at around 185,000, 177 local authorities have adopted and practise a nuclear-free declaration, and 12,000 people have been arrested during the last decade for acts of civil disobedience. There are currently around 750 local CND groups in Britain; the main office will be happy to give you a local contact, and CND's monthly magazine *Sanity* contains a list of regional contacts. Meg Beresford and Diana Shelley's recent booklet *For a Nuclear-Free Future*, available from CND for £1.95, is a good introduction to the organization's basic philosophy.

Membership brings you *Sanity* (if you choose to subscribe), a colourful sales catalogue with the usual badges, posters and T-shirts, and details of local and national activities.

The CND London office plans to move at the end of 1990 to new premises in north London, though all enquiries to the address below will be forwarded. Scottish and Welsh CND are autonomous but linked organizations; contact them at 420 Sauchiehall Street, Glasgow G2; Tel: 041 331 2878, or 56 Bryn Eron, Dunvant, Swansea SA2 7UX: Tel: 0792 206617.

Campaign for Nuclear Disarmament
22-24 Underwood Street
London
N1 7JG
0(7)1-250 4010

CND Scrapbook

This large format highly illustrated book will bring fond memories and tears to the eyes of anyone who was involved in any of the activities it describes. Aldermaston marches, the Committee of 100, anti-Vietnam War demonstrations, the Holy Loch Peace Cruise, Greenham, Molesworth, Barrow, shadow-painting, Snowball — all are here.

CND Scrapbook
Joan Ruddock
Optima, 1987
£9.95

The National Peace Council

Founded in 1908, the NPC is now in its 81st year of acting as the liaising and co-ordinating network of the British Peace Movement. The NPC doesn't instigate campaigns itself: its task is to keep its membership of over 160 groups and organizations (together with a number of interested individuals) informed of what is going on in the British peace movement. It does this mainly by means of its highly respected *NPC Newsletter*, which contains a regular round-up of peace movement news, contacts, useful resources and forthcoming events. The NPC also helps groups to co-ordinate peace activities, doing its best to ensure that nearby events don't coincide with each other and running a crisis response network. Write or phone for details of membership.

Declan McHugh, the NPC's Peace Information Project Officer, is building up a formidable information base of peace reference resources together with a comprehensive British peace organisation register.

National Peace Council
29 Great James Street
London WC1N 3ES
0(7)1-242 3228
0(7)1-242 4817 (Peace Information Project)

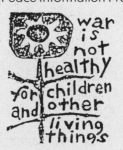

The Peace Pledge Union

'I renounce war and I will never support or sanction another.' So runs the peace pledge, the foundation of the PPU, which since 1934 has been working for positive pacifist action to stop all violent conflict. The PPU is very active in the field of peace education, and produces a wide range of material for teachers and children, including books, posters and badges (see page 266). The PPU also sponsors the 'white poppies for peace' campaign as a substitute for the red poppies which all too often celebrate the exploits of war. The bimonthly magazine of the PPU, *The Pacifist*, is free to members but can also be subscribed to separately — it contains a stimulating mix of news, reviews, articles and details of forthcoming events.

Peace Pledge Union
6 Endsleigh Street
London
WC1H 0DX
0(7)1-387 5501

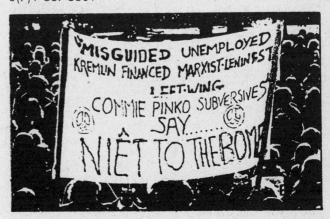

Nonviolence

One of Martin Luther King's most oft-quoted sayings is: 'We no longer have a choice between violence and nonviolence. The choice is either nonviolence or nonexistence.'

People who believe in the importance of moving towards a 'green' lifestyle almost always embrace nonviolence as one of their fundamental ethics, being convinced that there is always a better way of dealing with conflict and disagreement than fighting, and even killing, 'the enemy'.

Violence runs deep in our culture, however, especially among men, who are still often called cowards and worse if they refuse to condone overt aggression. When faced with personal violence in our lives (and institutional violence cannot be more than individual violence repeated many times over), it can be very hard to know what to do, which is why nonviolence training groups exist to explore violent behaviour and its alternatives. Such alternatives include:

▶ Recognizing feelings of anger when they arise, acknowledging their importance and validity, and channelling them into non-destructive activities.
▶ Keeping children (and especially little boys) away from pressures to be frightened into violence, and helping them to deal with their aggressive feelings.
▶ Recognizing that it is possible to be addicted to violence just as it is to alcohol or drugs, and dealing with that addiction.
▶ Exploring different ways of negotiating and working with potential conflict.
▶ Providing help and support for both the survivors of violence and its perpetrators (see the section on women and violence, page 201, and men's groups, page 205).

Nonviolence is a real alternative, and a crucial step on the road to real peace. As Aldous Huxley said as long ago as 1937: 'Nonviolence does not mean doing nothing. It means making the enormous effort to overcome evil with good. Nonviolence does not rely on strong muscles and devilish armaments; it relies on moral courage, self-control and the knowledge, unswervingly acted upon, that there is in every human being, however brutal, however personally hostile, a respect for goodness and truth which can be reached by anyone who uses the right means.'

Nonviolence Reading and Education

It's difficult to know what to recommend in the way of reading matter, partly because the situation (particularly the legal background) changes so quickly, partly because much of the best material is American and tends to be expensive. Even though it's rather out of date, try a *Peace News/CND* book called *Preparing for Non-Violent Direct Action* by Howard Clark, Sheryl Crown, Angela McKee and Hugh Macpherson (1984, £1.50) which includes case histories of the Torness nuclear power station action in 1979 and the successful Luxulyan protest in 1981.

Most people who are involved with nonviolent direct action (NVDA) think very highly of *Resource Manual for a Living Revolution*, a very readable and stimulating American book with many excellent ideas (New Society, distributed in Britain by Turnaround, 1977, £9.95), while *Peace News* (see page 267) still has available a 1983 broadsheet called *An Intro-duction to Nonviolence Training*.

Aldous Huxley's *Encyclopedia of Pacifism* (originally published in 1937) has recently been reissued, tripled in size by new entries to create *The Handbook of Nonviolence*, edited by Robert Seeley (Lawrence Hill, distributed in Britain by Third World Publications, 1986, £8.95). This is a book full of information and ideas to complement the very practical nature of the previous book.

David Polden at CND (see page 263 for the address) co-ordinates the CND Nonviolent Resistance Network. The network embraces nonviolence trainers in many parts of Britain who are willing to offer their services free (they ask only for their expenses) to train people in many aspects of nonviolence.

The Peace Tax Campaign

The average adult in Britain spends £8 a week to support the military machine, yet nobody is asked whether or not they want to. The Peace Tax Campaign exists to exert pressure for the right of pacifists to withdraw conscientiously from that part of the government's tax demand which goes to pay for weaponry and the military bureaucracy. This money would be used to create a Peace Fund to be used exclusively for non-military peacebuilding initiatives. Although the number is still fairly small in comparison with the USA, at least thirty people have refused to pay 'war tax' in recent years. Apart from the bimonthly newsletter, one useful piece of literature produced by the Campaign is a 'How to Write to Your MP' kit.

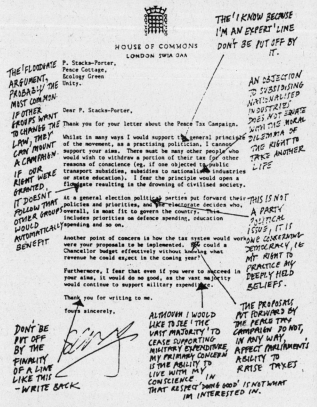

Peace Tax Campaign
1a Hollybush Place
London
E2 9QX
0(7)1-739 5088

Campaign Against Arms Trade

CAAT, founded in 1974, is a coalition of groups and individuals united in the effort to draw attention to Britain's key role in the world's arms trade (Britain is one of the top five arms traders), and to encourage the conversion of military industry to socially useful production. CAAT provides a useful information service about British companies actively involved in the arms trade and the countries they export to. CAAT produces a very good materials and publications list — write with a large sae for this and their information pack. There is also a bimonthly newsletter.

Campaign Against Arms Trade
11 Goodwin Street
London
N4 3HQ
0(7)1-281 0297

Civil Resistance

you read some of the nonviolent action literature on the last
age, you will see that nonviolent civil resistance can take
many forms. Much of it is symbolic: cutting one strand of fence
wire round a nuclear base causes little inconvenience to the
American air force, but it does make it clear that people will
not sit idly by while servicemen play at nuclear war; that great
example to nonviolent activists, Mahatma Gandhi, used
similar tactics to great effect.

There can be many different levels of involvement in peace
activism, from taking part in a candlelit vigil or making folded
paper birds in memory of Hiroshima, to standing in the way of
a missile carrier or padlocking the main gates of a military
base (both of which tactics cause enormous disruption without
actually doing very much at all).

To see what you can become involved in, your best way of
finding out is either through your local peace group (*Housmans Peace Diary*, see page 268, lists most of the active
groups in Britain) or by reading *Peace News* and the National
Peace Council *Newsletter*. It is not a good idea to take matters
into your own individual hands, however annoyed or excited
you are; if you are going to be successful in taking a stand
against the military powers that be you will need assistance,
company and support. Neither is it a good idea to be part of a
nonviolent action unless you have done some sort of nonviolence training (see the previous page); when provoked or
frustrated it is very easy to fall into violent ways of reacting to
violence.

The Snowball Campaign which had involved a gradually
escalating number of people symbolically cutting the wire
round military and nuclear bases, thereby indicating their
displeasure at Britain's 'defence' policies and attempting to
overload the courts was relaunched at Upper Heyford air
base on Hiroshima Day 1989 by an Oxford Christian CND
group. Their demand is for an 'abandonment of military
strategy based on the threat of genocide', and people are
encouraged to cut strands of the wire fence and take part in a
letter-writing campaign. There have been two rounds of Snowball actions so far, with a third planned for 1990. Each round is
accompanied by a statement of support by academics and
church people.

If you do 'fall foul' of the law during a nonviolent peace
action there is a free legal support service, an independent
group funded by CND, to give advice and prepare legal briefings if needed. The Legal Support Group can be found at the
Quaker International Centre, 1 Byng Place, London WC1E 7JJ
(tel: 0(7)1-388 9689 on Wednesdays only between 10 and 6).
Two other organisations involved with the legal side of
peace are Lawyers for Nuclear Disarmament, c/o 2 Garden
Court, Temple, London EC4; and the Institute for Law and
Peace (INLAP), Bryn-y-Mor, Parrog, Newport SA42 0RX.

Despair and Empowerment

The message of Joanna Macy's influential book *Despair and
Personal Power in the Nuclear Age* is that we have all allowed
ourselves to be pushed into a state of apathetic powerlessness
in relation to the terrible things that are happening in the world
because we refuse to deal with our despair. We repress the
pain because it hurts; but it hurts even more if we do nothing
about it. You may find her book a bit spiritual for your tastes,
but it will certainly get you thinking about what you need to do
to find the strength to be effective in the world — for the world.
This book contains many exercises, mostly for working in
groups, and some helpful (though very American) resources.
An index would improve this important book.

*

*As we allow ourselves to feel our pain for the world, we find our
connection with each other.*

Despair and Personal Power in the Nuclear Age
Joanna Rogers Macy
New Society, 1983 (distributed in the UK by Turnaround)
£9.50

Interhelp is a loose network of people working in the field of
environmental and peace politics and spirituality; Joanna
Macy's despair and empowerment work is central to its philosophy. It produces a quarterly newsletter called *Threads* and
organizes workshops and gatherings. As yet the network
seems rather unfocused and the newsletter bitty, but it fulfils an
important role in bridging the middle ground between activism
and a spiritual perspective.

The Interhelp Network
4a High Tenterfell
Kendal
Cumbria
LA9 4PG
0539 29256

Heart Politics

In *Heart Politics* Fran Peavey has brought together the personal
and the political in a unique and inspiring collection of essays
about her life as a front-line peace activist — using 'peace' in
its widest sense. Who else would travel the Third World, sitting
on park benches with a multilingual placard saying simply:
'American willing to listen'? This is a moving and honest
account of what can be done to make the world a more
humane and understanding place, written throughout in the
first person — one of the few books I would put in the
'absolutely essential reading' category.

In *Voices of Survival* Dennis Paulson has brought together the
personal peace testimonies of nearly two hundred well known
personalities, from Zhores Medvedev to Germaine Greer,
Dudley Moore to the Pope and the Dalai Lama. 'What can be
done?' asks Richard Pryor. 'Stop.'

Heart Politics
Fran Peavey
New Society, 1986
(distributed in the UK by
Turnaround)
£7.95

Voices of Survival in the Nuclear Age
edited by Dennis
Paulson
Wisdom Publications,
1986
£6.95

The Women's Peace Movement

Although a thousand women have been arrested at Greenham in the last two years, the women's peace camp which made history in the mid 1980s has ceased to be the 'real news' that it was. The first of the Cruise missiles have now been returned to the USA for dismantling, yet the camp continues nonetheless — and so does the official harassment. Donations of food, tents and money are welcome — and most important of all the support and visits of other women. There are a number of Greenham support groups throughout the country — contact the camp at the address below for details.

Lynne Jones' *Keeping the Peace* (Women's Press, 1983, £3.95) was written when Greenham was still front page news, and captures the spirit of those pioneering years very immediately. It contains a very good resource section on the women's peace movement, though not surprisingly the list of organizations is already a long way out of date. A more up to date and comprehensive source is the *Women's Peace Directory*, published in 1986 by Solid Women (£3.75 from bookshops or direct from Solid Women at Pump Close, Shilton, Oxfordshire OX8 4AB).

The long history of the women's peace movement in Britain is documented in Jill Liddington's carefully researched book *The Long Road to Greenham: Feminism and Anti-Militarism in Britain Since 1820* (Virago, 1989, £9.99). 'Greenham,' she writes, 'has provided us with an alternative icon for the 1980s,' and makes it very clear that after Greenham the relationship between feminism and pacifism can never be the same again.

Women For Life On Earth is the network that organized the 1981 march from South Wales to Greenham Common which resulted in the establishment of the Greenham Common Women's Peace Camp. WFLOE exists to promote the links between feminism, peace and ecology through direct action, education, and the exchange of information; it produces an occasional newsletter and organizes meetings and workshops. Other important womens' organizations working for peace and social change are the Womens' International League for Peace and Freedom (WILPF), 29 Great James Street, London WC1N 3ES, Tel: 0(7)1-242 1521; Change, PO Box 824, London SE24 9JS (a solidarity organization for women worldwide); and Women Working For a Nuclear-free and Independent Pacific (WWNFIP), 7 Furnace Cottages, Crow Edge, Sheffield S30 5HF, Tel: 0226 766310.

Greenham Common Women's Peace Camp
Blue Gate
outside USAF Base
Greenham Common
Newbury
Berkshire

Women For Life On Earth
2 Bramshill Gardens
London
NW5 1JH
0(7)1-281 4018

One of the most moving accounts of the action at Greenham Common is the oratorio *The Gates of Greenham*, written by Tony Biggin using words from the camp's history. Performed by the Quaker Festival Chorus and the LPO on a double album (Sain 1352R), it tells the story of the camp without romanticization yet with deep feeling.

Nonviolence and Children

The American organization Educators for Social Responsibility has compiled an excellent primer called *A Manual on Nonviolence and Children* (edited by Stephanie Judson, New Society Publishers (distributed in the UK by Turnaround), 1984, £9.95), full of ideas which can be used with children both individually and in groups. Another good resource is David Hicks' *Education For Peace* (Routledge, 1988, £11.95).

The Peace Pledge Union (see page 263) has a Peace Education Project which produces a magazine called *Peptalk* three times a year, designed for teachers and others involved with peace education. The PPU also publishes a *Children and War* newsletter.

Several excellent books written specially for children concerning these issues have appeared in the last couple of years. Jim Eldridge's *Save Our Planet: An Anti-Nuclear Guide for Teenagers* (Magnet, 1987, £1.95) is a very readable account of nuclear weapons and the link with the nuclear power industry. Any grown-up wanting a first primer on nuclear issues will also find this cheap paperback a very clear introduction.

Two novels in the growing specially-for-teenagers genre address the nonviolence issue in an immediate and gripping way. In Joan Lingard's *The Guilty Party* (Penguin, 1989, £2.25) Josie McCullough is determined to make her voice heard to prevent a Chernobyl in the Scottish seaside town where she lives, even to the lengths of breaking the law. Is she prepared to see it through to the bitter end?

In the wake of an international crisis America is threatened with nuclear attack. Suddenly life for Meredith and Barry, living in the Midwest town of Lombard, Illinois, have to come to terms with the possibility that next week may never come. Lynn Hall's *If Winter Comes* (Penguin, 1989, £1.99) is a chilling but immensely thought-provoking story.

Peace Studies

Although several universities offer courses in peace studies (the University of Ulster offers a BA and MA for example), only Bradford University has a Department of Peace Studies offering BA, MA and doctorates. The School of Peace Studies was established in 1973 and now has 100 undergraduates and 25 MA and 24 PhD students. The most important area of research at present is the nuclear issue, particularly Britain's involvement in it, though the School's interests cover the whole spectrum of peace issues from weapons control systems to arms conversion. It has close links with similar establishments in other countries, and has an extensive library which can be used by non-students with prior arrangement (see also page 331).

The Alternative Defence Commission, which used to be based at the University but has now been wound up, produced two important and still very relevant books on non-nuclear defence options for Britain, *The Politics of Alternative Defence* (Paladin, 1987, £3.95) and *Defence Without The Bomb* (Taylor and Francis, 1983, £4.45).

University of Bradford Department of Peace Studies
Richmond Road
Bradford
West Yorkshire
BD7 1DP
0274 733466 ext 260

Peace News

The first issue of *Peace News* appeared on June 6th, 1936, and PN soon became the official magazine of the Peace Pledge Union (see page 263). It continued right through the war years, providing an essential lifeline for those who could not endorse the violence in which Britain involved itself. In 1961 *PN* cut its direct links with the PPU and has since been doggedly independent, pointing out oppression, bureaucratic nonsense and woolly thinking wherever and whenever it occurs.

Peace News has now reached well beyond issue number 2,300, and its fortnightly mix of news, letters, very readable articles, small ads and intelligent editorials is something to be looked forward to. I like its honesty, courage and humour (the 'Earwig' column is a delight), and at £13 a year (£9 if you're unwaged) there can't be a much cheaper way of keeping in touch with interesting developments around the country.

Earwig is always pleased to hear of employers actually taking the needs of women employees seriously. Imagine her delight on hearing of one who is planning to introduce a nursery for the children of staff working in central London; to grant up to five years' maternity leave; and to give leave during school holidays (even if it's unpaid) to allow for the care of children. Imagine, also, her disappointment that this magnanimous employer is the Ministry of Defence . . .

PN, September 1989

Peace News
8 Elm Avenue
Nottingham
NG3 4GF
0602 503587

Achieving World Peace

'Once more we all owe Ted Dunn a debt of gratitude,' write's CND's Bruce Kent at the front of *A Step by Step Approach to World Peace*. A prolific author and tireless worker within the British peace movement, Ted Dunn has consistently managed to keep one step ahead of international developments, proposing both an ethical framework for achieving world peace and an eminently workable strategy for creating peace in each region where war and tension currently reign.

A Step by Step Approach, published in 1988, foresaw some of the recent developments towards stabilization — in South Africa and Central America for example. Ted Dunn also predicted the current debate about large-scale 'Marshall Plans' to redirect wealth and investment to the poorer regions of the world (though he could usefully have distinguished between sustainable and greed-motivated investment). It's rather a bitty book, but contains many thought-provoking ideas.

If we build the institutions of peace and security based on economic and social justice in the spirit of love and generosity within a viable structure, law and disarmament will follow, but if we insist on putting the cart before the horse by seeking disarmament without resolving social, economic and political problems we must not be surprised if peace remains a dream.

A Step by Step Approach to World Peace
Ted Dunn
Gooday Publishers, 1988
£4.95

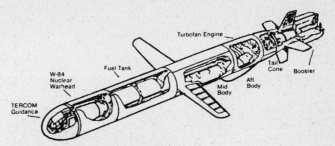

Professionals for Peace

In recent years a growing number of professions have organized their own campaigns for peace under the general umbrella of CND and the National Peace Council. Most of the organizations are featured in *Housman's Peace Diary* (see page 268); the list includes Mothers For Peace, Lawyers For Nuclear Disarmament, Pensioners For Peace, Architects For Peace, Clergy Against Nuclear Arms, Artists For Peace, Engineers For Nuclear Disarmament, Members of Equity For Nuclear Disarmament, Musicians Against Nuclear Arms, Scientists Against Nuclear Arms (SANA) (9 Poland Street, London W1V 3DG) who produce a very good newsletter, and the Medical Campaign Against Nuclear Weapons (MCANW) and the Medical Association for the Prevention of War (MAPW), who have moved into shared accommodation at 601 Holloway Road, London N19 4DJ; Tel: 0(7)1-272 2020 — both produce good newsletters. Then there are Psychologists For Peace (c/o 36 Dartmouth Road, London NW2 2EX), largely responsible for the British Psychological Society publishing the influential book *Psychological Aspects of Nuclear War* (Wiley, 1985, £3.95), Philosophers For Peace, Electronics And Computing For Peace (c/o GreenNet, see page 347), and many more. There's no need to think you're the only one that doesn't want the world to end.

Green Concern

Following the popular trend Stan Banks' Peace Concern recently changed its name to Green Concern, but what he does hasn't changed very much. Stan Banks has been running Green (ex Peace) Concern since 1982, selling the widest range of badges, postcards, leaflets, jewellery, keyrings, balloons and literature anywhere in the British peace movement. Green Concern is non-profit-making; all the money you spend goes into more resources. Send an A5 sae for your copy of the 'Give Peace a Chance' Campaign Catalogue.

Green Concern
113 Spetchley Road
Worcester
WR5 2LS
0905 360266

Local Groups

There are probably more than 2,000 local peace groups active in Britain today, and if you want to do something very practical about creating a more peaceful world you would be very unlucky not to find a group of like-minded people in your neighbourhood. The largest number of local groups are either CND (see page 263) or church-affiliated, most often associated with local Quaker meetings (see Quaker Peace and Service, page 176). In some parts of the country there are also lively regional peace networks (in Norwich and Dorset, for example), peace centres and councils, and local groups producing newsletters like West Midlands CND.

Though interest and activity has waned a little in recent months, the Dorset Peace Council is an example of a well organized regional network, which has been involved in running an impressive and exciting programme of festivals, fairs, conferences and public meetings, school and college visits, and publications. With more than fifty affiliated local groups and their regular monthly mailing, there is no excuse if you live in Dorset for not knowing what you can do for peace.

*

Of course the DPC is not utopian. We have moments of chaos; we get frustrated; some of us burn out; some ideas don't work; we have constant cash crises; we still get impatient with each other; we still waste a lot of time. But we have created something unique which reflects our aspirations as people and we know that slowly, inexorably, we are persuading people in Dorset that they can have some say in the kind of world they want for themselves, their children, their grandchildren, and that the peace movement is not a bunch of freaks but simply a group of extremely ordinary — and thus extremely wonderful — people attempting to deal with an extremely extraordinary situation in a peaceful and mindful way that reflects the kind of society they want.

Peace News, February, 1987

The Dorset Peace Council
53 Newberry Road
Weymouth
Dorset
DT4 8LP
0305 760758

Peace Information

For up to date information about the peace movement world-wide and a handy pocket diary you can't do better than buy *Housmans Peace Diary*, which appears early in September for the following year — it contains a comprehensive listing of British and international organizations, publications and bookshops, all with addresses and nearly all with telephone numbers. The 1990 *Diary* costs £4.25. Housmans bookshop in Caledonian Road, London, just round the corner from Kings Cross Station, has been intimately associated with the peace movement since it opened in 1954 and continues to sell the most complete range of books about peace that you will find. *Peace News* had its offices here until it moved to Nottingham in 1974.

In 1987 Declan McHugh of the National Peace Council (see page 263) compiled an excellent guide to 31 British libraries which hold specialist collections of books and other materials concerning peace. Called *Peace Information Resources*, it costs £1.50 (including p+p) and can be obtained from the NPC. Another excellent resource is *Teaching Resources For Education in International Understanding Justice and Peace*, compiled by Anne Brewer of the Surrey Library of Teaching Resources (6 Phoenice Cottages, Dorking Road, Bookham, Surrey KT23 4QG; Tel: 0372 56421). It costs £4.50 (including p+p) which covers the original volume published in 1988 and the 1989 supplement.

Housmans Peace Diary
Housmans Diary Group
(5 Caledonian Road
London
N1 9DX
0(7)1-837 4473)
£4.25

The Fate of the Earth

Jonathan Schell, who writes for *New Yorker* magazine, is a passionate, intelligent and fluent writer on the psychology of the nuclear stalemate — and on the breakthrough of consciousness which is necessary if we are to see the elimination of weapons of genocide.

In the much-acclaimed *The Fate of The Earth* he makes it very clear that the choice we have is fundamentally very simple — we must choose between life and death, since there is no tenable middle course; and we must acknowledge that we are potentially on the brink of annihilation: we must awaken to the truth of our peril, he says, 'break through the layers of our denials, put aside our fainthearted excuse, and rise up to cleanse the earth of nuclear weapons.'

The Abolition takes the argument a step further, showing what is actually necessary to rid the world of nuclear weaponry in a sane and reasoned mixture of hope and realism.

*

It needs to be said — once and for all, one would hope — that there is no need whatever to choose between short-term, moderate 'steps' that are within our immediate grasp and long-term, radical goals whose achievement would bring us real safety. . . Isn't it self-evident that both are needed?

The Fate of The Earth
Jonathan Schell
Picador, 1982
£1.95

The Abolition
Jonathan Schell
Picador, 1984
£2.50

WORK AND LEISURE

'There is an old Haitian proverb which I think should be our watchword through this period and it goes as follows: "If work were a good thing, the rich would have found a way of keeping it all to themselves."'
Barrie Sherman, in *The New Economic Agenda*

It is a fundamental green belief that people are not by nature lazy. If they have the choice, people will always prefer to be doing something worthwhile and fulfilling, something they really enjoy doing, something which produces results.

Yet mention the word 'work' to most people and they will utter at least an inward groan. A few people are fortunate enough to have work which is both rewarding and remunerative, but the sad fact is that most people don't enjoy doing what they are doing very much, and feel that what they are doing isn't producing anything very useful.

The American author Studs Terkel came very close to capturing the theme of the times in his study of American workers in the 1970s, *Working*: '"I'm a machine," says the spot-welder. "I'm caged," says the bank teller and echoes the hotel clerk. "I'm a mule," says the steel worker. "A monkey can do what I do," says the receptionist. "I'm less than a farm implement," says the migrant worker. "I'm an object," says the high-fashion model. Most of us have jobs that are too small for our spirit. Jobs are not big enough for people.'

Addiction to Employment

Because of convention and financial imperative, all the words to do with work — 'work' itself, 'employment', 'job', 'unemployment', 'living', 'leisure' — have become geared to one particular economic model of the world. It is a model in which 'real work' is a full-time paid job in a trade, occupation or profession, and anything other ('less') than that is second rate. 'It is extraordinary,' says economist Charles Handy, 'that we have people in this country fighting to preserve the right to crawl on their bellies underground hacking coal out of seams, particularly when their fathers were desperate to keep them out of the pits. But the reason why they are doing this is because we haven't yet offered any alternative to the employee society: they don't know any other way in which a decent able-bodied person can earn respectability and contribute to society.'

This may be bordering on the condescending, but it underlines the fact that the vast majority of people are well and truly hooked on rigid ideas about employment.

There are alternatives, however, and especially in areas where officially designated 'unemployment' is very high, individuals and groups of people, fed up with waiting, are exploring new ways of working.

Asking Difficult Questions

Whatever politicians and industrialists would like to believe, the future of work will inevitably be very different from its recent past. The fact is that well into the future the work required to be done is certain to decrease as Britain's population stabilizes, demand for goods and services peaks, and automation continues to replace human drudgery. Thus the number of people who find 'real work' will continue to fall, and any alleviation of 'unemployment' can come only from changing the definition of the term.

The most useful question to ask in these changing times is 'What is work for?' This must depend to a large extent on circumstances, but for a very large proportion of the working population 'money' must be very high on the list. If you currently have paid work, would you honestly go on working if you were guaranteed the same income for not working?

The related question is 'What should work be for?' A 1981 *Guardian* survey of job satisfaction gives some of the answers. When asked what they thought were the main elements in job satisfaction, people replied (in order): freedom, respect, learning, challenge, fulfilment, helping. How do your present circumstances rate?

Elements of the New Economic Order

If the foundations of the present system of work and employment had to be summed up in four phrases, they would be: personal and corporate competition; obedience and deference ('loyalty'); providing the cogs for an international economic machine; and the exploitation of whatever makes money fastest, whether people or material resources.

Big business is often referred to as a cut-throat world, its characters devoutly believing that you can't afford to be kind. The new way of working stresses co-operation, believing that we are in the world to help each other, not to do each other down whenever possible.

It involves small groups of people who enjoy working together, and who are producing the quality goods and services that people want to buy. Even the market has faith in co-operation: while in October 1987 the stock market was licking its wounds, the Industrial Co-Ownership Fund (see page 275) launched a share issue and had raised half a million within a few weeks.

People enjoy working much more if they know why they are doing it, and who is going to benefit. It helps even more if they can choose these criteria for themselves without excessive outside interference. It is naive to believe that centralized systems will ever have the interests of small communities, particularly peripheral communities, at heart. In hard times it is always the small ('uneconomic') branches that close first.

Control of local business must be in local hands, with people who will always put the local economy first, and will explore every possible way of providing flexible and imaginative ways of providing useful and fulfilling work. Co-operation, self-reliance and local initiative together create a sustainable economy to which people can relate, and which can weather the self-created storms of the international money market.

The Future of Work

Of several recent books which look at what we can expect in relation to work in the future, Charles Handy's is the most wide-ranging and probably the most pertinent for most people. As a visiting Professor at the London Business School he knows about business, yet isn't at all limited by conventional economic ideas, and in *The Future of Work* he has brought together many ideas about employment, pay, career structures, forms of organization, and relevant educational resources. He frequently uses examples of new initiatives to illustrate his arguments, and puts quotations and statistical summaries in clear boxes. Charles Handy is an enthusiastic and very human writer in an area which can easily be sanitized to the point of boredom, and he makes the need for radical change so clearly that only the blind can ignore it.

*

Lord Ritchie Calder used to tell the story of the sun-tanned youth lying on the beach at Naples who was confronted by the American businessman. 'Why do you just lie there doing nothing when you could be fishing? That way you could sell the fish and buy yourself a boat and then in time a proper trawler which might become an ocean-going fleet until you were as rich as Onassis.' 'And what then?' asked the youth. 'You could spend the day on the beach at Naples.'

*

We are fixated, both as a nation and as individuals, by the employment organization. Work is defined as employment. Money is distributed through employment. Status and identity stem from employment. We therefore hang on to employment as long as we can; we measure our success in terms of it; we expect great things from it, for the country and for ourselves; and we cannot conceive of a future without it. And yet, ironically, we are very bad at it because their is an individualist streak in all of us which agrees with Marx that it is alienating to sell ourselves or our time to another.

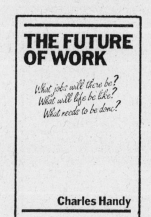

The Future of Work
Charles Handy
Blackwell, 1985
£5.50

Alternatives to Unemployment

If Charles Handy has produced an excellent and detailed overall map of the future world of work, James Robertson (on the next page) provides a description of the history of the landscape, and John Osmond the gazetteer of local street plans.
   Work in the Future takes us on a journey around the Britain of the late 1980s, showing us mostly local small-scale initiatives and the networks which operate to support and service them. John Osmond is very clear that a 'conventional jobs' scenario is untenable for the future, particularly for the growing numbers who will never have a regular job with a regular

income. After an introductory chapter about the New Economics, he looks at community initiatives, the co-operative movement, work based on materials recycling, and the alternative finance network (covered in *New Green Pages* under 'Money', pages 244-252). Finally, he peers into the crystal ball and sees a decentralized, small-scale, co-operative and ecologically-oriented society in which the emphasis is on the local economy and the wellbeing of the local community. The resource sections at the end of each chapter are excellent.

*

The growth of the New Economy is an evolutionary process: its projects and activities gradually filling the spaces left by the cracking of the old order. The New Economics does not offer a theoretical blueprint for the future; its very essence is to rely on the integrity and initiative of communities working out their own salvation. What the New Economics does offer is a global ecological concern combined with practical local action. It is our best hope for work in the future.

Work in the Future
Alternatives to
Unemployment
John Osmond
Thorsons, 1986
£5.99

Good Work

Many people find Schumacher's old-fashioned, almost biblical style hard to digest, but this, his last collection of essays, is short and easy to read. The pieces cover the need for a human scale technology and the impossibility of economic growth; the essay that gives the book its title examines the quality of work, pointing out that quality work can only be done by a person who is leading a quality life.

*

The question is raised: How do we prepare young people for the future world of work? and the first answer, I think, must be: We should prepare them to be able to distinguish between good work and bad work and encourage them not to accept the latter. That is to say, they should be encouraged to reject meaningless, boring, stultifying, or nerve-racking work in which a man or woman is made the servant of a machine or a system. They should be taught that work is the joy of life and is needed for our development, but that meaningless work is an abomination.

Good Work
E.F. Schumacher
Abacus, 1980
£1.95

Ownwork

In *Future Work*, ex-civil servant James Robertson puts the current crisis in employment firmly in its historical, philosophical and psychological context. If you want to know how things got to be the way they are, *Future Work* charts the different currents of thinking that have led to a situation where few people seem to realize that the old shibboleths of growth, full employment, and the prime importance of work have lost their magic.

James Robertson is particularly good at asking — and attempting to answer — the difficult questions like 'What is work for?', 'Who decides what work is worth?' and 'What is money anyway?' One useful expression he coins in this book is 'ownwork', meaning useful and fulfilling activity organized and controlled by its participants, though even here the insidiousness of preconceived ideas about work and selfishness battle it out among the various implications of the word 'own'.

*

It is, in fact, helpful to see the transition from employment to ownwork as the end of an empire — the breakdown of the employment empire and the liberation of its subjects from their present dependence on it. The process of transition will then have two different aspects, depending on where you stand. First, it will involve managing the breakdown of the old empire, in other words its decolonization. Second, it will involve liberating yourself — and helping to liberate other people — from being dependent on it.

Future Work
James Robertson
Temple Smith/Gower, 1985
£6.95

The Sane Alternative

Seven years before *Future Work*, and some time before the new economics bandwagon really started to roll, James Robertson put his ideas about the economic and political future together in a book called *The Sane Alternative: A Choice of Futures*. With his government service background and academic training, his radical ideas were not easily ignored, and reviewers paid it guarded compliments such as 'comprehensively considerate' and 'a reasonable revolutionary'.

In little more than a hundred pages, the book assesses (as clearly as the future can be assessed) the implications of the options available to us — 'Business as Usual', 'Disaster', 'Authoritarian Control', 'Hyper-Expansion', and (the Sane Alternative of the title and the author's very clear preference) a 'Sane, Humane and Ecological' future. Very little is side-stepped in this stimulating account — wealth, work, spirituality, revolution, peace, feminism, all are here. I'm not so sure about the utopian postscript, 'Teatime at Marshbeck'.

*

In Britain in the early 19th century, the Whigs and Tories for a long time refused to accept that an industrial society had replaced the old agricultural society. By delaying repeal of the Corn Laws and putting off the introduction of cheap food, they caused unnecessary hardship and distress to many working people. All the industrial countries are facing an equally profound transition now

— from an age of universal employment to a new work order. By refusing to recognise this and to ease the transition to a new paradigm of work, the various branches of today's establishment in these countries are imposing unnecessary hardship and distress on many millions of jobless people.

The Sane Alternative
James Robertson
James Robertson, 1983
(revised edition)
£2.95

Shadow Work

Ivan Illich is considered by many people to be one of the world's most original thinkers when it comes to the oppressive practices of modern society, but with rare exceptions he is hard going. This late collection of essays is easier and thinner than most; its subject is economic subservience and how certain sorts of work have come to be highly esteemed while others are ignored and unrewarded — 'shadow work'.

Using a range of historical sources, he shows how colonialism has always devalued traditional skills ('vernacular values'), and thus the subsistence work done by the peasantry, or women, or the poor, is always devalued and sentimentalized while the 'exciting' work on the leading edge of 'development' is exalted.

*

This sentimentalism is a dishonesty for which there is no known substitute in a society that has ravished its own environment for subsistence. Such a society depends on ever new diagnoses of those for whom it must care. And this paternalistic dishonesty enables the representatives of the oppressed to seek power for ever new oppression.

Shadow Work
Ivan Illich
Marion Boyars, 1981
£3.50

Unemployment

Unemployment can bring to people a threefold crisis: a crisis of poverty, a crisis of participation, and a crisis of purposelessness; little wonder that the suicide rate is eighteen times higher than amongst the rest of us. But a time of unemployment also brings a unique chance: to discover our real selves. With a little support, we can find true meaning, purpose, and new vision, in which our lives can be transformed.

Liz Shephard

Whichever way you count it there are more than three million unemployed people in Britain today, and probably another million (mostly women with young children) who would like to work if they could but who can't sign on. This doesn't include, of course, the people who aren't happy with the work they are doing but who feel they can't, or daren't, do anything about it.

That's a vast pool of people who are not happy with the role of work in their lives, and a vast pool of untapped skills, imagination, muscle and mindpower which costs the country (it has been estimated) more than £20 billion a year in benefits and lost taxes; this in a country crying out for essential work, both in caring for people and for the natural and built environment.

How can there be unemployment in a world where so much needs to be done? How many people are waiting to go to work at building the new creation, but no one has invited them yet? Breakdown is the surest starting point for breakthrough.

Matthew Fox

The Unemployment Handbook

First published in 1981 and now in its fourth edition, 70% rewritten, *The New Unemployment Handbook* is a treasure trove of ideas and resources for anybody who is unemployed, malemployed, unhappily employed, or (when they've read the book) can't wait to be unemployed. If you're at a loose end of any sort, you can hardly fail to be inspired by many of the projects and ideas described by Guy Dauncey and Jane Mountain in these 200 packed pages.

They cover virtually everything you might ever want to know about job opportunities, life directions, money and benefits, careers, special problems for women, ethnic minorities and the disabled, job clubs, co-operatives and much more. The resource sections are as long as the chapters, with hundreds of well-researched suggestions about what you can do to help yourself.

The National Extension College, who publish *The New Unemployment Handbook*, also produce several other useful resource books for unemployed people, so when you order your copy of the *Handbook,* ask them for a complete publications catalogue.

*

This book preaches. It bears no shame in doing this. We know how much pain there is out there, and we want to help you transform it. There is so much that can be done when people get together and start to help each other. We can support each other, have parties together, hunt for jobs together, establish local workshops together, set up arts and music groups together, organise festivals together, establish community projects together, set up co-operatives together, set up community businesses together, organise holidays together, plant trees together, petition city hall together, protest together. This book is a book of encouragement.

The New Unemployment Handbook
Guy Dauncey and Jane Mountain
National Extension College, 1987
(18 Brooklands Avenue,
Cambridge CB2 2HN)
£6.95

Signing On

THE VOICE OF THE UNEMPLOYED

Phillip Reilly is a journalist who, returning to Britain after working abroad to find himself unemployed, decided to set up a newspaper for himself and the other 3 million. The first issue of *Signing On: The Voice of the Unemployed* appeared in February 1988, and it has appeared monthly ever since. *Signing On* is available free to the unemployed and by subscription to anyone else (currently £10 for 6 bi-monthly issues). A mixture of news, reports, letters from readers, updates on changes in the law, and guides to dealing with questionnaires or interviews, it gives a balanced expression to the strength and courage involved in being unemployed.

Signing On
Workforce Publications Ltd
52 Queens Gardens
London
W2 3AA
0(7)1-724 5346

If you are signing on, or even better before signing on and facing the maze of restrictions, regulations and schemes, the Unemployment Unit publishes a number of excellent booklets to guide you through. *Your Rights on ET; Studying on the Dole; Signing On; Restart;* and *Where You Stand* are all free to claimants and trainees if you send an A5 sae to the Unit. If you're not a claimant they cost 50p each (£1 for *Restart*).

Unemployment Unit
9 Poland Street
London
W1V 3DG
0(7)1-439 8523

Ways of Working

As it becomes very clear that conventional ideas about what constitutes 'work' will never provide fulfilling activity for everybody, there has been a wave of new thinking about what constitutes work. A whole spectrum of ways of working has been identified, including part-time work, shared work, household work and voluntary work. Within this spectrum, the distinction between 'work' and 'leisure' has become blurred; after all, if you enjoy your work and can choose when to do it, doesn't that come close to fulfilling your 'leisure' needs too? While employment policies continue to hold sacred the idea of the 'real' fulltime job and make sharp distinctions between employment and unemployment, ways of earning money (and therefore ways of working) will be limited. Yet people are exploring alternative ways of working, and government and employers are gradually beginning to take account of the changes. We are waking up to the fact that there are as many ways of working as there are human beings.

Job Sharing

In a shared job one full-time post is shared between two people, each sharer doing half the work and receiving half of the pay and other benefits. Job sharing is most common in service industries and the professions, though some factories are also trying it. In many cases job sharing suits both the people who are working, giving them a guaranteed income and time to look after children or study, and the employer, who usually finds that the flexibility and reliability that two people can offer between them more than compensates for the slightly increased administrative work required.

As employers find it harder to recruit the staff they need due to a declining number of school-leavers, they are increasingly looking at job-sharing and other flexible ways of working. As it becomes a sellers' market the situation is getting easier for would-be job-sharers, and there is now even a job share agency called Gemini in Chelmsford. This and more can be discovered by contacting New Ways to Work, an organization which exists to advise people both about finding appropriate employment and organising their time. It also acts as a pressure group for the implementation of more flexible ways of working. Send for their information pack, which includes a newsletter and a publications list.

New Ways to Work
309 Upper Street
London
N1 2TY
0(7)1-226 4026

Volunteering

Twelve months after he was made redundant 44-year-old Graham Gill hit his lowest point. He had lost his job as a skilled worker in the declining engineering industry and a fruitless year-long search for work had completely sapped his confidence and self-esteem. The change in his life occurred when he turned in desperation to the volunteer bureau at Wythenshawe, a suburb of Manchester with high unemployment. After discussing with him the kind of work he was interested in, the bureau put him in touch with the local Victims Support Scheme where he helped crime victims fit new locks and fill in insurance claims, as well as providing emotional support. A few months later he took on an additional voluntary job delivering meals to handicapped people, work that soon led to a paid part-time job with the social services. Three years later he has completed his final term of a part time course at Manchester University prior to taking a diploma in community education at the city's polytechnic.

Jane Simms, *The Guardian*

If you would like to explore the potential of voluntary work (and voluntary work shouldn't affect your benefits), you can either go directly to your local volunteer bureau, of which there are 350 all over Britain, or contact The Volunteer Centre in Berkhamsted, who will be able to tell you what is available in your area.

The Volunteer Centre is an independent agency which provides information and advice about volunteers and community involvement. The Centre's library is comprehensive and the staff helpful; they also produce a very wide range of helpful literature covering volunteer work in different areas such as hospitals, children's play, and the natural environment. The Centre also organizes training courses on a wide variety of subjects, and produces an excellent journal called Involve.

The Volunteer Centre UK
29 Lower King's Road
Berkhamsted
Hertfordshire
HP4 2AB
04427 873311

Initiatives

Established in 1981, The Centre for Employment Initiatives is an independent non-profit-making organization which provides information and advice on ways in which employment can be created in novel and imaginative ways. By charging public authorities and the private sector at full rates, CEI is able to negotiate lower rates for community and voluntary bodies, and has helped projects all over Britain with financial and legal advice, feasibility studies, and evaluation of the initiatives. Possibly the most exciting thing about CEI is its research function — the Centre is constantly on the lookout for exciting new developments around the world. The bi-monthly magazine *Initiatives* is an excellent, thought-provoking and even witty survey of employment initiatives in Britain and abroad, and their associated publishing group, Ubique, has started publishing reports about employment initiatives in other countries — volumes on France and Canada have been published so far.

The Centre for Employment Initiatives
140a Gloucester Mansions
Cambridge Circus
London
WC2H 8PA
0(7)1-240 8901/2/3

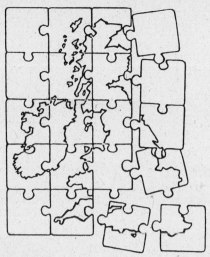

Co-operation

The new co-operative movement is flourishing with a small but strong base, and there are thus indications that workers' co-operatives could have an increasing part to play in the industrial development of our country. Their future role will depend on the existing co-operatives being able to demonstrate that it is possible to work to the co-operative ideal and earn an adequate wage at the same time. It will also depend upon politicians committing themselves to the co-operative ideal and being prepared to enact legislation which will encourage the growth of co-operative enterprises. It will depend on a changing of attitudes as people come to place more emphasis on democracy at work, on a pleasant working atmosphere, on quality rather than quantity.

Our hope is that democracy in the workplace will become as much a part of the fabric of our society as political democracy.

The Workers' Co-operative Handbook (see below)

Co-operative working began in Britain in the 1840s in the Pennine valleys of Lancashire, but although there have been co-ops of one sort and another ever since, the British co-operative movement really only started to grow quickly in the 1970s. In 1970 there were about a hundred co-operative businesses in Britain; by 1984 there were 900 and there are now between 1,400 and 1,600, with the early rapid growth having levelled out to about 300 a year.

Co-operatives are businesses in which every member has a financial and day-to-day organizational stake, and which operate for the benefit of all their members. There are different varieties — neighbourhood co-operatives, community co-operatives, marketing and service co-operatives, but all have the same basic idea — members' benefit and members' control.

Information About Co-operatives

If you want to know more about co-operative working or are thinking of setting up a workers' co-op, the best guide is *The Workers' Co-operative Handbook* (£4.50 from the Industrial Co-Ownership Movement — see below), which includes detailed information about the technicalities of setting up a co-op and a good resource section. A more recent guide in the form of a loose-leaf information pack, called *The Ins and Outs of Starting a Workers' Co-operative*, is produced by Hackney Co-operative Developments (16 Dalston Lane, London E8 3AZ; Tel: 0(7)1 254 4829). It costs £1.50 (free if you live in Hackney), and covers important issues such as racism and sexism as well as including an excellent resource section.

A Directory of Workers' Co-operatives was published in late 1988 by the Co-operatives Research Unit at the Open University. It covers co-ops by region and lists them by industrial sector at the back. Like any businesses in today's world of competitive 'enterprise' co-ops come and go with alarming regularity, but though it is already out of date this is the best

directory there is for England and Wales. Unfortunately the £25 price tag will put it out of the range of many potential buyers. The CRU publishes a number of books and pamphlets, so ask for a publications list. *Developing Successful Workers' Co-operatives* by Chris Cornforth, Alan Thomas, Jenny Lewis and Roger Spear (Sage Books, 1988, £10.95) is a very thorough study of the factors which make for a successful co-operative business.

SCDC's (see below) *Annual Report* includes the best directory there is of co-operatives in Scotland.

Co-operatives Research Unit
The Open University
Walton Hall
Milton Keynes
MK7 6AA
0908 652102/3

ICOM and ICOF

The Industrial Co-Ownership Movement was set up in 1971 to foster links between co-operatively run businesses, and is now the largest and most important national support organization for workers' co-operatives. ICOM has an extensive range of publications (send for their mail order catalogue), runs a series of training courses, and researches into different aspects of co-operative working, such as the role of women in co-ops and the implications of new technology. ICOM also produces a model constitution for co-operatives, which has been adopted by a large proportion of new co-operative ventures. Their magazine, *New Co-operation*, is available to non-members at £8 a year, and is a good source of up-to-date news and information about the co-operative movement.

In 1973 ICOM established a fund to assist new co-operative ventures called the Industrial Co-Ownership Fund. An independently run organization, it works with central and local government to provide loans for co-operative projects. On average the loans that ICOF can fund are around £7-10,000.

If you are wondering what happened to the government-sponsored Co-operative Development Agency set up by Act of Parliament in 1978 to promote co-operative working in Britain, well, it's being wound down because the government thinks that people ought to use their own initiative if they want to look at minority-interest fringe alternatives like co-ops. By the time you read this it won't exist any more. Typical.

ICOM
Vassilli House
20 Central Road
Leeds
LS1 6DE
0532 461737

ICOF
4 St Giles Street
Northampton
NN1 1AA
0604 37563

Co-ops in Scotland

Employee ownership in Scotland is booming, and the organization which co-ordinates the many exciting new initiatives is the Scottish Co-operatives Development Committee (SCDC). Formed in 1976, the SCDC can help with information and advice, practical help in the early stages of a growing business and follow-up training thereafter. More than one hundred projects have been helped so far, from handspinning in Shetland and graphic design and screen printing to home help on Deeside and ship repair on Clydeside. The SCDC's literature alone is an inspiration to anyone who thinks that 'co-operation' means inefficiency, inevitable failure, and something less than 'real work'.

SCDC
Templeton Business Centre
Bridgeton
Glasgow
G40 1DA
041 554 3797

Getting Started

The emphasis in many books about finding work is still on things like writing application letters, interview technique, career structures and lifetime vocations. As the reality of the economic situation in Britain has become increasingly obvious, however, so the number of handbooks and guides to work alternatives has increased, with a definite bias towards working for yourself, being your own boss, setting up your own business, and helping yourself if nobody else will.

Of the many titles currently available, I have chosen seven which have something particular and useful to offer.

Ideas For Young People

In *Working On It* Jenny Thewlis has written a short easy-to-read book for young people who are thinking about what they are going to do when they leave school. She's good at encouraging boys and girls to think about jobs not normally considered appropriate to their sexes, and gives plenty of attention to the fact that in your teenage years it's not easy to decide who you are, and therefore what you want to do. She starts by getting you to look at your relationships with your friends and family, your place in school and in the larger society. Having helped you sort yourself out a bit, Jenny Thewlis then moves you on to the choices available, from further education and training schemes to going out and getting a job. An excellent chapter on rights and responsibilities at work is designed to prevent you from being exploited and knowing what to do about it. The resources section gives addresses, organizations and further reading.

Working On It
Thinking About Jobs
Jenny Thewlis
Collins Lions, 1989
£2.25

Business Ideas

Most of these books give general ideas about starting your own business, but not many of them look in detail at imaginative possibilities. Alan Bollard's *Just for Starters* includes many of the more usual small business ideas, but also adventurous enterprises like brewing and servicing office equipment, and 'green' ones like recycled paper products and energy conservation.

The introductory chapters look at the present status of small businesses in the economy, then there are more than thirty business profiles which take you through all the things you need to consider in each line of work, together with a detailed resource list and sample balance sheet.

*

Just for Starters is designed to fill a precise and limited role: namely to stimulate business ideas, and provide back-up commercial information for counsellors. It can do no more than provide 'first stop' information, and then suggest where the serious reader should go to obtain more detailed help. And ultimately much of the know-how for a successful new business can necessarily come only from that business itself in the course of its tentative early steps. The reader should remember that most business enquiries do not lead to new small businesses, and most new businesses do not survive. But, while start-ups will always be risky operations, this handbook is dedicated to making them safer.

Just for Starters
A Handbook of Small-Scale
Business Opportunities
Alan Bollard
IT Publications, 1984
£6.95

A *Which?* book called *Starting Your Own Business* (1988, £7.95) is a concise guide to all the things you will need to consider if you are thinking of setting up a small business, including tax, insurance, product protection, buying and selling, and even bankruptcy if it all goes horribly wrong.

Your Own Boss

If you are seriously considering self-employment, three books which could save you a lot of bother and heartache are the *Be Your Own Boss Starter Kit* from the National Extension College (1986, £9.95), Godfrey Golzen's well-established *Working for Yourself* (Kogan Page, 1989, £9.99), now in its tenth edition, and Sidney Bloch's *The A-Z of Self-Employment* (Buchan and Enright, 1989, £5.95). The NEC kit is a cross between a self-assessment exercise and a training course, full of exercises and examples; a well-tested way of learning business skills (a *Be Your Own Boss Growth Kit* is also available at £9.95). *Working for Yourself* covers the same ground in more conventional book form, and includes sections on a range of possible work areas, while the *A-Z* looks at two dozen varied opportunity areas and some interesting case histories.

If you are thinking of self-employment as more of a part-time occupation, a *Which?* guide called *Earning Money at Home* (1988, £7.95) suggests ways in which you might develop a skill or hobby into a money-spinner, together with all the legal and financial considerations you will need to take into account. The suggestions range from candlemaking and bookbinding to taking in lodgers — you should find something here to inspire you.

Business and Society

Human beings are rich in varied interests and talents. There is a new requirement on the part of both employee and employer for talented individualism to be expressed through work. This means employers establishing a shared vision and allowing people to select for themselves that part of the contribution they feel they can make. It also means the giving of clear signals to employees that not only is it safe to act as individuals, but positively unsafe not to.
Business in Society: A New Initiative

To stand by Mansion House tube station at nine o'clock in the morning might give little indication that individuality and personal choice are important aspects of the city scene. Yet even in the city, even among bankers and stockbrokers, the chairpeople of multinationals and high-ranking civil servants, a new wind is blowing. It will have to blow hard for a long time to have any noticeable effect, but the seeds have already been sown.

The Business Network

The Business Network, now in its eighth year, holds a meeting each month in Central London. Members are drawn from business circles: consultants, directors and managers, but members also include academics, writers, journalists and therapists. Over the years the theme of the meetings has become increasingly international and environmental as contemporary understanding of moral values has expanded to include the planet as a whole. If you work in or near London and would like to come along to a Business Network meeting, or to find out more about the Network, drop Marilyn Rose a line at the address below.

At the same address is the Gaia Foundation, which works to highlight the importance of cultural and ecological diversity by helping to channel concern and funds towards the Third World. It works particularly through the Forest People's Fund, which is used according to the wishes of the forest peoples themselves, to ensure that money is used in the most sensitive and constructive way.

The Business Network/Gaia Foundation
18 Well Walk
London
NW3 1LD
0(7)1-435 5000

URBED

If 'the city' means only one thing to anybody involved with high finance, it means quite another if you are a small business trying to make a living in an inner city area where property developers threaten to turn the entire landscape into an enormous office complex.

URBED (Urban and Economic Development) was founded in 1977 to foster local economic development in urban areas. It specializes particularly in research, training schemes for the unemployed and people starting their own businesses. Studies undertaken by URBED's research trust include a survey of the potential for small enterprises in Covent Garden, and the possibilities of revitalizing Bradford's business quarter.

URBED have also pioneered 'managed workspace' for new enterprises, where for a small monthly sum you can have a room of your own, with a mailing address and answering service if you need it, then migrate to a larger space as and when your business requires. People who have trained with URBED are affectionately known as 'urbuds', and often keep in touch with each other long after their enterprises have successfully taken off.

URBED
3 Stamford Street
London
SE1 9NT
0(7)1-928 9515

The Conservation Foundation

It was difficult to decide whether to put The Conservation Foundation under 'Environment' or 'Work'; since their emphasis is on finding commercial sponsorship for environmental projects, the latter won by a short head. Since its launch in 1982, the foundation has encouraged big business to show how environmentally concerned it is, and recent and current projects include the Ford European Conservation Awards, the Trusthouse Forte Community Chest, the Bisto Kids' Wonderful World of Nature, and an acorn map of Britain sponsored by the aluminium industry.

Whatever you think of the ethics of industrial sponsorship to reclaim landscapes decimated by an industrial mentality which continues to pollute the environment, The Conservation Foundation has certainly been successful in raising resources for important conservation work.

The Conservation Foundation
1 Kensington Gore
London
SW7 2AR
0(7)1-235 1743

Keeping Green Businesses Informed

You can tell how seriously the business community is taking green issues from the coverage in the 'heavies' of the business publishing world. In its September 14th 1989 issue, for example (and well worth searching out in your main library), *Marketing* magazine ran an in-depth survey of the green phenomenon. Headlined 'Green about Green', the lead article started: 'Green has become the marketing bandwagon. But too few marketers have thought through the implications. Riding the first, superficial flushes may be easy. But the Greens and marketing may clash head on if marketing does not reform.'

One person who is very serious about providing business with the information necessary to such a reformation is Liv O'Hanlon, an experienced journalist who in September 1989 launched the fortnightly *GreenGauge* briefing newsletter. Knowing that busy people won't read more than two or three paragraphs on any topic or more than half a dozen pages of any publication, *GreenGauge* deliberately keeps its articles short and punchy, its size down to six A4 pages. Despite its brevity and because of its clarity, it provides a unique insight into the ways in which business is being pressed — and increasingly forced — to take green concerns to heart. It costs £165 for a year's subscription, and already more than a thousand companies and trade associations make use of Liv O'Hanlon's informed and up-to-the-minute researches and prognostications.

GreenGauge
Verdant Publications Ltd
40 Frith Street
London
W1V 5TF
0(7)1-734 6712

GREEN*GAUGE*

Green Businesses

Hardly a week goes by without another 'exciting, brand new and greener than green' business being announced. And I don't just mean the sorts of initiatives being dreamed up by advertising companies for multinationals which qualify instantly for Friends of the Earth's Green Con of the Year Award (see page 251). I mean small companies like Verdant, now operating two shops in Cumbria. Or Limited Resources in Manchester who deliver your green supplies by bicycle carrier. Or the Green Green Shop in Leamington, organized by the local Green Party.

Of course people's motives for offering this sort of service are mixed, but if the pattern of working, relating, buying and selling in Britain is to change in a green direction — as more and more people believe it must it we are to retain our sanity and guarantee ourselves a future — then small, community-based businesses offering a genuinely friendly and helpful service must be encouraged. To begin with it might seem a bit strange not to take the car to the supermarket, and while these small green businesses find their feet you may find yourself needing to be a less passive customer than usual, but the social and environmental rewards of doing businesses more meaningfully are potentially enormous.

Green Shops

Verdant in Kendal calls itself 'Britain's first green supermarket' (now where have I heard that before?). Sarah Howcroft, with several years' experience of running her Verdant shop in Kirkby Lonsdale (36 Main Street), has thought carefully about what such a concept might entail, and as well as being attractive and welcoming the Kendal shop offers more than just things to buy. Though only opened in November 1989, it has already become an environmental information centre of some importance as well as selling all the green items — from wholefoods to cleaning products — that you would expect.

On a much smaller scale, though a model for many a community-based green enterprise, is Leamington's Green Green Shop. Run by Warwick and Leamington Green Party, the GGS is a mixture of shop and resource centre, with books, magazines and information racks alongside the Ecover and Forestsaver.

After a long gestation, the Stroud-based Land and Food Company has now finalized its plans for a 'from-the-ground-up' green shop at Ryton Gardens, home of the Henry Doubleday Research Association (see page 78). The shop will stock a complete range of organic foods as well as 'green' non-food items, and if the L&F Company has its way will be the first of more than sixty retail outlets planned for the next five years. We shall see.

Verdant
34 Market Place
Kendal
Cumbria
LA9 4TN
0539 741188

The Green Green Shop
22 High Street
Leamington Spa
CV31 1LW
0926 339043

The Land and Food Company plc
PO Box 63
Stroud
Gloucestershire
GL5 1JF
0453 751515

Green Delivery Companies

If you would rather have your green goods delivered to you, several newly-sprouted companies offer such a service. First mention has to go to Limited Resources, where Danny Sofer and Di Rogan have set up the ultimate green machine, delivering a wide range of organic and environment-friendlier products by bike throughout central and southern Manchester. You don't just get things from LR; you get information about local events, advice and excellent service.

A similar job is done in London (though without the bikes) by Greenways in Hampstead and The Green Delivery Company in Chiswick — ring for their pricelists.

Limited Resources
215 Bonsall Street
Manchester
M15 5HA
061 226 4777

Greenways
Canada House
Blackburn Road
London
NW6 1RZ
0(7)1-625 7636

The Green Delivery Company
34 Dukes Avenue
Chiswick
London
W4 2AE
0(8)1-994 0855

Greenways

Buying Green

Kevin McGrother started producing *Buying Green*, 'The Newsletter for the Green Consumer', to keep ordinary concerned people informed about green initiatives both in products and in the way they are sold. It costs £6 for six bi-monthly issues — on recycled paper with a percentage of subscriptions going to FoE, Greenpeace and BUAV — and contains a mass of useful information and addresses.

Buying Green
PO Box 14
Stockton-on-Tees
Cleveland
TS18 3YL
0642 603910

Community Businesses

'Every community should have one' is the subtitle of a piece on the rapid growth of community business, written by the Director of Strathclyde Community Business, John Pearce. Community business is particularly lively in the economically depressed areas of central Scotland, showing what can be done when a whole community decides it has had enough of the status quo.

The main features of a community business are:

▶ It is owned and controlled by the people of a particular locality.
▶ It is non-profit-distributing; any surplus is reinvested in the community.
▶ It is limited by guarantee, and thus nobody stands to lose their personal resources.
▶ It is involved in a range of different activities, sometimes as many as ten or a dozen.

Castlemilk, on the south-east side of Glasgow, is a post war housing estate of 28,000 inhabitants. Castlemilk Community Business has grown from scratch to employing more than 50 full time workers in only 12 months. CCB's trading activities include neighbourhood security, landscaping and amenity improvements, painting and decorating, and security door installation.
SCB Annual Report

The community enterprise movement in England and Wales is not yet as advanced as it is in Scotland, though there are stirrings in London and the North East. Strathclyde Community Business is currently the coordinating centre for community business activity in Britain, and publishes an excellent magazine called *CB News*.

Strathclyde Community Business Ltd

6 Harmony Row
Govan
Glasgow
G51 3BA
041 445 6363

In 1986 *The Times* in conjunction with the Gulbenkian Foundation produced an excellent illustrated booklet of community initiatives in Britain, which also contains a very comprehensive resource list. For a free copy of *Community Enterprise* send an A5 sae to Community Enterprise (Dept JD1), The Beacon Press, 33 Cliffe High Street, Lewes, East Sussex BN7 2AN.

Business in the Community

BiC is a partnership of business, local and central government, chambers of commerce, the trade union movement, and voluntary organizations, working to help industry and commerce contribute to the health of local communities. BiC shows business how it can help, and for example has recently helped Barclays Bank to develop its youth action programme and British Rail how to work with the public on social and environmental projects.

If you are not part of the management of big business, you will probably be most interested in BiC's excellent publications, the quarterly *Business in the Community Magazine* and the bi-monthly *BiC News*, both sent free of charge to anyone interested in the involvement of business in community issues.

Business in the Community

227a City Road
London
EC1V 1LX
0(7)1-253 3716

LEDIS

LEDIS, the Local Economic Development Information Service, is one of the best sources of information about local employment, training and economic initiatives in the UK and abroad. Published by the Planning Exchange, a Glasgow-based organization providing information and research services in the areas of urban planning, housing and economic development, LEDIS provides readers with up-to-date information on individual employment and training initiatives, funding sources and resources on policy changes. The loose leaf format and indexes allow LEDIS to be used as a valuable database and reference tool.

The Planning Exchange

186 Bath Street
Glasgow
G2 4HG
041 332 8541

Community Information

The Community Information Project is a national resource for advice and information workers, helping people who work in community projects and advice centres to develop and improve their services. Computers are increasingly being used by community advice projects to gain rapid access to information, so CIP has paid particular attention to their use, producing several factsheets on the subject including *Storing Information on a Database* and *Programmes for Working with Money and Figures*. CIP also produces a useful bi-monthly newsletter called *Computanews*.

Community Information Project

Universal House
88-94 Wentworth Street
London
E1 7SA
0(7)1-377 2798

Leisure

We all know what leisure means for us — time off, relaxation, freedom, choice. 'Leisure' is a fascinating concept, however, and it is only recently that the vast majority of people have been able to choose how to spend a large portion of their lives. The word 'leisure' has the same root as 'licence', the Latin 'licere', to be allowed. 'Leisure' is traditionally the time when whoever claimed the bulk of your time allowed you to stop. As our ideas about work change, therefore, the 'bit left over' that has been given the label 'leisure' is certain to change as well. As more and more people are able to order their own lives, either from choice or from forced unemployment, the time that is theirs to use as they want will increase dramatically.

In this section I have concentrated on activities that refresh the mind and body: games, music, dancing, theatre and holidays, together with some ideas about buying presents to brighten up the lives of your nearest and dearest.

Because leisure is such an elusive idea, I thought I would start this section with series of quotations which raise questions that you can ponder on as you walk the Pennine Way or cycle through the vineyards of the Dordogne.

You can look at it like this. If most people ceased to care about work and concentrated on leisure, what would they do with their greatly increased leisure? If their leisure activities were of the kind that cost money, increasing leisure would increase their spending. But they won't be able to earn the extra money by doing more work. So how will they get it? Who will decide how much money everyone should get to support their leisure activities? On the other hand, if their leisure is of the kind that doesn't cost money, what will people be doing with it? If they are simply wasting time, they will get bored. On the other hand, if they are entertaining one another, looking after children and sick people, doing DIY activities in the garden or house or workshop, educating themselves, writing, playing music, and a whole range of other activities which are purposeful and satisfying, as well as being enjoyable, won't they think of some of these activities as work?
James Robertson, *The Sane Alternative* (see page 272)

It is true that the Greeks, the Romans, The Egyptians and even the English have had their leisured classes, but these were elites, and while they did no paid work, they all worked hard at governing, at the management of their estates, at patronizing the arts or at acting as benefactors to their communities. They seldom enjoyed real leisure: theirs was unpaid but glamorous work. When it did degenerate into pure consumption, as in Rome's last days, the civilization began to run down.

A leisured class at the bottom of society, however, rather than at the top, would have no glamorous but unpaid work to do. Bread and circuses, or their modern equivalents, dope and videos, have never proved to be the satisfactory basis for life or for society. On thee other hand, a leisured class at the top of society, with the masses working for it, would be incompatible both with democracy (which would never grant so much to so few) and with technology (which needs the brains and skills of the elite to harness its possibilities). It is hard not to conclude that the leisure-class scenario is either the false dream of the poets among us or a well meaning way to whitewash inevitable unemployment.
Charles Handy, *The Future of Work* (see page 271)

Large numbers of workers already do paid work for what averages out to only three or four days a week, or they take six months or a year off to pursue educational or recreational goals. This pattern may well grow stronger as two-paycheque households multiply. More people in the paid labour market — higher 'labour participation rates' as the economists put it — may very well go with reduced hours per worker.

This casts the whole question of leisure into a new light. Once we recognize that much of our so-called leisure time is, in fact, spent producing goods and services for our own use — prosuming — then the old distinction between work and leisure falls apart.
Alvin Toffler, *The Third Wave*, Pan, 1980, £2.95

How many hours do I spend on (a) housework, (b) occupation with the children, (c) cultural leisure pursuits? 'Leisure' is explained: radio and television broadcasts, visits to the cinema, theatre, etc., reading, sport, tourism, etc.

Ah, leisure, leisure . . . 'lei-sure'. Myself, I'm addicted to sport: running. I'm always running: to work, from work, shopping — a shopping basket in each hand . . . upstairs, downstairs, trolley bus — bus, into the underground — out of the underground. There aren't any shops near our new housing estate yet, we have been living there now for more than a year, but they still haven't been built.
A story from the Russian magazine *Novy Mir* quoted by Ann Oakley in *Subject Women*, Fontana, 1981, £2.75

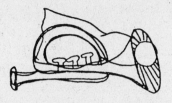

Playing

Play is a voluntary activity. If it is compulsory, then it is not play. J. Huizinga, in his famous study of the play element in culture, defined freedom as its major characteristic. The essential characteristic of play is fun. Play 'adorns life, amplifies it and is to that extent a necessity both for the individual — as a life function — and for society by reason of the meaning it contains, its significance, its expressive value, its spiritual and social associations, in short as a cultural function. The expression of it satisfies all sorts of communal ideas.' When did you last play? Was it fun? Play has been abolished in contemporary society — except in children, until we knock it out of them — and in its place there is recreation — human maintenance.

Richard Neville, *Playpower*, 1971

We are excited about the use of play and games to explore with people what a truly co-operative society might look like. Our vision of the world is that people are naturally co-operative, joyful, and playful beings but that many of us have been taught to act otherwise. . . You might be playing with five other people or five hundred other people — through co-operative play experience it is possible to create a sense of unified purpose, of connection to others, of belonging.

Matt Weinstein and Joel Goodman, *Playfair* (see below)

Non-competitive games may seem a ludicrous non-starter, but for many people, once they have taken part in a new games session and been given permission to have fun without the hassles of trying (or needing) to win, they become hooked and can't wait to do it again. The Californian-based New Games Foundation started the new games bandwagon rolling in the mid-1970s, dreaming up co-operative basketball and co-operative football alongside such new delights as schmerltz, pruie and boffing. Now new games are international.

If you need guidelines (and some gentle philosophy) about non-competitive games, try one of the books reviewed below. Here are instructions for a couple of such games below to give you a feel. Both are suitable for a group of between eight and thirty people, children and/or grown-ups.

Zoom (Racing Cars)

Everyone sits in a circle, and one person starts by turning to right or left and saying 'zoom' to the next person. This person passes the zoom to the next person as quickly as possible, and so the zoom passes round and round the circle. The first complication is to have more than one zoom, which can be passed round the circle in either direction. The second is that when you receive a zoom, you can choose either to pass it on, or to imitate the squeal of brakes (with gusto), in which case the zoom is turned in its tracks and the person who has just passed the zoom to the squealer has to turn the other way and pass the zoom back the other way round the circle. In a large group with half a dozen zooms whizzing round the circle this game needs considerable concentration, and is liable to dissolve in giggles.

Ourobouros (Catch the Dragon's Tail)

A fast and very physical game, named after the world snake of Norse mythology. Players hold hands in a long line, one end being the head of the snake and the other end the tail. The aim for the head is to touch the tail, the aim of the tail not to be touched by the head. Everyone up to halfway between head and tail helps the head to catch the tail, everyone else does their best to protect the tail. The head counts (slowly!) to ten while the tail does whatever it needs to, then the chase is on.

Keep the chain complete throughout, define your playing area or you may have boundary problems, and take off sharp watches and jewellery before you begin.

The New Games Foundation has a British 'subsidiary' which co-ordinates events and training sessions. New Games UK also sells books about non-competitive games, including some that are otherwise now out of print and unavailable.

New Games UK
PO Box 542
London
NW2 3PQ

Books of New Games

Although there have been some very good books about non-competitive games, they always seem to have been difficult to find and have gone out of print very quickly.

The most recent and readily available collection is Mildred Masheder's *Let's Play Together*, a collection of more than three hundred co-operative games and sports. It's divided into sections called 'Circle Games', 'Traditional Singing Games', 'Tag Games' and so on, and each game is given a short but adequate description and a 'blob rating' so you can see at a glance which are suitable for what sort of gathering. There are even games for playing outside in the dark like Night Trek and Walk in the Dark.

Playfair is decidedly American, and Californian at that. The book is written primarily for anyone who plans to lead co-operative games, and the descriptions of the eighty-odd games include much more than just the rules (sorry, guidelines). The authors are heavily into analysis and comment, and this and the 'come-on-everyone-let's-really-enjoy-ourselves' style may put you off — but there are some good games here and the photographs are helpful and inspiring.

Lets Play Together
Mildred Masheder
Green Print, 1989
£4.99

Playfair
Matt Weinstein and Joel Goodman
Turnaround, 1988
£8.95

Other co-operative games books which are relatively easy to buy in Britain are a good collection called *For the Fun of It* which has been reprinted in *A Manual on Nonviolence and Children* (New Society, distributed in Britain by Turnaround, 1984, £9.95), and Dale LeFevre's self-published *Playing for the Fun of It* (£4.95), available from the Findhorn Foundation Trading Centre (see page 183). What are to my mind the two best new games books are both out of print, but look out for secondhand copies of *The New Games Book* (The New Games Foundation, Doubleday, 1976) and *The Co-operative Sports and Games Book* (Terry Orlick, Writers and Readers, 1979).

*

At a UNESCO Peace Forum meeting, scholars from Europe, Africa, Asia, North and South America were discussing the problems of peace. On the last day of the four-day conference, discussion centred around how scholars could contribute to education. Some of the scholars had been protesting strongly that marginal things only were being discussed, and detente was being avoided. Elise Boulding . . . explained at some length that detente is precarious and difficult and that nothing was going to be solved by people sitting at a table, talking. Since the elements in detente have to do with interdependence, she wanted to illustrate her point metaphorically. She stood up and asked that everyone participate in playing Musical Laps. The scholars responded with varying degrees of puzzlement and enthusiasm. However, all played. It was an excellent experience for the scholars, who got the point of the metaphor. Afterwards the atmosphere was warmer and more responsive, and people listened more attentively to each other.

A Manual on Nonviolence and Children

Board Games for the Bored

New board games are big business if they can catch the popular imagination, but compared with what is available in the USA, Sweden or Germany, Britain is very poorly supplied with games that are interesting, informative, and provide an alternative to the competitive go-getting winning-is-all basis of most board games, and which are real value for money.

Considering how everyone from cosmetics manufacturers to publishers are rushing to manufacture 'green' product as fast as possible, I'm amazed that Christmas 1989 passed without at least two or three major 'green games' — I'll be even more surprised if we don't see them during the course of the next twelve months. The Conservation Foundation, however, has come up with one of the most unmitigated green disasters of modern times with their board game 'Save the World'. It's so bad that it's almost funny (though it wouldn't have been if I'd bought it myself).

'The most important game you will ever play,' says David Bellamy enticingly on the box. So we opened it all up, set out the pretty board, decided what colours we were all going to be and read the instructions. For a start it's decidedly not a co-operative game, and a for a second start most of it isn't made from recycled materials. But it's the question cards that are the downfall of this game. Not only are they a very odd mixture of the trite ('Oil pollution is a major threat to seabirds — true or false?') and the esoteric ('How many cubic kilometres of water are there in the world — 137,000,000, 1,337,000,000 or 1,337,000,000,000?'); the proofreading is appalling. You will be asked, for example, whether 'wage power' is a form of alternative energy, and be told that thanks to clean air legislation London no longer has to suffer from Sooty. I've rarely laughed so much, but I certainly wouldn't advise anyone to shell out £14.95 for this form of mental pollution. If you want a good recent board game go for Milton Bradley's 'Therapy' instead (£16.99ish, available almost anywhere) — it's original, well-researched, and will provide hours of fun and insight.

The first European Conservation Awards were sponsored by which large company?

a) Sony Corporation
b) Colgate–Palmolive
c) Ford Motor Car Company

Answer: (c)

Family Pastimes

Some cautions. We don't protect children from not making it to the summit or completing the space voyage. Our games are designed to offer realistic challenges. And the cultural habit of competing and confronting adversaries runs deep. Some players end up fighting the game itself. We suggest you'll get better results learning how to get along with Time, Winter, Gravity, Mountains rather than fighting them.

from the Family Pastimes catalogue

For really good co-operative board games you'll have to send to Family Pastimes in Perth, Ontario, where Jim Deacove has been designing co-operative games for more than ten years. If you can't stand 'Trivial Pursuits', where you're constantly finding out things that you don't need to know, try 'Untrivia' ($17.50, about £8.50, including postage). In 'Untrivia' the questions are practical and cover things like gardening, first aid, babyminding and household repairs; what's more, you play co-operatively. There are goof tokens to slow you down and surprise squares to speed you up, plus a box with thousands of questions and answers. Or you can try the original 'Community Game' ($16.50, about £8), where you work to create a happy and balanced community: if you succeed, you all win together (there is also an urban version called 'Our Town' ($19.50, about £9.50)). 'Earth Game' ($20, about £9.50) is a global peace game in which the players look after nations, manage resources, make co-operative trade agreements, and deploy peace armies. The catalogue alone is a good source of ideas, with a reading list and many helpful suggestions.

Family Pastimes

RR 4
Perth
Ontario
Canada
K7H 3C6
(010 1) 613 267 4819

Rainbow Warrior

'The world's first environment friendly software!' says the box, and in 'Rainbow Warrior' MicroProse has produced a computer game which is almost everything it claims — educational, thought-provoking, well-designed and fun to play. 'Rainbow Warrior' has been prepared with the co-operation of Greenpeace, and you can 'take part' in seven Greenpeace campaigns, from trying to prevent the dumping of nuclear waste to stopping the Antarctic whaling. Of course it's a bit simplistic — computer games always are — but if your youngster is spending hours hunched up over the screen wouldn't you rather have them playing 'Rainbow Warrior' than 'Barbarian the Ultimate Warrior'? It comes in an 8-bit version for the Commodore C64 at £9.99 (cassette) or £14.99 (disk), and a 16-bit version for the Atari ST and Amiga at £24.99.

MicroProse Software

Unit 1
Hampton Road Industrial Estate
Tetbury
Gloucestershire
GL8 8LD
0666 504326

Playworld

Reactions to Playworld events range from over-the-top enthusiasm to bored seen-it-all-before disappointment, but if you want to try something different and live in London, it's worth trying one of their 'alternative evenings out'. The emphasis is on enjoying yourself, using games, theatre, dancing and chanting. The evenings are thoroughly non-competitive and you don't need any special skills. Playworld quite often arranges courses in some of the conference centres mentioned on page 290.

Playworld
2 Melrose Gardens
New Malden
Surrey
KT3 3HQ
0(8)1-949 5498

PLAY·WORLD

Open Out

Open Out is a twelve-person London-based co-operative which gives training in the skills needed for living and working co-operatively. They use games in their training programme, together with team-building exercises, counselling, dance and drama. They work mostly with community groups and at senior management level in local authorities, where introducing an element of play helps people to open up, relax, and listen and work together co-operatively. The associated Play Train group works more with story telling, drama, co-operative games and singing to help people increase their self awareness and confidence, and to encourage both children and adults to enjoy sharing their lives. They offer their training to all sorts of groups and organizations from library staff to groups of parents.

Open Out/Play Train
27 Walpole Road
Tottenham
London
N17 6BE
0(8)1-888 9678/423 5540

Butterfingers

What a lovely name for a lively mail order catalogue of juggling equipment, books and miscellania. Butterfingers sell everything from juggling convention t-shirts to juffle bags; last summer's catalogue even included lettuces (yes, lettuces). If you are anywhere near Bath you are welcome to call in, see the Butterfingers range and share a cuppa.

Butterfingers
Puzzle Tree Cottage
Stoke St Micheal
nr Bath
Avon
BA3 5LB
0749 840107

Environmental Theatre for Children

There are few more direct ways of involving children in exploring environmental issues than encouraging them to take part in a theatrical happening, and in the last couple of years at least half a dozen small and often impromptu theatre groups have developed such repertoires. More established theatre groups, too (see page 287), are increasingly exploring green themes.

The Last of The Dodos is an Edinburgh-based theatre group which brings an awareness of environmental issues to schools through a mixture of play-acting and pantomime which lets the children comment on the message being projected. When in their 'Close Encounters of the Green Mind' the Acid Rain Dame asks 'Don't you think the earth will be so beautiful when all the trees are dead?' she invariably gets a resounding 'No!' from the youthful audience.

Surrey-based Rhythm Tree uses puppets to help children learn about environmental issues. They also provide back-up notes for teachers which are full of activities and ideas for greening the classroom.

The Last of The Dodos
c/o 43 Sandport Street
Edinburgh
EH6 6EP

Rhythm Tree Theatre Productions
The Barn
Festival Walk
Carshalton
Surrey
SM5 3NY
0(8)1-647 8141

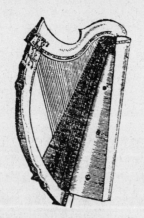

**Banks Music
Publications**
The Old Forge
Sand Hutton
York
YO4 1LB
090 486 472

Travis and Emery
17 Cecil Court
London
WC2N 4EZ
0(7)1-240 2129

Farringdon Records
52-54 High Holborn
London.
WC1V 6RL
0(7)1-831 2932 (shop)
0(7)1-831 4116 (orders)

**General
Gramophone
Publications Ltd**
177-179 Kenton Road
Harrow
Middlesex
HA3 0HA.
0(8)1-907 4476

Music

Music is very close to the heart of anything important, whether it be a Bach motet or a Bob Dylan classic, the ANC anthem or a Sufi chant, and a community that has pride in itself can invariably express itself in its own unique musical language. Sadly we live in a culture in which music has too often become something they do for us, a passive entertainment. This section concentrates on what you can do for yourself. It's a pity that the Edwardian drawing-room sing-song has no modern equivalent, that much modern music isn't considered to be music at all unless it's amplified so much that you can't hear the subtleties of the melody and the harmonies. In traditional cultures music mirrors the natural sounds of the environment; in learning to listen again to nature and join in with our own voices and simple instruments of our own making we can recreate the links of sound we have in common.

'Classical' Music

The twentieth century is the first when there was such a divide between 'art' music and 'popular' music, and when people were more or less forced by peer pressure to accept one at the expense of the other. Yet choral and instrumental traditions run deep, and modern music teaching in schools does its very best to bridge the chasm. Here are some resources for classical music that I have found useful.

If you are looking for music for vocal, choral or instrumental pieces, the best place I know is Banks of York. Their mail order service, based in Sand Hutton just outside York, will find quickly and efficiently any music that is in print; they are also very trusting and will send it to you with an invoice as soon as they find it. The upstairs floor of Banks' and Sons music shop in York's Lendal (they used to be related to Banks Music Publica-tions, but are no longer) is a treasure trove — the filing system is archaic, but they never put their prices up once something is in stock, so you can find sheet music marked 1/6d for which they will still charge 7.5p. There is a wonderful little shop called Travis and Emery, in Cecil Court off Charing Cross Road in London, which carries an enormous range of secondhand music and books about music; they usually have piles of sheet music on a shelf in front of the shop at 10p a time.

For classical records you can't do better than Farringdon Records; they have two central London shops in Cheapside and High Holborn and the mail order service operates from Lambs Conduit Street. Every record they sell is at discount price, even the new releases; they will also send a catalogue listing hundreds of bargains from 99p upwards, so it's easy to start a basic classical collection very cheaply. They are one of the few companies to recognise that the larger your order the more profit they make, and so charge no carriage on orders over £30. The best way to keep track of what recordings are currently available is to buy a copy of the *Classical Catalogue* published regularly by *The Gramophone* magazine; it lists every recording issued in the last three years by composer and artiste, and is also a very good reference source to the classical repertoire. The current edition costs £2.30, which is excellent value for nearly 450 pages.

'Popular' Music

The best single source for pop music — the actual printed music that you can play and sing from and so emulate your favourite artiste(s) — is Music Sales Ltd, who have a shop in Frith Street in London's Soho but run their mail order business from Bury St Edmunds. Their illustrated catalogue is a mine of goodies and nostalgia, with every kind of music from great shows of the 50s to the latest U2 or Billy Idol.

The Gramophone magazine (see above) produces a quarterly comprehensive listing of all pop LPs issued in Britain which are currently available; it's called *Pop Cat* and costs £2.50. There are now a number of specialist secondhand record shops that you'll no doubt hear about if you're heavily into a particular kind of music — in London, Ray's Jazz at 180 Shaftesbury Avenue and Daddy Kool (for reggae) at 94 Dean Street both do catalogues and mail order. Oldies Unlimited is an excellent way of building up a collection of music which is slightly past its prime, and as a result is a fraction of the price. Their mail order service is quick and efficient, they have over 3,000 7" records in stock, and do a very good range of bargain packages (3 Diana Ross or 3 Earth Wind and Fire for £1.50; 100 soul singles for a tenner . . .).

Music Sales Ltd
Newmarket Road
Bury St Edmunds
Suffolk
IP33 3YB
0284 702600

Oldies Unlimited
Dukes Way
St George's
Telford
Shropshire
TF2 9NQ
0952 616911

World Music

With the growing interest in music from places like Africa, the Caribbean and Eastern Europe, many people are waking up to the fact that the Western pop tradition isn't the only sound that can make it in the charts. But where can you get hold of Zairian soukous, Bulgarian folk song, Algerian rai and Nigerian juju, especially if you live out in the cultural sticks? Now that Totnes-based Offbeat Records has produced its mail order catalogue of records, tapes and compact discs it's no longer a problem. Nearly two hundred albums cover almost anything you could desire, from Ladysmith Black Mambazo to Music of the Intifada. Send an A5 sae for a catalogue.

Offbeat Records
10 Plymouth Road
Totnes
Devon
TQ9 5PH
0803 867366

Women's Revolutions

WRPM (Women's Revolutions Per Minute) is a one-stop solution to Christmas present problems for all your women (and probably most of your men) friends. Since 1977 WRPM have been building up an excellent list of recordings by women artistes which celebrate women's achievements and direct your attention to the fact that women have recently been recording some very exciting music. The WRPM list is still overwhelmingly American, with women like Holly Near and Chris Williamson, both very powerful performers, heading the list. There is a British contingent, however, with The Fabulous Dirt Sisters from Nottingham, and the versatile folk singer Frankie Armstrong. Every kind of music from rock and soul to classical and improvised is represented in the WRPM catalogue; send an A5 sae for your copy.

WRPM
62 Woodstock Road
Birmingham
B13 9BN
021 449 7041

Musical Instruments

Musical instrument making is on the increase all over the Western world. We haven't quite got as far as parts of the USA, where you can now buy anything from a marimba to a hammer dulcimer in many craft centres, but if you know where to look there are new little businesses springing up in many parts of the country making simple and fairly cheap musical instruments so you can indulge yourself (and your children) in sounds of your own making.

David Liggins makes traditional clay ocarinas at the Ocarina Workshop in Kettering: mini 4-hole ocarinas start at around £6; the big double bass weighs in at more than £20. The cimbala, a cross between a harp and a dulcimer (and a hundred tunes to go with it) is available from Musicopia in Dorset, and a range of wonderful ethnic wooden instruments from tongue drums to didgeridoos can be bought from the Leeds firm of Knock On Wood (they also have a shop under Leeds railway station in the Arches Craft Arcade).

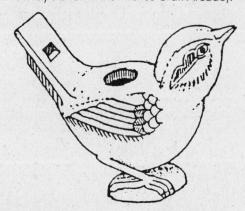

Ocarina Workshop
St Mary's Road
Kettering
Northamptonshire
NN15 7BW
0536 81547

Musicopia
12 Breach Lane
Shaftesbury
Dorset
SP7 8LE
0747 53176

Knock On Wood
Unit 1
30 Dock Street
Leeds
LS10 1JF
0532 429146

Street Bands

In recent years street bands have become a regular and welcome part of any political event, peace action, or street festival, and if you play an instrument reasonably well, preferably a loud one, you'll be most welcome. Street bands come in all shapes and sizes, and there are now more than two dozen of them in cities and towns the length of the country. Some, like London's Big Red Band, play from music; some, like Liverpool's Peacemakers, don't at all; others, like Sheffield's Celebrated Sheffield Street Band, do a bit of both. All the street bands in Britain try to get together once a year to have an almighty knees-up — it really is worth finding out about.

The Political Song Network is a group of radical songwriters and singers who organize the 'Red and Green Umbrella Road Show' and publish a regular *Red and Green Songbook* (the latest, for summer/autumn 1989, costs £3.50 + 25p p+p) — well worth getting hold of if you want to learn the latest ditties doing the rounds.

Street Band Information
The Peacemakers
Merseyside CND
24 Hardam Street
Liverpool
L1 9AX

Political Song Network
44 Roseneath Road
London
SW11 6AQ

Can't Find Your Voice?

If you think you can't sing, things are getting easier for you all the time. We can all make some sort of melodious sound: as we were told in one singing workshop I went to, 'you can't sing out of tune and at the wrong time, you can only sing in harmony and in syncopation.' Workshop centres like Laurieston Hall and Monkton Wyld (see page 289) sometimes run voice workshops, and if you're in or near London you might either try one of Jill Purse's voice workshops (she also runs work-shops on Mongolian and Tibetan overtone chanting), or a voice workshop at the Gale Centre in Loughton, where Derek Gale will help you find notes you never thought existed. Both produce leaflets about their work, and are relatively cheap for London.

Jill Purse
20 Willow Road
London NW3
0(7)1-607 5819 or
0(8)1-749 9841

The Gale Centre
Whitakers Way
Loughton
Essex
IG10 1SJ
0(8)1-508 9344

Dance

We are dancing on the brink of our little world
of which we know so little;
We are dancing the dance of life, of death;
Dancing the moon up in celebration of
dimly remembered connections with our ancestors;
dancing to keep the cold and darkness
of a nuclear winter from chilling our bones;
dancing on the brink of ecological awareness;
dancing for the sake of dancing
without analyzing and rationalizing and articulating;
without consciously probing for meaning
but allowing meaning in being to emerge into our living space.
Dancing has always been part of living for primal peoples.
For us, the dance may be a Ghost Dance for all that is lost:
condor, bison, redwood, watershed,
wolf, whale and passenger pigeon.
Or it may be the dance of a new revelation of Being,
of modesty and Earth wisdom on the turning point.
Bill Devall and George Sessions, *Deep Ecology* (see page 175)

There's no special magic about dancing, just ordinary magic. For a culture in which a great deal of dancing has become stylized and rather bored movement to overloud disco music in a setting where nobody can see each other, never mind hear each other, the magic of dance can seem far away. Go to a village ceilidh in the north of Scotland, however, or a midsummer circle dance on Glastonbury Tor, and dance takes on a new significance.

Dance is about patterned movement, movement which reflects the natural world, and most of us have forgotten how to move. We live lives where we spend hours almost motionless, flopped in chairs, behind the steering wheel, worn out though not with real physical effort. Then we wonder why our back aches, or why we can't run a hundred yards without getting a stitch.

You don't even need company to dance; it might overcome a few inhibitions to do it alone. Your own voice is enough to provide the accompaniment, though most people find the radio or cassette player helps. Everyone can dance.

Circle Dancing

Circle dancing is what happens when a group of people hold hands in a circle and dance together. Which sounds as though it should be easy to describe, but it's far easier to say what it isn't. We are doing folk dances, but it isn't folk dancing. We are not dancing to get the steps exactly 'right', or to be authentic, though some degree of accuracy is important in honour of the oral teaching tradition which has survived for hundreds of years. But we are not traditionalists either, for new dances are being created to music that particularly moves us — it could come from any culture. Basically we are doing folk dances with an aware-ness that something indefinable happens when we take the most ancient and simple way of expressing our togetherness — by being together in a circle. A connection with our distant past when everyone celebrated in this way; a simple way of expressing feelings of community, of wholeness; a way of healing and being healed and working for planetary healing.
Katya Gahlin, *Green Line*, September 1987

Circle dancing has taken root in Britain in a very big way in the last five years. Perhaps the most important link in this growth has been the 'sacred dancing' done at the Findhorn Commu-nity (page 183) from the teaching of Bernard Wosien, but there are now circle dance teachers and groups in every corner of the country, and though it can tend towards the spiritually wishy-washy, circle dancing is an excellent way of meeting people, moving your body and your spirit, and literally sensing yourself as part of the overall flow of things. Once you know some of the basic dances, you will always be at home in the circle dance wherever it is happening. The Circle Dance Net-work has a regular newsletter called *The Grapevine*, listing nearly a hundred teachers, seventy local groups, and a mass of local and national events. Circle dance is also being used very effectively with children, and with disabled and blind people. An sae to *The Grapevine* will put you in touch with a local group. Dancing Circles in Glastonbury are the centre for music tapes for circle dance; write to them for a list.

The Grapevine
75 Newtown Road
Eastleigh
Hampshire
SO5 4BX
0703 641632

Dancing Circles
PO Box 26
Glastonbury
BA6 9YA
0278 786307

Natural Dance

Dance doesn't have to be formal, stylized and 'correct'. Danc-ing can help you to relax and move, improve your posture and balance — and it can be fun. From a converted barge on the Thames Dancercise co-ordinates a national network of groups which use music as the framework of dance-like exercises. If you are more serious about your dancing, the people to contact are the Laban Centre, with their unique system of healing and creativity through movement, though this puts you deeply into the realm of personal and financial commitment. My recommendation is to start with circle dance if you want company and ritual; Dancercise if you want exercise and personal body awareness.

Many different sorts of dance classes are held in further and community education centres across Britain; ask at your local library or community centre for details. If you live in London and want to do tap dancing, explore movement in a trusting atmosphere or have a go at drumming and percussion, the Chisenhale Dance Space offers all these and more. You can become a Friend of Chisenhale for £4 and receive information about all the events happening there.

Dancercise
The Barge Durban
Lion Wharf
Old Isleworth
Middlesex
0(8)1-568 1751

**Chisenhale
Dance Space**
64-84 Chisenhale Road
Bow
London
E3 5QY
0(8)1-981 6617

**Laban Centre for
Music and Dance**
Laure Grove
London
SE14 6NW
0(8)1-692 4070

Theatre

As with music and dance, drama has become something we usually go to to watch them do it. Not that we don't enjoy it, but it is more of the same in terms of our own involvement — we have to sit still in our seats (or be whispered at). But this, too, is changing, as community theatre groups and experimental theatre projects which involve 'the audience' gain ground. 'Village plays' are now an established part of the Dorset scene thanks to the Colway Theatre Trust and its Director, Ann Jellicoe, who has written the handbook mentioned below. Hundreds of people were involved in the 1982 'Usk Valley Project' in Breconshire, and there are several regional theatre groups like the Northumberland Theatre Company and the Groundswell Farm Arts Workshop in Wiltshire who perform (and often involve their audience in) plays on regional and topical themes — Common Ground (see page 54) can often tell you about current projects in your area if you tell them what you want and enclose an sae. 'Green theatre' for children is explored on page 223.

Welfare State International

Probably the best-known of the radical theatre groups, Welfare State, founded in Yorkshire in 1968, have received enormous acclaim for their blend of popular theatre, visual spectacle and all-inclusive celebration. The troupe has been all over the world, including Tanzania, Poland and Canada, but they make a point of being relatively rootless so that nothing can stunt their originality and outrageousness. Look out especially for Welfare State performances in Glasgow for that city's Year of Culture, and at the summer Feast of Furness at Barrow in Cumbria.

They survive because they change, they are open to any suggestion, they'll go anywhere in the world, put on a massive performance, and then go back to Ulverston (have you heard of it?) and go down to the local school, the local hospital, the local centre for the mentally handicapped, or the Old People's Home. Then they'll make lanterns out of wire, bamboo, size, tissue and glue for the town's Lantern Festival, or send lanterns to Assisi for a world peace week. Later they will be making puppets, or taking their travelling theatre bus, the Lantern Coach, to community centres in Whitehaven or Carlisle.

Nick Jones, Resurgence, May-June 1987

Welfare State International
The Ellers
Ulverston
Cumbria
LA12 0AA
0229 581127

The Clown Jewels

When The Clown Jewels arrive in town in their converted double decker you can be sure of theatre with a difference. Clown Jewels produce an exciting mix of sketches, clowning and juggling, with a particular emphasis on important issues like nuclear dumping, yet with a deftness that involves everyone, especially children. Their regular two-month tours cover the north and west of Scotland, including the islands, and they also produce larger-scale integrated performances. Founded in 1984, Clown Jewels became a workers' co-operative in 1987.

The Clown Jewels
Ballintraid
Pelny
Invergordon
Ross-shire
0349 853943

Word and Action

Since 1972 Word and Action, based in Wimborne in Dorset, have combined theatre, audience participation and therapeutic groupwork in a unique mixture. If you don't like getting involved, being pushed, doing some real thinking, don't go anywhere near Word and Action. Word and Action perform in schools and community centres all over the south-west (and further afield if asked), and if your group (peace, trade union, co-operative . . .) is having problems, you can do worse than getting Word and Action in to explore the 'group process' with you.

*

Word and Action's performances and courses are for those who believe that imagination and language are the gifts of all people, and that the stimulation of their everyday use, without manipulation or deference to others' judgement, is one of the most important tasks facing this overcompetitive and examined age. Word and Action has a very different view of language, the arts, 'artistes' and people, than that of any other group. It is non-elitist, positive and hopeful in all its approaches; it can work with any age or range of people, bringing them to an awareness of language pleasures in themselves that they have not always been sure they possess.

Word and Action brochure

Word and Action (Dorset) 1983 Ltd
43 Avenue Road
Wimborne
Dorset
BH21 1BS
0202 889669

Community Plays

Ann Jellicoe of the Colway Theatre Trust in Dorset has written an extremely useful and practical manual about everything involved in staging a community play, from planning to performance, including extended samples of actual scripts. The first handbook to this emerging artform — and an excellent one.

Community Plays
How to Put Them On
Ann Jellicoe
Methuen, 1987
£5.95

Presents and Gifts

Go into any gifte-type shoppe and the amount of instant trash you can buy at exorbitant prices is overwhelming. So don't buy your Christmas and birthday presents in such places — you'll only be supporting an industry which should not exist, in places where the bulk of the stuff is made by slave labour and where the mark-up has to be at least 100% before they'll touch it.

So instead buy your presents from local craftspeople, or from places which sell Third World products which actually benefit their manufacturers. Or buy from co-operatives, or people whose products (like Leeds Postcards for example) will make people think. I'm not going to be purist and suggest you only buy strictly functional gifts, but if things aren't useful they just gather dust until they're thrown out or passed on to the next unsuspecting recipient.

Mail Order from Catalogues

There are many excellent catalogues to choose from. The ones you shouldn't miss are those from Traidcraft and OXFAM which I shall describe in more detail, but many smaller catalogues advertising worthwhile gifts are put out by campaigning organizations, and many of the suppliers mentioned elsewhere in *New Green Pages* produce mail order catalogues. My own selection (look in the index for page references) would include Greenpeace, CND, AA Enterprises, Friends of the Earth, Lynx, Co-operation, The Woodland Trust, Common Ground and the RSPB in the first category, and Clothkits, Tridias, The Body Shop and Culpeppers in the second.

Both OXFAM and Traidcraft trade directly with producer groups in Britain and the Third World, so you can be sure that the producers of the crafts in their catalogues are receiving a just reward. Both catalogues contain a wide range of crafts, the Traidcraft range being larger and in general more practical than OXFAM's. From the current Traidcraft catalogue you can buy a beautiful hand-embroidered rug from Bangladesh for £25.50, jewellery from Mexico and Peru, beautiful wooden boxes from India and basketware from the Philippines, plus tea and coffee, recycled paperware, and books and posters.

OXFAM
Oxfam House
274 Banbury Road
Oxford
OX2 7DZ
0865 56777

Traidcraft plc
Kingsway
Gateshead
Tyne and Wear
NE11 0NE
091 487 3191

Some Very Different Gift Shops

There are a growing number of retail outlets which sell products similar to those marketed by Traidcraft and OXFAM, some of which produce their own lines too, like Earthcare window transparencies. This is only a representative selection, but I can vouch that a visit to these shops will be well worth while.

Earthcare, Durham

Earthcare is a fascinating shop selling wooden toys, badges, stickers, toiletries, recycled paper products, posters, postcards, books and candles. Earthcare also has a catalogue and mail order service for the window transparencies that they manufacture and stock.

Earthcare
33 Saddler Street
Durham
091 384 5837

One World Shops, Woodstock and Cheltenham

Two shops founded in 1977 by the man who set up the trading side of OXFAM and became disillusioned with the scale of the OXFAM operation. The shops sell baskets, containers and bags, lampshades, bedspreads, cushions, leatherware and sandals. Music from all over the Third World is here as records, cassettes and CDs. A third of the turnover is carpets from Africa, Asia and South America. One Village specializes in importing direct from co-ops and community industries, and they also supply wholesale. No mail order catalogue.

One Village/The World Shop

Woodstock
Oxfordshire
OX7 3SQ
0993 812866

Regent Arcade
Cheltenham
Gloucestershire
0242 581944

Wayang Bazaar, Rawtenstall

Diane and Jim Gaffney worked in Indonesia for many years, and now run a small business buying a wide range of Third World crafts directly from the manufacturers. They sell masks, puppets, rugs, cushions, jewellery and textiles from their little shop in Rawtenstall.

Wayang Bazaar
5 Alexandria Street
Rawtenstall
Lancashire
0706 216418

One World, Edinburgh

Edinburgh's One World Shop is tucked away under St John's Church on the corner of Lothian Road and Princes Street, but it's well worth seeking out. It carries a wide range of Third World goods plus books, cards, wholefoods and recycled paper products.

One World Shop
St John's Church Centre
Lothian Road
Edinburgh
EH2 4BJ
031 229 4541

Other shops selling crafts and other items suitable for presents include Biashara in Bristol (see page 221), and the clothes shops listed on page 115, especially Tumi in London, Bath, Brighton and Oxford, and Ian Snow in Llanidloes and Newtown.

Leeds Postcards

All good radical bookshops stock Leeds Postcards, the fruits of a workers' co-operative set up twelve years ago to produce postcards with a political message as an alternative to 'wish you were here' seaside shots. They have turned postcards into an art form, and people now enthusiastically collect the early Leeds postcards. Postcards like 'Clouseau Fans Against The Beumb' and 'Nu Clear — Removes Unwanted Head and Shoulders' have become classics. You can become a subscriber and ensure you don't miss any new ones, or buy a complete set of everything still in print (250 cards) for only £20.00. Leeds Postcards will also print your postcards for you, or overprint theirs with your message.

Leeds Postcards
PO Box 84
Leeds
LS1 4HU
0532 468649

Holidays with a Difference

I have very mixed feelings about the whole idea of holidays, avoiding tourist resorts like the plague and resenting spending money on 'tourist attractions'. A lot of it is to do with not wanting to be thought of as a 'tourist' with all its connotations. An hour or so lying on a beach in the sun is fine, but then it needs to be balanced by doing something interesting, learning something new, walking up the nearest hill.

In the firm belief that a change is as good as a rest, the next three pages look at some of the holiday possibilities open to anyone who wants more from a holiday than a crowded beach, an amusement arcade, and a car park with an ice cream van.

WWOOF

If you want a weekend working in the open air, a chance to learn something about organic growing, and have very little spare cash, WWOOF is just the thing for you. Founded in 1971 by a London secretary, Sue Coppard, who wanted to combine her interest in the organic movement with weekends in the country, WWOOF brings much-needed assistance to organic farmers and smallholders, and provides helpers with a chance to enjoy country life. There is a small annual subscription to cover administrative costs, but the weekends themselves operate as a non-financial exchange: the WWOOFer provides two days of labour, the farmer or smallholder provides meals, mattresses, and transport from the local station if necessary. There are currently about 2000 active WWOOFers and 150 places offering work. Send an sae for details.

*

My first WWOOF was spent at Little Heartland with the Burtons. After being collected at the station by Charles, I was greeted by Judith with, 'Do you like apple pie? Great, here are the apples . . .'

Owen Early, WWOOF News, April-May 1987

Working Weekends on Organic Farms
9 Bradford Road
Lewes
Sussex
BN7 1RB
0273 476286

Conservation Working Holidays

The work programme organized through the British Trust for Nature Conservation now covers national parks, National Trust properties, and local authority schemes. The work can be building stone walls, repairing eroded footpaths, clearing litter or tree-planting, and in 1989 over 60,000 volunteers worked on more than 3,000 sites throughout Britain. Most working holidays are a week long, though some, especially in more remote areas, last for two or three weeks. There is a small annual membership charge (reduced rate for students and unemployed); prices for holidays start at about £20 a week for holidays with basic accommodation, rising to around £40 a week for projects with youth hostel or chalet accommodation. For most BTCV holidays no previous experience is needed, though there are a few — specially annotated in the brochure — which involve strenuous physical work. The Trust produces two brochures a year, in January and August, listing over 400 holidays. There are also special interest holidays (music in the Lake District, birdwatching), and family holidays in Northumberland, County Down and the Isle of Wight. BTCV runs an enormous range of training events, mostly one and two day, covering conservation skills from fencing and drystone walling to chainsaw technique — ask for their 'Developing Skills' brochure. BTCV Publications include practical guides to the construction and maintenance of footpaths, walls, etc., and a useful booklet called *Organising a Local Conservation Group* (£3.50).

British Trust for Conservation Volunteers
36 St Mary's Street
Wallingford
Oxfordshire
OX10 0EU
0491 39766

Scottish Conservation Projects

The SCP Trust was established in 1984 to encourage people to take part in the conservation of Scotland's scenic heritage and wildlife. The Trust organizes a range of projects — tree planting, fencing, drystane dyking, improving amenities in urban areas, managing wildlife areas — for people of all ages and from all walks of life, including the unemployed and disabled. Their Action Breaks are usually a week long, and there is a minimal donation. Membership of the Trust will bring you the quarterly magazine, details of the Action Breaks programme, and an opportunity to participate in their training programmes.

Scottish Wildlife Conservation Trust
Balallan House
24 Allan Park
Stirling
FK8 2QG
0786 79697

The Good Stay Guide

For many years the Council for Environmental Education produced a *Directory of Centres for Outdoor Studies*; now this information and more has been published in book form. *The Good Stay Guide* contains a comprehensive list of camping sites, hostels, outdoor activity centres, field study centres, conference facilities, hotels and guest houses which cater for the needs of groups with a particular interest in the environment, so whether you are a family, a group of friends looking for a suitable place to have a holiday together, or a school group wanting to look at a particular sort of habitat, *The Good Stay Guide* provides detailed information about environmental centres nationwide. A good resource guide (voluntary organizations, films and videos, sports bodies, special needs organizations) and a chapter of advice on groups with special needs are both useful additions.

The Good Stay Guide
A Guide to Environmental Centres in Great Britain Offering Accommodation, Leisure and Study Facilities to Groups and Families
Broadcast Books, 1987
£6.95

Communities-cum-Workshop Centres

There are several reasons why many of the larger intentional communities (see page 208) also run residential workshop programmes. For a start they have the space — both for people to stay and for large groups to work in. They also have the experience of working and living in groups, both the pros and the cons. They like to make a little money, and many communities survive on the cash brought in by workshops. And they like to share their skills and learn something in the process. One of the real plusses of community living is the flow of interesting people, a constant source of shared fun and stimulation.

Monkton Wyld

For more than forty years Monkton Wyld Court, not far from the sea in Dorset, was a progressive co-educational boarding school. When the school closed in 1982 Monkton Wyld began a process of transformation into a community involved in education in the widest sense, and the group (currently nine adults and seven children) organizes an ambitious programme of workshops and events, some for special groups and others which are open to anyone. Most of the workshops have a healing/therapeutic/self-exploration theme — 'Body Wisdom', 'Conflict and Integrity', 'Playweek', 'Breathing Space'. Monkton Wyld do a lot on the theme of sexual politics and on children's issues, putting a great deal of emphasis on what children really need. They have a graded charge scheme so that anyone can get there that really wants to, and offer their space to like-minded groups who want to use the house and its facilities.

Monkton Wyld Court
Charmouth
Bridport
Dorset
DT6 6DQ
0297 60342

Lower Shaw Farm

Lower Shaw Farm was established as a community fifteen years ago in a rural setting just west of Swindon. Roads and buildings have replaced the fields but Shaw continues regardless, a haven of sanity in the redbrick sprawl of suburban expansion. Six adults and seven young children make up the resident population, and the community runs weekend workshops throughout most of the year with a couple of week-long summer groups. These can be practical — 'Basketmaking' or 'Discovering Fungi', playful like the 'Easter Celebration', or growth-oriented like 'Exploring our own Death'. Some people like the place so much they go several times a year to see their 'other family' at Shaw. The *Lower Shaw Newsletter* lets you relive the event all over again, and gives an excellent insight into the intricacies of ecological communal living: 'Would you like to know why there are four waste bins under our kitchen sink . . .?'

Lower Shaw Farm
nr Swindon
Wiltshire
SN5 9PJ
0793 771080

Laurieston Hall

Laurieston Hall, one of the veterans of the communes movement, made a radical transition early in 1987 from communal household to housing co-operative, but this shift has meant no interruption to the operation of their People Centre, which offers a varied programme of events from Easter to the end of August. Being such a distance from most people's abodes, the events are generally longer than those at Monkton Wyld or Lower Shaw — 'Music Week', 'Healing Week' — so regular Lauriestonians make it one of their holidays. The beautiful Galloway countryside provides walking, canoeing and swimming in the loch; the residents have created a sauna, a hydro-electric scheme which provides a large proportion of the house's power supply, and a large, well-run and productive organic walled garden. Week-long events run from Thursday to Thursday to take advantage of cheap saver tickets on the train, and prices are flexible according to your ability to pay. An annual newsletter, produced in December, reviews the past year and looks forward to the events of the next — send £1 with your name and address and add yourself to the mailing list for the next couple of years.

Laurieston Hall
Laurieston
Castle Douglas
Kirkcudbrightshire
DG7 2NB
064 45 275

Hawkwood

Not a community, but an independent centre for adult education offering weekend courses on a wide range of subjects. Hawkwood is a large manor house at the foot of the Cotswolds, and aims to provide workshops which present an alternative to materialistic values. The 1990 programme includes all manner of courses from 'Chinese Brush Painting' and 'Understanding the Psyche' to trips around 'The Gardens, Houses and Villages of the Cotswolds'. Compared with the other centres on this page the charges are relatively high, but some bursaries are available.

Hawkwood College
Painswick Old Road
Stroud
Gloucestershire
GL6 7QW
0453 764607

Activity Holidays

As well as the holiday suggestions mentioned on the last two pages there are also an enormous and growing number of more mainstream activity holidays. Many British holiday-makers are no longer content just to lie on beaches, eat ice cream and play arcade games in the evening. Well, perhaps they never were, but there simply weren't the alternatives. There are today, though.

Tourist authorities now produce sheafs of literature about activity holidays, and if you do your homework carefully you can find parachuting holidays, art history holidays, snorkeling holidays, detective holidays, railway holidays, computer holidays, ballroom dancing holidays . . .

The English Tourist Board produces an annual handbook full of activity holidays. The 1990 edition, called *Let's Do It* (£2.95) contains thousands of original ideas for holidays under the headings 'Action and Sports', 'Childrens' Holidays', 'Arts and Crafts' and 'Special Interest'. Appetite whetted?

The Scottish Tourist Board puts together a similar *Adventure and Special Interest Holidays in Scotland* (which is free); lots of sporting holidays of course in the bracing Highland air, but also traditional crafts like spinning and weaving, pony trekking, and some real gems like Classic Motorcycle Tours.

For Wales the Welsh Tourist Board produces a brochure which contains a wide range of activity holidays including rally driving, marine biology and horsedrawn caravans.

English Tourist Board
Thames Tower
Black's Road
London
W6 9EL
0(8)1-846 9000

Wales Tourist Board
Brunel House
2 Fitzalan Road
Cardiff
CF2 1UY
0222 499909

Scottish Tourist Board
23 Ravelston Terrace
Edinburgh
EH4 3EU
031 332 2433

The Irish Organic Farmers and Growers Association have now been operating a scheme for four years whereby you are welcomed to visit Ireland and stay with one of eight of their members, either B&B or full board. Prices are very reasonable, with hostel accommodation starting at £4 a night up to luxurious full board in a guest house at £30; all the food is organic, and they will provide vegetarian meals. Write for a brochure.

Irish Organic Farm Guesthouses
Cranagh Castle
Templemore
County Tipperary
Ireland
(010 353) 504 53104

The Good Beach Guide

In 1976 the European Community issued a 'bathing waters directive', requiring that beaches where people traditionally swim in large numbers be monitored for pollution, and that those which failed to meet the standard be improved to the standard by 1985. Britain, true to form, designated 27 (even landlocked Luxembourg came up with 34!). After much protest and pressure from the European Commission 392 were designated, 40% of which do not reach EC standards for approved cleanliness of beaches used by the public. The main problems are untreated and partially-treated sewage, heavy metals from industrial discharge, agricultural fertilizer run-off and marine litter.

If you want to bathe and play safely at the seaside, *The Good Beach Guide* is as essential to your holiday as a bucket and spade. It lists and describes over 180 beaches all round Britain's long coastline, with maps and symbols identifying those that fail to meet the EC standards. Each beach has a short description, together with information about the facilities available like toilets and shops, access, seaside activities, local nature walks, bathing safety, and even what you can do nearby if the weather is wet.

The Good Beach Guide
Anne Scott
Ebury Press, 1988
£5.95

Green Guides

Green Print launched its series of Green Guides In 1989 with the intention of providing the green-tinted traveller with information about places of particular interest to anyone with a generally environmental bent, together with some thoughts about what travelling is really all about. My *Green Guide to England* was the first, to be followed in 1990 by *The Green Guide to Scotland* and Mary Davis's *Green Guide to France*.

The English and Scottish volumes follow a similar format: introductory chapters on the natural and peopled landscapes, the green movement, and practical advice about travel, accommodation and the like are followed by a region-by-region guide to the sorts of things other guidebooks don't usually mention — alternative energy initiatives, what interesting communities or green businesses there are, and where the best wholefood meals can be had. *The Green Guide To France* does a similar job, though it is organized by the type of place you might want to visit rather than by region.

If you are a travelling vegetarian, Green Print has also published *The Vegetarian Holiday and Restaurant Guide* (see page 46), while a forerunner of what could be done in other regions has been produced for the north of Scotland in the form of an excellent local guide called *The Vegetarian Guide to The Scottish Highlands*.

For those who just want a friendly healthy place to stay while on their travels (or just to get away for the weekend), I can't recommend Catherine Mooney's *Complete Healthy Holiday Guide* highly enough. This is the second edition of the guide, and contains a useful description and full details of more than 300 places in Britain where the food is good and the welcome warm. If what you really want is a good peaceful retreat and time to think about the world and your place in it, Geoffrey Gerard's *Away From It All* is a guide to more than a hundred retreat houses and centres for spiritual renewal throughout Britain.

The Green Guides to England and Scotland
John Button
Green Print,
1989 and 1990
£4.99 each

The Green Guide to France
Mary Davis
Green Print, 1990
£5.99

The Vegetarian Holiday and Restaurant Guide
Peter and
Pauline Davies
Green Print, 1989
£2.99

The Vegetarian Guide to the Scottish Highlands
Jane Clarke
Jane Clarke, 1989
90p

The Complete Healthy Holiday Guide
Catherine Mooney
Headway Books, 1989
£6.95

Away From It All
Geoffrey Gerard
Lutterworth Press, 1989
£4.95

Walks in Wales . . .

Laurence Golding organizes Head for the Hills, offering walking and camping holidays — a dozen walks every year, mostly in Wales but also as far afield as the Yorkshire Dales and the Northern Cotswolds. The cost is about £25 a day, and everything you need is provided except for your personal requirements — you don't need to even bring a book to read, since a library is included. The whole thing is very civilized, gets you to places where no other holiday could, and emphasizes being in harmony with the nature around you. Laurence Golding himself researches and accompanies each walk, and even not counting Laurence you can generally bank on stimulating company. In North Wales is Tom and Kay Culhane's Wild Wales Walks, guesthouse-based holidays with walking and cycling in the hills of Clwyd. They are open all year, with week-long holidays starting at around £198. Their specialities are the Wild Wales Way, coast to coast from Prestatyn to Barmouth, and the northern section of the Offa's Dyke Path.

Head for the Hills
The Recreation Hall
Garth
Builth
Powys
059 12388

Wild Wales Walks
Pen-y-Bont Fawr
Cynwyd
Corwen
Clwyd
LL21 ET
0490 2226

England . . .

In Cumbria, Paula Day of Skardi Women's Walking Holidays organizes walking holidays for women, with small friendly groups exploring the Yorkshire Dales or the Lakeland Fells. You are based in a comfortable house in a quiet valley where excellent vegetarian food is served. There are also courses on landscape photography and compass and map reading. The holidays run from Easter to October.

At the opposite end of Britain you can discover the magic of Cornwall with Adventureline. The walking (or occasional scrambling) is not strenuous, the aim being to really learn about and sense the depth of Cornish history and geography. Prices, from £115 to £290 a week, depend on whether you want to be booked into a traditional country house, do B&B or cater for yourself.

Skardi Women's Walking Holidays
High Grassrigg Barn
Killington
Sedbergh
Cumbria
LA10 5EH
05396 21188

Adventureline
North Trefula Farm
Redruth
Cornwall
TR6 53T
0209 820847

and Scotland

If you'd prefer Scotland, C'n'do (a pun on the skeandhu or Scottish hunting knife) organizes a wide range of camping and bothy based holidays in wild and rugged country, from Knoydart in the West Highlands to the Cairngorms, the Cape Wrath area in the north to the mighty Southern Uplands Way — 212 miles in 16 days. Prices start at around £90 for a week.

You can explore some real wilderness in the far north with North-West Frontiers. These are seven-day walking holidays, leisurely or more strenuous, around Wester Ross and Sutherland, based at the famed Ceilidh Place Hotel in Ullapool. The prices start from £185 and weeks run from May to October.

C'n'Do Scotland Ltd
Howlands Cottage
Sauchieburn
Stirling
FK7 9PZ
0786 812355

North-West Frontiers
19 West Terrace
Ullapool
Ross-shire
IV26 2UU
0854 2571

Bikes and Buses

Cycling in the beautiful south Devon countryside is the attraction of Celia and Ian Shields' Adventure Cycles. From around £150 a week they provide accommodation, midday picnics, bicycles (including hill bikes and child seats), sauna, plunge pool and tennis courts. Bicycle Beano organize week-long cycling holidays in Mid-Wales and the Welsh Borders, starting at around £170; the food is vegetarian.

Sussex-based Bob-a-Long organizes walking holidays based on youth hostels, plus French trips (Loire Valley Wine-Tasting, Running Holidays in Brittany) by strictly no-smoking coach. The walking holidays programme covers most parts of Britain and Europe, many of the walks following long-distance paths and other waymarked routes. Prices start at £180 a week for full board.

Adventure Cycles
2 Snow's Cottages
Mamhead
Kenton
Exeter
Devon
EX6 8HW
0626 864786

Bob-a-Long
Harbour Road
Rye
East Sussex
TN31 7TE
0797 226770

Bicycle Beano
59 Birch Hill Road
Clehonger
Herefordshire
HR2 9RF
0981 251087

And Finally . . .

It might not be your idea of leisure, but I couldn't finish this section without a mention of the Glastonbury Festival, the proceeds of which go to help a range of anti-nuclear and environmental causes. You'll need to buy a ticket well in advance of the solstice, and arrive in time to avoid the traffic jams in the narrow Somerset lanes, but once you're inside you can forget all your worries, listen to the music, check out all the new things on the Green Field. They say you haven't really experienced life until you've been to Glastonbury — as Mike Scott of The Waterboys has said, 'It's good and it's real and people come.' If you can't (or would rather not) make it to Glastonbury, get hold of Lynne Elstob and Anne Howes' book *The Glastonbury Festivals* (Gothic Image, 1987, £9.95); it catches a lot of the atmosphere and will help you to decide whether or not it's an experience you need in your life. Many thousands of ageing hippies (and even more cool young things) wouldn't miss it for anything.

Glastonbury Festivals Ltd
Worthy Farm
Pilton
Shepton Mallet
Somerset
BA4 4BY
074 989 254/470

TECHNOLOGY

'I am frequently asked if I believe that ordinary people are really able to cope with the complexities of advanced technology and modern industrial society. I have never met an ordinary person.'
Mike Cooley, *Architect or Bee?*

Two persistent myths colour the 'developed' world's thoughts about technology. The first is that the best technology is large scale, widespread, and complex: factories, power stations, pipework, cables, switchboards, keyboards, electronic arrays, satellites and missiles. The second is that modern technology is hard to understand, the realm of engineers and technicians; certainly not a world you could expect the average person in the street to comprehend.

Not surprisingly, those who are not involved with the business of 'modern technology', who are more or less consciously left out when it comes to the teaching of even basic technological skills, often turn against the whole concept of technology. Many people feel helpless, frustrated and angry when so much of the technology of their everyday world is beyond their understanding and control — and well they might.

The Appropriation of Technology

In its broadest and original sense, 'technology' means the exploration and application of useful skills. Writing is a technology, as is chopping wood, feeding a baby, or digging the garden. If you look up 'technology' in the dictionary, however, you will probably find something like 'the application of science to industry or commerce.'

But technology long ago ceased being concerned only with the useful; the quest for innovation, and particularly patentable and thus money-spinning innovation, has become a justifiable end in itself — almost regardless of the consequences for human beings or the environment. 'You can't stop progress' is the rallying call of the business of technology, used in the defence of motorways, nuclear power stations, supersonic aircraft and star wars.

In the early 1970s, and particularly with the publication of Fritz Schumacher's often-quoted *Small is Beautiful*, the myths of technology were opened up to scrutiny for the first time. 'If that which has been shaped by technology, and continues to be so shaped, looks sick, it might be wise to look at technology itself,' he said. 'If technology is felt to be becoming more and more inhuman, we might do well to consider whether it is possible to have something better — technology with a human face.'

Such a technology, he went on to say, would be at a scale where it could be understood and identified with by the people who were using it, and in general it would be small in scale. It would above all be in each case a technology which was entirely appropriate to the task in hand.

Appropriate Technology

In their *Appropriate Technology Sourcebook* of 1978, Ken Darrow and Rick Pam set out eleven important characteristics of a truly appropriate technology.

▶ An appropriate technology is as cheap as is consistent with the required quality and performance. Western economics is designed so that the more that goes into a technology the better, since it increases the cost and thereby the all-important turnover.

▶ An appropriate technology uses local materials wherever possible, saving the energy needed to transport goods long distances and maintaining local variety in skills and products.

▶ An appropriate technology creates employment and retains skills within the local area.

▶ An appropriate technology is small enough to be affordable by the people who can make real use of it, whether it be an individual or a group of households, farmers or craftspeople.

▶ An appropriate technology can be understood and maintained by the people who use it without needing a great deal of training and specialist education. Instructions are kept simple and clear, everybody knows the basic operation of it, and the technology is thus under the control of the people it is used for.

▶ An appropriate technology can be constructed without the need of massive investment in plant and machinery. Ideally it can be made in a small woodworking or metalworking shop without the need of specialist equipment.

▶ An appropriate technology is decided upon by the group of people who will be influenced by its introduction, who understand both the benefits and the drawbacks of introducing the technology and have the power to accept or reject it.

▶ An appropriate technology uses as little energy as possible, and whenever possible makes use of renewable energy resources.

▶ An appropriate technology is one that can easily be improved upon by the people who use it, since they understand what it is doing for them.

▶ An appropriate technology is flexible, so that it can be adapted or changed as circumstances vary.

▶ An appropriate technology does not involve any patent fees, royalties, consultants' fees, import duties, or financial management consultants. Plans from which to build the technology are easily and cheaply available, and no further cost is involved.

The final words can be Jonathon Porritt's: 'Ecologists are not hostile to technology *per se*, and the use of advanced technologies of many kinds is essential to the development of an ecological society. It is a matter of choice whether technology works to the benefit of people or perpetuates certain problems, whether it provides greater equity and freedom of choice or merely intensifies the worst aspects of our industrial society.'

Small Is Beautiful

This is the book that inspired a thousand fledgling Greens. Coming back to Schumacher after fifteen years, it is hard to understand what all the fuss was about — yet at the time there was precious little else along the same lines. The ex-adviser to the NCB tended to be long-winded, simplistic, sexist (though to be fair 'sexism' had hardly been invented) and too overtly religious, but *Small is Beautiful* also contains many gems which have hardly tarnished at all with age.

He went on to write several other books and be antholo-gized extensively, though too much Schumacher can rapidly become just too much. His philosophical treatise, *A Guide for the Perplexed*, leaves many readers more perplexed than they were before they read it. *Small is Beautiful*, however, retains its power, as long as you keep remembering the pioneering circumstances of its conception.

*

While the materialist is mainly interested in goods, the Buddhist is mainly interested in liberation. But Buddhism is 'The Middle Way' and therefore in no way antagonistic to physical well-being. It is not wealth that stands in the way of liberation but the attachment to wealth; not the enjoyment of pleasurable things but the craving for them. The keynote of Buddhist economics, therefore, is simplicity and non-violence. From an economist's point of view, the marvel of the Buddhist way of life is the utter rationality of its pattern — amazingly small means leading to extraordinarily satisfactory results.

Small Is Beautiful
A Study Of Economics As If People Mattered
E.F. Schumacher
Abacus, 1984
£2.95

Architect Or Bee?

Mike Cooley, designer and engineer, is an enthusiastic advocate of truly appropriate technology. His magnum opus, *Architect or Bee?* was first self-published in 1979 and rapidly made its way through the appropriate technology network, being lapped up by enlightened technologists in many spheres of interest. In this new edition Mike Cooley's message is still the same — new technologies can be used for good if we approach them with knowledge and insight. Intelligent mistrust of both processes and the way they are controlled is impor-tant, but so is subversion. He paves the way for a society which embraces new technologies without becoming slaves to them, though he is under no illusions that the path will be an easy one.

*

Socially irresponsible science not only pollutes our rivers, air a nd soil, produces CS gas for Northern Ireland, defoliants for Vietnam and stroboscopic torture devices for police states. It also degrades, both mentally and physically, those at the point of production, as the objectivisation of their labour reduces them to mere machine appendages. . . Science and technology cannot be humanely applied in an inherently inhumane society, and the contradictions for scientific workers in the application of their abilities will grow and, if properly articulated, will lead to a radicalisation of the scientific community.

Architect or Bee?
The Human Price of Technology
Mike Cooley
Hogarth, 1987
£5.95

An AT Sourcebook

The AT Reader from ITDG (see page 296) is a gem of a book: 450 pages, over 200 articles and extracts, good illustrations, useful quotations in little boxes to fill the spaces — you couldn't ask for more. What Marilyn Carr has done is comb the inter-national AT literature for basic sources, interesting stories, horrendous disasters and fascinating titbits, bringing them all together in such a way that one flows into the next to give an overview of the successes and failures (mostly the former) of the application of AT in the last twenty years. The scope is vast — worldwide, nearly as many authors as there are articles (including all the 'names'), and subjects from banana chips and soap to mud bricks and foreign aid — even the barefoot microchip gets a look in. This is truly a book to give you hope, not to mention practical ideas. £9.95 is a lot for a paperback, but it will certainly repay the investment with interest.

Another important collection of case studies, *The Barefoot Book*, has recently been published by IT Publications (1989, £6.95). Subtitled 'economically appropriate services for the rural poor', it describes ten varied examples of grassroots service provision from lawyers in Bangladesh to economists in Ecuador. Though the examples are all from the Third World, there is much that could be learnt from this book about how less-well-off communities in Britain might benefit from the more appropriate provision of important services.

*

Solar TV? The problem is most certainly not the technology. Certainly, solar-powered television receivers, for example, could be very useful in providing programmes to rural areas with poor electrification. But if we had them, would television programming for rural people improve? I believe not, at least judging by rural radio programming, which certainly has not improved in quantity or quality since the arrival of the cheap and relatively wide-spread transistorized receiver. In sum, all our experience leads me to conclude that the mere availability of cheap and appro-priate communication technology does virtually nothing to ensure its use for rural development.

The AT Reader
Theory and Practice in Appropriate Technology
edited by Marilyn Carr
Intermediate Technology
Publications, 1985
£9.95

The ITDG

![it]

The Intermediate Technology Development Group is almost one of the grandparents of the green movement, and certainly one of the best organized. From its main offices in Rugby, ITDG works hard to further the use of intermediate technology (an appropriate scale of technology between the primitive and the Western industrial), mostly in the Third World, though many of their initiatives have very practical applications in Britain. ITDG is now a network of linked companies (the main office will be happy to give you full details) providing practical advice and assistance to field workers and others involved in the introduction of IT, with specialized consultancies in the areas of energy, transport, and materials. ITDG produces a quarterly newsletter called *Small World*, the monthly journal *Appropriate Technology*, and for water engineers a specialist journal called *Waterlines*. Plans to create a network of local groups are well under way, and there is a youth section called Youth TAG (Technology Action Group) with its own newsletter. ITDG has its own publishing house, IT Publications, based in London, where you will also find the Intermediate Technology Bookshop. The IT Bookshop stocks a very wide range of titles about appropriate technology and development issues, and sends books all over the world. For 15p plus an A5 sae the IT Bookshop will gladly send you a copy of their comprehensive *Books By Post* list.

*

We are all increasingly aware that we are custodians of our environment. The poor of the Third World have never lacked that awareness; they simply lack what we have, the economic power to make the necessary changes. It is up to us to help them in that endeavour. Partnership, in all senses of the word, is essential to understanding how our support can be harnessed to their needs.
from the *1988-89 Annual Report*

ITDG	**IT Publications**
Myson House	103-105 Southampton
Railway Terrace	Row
Rugby	London
Warwickshire	WC1B 4HH
CV21 3HT	0(7)1-436 9761
0788 60631	

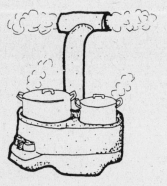

AHRTAG

The Appropriate Health Resources and Technologies Action Group is another well-established AT organization, whose concern is the promotion of good primary health care — mainly in the Third World — through the use of appropriate resources. Though AHRTAG is concerned mostly with the Third World, many of the ideas and some of the resources have relevance to disadvantaged groups in Britain, and any health worker interested in grassroots innovation would do well to subscribe to their publications, including *ARI News* on respiratory conditions, *CBR News* on community based rehabilitation schemes in the Third World, and *AIDS Action* on working with AIDS in developing countries. AHRTAG also produces a directory of primary health care courses in Britain, and has a resource centre to which visitors are welcome.

AHRTAG
1 London Bridge Street
London
SE1 9SG
0(7)1-378 1403   **AHRTAG**

TRANET

The Transnational Network for Appropriate and Alternative Technologies is run from a small town in upstate Maine, producing a bi-monthly newsletter and directory which wings its way to every corner of the world, listing AT initiatives and thus linking people involved in the fields of transport, communications, green politics, learning, womens' issues and much more. Each issue of the newsletter also contains a directory on a specific topic such as energy, or a particular region. TRANET also has an excellent library, and can refer enquirers to sources of information and advice. As long as you don't get hooked on AT networking for its own sake, the TRANET newsletter is a real inspiration — write now for subscription details.

TRANET
Box 567
Rangeley
Maine 04970
USA
(010 1) 207 864 2252   **TRANET**

Last But Not Least . . .

Since 1933 the Society of Dowsers has been pressing the case for this too-often overlooked appropriate technology. The Society organizes a series of events, can put you in touch with a local group, and publishes a quarterly *Journal* — a recent issue includes the story of how a dowser in Bolton found an old mineshaft which had completely eluded the site engineers under a supermarket building site. Still sceptical?

The Society's most recent initiative is their 'Water for Life' campaign, which funds experienced dowsers in the Third World to find and develop water sources; the first worker in southern India has so far helped to create more than 400 wells and boreholes.

British Society of Dowsers
Sycamore Cottage
Hastingleigh
nr Ashford
Kent
TN25 5HW
023 375 253

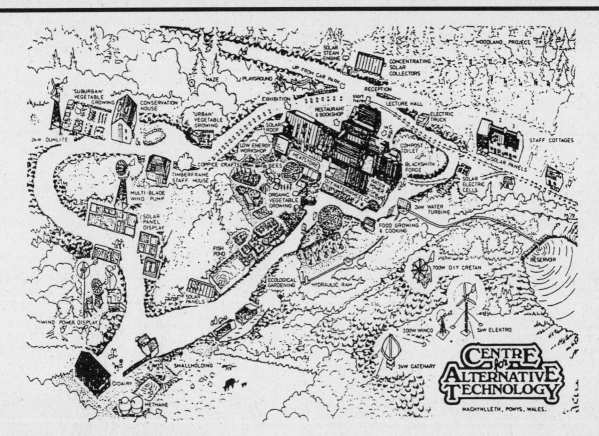

Centre for Alternative Technology

CAT has a whole page because it has probably done more than any other project to bring to people's attention the possibilities of environmentally benign technology. In a disused slate quarry in mid-Wales, CAT has spent fifteen years creating a community and a showpiece which demonstrates alternative technology in action — technology in its original and widest sense of the range of skills needed to live a sustainable and fulfilling lifestyle without harming the environment.

CAT has had its ups and downs, but its future now seems very rosy and it continues to provide a wide range of services from practical hands-on courses to delicious wholefood meals and a well-stocked bookshop. In its first twelve years nearly three quarters of a million people visited the old quarry, and on fine days during the summer it can be difficult to get near the more interesting displays of organic gardening, wind generation, blacksmithing, and the 'government maze'. There is an entrance charge (reduced rates for students, OAPs and claimants), but it is money well spent — allow several hours to see everything.

The bookshop, which stocks over a thousand titles and is probably the most comprehensive AT bookshop in Britain, also produces an extremely useful annotated booklist (50p plus postage). A wide range of weekend courses include self-build housing, low energy buildings, organic gardening, herbalism, woodland management and weekends for women — a flexible charge ensures that most people can afford to take part. Ask for a leaflet. Education is a very important aspect of the Centre's functions; as well as a resource room at the quarry the CAT will gladly send any teacher a copy of their educational visits information sheet and a list of resources available from them, which include books, posters, slide sets and project packs.

CAT also puts together comprehensive resource lists on a wide range of topics from solar energy to organic gardening. These are regularly updated, and are one of the most useful ways currently available of keeping up to date on particular aspects of appropriate technology. Resource lists currently available are: biofuels; buildings (energy and environmental factors); organic growing; renewable energy; solar energy; stand-alone electricity supply systems; water power; water supply and sewage treatment; and wind energy. These cost 30p each.

December 1989 saw the first issue of the CAT's very own quarterly magazine, *Clean Slate* (get it?), a very readable and newsy update of what's going on down at't'quarry. The CAT is also the home of the Alternative Technology Association; as well as supporting the work of the CAT members receive the magazine and join a network of like-minded people campaigning for the advancement of community-based alternative technology.

The bunkers you see on the other side of the railway line are where we compost domestic sewage. All waste from the toilets flow into a large concrete tank. The solids come to the surface as a sludgy crust, and from time to time we scoop off this crust — using very long-handled shovels! — into watertight wheelbarrows. It is then brought to these composting bunkers, which have walls of thick insulating blocks. The bunkers are filled firstly with a one-foot layer of straw, then a liberal covering of crust, more straw, more crust, and so on until the bunker is full. It is then sealed.

Within a week the bunker contents will heat up to 70°C, due to the activity of bacteria. Over the next three months the heap slowly cools down and the partially processed compost is then moved to another bunker, where it is remixed and left for a further year. The compost is then completely safe, free of smells, and ready for use. It is a crumbly, dark brown powder which can be put straight on the garden, and the cycle of life starts all over again.

from the CAT *Guidebook*
(50p plus an sae, available in English and in Welsh)

The CAT has grand plans for the future. It has just relaunched itself as a plc, and the million pounds' worth of planned developments include a new water-powered cliff lift to take visitors up from the car park to the centre. Write to them today and find out how you can invest in a truly sustainable future.

Centre for Alternative Technology
Llwyngwern Quarry
Machynlleth
Powys
0654 2400

Energy

Energy means vigour, vitality, force, life, movement. It wasn't until the early nineteenth century that the scientist Thomas Young used it to mean the doing of work by physical means, and not until this century that physicists put together an integrated model of the universe determined largely by different kinds of energy — gravitational, electro-magnetic and nuclear.

You will find the word 'energy' used in many different ways as you read about diet, healing, therapy and spirituality. The Chinese 'chi' and the Hindu 'prana' can both be translated as 'life-force' or 'energy', and nutritionists often talk about 'energy foods' and 'energy intake'. The commonest meaning of energy in the late twentieth century, however, and the meaning it has in this section, is the amount of portable power we use to make the machines in our life work for us.

Before we start looking at the energy needs of machines manufactured by human beings, though, it is important to recognize the context of the energy reservoir of the Earth and its place in the cosmos. It is vitally important to remember that although we can collect energy, control its release, and choose what uses it is put to, human beings can never actually create energy on a large scale. The most energy that we can create and exert on our own is our individual muscle power, and even that wouldn't be possible if the energy of the sun hadn't helped to create life, and food for the continuing nurturance of life.

Gaia

When you pull the plug out the television goes dead; much the same happens when your car runs out of petrol. On a larger scale a whole region can be plunged into chaos when storms bring down power lines. Yet the planetary energy system not only keeps going regardless of natural and human-manufactured hiccups; it has been going with very little marked fluctuation for the last three thousand million years. The Earth's average surface temperature has remained within a very narrow band in which life can thrive, and the constituents of the atmosphere, though inherently unstable, have nonetheless remained in roughly the same proportions for aeons of time. Have you ever wondered how?

In 1979 James Lovelock, a respected independent scientist, wrote a book called Gaia: A New Look at Life on Earth. His thesis is that the only way to explain this stability is to see the planet as a living system in which energy flows are carefully monitored and regulated, and in which the elements of the biosphere always thought to be fairly passive (the oceans, the atmosphere and the rocks) are actually alive, keeping everything running smoothly. Until now. Jim Lovelock argues that human activity is now threatening to throw off balance systems which have been perfecting themselves for millions of years. Gaia (Gaia was the ancient Greek name for mother earth) is a rare book, a well-written and passionate study by a scientist who cares about the future.

A companion volume to Gaia appeared in 1988 called The Ages of Gaia: A Biography of Our Living Earth. It expands upon the concepts discussed in the original book, introducing us for example to 'Daisyworld' and Martian mini-Gaias. The Ages of Gaia of necessity takes on today's pressing environmental concerns including the depletion of the ozone layer, acid rain and the greenhouse effect; also (and again perhaps out of necessity) a very personal chapter called 'God and Gaia'.

Gaia: A New Look at Life on Earth
James Lovelock
Oxford University Press, 1982
£3.95

The Ages of Gaia
James Lovelock
Oxford University Press, 1988
£4.95

Entropy

The second law of thermodynamics — the 'entropy law' — says that in any closed system the amount of disorder is constantly increasing. For at least the last three centuries, most human beings have been behaving as though this law did not exist, and that growth and progress can continue to proceed without the inevitable decay and disorder which must be created to balance the energy equation. Yet all around us are the signs of the decay — pollution, depleted resources, soil erosion, extinct species.

Jeremy Rifkin has pulled together ideas and examples from technology and science, industry and economics, politics and public life, to show that unless we start to recognize the importance of limits very soon, time will run out and we may well become part of the new global disorder.

*

Economists steadfastly cling to the idea that human labour and machinery create only value, because they believe in the paradigm of permanent and unlimited material progress. But we know from the second law that every time human energy or mechanical energy or any other form of energy is expended to make something of value, it is done at the expense of creating even greater disorder and waste in the overall environment.

Entropy: A New World View
Jeremy Rifkin with Ted Howard
Paladin, 1985
£2.95

The Breathing Planet

Many people are certain that what we are currently doing to our planet's atmosphere is bringing about marked changes in its composition and circulation. By polluting it with a cocktail of car exhausts and emissions from power stations and chemical factories, denying it oxygen by cutting down the world's forests, destroying the ozone layer and burning vast quantities of fossil fuels, we may be destroying the systems which provide one of our ultimate energy sources — breathable air.

The Breathing Planet is an important collection of pieces from the last ten years of the magazine New Scientist, covering all of these issues and more. Sometimes the articles are contradictory, sometimes reassuring, often frightening in their implications. The book often points out the parallels between the different issues, and has as its starting point James Lovelock's 'Gaia hypothesis' — that everything is connected to everything else in one global system.

The Breathing Planet
edited by John Gribbin
Blackwell, 1986
£7.95

Living In The Greenhouse

I spent the summer of 1988 in the American mid-west. For weeks on end there was no rain. Water levels in the Mississippi and the Ohio fell to record lows. Mid-western farmers stood by helplessly as their crops shrivelled and died. Raging fires in the forests of the Rockies sent their smoke as far east as Chicago and Detroit.

Some scientists held that the drought of 1988 was only part of a natural climatic cycle; others said it was the start of a global warming. As if to challenge the remaining doubters, the winter of 1988-89 turned into a series of often bizarre events: unseasonable mildness through much of Europe, record low temperatures in Alaska and northern Canada, and floods, Arctic chills and shirtsleeve weather alternately in the American mid-west.

John McCormick, Acid Earth (see page 57)

For those waiting for a sign, 1988 was the year they saw the greenhouse in action. If there was a moment that marked the sea-change in the view of scientists it came on 24 June 1988, at a hearing of the US Senate's Energy and Natural Resources Committee in Washington DC. 'It is time to stop waffling so much,' said Jim Hansen, the top climate investigator at NASA's Goddard Institute for Space Studies. 'We should say that the evidence is pretty strong that the greenhouse effect is here.'

Fred Pearce, Turning Up The Heat.

Yes, even conservative politicians now believe that global warming — the greenhouse effect — is for real. 1989 continued the general warmth of the 1980s, during which six of the ten warmest years in the 134 during which records have been kept have occurred. It was the fifth warmest year since 1856.

Why is the world getting warmer? Simply put, it's because over the last century we have been adding a 'blanket' of gases — mostly carbon dioxide, but also methane, carbon monoxide and a host of others — to the atmosphere. This lets the sun's heat to penetrate to the earth's surface but doesn't allow so much of it as before to be reflected back into space.

What will happen as a result of this warming? Scientists have predicted a range of effects, from major climatic shifts and increased incidence of freak weather conditions to widespread flooding as global sea levels rise, a result of polar ice melt and an increased volume of water as its temperature rises.

And what can we do about it apart from worry? Many of the solutions are obvious — reduce the burning of hydrocarbon fuels, travel less, reduce the numbers of cattle we keep — but they are politically almost unthinkable. The resulting dilemma, which encapsulates the green imperative that we change our collective behaviour very radically and very soon or suffer the consequences, is the subject of three recent books by well-known environmental authors.

First off the mark were Stewart Boyle and John Ardill with *The Greenhouse Effect*, closely followed by Fred Pearce's *Turning Up The Heat*. *The Greenhouse Effect* is strong on the political and economic context of global warming and the steps we need to take to avert ecological catastrophe; *Turning Up The Heat* is a more coherent story of how we have arrived at the present situation and of what repercussions we might expect in the coming decades — but there really isn't much between them.

In *Hothouse Earth* John Gribbin is more academic and less journalistic than the others, but though it contains more science this important book is very readable, and if forced to buy just one of the three this is the one I would choose. At present it is only available in hardback, but a paperback will follow soon. The title of the last section of *Hothouse Earth* sums up the whole question: 'Adapt,' it says, 'or die?'

The Greenhouse Effect
Stewart Boyle and John Ardill
New English Library, 1989
£3.50

Turning Up The Heat
Fred Pearce
Paladin, 1989
£4.99

Hothouse Earth
John Gribbin
Bantam, 1990
£14.95

NATTA

Whatever the answers are to keeping ourselves warm and comfortable, travelling and living in a more energy-efficient way, then NATTA is sure to have looked into it. NATTA, the Network for Alternative Technology and Technology Assessment, was established in 1981 as an independent coalition of people active in the 'soft energy' field — creating and using energy in a way which is as kind as possible to both us and our environment.

The Network now has around 500 members, and is administered by one of its affiliated organizations, the Open University-based Energy and Environment Research Unit. Membership (currently £10 and £8 if you are unwaged) is excellent value, and entitles you to attend NATTA's regular conferences as well as receiving the lively and attractive *NATTA Newsletter* every couple of months, packed with a wealth of news and information about everything from solar cars to nuclear threats. NATTA has also produced some important reports in this area, most recently Jo Robinson's timely survey of *Alternative Energy in Europe* (£5 from NATTA), probably the most comprehensive survey of its sort bar none.

NATTA
Energy and Environment Research Unit
Faculty of Technology
The Open University
Walton Hall
Milton Keynes
Buckinghamshire
MK7 6AA
0908 653197

natta

Thinking about Energy

The UK is rich in fossil fuels. It is often described as 'an island built on coal in a sea of oil and gas'. But it is also a very wasteful nation and is squandering these unique national assets at an alarming rate. At current rates of exploitation, the country's known oil and gas reserves will be seriously depleted within less than 30 years, forcing our children and their descendants to seek these commodities on the world market. We know a great deal about the problems; and we know what needs to be done to solve them. Why then is progress towards an energy-efficient future so slow?

Michael Flood, *Energy Without End*

The first thing to remember about energy is that it is not limitless. The money we pay for our energy reflects the cost of harnessing it, and that alone should spur us into using it as efficiently as possible, but there are physical limits too. Supplies of some fuels in some areas, as the above quotation shows, will not last more than another generation. We can be selfish and take everything for ourselves — that is seemingly what the energy supply industries want us to do — but using fewer resources now shows our responsibility to our children as well as saving us financial headaches in the immediate future.

Energy can be harnessed and used in many different ways, and we waste a great deal of energy by using it in inefficient and expensive ways. We have come to believe that anything can be made to work by plugging it in and switching it on, which works of course, but often isn't the most efficient way of producing the desired effect. We store hot water at temperatures much higher than we need; heat rooms with expensive electricity and lose half of the heat to the atmosphere due to poor insulation and draughtproofing. In technical terms, we use high-grade energy for low-grade uses when low-grade energy would do perfectly well.

We run inefficient transport systems, cars that even when carrying their full passenger load use three times as much energy per passenger mile as a train. We build houses that make inefficient use of sunlight for light and heat, then instal systems to compensate for that energy using scarce fossil fuels.

Coal-fired electricity generating stations rarely supply more than a third of the potential energy stored in the fuel they use, the other two-thirds being lost in heat, incompletely burned fuel and operating losses. When all the energy input is calculated, it has been estimated by some scientists that most nuclear power stations actually represent a net energy loss.

Taking all this into account, what can we as consumers of energy actually do to improve the situation?

Obviously we can use as little as possible, especially energy which comes from resources which are not renewable. Where electricity is concerned, unless you generate your own it is impossible to know exactly how the power you use is being generated, since we have a nationwide transmission grid. There are, however, still ways of making your preferences known, especially when it comes to nuclear energy (see page 302).

You can also do more to save energy, and this is the subject of pages 307 and 308.

Soft Energy Paths

Amory Lovins is a wise and fearless advocate of energy policies which ensure a sustained supply of energy for uses which are beneficial to both the environment and the people who inhabit it. As a consultant physicist he knows what he is talking about, and knows exactly how to get it over clearly and persuasively in a way that has a distinctly worrying effect on energy industry representatives.

His best known book, *Soft Energy Paths* (Penguin, 1977), is currently out of print, but it is well worth seeking out for the new perspective it gives on world energy needs, and how these can be achieved using 'soft' user-and-environment-friendly technologies rather than 'hard', heavy, multi-million pound technologies.

A recent book that covers much of the same ground is Michael Flood's *Energy Without End*, an illustrated introduction to renewable energy resources which makes it very clear that given the political will Britain need not remain dependent on heavy environmentally damaging technologies for its power supply. *Energy Without End* includes a good survey of British energy trends, showing among other things that energy needs are currently falling, and that as much as 70% of the energy generated in this country is currently being wasted in conversion, distribution and inefficiency. It then goes on to look at all the different energy options available, concluding with a nineteen-point action plan.

*

The obstacles we face may look formidable. Nevertheless they are neither insuperable nor insurmountable. Moreover, the opinion polls show that the public wants change: with every nuclear leak or accident, and with every report of dying forests and lakes, its resolve grows. The position of those who seek to continue squandering our national resources and ridiculing the renewables becomes more and more untenable.

Energy Without End
Michael Flood
Friends of the Earth, 1986
£2.40

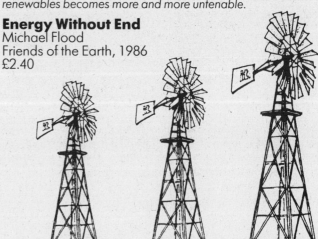

Nuclear Energy

Sixteen months after the Chernobyl disaster, restrictions are still in force in several European countries on the sale of certain contaminated food products, despite earlier pronouncements that the radioactivity would rapidly fall to harmless levels. In Britain, restrictions on the movement and slaughter of sheep have been renewed in Cumbria and re-imposed in Scotland and Wales, after levels of caesium in sheep meat were found to be above the 1000 becquerel per kilo safety limit set after Chernobyl. A total of 559,000 sheep on 564 hill farms are affected.

*

One of the two Magnox reactors at Trawsfynydd in Wales has been closed following an explosion at the plant. The shutdown will cost more than £350,000 a week, with an additional £100,000 in repairs. At first, the Central Electricity Generating Board denied that an explosion had taken place. Later, it acknowledged that there had been 'a loud noise'.

*

The United Kingdom Atomic Energy Authority has announced that 18 grams of weapons grade uranium, enriched to 93 per cent, has been lost en route from Winfrith in Dorset to Dounreay in Scotland.

*

Just isolated incidents in the ups and downs of Britain's beleaguered nuclear industry? Not at all. These news stories appeared in the *Telegraph, Times, Guardian* and *Independent* in just one week in late August 1987. Yet despite the fact that nuclear power stations have now been acknowledged as the financial and environmental liabilities they are, the industry still can't understand why 83% of Britons are opposed to the building of new nuclear power stations. They even resort to full-page adverts telling us how very green nuclear energy is 'because it doesn't pollute the atmosphere' — Friends of the Earth have been very quick to demolish that perverted line of argument.

Heralded in the 1950s as the source of energy which would be 'too cheap to meter', even the Chairman of the Central Electricity Generating Board has admitted that nuclear power in Britain has not yet started to pay its way. At the same time it is becoming clear that the development of this country's 'civil' nuclear programme was always contingent upon its ability to provide weapons grade materials, and that while Britain continues to import nuclear waste from around the world for 'reprocessing', it is unlikely that any completely safe way will ever be found to store it.

Studies show repeatedly that the incidence of childhood cancers is highest around nuclear testing establishments; that the Irish Sea is the most radioactive in the world; that caesium levels in Chernobyl 'hot spots' are not going away as predicted. Is it enough that we simply wait for the next nuclear accident to happen and hope it isn't here? Or do we raise our voices now to say that nuclear energy isn't worth the risk, and that there are cheaper and infinitely safer ways of producing the energy we need?

Nuclear Power

Veteran campaigner Walt Patterson has recently added a new postscript to his outstanding primer on nuclear power, first published in the mid-seventies. Nuclear jargon can be daunting, but this book will lead you gently and confidently through the history of nuclear power, the nuclear fuel cycle, different sorts of reactors, and the real economics of nuclear energy. By the end you will know the difference between becquerels and curies, radiation and radioactivity, PWRs and HTGRs. The book includes a very clear glossary of nuclear terms, and a helpful 'nuclear bookshelf'.

*

Plutonium is man-made, an element which essentially did not exist in nature until 1940. Glenn Seaborg and his colleagues at the University of California, using a particle accelerator, first created plutonium, effectively one atom at a time. Seaborg later recalled keeping the world's entire stock of plutonium in a matchbox on his desk.

Nuclear Power
Walter C. Patterson
Penguin, 1986 (revised edition)
£3.95

No Immediate Danger

While politicians and the nuclear industry keep telling us that we have nothing to fear from nuclear power stations and the testing of nuclear weapons, scientist Rosalie Bertell estimates that as many as sixteen million people may already have died from radiation overdoses in the last 45 years. In this vitally important and compelling study of the effects of radiation on human beings and their environment, Dr Bertell makes it very clear that there is no solution to the nuclear waste problem — once created, radioactive material cannot be made safe. In *No Immediate Danger*, detailed and often confidential information from all round the world has been carefully pieced together to spotlight aspects of the nuclear industry that have been kept hidden for too long.

*

Dr Alice Stewart carefully collected information on children born in England and Wales and through rigorous analysis showed damage from radiation at levels of 1/50 to 1/100 the levels being assumed as 'safe' by the nuclear military-commercial establishment. In spite of efforts to cut her research funds, attack her scientific reputation and weary her spirit, Alice Stewart continued methodically to prove her points about the seriousness of human exposure to radiation. She also just as methodically unravelled the carefully constructed 'proofs' and non-findings of the official radiation health experts.

No Immediate Danger
Prognosis for a Radioactive Earth
Rosalie Bertell
Women's Press, 1985
£5.95

Handbooks For The Nuclear Age

'Whether we like it or not,' says the back cover blurb of Peter Bunyard's *Health Guide*, 'we live in a nuclear age. These two important books, one by the co-editor of *The Ecologist* and the other by Greenpeace's nuclear research team, open up much of the nuclear debate to detailed public scrutiny for the first time. The *Health Guide* brings together a wealth of practical information about the nature of nuclear energy and its attendant radiation risks, while the main function of the Greenpeace book is to chronicle in a terrifyingly compelling form the many thousands of accidents, mishaps, cover-ups and downright lies which have been the hallmark of the nuclear business for the last half century.

Considering their often technical and frightening subject matter, both books are clear and fluent, opening our eyes to the risks we run daily from the supposedly 'safe' installations in our domestic backyards.

*

The Nuclear Age has taken us a long way down the path of despair. Beginning with false promises and naïve faith, and continuing through disappointment, disillusion and cynicism, it has left us with a legacy of fear. Fear of the sudden siren blast. Fear of evacuation from our homes at night. Fear of the insidious stealth of cancer and genetic damage. Fear of what a technology out of control can do. Fear of the Holocaust. Yet it is with these fears that age-old patterns are beginning to crumble. Our loss of innocence has brought new hope and new ideas. The scale of the challenge that now faces us is bringing forth a new vision.   The Greenpeace Book Of The Nuclear Age

Health Guide For The Nuclear Age
Peter Bunyard
Macmillan; 1988
£7.95

The Greenpeace Book Of The Nuclear Age
John May
Gollancz, 1989
£6.99

The Industry Viewpoint

The nuclear industry in Britain puts a great deal of money and effort into public relations to convince people that nuclear energy is a Good Thing — even though their task gets harder with each passing year. Whatever your views about nuclear energy, it is always a good idea to find out how the industry is presenting itself in the light of recent setbacks.

The United Kingdom Atomic Energy Authority is the main nuclear agency in Britain, and if you ask them they will send you their free monthly magazine *Atom*, together with a full publications list. The UKAEA also has a comprehensive library (including photographic prints and slides), which can be visited with advance notice.

Nuclear reprocessing in Britain is controlled by British Nuclear Fuels plc (Risley, Warrington WA3 6AS; Tel: 0925 832000), and nuclear waste by UK Nirex Ltd (Curie Avenue, Harwell, Didcot, Oxfordshire OX11 0RH; Tel: 0235 833009). Both have public relations and information departments which will send literature giving the official line. A consortium of industry interests called British Nuclear Forum, in a last-ditch effort to sell nuclear to the British public, is currently spending millions in a publicity campaign — if you want to know what they are saying in defence of their white-elephantine interests, send for their free 'fact' pack.

UKAEA
Harwell Laboratory
Information Office
Building 465
Harwell
Didcot
Oxfordshire
OX11 ORA
0235 821111 ext 5579

British Nuclear Forum
22 Buckingham Gate
London
SW1E 6LB
0272 217333

The End Of The Dream

Major changes and cutbacks are the order of the day in the British nuclear industry, especially now that expected decommissioning costs have spiralled to a point where the nuclear programme has been considered to threaten the success of impending electricity privatization. The UKAEA is likely to be an early casualty, and a recent Friends of the Earth report, *The End Of The Nuclear Dream*, takes a hard look at where Britain now stands in the context of global disaffection with all things nuclear. The last chapter looks at where we go from here, making a large number of practical suggestions as to how the halting of the nuclear industry should be implemented and monitored.

Another important Friends of the Earth report, *Magnox: The Reckoning*, makes it clear that almost every reassurance that was made about the purpose, safety and performance of Britain's earliest nuclear power stations was a more or less blatant untruth.

*

'The next few years will not be easy'
John Collier, Chairman of UKAEA, 1988

The End Of The Nuclear Dream
Michael Flood
Friends of the Earth,
1988
£7.00

Magnox: The Reckoning
Philip Davies
Friends of the Earth,
1988
£5.50

SCRAM and CANE

We have the power to say NO

Established in 1975, the Scottish Campaign to Resist the Atomic Menace is one of the most active and enterprising anti-nuclear groups in Britain; its bi-monthly journal *Safe Energy* will keep you up to date on green energy issues throughout the country, with a special emphasis on Scotland.

Consumers Against Nuclear Energy works in much the same way as the Peace Tax Campaign (see page 265), supporting members who temporarily withhold a symbolic proportion of their electricity bill to show the electricity authority that they do not approve of their activities. Less extreme actions include writing your cheques on an anti-nuclear cheque book, and distributing stickers and leaflets saying 'We have the power to say no'.

SCRAM
11 Forth Street
Edinburgh
EH1 3LE
031 557 4283/4

CANE
PO Box 697
London
NW1 8YQ
0(8)1-854 6390

NUCLEAR POWER? NO THANKS

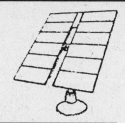

Solar Energy

The UK receives a significant solar contriution over the course of the year, in theory sufficient to provide all of the space- and water-heating of a well-designed dwelling. In practice, seasonal swings in the availability of solar energy make year-round solar heating impractical in small installations because of the high cost of interseasonal storage. However, costs are scale dependent. Swedish engineers have demonstrated that they need not be a major barrier if very large underground rock heat stores are used.
Michael Flood, *Energy Without End* (see page 299)

Virtually all the energy we use can be traced back to the sun, that enormous nuclear reactor which deals with all its own waste at a safe distance from life on Earth. The only possible exception is the energy we can harness from the tides, which is mostly lunar energy. 'Solar energy' is usually used in a more limited sense to mean direct solar energy — the energy contained in the heat and light of sunshine.

Good solar engineering depends as much on conserving energy as it does on generating it; the concept of 'solar architecture' is now well advanced, with hundreds of thousands of buildings all over the world (even in Alaska and Lapland!) being designed to make the most of the sunlight that falls on them. Large south-facing windows and high levels of insulation can trap more of the sun's energy and store it as heat within the fabric of the building.

Sun Traps

In *Sun Traps*, John Elkington has produced an excellent and well illustrated survey of energy options for the future at the same time as writing a very readable history of energy. He cleverly links the different forms of 'solar' energy, including nuclear and fossil fuels alongside the renewables. Energy traditionalists may write many of the ideas in *Sun Traps* off as wishful thinking, some radical greens may think some of them yet more inappropriate technology, but John Elkington probably comes as close to an accurate assessment of the global energy future as anyone.

*

Applying what he called the 'principle of the baked potato', Shao Yuan, engineering professor at George Washington University, was trying out a solar heat-storage method which he had developed and patented. From April to November, Professor Yuan was collecting the sun's heat in an array of water-filled collectors connected to an underground system of coiled plastic piping that heated the surrounding earth. By the beginning of November, the temperature of the ground surrounding the coils had risen to 77-82°C, creating an underground reservoir of heat — with the normal underground temperature varying between 13° and 18°C. This reservoir stayed hot enough through the winter, said Professor Yuan, to heat the water in the plastic piping, and thence the water in the domestic supply system, until the spring.

'The ground,' he explained, 'will hold heat longer than water will. It's something like the difference between a cup of coffee and a baked potato. When you go out to dinner, order a coffee and a baked potato with your meal and set them aside. At the end of the meal, the potato will still be hot, but the coffee will be lukewarm. The ground under the house is like the baked potato, storing the heat all winter.'

Sun Traps
John Elkington
Penguin, 1984
£3.95

Practical Information About Solar Energy

Technologies and suppliers change so rapidly in the solar energy business that it can be hard to track down the suppliers that might be offering the sort of system you are looking for. Any address list more than a couple of years old might as well be thrown away. There are two reliable sources of general information, however — the Solar Trade Association and the Centre for Alternative Technology. The Building Centre (page 88) is a good place for books and technical information about solar architecture.

The Solar Trade Association represents about twenty companies specializing in solar technology, and will send you an up to date membership list which includes the names of people to contact. They also produce a useful pamphlet called *Solar Water Heating: What's In It For Me?*. Members of the association agree to abide by high standards of marketing and installation, and the association also acts as a lobby for solar technology.

CAT (see also page 297) produces a *Solar Energy Resource List* which lists around forty firms involved in solar energy, and which includes a list of relevant books obtainable from the CAT bookshop.

The Solar Trade Association Ltd
Brackenhurst
Greenham Common
South
Newbury
Berkshire
RG15 8HH
0635 46561

Centre for Alternative Technology
Llwyngwern Quarry
Machynlleth
Powys
SY20 9AZ
0654 2400

Solar In The City

If you want a good idea of the various solar options currently available in Britain, you can either visit the solar displays at the Centre for Alternative Technology (see above), or you can wander round the new town of Milton Keynes, where over the last twenty years or so Milton Keynes Development Corporation has sponsored a range of energy efficient house designs. NATTA (see page 300), together with Milton Keynes Urban Studies Centre, has put together a guide to more than a dozen of these novel buildings: it is called *Solar In The City* and can be obtained from NATTA for 50p plus an A4 sae.

The projects include such hi-tech-sounding buildings as the Low Energy Adaptable Dwelling, Solaire Court, and Futurehome 2000, and while they can all be viewed from the outside, do remember that they are people's homes, so respect the occupants' privacy and keep to public paths and pavements!

Solar Water Heating

It was in the late 1970s that solar panels started to appear on roofs across the country as many small companies were formed in response to a grassroots interest in solar energy. Typically these solar collectors consist of connected pipes sandwiched between an insulated backing and a glazed front, water being pumped through the pipes with a low-power pump. To begin with these panels were not very efficient, but the technology has developed by leaps and bounds in recent years.

Advanced vacuum tube collectors can now generate temperatures as high as 200C with efficiencies in excess of 50%. They can even convert sunlight into useful heat when the temperature is below freezing. Another development is integral solar absorption panels, through which water trickles between layers of stainless steel. The big problem is that vacuum tube collectors, solar absorbers and their associated heating systems cost a lot of money — at least £2000 for a small house — so the payback time is in the order of ten years. Prices are beginning to come down, however, as manufacturers recoup their development costs.

Thermomax are the leaders in evacuated tube solar heating. From their factory in Surrey, this Design Council and Queen's Award winning firm exports solar collection and conversion equipment all over the world. One important advantage of the Thermomax system is that it is extremely flexible and easily transported. Systems start at around £1,100, and most items can be obtained from stock.

Filsol in South Wales specializes in small-scale systems for individual houses and swimming pools, based on solar absorption panels. They market the Stamax stainless steel collectors, and Pilkington's range of Sunsense small-bore collector panels. Their domestic solar heating kits start at around £750.

Alan Parsons has recently relaunched Natural Energy Systems, a Norwich-based company specializing in domestic solar hot water systems using the Thermomax evacuated tubes. He has also written a very practical guide called *The Practical Solar Handbook* (available from Anthony Bushell Publications, Opal Cottage, Colby Road, Banningham, Norwich NR11 7DY; Tel: 0263 733294, for £3.95 including p+p). The *Handbook* is for hands-on DIY plumbers rather than the interested layperson, though it does give a good overview of what is involved in converting your domestic hot water system to solar.

Thermomax Ltd
15 Stockwood Rise
Camberley
Surrey
GU15 2EA
0276 66672

Filsol Ltd
Ponthenri Industrial
Estate
Ponthenri
Dyfed
SA15 5RA
0269 860979

Natural Energy Systems
2 Arderon Court
Adelaide Street
Norwich
Norfolk
NR2 4ER
0603 661863

Solar Cells

The photovoltaic effect has been known for more than a hundred years, but it is only in the last thirty years that the technology has been explored in detail, and only in the last five that photovoltaics have promised to supply sufficient amounts of energy to provide a viable and economic alternative to other renewable resources.

The effect takes place at the junction of two different semi-conducting materials, but only a minute charge is produced, which means that large areas of cells are needed to provide a usable current. If only a very small current is needed (as in a calculator, for example) photovoltaics are an ideal solution, but at the present state of the art it needs more than six square feet of cells to produce enough current for one light bulb.

On the other hand, the basic material — silicon — is the commonest element on earth, and once manufactured, the technology is totally non-polluting. Each array of cells has a long life, so that although the initial cost is high, a module will typically last for more than twenty years. Moreover, the cost is rapidly decreasing, and each installed module now costs less than a third of the price ten years ago.

As yet the commonest applications of solar cell technology are for small isolated installations like telecommunications relays, navigation buoys, sailing boats and isolated road signs. As their efficiency increases and prices fall, however, they will increasingly become a viable option for low power uses in any location.

The two leading British manufacturers of solar cells are Chronar in South Wales and PAG in Abingdon. Chronar pioneered LCD displays for watches and calculators, but their main interest is in photovoltaic panels which can be built up into arrays of any size. For small-scale applications the array passes current through a trickle charger to a battery; larger arrays can power electrical products directly.

PAG specializes in photovoltaic panels for yachts and caravans — their stylish designs won a Design Council award early in 1987. PAGPanels have also been used to recharge the batteries of a small electrically-driven car.

The American firm ARCO (a division of Atlantic Richfield — an oil company hedging its bets) is the big boy of solar cell technology — their pride is the 6 megawatt Carissa Plains solar power plant in California which generates sufficient electricity for 2,300 houses. In 1985 the company opened a European operation based in Maidenhead. ARCO produce a wide range of modules, and if you are interested in solar technology they will happily send you a copy of their magazine, *ARCO Solar News*.

Chronar Ltd
Unit 1
Waterton Industrial
Estate
Bridgend
CF31 3YN
0656 61211

ARCO Solar Europe Inc
McGraw Hill House
Shoppenhangers Road
Maidenhead
Berkshire
SL6 2QL
0628 75011

PAG Solar Technology Ltd
Unit 11
Thames View
Industrial Park
Station Road
Abingdon
Oxfordshire
OX14 3LD
0235 33367

LESS

Richard St George started Low Energy Supply Systems in 1984 to make small scale renewable energy equipment easily available to the general public. LESS can advise on a wide range of options, including solar panels and cells, low voltage windmills, micro-hydro and low-voltage appliances. They supply only equipment made in Britain, and visitors are welcome for a chat and a cup of tea — the human face of human-scale technology! Two of LESS's windmills supplied to the Ecological Development Centre in Ladakh have been blessed by the Dalai Lama.

Low Energy Supply Systems
84 Colston Street
Bristol
BS1 5BB
0272 272530

Wind Energy

Harnessing the energy of the wind seems an obvious way of providing electricity easily, cheaply and sustainably — windmills have after all been pumping water and grinding corn for centuries. In the last twenty years the technologies associated with wind generation have improved dramatically, though there is still a great deal of debate about some of the basic issues involved.

The main debate is one of scale. Companies like Boeing and General Electric have built and commissioned enormous wind generators with towers 200 feet high and rotors which are 300 feet from tip to tip. Such machines produce a lot of electricity — this size of machine is designed to generate 7 million kilowatt-hours a year or sufficient electricity for about 800 households.

The problems of wind generation at this scale can be correspondingly gigantic — noise, stress and turbulence among them. Large generators have a very high failure rate. Small generators, on the other hand, are extremely reliable, and the obvious inference is that wind generation is ideal for relatively small installations, right down to the individual isolated dwelling.

*

One small company which believes it has the answer and that, not to put too fine a point on it, companies like Boeing have taken the wrong turning, is US Windpower. At its Crotched Mountain wind farm in New Hampshire, US Windpower was using 40-foot rotorspan machines mounted on 60-foot steel tripods. Each of these relatively small windmills can generate 30kW in winds of 25 miles per hour, and while Boeing was talking about driving the price of wind-generated electricity down from $10 to $1 per peak watt, US Windpower was claiming that its machines had been built at a capital cost of $1 per peak watt. The main reasons for this low cost was the use of off-the-shelf components such as a 50-horsepower motor, run backwards as a generator, and of commercially available transmission equipment. The only custom-made bits were the fibreglass blades and a microprocessor used to control the entire operation.

John Elkington, *Sun Traps* (see page 274)

Medium-scale installations have already been commissioned in several parts of Britain — Devon, South-West Wales, Orkney and Shetland. In addition there are small-scale generators all over the country; since this is the technology that will interest you most if you are thinking of installing wind generation for your own use, it is small-scale equipment which is emphasized in this section.

The advantages of small-scale wind generation include ease of installation, relatively low capital cost (as renewable energy systems go), and pollution-free operation. Possible difficulties include the enormous variability of wind speed, requiring fairly complex control mechanisms, and the fact that aero-generators usually need more maintenance than solar or hydro installations.

General Information About Wind Energy

The Centre for Alternative Technology (see page 297) produces a comprehensive list of suppliers and organizations concerned with wind energy (send an sae with your enquiry); the CAT bookshop also carries an extensive range of books on the subject.

Two national alternative technology networks which have concentrated on wind as a source of energy are the Network for Alternative Technology and Technology Assessment (see page 300), whose publications include the comprehensive 1988 report *Windfarm Location and Environmental Impact* by Alexi Clarke (£10 from NATTA), and the British Wind Energy Association (4 Hamilton Place, London W1V 0BQ), which publishes the quarterly *Windirections*.

Aerodyn

Engineer John Shore has worked in alternative technology for twenty years, and in 1981 started production of his Aerodyn wind turbines. A complete system starts at around £900, and as long as the average wind speed exceeds 9mph (which includes most of Britain), can produce a continuous 12 or 24 volt supply, which can be inverted to power standard 240 volt appliances. John will happily advise on specific requirements (though as he says, wind power enthusiasts are great talkers and talk never yet built a windmill). The introductory leaflet he sends out (sae please) is a good overview of the potential for small-scale wind power in Britain.

Aerodyn Windturbines
PO Box 2
Wellington
Somerset
TA21 0AW
082 366 6177

Dulas Engineering

Founded in 1982, Dulas Engineering is based at the Centre for Alternative Technology (see page 297), and specializes in control and instrumentation systems for small renewable energy supplies, especially wind generators. Among other innovations, Dulas manufactures and markets the Unitemp Air Recirculator, a low energy air pump which recirculates warm air from ceiling level through a polythene vent to the floor — at less than £50 it could make all the difference to heating a tall room like a church hall or community centre.

Many Dulas orders have been for developing countries. In 1983 sixty portable wind-powered battery management systems were exported to Mongolia for use by nomadic herders. This gave them enough electricity for lights, radios and the occasional brew-up.

Dulas also make high efficiency fridge/freezers which operate on the 12/24 volt output of a small wind energy system; following successful field trials the first large order was shipped to hospitals in Eritrea early in 1989.

Associated with Dulas is the Aberystwyth firm of Aber Instruments, the hived-off electronics arm of the CAT. In 1988 Aber moved into the new Aberystwyth Science Park, where its first major project is the 'Bugmeter', a device which monitors the proportion of living organisms present in a liquid.

Dulas Engineering Ltd
Llwyngwern Quarry
Machynlleth
Powys
SY20 9AZ
0654 2782

Aber Instruments Ltd
Aberystwyth
Science Park
Cefn Llan
Aberystwyth
Dyfed
0970 615284

Wind And Sun

Steve Wade's Wind And Sun supplies renewable energy systems of all kinds, but specializes in small wind and solar installations. His travelling exhibition is well known among AT people in southern England, and a recent achievement was providing the power for lighting and a full public address system for a big marquee at the Glastonbury Festival (see page 264) — all from windmills. Based near Oxford, Steve is happy to give advice on suitable systems for any application.

Wind and Sun
The Howe
Watlington
Oxford
OX9 5EX
049161 3859

Marlec

Marlec Engineering in Corby manufactures and markets a range of wind generators, with systems starting at around £250 suitable for a caravan, boat or isolated farm building. They manufacture the popular Rutland range at what are probably the lowest prices you will find, and also sell a range of low-energy appliances, including the Leisure Light 2D range of 12/24 volt light fittings which have all the illumination characteristics of a hundred watt bulb but use an eighth of the energy and last five times longer.

Marlec Engineering Co Ltd
Unit K, Cavendish Courtyard
Sallow Road
Corby
Northamptonshire
NN17 1DZ
0536 201588

Hydro Power

Falling water is the source of one quarter of the world's electricity. Whether harnessed by a slowly turning water wheel on a tiny stream in Nepal or by a hundred ton steel dynamo at Aswan on the mighty Nile, all hydropower comes from the ceaseless cycle of evaporation, rainfall and runoff set in motion by the sun's heat and the earth's pull.

Daniel Deudney, Worldwatch Paper 44

If you have access to a continuous stream of water falling at least ten feet, then you have the potential for a mini-hydro scheme. Ideally, though, you need a head of fifty feet or so before a system becomes at all cost-effective, and even then you are looking at a pay-back period of at least ten years. There are locations, however, which are ideally suited to small-scale hydro power, and new schemes are currently being installed in several locations in Britain, mostly in the West Highlands of Scotland.

Again, the Centre for Alternative Technology (see page 297) produces a resource sheet and a booklist.

Two helpful companies when it comes to assessing the potential for small-scale hydro power are MacKellar Engineering at Grantown-on-Spey, who manufacture turbine generators to your requirements (systems start at around £8,000); and Gilbert, Gilkes and Gordon in Kendal, who are extremely helpful and will give advice and assistance at every stage of the process. They market and install a wide range of small hydro equipment, including turbines, pumps, piping and control equipment.

MacKellar Engineering
Grantown-on-Spey
Morayshire
0479 2577

Gilbert Gilkes and Gordon Ltd
Kendal
Cumbria
LA9 7BZ
0539 720028

Energy Saving

Britain has some of the coldest homes in Europe. People living in these properties face enormous problems every time the cold season approaches. More and more often, advice workers, housing staff, social services and energy projects are called upon to help clients who have difficulty paying their fuel bills or keeping warm. Giving advice on welfare benefits and helping resolve fuel debt problems obviously solve an immediate crisis faced by a client. It may not, however, do anything to tackle the underlying causes of fuel poverty. To give effective heating advice means being aware of the factors that cause fuel poverty and how they can be resolved. This means knowing about heating systems, how much they cost and how to control them; advising on alternative ways of paying for fuel or paying off a fuel debt; identifying the most appropriate energy efficiency measures to be taken or campaigned for; or referring clients to special projects that are operating locally.

Heating Advice Handbook (see below)

*

Currently, the economic efficiency with which we use energy is far lower than the economic efficiency with which we supply it. This means that typically the marginal investment in nuclear power supply costs 80-100p/therm, whereas in the domestic sector energy can be saved through loft insulation, cavity wall insulation, draughtstripping etc. for a capital investment of 5-40p/therm. The domestic sector accounts for 30% of our national energy usage. Over a quarter of the energy used in the sector could easily be saved through simple and proven measures. By wasting this energy we are losing over £1 billion of the national income needlessly. It also means misery for millions of households. In all sectors, £7 billion could be saved on the current £35 billion energy bill.

Local Alternatives to Nuclear Power (see below)

Advice on Heating and Energy Conservation

Measure	Average U-Value reduction (W/m²°C)	Typical extra cost	Typical Payback Period
Solid Wall Insulation			
Adding 50mm external insulation to a solid wall	21–0.55	£13.50 per m²	11–12 years
Insulating wall internally using 50mm plasterboard laminates	21–0.64	£11.50 per m²	9 years
Insulating wall internally using batten method and 60mm mineral fibre quilt	21–0.6	£6.75 per m²	5 years
Floor Insulation			
Insulate timber ground floor with 60mm mineral fibre quilt	0.85–0.39*	£4.00 per m²	6–8 years
Insulate timber ground floor using 50mm polystyrene board	0.85–0.4*	£7.50 per m²	9–14 years
Insulate a solid ground floor using 'floating floor' technique with 25mm polystyrene board	0.89–0.54*	£4.50 per m²	7–9 years
Flat Roof Insulation			
Add 50mm polystyrene insulation board on top of flat roof	1.7–0.49	£3.50 per m²	9–12 years
Add 100mm mineral fibre insulation between joists underneath flat roof	1.7–0.3	£6.00 per m²	7–10 years
Double Glazing			
Install secondary glazing system (hinged or sliding) in main windows [wood frame] / [metal frame]	4.3–2.5 / 5.6–3.2	£750 (total cost)	30 years

The *Heating Advice Handbook* from the now-defunct London Energy and Employment Network tells you virtually everything you could ever want to know about energy conservation. There is the information you might expect on different heating systems and how they compare; insulation options; dampness and ventilation. Then there are the introductory chapters on how to read your fuel bill, different ways of paying (both current bills and arrears), and the health risks of cold houses. Each section includes detailed references and resource lists; appendices cover metric conversions, a definition of heat, the relevant building regulations and a complete list of organizations. There is a very good index, pages you can fill in with local information about prices and climate, and even a clear diagram at the beginning to show you which part of the book is relevant to your problem. Excellent illustrations and well laid out statistics fill out this outstanding handbook, a model of clarity and relevance.

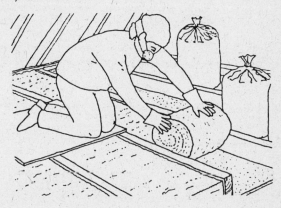

Heating Advice Handbook
LEEN, 1987 (available from Energy Inform, see below)
£5.95

Optima

Optima Partnership Limited, which recently took over the activities of ECSC (The Energy Conservation and Solar Centre), is primarily a technical advice agency which conducts surveys and energy audits of buildings for local authorities and tenants' organizations, and provides short courses on technical aspects of energy conservation.

The Tenants' Heating and Insulation Service (0(7)1-387 8906) provides management services for energy-saving schemes, and encourages local authorities to give tenants the opportunity of having a package of simple improvements installed in their homes, paying for them by weekly installments which are normally more than offset by savings on fuel bills.

Another associated service (address and phone as Optima) is the Tenants' Energy Advice Scheme, which can provide information and research facilities for tenants' groups.

Two important reports which relate to Optima's work can be obtained free from the London Strategic Policy Unit, Room 308, Middlesex House, 20 Vauxhall Bridge Road, London SW1V 2SB. The first is *The People's Plan for Combined Heat and Power*, which looks at the potential for CHP schemes in densely populated urban areas, specifically two schemes in Southwark and Tower Hamlets; the other is *Local Alternatives to Nuclear Power*, which expands on the CHP report and gives a brief introduction to other energy-saving initiatives in London.

Optima Partnership Limited
1 Goods Way
London
NW1 1UR
0(7)1-833 2253

Energy Inform

*energy*INFORM

Founded in 1980, Energy Inform is a co-operative business which provides advice and information about energy saving on a consultancy basis to organizations, local authorities and fuel utilities.

Energy Inform Ltd
9-10 Charlotte Square
Newcastle upon Tyne
NE1 4XF
091 232 7826

ACE

Established in 1981, the Association for the Conservation of Energy is a pressure group which stresses the importance of national policies for energy conservation. ACE has published some important academic studies of the potential for energy saving in Britain, and produces a good free quarterly newsletter called *The Fifth Fuel*.

Association for the Conservation of Energy
9 Sherlock Mews
London
W1M 3RH
0(7)1-935 1495

Trade Organizations

The manufacturers of different types of insulation products belong to one or more of the four trade organizations within the industry:
   The National Cavity Insulation Association Ltd
   The External Wall Insulation Association
   The Draught Proofing Advisory Association Ltd, and
   The National Association of Loft Insulation Contractors
Luckily all four use the same public relations company to disseminate information and up to date lists of members, which makes it very easy to find out which firms in your neighbourhood offer these services. None of the associations guarantees its members' work, but the fact that they appear in the association lists tends to suggest that they are at least reasonably reputable, and nearly all the largest manufacturers and installers are represented. As well as a list of members, each association also produces promotional literature which you can request at the same time.

National Cavity Insulation Association Ltd
External Wall Insulation Association
Draught Proofing Advisory Association Ltd
National Association of Loft Insulation Contractors
c/o Corporate Public Relations Ltd
PO Box 12
Haslemere
Surrey
GU27 3AH
0428 54011

Local Initiatives

Neighbourhood Energy Action, based in Newcastle upon Tyne, were the pioneers of community action on energy conservation, and there are now more than 320 local energy saving schemes running in Britain, largely using the resources of the government Employment Training scheme. NEA provides advice and information about community projects, and produces a wide range of literature, including a bi-monthly *Energy Action Bulletin*.

Neighbourhood Energy Action
2nd Floor, Sunlight Chambers
2-4 Bigg Market
Newcastle upon Tyne
NE1 1UW
091 261 5677

Still in the North-East, Newcastle's Energy Management And Information Unit (091 281 1303), which is funded by the City Council, provides an independent and impartial energy information and advice centre for individuals, groups and businesses; in the winter of 1986-7 the centre distributed thousands of leaflets and thermometers to old people in the city. There are also energy information centres in Aberdeen, Bathgate, Birmingham, Bristol, Glasgow, Hull, Liverpool and Sunderland; addresses and telephone numbers are given at the end of the Heating Advice Handbook, or your local Citizen's Advice Bureau will be able to direct you to it.

If energy consumption is a problem in the city, it can be even worse in the countryside, where houses often receive the full force of wind and rain and winter power cuts can be frequent and prolonged. In South-West Wales the Newport and Nevern Energy Group has shown what concerted community action can achieve.

Newport and Nevern are two small villages near the coast in Pembrokeshire. The population of the whole district is no more than 1,500. In 1980 a small group of a dozen people, conscious of environmental issues, came together to form the Newport and Nevern Energy Group. They began thinking about the impact of high energy costs on the local community not just in terms of the amount individual families were spending but also in terms of the impact on local employment structures and local self-reliance. They calculated that the 560 householders in the district were spending £250,000 a year on energy bills. Even a 20 per cent reduction in demand would produce £50,000 that could be used to benefit the community, money that could be recirculated rather than draining straight out of the area.

So the Group set about encouraging the efficient use of existing energy resources and promoting small-scale power-generating projects such as stream turbine generators, solar panels, windmills and even a water wheel to power an old flour mill. Bulk purchase of loft insulation material halved the cost and a full-scale scheme was inaugurated with the assistance of the local council, which soon appreciated that its grant aid was achieving more. By 1985 the Group's membership had passed 200 and they reckoned they had more than achieved their aim of reducing the community's total energy bill by 20 per cent.
          John Osmond, *Work in the Future* (see page 272)

The Group now has an Energy Van which travels round South Wales carrying the energy-saving message, with a small wind generator, a photovoltaic array, and two independent solar heating systems. The Energy Group's occasional *News-letter* will keep you up to date with the Group's imaginative schemes.

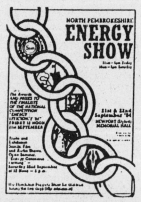

Newport and Nevern Energy Group
Trefelin
Cilgwyn
Newport
Pembrokeshire
Dyfed
SA42 0QN
0239 820470

Transport

Chris Winn, from *Friends of the Earth Handbook* (see page 65)

Transport

All city transportation contributes to pollution. Trains run on electricity generated in plants by fossil fuels or deadly atomic reactors. But as anyone who has been lucky enough to live through a taxicab strike or vehicle ban knows, cars and buses are the real problem. I shall never forget a winter many years ago when a friend and I came driving into New York City late at night after a holiday in Canada. To my amazement, the lights of the city shone like jewels and each building was clear and distinct. From the west bank of the Hudson River I could for the first (and perhaps only) time in my life see Manhattan and the Bronx in perfect detail from beginning to end, and even beyond to Brooklyn and her bridges. As we crossed the George Washington Bridge the air was clean and fresh, and the city, usually an object of horror and revulsion, was astoundingly beautiful and iridescent. The explanation was simple: enough snow had fallen to effectively eliminate vehicle traffic for a couple of days. No vehicles, no junk in the air. A better world.

Richard's Bicycle Book (see page 282)

Most people would think that mobility is desirable and that to provide for it should be one of the main aims of urban planning, but agreement breaks down when it comes to proffering a definition. In common parlance, one person would be called more mobile than another if they can and do travel more; in transport planning there has been a further tendency to equate mobility, at least in its higher forms, with travel by car. But a satisfactory approach must recognise the purpose of travel, which is to obtain access to other people and to facilities. Otherwise, we are in danger of regarding movement as desirable in itself — a proposition contrary both to common sense and to the theory of transport economics, which both rightly regard the time and expense of travel as costs to be avoided wherever possible.

Stephen Plowden, *Taming Traffic* (see page 287)

Few people would choose to travel simply for its own sake. The main reason why most of us do it is to get to what is at the other end, though we appreciate it if the journey is as pleasant as possible.

Travelling uses a great deal of energy, both physical and emotional, and the faster and further we travel the more energy it uses. 27% of all delivered energy in Britain is used to transport people and things; we spend 15% of our income on personal transport and probably another 10% on the hidden costs of transporting things to us. Perhaps not surprisingly, it has been estimated that regardless of advances in transport technology, the amount of time the average Westerner spends en route to wherever he or she wants to go has increased steadily over the last hundred and fifty years.

The two fundamental questions to ask when it comes to transport are: Is your journey really necessary? and Is this the most efficient way of getting there?

We are often in danger of taking the availability of machines for transporting us so much for granted that we don't stop to think about whether we really want to go wherever it is we had planned to. Accessibility is a two-edged concept, especially in modern cities where the supposed benefits of accessibility are constantly thwarted by the sheer quantity of human beings and their vehicles. Large out-of-town shopping centres and facilities — 'designed for convenience' — can only add to the problems as city dwellers travel to them en masse and struggle back with their purchases.

A great deal of the solution must be neighbourhood services and employment initiatives which reduce the time that people need to spend travelling, together with integrated transport systems which encourage people to use transport facilities efficiently, which in turn means less time and frustration expended in travelling.

Transport 2000

Transport 2000 is Britain's most important transport pressure group, taking both consumer and environmental aspects of the issue into account. Since 1973 it has been working very actively for an integrated transport system with a heavy emphasis on public transport. T2000 produces useful reports and statements on many aspects of British transport policy including *Roads To Ruin*, a critique of the government's recent white paper on road investment (for a free copy send an A4 sae). Their monthly magazine *Transport Retort* will keep you up to date with the latest news and plans, including all major road improvement plans (and where to lodge your objections).

Transport 2000
Walkden House
10 Melton Street
London
NW1 2EJ
0(7)1-388 8386

TRANSPORT
2000

Transport for the Disabled

Many disabled people may find that there is a great deal more going on than they had imagined; journeys which would have been out of the question a few years ago may now be quite possible as more links in the chain, which must lead quite literally from door to door, are completed.

The Department of Transport published the first edition of *Door to Door* in 1982, listing the many services now available for disabled people both financial and physical. The free guide covers using your own car and public transport, community buses and holiday schemes, wheelchairs and walking aids, aids and benefits. Appendices list all the addresses and phone numbers (both local and national) that you might need. For a copy of *Door to Door* write to the Department of Transport, Door-to-Door Guide, Freepost, Victoria Road, South Ruislip, Middlesex HA4 0NZ.

Walking

Buckminster Fuller has estimated that the average Westerner in 1914 travelled 1,640 miles a year, 1,300 of them by foot. Today the figure is something like 16,000 miles a year, of which perhaps 300 are on foot. We now live such a strange existence that many people will get up early to jog, then drive the couple of miles to work.

Everybody knows that exercise does you good, keeps muscles in trim, is good for your heart. Then why do they imagine that if wheels aren't available, wherever they want to get to is inaccessible? I remember the oft-told Shetland story of the man from the Westside who told his wife he was just going for a 'peerie waalk', and got home six hours later having decided he'd just 'stramp it tae Lerrook to buy a twist o' bakky', a round journey of twenty-five miles. But then, many of early white settlers in California had walked the best part of three and a half thousand miles to reach their new home.

Part of the problem is not having enough safe places to walk. In many parts of the country access to land away from roads and traffic is difficult, and priority on Britain's roads is always given to motor traffic. In some town and city centres pedestrian precincts have been designated despite loud protests from the road lobby, but elsewhere roads are primarily for vehicles, which makes life difficult for walkers. Not only do they take their life into their hands every time they cross territory which drivers guard with a vengeance; they are by no means safe even when walking on the pavement.

Department of Transport officials are pleased to tell us that pedestrian casualties in Britain have been falling since 1974 — what they don't say is that the number of people who dare to walk along Britain's roads and pavements has decreased at an even faster rate. The accident figures for walkers are still pretty horrific:

▶ Over 60,000 walkers are killed or injured by road traffic every year.
▶ A walker is four times as likely to be killed as a car traveller per mile travelled, three times as likely to be seriously injured, and twice as likely to be slightly injured.
▶ Deaths and serious injuries among teenage pedestrians have risen every year since 1980 — the rate is now double what it was twenty-five years ago.

Walking is still the most efficient and pollution-free way of travelling short distances, and pedestrians deserve better treatment. 'Pedestrians colliding with moving cars' jokes may be funny when read in court reports, but when the two do collide it is invariably the walker who comes off the worst. Let's reclaim our right to walk, to walk where we want as long as we don't harm anything. As the Pedestrians Association says, 'Walking is free, and it's not illegal (not yet anyway).'

The Pedestrians Association

Founded in 1929 and still going strong, the Pedestrians Association works hard to make the majority viewpoint (there are far more pedestrians than motorists) heard against the mighty road lobby. Membership will bring you the magazine *Walk* three times a year, and the association has a range of posters, cards and stickers, including a useful card that you can put on dangerously-parked cars saying 'Think before you park', reminding drivers of their legal obligations, and another to send to your local authority to tell them about dangerous pavement surfaces you encounter. Their literature gives plenty of useful advice, and *Women's Movement* points out that pedestrian problems are frequently women's problems, since women walk half as many journeys again as men.

*

It is an offence for a motorist not to give you priority at a zebra crossing, and you have this priority while the motor vehicle is within the zigzag lines. But do not rely too much on the motorist remembering this. If you intend to assert your rights, watch carefully how he behaves: he has more power under his foot than you have!

Pedestrians Association
1 Wandsworth Road
London
SW8 2LJ
0(7)1-735 3270

The Ramblers

'The Ramblers Association promotes rambling, protects rights of way, campaigns for access to open country and defends the beauty of the countryside'. So it says on its letterhead, and while the Pedestrians Association works to make walking safer, the Rambler's Association works to provide walkers with alternatives to walking along roads to get their exercise. Like the Pedestrians, the Ramblers have been going a long time — since 1935 — yet with a membership of over 75,000 and a knack of appearing fresh and up-to-date there is nothing old-fashioned about them. Membership gives you automatic membership of one of 330 local groups; a quarterly magazine; a copy of the invaluable *Ramblers' Yearbook* (now available to non-members for £2.95) listing over 2,300 selected bed-and-breakfasts and a wealth of practical information on equipment, transport and footpaths; access to their map library; and discounts in selected outdoor equipment shops. The normal subscription rate is a bargain; the reduced rate for claimants, under-eighteens, retired people, disabled and students not to be missed. One of the Association's major current campaigns is called 'The Right To Roam', and is seeking the legal right of access to all open countryside (see also page 52).

The Ramblers Association
1-5 Wandsworth Road
London
SW8 2XX
0(7)1-582 6878

The Countryside Commission (see page 69) produces a range of publications which will help you to enjoy your countryside walking, including an informative free booklet called *Out In The Country: Where You Can Go And What You Can Do*. The *Countryside Access Charter* is a neat double-sided card reproduced from the booklet which outlines the countryside code and gives basic (but very useful) information about access rights in England and Wales.

Cycling

The world will pedal into the twenty-first century on billions of bicycles. From remote semi-arid high plains to teeming cities the bicycle has emerged as the most efficient, convenient and pleasant form of personal transport. Global production of bicycles, nearly 80 million units in 1981, is steadily increasing by about 10 per cent annually.   Richard's Bicycle Book (see below)

In a world preoccupied with high-tech and hyped tack, it's often the simple and sensible things that get lost. In transport policy terms, that's exactly what seems to have happened to the bike. You'd think that if politicians were told how they could save 14 million barrels of oil a year (at a saving of £200 million), reduce dangerous pollutants from car exhausts, create up to 100,000 jobs, mainly in urban areas, help relieve traffic congestion, promote fitness and health, reduce road accidents, and thus bring about a better environment for thousands of people — well, you'd think they'd jump at the chance!

Jonathon Porritt, in *Pro-Bike: A Cycling Policy for the 1990s*
(Friends of the Earth, 1987, £1)

There are fifteen million bicycles in Britain, and in 1983 and 1984 more new bikes were sold than new cars. People are using them, too. Between 1974 and 1984 cycle mileage rose by 56% compared with an overall growth in vehicle traffic of 31% — in London the increase in cycling was a massive 300%.

Yet cyclists are seventeen times more vulnerable as road users than car drivers. The road lobby likes to blame cyclists for accidents, but the truth is that cycling is inherently very safe. It is usually the drivers of other vehicles ignoring cyclists that causes accidents involving cyclists. In Holland, a country where cyclist are considered when roads are planned, the death rate for cyclists is a quarter of Britain's.

As long as the car remains the paramount ruler of Britain's roads, and particularly urban roads, cycling will be dangerous and the considerations which prevent people cycling will outweigh the mobility and freedom which bicycles offer. Andy Clarke, Friends of the Earth's cycling campaigner, points out the nonsense of perfectly able-bodied children being ferried to school in cars by parents who dare not let them cycle because of busy and dangerous roads filled with private cars.

There are local initiatives taking place all over Britain, however. Cycle routes have been designated in many cities, and twenty-three local authorities now have capital allocations for cycling facilities. A typical project is the Hastingsbury Cycle Route in Bedford, a three-mile route from the town centre to a large residential area including a riverside section, cycle tracks and signalled cycle crossings. It cost around £100,000 a mile to construct, compared with £23 million a mile for the four miles of the Hackney Wick M11 Link in east London.

Richard's Bicycle Book

Richard Ballantine's *Bicycle Book*, first published in 1972 and now in its third and even more expanded edition, is considered to be the Bible of basic cycling information — the *New York Times* called it 'the only good book ever written for the serious amateur cyclist.'

The style is chatty but clear, and the illustrations helpful (the technical ones) and witty (the period cartoons). It starts by assuming that you know nothing at all about bicycles, explaining the difference between ordinary valves and pressure valves, derailleur changers and freewheel sprockets, lugs and cotter pins in language that anyone can understand but without simplifying it to the point of practical uselessness. The seasoned and experienced cyclist still keeps an oily copy of *Richard* around the place to check standard tyre descriptions, gear ratios, or taking the power train apart (and putting it back together!).

A *New Bicycle Book* by Richard Ballantine has recently been published by Oxford Illustrated Press at £14.95, but that's an awful lot to pay for a workshop manual; look out for the paperback late in 1990.

*

Riding successfully and comfortably in traffic requires a blend of determination and knowing when to give in. For example, try never to block overtaking cars. But if it is unsafe for you to let them pass, then do not hesitate to take full possession of your lane so that they can't pass. Both you and the other human have exactly the same right to use the street or highway. Possession of a motor vehicle confers no automatic additional rights or privileges. If anything, it is the other way round.

Richard's Bicycle Book
Richard Ballantine
Pan, 1986 (3rd edition)
£2.95

Vehicle For A Small Planet

This timely report from the Worldwatch Institute (see page 237) makes a fascinating and compelling case for the bicycle as one of the best means of transport available to the citizens of a crowded planet. It makes detailed comparisons between the policies of different countries towards the bicycle, and at how these reflect upon the nation's varying attitudes towards society as a whole.

*

Chinese commuters have little choice but to make use of their bikes; nationwide, only 1 person in 74,000 owns an automobile. Bicycles are also popular because, like cars in industrial countries, they offer the luxury of individual mobility and door-to-door travel, without detours or extra stops for other passengers. When the same trip takes equal time by cycle or mass transit, most Chinese commuters prefer to bike.

The Bicycle: Vehicle For A Small Planet
Marcia D. Lowe
Worldwatch Institute, 1989
(available from *The Ecologist* magazine)
£2.95

Bicycle Books

Rob Van der Plas is a walking encyclopedia and single-minded campaigner on behalf of the West's beleaguered cyclists. He teaches courses on cycle repair and riding techniques, cycles as often as he can, and writes. And how he writes! California-based Bicycle Bicycle Books alone has eight of his titles in print.

The first of Rob Van der Plas's books written specifically with British readers in mind is *The Bicycle Commuting Book*, which covers everything you might need to know about day-to-day cycling on busy urban roads. The style is informal but informed, the many illustrations clear and helpful, the proof-reading pretty appalling, but if you use your bicycle on a regular basis for work or shopping then it is well worth looking out for this practical and thought-provoking book.

The Bicycle Commuting Book
Rob Van der Plas
Bicycle Books, 1989
£4.95

Cycle Friendly Motoring

Many guides have been produced advising cyclists how to behave on the road and what to wear to ensure maximum visibility to other vehicle drivers. Campaigns to cut accident figures among cyclists have all tended to warn the cyclist to be wary. This guide is aimed at informing the conscientious motorist about sharing the road with the bicycle.

*

If you cycle on busy roads, you learn very quickly to gauge how motorists are going to behave. Many motorists, however, have never ridden a bike on a busy urban road, and often have no clear idea about where bicycles are supposed to be on the road, or how a cyclist will behave. The Friends of the Earth's *Guide to Cycle-Friendly Motoring* (free if you send an sae to FoE at 26-28 Underwood Street, London N1 7JQ) sets out very clearly where the main dangers lie, and shows how you as a motorist can look out for and avoid potential accidents.

New Cyclist

New Cyclist, now approaching its second birthday, calls itself 'the cycling magazine for grown-ups', and is crammed with fascinating and well-written articles about every conceivable aspect of cycling, from reviews and holidays to history and sexism in cycling circles. Plenty of interesting adverts and offers and a regular Young Cyclists page round off one of the cycling world's best and most exciting publications. *New Cyclist* is produced from a lively community in the Scottish Borders, is published quarterly, and a subscription costs £7 a year. Also at The Lees is Neatwork, a small company selling specialist bicycles such as the Rollfiets cycle-cum-wheelchair.

New Cyclist
The Lees Stables
Coldstream
Berwickshire
TD12 4NN
0890 3167/2709

Cyclists' Touring Club

The CTC has been looking after the interests of cyclists since 1878, which must make it one of the longest-established ennvironmental pressure groups in Britain. With more than 200 local groups, membership of the CTC provides companion-ship and support to cyclists. The *Handbook* (which is updated every two years) includes lists of suppliers and repairers and a comprehensive list of bed and breakfast accommodation; their mail order service is excellent (especially for books, of which they carry an enormous range); and they can offer competitive insurance rates. The bi-monthly magazine *Cycletouring and Campaigning* is an attractive and informative publication, always full of adverts and advance information about cycling events, both local and national. The CTC has also developed a Cyclists' Rights Network of members interested in improving conditions for cyclists in their area. To support this network, a range of technical information sheets has been prepared so that the Club can help local authorities and central government to plan for cyclists' needs.

Cyclists' Touring Club
69 Meadrow
Godalming
Surrey
GU7 3HS
04868 7217

British Rail and Bicycles

For many years British Rail seemed determined to rid trains of bicycles, designing trains without spaces where they could conveniently be stood during journeys. In recent years, however, and under constant pressure from the cycling lobby, BR are now beginning to realise that the cyclist and the railways are on the same side of the great transport debate.

You can take your bicycle free on most British trains; on 125 trains you need to book in advance and it costs £3 (though some have no cycle space). Taking a bike on London local services isn't allowed at peak times for fairly obvious reasons. If you plan to take your bike on a route that you haven't done before it's always a good idea to check in advance that you will have no problems. Your local station should be able to give you the necessary information, together with a leaflet called *The Rail Traveller's Guide to Biking By Train*.

And When You've Finished With It

Bikes Not Bombs is a most worthwhile project, similar to Tools For Self-Reliance (see page 91), which renovates donated second-hand bicycles and sends them to Nicaragua to be used by health and educational workers. So far BNB has shipped more than 300 bikes to Central America, and is in the process of setting up support groups throughout Britain. If you have an old bike you don't need, or are interested in helping to recondition bikes for Nicaragua, get in touch with BNB.

Bikes Not Bombs
34 Bellevue Road
Easton
Bristol
BS5 6DR
0272 522131

A Future for Railways in Britain?

The new South Wigston station, opened on the Leicester-Birmingham line, has proved to be more successful than even the Railway Development Society predicted. Since opening in May 1986 the station has been extensively used, so much so that BR have been embarrassed by the demand. The original 16 or so trains have now increased to 30-odd. More additions are likely and the station is expected to make £80,000 for BR in a year.
RDS *Railwatch, July 1987*

Between 1963 and 1965 Britain lost nearly 30% of its rail network in the infamous 'Beeching cuts'; more than 5,000 route miles were axed, together with 2,350 stations and a high proportion of local and stopping passenger services. This scale of closures, unique in Europe, turned rail travel into the poor relation of road transport, and despite renewed and growing support from the general public for rail travel there is little official support for a way of transporting people and goods which is much less harmful to both the environment and to human life and limb than road transport. It is true that nearly 150 stations have been opened or reopened since 1965, and that there has been large-scale investment in the electrification of some important main lines, but compared with rail investment in countries like Germany, Sweden or Japan, Britain is way behind.

As an individual there is probably little you can do to affect the transfer of heavy freight from road to rail beyond campaigning, lobbying, and in general consuming as little as possible which needs to be carried long distances. You can, however, do a great deal about choosing how you travel, especially when it comes to travelling long distances.

Always at least consider whether your journey can be made by train rather than by road, especially if you are thinking of taking your own car rather than going by coach. If you are eligible for a railcard (Young Persons, Senior Citizen, Disabled Persons, Season Ticket Holders, or Family), get one now so you don't have the excuse of not having one next time you need to travel. Whenever you can, avoid Fridays and other 'white days' so you pay less on your saver tickets (except in Scotland where there is no difference), and take full advantage of British Rail's special bargains, calling in at your local station's information centre every so often to check what's on offer. Remember you can take your pushbike for nothing on most trains (see page 311). Get a local train timetable (or buy the national one — see opposite) so you know when the trains run (or at least when they're supposed to). Make faces at the people stuck in traffic jams . . .

Railway Development Society

The RDS was founded in 1978 to encourage the greater use of the rail system and thus help to preserve Britain's environment. Fifteen branches and numerous affiliated rail users' groups work hard to point out the advantages of rail transport for freight and passengers, and the RDS has had several successes in the last year or so. Passenger trains run once more from Kettering to Corby and from Oxford to Bicester, the future of the Carlisle-Settle line has been assured, and new stations are being opened in Yorkshire and Lancashire at the rate of three or four a year.

The RDS publishes a quarterly magazine, *Railwatch*, and a useful summary of rail-related happenings in Whitehall called *In Parliament*. A series of ten RDS Railguides covers the country; costing between £1.95 and £2.75 they are full of information about a region's railways and what can be seen from and near them. At £7.50 a year for membership the RDS is altogether a good thing for anyone actively interested in changing the direction of Britain's transport policy.

Railway Development Society

(Membership Secretary)	(General Secretary)
49 Irnham Road	15 Clapham Road
Four Oaks	Lowestoft
Sutton Coldfield	Suffolk
West Midlands	NR32 1RQ
B74 2TH	0502 581721

How To Fight A Rail Cut is a useful little twelve-page leaflet available from RDS (20p + postage from RDS Sales: 35a Clarendon Road, Luton, Bedfordshire LU2 7PQ) with all the practical details about how to organize a campaign to stop BR meddling with your rail service.

Railways — A Public Service

In the dubious scramble to sell even more of the assets which already belong to the British public, the government now has its eye on British Rail. BR currently receives less subsidy than any other rail network in the western world, and privatization would almost certainly mean a further rapid increase in the price we shall have to pay to travel ecologically. This might be more reasonable if public subsidy for the road system were done away with at the same time, but you can imagine the hue and cry that would result from that sort of suggestion.

Two important recent reports look at the likely results of privatization, and at alternatives which might better achieve the joint objectives of efficiency and public service. Transport 2000's *Rails For Sale?* looks at arguments both for and against privatization and 'remains to be convinced'; the report puts the discussion in the wider context of British transport policy in general and stresses the importance of safeguards for rail travellers.

The Manchester-based Centre for Local Economic Strategies has produced *The Radical Alternative to Privatisation*, seeing BR's brightest future as a 'public enterprise' — best of both worlds? A readable thought-provoking study with an excellent bibliography.

British Rail: The Radical Alternative To Privatisation Paul Salveson CLES, 1989 £3.95	**Rails For Sale?: The Privatisation Of British Rail** Transport 2000, 1989 £2.50

Getting About Britain

Clive Lewis's monthly magazine is highly recommended for anyone who has an interest in the present and future of public transport in Britain. Colourful and lively, it presents an attractive mix of travel stories, detailed fare and timetable information, letters, reviews and advertisements. For anyone who uses public transport regularly, the cover price of £2 will be reimbursed almost immediately if you take account of the information in *Getting About Britain*.

Getting About Britain
21 Church Walk
Thames Ditton
Surrey
KT7 0NP
0(8)1-398 8332

Inland Waterways

Canals today are enjoying a boom in popularity unrivalled since the halcyon days of the 1790s. More and more people are realising what a minority has known for a long time — that canals provide beautiful and interesting walks, a means of travel for enjoyment and for the pollution-free carriage of bulk freight, and a positive attraction for wildlife. A two-thousand mile network woven across the country, the canal system, with its little bridges, lock systems and colourful narrowboats, enhances the countryside like no other form of transport.

British Waterways Board

The BWB is a useful point of reference for anyone interested in canals. They produce several worthwhile (and free) publications, including a 40-page canal bibliography, educational packs, and a sales and hire catalogue. BWB also sell Nicholson's *Guides To The Waterways* in three paperback volumes (South, Central and North, £6.95 each), which contain information about navigation, lock widths, history, canalside pubs and a lot more which is vital to the narrowboat user and useful to anyone who spends time near Britain's canals.

British Waterways Board
Melbury House
Melbury Terrace
London
NW1 6JX
0(7)1-262 6711

If you are interested in buckling down to some hard work restoring one of Britain's disused canals, you might like to contact the Waterway Recovery Group, which coordinates the work of voluntary restoration groups throughout the country and publishes a quarterly magazine called *Navvies*.

Waterway Recovery Group
47 Melfort Drive
Leighton Buzzard
Buckinghamshire
LU7 7XN
0525 382311

Timetables

It's all very well having a public transport system, but if you live somewhere that doesn't have a ten-minute service and you don't know when the bus or train is likely to turn up you might as well not have the service at all.

Across Europe from Norway to Greece bus stops display a current timetable (and often an indication of the name of the stop so you can relate the timetable to your current predicament). With rare exceptions British bus operators spurn such logic, often preferring to leave you wondering where the bus stop is, never mind when a real live bus might deign to pass by. Deregulation hasn't helped, pushing local rail patronage up by 20% in some areas. But you can still get decent timetables in some areas, so go to your nearest bus station and persevere. In some places local bus timetables are a model of clarity (Leicester and Brighton are just two places I have been recently which have excellent printed information available), but the general standard, though improving, is still pretty dire.

British Rail is much easier. The complete passenger timetable is probably the best book value there is in terms of weight per £, and is £3.50 well spent — your travelling friends will never stop ringing you up if you put it about that you have it and understand all the codes. Area timetables are free, and much more readily available than they once were. The complete BR timetable also includes useful information about private railway companies, shipping services, and much else.

In 1984 the London Transport Passengers Committee (1 King Street, London WC2E 8HN) commissioned a report on the design of passenger transport information, to see how public transport information can best be conveyed to potential travellers. John Cartledge's *See How They Run* gives a fascinating overview of the various ways in which this problem has been tackled, with examples from North America and Europe as well as many parts of Britain.

Service	979 ●	981	980	929 ●	984 ‡	981
PARK WOOD, Parade	0545	—	0630	—	—	—
Shepway, Plains Avenue, Roundabout	0550	—	0635	—	—	—
BEARSTED, Yeoman	—	—	—	—	—	0630
Bearsted, Green	—	0600	—	—	0620	0635
Madginford, Madginford Rd/Lambourne Rd	—	0605	—	—	0625	0640
Downswood, Horton Downs	—	—	—	—	0627	—
Vinters Park, Emsworth Grove	—	0612	—	—	0642‡	0647
Penenden Heath	—	—	—	—	0645	—
Running Horse	—	—	—	—	0647	—
MAIDSTONE, Bus Station	0600	0620	0645	0647	—	0655
Maidstone, Allington Way	0605	0625	0650	0652	—	0700
Larkfield, Spotted Cow	0612	0632	0657	0700	—	—
Lunsford Park, Chaucer Way/Masefield Way	0615	0635	0700	—	—	—
non-stop to:				●		
Lewisham, Duke of Cambridge	0725			0815		
New Cross, Queens Road	0733			0826		
Peckham, 28 Hanover Park	0737			—		
Camberwell, 50 Church Street	0741			—		
Kennington Oval, Underground Station	0746			—		
Old Kent Road, Dun Cow	—			—		
Elephant & Castle, New Kent Road	—			—		
Millbank, Thames House	—			—		
Pimlico, St. Georges Square	0751			0848		
London Bridge, Tooley Street	—	0745	0800	—	0805	0815
Cannon Street, Rail Station	—	0748	0803	—	0808	0818
Blackfriars Rail Station	—	0752	0807	—	0812	0822

Getting Around the Highlands and Islands

This regional timetable and directory for the Highlands and Islands of Scotland, together with its associated Travelpass scheme, deserves a medal for its services to public transport. You might think that combined public transport timetable for a whole area was an obvious way to promote tourism, keep the transport system flourishing, and advertise local attractions, but although there have been brave attempts elsewhere, only *Getting Around* appears regularly, twice a year, every year. With colour-coded sections for rail, sea, road and air travel, a services directory, and really useful maps, *Getting Around* is a model for what could easily be done elsewhere in the country given minimal resources and political will.

Getting Around the Highlands and Islands
FHG Publications in association with
The Highlands and Islands Development Board
published annually (1989 edition £2.95)

Air Travel

Advice about air travel for green-minded people is simple: don't unless you absolutely must. Aeroplanes are certainly the most convenient and rapid way of travelling long distances, but so many (rich) people take them completely for granted and don't think twice before using all that highly-refined non-renewable aircraft fuel, making a horrible noise over the suburbs and countryside around the airport, killing the odd bird that gets in the way, and damaging the earth's ozone layer with high-level vapour trails.

If you must, however, here are a few tips for keeping your costs down and your spirits up:

▶ Shop around until you find a good travel agent, then stick with them. If you travel a lot, a good travel agent can be invaluable, even for things you might usually book yourself like train tickets and reservations — it should cost you no more, and bring some money back into your local economy.

▶ Get hold of A Consumer's Guide to Air Travel by Frank Barrett (Telegraph Publications, 1986, £3.95), which tells you about the complications of (and ways round) denied boarding and compensation, MPM, refunds, charters and bucket shops. Lots of good advice, too, about the best seats to reserve, what to carry with you, how to visit other places en route at no extra cost.

▶ If you like timetables, ask your travel agent to give you their most-recent-but-one (they'll have no further use for it) issue of the ABC World Airways Guide. The thousand-odd pages of Part One give information on airline codes, aircraft types, flight routings and (most importantly) fares; the 2,500 pages of Part Two list every scheduled route in the world: did you know there was a Saturday-only flight from Gewoya to Safia that leaves at 8.30 in the morning (Papua New Guinea time)? Or you can always use the ABC to reach those awkward top shelves.

Roads and What Goes On Them

The words Okehampton Bypass have entered the national consciousness . . . Michael Howard QC, MP, told the inspector that . . . 'In terms of quality of scenery and extent of recreational use, the countryside through which the published route would pass is precious, and it would be a monstrous act of vandalism to destroy it as it would undoubtedly be destroyed.' . . . Work has now started on the 'monstrous act of vandalism' . . . Dartmoor knows how to fight back, and volumes of polluted water were recently observed cascading into the East Okement, unchecked by the newly excavated diversion pits and sandbag redoubts, and extensively discolouring the river. The madness of it all is now painfully evident. A high-pressured tree felling operation has cut a vast swathe through the 'thick woods of almost every kind of trees' that once enchanted the Rev. John Swete; about 2,000 of those trees are to go. Their trunks litter the valley floors, and are being crane-lifted into heavy transporters, churning the ground into a morass. There is lamentation and recrimination in Okehampton.
Sylvia Sayer, The Guardian, March 28, 1987

Covering large areas of land with concrete and tarmac is one of the best ways of disguising the fact that the surface of the earth is alive. Putting large numbers of fast-moving vehicles on those areas bars those areas from all living things that aren't

protected by metal cages — or kills them. Ensuring that these vehicles burn vast amounts of non-renewable hydrocarbons leads to fuel shortage and price hypes, massive air pollution, and constant noise. So why do we do it?

We do it because it 'makes money' for the people who 'own' the resources that go into the making of roads, cars, lorries and fuel. And we do it because we're used to thinking in terms of easy and relatively cheap transport, and can't imagine any other way. In the 1750s the only regular freight transport between Glasgow and Edinburgh, for instance, was a weekly stagecoach — most people in eighteenth century Scotland wouldn't have expected more; now the M8 carries more than 20,000 vehicles a day, a state of affairs we take for granted.

Wheels Within Wheels

Few people in Britain realise just how powerful the road lobby is, and just how many politicians have a stake in the continuing expansion of Britain's road-building programme and its lucrative financial spin-offs. Under any guise they can dream up, the British Road Federation extols the virtue of new roads — by-passes to 'save' historic towns, motorways to 'keep heavy lorries clear of residential areas'. Yet every forecast has underestimated the relentless ability of a consumer-oriented economy to fill new roads with more vehicles, so while the bored rich youth of London see how fast they can circumnavigate the crowded M25, the North Circular (which the M25 was designed to relieve) is as congested as ever. 'The road lobby is insatiable,' says Mick Hamer in this important study of vested interests, 'as it has to be if its industries are to grow . . .'

*

In 1982 a West German government study showed that cutting the speed limit from just over 30mph to slightly under 20mph could cut road deaths by half. Researchers in countries as far apart as Sweden, the Netherlands and Japan have found that lower speeds save lives. In Britain the lowest speed limit is 30mph. Even this limit is widely flouted. Most roads in Britain's built up areas have a 30mph speed limit. Roughly 55 per cent of the country's road deaths occur on these roads. Many victims are pedestrians, often elderly people or children. Britain has a poor record for pedestrian safety, in comparison to its safety record for motorists, which is quite good. And Britain's child safety record is appalling. A British child is twice as likely to die on the roads as one in the Netherlands, and three times as likely as one in Sweden.

*

The road lobby is a network of vested interests: the people who make the cars that clog the roads; the people who fuel those cars; the people who build the roads to relieve the traffic jams (and create them a few miles down the road); the people who own the lorries that cause the roads to crumble; and the people who patch them up. The road lobby exists for the sole purpose of influencing government policy, so that it can sell more cars, lorries, oil, rubber and concrete.

Wheels Within Wheels
A Study of the Road Lobby
Mick Hamer
Routledge, 1987
£5.95

Cars

About thirty million cars are made every year. Each one will offer its owner complete freedom of movement. In exchange it will get through about three tonnes of petrol, will grossly pollute the atmosphere, will kill wildlife and perhaps pedestrians, and will offer its driver a chance to kill him or herself into the bargain. It may not sound like a very good bargain, but it is the one that has been struck. Despise the car though we may, we have come to depend on it. We think nothing of travelling a hundred miles to visit friends. We take it for granted that, through the car, our homes and workplaces are far apart, and that the supermarkets where we shop cannot be reached on foot. We even accept (although we may not like it) that the car is a social yardstick by which we will be judged. As a means of travel, the car is undoubtedly a mixed blessing. We have to live with it, but at the same time we have to do a lot more to bring the car's worst effects under control. Blueprint for a Green Planet (see page 100)

The motor car is not only a method of travel, a status symbol, or a demonstration of masculinity. It is also the source of a wide range of pollutants which damage the environment as well as people's health. The number of cars in the world has already increased from 38 million to 350 million in the last forty years, and the pollution from road traffic is continuing to increase with extreme rapidity. Acid News, December, 1986

Suppose the course of technological development had been different, so that initially it had been possible to build only a slow electric car, and only after its use had become firmly established had the kind of cars we know today been invented. If anyone had then suggested that cars of our present type should be permitted, not only on purpose- built inter-urban roads, but generally in towns, and had made this suggestion in the full knowledge of the deaths, injuries, anxiety, discouragement to pedestrians and cyclists, and the extra noise and air pollution that would have resulted, what would society's reaction have been? Would he not have been locked up as a dangerous madman? Taming Traffic (see below)

Taming Traffic

The 1972 Plowden Report, *Towns Against Traffic*, was the catalyst for many of the pedestrian and traffic control schemes which have been created in many of Britain's towns and cities. If as much notice were being taken of his most recent book,

Taming Traffic, Britain could begin to deal with some of the worst symptoms of our current addiction to the private car. While most commentators look at the mess we are in and wring their hands, Stephen Plowden — whose traffic consultancy firm has been looking at these issues for twenty years — has surveyed the situation and come up with a host of suggestions for alleviating the problems. His is an integrated and gradualist approach to change in transport priorities, but he is convinced that in the end we must come to our senses and realise that methods of transport must be related to the varying needs of people much more than they are today.

If we were to take the suggestions in *Taming Traffic* seriously, we could foresee a time when people had access to a wider variety of forms of transport, each suitable for the journey being undertaken. Private cars — non-polluting, quiet, relatively slow (he suggests a maximum design speed of 30mph), and cheap — would be used for local journeys, with the option of public transport or hiring fast cars for long journeys. It only seems pie in the sky because our addiction has blinded us to the alternatives, but read *Taming Traffic* and see how much of Stephen Plowden's argument makes sense to you.

*

These principles suggest that road building, once seen as the urban transport planner's sole concern, is one of the last things he should consider. It does nothing directly to help the people whose needs have first claim on our attention, it is expensive and it is completely inflexible. Apart from road building required to serve new development, it would appear that the only circumstance in which roads should be built in towns, in the near future at least, is when it can be shown that schemes to improve either the environment or conditions for pedestrians, cyclists, buses and essential lorries cannot otherwise be introduced. It would need to be shown in each case that the improvement was worth the extra cost and environmental damage caused by the road building itself. The construction of relief roads should be accompanied by the introduction of restraint measures on the roads they are intended to relieve; otherwise, it is likely that the relief will not be achieved but that the effect of the new road will simply be to increase the total flow of traffic.

Taming Traffic
Stephen Plowden
Andre Deutsch, 1980
£7.50

Objecting to Roads

Before any major trunk road proposal is rubber stamped, the Department of Transport must go through a statutory public participation process, usually involving an informal participation stage and a public inquiry. The Department of Transport (2 Marsham Street, London SW1P 3EB; Tel: 0(7)1-276 3000) produces a booklet called *Public Enquiries into Road Proposals: What You Need to Know*, but if you do find yourself in the thick of the road proposal participation process, you will find the really helpful advice in *The Objector's Guide to Trunk Road Enquiries*, which costs £2 from Transport 2000 (see page 309).

Road Safety

Today about 16 people will die in traffic pile-ups in Britain. This tragedy will be largely unreported. The reason is simple: the event is so commonplace that it is not news. In addition, some 78,000 people every year are maimed and mauled by the vehicles that use our roads. Most of them will bear the scars for the rest of their lives. This is what in the 1930s was called the 'toll of the road', then considered a scandal. It is now, despite road safety policies, accepted as part of the British way of life — the price we pay for 'progress'.

Why We Have to Control the Car, FoE Transport Paper No. 1

The official body which deals with all aspects of safety is the Royal Society for the Prevention of Accidents; they produce a monthly newspaper called *Care on the Road*, and run training schemes and educational projects on road safety. One of the best sources of information on all aspects of road safety, however, is Friends of the Earth's London Road Safety Alert; their *Road Safety Information Pack* covers many aspects of road safety, including planning, drinking and driving, the effect of speed limits, and pavement parking. The pack of two booklets and thirteen leaflets contains a very good resource list for further information.

Royal Society for the Prevention of Accidents
Cannon House
The Priory
Queensway
Birmingham
B4 6BS
021 200 2461

London Road Safety Alert
Friends of the Earth
26-28 Underwood Street
London
N1 7JQ
0(7)1-490 1555

Cars and Air Pollution

Cars may be useful for getting us where we want to go; at the same time it would be harder to imagine a more efficient way of polluting the atmosphere. Here is a rundown of the contents of your car's exhaust fumes:

▶ carbon dioxide, known to contribute to the 'greenhouse effect' which is gradually warming the atmosphere.
▶ water vapour, possibly the only non-polluting waste product (though it is implicated in the greenhouse effect).
▶ nitrogen oxides, which in warm dry conditions combine with hydrocarbons to form a photochemical smog with a large ozone content, responsible for the death of trees and plants. Ozone is also poisonous for people.
▶ unburned hydrocarbons, which are carcinogenic and react with nitrogen oxides to form photochemical smog.
▶ carbon monoxide, poisonous to people and other living things.
▶ tetraethyl lead, known to be taken up by the human body and enter the bloodstream; a known carcinogen.

All this is well-known and, moreover, the technology exists to reduce car exhaust pollution dramatically. US legislation calling for catalytic converters to be fitted to new car exhausts has reduced carbon monoxide emission to a tenth of previous levels, and hydrocarbons and nitrogen oxides to a quarter.

Nearly half the world's supply of catalysts, over 15 million a year, are made by the British firm Johnson Matthey (Johnson Matthey Catalytic Systems Division, Orchard Road, Royston, Hertfordshire SG8 5HE; Tel: 0763 244161), who will gladly send you a free leaflet called *Cutting Car Pollution: The Role of Catalytic Converters*, together with a list of the UK availability of catalyst-equipped cars.

The facts about catalytic converters are that catalysts are still falling in price and now cost between £100 for a small car and £370 for a large one; that a small but growing number of manufacturers are now fitting them as standard (Audi, VW and Volvo are currently the leaders in this field); that catalysts are completely compatible with lean burn engines, of which more soon; that engine performance and fuel economy are maintained; and that the British car industry would not be threatened by the introduction of legislation requiring catalysts since imported cars would need them too (and the technology has largely been developed in Britain).

For a very long time the British government refused to ratify the EEC Vehicle Emissions Directive, saying it would damage the domestic car industry; at the same time British car manufacturers were producing literature for the US market bragging about the pollution reductions that have been achieved using catalysts — what a double standard. Belatedly Britain is now following Europe, and by the end of 1992 all new cars will have to have a catalytic converted fitted as standard. But by then pollution from vehicle exhausts will already have risen a further 5% above current levels. Too little too late?

Meanwhile car manufacturers, Ford in particular (write for details to Ford of Europe Ltd, Eagle Way, Brentwood, Essex CM13 3BW; Tel: 0277 252662) are making a great deal of their lean burn engine technology. Lean burn engines do produce less nitrogen oxide — but only at low speeds. Hydrocarbons and carbon monoxide emissions are virtually unaffected.

Lorries

European legislation now allows lorries of up to 38 tonnes to use all but a few restricted roads in Britain, and there are plans to raise the maximum weight yet again. Little known facts about heavy lorries include:

▶ One fully laden 32t truck can do more damage to a stretch of road than 24 hours' worth of cars.
▶ HGVs are 24 times more likely to kill if involved in an accident than all other vehicle types put together.
▶ No records are kept of local authority expenditure on HGV damage, and although HGV drivers are required under the 1974 Road Transport Act to report any damage they cause to property no figures have ever been published.

Transport 2000 (see page 309) produces a campaign guide called *Lightening the Load: What You Can Do About Heavy Lorries* (85p), and a free (sae please) *Heavy Lorry Fact Sheet*.

Cars That Last

It is generally agreed that the two most important financial commitments that anyone is likely to get involved in during their lives are home and car ownership. Both can swallow up an equally large part of their owner's taxed income, and yet society attaches such very different financial values to them that buying a house is a recognized way to save money whilst owning a mass produced modern car is an unavoidable way of losing it.
Durable Car Ownership (see below)

Twelve years ago Charles Ware opened the Morris Minor Centre in Bath to prove that buying a new car every few years is not an annoying but necessary fact of life in the late twentieth century. He chose the Morris Minor as a well-designed classic that may have its idiosyncrasies, but with proper care and maintenance was made to last for a very long time.

In 1985 the Series 3 Minor was launched, a fully reconditioned and respecified car which costs between £3,300 and £8,000, depending on how much work is required. The most important point about it, however, is that running costs on one of Charles Ware's cars are around 13p a mile compared with 24p for an average new small car, and over a twenty-year period running a well-maintained Minor might cost £3,000 in depreciation while a series of new cars could well cost £19,000.

All of these arguments are well presented in a book called Durable Car Ownership (£2.95 from the Morris Minor Centre). Illustrated with diagrams, photographs and tables, the concept of the durable car makes a great deal of sense for anybody who wants to opt out of the financial carousel of new car ownership, but doesn't want all the headaches that normally go with owning an old car. And think of the ecological arguments, too.

Charles Ware's cars now run on unleaded and can have catalytic converters fitted. His latest plans are to work with a Sri Lankan company to start production of the Morris Minor in that country.

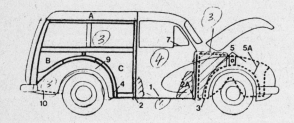

Morris Minor Centre Ltd
Avon House
Lower Bristol Road
Bath
Avon
BA2 1ES
0225 315449

Lead in Petrol

Unleaded petrol was introduced onto the Swedish market in January 1986. With its introduction further importation and production of Regular leaded 93 octane petrol was prohibited. The Act of Parliament concerning the changes required that all petrol stations with more than one pump have unleaded petrol by 1 July 1987. By the summer of 1986, unleaded petrol was available practically throughout the country. To encourage drivers to change to unleaded, it was also decided to introduce a tax reduction of 16 öre per litre (about 4 per cent) as compared to leaded petrol of the same octane. A questionnaire in October 1986 showed that about two thirds of the public who could use unleaded petrol were doing so.
Acid Magazine, 1987

Would that it was happening so quickly here, and that the Prime Minister had not been lying when she told Michael Buerk in a famous television interview that Britain had led Europe in the push for unleaded. Though 90% of petrol stations now sell unleaded and more than 27% of drivers are using it, that's still not good enough. Nearly all new cars now on sale can run on unleaded, three-quarters of them without any adjustment, and by the end of 1990 it will be illegal to sell a new car that can't use unleaded. So why are three-quarters of drivers still using leaded? The benefits of a shift to unleaded are enormous: one survey in New York showed that levels of lead in children's blood dropped 37% within months of a state-wide 50% reduction of lead in petrol.

The Campaign for Lead-Free Air (CLEAR), established in 1982, was one of Britain's most vociferous campaigning groups, monitoring the effects of lead in the atmosphere and working hard for the rapid introduction of lead-free petrol and cars that can use it. At last it seems that most of its job is done, and in March 1990 CLEAR wound down its operations and recycled its staff into other important campaigns (like Parents Against Tobacco, see page 218). Belatedly, information about the conversion of cars to unleaded is available from the Departments of Transport and the Environment — look out for their booklet *Adjust to Unleaded*, available from most libraries and garages. Most of the oil companies now produce information leaflets about lead-free petrol and which of their stations stock it.

Diesel Fuel

In recent years there has been a great deal of debate about whether diesel engines are more or less polluting than petrol engines. The main conclusions are that the type of pollution is different, black smoke and sulphur dioxide replacing much of the carbon monoxide and unburned hydrocarbons, and that diesel engines must be kept clean to reduce pollution to a minimum. It is certainly the case that diesel fumes that cause most of the smoke and fumes on our roads. On the other hand, well-maintained diesel vehicles can be extremely fuel-efficient as well as relatively clean. Friends of the Earth (see previous page for address) has produced a detailed report on the environmental impact of diesel engines, *Particulate Pollution from Diesel Vehicles*, a worthwhile read if you are thinking of investing in diesel.

Recycling Waste Oil

Each year over 100,000 tonnes of waste sump oil from DIY oil changes is unaccounted for. Many motorists still seem unaware that most garages will accept used oil for safe disposal, and that many local authorities have special schemes for the collection and disposal of used oil. The oil from one oil change can form a visible film over four acres of water, so don't dump your oil — it's illegal and environmentally irresponsible.

Sharing Your Car

What a nonsense it is to cart a large metal box around with you whenever you want to go somewhere, especially if there's only you in it and it joins thousands of other almost-empty boxes in a convoy of smelly slow-moving traffic. And what of the 37% of households that don't have a car, people who would love to share the good fortune of those with their own wheels if only there was a better way of organizing things?

Car-sharing is such an obvious solution to many of our transport problems that it's a wonder it isn't more widespread, yet there are a great many preferences, prejudices and pure bad habits to be dealt with when it comes to sharing 'your' car with 'them'.

Hitch-hiking is one way of sharing cars, offering company, and keeping the resource cost (not to mention the personal cost) of journeys to a minimum. There is a definite art to hitching, not the least of which is to look as though you really want to go somewhere, and now that fewer people are hitching Britain's roads it is — contrary to popular belief — much easier to hitch now than it was ten years ago. Also, contrary to popular belief and as far as the crime statistics can be interpreted, it isn't any more dangerous.

If you can't afford public transport and would like a more organized way of sharing medium to long distance journeys, Britain has a widespread network of Interstop members. Interstop is an international federation of car-sharing centres in thirteen countries, so wherever in Europe you want to go it can usually find somebody to share the journey with you. Membership of British Interstop, a non-profit-making collective, currently costs £12.30 a year — this gives you access to the Interstop helpline staff, who will give you the telephone numbers of anyone wanting to make a similar journey at a similar time. The petrol costs of the journey are shared between all the travellers, so if you're the car owner you recoup some of your costs and if you're a passenger you get cheap long-distance travel without the hassle of owning a car. 1980 changes to the Transport Act make car-sharing perfectly legal and extend insurance to any passenger making use of car-sharing facilities.

Car-sharing, usually for sick or older people who don't have their own cars, is also an important part of what has become known as 'community transport'. The National Advisory Unit (see below) has recently produced a useful guide which covers a wide range of practical, legal and financial aspects of car-sharing; called *Social Car Schemes*, it costs £3.50 (plus 59p p+p) from the NAU.

Interstop
Freepost
Glasgow
G1 4BR
0898 654123

Share your car
Share your costs

Community Transport

If our transport systems, public and 'private', were used more efficiently and in a more integrated way, we could alleviate a wide range of transport problems from congestion to air pollution. At the same time it would encourage a sense of community and shared experience which more and more people are lacking in their lives. On the wider canvas this is what community transport is all about, though being in its infancy it tends to see its remit solely as providing transport facilities for those without easy access to cars and buses.

The two main organizations involved in the exploration and implementation of social transport schemes in Britain are the National Advisory Unit (the research and information side of things) and the Community Transport Association (which deals more with training and advice about the day-to-day running of community transport projects). The NAU's publications include *Setting Up* (£7.50), a very practical looseleaf manual for anyone thinking of starting a non-profit-making transport scheme, and the equally practical *How To Start a Dial-a-Ride* (£5.50). The CTA runs regular training courses for drivers, mechanics and operators of community transport schemes, and produces the bi-monthly newsletter *Community Transport*, which includes adverts for jobs and vehicles.

National Advisory Unit for Community Transport
35 Fountain Street
Piccadilly
Manchester
M2 2AF
061 236 5581

Community Transport Association
Highbank
Halton Street
Hyde
Cheshire
SK14 2NY
061 351 1475/366 6685

Sustrans

Sustrans is short for 'sustainable transport', and for the last ten years this very active company has been planning and building a nationwide network of long-distance cycle/bridle/walkways, demonstrating in a very practical way that transport — especially the transport of the future — isn't just about more and more roads.

Sustrans has now built nearly 200 miles of paths in Bristol, Derby, York, Liverpool, Consett, Glasgow, and a score of other places. One of its earliest routes, the disused railway between Bristol and Bath, is now used by a million people each year. Sustrans has much greater ambitions, however, with plans on the drawing board for nearly a thousand miles of new routes throughout the country — and they're far more than vague fantasies. The company is currently working with more than a dozen local and regional authorities to prepare proposals for long-distance paths, which include a 200-mile route from Liverpool to Leeds and a 60-mile Thameside cycle path. The grand vision is to have a continuous route all the way from Inverness to London, and if anyone can do it, Sustrans can. Write for a full list of reports and studies — and a membership application form.

Sustrans Ltd
35 King Street
Bristol
BS1 4DZ
0272 268893

Sustrans Scotland
53 Cochrane Street
Glasgow
G1 1HL
041 552 8241

319

Microtechnology

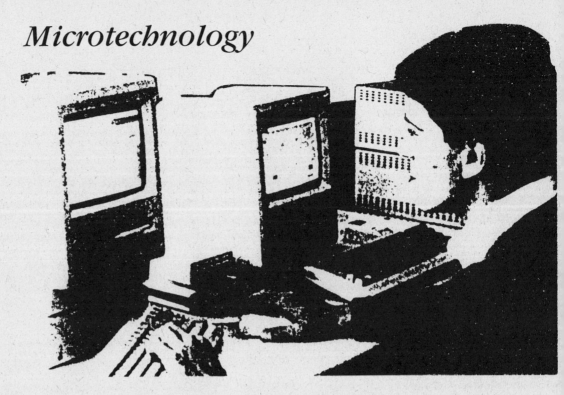

Microtechnology

We all know how we couldn't manage without microtechnology — how we depend on calculators, telephone systems, control mechanisms in household gadgets, and less directly on complex industrial and commercial processes.

Of course computers and their associated technologies have their place in the modern world, but there are a great many considerations to take into account before embracing them wholeheartedly.

In the end it all comes down to appropriateness — using the best means to achieve truly fulfilling ends. Immediately a great many uses of microtechnology show their true colours. Many people are indeed using computers to improve the world — to design less polluting transport systems, to test the oceans to assess the complex cocktails we have dumped in them, to help disabled people to communicate. But most computers — certainly the most costly and 'advanced' systems — are used for weapons control, defence intelligence gathering, price fixing in world markets, and speeding the flow of resources from poor to rich. You would find it well nigh impossible to buy computer hardware from a firm that wasn't involved in military activities.

Computer systems are also used to store a great deal of personal information about each of us, the existence of which you may not know about until you are refused a loan. Nor do we have the same degree of 'freedom of information' as they do in the USA, so you may never know whether the information stored about you in one of the many data bases — from the Inland Revenue and the DHSS to banks and private information services — is accurate, inaccurate, or inferred.

'Ah but,' they say, 'it's not the computer that's good or evil, it's what you do with it.' This is as much nonsense as saying that nuclear technology or the research that goes into star wars is intrinsically 'neutral'. Research into any technology — and the resultant hardware — must be coloured by the original purpose of the research. And is it really true that we would have no teflon pans if it were not for the space programme, or that communications satellites were developed solely as a result of military research?

We often forget that computers can only do what human beings programme them to do — the worst imaginings of sci-fi authors can never come about because microsystems will never be able to create more energy than they consume.

However complex the switch or frightening the application, a computer can always be relied on to fail if you pull the plug out.

It's true that computers can save a great deal of drudge, yet despite all the promises, computers create an awful lot of unnecessary work, a great deal of waste paper, and quite a lot of pollution.

If an accountant wanted to make a cash forecast in the days before computers, they did it once and if it looked roughly right they presented it to the client; if it didn't they made a few adjustments and then presented it. Today no business plan is complete without alternative computer-generated spreadsheets with complex ifs and buts built in. I am not at all convinced that the existence of all this additional paper actually increases either efficiency or the sum of human happiness. It does, however, increase the profits accruing to the computer world.

On the pollution front, the computer industry still uses a lot of solvents containing CFCs and other 'ozone-hungry' ingredients, and the plastic packaging used to house and protect computers are further sources of CFC pollution. In a recent incident in northern California two electronics firms admitted considerable leakages of two toxic and carcinogenic chemicals, trichloroethane and trichloroethylene. The October 1989 issue of *Practical Computing* carried a full-scale investigation of this important issue under the title 'How Green is Your PC?'.

Some of the applications of microtechnology are dealt with under household appliances (pages 98-104), energy (298-308) and transport (309-318); this section concentrates on computers — specifically the 'micro' systems used in most offices and in an increasing number of homes.

What Are Computers Good At?

However complex they appear to be, there is only one thing that computers do well — 'crunch' numbers, or in everyday language, sort out lots and lots of *very* simple calculations extremely quickly. They can translate these numbers into letters, patterns, colours or sounds, but it is vitally important to remember that this is *all* they can do. Though we may believe otherwise, computers can never feel, heal themselves, appreciate, be self-sustaining or original.

So for what purposes can you usefully use this number-crunching capability?

What's a shorter way of storing "CENTRAL INTELLIGENCE AGENCY"?

Education

Much has been made of the potential for computers in education, and no self-respecting school would be anything without the odd BBC micro. There are a few things that computers teach very well, but not very much beyond those things.

They do teach you to think carefully and rationally, checking each step as you go. If you miss out just one step (a step that most human beings might automatically assume and carry on functioning) your screen will blink 'syntax error' (or some such message) at you — it's sometimes hard to remember that this is not bloodymindedness on the part of the micro, just that a computer is basically very simple.

They are also good at teaching things that are either right or wrong, like arithmetic, or typing, or learning about computers, but because they can only accept answers foreseen by the programmer they are limited even here. If Shakespeare had used spellcheck we may never have been heirs to modern English. If the primary school computer says 'What is 99 divided by 11?' and, not being absolutely certain, you type in 'something between 9 and 12', it won't say 'Hmm, how did you think that out?'. It will say 'Wrong. Try again.' A poor substitute for a human teacher. If you then type in 'You are a very stupid computer,' it will wink nonchalantly at you and say 'Wrong. Try again.'

Then there are computer games. I'm not above an occasional fling at Grand Prix or Flight Simulator, and they do help both quick thinking and manual dexterity, but it's hard to see how Space Invaders or Pacman, let alone Terrorpod and Ikari Warriors, will ever increase the sum of human fulfilment, appreciation of the natural world, or mutual love and compassion.

Figures, Money and Accounting

If you run a large company and have many cash transactions, PAYE calculations and financial forecasts to do, a computer is now almost essential. But it may not surprise you to learn that around 70% of business computers are underused, and around a third of the computers bought by small businesses and organizations are currently not being used at all.

Even fairly complex accounts can easily be accommodated in accounts books and invoice files, where they are instantly accessible, do not depend on someone knowing how to use the computer system, and use the brainpower of the compiler rather than electricity and the blinking screen. It's not that professional accountants should go back to working without computer assistance, simply that if you are thinking of buying a computer system primarily for your own personal accountancy use you probably don't need to.

Address Lists and Information Files

An increasing number of organizations are keeping their membership address lists on computer disk with the idea of using it to print out up-to-date lists, particularly for address labels for magazines and newsletters. Whether or not this is really appropriate depends on the amount of information you need to store, how often this information changes, and what else you plan to use the computer for. If this is the main or only use, it is unlikely that you need a computer until your mailing list reaches a thousand or more.

One thing to keep in mind if you store personal information on disk is that you may well be subject to the provisions of the 1984 Data Protection Act. For more information on these requirements contact the Data Protection Registrar, Springfield House, Water Lane, Wilmslow, Cheshire SK9 5AX (0625 535777).

Word Processing

Word processing is where computers really do come into their own, and many people who work with words find that word processing on a personal computer has revolutionized the way they work, making their job far more flexible and efficient.

Even here, though, it is important to remember about appropriateness. Word processing is what enables companies to send you those ridiculous circulars that say things like 'Just imagine what your neighbours in *Acacia Avenue* will think, *Mrs Higginbtotom*, when they see . . .'. Word processing should never be about creating paperwork for its own sake.

It can, however, save hours and hours of tedious retyping. If you are the one who has done those hours, your heart will leap at the idea of being able to correct and change text at any stage. And when it comes to sending masses of text by post, think how much energy and money you can save (assuming that you are communicating with somebody with a compatible system) by sending a couple of floppy disks instead of a bulky manuscript.

Signals

I tried very hard for this edition of *New Green Pages* to find a book or books that explored the new microtechnology from a green-tinted perspective, and so far I've come up with very little. As a fellow Green Party member who is also a computer consultant said to me recently, it seems that green people are either very (and rather unquestioningly) into computers, or they are emphatically (and rather blinkeredly) not.

What I did discover, however, is that one of the most recent volumes compiled by the American *Whole Earth* people (see page 346) deals with almost every aspect of information technology that you could think of. It's called *Signal: Communication Tools for the Information Age*, and its 240 pages cover in inimitable *Whole Earth* fashion everything from learning how to write to worldwide telecommunications. The *WE* folk are far more enchanted with the new technology than I ever want to be, but this is a fascinating and absorbing ragbag of a book.

*

Information technology is a self-accelerating fine-grained global industry that sprints ahead of laws and diffuses beyond them. It has done so for twenty-five years and shows every sign of being able to keep dodging for another twenty-five, if not indefinitely. Hence Whole Earth's abiding, and now focussed, interest.

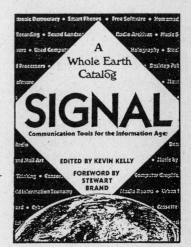

Signal
Communication Tools for the Information Age
edited by Kevin Kelly
Harmony Books, 1988
about £14.95

Hardware

When the Plowshare peace activists in the USA hammered nuclear warheads and poured blood round them to symbolize the annihilistic implications of such weaponry, they were told in court that they couldn't use the word 'warhead' — the correct word was 'hardware'. Remember this euphemism as you decide which computing machinery you want to buy.

Nowadays several 'beginner's' systems come complete with keyboard, screen (VDU or visual display unit), disk drive (to store the information) and printer. Many have a certain amount of 'software' (programmes on disk) thrown in too. You can expect to pay around £1000 for a system like this.

The most useful system to go for is one which is IBM 'PC' ('personal computer') compatible. Though I was disparaging about the importance of PC compatibility two years ago, it is now abundantly clear that it has become a widespread industry standard. Thus although there are currently some tempting offers on, for example, the Amstrad PCW and Amiga 500 ranges, it is hardly worth buying a non-PC machine if you might ever want to communicate with other people who use computers.

Buying IBM PC-compatible doesn't, however, mean buying an IBM machine (which are on the expensive side); there are now a number of cheaper 'clones' like the Amstrad, Tandon, Epson or Atari PCs, all of which will allow you to run the same software. There isn't a great deal to choose between the more reputable brands. A machine like the Amstrad 2086 with a hard disk and black-and-white screen at around £800 is good value, especially now that Amstrad appear to have solved the technical problems which had given them a less than good reputation for reliability. The Tandon PCA and Epson AX2 series both have their devotees; they will set you back around £1000-£1100.

Many people continue to swear by their Apple Macintoshes, which work largely with a handheld 'mouse' rather than using the keyboard. Macs are certainly user-friendly, but with a system starting at around £2000 you have to be pretty rich to join the club.

Printers

If you are doing a lot of word processing then you will need a decent printer. There are three basic types: a daisy wheel printer uses individual characters like a typewriter, a dot matrix printer makes up letters using a series of dots, and a laser printer produces images using technology similar to a photocopier.

A daisy wheel printer will make your text look as if it had been typed, but will probably do so rather slowly and can't be used with graphics software. Dot matrix printers come with a varying number of dots to the letter: a 9-pin NLQ ('Near Letter Quality') machine like the Epson LX800 costs around £160; a 24-pin LQ ('Letter Quality') like the NEC P2200 around £290.

Unless you are producing quantities of literature which really do need to be high-quality, laser printers tend to be used to show off rather than as a truly appropriate technology. A laser printer will cost a lot to buy (in excess of £1000) and is expensive to run.

Software

Software comes as programmes on disks, designed to do specific jobs. If you buy mainstream software (rather than shareware, for which see the next page), you will also get a manual — or three — as well.

You will probably find most use for word processing, spreadsheets (for calculations like accounts), databases (electronic filing systems), and communication between different computer systems (see page 348). You can either buy separate programmes to do each of these functions, or you can buy an 'integrated package' which combines most or all of these functions. Look out for packages such as Smart or Symphony (if you've got money) or 8-in-1 if you haven't.

Where To Buy From

If you decide you really must have a computer system, then think about the following:

▶ Do you need a new system? There is plenty of second hand equipment around, and although people may warn you off buying secondhand I have had nothing but good experiences. If a computer is going to fail, then it will do so very early on. You can find any number of secondhand computers on offer through the small ads in computer magazines, or you can ask local computer suppliers — they will try to sell you a new one, but may relent if you persist.

▶ Make sure that you can get technical backup if you need it. The chain stores or mail-order 'box shifters' who advertize in the computer magazines will be only too pleased to sell you the equipment, but make sure they have a decent customer help department. It may well be worth spending a little extra on equipment bought from a local supplier who can offer training and technical support.

The more you know before you buy the better. You can learn a lot from magazines: two of the best are *Personal Computer World* (monthly, £1.50) and *What Personal Computer?* (monthly, £1.95). These magazines carry regular reviews of equipment and software as well as a plethora of adverts from mail order firms and shareware distributors.

Systems Exchange, established by Geoff Cohen in 1986, is a computer company which specializes in supplying and servicing the microtechnology needs of green organizations and individuals. It does this by having two parallel operations, a non-profit-making side for green projects and a mainstream side which cross-subsidizes the green work. Systems Exchange can supply both hardware and software, especially network systems, and organizes training and maintenance contracts. They are very approachable, and welcome difficult questions and tentative enquiries.

For software and computer bits and pieces like disks and ribbons, two firms that I have found particularly reliable are PW Computer Supplies and Action Computer Supplies. Both produce very clear catalogues (Action's full-colour glossy version is a bit too comprehensive for my sensibilities), and Action will send stuff carriage free next day if you phone them on their Freefone number with your credit card details.

Systems Exchange
16 Crawford Street
London
W1H 1PF
0(7)1-224 6333

PW Computer Supplies
Dawlish Drive
Pinner
Middlesex
HA5 5LN
0(8)1-868 9548/
866 2258

Action Computer Supplies
5-6 Abercorn
Commercial Centre
Manor Farm Road
Wembley
Middlesex
HA0 1BR
0800 333 333

Public Domain and User-Supported Software

You don't have to pay large sums for all the software you buy. Especially in the USA there are a lot of computer enthusiasts who like writing programmes and are quite happy for other people to use the products of their efforts. This is done either by declaring the software free of copyright ('public domain software'), or by allowing copyrighted software to circulate freely on the understanding that if you like a piece of software enough to want to use it, you will be sufficiently honest to pay a small sum to the author ('shareware' or 'user-supported software'). In return for this payment (usually between £8 and £30) you can normally obtain full documentation and technical support for the shareware, together with updates when they appear.

There are many companies specializing in public domain and user-supported software. They charge a small amount (in the region of £1-£2.50) for each disk supplied to cover the cost of the disk and handling charges, though some charge more — up to £8 a disk — and include documentation and backup. In general the programme will come with instructions about how to use it on the disk. The range of programmes covered in this way is enormous, and there are even such green-tinted programmes as ones to help calculate heating losses in the home or work out the most energy-efficient way to travel to work.

There is always a risk of your computer getting infected by a 'virus' (a programme specifically written to destroy your system by deleting chunks of data) if you copy unreliable software, though the main shareware companies, knowing how much their reputation depends upon reliable software, are very careful indeed. As one shareware supplier, Steve Townsley of Shareware Marketing, writes: 'The plain fact is that no vendor of any kind of software can be sure that a product is virus free. There is an overwhelming feeling that using commercial software gives much greater protection than using shareware. To try out this belief I telephoned Microsoft, creators of the MS-DOS operating system. I asked "Can you guarantee that your Microsoft disks are virus free?" "There are no guarantees;" they replied, "there are no viruses on Microsoft disks." We can offer the same guarantee as Microsoft.'

You will find addresses for firms supplying this kind of software in computer magazines: two reputable suppliers are College Shareware in Derby and Advantage Shareware in Cheltenham. Slightly more upmarket, with a very full and instructive catalogue (*The Shareware Book*), is Shareware Marketing in Devon, which also specializes in superceded and cut-price software.

4100 series		EXPLORING . . .
4101	C	EXPLORING WORDS Norland Hangman, Spelling Bee, Letterfall, Word Processor For Children (Age 6-12)
4102		EXPLORING MATHS Funnels & Buckets, Math, Algebrax, Prime Number Calculator (Age 8-16)
*4103	C	EXPLORING TIME Telling Time, Speaking Clock, World Time Zones, Easters Calculator, Perpetual Calendar (Age 4-12)
*4104		EXPLORING SCIENCES Physicalc, Equator, Planets – large collection of formula solutions and info, Operating Engine simulator, 3D Surface Modelling (Age 10-Adult)
4105		EXPLORING YOUR IQ Number Sequences, Antonyms, Synonyms, Analogies, Memory Tester, Anagrams, Hexadecipals (Age 8-16)

College Shareware
The College
Business Centre
Uttoxeter New Road
Derby
DE3 3WZ
0332 294447

Advantage Shareware
56 Bath Road
Cheltenham
GL53 7HJ
0242 224848

Shareware Marketing
Beer
Devon
EX12 3HW
0297 24088

Advice and Training

Most colleges and education authorities run evening classes in basic computing and word processing. Unless you have a knowledgeable and patient friend, this is by far the easiest and cheapest way to learn. At the next level, the government-sponsored network of Information Technology Education Centres provide training in computing and information technology to a high standard in some sixty towns and cities throughout Britain. Phone Freefone ITEC for more information.

There is a growing network of computer groups for women, many of which offer training — see page 199 for information on initiatives such as Microsyster and the *Women and Computing Newsletter*. The Community Information Project (see page 279) publishes a quarterly newsletter called *Computanews* which deals specifically with ways in which computers can be used in voluntary and community activities.

GreenNet (see page 347) is a computer network specifically set up to exchange environmental, peace and other green information; they can also supply the necessary communications equipment and software.

For those working in computing, Exchange Resources in Bath run a recruitment agency for people looking for socially and environmentally sound employment. They are also computer consultants, and produce a regular newsletter containing articles about such topics as the ethical use of computers.

There are now a number of specialist firms which will take your word processor disks and produce neatly typeset artwork from them; check their prices carefully before committing yourself. Saxon Printing in Derby are as knowledgeable as any and more helpful than most (though confusingly they only do typesetting, not actual printing). If you are involved in producing a magazine or book, talk to them before you begin about the most economical way of doing it.

Two years ago, when desktop publishing (DTP) was in its infancy, I was a bit scathing about it, saying that you would get similar results far more cheaply using a word processor, a photocopier, glue, scissors and imagination. Since then DTP has become cheaper, easier to use and more widely available, but a quality DTP software package like Pagemaker or Ventura will still set you back more than £500. There is cheaper software available, like Fleet Street Publisher at around £99, but you may find its limitations frustrating.

If you live in the south-east and want to learn to use desktop publishing for your organization's printed material, Neal's Yard DTP will train you and provide equipment for you to work on. Charges range from £5 per hour for unassisted use of a Macintosh workstation (after training) to £20 per hour for disk translation. You can also include drawings and photos in your work, using their scanner. Camera ready artwork can thus be created from around 50p per A4 sheet.

EXCHANGE RESOURCES

Exchange Resources
28 Milsom Street
Bath
Avon
BA1 1DP
0225 469671

Saxon Printing Ltd
Saxon House
Heritage Gate
Derby
DE1 1DD
0332 361370

Neal's Yard DTP
Neal's Yard
London
WC2H 9DP
0(7)1 379 5113

Biotechnology

Biotechnology and You

While the nation has begun to turn its attention to the danger of nuclear war, little or no debate has taken place over the emergence of an entirely new technology that in time could very well pose as serious a threat to the existence of life on this planet as the bomb itself. With the arrival of bioengineering, humanity approaches a crossroads in its own technological history. It will soon be possible to engineer and produce living systems by the same technological principles we now employ in our industrial processes. The wholesale engineering of life, in accordance with technological prerequisites, design specifications, and quality controls, raises fundamental questions.

Jeremy Rifkin, *Algeny*, Penguin, 1984, £2.95

Once manipulated by people, nature loses its neutrality. Elite research institutes will produce new seeds that work — at least in the short term — for a privileged class of commercial farmers. Genetic research that involves ordinary farmers themselves will produce seeds that are useful to them. A new seed, then, is like any other technological development; its contribution to social progress depends entirely on who develops it and who controls it.

Frances Moore Lappé and Joseph Collins, *Food First*, Abacus, 1982, £3.50

Newspapers assure us that such new reproductive technologies as embryo transfer, in vitro fertilization and artificial insemination of breeder women (usually known as 'surrogate mothers') are merely 'therapies' which kindly physicians provide for infertile women. Of course there is more to it than that. Through the years, with widespread use of the technologies, social institutions will be restructured to reflect a new reality — tightened male control over female reproductive processes.

Gena Corea, in *Man-Made Women*, Hutchinson, 1985, £3.50

Nearer to home similar concerns have been expressed about secret trials of the hormone [bovine somatotropin] carried out by the Ministry of Agriculture, Fisheries and Food on behalf of a number of drug companies. The product is presently being used on several farms with the increased milk yield entering the normal milk supply — something that Rifkin and his coalition managed to stop in the States. 'The first thing you've got to do [says Rifkin] is to stop calling it BST. It's bovine growth hormone and once the public realise that it's a growth hormone they won't want it. This product is entirely without social value. You can't use it in the Third World for example, it doesn't work in hot climates. The only place it works is in the northern hemisphere which is awash with surplus milk. This is the craziest product to come down the pike in a long while.' BGH is clearly a test case for the bio-tech industry — if it comes to fruition the industry will have gone a long way towards massaging public opinion into accepting genetically-engineered products and turning a blind eye to the longer-term consequences. According to Rifkin, 'if this one gets through, the floodgates will open', with scores of products waiting n the wings and with even more profound effects.

Julie Sheppard, *London Food News*, Summer 1987

The US and Mexican governments are to spend millions of dollars in an effort to combat the so-called 'killer bees' which escaped six years ago during genetic engineering trials in Brazil and now threaten the native bee population of North America.

The Guardian, September 1987

All over the USA in the 1960s and 1970s, vivisectors were deliberately transmitting simian AIDS from animal to animal, species to species, laboratory to laboratory, watching it develop in severity and speed of action. No attempt at all was made to contain the viruses, for at this stage the human consequences of such work were unknown.

The Campaigner magazine (see page 72), March-June 1987

What happens if for instance someone implants into the human embryo a gene for longevity . . .? Or will crazy scientists instead concentrate on producing a race of immensely strong but mentally quiescent people to do the heavy manual work, and at the other extreme produce super-intelligent humans to plan society — intelligent but without ethics? Is all of this wild scaremongering? Bear in mind that man will do anything for money. While the American Commerce Department has approved the patenting of higher life forms, it has specifically banned the patenting of new genetic characteristics in humans — for the time being.

Agscene (see page 71), June 1987

Mr John MacGregor, the Agriculture Minister, said he would consider the best scientific evidence and advice before deciding to licence bovine somatotropin. He also said: 'No industry can be expected to prosper if it does not take every advantage of new technology to keep abreast of the competition.'

Environment Digest, June 1988

'Biotechnology' is one of those areas which are so complex and all- embracing that it's very easy to be cowed by scientific jargon and the reassurances of industrialists, then when you open your mouth to object, be told that 'biotech' is nothing really new, that it opens up enormous potential 'for the benefit of mankind', and that you don't know what you're talking about anyway. Which hides a great deal that should concern all of us enormously, for it has implications for the future of life itself — yours, mine, and the planet's.

We have used aspects of biotechnology for centuries — selective breeding of domestic animals and crops, the technology of yeast to raise our bread and ferment our drinks — but the current threat is something new which must be understood and challenged. The Scottish Milk Marketing Board has come out against bovine somatotropin — you can help to build on that opposition and extend it to an outright ban. Watch out for industry propaganda and object to it.

INFORMATION

'The chief limitation of all information systems, electronic or otherwise, is that essentially they confirm pre-existing ways of looking at the world, simply adding more detail.'
David Andrews, *The IRG Solution*

Until the beginning of this decade, economics students learned that there were three sectors within the economy — agriculture and mining, industry, and services. In the early 1980s, and particularly with the publication of Professor Tom Stonier's book *The Wealth of Information* in 1983, a fourth sector was identified, one which is growing rapidly and may well be the only area of growth in the Western economy in ten years' time: the information sector.

At its most neutral, information is knowledge about something or someone. It is being able to find the answers to simple questions, answers which affect the way we choose to live. Ideally such questions would find answers quickly and easily, though in practice it can be difficult to know what the appropriate question is, let alone where you might go to find the answer.

Information activities include teaching and research, libraries, writing and book production, word processing and data retrieval, advice services, postal services and telecommunications, the media; it can be extended to include advertising, banking and insurance, management, and even government and social work. It has been estimated that these activities now employ a third of Britain's workforce, and the proportion is still rising rapidly at a time when all other forms of employment have already peaked. Some observers have suggested that we now live in an Information Age.

Information Overload?

In his influential book *Future Shock*, Alvin Toffler talks of the overstimulation and inability to think clearly that we can experience when we are presented with more information at one time than we can handle.

Technical writer David Andrews quotes a Glasgow University lecturer who has high praise for computer based information retrieval systems: 'I spent half an hour with the librarian, discussing my research and producing a short list of key words. My colleague dialled a number, pressed a key and teleprinted our words — interdisciplinary, multidisciplinary — via satellite to California. In seconds we had sample titles of relevant articles, and promises of delivery by air mail of a further 492 titles. The operation cost £19.' 'Impressive,' comments David Andrews, 'and yet has he really got the right information? Has he used the correct key words? How does he select from the 492 papers? Has he got time to read them all? Are they worth reading?'

The danger is that information can become a commodity in its own right, regardless of what it is needed for. Thus lists of names and addresses can be sold by the thousand; trade figures by the page. Being able to root out important information is a crucial skill, but almost anyone can copy down (or print out) strings of facts from a computer screen. To be of any real use facts must be assessed against personal experience and integrated into a thoughtful consideration of their significance and usefulness.

Information or Knowledge — or Both?

In his book *Megatrends* John Naisbitt explores the growing information society. He points out that scientific articles are currently being written at the rate of 7,000 a day, and that the amount of data available will soon be doubling every two years — and that is just in science and technology.

'This level of information is clearly impossible to handle by present means,' he goes on. 'Uncontrolled and unorganized information is no longer a resource in the information society. Instead, it becomes the enemy of the information worker. Scientists who are overwhelmed with technical data complain of information pollution, and charge that it takes less time to do an experiment than to find out whether or not it has already been done.'

The emphasis must thus shift from quantity and specificity to selection and imagination. It becomes as important to know what you don't want to know as what you do, and equally important to happen upon things you didn't think you needed to know until you came upon them. Computers may be able to do some of the work, but can never think laterally like the human brain.

NASA scientists worked for decades on the design of space suits which would cover the whole body yet be flexible enough to allow every part of the body to move freely. A detailed literature and information search was carried out to ensure that no angle was missed, whether it was research into materials in Japan or ergonomics in Sweden. Then somebody had the sort of brainwave that no amount of information technology would have supplied, but which centuries-old knowledge had filed at the back of a human brain.

Within weeks, a specialist team had been despatched to the Tower of London to examine a suit of armour made for Henry VIII in the Royal Workshops at Greenwich in the 1520s. As the Keeper of Armour explained, 'This armour is exceptional in that it covers every part of the body, including buttocks, groin, the insides of the elbows, the armpits and the backs of the knees. The way in which every plate links to the next, and the wearer's movements are allowed for, is marvelously ingenious, yet simple and effective. When the NASA team saw this armour they observed that they wished they had seen it earlier on in their development programme, since it would have saved them a lot of time and money.'

Appropriate information is just as important as appropriate technology.

Reference Books

If you go into the reference section of any good library you will find shelf upon shelf of important-looking reference books. Reference books are very big business, and dictionaries, directories, yearbooks, indexes and abstracts are very useful if you are looking for detailed information about a specialist subject. The trouble with most reference books, however, is that you have to have a lot of information in them to be of any use, yet you never need the vast bulk of that information. It just sits there, unused, filling up paper that trees were chopped down to make and space that has to be kept warm and dry so the silverfish and booklice don't take hold.

For this reason, if not simply because of the price of good reference books, it is best to use libraries wherever possible for your reference books. Yet if you work with words and information, you will almost certainly find that there are certain reference books that you consult every day. Here is a selection for the researcher interested primarily in things green and ecological.

English Dictionaries

I have to start with the Oxford English, which comes as a whole family of dictionaries from the massive fourteen-volume-plus-four-supplements *OED* proper to the *Mini Oxford* at £1.75. The cheapest way to buy the full-blown OED is in the photographically-reduced edition, which consists of two volumes of main dictionary and one of supplement, which brings it right up to 'yuppie', coined only in 1984. That will set you back £295, but you'll never have a dull moment thereafter, and you'll always win at Scrabble.

> **yuppie** (yʊ·pi). *colloq.* (orig. U.S.). Also **Yuppie**. [f. the initial letters of *young urban professional*: see -IE.] A jocular term for a member of a socio-economic group comprising young professional people working in cities. Also *attrib.* Cf. *YUMPIE.
> **1984** PIESMAN & HARTLEY (*title*) The yuppie handbook. **1984** [see *YUMPIE*]. **1984** *Times* 21 Mar. 14/2 A new term has been introduced into the American political lexicon... It is 'Yuppie', which stands for Young, urban professional people. **1984** *Observer* 8 Apr. 12/1 We have got to break this yuppie image. **1984** *Guardian* 22 Oct. 6/6 The yuppies themselves, in the 25-34 age group, supported Senator Gary Hart in the primaries.

For a mid-price English dictionary, the *Collins English* is good, published in 1986 at £14.50. It's clear, as unbiased as any, contains both general words and encyclopedic entries (people and places), and up to date ('green: 21. concerned with or relating to conservation of the world's natural resources and improvement of the environment: used esp. in a political context'). For a slightly different perspective you might try *Webster's Collegiate* (£14.95), the American mid-price equivalent of the *Collins English*; it has American and British usages, the first recorded date of each word, and a free service whereby you can write to Websters Language Research Service and they'll search their collection of 13 million citations for examples of the word you're interested in.

Some Alternative Dictionaries

There have always been alternative dictionaries, from Ambrose Bierce's *Devil's Dictionary* to Monique Wittig and Sande Zeig's *Lesbian Peoples: Materials for a Dictionary*. Here are two recent dictionaries, both of which look deeply and fundamentally at the language we use, and both of which fall fairly and squarely into the category of reference books. I'll warn you in advance that one of them was compiled by me.

A Dictionary for Feminists
A big book, nearly 600 pages long and with over 1,500 sources in the bibliography, *A Feminist Dictionary* breaks new ground in many ways. First, it lets women speak (and only women with rare exceptions). Second, it lets them speak for themselves with only minimal editorial linking material. In this way it by and large succeeds in letting ideas define themselves, even when there is considerable disagreement about what a word really means. *A Feminist Dictionary* is an excellent sourcebook, not only for quotations but for cultural and social history too, and putting quotations side by side in this way shows how ideas often develop in parallel ways in different countries and cultures. This way of setting things out does have disadvantages, though. Sometimes it is difficult to see why a word is in beyond the fact that the editors happened to have a quotation containing it and couldn't think where else to put it. It is very noticeably American, even though published in Britain — 'button' is in, for example, but no cross reference from 'badge'. There are a few important words which are noticeable by their absence: 'couple', 'relationship' and 'single' for example, and I find it a bit humourless — but then, you might say, I would.

FEMINISM
(See all entries above and below)
A movement with a long history. Three basic positions of feminism during 1400-1789: (1) a conscious stand in opposition to male defamation and mistreatment of women; a dialectical opposition to misogyny. (2) a belief that the sexes are culturally, and not just biologically, formed; a belief that women were a social group shaped to fit male notions about a defective sex. (3) an outlook that transcended the accepted value systems of the time by exposing and opposing the prejudice and narrowness; a desire for a truly general conception of humanity. (Joan Kelly 1982, 6-7)

Has as its goal to give every woman "the opportunity of becoming the best that her natural faculties make her capable of." (Millicent Garrett Fawcett 1878, 357)

Has as a goal: The liberation of women for women. "We don't have to have anything to do with men at all. They've taken excellent care of themselves." (Jill Johnston 1973a, 91)

"May be defined as a movement seeking the reorganization of the world upon a basis of sex-equality in all human relations; a movement which would reject every differentiation between individuals upon the ground of sex, would abolish all sex privileges and sex burdens, and would

A Feminist Dictionary
Cheris Kramerae and Paula Treichler
Pandora, 1985
£6.95

A Dictionary for Greens
When I started working on *A Dictionary of Green Ideas* three years ago, it had been in my mind for a long time that it would be useful to bring together and examine all the words used by people involved in the green movement, from appropriate technology to peace work, ecology to feminism. When Routledge said they liked the idea enough to want to publish it I was delighted. I wasn't quite so delighted when the dictionary turned into a six-month-long megawork with more than 1,300 entries and more than 500 closely-printed pages!

To my mind a great deal of what the green movement is about is reclaiming language and ideas from those in power who have distorted and used them to their own ends. I hope you will find the lines of thought opened up by the dictionary both stimulating and thought-provoking.

Green
[c.1978 in this sense]
A set of beliefs and a concomitant lifestyle that stress the importance of respect for the EARTH and all its inhabitants, using only what resources are necessary and appropriate, acknowledging the rights of all forms of LIFE, and recognising that all that exists is part of one interconnected whole. The concept of being 'green' arose in the late 1970s, though since the 1950s 'green' had been used as a qualifier for environmental projects such as The Green Front, a tree-planting campaign initiated by The Men of the Trees in 1952, and GREENING was already in use in the late 1960s. The Green Alliance, an ecological pressure group, was founded in Britain in 1978; at this time 'green' was used to describe an ecological perspective, and many of the social and economic implications of such a perspective had yet to be looked at. The rise of die Grünen (the Greens) in West Germany and their first parliamentary success in 1983 brought the word 'green' to many people's attention. By this time die Grünen had formulated many far-reaching policies, and

A Dictionary of Green Ideas
John Button
Routledge, 1988
£12.95

Whitaker

AN
Almanack
For the Year of Our Lord
1990
ESTABLISHED 1868
BY
JOSEPH WHITAKER F.S.A.

The first *Whitaker's Almanack* appeared in 1868 and it has been published every year since, containing 'Astronomical and other Phenomena, and a Vast Amount of Information respecting the Government, Finances, Population, Commerce, and General Statistics of the various Nations of the World with an Index containing nearly 20,000 References.' At £17.95 for its 1,236 pages (you can get a shorter, paperback version for £9.50) it isn't something you need to buy every year, but it does encapsulate a vast amount of information that no other single volume will give you, including every candidate in the last general election, all the trades unions with addresses and membership numbers, every university in the Commonwealth, sunrise and sunset times for every day in seven different cities, the opening times of houses open to the public, the coin and note denominations of every currency in the world, and full legal notes — and that's a minute proportion of the contents.

Whitaker's Almanac
Whitaker's, 1989
£17.95

Some Specialist Dictionaries

There are an enormous number of specialist dictionaries, most of which are too expensive, too narrow, too biased or too boring to stay anywhere but in the reference library. From the green perspective, however, there are a few that are worth considering for your own shelves.

Two of the dictionaries in the paperback Macmillan series look promising — Michael Allaby's *Dictionary of the Environment* and Malcolm Slesser's *Dictionary of Energy*. Despite expectations, perhaps, it is the latter that stands out. Together with a team of seven other knowledgeable people, Malcolm Slesser uses 'energy' in a wide sense, so *A Dictionary of Energy* contains good and useful entries on meteorology, economics, agriculture (where it is particularly helpful) and ecology, as well as the entries you might expect from nuclear physics and energy studies. It has useful entries on all the renewables (hydro, solar, wave, etc.), and includes some marginally provocative entries like 'Three Mile Island' (the US nuclear power station which suffered a partial meltdown in 1979.

Michael Allaby, for all his experience, is rather a disappointment. *A Dictionary of the Environment* gives straight dictionary definitions of hundreds of words you'll come across in biological ecology and related fields, and for that alone it is well worth consulting, but it rarely makes you think, and there are some most surprising omissions, including 'energy', 'land', and 'nature'.

The Dictionary of Human Geography is, despite its specialist feel, an extremely useful — and readable — resource. It has abolished sexist language, isn't afraid to tackle 'feminist geography', 'marxian economics' or 'global futures', and presents a balanced view of controversial issues. It's very good when it comes to disentangling philosophical ideas like 'existentialism' and 'phenomenology', and at nearly 600 pages is good paperback value.

For something completely different, David Harvey's *Guide to Alternative Living* is rather a misleading title for a guide to all the weird and not-quite-so-weird ideas you might come across in the areas of healing, spirituality, fringe therapy and 'psi' activities. When David Harvey is good he is very good; when he's not he tends to be careless and superficial — in general the healing entries are very good, the therapy entries good, the 'magical' entries shallow. The resource section at the end is not particularly helpful; non-annotated entries for health organizations are useless.

Dictionary of Energy
edited by Malcolm Slesser
Macmillan, 1982
£7.95

The Dictionary of Human Geography
edited by R.J. Johnston
Blackwell, 1986
(2nd ed.)
£9.95

Dictionary of the Environment
Michael Allaby
Macmillan, 1985
(2nd ed.)
£8.95

Thorson's Complete Guide to Alternative Living
edited by David Harvey
Thorsons, 1986
£6.99

Directories

Two useful directories for any green activist's library are Monica Frisch's *Directory for the Environment* and Rose Heaword and Charmian Larke's *The Directory of Appropriate Technology*. For basic information about organizations, publications, and the range of resources available in Britain in the late 80s, they are excellent sources.

Directory for the Environment lists nearly 1,400 organizations in Britain concerned with various aspects of the environment — Monica Frisch has undertaken a thorough and much-needed task in updating Michael Barker's database, adding a useful 'How to Use this Directory' section at the beginning. As well as full details of addresses, telephone numbers, contact names and publications, most entries also give the year of establishment of the organization, aims and activities. A most welcome addition to the green reference shelf.

The Directory of Appropriate Technology contains annotated entries for organizations, businesses, books, journals and other publications covering a wide range of subject areas like work and employment, transport, energy, and building. It's a pity that this important book was so long in the making, since many of the addresses and telephone numbers were out of date even before the book was published. The price is a bit steep too; surely a paperback would have been more appropriate. Where this directory is excellent, however, is as a record of important resources (books, magazines, etc.) and ideas. Thus if you can vaguely remember reading a book about earth-covered houses written by someone whose name began with C sometime in the mid-1970s, this volume is just what you need.

Directory for the Environment
Monica Frisch
Green Print, 1990
(3rd ed.)
£15.95

The Directory of Appropriate Technology
Rose Heaword and Charmian Larke
Routledge, 1989
£40.00

Maps

Judging from sales, the use of maps in Britain is increasing very rapidly. Part of this must be to do with increasing leisure time, part with more of this time being spent in the open air, and part with recent sales drives by the publishers of maps, especially the Ordnance Survey, which means you can now buy maps in almost every newsagents and tea-shoppe in the country.

The Ordnance Survey

The first OS maps were made at the turn of the nineteenth century to thwart the expected French invasion. The Board of Ordnance surveyed and mapped the south coast so well that it wasn't long before everyone who owned and used land wanted such high-quality mapping for their area. The OS dropped its military links after the Second World War, and from its Southampton base organizes an efficient team of surveyors and cartographers, and an increasingly commercially-minded marketing operation.

The OS is also very helpful if you ask them for information. Every year they publish a catalogue which lists all their publications and services, and tells you how to order maps from them if you have any problem getting them locally. In addition to the catalogue, they have a series of leaflets describing various aspects of their work — No. 2 on the history of the OS is interesting, and there are others on such obscure but fascinating subjects as the edition letters you find in the corner of OS maps, the land parcel numbers on large-scale maps, and how high and low water levels are worked out.

The Maps

Nobody produces better maps of Britain than the Ordnance Survey (though some local large-scale maps produced especially for climbers and orienteerers come close), and OS maps get better all the time. I was sad to see the end of the familiar red-covered one inch maps, especially when the new 1:50,000 maps (2cm to 1km) turned out to be more expensive (and rather bad) enlargements of the same material. But the new (second edition) 1:50,000 maps are clearer and even more accurate than their predecessors. The new green-covered 'Pathfinder' 1:10,000 maps are excellent too, so much clearer than the old blue ones, though when it comes to the quarter-inch (1:250,000) I don't think the new style is so much better: yellow isn't right for built-up areas (grey or dirty orange is much more descriptive), and the new squashed-up typeface for placenames is no improvement.

The bad news is that Ordnance Survey maps are now so

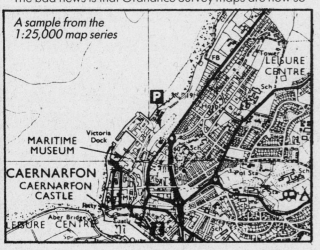

A sample from the 1:25,000 map series

MARITIME MUSEUM
CAERNARFON
CAERNARFON CASTLE
LEISURE CENTRE

expensive you probably won't be able to afford the ones you'd like. When the OS started publishing the new edition of the 1:50,000 maps in 1976 they cost £1.15; now the same sheets cost £3.35, a 291% increase in thirteen years: rather higher than the even the current rate of inflation.

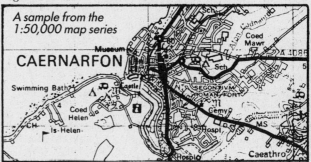

A sample from the 1:50,000 map series

CAERNARFON

The Atlases

The OS do three atlases of Britain, all based on the quarter-inch sheets. The *Motoring Atlas* is published annually (it currently costs £5.95) and is an ordinary sort of large-format paperback book of road maps (you can also buy a spiral-bound version at £7.95). *The Atlas of Britain* (co-published, like the road book, with Temple Press) is a £12.95 hardback with a few climate and geology maps added at the front and thirty pages of history at the end. The latest addition to the range is the *National Atlas* (co-published with Country Life Books at £20.00), which prefaces the maps with eighty pages of text, maps and illustration which are informative and very well written (including a section on 'Politics, Power and the State' by Duncan Campbell of banned television programme fame). The two hardback atlases include a complete index to the placenames on the maps, which is very useful. Again the problem is their cost, though the big book clubs (see page 340) have the OS atlases in their 'backlists', and this is one of those times when book clubs can be a really good idea.

Following the Map

For many years map-reading guides were rather boring and pedantic. John Wilson's guide to Ordnance Survey maps is neither. With plenty of colour photographs and extracts from maps he tells you a great deal about maps, and a great deal about the countryside, its history, geology and geomorphology. Starting with signs and symbols and leading you gently through grid references, direction-finding and contours, you gradually build up an understanding of how the landscape is encapsulated in a map. Soon you'll understand why some people prefer to stand on the top of a mountain looking at the map rather than at the view (but don't join them).

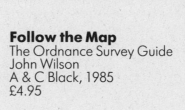

Follow the Map
The Ordnance Survey Guide
John Wilson
A & C Black, 1985
£4.95

Atlases

Good atlases cost a lot of money, but inexpensive atlases are in general pretty useless. The best advice is probably to wait until you (or a group of friends) can buy a decent one, and use the public library's reference room till then. The other problem with atlases is that things change all the time — not so much the rivers and mountains, but the names of countries and towns and the lines of roads and railways.

The best world atlas is indubitably the big *Times Atlas of the World*, whose 500 massive pages are updated every couple of years; the current edition will set you back £55. One level down is the *Philip's Great World Atlas* at £29.95; it's pretty clear and even, though some larger-scale maps of the areas most in the news would be useful. 1989 saw the publication of the *Peters Atlas of the World* (Longman, £29.95), which covers the whole world at the same scale and using a projection which does not distort areas in favour of the middle latitudes as so many atlases do. Topographical, political and vegetation information are all given, based on the latest satellite photography.

For something completely different in the way of world atlases look out for some of the following green-tinted atlases.

The Gaia Atlas

It can be criticized for its emphasis on official figures and technofix solutions, but the *Gaia Atlas of Planet Management* (Gaia was the Greek mother earth goddess — see page 298) is an excellent compilation of all the environmental challenges currently facing us. Illustrated throughout in full colour, it looks at what we are doing to the land, the seas, the atmosphere and each other — and what we can do about it all. For a packaged book the text is remarkably uniform, even though there is a bit of padding here and there, especially in the section introductions. The Foreword by David Bellamy and a good list of sources at the end sandwich 250 pages of easily-assimilated text, diagrams and photographs — a book which should be in every school library, and in daily use by aware teachers. Already five years old, I hope an updated version is in the offing.

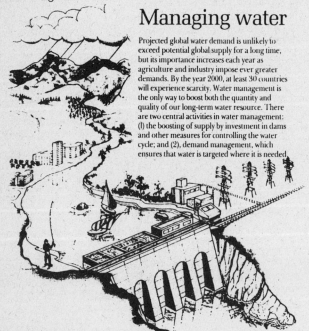

Managing water

Projected global water demand is unlikely to exceed potential global supply for a long time, but its importance increases each year as agriculture and industry impose ever greater demands. By the year 2000, at least 30 countries will experience scarcity. Water management is the only way to boost both the quantity and quality of our long-term water resource. There are two central activities in water management: (l) the boosting of supply by investment in dams and other measures for controlling the water cycle; and (2), demand management, which ensures that water is targeted where it is needed.

The Gaia Atlas of Planet Management
edited by Norman Myers
Pan, 1985
£7.95

The State of the World Atlas

The original *State of the World Atlas* appeared in 1984, an original, provocative and disturbing survey of our world; a very necessary antidote to the conventional stance of most atlases. Now there is a new edition, with some of the same but a lot of additional information, all as up-to-date as it is possible to obtain. The two volumes are an excellent source of straightforward facts about the world, and the extensive notes give much useful background.

The atlas uses a variety of different mapping techniques and symbols to compare the nations of the world, with subjects ranging from military spending to multinationals, urban blight to desertification. New features in the 1987 atlas include an overview of threatened species and a world survey of 'green' concern — though because it is much easier to sign international conventions than abide by them Britain comes out looking much rosier than the reality.

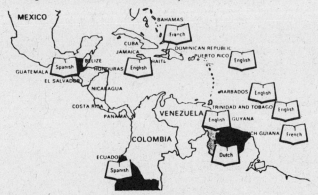

The New State of the World Atlas
Michael Kidron and Ronald Segal
Pan, 1987
£8.95

Women's Worlds

A companion volume to *The State of the World Atlas*, this important source of information makes visible women's experience worldwide. The forty maps cover subjects from violence against women and migrant workers to pornography and protest, with a fascinating final map showing how difficult it is even to get information, since many aspects of women's lives are not considered important by official agencies. There are full notes to each map, and a useful country-by-country statistical table (though the amount of information 'not available' on issues such as education and health is frightening).

Women in the World: An International Atlas
Joni Seager and Ann Olson
Pan, 1986
£7.95

The Peace Atlas

From the team that produced *The Gaia Atlas of Planet Management* comes *The Gaia Peace Atlas*, another essential 270-page megawork. The illustrations are sometimes a little crude and the celebrities rather packed in, but even recent disarmament talks and developments in eastern Europe haven't dated the central message of this illuminating book. If you think war is just about soldiers in foreign countries, *The Peace Atlas* will make you think again about how central war is to the present global economy.

The Gaia Peace Atlas
edited by Frank Barnaby
Pan, 1988
£10.95

Libraries

A good library fulfills a very important role in any community, giving people access to an enormous range of books and other material. Every local authority in Britain provides a library service, which with the back-up of the inter-library loan service and the lending division of the British Library should be able to find you any book or article you request. Items held in stock usually cost nothing to borrow, items which the library does not hold need to be requested from elsewhere — at a cost to you (usually around a pound), and often after a considerable period of time. Most libraries welcome suggestions from readers for books which you would like to see in the library.

Every university and college also has a library or libraries, and many of them allow the general public to use their facilities (though usually not to borrow books) with the written permission of the librarian or a member of staff.

Libraries of Deposit

Under the provisions of the 1911 Copyright Act, six libraries in the British Isles are entitled to receive free copies of any new book published in Britain. It is useful to know about this provision since these libraries hold an almost complete collection of recent books, and since they are not lending libraries it also means that the books are always there to be consulted.

These libraries are the Bodleian Library in Oxford, Cambridge University Library, Trinity College Library in Dublin, the National Library of Wales, the National Library of Scot- land, and the British Library in London. Of these, the most convenient places for members of the public to have access to such a complete collection of material are the British Library and the National Libraries in Edinburgh and Aberystwyth.

Each of these three libraries has a large reading room open to the public, for which you will need to ask for a reader's ticket. You then have access to the library's catalogue (held on microfiche which you use yourself on a special viewer, or for older material still held in bound catalogues); when you have found the material you want to look at, you make your requests and the books are brought to you. The only problem is that the quantities of material each library holds are such that all the books are not kept at the central location.

Founded in 1973, The British Library was created to bring together the British Museum Library, the Colindale Newspaper Library, the Science Reference Library and the National Sound Archive. With a stock of over sixteen million books and countless other collections, this is an invaluable reference source for any London-based researcher. The main humanities reading room is in Great Russell Street (this is where the exiled Karl Marx wrote *Das Kapital*).

The Science Reference and Information Service, formerly the Science Reference Library, at 25 Southampton Buildings (near Chancery Lane tube station) is the British Library's main focus for environmental information. They hold over 200,000 books and 30,000 journals, all of which can be consulted by interested researchers.

The British Library also operates the Lending Division in Boston Spa, South Yorkshire, where there is a reading room. You can't order books directly from them, but your local library will be able to. For a booklet about all of the British Library's many services, write to the main administrative office in Sheraton Street.

The National Library of Scotland holds over three million books, including (like the British Library) virtually everything published in recent years; it has an unrivalled Scottish collection, much of it dating from library's early days as the Advocates' Library. The National Library of Wales has nearly as large a collection, including specialist collections relating to Wales and the Celtic peoples.

The British Library
2 Sheraton Street
London
W1V 4BH
0(7)1-636 1544

National Library of Scotland
George IV Bridge
Edinburgh
EH1 1EW
031 226 4531

National Library of Wales
Penglais
Aberystwyth
Dyfed
SY23 3BU
0970 623816

Some Other Libraries Worth Knowing About

Centre for Human Ecology Library
15 Buccleuch Place, Edinburgh EH8 9LN (031 667 1011 ext 6799)
For ecology and related issues the Centre for Human Ecology at Edinburgh University holds an excellent collection of nearly two thousand books and over two thousand magazines from the 1950s to the present day. Books may now be borrowed; you need to apply in advance to use the library, which is open on weekdays from noon-5pm.

The Fawcett Library
City of London Polytechnic, Old Castle Street, London E1 7NT (01-283 1030 ext 570)
A library specializing in the recent history of women, both in Britain and in the rest of the world. The Feminist Library (5 Westminster Bridge Road, London SE1; Tel: 0(7)1-928 7789) is a women's lending library and resource centre; the Feminist Archive in Bristol (Trinity Road Library, Bristol BS2 0NW; Tel: 0272 350025) is an excellent place to research women's issues.

The Commonweal Library
University of Bradford, Bradford BD7 1DP (0274 733466 ext 8477)
A library of books on nonviolence and nonviolent social change, including a comprehensive collection of Gandhi's works. Also at Bradford is the library of the Bradford School of Peace Studies, a reference library which is possibly the most up-to-date in the country when it comes to materials about current defence issues. For other peace collections consult Declan McHugh's *Peace Information Resources* (see page 268).

Concord Videos and Films

Every teacher and group organizer worth their salt knows about Concord, Britain's largest educational video and film library. An educational charity established in 1959, Concord carries well over 5,000 titles covering an enormous range of contemporary issues; many have been shown as television documentaries. It costs between £8 and £20 to hire a Concord video; £30-70 to buy. Bookings are usually made by letter (as far ahead of the screening date as possible); Concord then sends the titles by first class post in plenty of time for the showing. Their massive catalogue is a fascinating read.

Concord Video and Film Council
201 Felixstowe Road
Ipswich
Suffolk
IP3 9BJ
0473 715754/726012

CONCORD VIDEO AND FILM COUNCIL

Citizens Advice

I was in a real state. I was laid off work with no warning and I was up to my ears in debt. With a young family, all the bills coming in at once and my son in trouble at school, I didn't know where to start. Someone suggested the local CAB and they were terrific. They stopped the gas and electricity being cut off, sorted out my housing benefit and put me on to someone at the social services. I've still got problems, but at least my head is above water.

from a CAB leaflet

In 1989 more than a thousand Citizens Advice Bureaux handled nearly eight million queries. 21% were to do with social security, 19% with consumer problems, 14% with housing, and 11% with family and personal problems. As with the client quoted above, Citizens Advice Bureaux provide a lifeline for many people who feel so bogged down with problems that they don't know where to turn to, as well as answering millions of straightforward questions from people who know that the CAB is probably the best single source of information on a wide range of subjects.

Citizens Advice Bureaux were set up at the beginning of the second world war to provide help and advice in the midst of a welter of new rules and regulations. After the war it was clear that the CABs had become an essential part of helping people deal with the vicissitudes of bureaucracy, and the National Association of CABs (NACAB; Citizens Advice Scotland – CAS – in Scotland) now acts as an advisory (and where necessary pressure) group in important areas of official policy making.

You will find your local CAB in your telephone directory. Check the opening hours, as some smaller ones are not open every day. Don't worry about whether or not they will be able to help you; the service is free and confidential. If they cannot help, they will at least advise you about what you might do next. The subjects they cover include employment, relationship problems, housing and social services, legal problems, debt and other financial problems, and grants and benefits. With laws and regulations changing all the time such areas can be nightmares, and the CAB will almost always be able to help. For general information about CABs contact:

NACAB
115-123 Pentonville
Road
London
N1 9LZ
0(7)1-833 2181

CAS
26 George Square
Edinburgh
EH8 9LD
031 667 0156

How To Complain

How often have you been annoyed when a first-class letter arrives a fortnight late, the bus simply doesn't arrive, the toaster your Aunty Mabel gave you for Christmas keeps setting itself alight, or HM Tax Inspector sends you an assessment for more than you earned last year? And how often have you known what to do about it beyond stamping on the cat and boring the rest of the household sick with the story?

Steve Wiseman's *How to Complain Effectively* is based on years of experience working in the Norwich CAB, so he should know how to do it. Part One of the book gives you some basic principles (What do you actually want? Where do you stand? Who should you go to?); Part Two takes you alphabetically through a range of different areas from airlines and banks to telephone and water services, in each case suggesting what you can do and giving a list of useful addresses. But why does such an important reference book have no index?

*

If a public payphone takes your money but does not allow you a phone call or if you are given a bad line or get cut off, complain to the operator. Your call will either be connected for you, or a refund will be sent to you or credited to your telephone account if you have one. If you cannot get money into the public payphone you could ask the operator to ask the person you are phoning to pay for the call. For inland calls only, this person will be charged at the same rate as for a normal dialled call and not have to pay at the 'reverse charges' rate.

How to Complain Effectively
Steve Wiseman
Optima, 1987
£3.95

Law Centres

Citizens Advice Bureaux usually have legally trained advisers who ca n help you if you need legal advice. Another place to turn to is your local Neighbourhood Law Centre, if there is one. There are currently nearly sixty Law Centres operating in Britain, mostly in inner city areas, and they exist to provide free legal advice and representation to individual groups and people who would otherwise have problems in finding proper legal help. Law Centres have always been under-funded for such a vital service, but continue to provide valuable assistance and a worthwhile challenge to law graduates who want more than a high-sounding title and lots of money.

Law Centres Federation
Duchess House
18-19 Warren Street
London
W1P 5DB
0(7)1-387 8570

If you can afford a solicitor's services with little problem, the chances are that you already have one. If you are looking for one, it is best to take local advice, though the national Law Societies (50-52 Chancery Lane, London WC2A 1SX, Tel. 0(7)1-242 1222; 26-27 Drumsheugh Gardens, Edinburgh EH3 7YR, Tel. 031 226 7411) will be able to help you if you have a problem. If you think you may be eligible for Legal Aid do ask your solicitor before you go ahead with any action.

Civil Liberties

What is a civil liberty?

The National Council for Civil Liberties, for fifty years Britain's foremost watchdog body where domestic civil rights are concerned, lists our basic liberties as:

▶ The right to live in freedom and safe from personal harm.
▶ The right to protection from ill-treatment or punishment that is inhuman or degrading.
▶ The right to equality before the law and to freedom from discrimination on such grounds as disability, political or other opinion, race, religion, sex, or sexual orientation.
▶ The right to protection from arbitrary arrest and unnecessary detention; the right to a fair, speedy and public trial; to be presumed innocent until proved guilty; and to legal advice and representation.
▶ The right to a fair hearing before any authority exercising power over the individual.
▶ The right to freedom of thought, conscience and belief.
▶ The right to freedom of speech and publication.
▶ The right to freedom of peaceful assembly and association.
▶ The right to move freely within one's country of residence and to leave and enter it without hindrance.
▶ The right to privacy and the right of access to official information.

The NCCL works to ensure that these rights are upheld and are not eroded, especially at a time when invasion of personal privacy and official harassment seem to be on the increase. In recent months they have been successful in allowing a young mother in prison to keep her baby rather than handing it to the authorities at four weeks old; travellers in Dorset have been helped to keep the vehicles which are their homes, rather than the police being allowed to sell them; and NCCL have helped Gay's the Word Bookshop to make the customs and excise drop charges against them. Who knows when you might not need their help?

The NCCL publish several invaluable guides (send an sae for a publications list), and a bi-monthly journal called *Civil Liberty*.

National Council for Civil Liberties
21 Tabard Street
London
SE1 4LA
0(7)1-403 3888

Freedom Of Information

How can anybody make informed decisions about major issues without access to appropriate and necessary information? In the USA, where freedom of information legislation is an important aspect of human rights, businesses and government agencies have come to terms with accessibility and accountability; in Britain official and trade secrecy too often results in criminally reprehensible protection for the oppressor and the polluter.

So thank goodness we have the Campaign for Freedom of Information, established in 1984 with the primary goal of replacing current Official Secrets legislation with a US-style Freedom of Information Act. The Campaign is a coalition of more than fifty national organizations, all agreed that unnecessary secrecy must end. Supporters receive the monthly *Secrets* newsletter and access to CFI's well-organized information base and accumulated expertise in prising open the recesses of officialdom.

Campaign for Freedom of Information
3 Endsleigh Street
London
WC1H 0DD
0((7)1-278 9686

Which Organization?

When you have decided that you really need a particular piece of gadgetry or equipment, or that you need to know how best to assess your tax situation or work out where to go on holiday, you may well be thankful for the Consumers' Association, thirty years old this year.

Whatever you think of consumerism (more of which soon), it cannot be denied that the CA with its 'best buys' set against damning criticism for shoddy, dangerous and expensive goods and services has raised the awareness of consumer affairs in Britain to new heights. More than a million people now belong to the association, which has a staff of 400 people working on consumer affairs. The CA is independent, and buys all the products it tests from ordinary shops to ensure that they are selected at random. A large part of the testing is done by members, who send in reports of their experiences — invaluable when it comes to services like insurance and foreign holidays.

The first CA publication was the monthly magazine *Which?*, still going strong. Various supplements and annual bulletins complement the magazine, covering areas such as holidays, cars, gardening and drugs. Most public libraries carry a complete set of back issues of *Which?*, so you should have no problem looking up which iron or washing machine they recommended most recently.

Along with everyone else, the CA is now beginning to take account of consumer interest in green issues: recent *Which?* magazines looked at 'green presents', catalytic converters and acid rain. It will be interesting to see how long it takes them to incorporate details about energy use, recyclability and resource use routinely into their reports. When that happens, and blinkered consumerism gives way to aware conservation, the CA will be doing an even more important job.

Consumers' Association
2 Marylebone Road
London
NW1 4DX
0(7)1-486 5544

Consumer Law

The updated version of the Consumers' Association's *Handbook of Consumer Law* is a very useful book to have at hand if you are frequently involved in buying and selling goods. With the help of a clutch of imaginary buyers and sellers called things like Mr Watercress and Mrs Onion this guide takes you by the hand through the morass of consumer law.

*

If you order goods and want to be able to cancel your order if they do not arrive quickly, you should say when ordering by telling the salesman, mail order firm, or whoever it might be: 'I must have the goods by such and such a date.' The legal phrase is 'time is of the essence'. If the trader does not object, the time of delivery then becomes an essential part of the contract.

A Handbook of Consumer Law
National Federation of Consumer Groups
Hodder and Stoughton, 1988
£6.95

Environmental Information

The London Ecology Centre in Covent Garden is a pleasant place to stop for a drink and a light meal during a day out in the capital; there is a small bookshop, a leaflet rack, and a gallery which houses some fascinating exhibitions. The Ecology Centre Trust also manages a building near Kings Cross, the home of The Environment Council. The Council co-ordinates the activities of voluntary conservation bodies in Britain; it organizes forums for the discussion of important issues and publishes a range of material including a *Directory of Lecturers in Natural History and Conservation* (£3.50).

There is also an Environment Centre in the old Drummond High School in Edinburgh, seedbed of many green activities including a comprehensive computer database of Scottish environmental initiatives called IDEAS (Information Database for Environmental Action in Scotland). Ecoropa, based in mid-Wales, is known mostly for its series of leaflets on important environmental issues from nuclear war and nuclear power to food and health. These readable leaflets, set out in question and answer form, are ideal for handing out to people on the street or leaving in libraries or waiting rooms. Bedford Square Press, the publishing imprint of the National Council for Voluntary Organizations, publishes a number of directories which provide detailed and up-to-date information about green-tinted groups and organizations in Britain. Perhaps the most useful is their *Voluntary Agencies Directory* (1989, £8.95) — it's well worth writing for their catalogue.

The enlightened London borough of Sutton is the first British local authority to provide money for a local environmental information service. The Sutton Centre For Environmental Information deals with requests for information from local schools, businesses and voluntary organizations, and acts as a focus for the setting up and implementation of environmental policies.

London Ecology Centre
45 Shelton Street
London
WC2H 9HJ
0(7)1-379 4324

The Environment Council
80 York Way
London
N1 9AG
0(7)1-278 4736

The Environment Centre
Drummond High School
Cochran Terrace
Edinburgh
EH7 4DP
031 557 2135

Ecoropa
Crickhowell
Powys
NP8 1TA
0873 810758

Bedford Square Press
26 Bedford Square
London
WC1B 3HU
0(7)1-636 4066

The Centre For Environmental Information
24 Rosebery Road
Cheam
Surrey
SM1 2BW
0(8)1-642 3030

Green Publicity

Environmental groups are increasingly wanting to communicate their campaigns and ideas in a more professional manner, but lack the necessary skills and facilities to do so. MediaNatura, a group of environmentalists and media professionals, has been formed to meet this need. It acts as an agency for environmental groups needing professional assistance, and as broker for the expertise and resources of people in the media industry who want to help the green cause.

If your group or business wants to learn about publicity skills from an experienced green activist of many years' standing, Moira Adams offers her Publicity Workshop to groups and individuals, tailoring what she offers to suit her clients' needs.

MediaNatura
45 Shelton Street
London
WC2H 9HJ
0(7)1-240 4936

The Publicity Workshop
36 Belle Vue Drive
Lancaster
LA1 4DE
0524 37592

Environmental Grants

The London-based Directory of Social Change is a useful organization to know about when it comes to money and the green movement, since it publishes a number of useful handbooks and runs training courses in fund-raising and financial management. One of their most recent guides, *Environmental Grants* (1989, £12.50), looks at ways of staking your claim on some of the £180 currently being offered by businesses and grant-making trusts for green initiatives.

Directory of Social Change
Radius Works
Back Lane
London
NW3 1HL
0(7)1-435 8171

Green 'Think-Tanks'

Think-tanks are a quintessential element of late twentieth century life, and the green movement isn't without its own. One of the best known is The Institute For Social Inventions, masterminded by the irrepressible Nicholas Albery, which dispenses with the conventional passive approach of simply dreaming up ideas and works hard to promote initiatives which improve the quality of life in a practical way. The fact that there are always far more ideas than actions may indicate either a slight greenish-ivory-tower mentality or that the world simply isn't yet ready for flashing brake lights and orbiting peace symbols. The Institute holds regular meetings and produces a thought-provoking quarterly journal which costs £12 a year.

And Turning Point is back with us, resurrected as TP2000 so we can all focus on what sort of future we really want. Turning Point is a feast of green information published twice a year in March and August by James Robertson (see page 272) and Alison Pritchard — a subscription costs £5 a year and is well worth it.

The Institute For Social Inventions
24 Abercorn Place
London
NW8 9XP
0(7)1-229 7253

Turning Point 2000
The Old Bakehouse
Cholsey
nr Wallingford
Oxfordshire
OX10 9NU
0491 652346

Environmental Data Services

ENDS' main activity is the publication of a monthly report about new environmental developments, aimed at the business sector but very useful for environmental specialists wanting to stay in touch with corporate environmental policy and practice. Each report provides information on many topics, including early warning of legislative initiatives and case studies of good industrial practice. Subscription rates are currently £145 a year for businesses and organizations, £70 for individuals.

Environmental Data Services
Unit 24, Finsbury Business Centre
40 Bowling Green Lane
London
EC1R ONE
0(7)1-278 4745

ENDS

Right Livelihood

Since 1980 the Right Livelihood Award (often called the Alternative Nobel Prize) has been awarded 'to honour and support work in the most vital areas of human endeavour, beginning with our needs for food and shelter, for a clean environment, for the education of the human spirit and for the preservation of the planet'. The award has now been given to over thirty individuals and organizations: you can read the inspiring speeches of the 'winners' in a book called *People and Planet*, edited by Tom Woodhouse (Green Books, 1987, £6.50).

The Right Livelihood Award
School of Peace Studies
University of Bradford
Bradford
BD7 1DP
0274 737143

Publishers

There are currently more than two thousand active book publishers in Britain, and many more publishers of magazines, journals and periodicals. Even a good bookshop only carries publications from a small selection of publishers, and although many bookshops will make a real effort to order what you want, it isn't uncommon to be told that a book you have seen at a friend's house simply doesn't exist, or to wait so long for a book to arrive that when it does turn up the need or desire for it has faded long ago.

If books are an important part of your life, there are several things you can do to ensure that you know what is currently available, and what is coming up in the near future.

As well as producing what they consider to be important books, publishers also want to sell them. To this end, most publishers (and especially the smaller ones) will be happy to put your name on their catalogue mailing list. This means that once or twice a year you will be able to see what is forthcoming, be able to order a copy if you want to, or be first on the request list at your local public library.

To request their catalogues, you need to know where the publishers who produce your sort of book have their main offices. Your library will have a copy of *The Writers and Artists Yearbook*, published each October by A&C Black (£6.95 for the 1990 edition). This contains the addresses and phone numbers of the major publishers, but for a more detailed listing of nearly 2,000 publishers in Britain you will need Whitaker's *Publishers in the United Kingdom and Their Addresses* (£4.25 for the 1989 edition). As well as addresses and numbers, this tells you the areas in which each publisher specializes, and the International Standard Book Number codes for each publisher (which can help you to find a publisher if you only know the ISBN, of increasing value as computers take over in the book trade).

Your public library will also subscribe to *The Bookseller* magazine, and if you ask for it by name the librarian will almost certainly let you look at the latest six-monthly *Bookseller* forthcoming books issue, published each February and August. This consists of a review of the next six months' new books, listed by subject, followed by publishers' advertisements for their new books — much more comprehensive and forward looking than waiting for the reviews in the Sunday papers.

If you are passionately interested in a particular subject, and have both a detailed knowledge of it and the ability to write interestingly, the chances are that your local paper or regional magazine could use your services as a reviewer. This is also the case if you are involved with the production of a specialist publication. Publishers are understandably wary of handing out free review copies of books to anybody who asks, but are nearly always very helpful if they know that the donation of a copy will result in a review. It is standard practice for a reviewer to keep the book in question if the review is accepted for publication.

If you buy books fairly regularly, you will already know some of the names you can trust in your particular fields of interest. Here (in alphabetical order) are some of the publishers currently producing important books in the areas covered by *The New Green Pages*. This is, of course, only a very small selection.

Ashgrove Practical books on health, education etc.

Blackwell Good on current affairs, especially under the Polity imprint.

Century In recent years Century has become particularly daring in the fields of health and diet, publishing for example many of the standard works on alternative cancer treatment. The Rider imprint is a strong spiritual and esoteric list.

Earthscan The recently-established publishing arm of the International Institute for Environment and Development (see page 242), with an exciting and rapidly-growing green list.

Element Spiritual and practical alternatives; also an important distributor of small UK and US houses.

Gollancz Traditionally a socialist publishing house, rapidly becoming known as publishers of green titles; recently managed to maintain its independence against heavy odds.

Green Books A slightly heavy and artsy green publisher, but with a growing list of interesting titles.

Green Print Britain's most exciting publishers of green titles, with a rapidly-expanding list; an imprint of Merlin Press, who publish heavy politics and culture.

Kogan Page Publishers of very practical books on careers, setting up in business, and similar themes.

Macmillan An extensive list, strong on reference and current affairs.

Methuen A strong list in the social sciences, and their women's list is a good one, especially in feminist fiction.

Optima An imprint of Macdonald, specializing in practical alternatives, health and environmental issues.

Penguin The long-established publishers of quality paperbacks; Viking is their hardback imprint, with some interesting environmental titles. Arkana is their spiritual/esoteric imprint.

Pluto An important publisher in the fields of politics, current affairs and feminism.

Routledge A long-established house, very strong on reference books.

Souvenir Some good practical books and thought-provoking popular philosophy.

Thorsons The market leaders in alternative health and popular esoterics; tend to publish too many books but the gems are worth searching for.

Unwin Hyman A marriage of two long-established houses. A mixed list, strong on practicalities, with good spiritual and feminist lists under the Mandala and Pandora imprints.

Virago An important women's list, now independent again after a flirtation with Chatto, Cape and Bodley Head. The new independence sadly meant the demise of the Covent Garden Virago Bookshop.

Women's Press Publishers of books by women for women, with a strong fiction list and some important non-fiction titles too.

Zed Very good on international current affairs.

Book Distributors

Large publishers operate their own distribution networks; smaller ones obviously can't support their own salespeople and warehousing, so they use distribution services. Here are three that carry a large and important range and who will be happy to send you copies of their catalogues.

Turnaround in London started life as the Publications Distribution Co-operative, a distribution service for many small, alternative and radical book and magazine publishers. After a reorganization five years ago it moved into its current premises and changed its name; now it carries a wide range of publications from 150 publishers, including a number of foreign houses. It distributes the publications of many of the important British voluntary organizations, from Amnesty and CND to Shelter and the SHAC Housing Aid Centre. It also acts as a wholesaler for many titles from larger publishers.

In the first five years of its life Edinburgh-based wholesalers and distributors Bookspeed have built up a formidable reputation for speed and efficiency. They carry a wide range of titles, both hardback and paperback, specializing in green issues, mind/body/spirit, women's and gay book, health and cookery, children's books and Scottish titles.

Both Turnaround and Bookspeed will be happy to consider opening a wholesale account with bona fide groups wanting to sell books on a regular basis, such as local peace groups or wholefood co-operatives — Bookspeed, for example, simply asks for a minimum order of twenty books.

Airlift have been importing independent press American books into Britain for eight years, and have an impressive list with an emphasis on women's books, and spiritual and personal growth. They are also the distributors of the two British feminist publishers, Sheba and Onlywoman.

Turnaround Distribution
27 Horsell Road
London
N5 1XL
0(7)1-609 7836

Airlift Book Company
26-28 Eden Grove
London
N7 8EL
0(7)1-607 5792/5798

Bookspeed
48a Hamilton Place
Edinburgh
EH3 5AX
031 225 4950

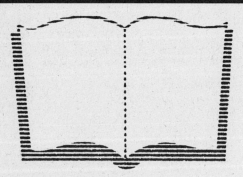

Specialist Bookshops

With so many different book titles currently available, it is getting harder and harder to go into a general bookshop and find the particular book you are looking for. This is why it is important — if books are any part of your life — to know which bookshops are likely to have the book you want. Almost all specialist bookshops will happily send you any book they have in stock (once you've paid for it, of course), and this way you'll get what you want much faster. Many of them also produce catalogues, which provide excellent reference sources for books in your area of interest.

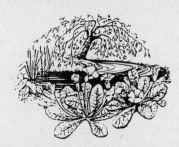

Environment, Green Interests and World Development

Books for a Change in London's Charing Cross Road is *the* shop for green books. Jointly owned by CND, Friends of the Earth, the United Nations Association and War on Want, it carries a very good range of books for quite a small shop, plus recycled commercial stationery. A very comprehensive catalogue lists hundreds of books (send an A4 sae please).

A growing number of bookshops specialize in a combination of green and associated issues from Third World issues and health to personal development. Oxford's Inner Bookshop carries a very good range of books on the environment, green politics, the Third World and radical politics, including American and Australian titles which are hard to get elsewhere; since the last edition of *Green Pages* the Inner Bookshop has taken over the running of EOA Books.

Body and Soul in Edinburgh, the retail side of Bookspeed (see under wholesalers), provides a similar service to the Inner Bookshop. It's a small but very welcoming shop, down by the water of Leith in Stockbridge; B&S also organizes a lecture programme.

For Third World books, Third World Publications (see page 340) provides an excellent mail order service and has a small shop in London's Africa Centre at 38 King Street, WC2; back in Oxford again Worldwise have a very good range of books, plus crafts, tapes and stationery. They are particularly good for children's books; their mail order catalogue is very helpful, and they have also distribute a guide to multicultural fiction for young people called *Books to Break Barriers* (£2.25 plus 50p p+p).

Books for a Change
52 Charing Cross Road
London
WC2H 0BB
0(7)1-836 2315

Body and Soul
52 Hamilton Place
Edinburgh
EH3 5AX
031 226 3066

The Inner Bookshop
34 Cowley Road
Oxford
OX4 1HZ
0865 245301

Worldwise
72 Cowley Road
Oxford
OX4 1JB
0865 723553

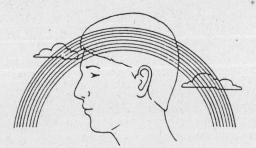

Health, Spirituality and Therapy

For alternative health the best place I know is the Robert Chris part of what is now Watkins and Robert Chris in London's Cecil Court, where the two proprietors know both their books and the subject inside out, Val Chris being knowledgeable in nutrition and relaxation and Peggy Last a homeopathic nurse.

The equivalent for therapy is Brian Wade's Changes Bookshop in Belsize Park; for £1 you can be put on their catalogue mailing list, which will bring you details of hundreds of titles on psychology, psychotherapy, counselling and personal growth. If Changes doesn't have it the chances are that nobody will.

And for spirituality and esoterica there is the famous Watkins, now incorporating Robert Chris, though I think you get a better service from the Inner Bookshop in Oxford (see above) — you could certainly not wish for a more complete catalogue, with 64 closely printed pages covering books on every conceivable aspect of religion and spirituality, occult and yoga. Two bookshops in the south-west offer a very wide range of books on health, spirituality, the occult, ancient Britain and the like, together with a wide range of green titles. These are Gothic Image in Glastonbury, whose mail order catalogue is very comprehensive, and Arcturus in Totnes, shortly to move into a 'green shopping complex' with several other green-tinted retail businesses.

For second-hand books in these esoteric areas, I must also mention Nick Rose's Greensleeves in Cheltenham, which publishes regular catalogues.

Watkins Books Ltd and Robert Chris Books
19 and 21 Cecil Court
London
WC2N 4EZ
0(7)1-836 2182

Changes Bookshop
242 Belsize Road
London
NW6 4BT
0(7)1-328 5161

Gothic Image
7 High Street
Glastonbury
Somerset
BA6 9DP
0458 31453

Arcturus
47 Fore Street
Totnes
Devon
TQ9 5NJ
0803 864363

Greensleeves
23 All Saints Villas Road
Cheltenham
Gloucestershire
GL52 2HB
0242 516273

Women's and Gay

There are two specifically women's bookshops in London, Sisterwrite in Upper Street and the younger of the two, Silver Moon, in Charing Cross Road. Sisterwrite, on two floors, probably has the largest selection of women's titles anywhere in Britain. Silver Moon is more central for visitors to London, and carries a wide range of women's titles. They produce a *Silver Moon Quarterly* with reviews of the important new titles, and the shop boasts its own dog called Biff (after the cards), with her own fan-club.

Since 1979 Gay's the Word has been selling books to the gay and lesbian community, and making the news from time to time as HM Customs seize yet another parcel of gay books which have already been on sale for years. They produce a bi-monthly review which includes reviews of the new books. Complementing Gay's the Word's London-based service is West and Wilde (formerly Lavender Menace) on the edge of Edinburgh's new town.

Sisterwrite
190 Upper Street
London N1 1RQ
0(7)1-226 9782

Silver Moon Women's Bookshop
68 Charing Cross Road
London
WC2H 0BB
0(7)1-836 7906

Gay's the Word
66 Marchmont Street
London
WC1N 1AB
0(7)1-278 7654

West and Wilde
25a Dundas Street
Edinburgh
EH3 6QQ
031 556 0079

Peace and Politics

The most comprehensive range of books on peace and related issues is to be found at Housmans Bookshop in London (see page 268), while the CND Bookshop (page 263) sells a wide range of their own publications.

For socialist and communist books, Central Books in London's Grays Inn Road carries a comprehensive stock specializing in labour history, marxism, development and aid issues, feminism and peace; they also produce useful lists on specific subjects. You can find a wide range of anarchist books at the Freedom Bookshop off Whitechapel High Street; they also publish the fortnightly magazine *Freedom*. A very friendly shop.

Central Books
37 Grays Inn Road
London
WC1X 8PS
0(7)1-242 6166

Freedom Bookshop
Angel Alley
84b Whitechapel High Street
London
E1 7QX
0(7)1-247 9249

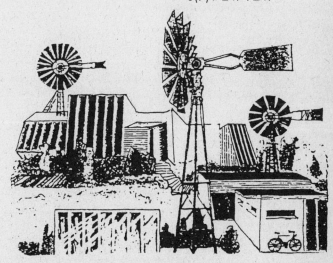

Appropriate Technology

The two best AT bookshops in Britain are the Intermediate Technology Bookshop in London (see page 296) and the Quarry Bookshop at the Centre for Alternative Technology in Mid-Wales (see page 297); both produce catalogues and run a mail order service.

Alternative Bookshops in Britain

From the early 1970s onwards, groups of people throughout the country who were becoming frustrated with the problems of obtaining good and important books decided to take matters into their own hands. Starting with Compendium in North London and followed closely by shops like Mushroom in Nottingham and Grass Roots in Manchester, a chain of alternative bookshops developed rapidly, most of them being organized along co-operative lines and becoming members of the Federation of Radical Booksellers (see opposite).

Mainstream booksellers are certainly getting better at providing a wide range of books, including the areas covered in *The New Green Pages*, but for the more unusual books, a wide range of small press books and magazines, and the services of bookselling staff who really know and love their books, I would recommend that you make the acquaintance of your nearest bookshop in the following list. You will also be putting your money into a co-operative venture which is actively supporting vital small press publishing in Britain.

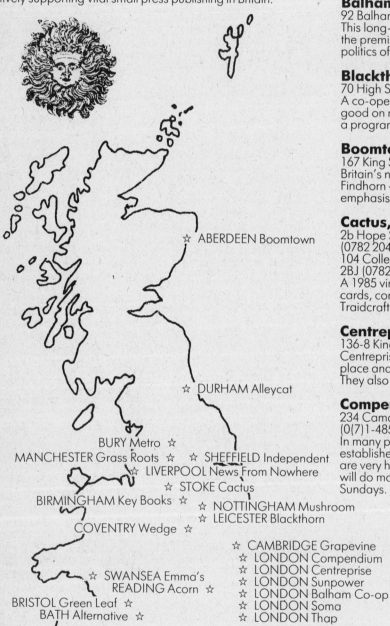

☆ ABERDEEN Boomtown

☆ DURHAM Alleycat

BURY Metro ☆
MANCHESTER Grass Roots ☆   ☆ SHEFFIELD Independent
☆ LIVERPOOL News From Nowhere
☆ STOKE Cactus
BIRMINGHAM Key Books ☆
☆ NOTTINGHAM Mushroom
☆ LEICESTER Blackthorn
COVENTRY Wedge ☆

☆ CAMBRIDGE Grapevine
☆ LONDON Compendium
☆ LONDON Centreprise
☆ SWANSEA Emma's   ☆ LONDON Sunpower
READING Acorn ☆   ☆ LONDON Balham Co-op
☆ LONDON Soma
BRISTOL Green Leaf ☆   ☆ LONDON Thap
BATH Alternative ☆
☆ SOUTHAMPTON October
☆ BRIGHTON Public House
☆ PLYMOUTH In Other Words

Acorn, Reading

17 Chatham Street, Reading RG1 7JF (0734 584425)
A co-operative founded in 1984. Wide range of subjects, plus badges, books, posters, t-shirts, records, recycled paper, community notice board, and a printing service. Mail order.

Alleycat, Durham

85a New Elvet, Durham DH1 3AQ (091 386 1183)
Its full name is the Durham Community Co-op Bookshop, a co-operative founded in 1983. Full range, particularly good on children's books and labour history. Mail order.

Alternative Bookshop, Bath

15 Margaret's Buildings, Bath BA1 2LP (0225 334299)
This pleasant open-plan bookshop in a pedestrian precinct near Bath's famous Royal Crescent is a model for all green bookshops — welcoming and well-stocked, especially strong on health issues.

Balham Food and Book Co-op, London

92 Balham High Road, London SW12 9AA (0(8)1-673 0946)
This long-established co-op sells both food (vegan, cooked on the premises) and books, mostly to do with nutrition and the politics of food.

Blackthorn, Leicester

70 High Street, Leicester L1 5YP (0533 621896)
A co-operative founded in 1981, with a large stock; especially good on modern politics and fiction. Blackthorn also organizes a programme of artistic and literary events.

Boomtown, Aberdeen

167 King Street, Aberdeen (0224 645433)
Britain's northernmost alternative bookshop (if you don't count Findhorn — see page 183); a good general stock with an emphasis on conservation and Scottish issues.

Cactus, Stoke

2b Hope Street, Hanley, Stoke-on-Trent, Staffordshire ST1 5BS (0782 204449)
104 College Road, Shelton, Stoke-on-Trent, Staffordshire ST4 2BJ (0782 744740) (only open during college term time).
A 1985 vintage co-operative; wide-ranging book stock plus cards, community notice board and meeting rooms, and Traidcraft goods (see page 240). Mail order.

Centreprise, London

136-8 Kingsland High Street, London E8 2NS (0(7)1-254 9632)
Centreprise is now nineteen years old and provides a meeting place and projects centre as well as a very good bookshop. They also run a coffee bar and takeaway.

Compendium, London

234 Camden High Street, London NW1 8QS (0(7)1-485 8944/267 1525)
In many people's opinion Britain's best bookshop, this long-established shop has a very large stock on two floors. The staff are very helpful, and Compendium produces catalogues and will do mail order. Well worth a special effort to visit it. Open Sundays.

Emma's Community Bookshop, Swansea

19 Bryn-y-Mor Road, Brynmills, Swansea SA1 4JH (0792 476901)
Opened in 1987 and named after 'Red Emma' Goldman, Emma's specializes in anarchist and socialist titles, though with a good general stock of other green-tinted titles too.

Grapevine, Cambridge

Unit 6, Dales Brewery, Gwydir Street, Cambridge CB1 2LJ (0223 61808)
Largish general stock, specializing in women's and Third World issues. Also has records, magazines and tapes.

Grass Roots, Manchester

1 Newton Street, Piccadilly, Manchester M1 1HW (061 236 3112)
One of the first co-operative bookshops, opened in 1976, now a women's co-op with a wide-ranging stock especially strong in feminism, socialism, black and Third World issues. Knowledgeable staff.

Green Leaf, Bristol

82 Colston Street, Bristol BS1 5BB (0272 211369)
A small bookshop, particularly good on books about health and nutrition. Has an excellent café attached.

Independent, Sheffield

69 Surrey Street, Sheffield S1 2LH (0742 737722)
A co-operative founded in 1979 to provide an outlet for radical left-wing literature; good on green and women's issues and children's books. Community notice board.

In Other Words, Plymouth

72 Mutley Plain, Plymouth PL4 6LF (0752 663889)
A large stock (best in the south-west) of interesting books, particularly strong on feminism, the politics of food, ecology, health and New Age. Community notice board and a children's section.

Key Books, Birmingham

Makepeace House, 136 Digbeth, Birmingham B5 4TR (021 643 8081)
The alternative bookshop in Birmingham, with a particularly good range of green, Third World, black and women's titles. Key Books also sells a range of Traidcraft products (see page 240), cards, posters, t-shirts, mugs, records and recycled paper products.

Metro, Bury

Derby Hall, Market Street, Bury, Lancashire BL9 OAJ (061 761 7584)
Recently moved to larger premises, Metro, a workers' co-op, has a good range, particularly strong on arts, women's issues and poetry.

Mushroom, Nottingham

10-12 Heathcote Street, Nottingham NG1 3AA (0602 582506)
Another early starter, Mushroom has been going since 1972. Their large stock covers a wide range of subjects, especially strong on fiction, travel and esoterica. Postcards, badges, notice board, and a good Christmas catalogue. Mail order.

News from Nowhere, Liverpool

112 Bold Street, Liverpool L1 4HY (051 7087270)
A women's co-operative which is a treat to visit, with a big toybox for children and a completely hassle-free atmosphere — people who can't afford to buy books often come in and read a chapter at a time. Specializes in Irish books.

October, Southampton

4 Onslow Road, Southampton SO2 0JB (0703 224489)
A 1977-founded co-operative; a good range of books plus postcards, posters, badges, t-shirts and mugs. Community notice board and occasional booklists.

Public House, Brighton

21 Little Preston Street, Brighton, East Sussex BN1 2HQ (0273 28357)
An early starter (1973), Public House (it was before it was a bookshop) has been called 'the finest bookshop for its size in the UK'. A wide range of alternative visions, it is also the biggest European outlet for American Indian titles. In addition it runs Dark Horse Press and is involved in the production of educational materials on American native culture.

Soma, London

38 Kennington Lane, London SE11 4LS (0(7)1-735 2101)
Soma specializes in books from and about Asia, Africa and the Caribbean; it co-publishes with Indian publishers and is the UK distributor for a number of them. As well as books the shop sells crafts, cards and posters.

Sunpower, London

83 Blackstock Road, London N4 2JW (0(7)1-226 1799)
Sunpower sells books and much more — wholefoods and crafts too, many of them made locally. Community noticeboard and leaflet counter.

Thap, London

178 Whitechapel Road, London E1 1BJ (0(7)1-247 0216)
Thap's specialist areas include Afro and Caribbean history and writing, Bengali language, multi-cultural children's books and the largest available selection of books about London's East End. Thap also organises writing workshops and local history displays.

Wedge, Coventry

13 High Street, Coventry CV1 5RE (0203 225634)
A very wide-ranging book stock, especially good on green issues, with a good café attached.

Making The Connections

In the past year mainstream bookshop trade has 'hotted up' considerably. It is virtually impossible to know how much new bookshops have affected our sales. We certainly haven't seen a decline. The loyalty of our committed customers is more important than ever — people who come here for books they could get anywhere for the sake of the ones that only we sell. We've kept a steady watch on our sales mix, and radical sales have gone up with the others. While fiction has grown slightly faster, nothing has suffered. We still get people recommended by friends to try us for a book on South Africa or a copy of Engels on the family; there are still people just discovering us.

Independent Bookshop, Sheffield

Making The Connections is a celebration of the first couple of decades of radical publishing and bookselling: a couple of dozen articles by the people who are doing it about the hows and whys, together with a full and detailed directory of nearly 200 bookshops in Britain and Ireland where you can buy a wide range of real books by a variety of authors. The collection chronicles both the highs and the lows — achievement and solidarity, censorship and physical attack — providing real insight into the radical book trade in the late 1980s.

Making The Connections: Radical Books Today

Federation of Radical Booksellers (c/o Housmans Bookshop, see page 268), 1988
£2.50

Book Clubs

If you live far from bookshops, or you like to know which new books are available in a particular subject, you might consider joining a book club. There are nearly seventy book clubs active in Britain, all of which offer books to their members at special or discount prices — a great many of them are in fact subsidiaries of Book Club Associates (owned by W.H. Smith) or The Readers Union (owned by David and Charles). If you know exactly what you want and are on the ball enough to send your form back promptly saying that you don't want the monthly horror or guts-and-thunder 'editor's selection' you can do quite well out of a mainstream book club. After your virtually free first selection and as long as you take the required number of books (usually four) in the first year, you are then free to pick and choose at will, though remember that a hefty postage fee is extra.

As well as the mainstream book clubs, here are a couple that are worth a special mention in *The New Green Pages*.

The Women's Press Bookclub

In the eight years it has been running, The Women's Press Bookclub has built up a membership of seven thousand and is still growing. Virtually every worthwhile new book of interest to women (and many of interest to men too) finds its way into the book club catalogue, and the latest catalogue lists over 150 titles, all at savings of between 25% and 75% on the cover price. You join by paying an initial membership fee (reduced rates for students, claimants and OAPs; special bargains for 'life membership'), then receive a new catalogue every three months listing eighteen selected new titles and a large selection of back titles. You only get the books you order, and they never send anything 'on approval'. A fair sprinkling of the membership is male — they believe that many men give only their initials to avoid embarrassment. Who for?

The Women's Press Bookclub
34 Great Sutton Street
London
EC1V 0DX
0(7)1-253 0009

Readers International

Less than 1% of the novels published each year in English originate outside the 'developed' Western world. If you are interested in hearing the voices of the rest of the world at first hand you might like to subscribe to Readers International who publish a new book every two months, available to subscribers at considerable savings. Novels by some of the world's most gifted writers grace the RI list — Nicaragua's Sergio Ramirez, Linda Ty-Casper from the Philippines, Njabulo Ndebele from South Africa as well as important East European writers such as Czechoslovakia's Ludvick Vaculik. If you take out a year's subscription each hardback novel costs only £6.00 including postage — an excellent way of supporting worthwhile yet 'commercially marginal' literature and a guarantee of at least one good read every couple of months.

Readers International
8 Strathray Gardens
London
NW3 4NY
0(7)1-435 4363

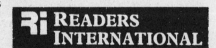

As well as the specialist book clubs, there are also some specialist book services — as distinct from bookshops — worth knowing about.

Schumacher Society Book Service

Part of the Resurgence empire (see page 344), the Book Service includes in its list some otherwise very difficult-to-obtain American-published titles which are well worth reading, like Hazel Henderson's *Creating Alternative Futures* and Kirkpatrick Sale's *Dwellers in the Land*. On the other hand, to cover post and packing they ask for a hefty 20% of cover price on all orders, however large, and only have some titles in stock and will therefore keep you waiting while they order another copy. It's worth having their catalogue to hand, though, which contains more than a hundred titles of general 'green' interest.

Schumacher Society Book Service
Ford House
Hartland
Bideford
Devon
EX39 6EE
023 74 293

Third World Books

Since 1972 Third World Publications has been distributing books from and about the Third World, and are the best single source for books by post on development issues. They produce a range of catalogues — South Africa, Asia, Fiction, Education — packed full of interesting titles from many Third World publishers, aid organizations, radical publishers and campaigning groups. Send an sae for their current catalogues. A large selection of Third World's titles, together with a range of other African books, can be found at The Africa Book Centre in London's Covent Garden; alongside the bookshop is an African art gallery and restaurant.

Third World Publications (Co-op) Ltd
151 Stratford Road
Birmingham
B11 1RD
021 773 6572

The Africa Book Centre
38 King Street
Covent Garden
London
WC2E 8JT
0(7)1-240 6649

Concord

Concord is a Nottingham-based green book supplier specialising in wholesale distribution to small book and wholefood shops, though David Lane will supply books to ordinary mortals too. Concord carries a full range of titles from publishers like Green Print and Green Books, and from organizations including the Green Party and the Vegetarian and Vegan Societies. Orders of over £65 qualify for 35% discount, postage free. Good catalogues.

Concord Books
9 North Road
West Bridgford
Nottingham
0602 816049

Eco-Logic

Sustainable agriculture and holistic housing are two subject areas in which it can be hard to find a good range of books, which is why Andy and Verity Langford have started Eco-Logic Books, a small mail order business. They started Eco-Logic as an eco-logical addition to their permacultural interests (see page 60), subsequently expanding their range to include building and business titles. Eco-Logic 'look for books which offer solutions and don't just state the problems'.

Eco-Logic Books
8 Hunters Moon
Dartington
Totnes
Devon
TQ9 6JT
0803 867546

Directories

A directory is a book or booklet that lists suppliers of goods or services, usually giving full addresses and telephone numbers so that you can easily get hold of whoever or whatever you need. The directory that most of us are familiar with is *The Phone Book* (the new name for telephone directories) which comes in 104 volumes covering the country. A further 23 *Community Phone Books* cover areas of London, and 64 volumes of *Yellow Pages* list businesses and organizations under a wide range of headings. Most libraries hold a complete set of telephone directories, or at least *Yellow Pages*, and of course you have access to any phone number you need by ringing directory enquiries on 192 (142 for London numbers if you're dialling from London; 153 for international directory enquiries). Computerization of directory enquiries might make it quicker to find a number if you've got all the details right, but it makes it very hard to do intelligent lateral thinking.

There are now any number of specialist business directories, most of which cost a lot and don't tell you much more than you already knew. There are also, however, a growing number of local and regional directories in Britain designed to give people access to the sorts of things contained in *The New Green Pages*, but on a local level.

Some only ever happen once, then apparently disappear, like the *Alternative Merseyside Directory*. Some projects, like *Green Pages South-West* (listed in the first edition of *Green Pages*) start collecting data but never get into print. There have been several national 'alternative directories', like the various editions of Nick Saunders' *Alternative England and Wales* in the 1970s, Brian John's *Alternative Wales* and the idiosyncratic *Alternative Scotland* of 1975. The directories listed on these pages are ongoing projects designed to keep you up-to-date with all the good things that are happening in your area.

The Birmingham Green Guide

Friends of the Earth (Birmingham), 54 Allison Street, Digbeth, Birmingham B5 5TH (021 632 6909)
Here is the bees' knees of green guides. Compiled by the local Friends of the Earth group and financially supported by the City Council, *Birmingham Green Guide* is a comprehensive 84-page listing of everything in the city that you might think of as being green — and more. There are excellent sections on green businesses, environmental problems, health, and many other areas. This is a truly professional production, carefully thought out and very user-friendly (though the index is a bit of a disappointment); lots of photographs and informative adverts complement the text. If you're thinking of producing a directory for your city and can get the support of your local authority to help you, get hold of a copy of the *Birmingham Green Guide* to inspire you. It costs £4.95, and really is worth it.

Environmental action

Working with the City Council

Although we can all make our individual contribution towards maintaining the quality of our local environments, ultimate responsibility for care and maintenance of the local areas does rest with Birmingham City Council. They have the statutory responsibility and the resources to implement that duty. This section outlines the various ways in which you can contact the Council, offer ideas, suggestions or complaints to the Council representatives, and perhaps take part in the decision-making process which works for the benefit of local people and the improvement of the local environment.

ideas and views into the main service committees of the City Council.

COMMUNITY DEVELOPMENT OFFICERS

The Recreation and Community Services Department have a Community Development Officer at each of their 12 area offices. Their role is to provide assistance and support to community groups, enabling them to become more active locally. The Community Development Officers are also a good source of information on what community activities are happening in the local area. Find out where your nearest area office is from the phone book, library or Neighbourhood Office. If you live in Council accommodation, the

The Gloucestershire Directory

Co-operative Elements Ltd, 20 Gloucester Place, Cheltenham, Gloucester GL52 2RN (0242 577836)
The 1989 edition of *The Gloucestershire Directory* is the fourth, listing hundreds of addresses and phone numbers of people and organizations involved in a wide range of worthwhile activities. It includes community information like local and regional councillors, resources on work and unemployment, women's groups, facilities for children, alternative health and therapy, and much more. Available in all local bookshops (or from the publishers if you have problems finding it), the *Directory* costs £1.50 (£1 for the unemployed if bought at an unemployment centre). The *Directory* people have opened an information centre at the above address in Cheltenham town centre, open all day on Wednesday, Thursday and Friday, and Saturday mornings — look out for them.

CONSERVATION AND THE ENVIRONMENT NATIONAL ADDRESSES

DIRECTORY FOR THE ENVIRONMENT
"..is the most wide-ranging and detailed guide of its kind in Britain..it provides up-dated information on nearly 1,000 organisations involved in activities concerned with the physical and human environment..

WORLD WILD FUND FOR NATURE	04834 26444
Panda House, Weyside Park, Guildford GU7	
FORESTRY COMMISSION	031 334 0303
231, Corstorphine Road, Edinburgh EH12 7AT	
MEN OF THE TREES	0342 712 536
Turners Hill Road, Crawley Down, West Sussex	
WOODLAND TRUST	0476 74297
Autumn Park, Dysart Road, Lincs NG31 6LL	
RAMBLERS ASSOCIATION	01 582 6878
1-5 Wandsworth Road, London SW18 2LJ	
PEDESTRIANS ASSOCIATION	01 735 3270

Oxford Grapevine

PO Box 0, 34 Cowley Road, Oxford OH4 1HZ (0865 240090)
Inspired by *The Gloucestershire Directory* and similar in format, the 1989-90 *Oxford Grapevine* is the third edition of an annual publication. Tastefully printed on recycled green paper, the 84-page booklet costing 95p covers health and therapy, peace and green groups, food, community organizations, women's groups, Third World, a good section on alternative goods, shops and services, publications and further information. As it says on the back cover, it 'finds the people the other Pages don't reach!' An invaluable resource if you live in Oxfordshire.

GREEN & ENVIRONMENTAL GROUPS

BBONT Protection of wildlife in Berks, Bucks & Oxon. 3 Church Cowley Rd, Oxford:........775476 [+ appeals office: 715835]
British Trust for Conservation Volunteers Midweek, w/end & week long conservation projects. 36 St Mary's St, Wallingford OX10 0EU:.................................39766
Conservation Society. John Herrivel, 75 Lonsdale Rd, Oxford:..................50558
Earth'n'Wear Non polluting, recycled & cruelty free products. 15 Cowley Rd, Oxford:..................250273
Fauna & Flora Preservation Society (Oxford Branch). Meetings & fundraising for wildlife in danger. c/o Louise Butler, Zoology Dept. South Parks Rd, Oxford:..................56788
Friends of the Earth, Oxford Branch. More rational use of earth's resources. 26 Church View, Freeland:..................882148
Green Anarchist. National magazine. 19 Magdalen Rd, Oxford OX4 1RP
Green C N D. Jenny Linsdell, 14 Alexandra Rd, Oxford:..................246079
Green Line. National mag. of green politics & lifestyle. 34 Cowley Rd, Oxford:..................245301
Greenpeace Campaign against pollution. c/o Sandy Kennedy, 17 Western Rd, Oxford:..................249020
Greenpeace Support Group. c/o Mike Carter, 10 Hurst St, Oxford:..................728120 [or J.Fitzwilliams:..................250392, or S Billings: 240090]

Sheffield Green Pages

Systemic Issues, 34 Four Wells Drive, Sheffield S12 4JB (0742 474540)
This wide-ranging directory, published in November 1988, covers everything from choices in education to spirituality based groups, via health, shopping and a couple of dozen other green-tinted categories. *Sheffield Green Pages*, with its colourful cover and 56 pages printed (of course) on recycled paper, is neat and handy, indispensable for any Sheffield Green, though the tiny print size which is used to squeeze in as many groups as possible is a little hard on the eyes. Due to be updated in 1990, *Sheffield Green Pages* costs a very reasonable £1.30. Systemic Issues are also working on a *Norwich Green Pages*, to be published early in 1990.

CONSERVATION/ENVIRONMENTAL GROUPS

British Trust for Conservation Volunteers, 14-18 West Bar Green, S1 (755087)- pond clearance, tree planting.......
Chestnut Centre, Country Park, Otter Haven & Owl Sanctuary, Castleton Rd, Chapel-en-le-Frith, Derbyshire (0298 814099)
Clean Rivers Campaign, Chaucer Yard, Countess Rd, S1 4JE
Conservation Corps, c/o University Students Union, Western Bank, S10 3EF (724076) not restricted to just students.
Council for the Protection of Rural England (Sheffield branch),22 Endcliffe Crescent S10 3EF (665822)
Dronfield Natural History Society, Anne Toomey (95-412279)
The Fulwood Society, 44 Chorley Rd, S10 3RJ (302551), to protect the area around Fulwood

Gleadless Valley Wildlife Group, Sheila Walker (585217)
Grenoside Conservation Society, 11 Greno Gate, Grenoside, S30 3PY (465365)
Hallam Conservation Volunteers, 18 Foxwood Grove, S12 2FN (748548)·practical projects not just Hallam

The Green Guide to London
May Tree Cottage, Crossways, West Chiltington, West Sussex RH20 2QY (07983 2167/0(7)1-834 0421)
I've been hearing about putative London green guides for years, but this one, to be published by Simon and Schuster in the early summer of 1990, looks like being both comprehensive and eminently practical. It has been compiled with the active involvement of Friends of the Earth and London's 33 borough councils, and is edited by writer and broadcaster Bill Breckon. A full review in the next *Green Pages*. . .

Green Leaves
North East Environment Network, 6 Higham Place, Newcastle upon Tyne NE1 8AF (091 232 8183)
Produced for European Year Of The Environment with financial assistance from EYE and the Countryside Commission, *Green Leaves* shows the wealth of green organisations which exist in the North East, some of which are very pioneering in their approach. Nearly 450 organizations are listed, from railway preservation societies to mountaineering clubs; each entry gives details of the organization's aims and activities, with full contact names, addresses and telephone numbers. The arrangement is alphabetical, with a subject index so you can find what you need. Critical it isn't (entries are based verbatim on questionnaire returns), but comprehensive it certainly is. For 160 pages the price, at £3.95, is very reasonable.

Tyneside Urban Wildlife Project
Centre for Continuing Education, University of Newcastle upon Tyne,
1A Windsor Terrace, Newcastle upon Tyne NE2 4HE
091-232 8511 x2792

Tutor/Organiser Dr Veronica Woolley
Status Educational

Aims To provide educational courses at all levels in urban ecology.

Activities Offering short courses, depending on demand, along the following lines: elementary wildlife courses (animals and plants found in the area and their niche in the local environment); wildlife workshops, including practical projects and guided

Green Fax
Green Crane Press, 17 Queen's Crescent, Glasgow G4 9BL (041 332 4924)
Green Fax, 'A Holistic Handbook for Alternative Scotland', appeared early in 1990. If you're just looking for names and addresses then *Green Fax* may be just what you need, but 'Handbook' it isn't. Though the number of entries looks impressive there are, for example, scores of identical references to the same few natural health centres listed under all the different therapies they offer. It's very heavy on the health and personal growth front, to be expected from authors also involved with the Glasgow Natural Health Centre. Just worth the outlay if you live in Scotland, I hope the second edition will be more balanced and user-friendly.

CONSERVATION
1550 *AYR ROAD COMMITTEE (environmental group against new road)*, Alice Mosley, 58 Norham Street, Glasgow G41.

1551 *BELLARMINE ENVIRONMENTAL COMMUNITY RESOURCE CENTRE*, 42 Cougler Road, Glasgow G53 6EW. Tel: 041 880 7630.

Cruelty-Free Nottingham
The Rainbow Centre, 180 Mansfield Road, Nottingham (0602 585666)
People come to green issues from a range of concerns; Nottingham's green guide arose from a concern with animal welfare and healthy cruelty-free eating. *Cruelty-Free Nottingham*, produced in March 1989, is based on the painstaking researches of the folk at The Rainbow Centre, a peace and environment information centre which has also produced useful guides on recycling and women's rights in Nottingham. In this 52-page A5 guide, details about vegetarian restaurants, alternative health, cruelty-free cosmetics and much more local information is interleaved with articles about 'What's Wrong With McDonalds' and 'Don't Bother With Boots'. *Cruelty-Free Nottingham* costs £1.

The Green Guide To York
One World, 17 Goodramgate, York YO1 2LW (0904 32896)
The Green Guide to York, published in May 1988, is an easy-to-use sixteen-page guide to green resources in the city, covering fifteen subject areas from wholefoods and recycling to furniture and clothing. I didn't know whether to be flattered or annoyed that the York guide quotes *Green Pages* book reviews verbatim without acknowledgement, but I chose to be flattered. The guide costs 30p; the compilers are hoping to produce a revised edition in the near future.

The Avalonian Guide to Glastonbury
5 High Street, Glastonbury, Somerset BA6 9DP (0458 34786)
Similar to the above directories, but doubling as a guidebook too, is the *Avalonian Guide to Glastonbury*. Forty pages of annotated entries covering everything you'd expect from healing to esoteric tools via food and 'kidz', plus articles on the Tor, the Chalice Well, the Glastonbury Thorn and so on, photos and maps. At £2.30 this is excellent value; the 1989 guide is the third edition.

Greenwave
69 Cambridge Road, Oakington, Cambridge CB4 5BG (0223 233200)
A full-scale directory, updated every year or couple of years, is one way to provide local green information. With everything changing so rapidly, however, another way is to include this information in a regional green magazine, where it can be updated bi-monthyl or quarterly. *Greenwave*, the green magazine for the Cambridge area, has been published regularly every three months since 1984, blending articles on a wide range of issues with an up-to-date and comprehensive listing of events, networks and alternative health services. The combination works extremely well. *Greenwave* costs 50p an issue from green outlets in and around Cambridge, or an annual subscription costs £2.50.

Bodymind
18 Sawkins Avenue, Great Baddow, Chelmsford, Essex (0245 356056/469158)
Bodymind is a magazine-cum-directory published quarterly by a network of green-minded people in the Chelmsford area. The magazine (40p an issue, tastefully produced on recycled paper) contains articles on a range of subjects from health and wholefood cookery to green politics and lifestyle, and at the end of each issue lists a wide range of green resources together with a calendar of activities in the forthcoming three months. Bodymind also organize a range of events, workshops and exhibitions — a very lively group of people.

Green Umbrella
34 Quebec Road, Ilford, Essex IG1 4TT (0(8)1-554 2553)
Green Umbrella is a friendly and informative bi-monthly newsletter and green directory for the north-east edges of London, very similar in format to *Bodymind*. As well as articles and local adverts it carries reports from local green groups, a diary of green events, and 'Green Friend', a means for readers to get in contact with local like-minded people. Each issue costs 30p for 32 pages; an annual subscription costs £2.70.

Cahoots

PO Box 12, Levenshulme PDO, Manchester M19 2EW
(061 225 0670)
Cahoots, which has recently celebrated its seventh birthday, is an excellent magazine: professional, regular, informative and well edited and designed. Subtitled 'North West Guide to Alternatives', it covers an area roughly from Chester to Lancaster with forays eastwards into Yorkshire and Derbyshire. As well as articles and newsshorts on a wide range of subjects, each issue incorporates a directory subdivided into the usual 'body and mind', 'creativity and fun' and so on, and a diary of forthcoming events. At £1.25 an issue, *Cahoots* is very good value, and provides an excellent model for other regional publications.

CENTRES & COMMUNITIES

BEECHWOOD COLLEGE LTD.
is a co-operatively managed residential venue aimed at a wide audience with related interests. These include group development, the examination of alternative structures for the organisation of work; and involves the work of national organisations who are interested in social welfare and development. There are residential facilities for 43 people, mostly in twin rooms, and other amenities include a bar, sauna, seven acres of gardens and woodland, and a walled garden cultivated organically. For more details,

in exchange for part-time work in garden. Committed persons taken for year-shorter periods negotiable.
Contact: Send sae to Mehr Fardoonji, Oakcroft, Malpas, Cheshire. Tel: 0948-860213.

THE PAVILION NEIGHBOURHOOD CO-OPERATIVE
is a Tennis and Social Club which is aiming to provide a friendly centre for sports and social events in the Chorlton and Whalley Range area. Tennis, Table Tennis, regular folk-music evenings and a wholefood snack/catering service both on/off the premises. New members welcome. Closed Mon. and Tues. during Autumn and Winter.
Contact: 299 Brantingham Road, Chorlton, Manchester 21. Tel: 881 0819.

SPAIN — CORTIJO ROMERO
A self-development centre in the foothills of the Sierra Nevada running 1 and 2 week courses throughout the year in Rebirthing, Yoga, Music and Dance. Luxury accommodation, swimming pool, excellent value.
Contact: Marie Fraser-Nash, 9 Hatchpond Road, Poole, Dorset BH17 7LQ. Tel: 0202 699581.

Connections

128 Byres Road, Glasgow G2
A twice-yearly magazine which tries valiantly within the resources available to be like *Cahoots*, with an emphasis on healing, therapy and the arts, though it does make forays into politics now and then. The directory section included in each issue is the best guide there is to the alternative scene in Scotland. 95p an issue; subscriptions £2.30 a year.

CENTRES/RESOURCES

BRAMBLES WHOLEFOODS
45 Huntly Street
Inverness
(0463) 223550
Wholefoods, herbs and spices, books and periodicals.

CENTREPEACE
143 Stockwell Street
Glasgow G1 4LR
041-552-8357
Third World craft shop, Development Education, Lending Resource, Library, Information Centre.

CHANGES BOOKSHOP
340 West Princes Street
Glasgow G4 9HF
Fiction, Left, Women, International, Gay, Anarchist, Health, Rights, Ecology, Therapy, etc. Plus Mags, Cards, Posters, Badges. Open 10-6, Mon.-Sat.

FRIENDS OF THE EARTH
16 Newton Terrace
Glasgow G3
041-339-8677

LOTHLORIAN
Corsock
Castle Douglas
Kirkcudbright
Organic gardening and smallholding, therapy.

ONE WORLD CENTRE
Lothian Road
Edinburgh
Wholefood, books, Third World crafts etc.
Drop in cafe.

SALISBURY CREATIVE HEALTH CENTRE
2 Salisbury Road
Edinburgh EH16 5AB
031-667-5438
Classes in pottery, meditation, yoga, t'ai chi, dream groups.

SAMYE DZONG
1416 Dumbarton Road
Glasgow G14
Tibetan Buddhist Centre

CAMPAIGN FOR NUCLEAR DISARMAMENT
420 Sauchiehall Street
Glasgow G2
041-331-2878

Community Directories

In recent years several local authorities in Britain, recognizing that access to information is a crucial part of involvement in community affairs, have published resource guides of their area. Of course, you can find out about local authority services anywhere if you are determined enough, and many authorities publish leaflets and booklets about their services, but not many have gone the whole way and produced a comprehensive and accessible guide.

One such guide, which provides a model for what can be done, was *The Calderdale Resource Guide*, sponsored by Calderdale Metropolitan Borough Council and compiled by the Halifax-based Community Education Training Unit (CETU). Produced in loose-leaf format in a binder (so that it can easily be updated), it covered a wide range of resources available to anyone involved in setting up or running a community group or voluntary organization in the Calderdale area of West Yorkshire. The sections covered 'Getting Started', 'Getting Organized', 'Getting Yourselves Known', 'Getting Involved' and 'Getting Training and Support', and the clearly-written advice was detailed without being overwhelming.

CETU would be glad to hear from any other local authority or community group interested in producing a community directory and resource guide, and is planning to produce a handbook on the subject.

Community Education Training Unit

Trinity Royd Cottage
Blackwall
Halifax
HX1 2EH
0422 357394

Survivors London

Many ageing hippies who were around the country's capital in the early seventies will remember the eccentric but helpful *Alternative London*. With the individualistic enterprise culture of the eighties I half suspected that the reincarnation of such a project was now beyond the realms of possibility. But no.

In November 1989 Alternative Press published *Survivors London*, a comprehensive and common-sense handbook about how to get the most out of London using the minimum of resources (meaning, in most cases, money). Thirty-six tight-packed (but very readable) sections cover everything from finding somewhere to live to appropriate technology in the city, via sex, drugs, food, computers, green politics, agitation and masses more. *Survivors London* is a model of how important information can be made as accessible as possible; if every British city had such a guide the changes needed to rebuild a sane and sustainable future would be so much the easier to implement. A few things are missing — why the London Food Commission doesn't feature in the 'Food' section I can't imagine — but tiny potential improvements apart I have nothing but praise for this vitally important handbook.

Survivors London

Mike Considine, Kate Brady and Marijke Acket
Alternative Press, 1989
£4.95

Magazines

1989 was the year of the green magazine, when it dawned on publishers large and small up and down the country that there were important things to be said and people out there (they hoped) just waiting to fork out to hear them. 1990 will be the year when some of these dreams are shattered, and it may well be that some of the newer publications never see their first anniversary.

Books may be able to teach you much of what you can learn by way of the written word, yet by their nature they cannot keep you informed of the latest developments in your particular field of interest. They may well also go into more detail than you need, as well as being beyond your financial means.

These considerations can often be fulfilled by good magazines and journals, and to my mind a good magazine should fulfill several important functions:

▶ It should fulfil an obvious need, and know the sort of person it is aimed at.
▶ It should always be readable, and sometimes fascinating. It should know what it's talking about.
▶ It should give space to different points of view on whatever subjects it covers, but be clear about where it stands on such issues.
▶ Ideally it should give space to readers' letters, lively reviews, relevant illustrations and imaginative advertising.

Not much to ask . . .

In *New Green Pages* you will find magazines dealing mostly with specific issues within the relevant sections. On the following two pages are listed in alphabetical order a dozen or more magazines which cover a wider range of issues, all of which (if you can afford them) are worth subscribing to. Subscription rates apply to early 1990 and are for comparison; don't assume that they haven't gone up since.

The Ecologist

The Ecologist
Worthyvale Manor Farm, Camelford, Cornwall PL32 9TT (0840 212711)
The old faithful bi-monthly, first published in 1970 (one of the first issues contained the famous 'Blueprint for Survival') and still going strong, though it has definitely moved upmarket in recent years to appeal to a more academic and international clientele. Good long readable articles, usually on a theme; reviews; letters; classified adverts (the fact that the 'Call for Papers' section is often the longest shows the emphasis of the magazine). Very male-dominated, but important reading for any professional in the field of ecology and conservation. £18/year (students £15).

Ecos: A Review of Conservation
Packard Publishing Ltd, 16 Lynch Down, Funtington, Chichester, West Sussex PO18 9LR (0243 575621)
The magazine of the British Association of Nature Conservationists (see page 63), which is worth joining (£12.50/year; £10 if you're unwaged or a student) for the magazine alone. *Ecos* is the liveliest little magazine on the conservation scene, a bulky 64 pages to each issue full of very readable articles, reviews, letters, and invariably a good and thoughtful editorial. It specializes in controversial environmental and conservation issues like acid rain, the trade in wild animals and plants, deforestation and the like, but does not wallow. *Ecos* is always a welcome ray of light in what could be a very depressing area.

The *Environment* Digest

Environment Digest
Worthyvale Manor Farm, Camelford, Cornwall PL32 9TT (0840 212711)
From the same stable as *The Ecologist* comes this incredibly useful digest of environmental news. You don't have to scour the papers and journals for every interesting news story, because the researchers at *Environment Digest* do it for you. Twelve closely-printed pages every month bring you the latest stories in the fields of land use, countryside, food and health, nuclear power, politics, pollution, and Third World issues, culled from a couple of dozen newspapers and weeklies. £15 a year (£12 for the unwaged).

environment now

Environment Now
Hyde Park Publications, 27 Kensington Court, London W8 5DN (0(7)1-937 3535/7)
Now in its third incarnation, *Environment Now* has turned into a lively large-format full-colour environmental news magazine. The design and layout still leave something to be desired, but the content is generally informative and stimulating. Regular columns cover Building, Consumer Choices, Countryside, Energy, Farming, Fashion, Food and Drink, Green Home, Health, Money and Motoring, while Marion Shoard's 'Lie of the Land' column and Roger Smith's view from Scotland are always worth reading. The editorial opinion can sometimes veer towards the opinionated, but I'd rather have it that way than bland. You can buy it for 95p a month from health food shops, Safeway supermarkets and other selected green-tinted outlets; an annual subscription costs £12. Very good value.

The Globe
PO Box 519, Sheffield S11 8EQ (0742 420379)
The first issue of *Globe: The Magazine For The Green Future* appeared in November 1989, and its mixture of informed news coverage, humour and zappy design appealed to me immediately. Though targeted primarily at the north of England (the subtitle is '8 weeks of sustainable living in and around Leeds, Sheffield, Manchester and The World'), it isn't afraid to take on any and every green issue. *Globe* incorporates a useful eight-page 'Green Pages' directory of organisations and events and a lot of fascinating adverts. I sincerely hope that this one makes it through to the next edition of *Green Pages*. Bi-monthly £1 from northern green outlets, or an annual subscription costs £6 (£5 unwaged).

Green Anarchist
Box H, 34 Cowley Road, Oxford OX4 1HZ

A necessary and constant prod to complacent greens, *Green Anarchist* raises important issues and stirs them. *GA* tends to be confrontative, and involves itself in a great deal of infighting, but it still makes for interesting and worthwhile reading. I like the first-person directness, and could do with less of the 'This is in reply to the two dumb letters slagging off the . . .'. £8 for 10 issues.

Green Drum
18 Cofton Lake Road, Birmingham B45 8PL

A lively and long-lived quarterly, now in its fifteenth year, *Green Drum* airs a wide range of green issues with an emphasis on the practical. Based in the Midlands, the 'what's on' and advert sections tend to be regionally-oriented towards that area, but the coverage of important issues is excellent. The reviews are good, and in each issue is a 'Green-Eye' data card, which build up to create a very useful environmental reference library. 70p a copy; subscription rates are £3.50 for four issues (£3 for the unwaged).

Green Line
34 Cowley Road, Oxford OX4 1HZ (0865 724315)

Essential reading for anybody interested in green issues, *Green Line* is the most lively and readable guide to current events on the leading edge of the green movement. The standard of writing is high, the reviews good, the debate generally excellent, though of recent months the editorial anti-waffle department seems to have been slipping a little. Lots of small ads and little titbits of news to whet your appetite. Being a monthly, its events calendar is actually useful, and at £6/year (£5 unwaged) *GL* is very good value.

Green Magazine
Northern and Shell plc, PO Box 381, Millharbour, London E14 9TW (0(7)1-987 5090)

Coming from the same stable as *Penthouse* and *Forum*, *Green Magazine* is glossy, colourful and packed with information and adverts. It's good to see a new environmental title in newsagents and station bookstalls, though it reads and looks rather like a wildlife magazine and doesn't yet have much of an identity. I wasn't impressed with mistakes like the confusion between John and Chris Patten in the first issue, or with their silly review of *How To Be Green*; it also makes a great deal of being 'printed on environment friendly paper', which unlike most other green magazines *doesn't* mean recycled. The magazine runs a Green Gremlin Award for companies, products and services which fall noticeably short of the green ideal; the magazine could be in danger of becoming a candidate. £1.95 every month; subscriptions £19.95 for 13 issues (must go by lunar months . . .).

Green News
PO Box 708, Bradford-on-Avon, Wiltshire BA15 1FA

Like *Globe*, the first issue of *Green News* appeared late in 1989. Also like *Globe*, *Green News* is essentially a regional magazine with wider horizons, this time concentrating on news and events from central southern England and the Bath/Bristol area. The magazine (really more of a newsletter) is well-written and attractively designed, and in its 'help needed' section could perhaps afford to be slightly less apologetic about what has been and what can be achieved by a regional publication of this sort. The Local News Insert and local adverts are useful, and *Green News* hopes to expand its size and readership as more money becomes available. 50p an issue; subscriptions £3.00 for four quarterly issues.

I-to-I
92 Prince Of Wales Road, London NW5 2NE (0(7)1-267 7085)

Another late 1989 birth, this time the brainchild of Anglo-Greek entrepreneur and visionary Yannis Andricopoulos (one of the founders of the well-known 'holistic centre' on the island of Skyros), *I-to-I* has grand plans. Subtitled 'The Alternative Monthly', this large-format magazine comprises an engaging mixture of green-tinted features covering the whole spectrum of art, health, environment, personal growth and consumer concerns. In an attempt to find its place alongside the *Spectators* and *New Statesmans* of the publishing world it has had to start big and brave; being as yet but new-born it must find its feet in terms of content and style, but if it can keep going there's certainly a place for it. £1.85 a copy or £20 for an annual subscription.

New Internationalist
120-126 Lavender Avenue, Mitcham, Surrey CR4 3HP (0(8)1-685 0372)

'*New Internationalist* exists to report on the issues of world poverty and focus attention on the unjust relationship between rich and poor worlds; to debate and campaign for the radical changes necessary within and between nations if the basic needs of all are to be met; and to bring to life the people, the ideas and the action in the fight for world development.' So it says on page 1 of each monthly issue, and *NI* certainly makes the practical concerns of the real world very accessible. Each issue deals with a theme — population, South Africa, sexual politics, health — with articles, *NI*'s inimitable graphics, well-laid-out pages giving The Facts, and A Second Look, a devil's advocate critique of one of the leader articles. Plus a regular Update feature, letters, reviews, classifieds, and a profile of a particular country each month. £18.40 for twelve issues, though they run a continuous 'special offer' of three free issues plus a world map for first-time subscribers.

Resurgence

Ford House, Hartland, Bideford, Devon EX39 6EE (023 74441 293)

Now in its tenth year, *Resurgence* is the only general-interest 'green' magazine to have survived intact right through the last decade, *Vole* having died a fairly early death and *Undercurrents* taken within the *Resurgence* fold. With a fat 48-page issue every other month, the magazine is getting more interesting and less esoteric by the issue, recovering some of the humour and lightness that *Undercurrents* had when it was on form. The articles cover all sorts of alternative subjects, with regular features from 'names' like Kirkpatrick Sale and Maurice Ash. Very male still, and overly self-congratulatory; good reading nonetheless. The reviews and ads (especially the small ads) are particularly good. Part of the Satish Kumar empire, which also includes Green Books, The Schumacher Society and the Schumacher Book Service, and has a strong involvement in The Small School. *Resurgence* costs £14/year, with a free book for first-time subscribers.

Whole Life

Sanctum Outdoor Services Ltd, 393 Station Road, Wallsend, Tyne and Wear NE28 8DT (091 234 0259)

Now in its second year, *Whole Life: The New Magazine of Alternative Choices* has found its niche and deserves to flourish. Forty pages of informed writing and attractive graphics cover the whole range of what are these days called 'lifestyle issues': environment, healthy eating, personal growth and alternative health, but unlike some lifestyle magazines *Whole Life* has a clear political conscience too. Fascinating classified adverts, informed reviews and a discriminating 'Grapevine' section on new products add to an already vital and useful bi-monthly. 70p an issue; subscriptions £4.20 for six issues.

Magazines from Abroad

There are of course many magazines worth dipping into if they come your way, especially from North America and Australia, but there's no room here other than to mention a couple of quarterly titles that I look forward to reading each issue.

SOCIAL ALTERNATIVES

Social Alternatives

Department Of Government, University of Queensland, St Lucia, Australia 4067

A stimulating and well-edited journal which usually takes a theme (peace education, for example, or health) and looks at it in depth with articles, reviews, poems and stories. An Australian/New Zealand slant, but it's good to have a slightly different perspective. $24 Aust/year ($16 Aust unemployed); single issues available in Britain from Housmans and Freedom (see page 337).

Whole Earth Review

27 Gate Five Road, Sausalito, California 94965, USA

The current reincarnation of the *Whole Earth* magazine, a quarterly full (144 pages) of titbits covering a wide range of subjects — the latest issue had pieces on plantwatching, mountain sleds, running a one-person business, the honey bee, fascism and child abuse, educational software and Australia by rail; get the idea? And no advertizing! You'll need to see it before you know whether it's for you, but I always find nuggets of wisdom and information lurking in its straight-talking pages. $20/year.

Computer Networks

On Saturday afternoon, 17th September 1988, there was a fatal car accident near Ilminster in Somerset involving an RAF convoy carrying nuclear weapons, which was being tracked by Nukewatch. The accident was reported to GreenNet, and was picked up by the Media Transcription Service, which posted updated transcripts of local news stories throughout the weekend. GreenNet also happened to be supporting a North Atlantic Network Conference in Glasgow that weekend, and so had immediate access to a number of prominent experts on nuclear defence. By the Monday all this information had been passed through the computer network to national television and the daily newspapers: ITV ran the story ahead of coverage of the Olympic Games on their news bulletins and all the quality papers covered the story extensively. Thus a potential nuclear disaster received the coverage it deserved rather than being relegated to a minor item in the local papers.

Efficient information and communications links are vital to a global green movement, and computer networks have an important part to play in allowing ordinary people to talk to each other. Used wisely, computer networks augment postal and telephone systems to enormous benefit. It's easy, however, to get hooked on giving out and receiving information for information's sake, and one of my favourite modern maxims comes from John Naisbitt's *Megatrends*: 'We are drowning in information but starved for knowledge.'

GreenNet

GreenNet's aim is 'to provide to the green movement in the widest sense the sort of communications normally available only to the government, military or multinationals', and in its first four years of operation GreenNet has done amazing things. It now has more than 5,000 regular users, including all the major green organizations, and its 40,000 pages of regularly-updated information can keep subscribers up to date on anything from wind energy to indigenous peoples.

GreenNet is an information and communications service which many a spymaster might envy. It has regular links with similar networks in North and South America, Australia and Europe, and is one of the founder members of the Association for Progressive Communications, a federation of seven green networks covering Canada, the USA, Nicaragua, Brazil, Australia and Sweden as well as Britain (links are planned with Kenya, Italy, Germany and the Soviet Union). GreenNet works closely with Poptel (a labour organization network), whose premises it shares.

Individuals are welcome to join GreenNet for a low fixed monthly sum (currently £5) plus one of the lowest 'connect rates' in the business — send an sae for current rates and an application form. I put all my misgivings about microtechnology on one side when it comes to GreenNet: it is an excellent example of complex technology used in an entirely appropriate way, and deserves every success.

GreenNet
25 Downham Road
London
N1 5AA
0(7)1-249 2948

HoneyTree and Friends

The HoneyTree system migrated to Wales from the USA in 1984 and took root in a craft shop and café in the Welsh borders, where it has been carefully tended and nurtured by the one of the few female 'sysops' (systems operators) in Britain, Eluned Hurn.

HoneyTree is a system designed to provide information to a widely- spread community of green-tinted computer operators. The various 'menus' you can access include Peace Network, Alternative Medicine and Dietary Therapy.

Loosely linked with the HoneyTree is a group of people called collectively NetReach, all interested in using computers to facilitate life-enhancing communication between people worldwide — NetReach meets fairly regularly, and Eluned Hurn will be glad to send you details. Other live wires within NetReach include Sabine Kurjo (who also organizes the London-based Turning Points programme) and Len Stuart, the secretary. NetReach was also involved in the novel but rather navel-gazing 'Networking of Networks' at the 1987 Festival for Mind/Body/Spirit (page 184).

HoneyTree
The Honey Café
Bronllys
Brecon
Powys
LD3 0LH
0874 711382

NetReach
89 Mayfair Avenue
Worcester Park
Surrey
KT4 7SJ
0(8)1-337 3747

TACIN

TACIN

Barry Cooper runs his information service — the Town and Country Information Network — from his home in the Herefordshire countryside. His database contains information on green and community related issues, and Barry also co-ordinates the services of a number of freelance consultants. A quarterly index lists what is available within the network. Send an sae and details of what you need; Barry is extremely helpful.

TACIN
Orcop
Herefordshire
HR2 8SF
0981 540263

Bulletin Boards

Bulletin boards are privately organized public access information services, computerized notice boards which are continuously updated — a sort of People's Prestel. Eluned Hurn's 'Faith' provides a bulletin board service on 0874 711147 (modem speed V21 — you'll know what that means if you're into computers); Organic Garden another on 0(8)1-464 3305 (modem speed HST) which calls itself 'Britain's first green bulletin board' and pops the message 'Think Green, Clean and Safe' on your screen at every opportunity.

There are far more bulletin boards than their sysops know what to usefully do with them, but it's an idea that can be used imaginatively — Protocol Communications in Totnes have developed a local bulletin board system for local schools to use, and several local authorities use them in libraries and information centres. *Personal Computer World* carries a complete list of operational bulletin boards every other issue, together with their numbers and operating characteristics.

AFTERWORD

'Change and movement are judged according to their consequences. When closely related things do not harmonize, misfortune is the result.'
I Ching: The Great Treatise

Everything changes all the time. Which is a good thing, since without change there is neither growth nor development. Yet we live in a world where change often happens faster than we can cope with it — Alvin Toffler has called this phenomenon 'future shock', a future which arrives before we are really ready for it. The main reason for the shock is that most people feel that the changes taking place are completely outside their control, and that they can do nothing to influence them. *New Green Pages*, on the other hand, looks at the sort of changes that *are* within our control, and for which the world is crying out more than ever. The keyword for these changes is 'harmony': the ancient wisdom of the *I Ching* is as relevant now as it was three thousand years ago.

Harmonious change — the greening of our collective lifestyle — is taking place much faster than is immediately apparent, partly because good news rarely makes the headlines, partly because few people have made the links between all its various aspects. But the change towards a green-tinted lifestyle is gathering momentum month by month. I wrote two years ago that this movement was 'already a stream large enough for advertisers and multinationals to have taken notice of it; before long it will have enough force to move sizeable political and economic boulders'. It is happening: from the prime minister to the boardrooms of multinationals they know they can't get away with platitudes and minimal action for much longer.

Things are now moving so quickly that it is impossible to keep up with every new green development; indeed, to do so would be counterproductive, since you could easily spend more time keeping up to date than actually living and enjoying your life.

I certainly had a problem keeping up with the new developments of the last couple of years, though nearly all the information in *New Green Pages* was carefully checked between November 1989 and January 1990. Despite the effort, I cannot imagine that every single address, telephone number, reference and fact is absolutely accurate, and this is where I welcome your help. If you come across an inaccuracy, if you are involved with one of the organizations or businesses mentioned and your circumstances change, or if you think you should be included in a future edition, then please do write to me, care of the publishers (their address is on page 2).

The Ultimate Green Consumerism

Yes, at last there is a shopping catalogue that you can trust to be as green, as aware and as inspiring as even the purest purist could demand.

'Welcome,' it says on the back cover, 'to *The Whole Universe Catalog*, your resource guide for new age clothing, equipment and accessories. We're sure you'll find everything you need to make your transition into cosmic consciousness because our products are truly out of this world!'

This fully-illustrated slim but fascinating volume shuns pointless yuppie playthings like calculators that translate into six languages and plastic flowers that dance when you sing to them.

Instead you will find *truly* natural products. The all-natural-fibre ribknit white light converter can harness your body's excess energy to run small household appliances so you no longer need to pollute the atmosphere to see in the dark. Celibacy capsules eliminate bodily urges and help solve the population crisis. You can now mend those unsightly holes in your aura with newly-developed aura putty. All this and much *much* more . . .

Shopping For Enlightenment
The Whole Universe Catalog
Laura Eisen and Mark Frey
Celestial Arts (distributed in the UK by Airlift)
£4.95

INDEX OF SUBJECTS

For main subject areas, look first at the contents page (page 3), which will give you a good idea of where to find a general overview of a subject.

INDEX OF SUPPLIERS AND ORGANIZATIONS

This index comprises all the the suppliers and organizations listed in New Green Pages, *with the exception of publications and bookshops (which will either be found on pages 336-345 or on the pages covering their field of interest), and some professional organizations covering specific alternative therapies, the reference for which you will find by looking up the relevant therapy (acupuncture, homeopathy, etc.) in the subject index.*